Romans

Volume 1

The Gospel Freedom

Romans 1–8

P. G. Mathew

GRACE & GLORY
MINISTRIES

GRACE & GLORY MINISTRIES
Davis, California

ISBN: 9780977114955
Library of Congress Control Number: 2011938959

I dedicate The Gospel Freedom
to the saints of God at Grace Valley Christian Center
in California, where I have been preaching this gospel
of freedom for many decades.

These saints have experienced the saving
and reviving power of the gospel.
I appreciate their love for their pastor
and especially their love for the gospel
of our Lord Jesus Christ.

Contents

CONTENTS

About the Author

P. G. Mathew, who holds three graduate degrees in theology from Central and Westminster theological seminaries (USA), is the founder and senior minister of Grace Valley Christian Center in California. Originally a scientist from India, he is also a former professor of Greek and systematic theology and has traveled widely for Christian mission interests. He is the author of *The Normal Church Life* (1 John); *Victory in Jesus* (Joshua); *The Wisdom of Jesus* (The Sermon on the Mount); *The Lawless Church*; *Muscular Christianity* (Hebrews) and several other books, including commentaries on Isaiah, Matthew, and Acts. He is also the founder and president of Grace Valley Christian Academy. For more information, visit *www.gracevalley.org*.

Foreword

*From the saints of Grace Valley Christian Center in California
and their friends who are experiencing the power
of this preached word throughout the world*

When you feel the pulse of most of today's evangelical and charismatic churches in the light of *sola scriptura*, those who worship God in spirit and in truth have reasons for deep sorrow. Such present day "Christianity" can be likened to the lukewarm church of Laodicea, of which the Lord said, "You say, 'I am rich; I have acquired wealth and do not need a thing.' But you do not realize that you are wretched, pitiful, poor, blind and naked" (Rev. 3:17).

The modern church has grown rich and famous, but it is no longer holy and powerful to declare the truth of the gospel. The church is full of false prophets, such as those spoken against by the prophet Jeremiah:

- Jer. 2:13: "My people have committed two sins: They have forsaken me, the spring of living water, and have dug their own cisterns, broken cisterns that cannot hold water."
- Jer. 5:13, 31: "The prophets are but wind and the word is not in them; so let what they say be done to them. . . . The prophets prophesy lies, the priests rule by their own authority, and my people love it this way. But what will you do in the end?"
- Jer. 6:13–14: "From the least to the greatest, all are greedy for gain; prophets and priests alike, all practice deceit. They dress the wound of my people as though it were not serious. 'Peace, peace,' they say, when there is no peace."
- Jer. 8:11: "They dress the wound of my people as though it were not serious. 'Peace, peace,' they say, when there is no peace."
- Jer. 14:14: "Then the LORD said to me, 'The prophets are prophesying lies in my name. I have not sent them or

appointed them or spoken to them. They are prophesying to you false visions, divinations, idolatries and the delusions of their own minds.'"

Amos prophesied of a famine, "not a famine of food or a thirst for water, but a famine of hearing the words of the LORD" (Amos 8:11). Pastor P. G. Mathew's book *The Gospel Freedom* is the bread of life to revive the famished and refresh the thirsty. *In fact, it was during the preaching of these sermons from Romans that God began a revival in our church that still continues.*

When you read this book, you will notice that Pastor Mathew stands in the Puritan tradition. Like the Puritans, Pastor Mathew insists that all aspects of life must become "Holiness to the Lord." He preaches a gospel that justifies, sanctifies, and glorifies all elect sinners. He refuses to preach a compromised, corrupt gospel that entertains people, meets their "felt needs," and shows them how to get rich and famous in this world. He calls sinners to repent and believe in the Lord Jesus Christ, the only Savior of the world.

Pastor Mathew powerfully proclaims the gospel of peace that alone can usher in living hope and great joy to those who have been set free by it. People throughout the world have been set free from all bondage through this liberating gospel.

We praise God that we have experienced this gospel power. May God revive you as you read *The Gospel Freedom.*

Preface

I thank God for granting me grace to preach through Romans chapters 1–8 at Grace Valley Christian Center from January 6, 2008 to August 1, 2010. I agree with my late professors John Murray of Westminster Theological Seminary in Philadelphia and Dr. Martyn Lloyd-Jones of Westminster Chapel in London, along with a number of other scholars whose views on Romans are cited below:

- John Murray: "The grand theme of the early part of the epistle is justification by grace through faith. And human righteousness is the essence of the religion of this world in contradiction to the gospel of God. Only a God-righteousness can measure up to the desperateness of our need and make the gospel the power of God unto salvation."
- Martin Luther: "This Epistle is really the chief part of the New Testament and the very purest Gospel, and is worthy not only that every Christian should know it word for word, by heart, but occupy himself with it every day, as the daily bread of the soul. It can never be read or pondered too much, and the more it is dealt with the more precious it becomes, and the better it tastes."
- D. Martyn Lloyd-Jones: "It has been the universal opinion in the Christian church throughout the centuries that Romans is the Epistle above all which deals with fundamentals, and if you look at the history of the church I think you will see that that has been borne out time and time again. There is a sense in which we can say quite truthfully that the Epistle to the Romans has, possibly, played a more crucial part in the history of the church than any other single book in the whole of the Bible."
- James Boice: "Christianity has been the most powerful, transforming force in human history—and the book of Romans is the most basic, most comprehensive statement of true Christianity."
- John Stott: "Paul's letter to the Romans is a kind of Christian manifesto. . . . It remains a timeless manifesto, a manifesto of

freedom through Jesus Christ. It is the fullest, plainest and grandest statement of the gospel in the New Testament. Its message is . . . that human beings are born in sin and slavery, but that Jesus Christ came to set us free."

This volume is entitled *The Gospel Freedom* because it is good news to the worst sinners of the world, who are under slavery to sin, Satan, and death. Those under the just wrath of God can enjoy peace with God. The good news is that God justifies the ungodly and makes them godly and glorious through the redemption and righteousness of Jesus Christ (Rom. 3:21–26). There is no atonement, no righteousness, and no redemption outside of Jesus Christ. Life eternal is found only in the Son, who is righteousness, holiness, and glorification.

In his epistle to the Romans, Paul declares that through faith in the gospel of Jesus Christ, fallen, sinful, dying man can be set free from the dominion of sin, the flesh, and the devil. Enemies of God by divine power can become children of God who love God and live victorious Christian lives in the power of the Holy Spirit.

I thank my wife Gladys, with whom I have experienced this glorious gospel freedom. I am also grateful for Mrs. Margaret Killeen, Mr. Gregory Perry, Dr. Lisa Case, Mr. Marc Roby, Mr. Matthew Sanders, Mr. Michael Ishii, and Mr. Daniel Washabaugh for their help in preparing this manuscript for publication and Mrs. Lorraine Smith for her work on designing the cover. It is my prayer that by reading this book you will also be set free to love God and live all your life for God's glory. *Soli Deo Gloria!*

P. G. MATHEW

1

The Gospel of God

¹Paul, a servant of Christ Jesus, called to be an apostle and set apart for the gospel of God— ²the gospel he promised beforehand through his prophets in the Holy Scriptures ³regarding his Son, who as to his human nature was a descendant of David, ⁴and who through the Spirit of holiness was declared with power to be the Son of God by his resurrection from the dead: Jesus Christ our Lord. ⁵Through him and for his name's sake, we received grace and apostleship to call people from among all the Gentiles to the obedience that comes from faith. ⁶And you also are among those who are called to belong to Jesus Christ.

⁷To all in Rome who are loved by God and called to be saints: Grace and peace to you from God our Father and from the Lord Jesus Christ.

Romans 1:1–7

Paul wrote the Epistle to the Romans around 57 AD from Corinth to the believers in Rome. Luther called this book "the chief part of the New Testament, and . . . truly the purest gospel."[1]

God has used this epistle throughout church history in mighty ways. In the fourth century, Augustine of Hippo, a teacher of literature and rhetoric, was led by the Holy Spirit to read Romans 13:13–14: "Let us behave decently, as in the daytime, not in orgies and drunkenness, not in sexual immorality and debauchery, not in dissension and jealousy. Rather, clothe yourselves with the Lord Jesus Christ, and do not think about

---

1   Quoted by Stott, *Romans: God's Good News*, 19.

how to gratify the desires of the sinful nature." As a result of these words, Augustine found grace, peace, and eternal salvation. In the early sixteenth century, while the Augustinian monk Martin Luther was teaching the Bible at Wittenberg University, he found salvation through the righteousness of God that justifies the ungodly, as set forth in this letter. Luther's discovery sparked the Protestant Reformation. In 1738, John Wesley found the joy of salvation as he heard someone reading Luther's preface to his commentary on Romans. Wesley said, "I felt my heart strangely warmed. I felt I did trust in Christ, Christ alone, for salvation; and an assurance was given me that he had taken away *my* sins, even *mine*, and saved *me* from the law of sin and death."[2] Günther Bornkamm calls Romans "the last will and testament of the Apostle Paul."[3]

Born a Roman citizen, Saul of Tarsus was a highborn, highly educated, high achiever. Tradition describes him as "an ugly little [man] with beetle brows, bandy legs, a bald pate, a hooked nose, bad eyesight and no great rhetorical gifts."[4] But he was God's apostle, a great genius who gave us this amazing theology revealed in this longest of his letters, the Epistle to the Romans. Paul introduces himself in this letter to the Roman Christians and sets forth his apostolic understanding of the gospel. He discloses his plan to evangelize Spain after visiting Rome and being refreshed by the believers there. The theme of Romans is the gospel of God: God's good news to a sinful world under his wrath. This letter was written down by Paul's secretary Tertius (Rom. 16:22).

Paul's Introduction

"Paul, a servant of Christ Jesus, called to be an apostle and set apart for the gospel of God" (v. 1). Paul introduces himself as a slave of Christ Jesus, just as Moses, Joshua, and David were slaves of God before him. Though Paul was a rich, famous, and brilliant Roman citizen, this highly educated super-achiever glories in the fact that he is a slave of Jesus.

2　Examples cited by Stott, *Romans: God's Good News*, 20–22.
3　Morris, *Epistle to the Romans*, 8.
4　Stott, 58.

The Greek world considered it shameful to be a slave, but Paul considered it a great honor to serve the Lord of the universe as his slave. Wholly owned by Christ, Paul delighted to serve Jesus with all his heart. The chief of sinners became Christ's slave to think Christ's thoughts and do Christ's will alone. To serve Jesus as a slave was Paul's greatest joy and honor.

Paul was also chosen by the risen Christ to be his apostle. He was directly called and appointed to be Christ's authorized delegate, empowered to act in his behalf. "Apostle" was a title of great authority. Paul was one of the primary apostles authorized to proclaim and write the word of God. When the apostles spoke, Jesus was speaking, and their writings became the Holy Scriptures (1 Thess. 2:13; 2 Pet. 3:1–2).

God chose Paul from all eternity and separated him from his mother's womb (Gal. 1:15). In Damascus, Christ called and separated him to believe and proclaim the gospel of God. He later appointed him to the gospel ministry through the church in Antioch (Acts 13:2).

Even before his conversion, Paul was a "separated one," for that is what Pharisee means—one who is separated to observe the traditions of the elders. But Christ called him and set him apart to proclaim the gospel. God separated Paul from all other loyalties to be loyal to Christ alone so that he could believe, defend, and declare the gospel of God.

The Gospel of God

This passage articulates seven aspects of the gospel of God.

1. THE ORIGIN OF THE GOSPEL

God the Father is the author of the gospel. The apostles did not invent the gospel, but God entrusted it to them (2 Pet. 1:20–21). They received and proclaimed it, but they did not add to or subtract from this message entrusted to them. The gospel is the Father's good news to a lost world under God's wrath. John Murray writes, "The gospel as the power of God unto salvation is meaningless apart from sin, condemnation, misery, and death. To be subjected to the wrath of God is the epitome of human misery."[5] The gospel of God puts an end to this misery.

It is the gospel of *God*. "God" is the most important word in this letter to the Romans, appearing about 153 times. This God, who is with us, is the heart of the gospel, as Isaiah declared: "You who bring good tidings to Zion, go up on a high mountain. You who bring good tidings to Jerusalem, lift up your voice with a shout, lift it up, do not be afraid; say to the towns of Judah, 'Here is your God!' . . . How beautiful on the mountains are the feet of those who bring good news, who proclaim peace, who bring good tidings, who proclaim salvation, who say to Zion, 'Your God reigns!'" (Isa. 40:9; 52:7).

The gospel speaks of God's intervention in human affairs as a king who defeats all his enemies and brings salvation to his people. The gospel of God spells hope, life, peace, and joy to all sinners who are chosen by him.

2. THE GOSPEL WAS PROMISED BEFOREHAND

Paul was set apart for the gospel that God *"promised beforehand through his prophets in the Holy Scriptures"* (v. 2). The gospel is not something new; it was promised long before the coming of Christ. The promise of the gospel came through the holy prophets of old, like David and Moses (Acts 2:30; 3:21–22). There is continuity between the Old and New Testaments. The promise of a Savior coming as the seed of the woman (Gen. 3:15), the seed of Abraham (Gen. 22), and the seed of David (2 Sam. 7) was fulfilled in the son of Virgin Mary, Jesus Christ.

God always fulfills what he promises; therefore, God's word can be fully trusted. Paul writes, "But as surely as God is faithful, our message to you is not 'Yes' and 'No.' For the Son of God, Jesus Christ, who was preached among you by me and Silas and Timothy, was not 'Yes' and 'No,' but in him it has always been 'Yes.' For no matter how many promises God has made, they are 'Yes' in Christ. And so through him the 'Amen' is spoken by us to the glory of God" (2 Cor. 1:18–20). The same idea is found in Joshua: "Not one of all the LORD's good promises to the house of Israel failed; every one was fulfilled" (Josh. 21:45); "Now I am

---

5   Murray, *Epistle to the Romans*, xxiii.

about to go the way of all the earth. You know with all your heart and soul that not one of all the good promises the LORD your God gave you has failed. Every promise has been fulfilled; not one has failed" (Josh. 23:14). Let God be true and all men liars!

This promised gospel of God is embodied and enshrined in the Bible. Because God is holy, his word is holy. It is also unique. Only in the Bible do we discover the good news of God. The author of the Holy Scriptures is the Holy Spirit, so the Scriptures are holy, infallible, and inerrant.

Both the Old and New Testaments are holy. The New Testament Scriptures are written by the apostles, Christ's delegates, under the guidance of the Holy Spirit. When the apostles speak, God speaks; thus, the word of the apostles of Christ is the word of God (2 Tim. 3:16; 2 Pet. 1:19-21; 3:16).

To hear the good news of God, go to the Scriptures. Read them, believe them, and be saved. Paul concluded this epistle: "Now to him who is able to establish you by my gospel and the proclamation of Jesus Christ, according to the revelation of the mystery hidden for long ages past, but now revealed and made known through the prophetic writings by the command of the eternal God, so that all nations might believe and obey him—to the only wise God be glory forever through Jesus Christ! Amen" (Rom. 16:25-27).

3. THE GOSPEL CONCERNS HIS SON

Paul says this gospel of God is *"regarding his Son, who as to his human nature was a descendant of David, and who through the Spirit of holiness was declared with power to be the Son of God by his resurrection from the dead: Jesus Christ our Lord"* (vv. 3-4). The substance of the gospel is God's eternal Son; therefore, the key to understanding Scripture is Christ. John Calvin said, "The whole gospel is contained in Christ. . . . To move even a step from Christ means to withdraw oneself from the gospel."[6]

Jesus declared that the whole Bible speaks of him (Luke 24:25-27, 44-47). Paul told the Corinthians, "When I came to you, brothers, I did not come with eloquence or superior wisdom as I proclaimed to you the testimony about God. For

---

6   Quoted by Stott, *Romans: God's Good News,* 49.

I resolved to know nothing while I was with you except Jesus Christ and him crucified. I came to you in weakness and fear, and with much trembling. My message and my preaching were not with wise and persuasive words, but with a demonstration of the Spirit's power, so that your faith might not rest on men's wisdom, but on God's power" (1 Cor. 2:1–5). A minister who refuses to preach Jesus Christ and him crucified is a fraud, a deceiver, and under God's severe judgment.

The gospel concerns God's Son—the pre-existent, second Person of the Trinity. Paul says, "For if, when we were God's enemies, we were reconciled to him through the death of his Son, how much more, having been reconciled, shall we be saved through his life!" (Rom. 5:10). He also says, "For what the law was powerless to do in that it was weakened by the sinful nature, God did by sending his own Son in the likeness of sinful man to be a sin offering. And so he condemned sin in sinful man. . . . He who did not spare his own Son, but gave him up for us all—how will he not also, along with him, graciously give us all things?" (Rom. 8:3, 32). Elsewhere Paul declares that Jesus is God himself: "Theirs are the patriarchs, and from them is traced the human ancestry of Christ, who is God over all, forever praised!" (Rom. 9:5; see also Col. 2:9). The Son is God, co-equal with the Father.

This gospel speaks of the eternal Son entering into a state of humiliation by taking upon himself human nature and becoming man. The name "Jesus" speaks of the One who is the Savior of the world, the promised King of David's line. The Son became incarnate that he might die for our sins and be raised for our justification. The gospel of God is about the Son's incarnation, life, death, burial, resurrection, ascension, session, and sovereign rule over the entire cosmos. It is about Jesus as our substitute, representative, and only mediator between God and man. The gospel speaks of the person and work of Christ.

The gospel of God speaks not only of the Son's pre-resurrection incarnational life of humiliation, but also of Christ's post-resurrection incarnational life of exaltation. Jesus was the Son of God incarnate in weakness, but God also appointed him to be the Son of God incarnate in power. He did so by raising him from the dead. Paul writes: "[Christ Jesus], who, being in very nature God, did not consider equality with God something to be grasped, but made himself nothing, taking the very nature of a servant, being made in human likeness. And being found in appearance as a man, he humbled himself and became obedient to death—even death on a cross! Therefore God exalted him to the highest place and gave him the name that is above every name, that at the name of Jesus every knee should bow, in heaven and on earth and under the earth, and every tongue confess that Jesus Christ is Lord, to the glory of God the Father" (Phil. 2:6-11). The incarnational life of Jesus consists of two stages: humiliation and power.

By saying that Jesus has been given a name above every name, Paul is declaring that the Lord Jesus has conquered all his enemies and now rules with power. He is mighty to both save and judge. After resurrecting Christ by the Spirit (Rom. 8:11), God the Father installed his Son as King of the universe. So Peter says, "Therefore let all Israel be assured of this: God has made this Jesus, whom you crucified, both Lord and Christ" (Acts 2:36). Jesus himself said, "All authority in heaven and on earth has been given to me. Therefore go and make disciples of all nations, baptizing them in the name of the Father and of the Son and of the Holy Spirit, and teaching them to obey everything I have commanded you. And surely I am with you always, to the very end of the age" (Matt. 28:18-20). John writes in Revelation that Jesus is the King of the universe. The gospel of God proclaims, "Surrender to Jesus and be saved; or resist him, and be condemned."

Peter had said, "God has made this Jesus, whom you crucified, both Lord and Christ" (Acts 2:36). Jesus earlier had told his disciples, "I tell you the truth, some who are standing here will not taste death before they see the kingdom of God come with power" (Mark 9:1). Christ was crucified in weakness, yet he lives by God's power. Paul speaks of these two stages in the incarnational life of the Son: "For to be sure, he was crucified in weakness, yet he lives by God's power. Likewise, we are weak in him, yet by God's power we will live with him to serve you" (2 Cor. 13:4). He writes about the lordship of Christ: "That power is like the working of his mighty strength, which he exerted in Christ when he raised him from the dead and seated him at his right hand in the heavenly realms, far above all rule and authority, power and dominion, and every title that can be given, not only in the present age but also in the one to come. And God placed all things under his feet and appointed him to be head over everything for the church, which is his body, the fullness of him who fills everything in every way" (Eph. 1:19–23).

Jesus Christ is Lord of the universe, including all humans and angels. The psalmist declares,

> The One enthroned in heaven laughs; the Lord scoffs at them. Then he rebukes them in his anger and terrifies them in his wrath, saying, "I have installed my King on Zion, my holy hill." I will proclaim the decree of the LORD: He said to me, "You are my Son; today I have become your Father. Ask of me, and I will make the nations your inheritance, the ends of the earth your possession. You will rule them with an iron scepter; you will dash them to pieces like pottery." Therefore, you kings, be wise; be warned, you rulers of the earth. Serve the LORD with fear and rejoice with trembling. Kiss the Son, lest he be angry and you be destroyed in your way, for his wrath can flare up in a moment. Blessed are all who take refuge in him. (Ps. 2:4–12)

Paul writes, "For he must reign until he has put all his enemies under his feet. The last enemy to be destroyed is death" (1 Cor. 15:25–26). God has installed his Son as the powerful King to whom we must surrender.

This One is the eternal Son of God. He is Jesus, the Savior of the world. He is Christ, anointed and fully qualified. He is Lord and Conqueror of the universe, mighty to save and to judge. He has emerged victoriously from the state of humiliation to the state of exaltation and power.

John describes this exalted Lord after beholding him in all his brilliance and glory:

> I turned around to see the voice that was speaking to me. And when I turned I saw seven golden lampstands, and among the lampstands was someone "like a son of man," dressed in a robe reaching down to his feet and with a golden sash around his chest. His head and hair were white like wool, as white as snow, and his eyes were like blazing fire. His feet were like bronze glowing in a furnace, and his voice was like the sound of rushing waters. In his right hand he held seven stars, and out of his mouth came a sharp double-edged sword. His face was like the sun shining in all its brilliance. When I saw him, I fell at his feet as though dead. Then he placed his right hand on me

and said: "Do not be afraid. I am the First and the Last. I am the Living One; I was dead, and behold I am alive for ever and ever! And I hold the keys of death and Hades." (Rev. 1:12–18)

John later speaks of a vision of the glorious coming of the Lord:

> I saw heaven standing open and there before me was a white horse, whose rider is called Faithful and True. With justice he judges and makes war. His eyes are like blazing fire, and on his head are many crowns. He has a name written on him that no one knows but he himself. He is dressed in a robe dipped in blood, and his name is the Word of God. The armies of heaven were following him, riding on white horses and dressed in fine linen, white and clean. Out of his mouth comes a sharp sword with which to strike down the nations. "He will rule them with an iron scepter." He treads the winepress of the fury of the wrath of God Almighty. On his robe and on his thigh he has this name written: KING OF KINGS AND LORD OF LORDS. (Rev. 19:11–16)

4. THE SCOPE OF THE APOSTLE'S MINISTRY

"Through him and for his name's sake, we received grace and apostleship to call people from among all the Gentiles to the obedience that comes from faith" (v. 5). The apostle's ministry reaches the whole world because Jesus is Lord of all. He received all authority in heaven and on earth (Matt. 28:18). The scope of Paul's ministry especially included the world of Gentiles. Yet he also ministered to Jews: "I am not ashamed of the gospel, because it is the power of God for the salvation of everyone who believes: first for the Jew, then for the Gentile" (Rom. 1:16).

The church is to be engaged in world missions. We must love the world so that we can proclaim to the world the good news. We must rule out all pride of race, caste, and nationality, knowing that all have sinned and fall short of the glory of God. God loves the world, so all must hear the gospel. We must proclaim that our God reigns, and that he is mighty to save all who surrender to his lordship.

The scope of Paul's ministry reaches even us. This letter to the Romans is the authoritative presentation to all mankind of the gospel of God concerning his Son, the crucified, risen, and reigning Lord Jesus.

5. THE GOAL OF THE GOSPEL

"Through him and for his name's sake, we received grace and apostleship" (v. 5). The ultimate purpose of the gospel proclamation is not our salvation, but, as stated here, "for his name's sake," meaning for the glory of the name of the Son.

The Father is zealous for his Son's honor. When we do not believe in God or obey him, we are refusing to honor the Lord Jesus Christ. He who refuses to believe in God's Son and confess him as Lord dishonors both Christ and his Father.

God not only saves people for his glory, but he also judges them. Jesus says, "Moreover, the Father judges no one, but has entrusted all judgment to the Son, that all may honor the Son just as they honor the Father. He who does not honor the Son does not honor the Father, who sent him" (John 5:22–23). Paul writes, "For the Scripture says to Pharaoh: 'I raised you up for this very purpose, that I might display my power in you and that my name might be proclaimed in all the earth'" (Rom. 9:17; see also Eph. 1:6, 12, 14). The ultimate purpose of proclaiming the gospel is to bring glory to God's name.

It may be disappointing to think that our salvation is only God's penultimate purpose, yet we delight in this truth. The catechism teaches that the chief end of man is to glorify God and enjoy him forever. Paul declares that "at the name of Jesus every knee should bow . . . and every tongue confess that Jesus Christ is Lord, to the glory of God the Father" (Phil. 2:10–11). Everyone must confess and bow their knees to the exalted Lord.

6. THE PURPOSE OF THE GOSPEL PROCLAMATION

"We received grace and apostleship to call people . . . to the obedience that comes from faith" (v. 5). As King of kings and Lord of lords, Christ demands that all people trust and obey him. The purpose of proclaiming the gospel to all nations is that all may do just that: "How, then, can they call on the one they have not believed in? And how can they believe in the one of whom they have not heard? And how can they hear without someone preaching to them? And how can they preach unless they are sent? As it is written, 'How beautiful are the feet of those who bring good news!'" (Rom. 10:14–15).

When Jesus is proclaimed as the only Savior and Lord, we must respond. Paul told the Athenians, "In the past God overlooked such ignorance, but now he commands all people everywhere to repent" (Acts 17:30). The gospel proclamation demands the obedience of faith, meaning saving faith in Jesus that issues in total obedience to Christ the King.

Paul declares, "If you confess with your mouth, 'Jesus is Lord,' and believe in your heart that God raised him from the dead, you will be saved" (Rom. 10:9). When we confess Jesus as Lord, we are saying that we are his slaves. How glorious to be a slave of the King of kings and Lord of lords! We are his property. He owns, guides, and protects us. This is not the dead faith of the devil that refuses to repent and obey; it is the living faith of Abraham: "By faith Abraham, when called to go to a place he would later receive as his inheritance, obeyed and went, even though he did not know where he was going" (Heb. 11:8). Paul explains this faith: "But thanks be to God that, though you used to be slaves to sin, you wholeheartedly obeyed the form of teaching to which you were entrusted. . . . Therefore I glory in Christ Jesus in my service to God. I will not venture to speak of anything except what Christ has accomplished through me in leading the Gentiles to obey God by what I have said and done" (Rom. 6:17; 15:17–18).

We must respond to the gospel in faith and obedience. Trust and obey—there is no other way. Our lives must be characterized by self-denial and Christ-dependence. To not trust and obey Jesus is to dishonor God and his Son. Paul writes, "For Christ's love compels us, because we are convinced that one died for all, and therefore all died. And he died for all, that those who live should no longer live for themselves but for him who died for them and was raised again" (2 Cor. 5:14–15).

7. THE RECIPIENTS OF THE EPISTLE TO THE ROMANS

"You also are among those who are called to belong to Jesus Christ. To all in Rome who are loved by God and called to be saints: Grace and peace to you from God our Father and from the Lord Jesus Christ" (vv. 6–7). Let us look at some characteristics of the recipients of this epistle.

CALLED TO BE HIS SAINTS

"To all in Rome who are loved by God and called to be saints" (v. 7). Calling speaks of an effectual, divine action. When God

calls us, he also creates in us what he demands. To the stinking corpse Lazarus, Jesus commanded, "Lazarus, come forth!" and he emerged from the tomb (John 11:44). When Paul preached by the riverside, God opened Lydia's heart to respond properly to the gospel and she believed (Acts 16:14).

There is a general call and an effectual call. Jesus says, "No one can come to me unless the Father who sent me draws him, and I will raise him up at the last day. . . . No one can come to me unless the Father has enabled him. . . . But I, when I am lifted up from the earth, will draw all men to myself" (John 6:44, 65; 12:32).

The Father, the Son, and the Holy Spirit draw us powerfully and effectually. When that happens, we will come and surrender, repent, believe, confess, obey, and worship our Lord Christ. He makes us able to do these things. God himself calls us "into fellowship with his Son Jesus Christ our Lord" (1 Cor. 1:9).

God calls us out of the world and away from all other loyalties to come and belong to him and be his saints. He changes our nature and behavior, making bad trees into good trees so that we will live holy lives.

BELOVED OF GOD

The Father loved us from all eternity and gave us to his Son to save us. The Son also loved us and gave himself for us to cleanse us from all our sins and make us glorious. Paul speaks of this in his instruction to husbands: "Love your wives, just as Christ loved the church and gave himself up for her to make her holy, cleansing her by the washing with water through the word" (Eph. 5:25–26). He alludes to it elsewhere: "I have been crucified with Christ and I no longer live, but Christ lives in me. The life I live in the body, I live by faith in the Son of God, who loved me and gave himself for me" (Gal. 2:20).

The Father loves us just as he loves his Son. Jesus spoke of this in his high priestly prayer: "I have given them the glory that you gave me, that they may be one as we are one: I in them and you in me. May they be brought to complete unity to let the world know that you sent me and have loved them even as you have loved me" (John 17:22–23). God's love is eternal. He never stops loving us. And because he loves us, he also chastens us to rid us of our foolishness (Heb. 12:4–11). With God's love, we love one another.

GRANTED GRACE AND PEACE

"Grace and peace to you from God our Father and from the Lord Jesus Christ" (v. 7). What evidence do we have that God loves us? He called us effectually and gave us grace, which is unmerited favor. We merited wrath and death, but God gives us love and life. Grace is God's power to save us. Grace turns our mourning into dancing forever. Grace causes us to rejoice, not only in good times, but in tribulations also. Grace turns our death to life, our midnight to midday, our poverty to riches, and our weeping to joy.

By nature we were enemies of God and under his wrath. But God reconciled us to himself through Christ. Now we have peace and hope: "Therefore, since we have been justified through faith, we have peace with God through our Lord Jesus Christ" (Rom. 5:1). All enmity is gone and God is now our heavenly Father. We have fellowship with the Father and the Son in the Holy Spirit. This peace is eternal salvation. And because we have peace with God, we can experience in our hearts the peace of God that guards us from all fear and anxiety. Paul says this peace flows to us *"from God our Father and from the Lord Jesus Christ."* As God, Jesus is the co-author of the grace and peace God gives us. So we worship the Father and the Son in the Holy Spirit.

Application

The gospel is the great news of God's goodness to sinners. Found only in the Bible, the gospel concerns God's Son: his incarnation, his sinless life, his substitutionary death, his burial, his resurrection, and his exaltation. This book of Romans is the exposition of God's gospel, written by Christ's apostle, to tell us how God fulfilled his promise of a Savior in Jesus Christ.

Have you heard this gospel of God's Son? Have you responded with the obedience of faith? Have you confessed Jesus as Lord and yourself as his slave? If so, may grace and peace be with you, and may you live for his glory all the days of your life.

2

The Blessing of Christian Fellowship

⁸First, I thank my God through Jesus Christ for all of you, because your faith is being reported all over the world. ⁹God, whom I serve with my whole heart in preaching the gospel of his Son, is my witness how constantly I remember you ¹⁰in my prayers at all times; and I pray that now at last by God's will the way may be opened for me to come to you.

¹¹I long to see you so that I may impart to you some spiritual gift to make you strong— ¹²that is, that you and I may be mutually encouraged by each other's faith. ¹³I do not want you to be unaware, brothers, that I planned many times to come to you (but have been prevented from doing so until now) in order that I might have a harvest among you, just as I have had among the other Gentiles.

¹⁴I am obligated both to Greeks and non-Greeks, both to the wise and the foolish. ¹⁵That is why I am so eager to preach the gospel also to you who are at Rome.

Romans 1:8–15

In Romans 1:8–15, Paul speaks about the blessing of Christian fellowship. If we are Christians through the miracle of new birth, and have repented truly of our sins and savingly trusted in Christ through hearing the gospel of God's Son, then we belong to the family of God through Jesus Christ our Lord. As members of God's family, we have fellowship with the Father and the Son and with all true people of God throughout the world.

All true believers are our brothers and sisters; therefore, we are obliged to love them, suffer with them, rejoice with them, and pray for them. We are part of the one great family of God, the international body of Christ that knows no racial, gender, or class discrimination. In this passage Paul reveals his intense love for the saints in Rome. Though he did not know most of them personally, he was in fellowship with them. The gospel of God concerning Jesus our Lord creates a worldwide Christian community.

The word "fellowship" (*koinônia*) appears in the New Testament first in Acts 2:42: "They devoted themselves to the apostles' teaching and to the fellowship." Where there is doctrine, there is necessarily fellowship. Where there is the preaching of the gospel, there is God's church. Such Christian fellowship results in great blessings.

Paul's Thanksgiving

"I thank my God through Jesus Christ for all of you" (v. 8). Paul first gives thanks for these Roman Christians. Although Paul did not found this church, he praises God for calling it into existence in the capital city of the empire. He is not thanking the believers; he is thanking God for them, specifically for their faith.

Notice, he says, "I thank *my* God." He is thanking the God with whom he enjoys intimate relationship. He says elsewhere, "My God will meet all your needs" (Phil. 4:19). David spoke often of his similar relationship with God: "I love you, O LORD, my strength. The LORD is my rock, my fortress and my deliverer; my God is my rock, in whom I take refuge. He is my shield and the horn of my salvation, my stronghold. . . . The LORD is my shepherd" (Ps. 18:1–2; 23:1). If we cannot say, "I thank *my* God," our profession of faith is empty and we are not born of God. We should have such a personal relationship with God that we are able to say, "My Father and my God," with an infinitely greater intensity than we have when we refer to "my wife" or "my children."

Do you love God with all your heart, soul, mind, and strength, so that you can say with Paul, "I thank *my* God through Jesus Christ"? I hope we will all love and know God in this way. Jesus said, "This is eternal life: that they may know you, the only true God, and Jesus Christ, whom you have sent" (John 17:3). Our knowledge of God should be experimental, personal, and intimate.

Through Jesus Christ

Next, we notice that Paul is thanking God *"through Jesus Christ"* (v. 8). This is the only time we find this phrase in Romans. We have access to the Father only through Jesus, our only mediator and atonement. Only as we are robed in Christ's righteousness may we come to God and enjoy fellowship with him. So we worship God *through Jesus Christ.* All of life is worship. "Whether you eat or drink or whatever you do, do it all for the glory of God" (1 Cor. 10:31). Speaking of Jews and Gentiles, Paul says, "For through [Christ] we both have access to the Father by one Spirit" (Eph. 2:18). This tells us there is no access to the Father except through his Son, who died for our sins and was raised for our justification. Only vital Christianity shows the way to the Father. Salvation is found in no one except Christ. If anyone rejects Christ, he rejects God's eternal salvation and welcomes his own eternal damnation. Jesus alone is our atoning high priest who ever lives to make intercession for us. May we come to God through him!

The Faith of the Roman Christians

"I thank my God through Jesus Christ for all of you, because your faith is being reported all over the world" (v. 8). Paul is giving thanks to God through Jesus Christ because of the faith of the Roman Christians. They heard the gospel, believed it, and were saved. We must note, though, that God was the author of their faith. Repentance and faith are divine, miraculous gifts.

The faith of these believers was a vibrant, flourishing faith, visible to all Christians in the Roman Empire. Though saving faith is an invisible, interior reality, like the root of a tree, it manifests externally by obedient works, like the fruits of a tree.

Faith without works is dead. It is the devil's faith. We know the faith of the Romans was authentic and visible because other Christians observed and spoke about it throughout the Roman Empire. Paul writes about the similar faith of the Thessalonians: "We always thank God for all of you, mentioning you in our prayers. We continually remember before our God and Father your work produced by faith, your labor prompted by love, and your endurance inspired by hope in our Lord Jesus Christ" (1 Thess. 1:2–3). Faith, love, and hope are internal and invisible, but they necessarily manifest themselves in work, labor, and endurance. So Paul says, "The Lord's message rang out from you not only in Macedonia and Achaia—your faith in God has become known everywhere" (1 Thess. 1:8). Dr. Lloyd-Jones says, "A revival never needs to be advertised; it always advertises itself."[1]

Faith always issues in obedience to God. Paul received the apostolic call "to call the Gentiles unto the obedience of faith." Is your faith visible to others through your good works? Is your faith proclaimed everywhere?

God Is My Witness

Paul next says, "God . . . is my witness" (v. 9). Paul loved the Roman Christians, and to persuade them of that truth, he calls on God to witness the reality of his love for them. He takes an oath so that the Romans will know that Paul truly loves them and prays for them.

It is not sinful to take an oath. If we are telling the truth, we can call upon God to be a witness to that truth. Paul does this often: "I speak the truth in Christ—I am not lying, my conscience confirms it in the Holy Spirit" (Rom. 9:1; see also 2 Cor. 1:23; 11:31). In this epistle, Paul is invoking the all-seeing God to witness to the Romans about his love for them. He is saying, in essence, "My God guarantees the veracity of my love for you."

Do we love God's people whom we see with our eyes? Can we call God as our witness that we love them, pray for them, and care for them?

Whom I Serve in My Spirit

Paul defines God as the One "whom I serve with my whole heart" (v. 9), or "whom I serve in my spirit" (author's translation). For the Christian, all of life is serving and worshiping God

---

1   Lloyd-Jones, *Romans*, vol. 1, *Gospel of God*, 179.

(Rom. 12:1; Gal. 2:20; Phil. 1:21). There is no sacred and secular distinction; we live *coram Deo*, in the presence of God.

Joseph told Potiphar's wife: "How then could I do such a wicked thing and sin against God?" (Gen. 39:9). He was living coram Deo. Jesus also always lived in God's presence, resisting all the devil's temptations and doing what was pleasing in God's sight.

Paul is saying that he served God sincerely with all his heart. He was not a hypocrite, putting on an air of spirituality to fool people. About his plans to visit the Corinthian church he wrote, "When I planned this, did I do it lightly? Or do I make my plans in a worldly manner so that in the same breath I say, 'Yes, yes' and 'No, no'?" (2 Cor. 1:17). Then he explained, "Rather, we have renounced secret and shameful ways; we do not use deception, nor do we distort the word of God. On the contrary, by setting forth the truth plainly we commend ourselves to every man's conscience in the sight of God" (2 Cor. 4:2). There were false ministers in the church who were masquerading as ministers of truth. Of them Paul said, "For such men are false apostles, deceitful workmen, masquerading as apostles of Christ. And no wonder, for Satan himself masquerades as an angel of light. It is not surprising, then, if his servants masquerade as servants of righteousness. Their end will be what their actions deserve" (2 Cor. 11:13–15; see also 2 Cor. 10:1–5). Paul knew that God looks at the heart and desires truth in our inward parts.

Paul served God by proclaiming the gospel of his Son, the unsearchable riches of Christ, the whole counsel of God. Not only did he proclaim the whole gospel, but he also lived it. So he could say, "I serve [God] with my whole heart in preaching the gospel of his Son." That was the sphere of Paul's ministry. To the Corinthian church he wrote, "When I came to you, brothers, I did not come with eloquence or superior wisdom as I proclaimed to you the testimony about God. For I resolved to know nothing while I was with you except Jesus Christ and him crucified. I came to you in weakness and fear, and with much trembling. My message and my preaching were not with wise and persuasive words, but with a demonstration of the Spirit's power, so that your faith might not rest on men's wisdom, but on God's power" (1 Cor. 2:1–5).

Most ministers today refuse to serve God by declaring the gospel of his Son. They preach a synthetic gospel of their own creation that makes them rich and famous. They seek man's approval, not God's.

Paul's Constant Prayer

Paul's love for the Roman Christians is revealed by his continual prayer for them: *"God . . . is my witness how constantly I remember you in my prayers at all times; and I pray that now at last by God's will the way may be opened for me to come to you"* (vv. 9–10).

Paul was a man of prayer. God witnessed his love for the Romans expressed by his constant prayer for them. He prayed for them on all occasions, making mention of them continually in his prayers. As Daniel prayed three times each day, so also Paul prayed many times a day. Acts 16 speaks of him praying even at midnight in the Philippian jail. In these prayers he would mention the names of all these believers in all places.

We have to pray beyond ourselves and our own needs. Paul prayed not just for himself but also for others, even for those he did not know by name. Intercession for others demonstrates our love in Christ for them. As Christians, we are to pray for others, even for our enemies. In Romans 8 Paul tells us that not only does Jesus pray for us, but the Holy Spirit also intercedes for us. We likewise must pray for one another. Robert Haldane says, "To pray without labouring is to mock God: to labour without prayer is to rob God of His glory."[2] Prayer directs our service and makes it effectual.

Praying in the Will of God

Paul prays that in the will of God he might be able to go to Rome so that he can see these believers and bless them through his gospel ministry: *"I pray that now at last by God's will the way may be opened for me to come to you"* (v. 10). As a slave of Christ, Paul certainly would not demand anything of his Master but was waiting to know God's will about going to Rome.

---

2   Haldane, *Exposition of Romans*, 40.

God commissions his people to preach the gospel to the whole world. Yet we must seek God's will about where and when we must do so. God has both a general and specific will, so we must pray that God will make his will clear to us. We should not pray, "My will be done," but "Thy will be done," and surrender ourselves completely to his will. That is what it means to confess Jesus Christ as Lord.

Jesus himself prayed in Gethsemane, "Thy will be done" (Matt. 26:39, 42, 44). Paul told the believers, "I urge you, brothers, by our Lord Jesus Christ and by the love of the Spirit, to join me in my struggle by praying to God for me. Pray that I may be rescued from the unbelievers in Judea and that my service in Jerusalem may be acceptable to the saints there, so that by God's will I may come to you with joy and together with you be refreshed" (Rom. 15:30–32). We are to pray and God will answer either "Yes," "No," or "Wait." When Paul prayed about going to Rome, God told him to wait, so Paul kept on praying. Paul speaks of this interval: "*I do not want you to be unaware, brothers, that I planned many times to come to you (but have been prevented from doing so until now) in order that I might have a harvest among you, just as I have had among the other Gentiles*" (Rom. 1:13).

As the apostle Paul prayed and planned to go to Rome, he sought God's counsel. Yet he was prevented from going for several years. At the end of this epistle, he reveals the reason to the Roman Christians:

> It has always been my ambition to preach the gospel where Christ was not known, so that I would not be building on someone else's foundation. Rather, as it is written: 'Those who were not told about him will see, and those who have not heard will understand.' This is why I have often been hindered from coming to you. But now that there is no more place for me to work in these regions, and since I have been longing for many years to see you, I plan to do so when I go to Spain. I hope to visit you while passing through and to have you assist me on my journey there, after I have enjoyed your company for a while. (Rom. 15:20–24)

God wanted Paul to evangelize the eastern Mediterranean region, specifically Asia, Macedonia, and Achaia. Having completed that task, Paul now begins to think that God will allow him to go to Rome.

God guides us to do his will in his time. Acts 16:6–10 describes how the Holy Spirit prevented Paul from preaching in certain places, and then guided him to preach in Macedonia. God even permits Satan to stop us (1 Thess. 2:18). God also permits circumstances, such as sickness, to prevent us from doing certain things. But in his time God will guide us to work where he wants us to. A Christian is led by the Spirit of God.

Eventually, in God's time, Paul arrived in Rome. But he did not get there exactly as he expected. He had planned to go after visiting the church in Jerusalem: "Paul decided to go to Jerusalem, passing through Macedonia and Achaia. 'After I have been there,' he said, 'I must visit Rome also'" (Acts 19:21). But in Jerusalem he was arrested, beaten, and bound. The day after he was thrown into the barracks in Jerusalem, God encouraged him: "The following night the Lord stood near Paul and said, 'Take courage! As you have testified about me in Jerusalem, so you must also testify in Rome'" (Acts 23:11). After this, Paul was sent to Caesarea, where he languished in prison for two years. Then he was put on a ship bound for Rome, but on the way the ship was caught in a great storm. Even then God ministered to Paul, who declared to the sailors, "Last night an angel of the God whose I am and whom I serve stood beside me and said, 'Do not be afraid, Paul. You must stand trial before Caesar'" (Acts 27:23). The ship was wrecked on Malta, and Paul and his companions had to wait three months until they could sail. Yet, finally, in God's will, Paul arrived in Rome. He came in shackles, as a prisoner of Caesar. We may not like the way God guides us, but if we are slaves of Christ, we will surrender totally to our Master to do whatever he wants.

The Purpose of His Visit

"I long to see you so that I may impart to you some spiritual gift to make you strong" (v. 11). Paul loved these Roman saints. Even though he had not met many of them, they were his brothers and sisters in Christ. Additionally, most of them were Gentiles, and he was called to be an apostle to the Gentiles. So he longed to see them that he might bless them, pray with them, pray for them, preach to them, teach them, counsel them, and enjoy their fellowship.

Paul was always a giver. He wanted to give these Roman Christians what he had received from God, especially the gospel. He wanted to strengthen and establish them in their faith by revealing to them the unsearchable riches of Christ as outlined in this letter. Babes must grow up and become adults. Miracles do not make us strong; it is the knowledge of God that strengthens us by rooting us in God and his great love. Dr. Lloyd-Jones says that those who are ignorant of God's word will remain spiritual butterflies[3]—ignorant, emotional, vacillating, self-focused, miserable, complaining, anxious, and silly. The Bible says God has gifted the church with apostles, prophets, evangelists, pastors and teachers, so that we may grow up and become strong spiritual adults, able to endure hardship and persevere to the end in the faith, fighting the good fight, running the race, and keeping the faith (Eph. 4:11–15; 2 Tim. 4:7; Heb. 12:7–11).

Christian fellowship is crucial because whenever we come together, we impart spiritual gifts that strengthen others. To each of us God has given grace that we may enrich one another. The church is a body with many members, each having a function designed to help the others. What we have received freely, we freely give. It is more blessed to give than to receive; when we receive more, we give more. Christian fellowship is giving and receiving for the edification of the whole body, both local and international.

As weak and easily discouraged people, we all need strength and encouragement from the Lord. We need to grow in the grace and knowledge of Jesus Christ. So we come together to strengthen and encourage one another with the grace God gives us.

Paul told the Ephesian elders: "Now I commit you to God and to the word of his grace, which can build you up and give you an inheritance among all those who are sanctified" (Acts 20:32). It is the word of God's grace that builds us up. He also wrote to the Thessalonian believers: "We sent Timothy, who is our brother and God's fellow worker in spreading the gospel of Christ, to strengthen and encourage you in your faith, so that no one would be unsettled by these trials" (1 Thess. 3:2–3). Spiritual gifts are designed to edify the body of Christ. Paul exhorts, "He who prophesies is greater than one who speaks in tongues, unless he

---

3   Lloyd-Jones, *Romans*, vol. 1, *Gospel of God*, 227.

interprets, so that the church may be edified. . . . So it is with you. Since you are eager to have spiritual gifts, try to excel in gifts that build up the church" (1 Cor. 14:5, 12; see also vv. 26, 31).

The writer to the Hebrews also speaks of the importance of maintaining Christian fellowship so that we may be built up: "See to it, brothers, that none of you has a sinful, unbelieving heart that turns away from the living God. But encourage one another daily, as long as it is called Today, so that none of you may be hardened by sin's deceitfulness" (Heb. 3:12–13).

We all need encouragement, including the apostle (see 1 Cor. 2:3; 2 Cor. 4:8–9; 11:28). So Paul adds that he longs to see the Romans *that you and I may be mutually encouraged by each other's faith* (v. 12). We encourage each other through our faith. If our faith is weak because we do not want to read and meditate on God's word and do what it says, then we cannot be of much use to others. Strong faith enables us to make others strong. The Bible says that without faith it is impossible to please God. Faith is the victory that overcomes the world. The strong faith of one person ministers to the little faith of another. Paul wanted to go to Rome, not to see the sights, but to see the saints. He wanted to fellowship with them and, through his gospel ministry, strengthen them and be strengthened by them. Do you have such craving to see and fellowship with God's people?

Paul said he wanted to visit the Roman believers to *have a harvest* among them (v. 13). He wanted to convert unbelievers in Rome, as well as encourage spiritual growth in believers. We serve God by serving one another, with the ultimate purpose that God the Father, the gardener, may receive fruit, more fruit, and much fruit, and be greatly pleased.

Paul planned to come to Rome in God's will at God's time to preach the gospel to the Roman Christians. In verse 15 he declares he is ready to come. He would go to Rome as a slave of Christ, separated unto the gospel of God as an apostle, especially to the Gentiles.

A Debtor to All the World

Paul says he is a debtor to the world: *"I am obligated both to Greeks and non-Greeks, both to the wise and the foolish. That is why I am so eager to preach the gospel also to you who are at Rome"* (vv. 14–15). The people called by God may be cultured or uncivilized, intelligent or ignorant—God does not discriminate. Grace pays our debts to God and makes all of us debtors to others.

Imagine that someone entrusts you with medicine to give to a person who will die without it, but you do not give the medicine to the person. That would be criminal. It would be a clear demonstration of the unloving nature of the human heart.

How dare we keep the gospel to ourselves when we are surrounded by starving multitudes! We owe them this bread of life. Not only were Paul and the other apostles debtors, but also pastors are debtors entrusted to preach the gospel. In fact, every believer is a debtor who needs to give the gospel message to those around him. We must say with the lepers who discovered bread during the famine of Samaria, "We're not doing right. This is a day of good news and we are keeping it to ourselves. . . . Let's go at once and report this to the royal palace" (2 Kings 7:9).

All must hear the gospel. "God so loved the world that he gave his one and only Son, that whoever believes in him shall not perish but have eternal life" (John 3:16). We are to be channels of blessing, not dams. We are to be like the River Jordan, blessing the land all around us, not like the Dead Sea. Let us, therefore, be eager to pay our debts. It is a great shame not to pay this debt of the gospel, because there is no other Savior but Jesus Christ, the crucified and risen Lord.

God has entrusted the gospel to us for the benefit of others. To Cornelius God said, "Go and call Peter. He will tell you the gospel" (Acts 10). To the disciples Jesus said, "Go and make disciples of all nations, baptizing them in the name of the Father and of the Son and of the Holy Spirit, and teaching them to obey everything I have commanded you. And surely I am with you always, to the very end of the age" (Matt. 28:19–20). The One who received all authority in heaven and on earth is with us to guide us, to protect us, to empower us, to provide for us, and to bring us safely home. So Paul says, "I am ready, eager, and willing to preach the gospel to you who are in Rome." He desires to pay his debt to the Romans.

I also was called to be a missionary and went from my home to the other end of the world. In God's will I came to this country, this state, this county, and this city to preach the gospel. God wanted me to impart some spiritual gift to you so that we may be strengthened by each other. Let us all, therefore, determine today to pay our gospel debt to all God brings our way. Let us do so for the glory of God, knowing that the gospel alone is the medicine for human sin. It is "the power of God for the salvation of everyone who believes: first for the Jew, then for the Gentile" (Rom. 1:16). May we love all God's people everywhere by interceding for them, rejoicing with them, suffering with them, and supporting them. May we enjoy our salvation and proclaim it to others through Jesus Christ our Lord.

3

The Glory of the Gospel

¹⁶I am not ashamed of the gospel, because it is the power of God for the salvation of everyone who believes: first for the Jew, then for the Gentile. ¹⁷For in the gospel a righteousness from God is revealed, a righteousness that is by faith from first to last, just as it is written: "The righteous will live by faith."

Romans 1:16–17

The moment we are saved by the gospel of Jesus Christ, we become indebted to all the peoples of the world to preach the gospel to them. Paul declared himself such a debtor and said that was why he was so eager to preach the gospel in the mighty city of Rome (Rom. 1:14–15). Now he gives the reason for his eagerness: *"I am not ashamed of the gospel, because it is the power of God for the salvation of everyone who believes: first for the Jew, then for the Gentile"* (v. 16).

The Offense of the Gospel

Paul probably had been tempted to be ashamed of the gospel at some point, for the gospel is "a stumbling block to Jews and foolishness to Gentiles" (1 Cor. 1:23). Sinful man minimizes his sin and maximizes his ability to save himself by his own righteousness. He glories in his homemade salvation—his philosophy, religion, materialism, science, asceticism, hedonism, morality, and social action. He hates to cry out, "Have mercy upon me, a sinner!" He refuses to confess that he is born a sinner and can only sin. He will not admit that he can do nothing before God to save himself and that he must be saved from God's wrath by God himself. But it is God alone who plans, accomplishes, and applies salvation effectually to every elect sinner.

Sinners hate and mock the gospel because it declares that there is none righteous. It says all have sinned and come short of the glory of God. The gospel declares that every sinner is born under the wrath of God and remains the object of his wrath. The wages of sin is eternal death, and man is dead in trespasses and sins. He cannot save himself because of his moral inability. He must repent of his sins and believe in God's plan of salvation by trusting in God's Son, who died on the cross for our sins. But sinful man resists this because he is offended by the gospel that first and foremost declares that he is born a sinner, practices sin, and is an enemy of God. Anyone who proclaims the gospel will experience persecution from such men.

Though Paul may have been tempted to be ashamed of the gospel, in fact he was not. He was ready to go to Rome, where powerful, civilized, educated, rich people such as Caesar and the Roman senators lived. Paul knew these were all sinners under God's wrath. Therefore, Paul was eager to go to the very heart of Rome to give them the gospel they so desperately needed.

If we preach the gospel, the world will heap shame upon us. If we speak about Jesus Christ in our school or university, we will experience instant mocking and persecution. If we are not mocked and persecuted, perhaps we have been ashamed of the gospel and are glorying in the world, with its power, pleasure, philosophy, and values.

What should we do when people mock and despise us? Jesus demonstrated how we should live. Hebrews 12:2 tells us that he despised the shame of the cross. That means he refused to let shame control him. In the same way, we too must despise the shame that comes to us from the world. Jesus counseled: "If anyone is ashamed of me and my words in this adulterous and sinful generation, the Son of Man will be ashamed of him when he comes in his Father's glory with the holy angels" (Mark 8:38). I am not worried about what the world says about the gospel and about me. I despise that shame. But I am concerned about the Son of Man being ashamed of me when he comes. I want my Lord Jesus to confess my name to the Father.

Young Timothy was ashamed of the gospel because he did not want to suffer for the cause of Christ. So Paul exhorted him, "Do not be ashamed to testify about our Lord, or ashamed of me his prisoner. But join with me in suffering for the gospel, by the power of God, who has saved us and called us to a holy life" (2 Tim. 1:8-9). Living and proclaiming the gospel will bring suffering to us, but we can endure that suffering by God's power. Paul also encouraged Timothy, saying, "For God did not give us a spirit of timidity, but a spirit of power, of love and of self-discipline" (2 Tim. 1:7). Jesus told his disciples, "You will receive power when the Holy Spirit comes on you; and you will be my witnesses" (Acts 1:8). A true child of God despises the world's shame and is eager to suffer for Christ's name, enabled by the Spirit of God upon him and knowing that God has given him eternal life. The world can only kill us, but our death will not destroy our eternal life. Jesus said, "I give them eternal life, and they shall never perish; no one can snatch them out of my hand. My Father, who has given them to me, is greater than all; no one can snatch them out of my Father's hand" (John 10:28-29). Secure in our salvation, we are not ashamed of the gospel.

Paul told Timothy: "That is why I am suffering as I am." Living, proclaiming, and sharing the gospel involves suffering, mocking, and shame. Suffering is inherent in the gospel. But he continued, "Yet I am not ashamed, because I know whom I have believed, and am convinced that he is able to guard what I have entrusted to him for that day" (2 Tim. 1:12). God will take care of us. We are secure in Christ, to whom we have committed our lives. Then Paul gives an illustration of a brother named Onesiphorus, who was not ashamed: "May the Lord show mercy to the household of Onesiphorus, because he often refreshed me and was not ashamed of my chains. On the contrary, when he was in Rome, he searched hard for me until he found me" (2 Tim. 1:16-17).

The gospel offends the pride of sinners. Yet we are not at liberty to remove the offense of the gospel as anti-supernaturalist theological liberals have done. They say, "Do not worry about that statement that Jesus is God. He was only a good man—the best man who ever lived." They have also removed all miracles from the Bible because they offend rationalist man. They would say man is not at all sinful, that man can save himself by doing social work, that there is no eternal hell, and that God is not wrathful but all love. They would say, in fact, that all are saved already; they only need to realize it. These people have taken away the offense of the gospel.

Those who preach the health and wealth gospel have also taken away the offense of the gospel. Such churches never say that man is a sinner under the wrath of God and that he must repent of his sins and believe in Jesus Christ who died on the cross for our sins. They only speak about how to make more money.

Surprisingly, many modern evangelical churches have also taken away the offense of the gospel. Such churches even take polls to find out what the people want the pastor to do. The results of such polls indicate that many people are more interested in certain styles of music than in preaching about sin, repentance, hell, the blood of Jesus, and living a holy life.

But when we take away the offense of the gospel, we are left with a gospel that will not save anyone. It is an impotent gospel that entombs people in their hell. Therefore, let the Athenians mock and call Paul a babbler for speaking about a poor carpenter who lived in Judea, was crucified by Roman soldiers, was raised from the dead, and is the Savior and Judge of the world. When Paul says, "I am not ashamed of the gospel," he means, "I am proud of the gospel. I glory in this glorious gospel." Romans 1:16–17 is the theme of this great epistle. Dr. Lloyd-Jones states, "I suppose that, in a sense, there are no two verses of greater importance in the whole Scripture than the two verses which we are now considering."[1]

Paul was not ashamed of the gospel. Are we? Those who are ashamed of the gospel are respectful of the world. They cannot and will not say, as Paul did, that "the world has been crucified to me, and I to the world" (Gal. 6:14). They love the world and are alive to it. Since they follow the world's ways, values, and pleasures, they are ashamed of the gospel.

The people of the world mock the Bible truths that affirm that the infinite personal God created all things. Instead, they believe in evolution. We affirm that there has been a moral fall, but again

---

1   Lloyd-Jones, *Romans*, vol. 1, *Gospel of God*, 257–58.

these people disagree and state that man is getting better all the time. They do not believe in the fall of man but in his ascent. We declare that God is redeeming the lost world, but these people say there is no need for redemption because there was no fall. We say there is a heaven and a hell; they say not only is there no heaven or hell, but that death is the end of our existence.

I hope we will not be impressed by the world, but will listen to what God says about this fallen world and its glory, rulers, powers, and philosophies. Paul writes, "We do, however, speak a message of wisdom among the mature, but not the wisdom of this age or of the rulers of this age, who are coming to nothing" (1 Cor. 2:6). Paul also asks, "Where is the wise man? Where is the scholar? Where is the philosopher of this age? Has not God made foolish the wisdom of the world?" (1 Cor. 1:20).

"This world in its present form is passing away" (1 Cor. 7:31). How many people are like Lot, buying real estate in Sodom! He pitches his tent near Sodom, then he moves closer to Sodom, and now he is living in Sodom as a judge. John warns, "Do not love the world or anything in the world. If anyone loves the world, the love of the Father is not in him. For everything in the world—the cravings of sinful man, the lust of his eyes and the boasting of what he has and does—comes not from the Father but from the world. The world and its desires pass away, but the man who does the will of God lives forever" (1 John 2:15–17). Peter also writes: "But the day of the Lord will come like a thief. The heavens will disappear with a roar; the elements will be destroyed by fire, and the earth and everything in it will be laid bare. . . . But in keeping with his promise we are looking forward to a new heaven and a new earth, the home of righteousness" (2 Pet. 3:10, 13). This world is going to be destroyed and a new world is coming. May we invest in the world to come!

Why was Paul glorying in the gospel and so eager to evangelize the whole world, including the capital of the Roman empire? He gives several reasons for not being ashamed of the gospel.

1. THE TRANSFORMING POWER OF THE GOSPEL

Paul experienced the power of the gospel in his own life. We will not witness to the gospel if we have never experienced its transforming power in our lives.

Paul had earlier considered himself, not a sinner, but a good man who was perfectly righteous by keeping the law. He did not think he needed a Savior. Yes, Paul had heard Stephen and others speak of Jesus crucified, buried, risen, and reigning. He opposed them all, persecuting and even killing some of them out of his hatred for Jesus. But on the road to Damascus, the risen Lord arrested and saved Paul, opening his eyes to the truth of his sinfulness and need of salvation. Now Paul acknowledged the Savior, Jesus of Nazareth, and God forgave all his sins. Jesus justified Paul by his own perfect righteousness and commissioned him to be his apostle to the Gentiles.

Paul speaks of this experience in his letter to the Philippian church: "If anyone else thinks he has reasons to put confidence in the flesh, I have more: circumcised on the eighth day, of the people of Israel, of the tribe of Benjamin, a Hebrew of Hebrews; in regard to the law, a Pharisee; as for zeal, persecuting the church; as for legalistic righteousness, faultless" (Phil. 3:4–6). This describes Paul before he was apprehended by Jesus. "But whatever was to my profit I now consider loss for the sake of Christ. What is more, I consider everything a loss compared to the surpassing greatness of knowing Christ Jesus my Lord, for whose sake I have lost all things. I consider them rubbish, that I may gain Christ and be found in him, not having a righteousness of my own that comes from the law, but that which is through faith in Christ—the righteousness that comes from God and is by faith" (Phil. 3:7–9). He also told the Galatians, "I have been crucified with Christ and I no longer live, but Christ lives in me. The life I live in the body, I live by faith in the Son of God, who loved me and gave himself for me. I do not set aside the grace of God, for if righteousness could be gained through the law, Christ died for nothing!" (Gal. 2:20–21). After being confronted and saved by Christ, "Saul spent several days with the disciples in Damascus. At once he began to preach in the synagogues that Jesus is the Son of God" (Acts 9:19–20). When we are saved and transformed by this mighty Christ, we too will open our mouths and declare the gospel.

If we are ashamed of the gospel, it is because we respect the world and its philosophies. But we must realize that this is a fallen world, destined to be destroyed. In fact, if we are ashamed of the gospel, we may not be Christians. If that is the case, we must believe on the Lord Jesus Christ and confess our sins, and he will save us from his wrath. When Jesus sets us free, we shall leap for joy and gladly proclaim the gospel, declaring, "I was blind but now I see; I was bound but now I am free; I was dead but now I live; I was depressed and helpless but now I rejoice in God my Savior, all because of Jesus." May all of us who have experienced this great salvation open our mouths to proclaim the gospel.

What type of sinner did Jesus save? We all have a tendency to minimize our sin. But when we minimize our sin, we also minimize the glory of Christ. Paul writes, "Here is a trustworthy saying that deserves full acceptance: Christ Jesus came into the world to save sinners—of whom I am the worst. But for that very reason I was shown mercy so that in me, the worst of sinners, Christ Jesus might display his unlimited patience as an example for those who would believe on him and receive eternal life" (1 Tim. 1:15–16). Paul says he is the worst of sinners. Yet Jesus saves the worst of sinners. Jesus Christ is a great and sufficient Savior. Elsewhere Paul asks, "Who shall separate us from the love of Christ?" (Rom. 8:35). The answer is nothing: "Neither death nor life . . . nor anything else in all creation, will be able to separate us from the love of God that is in Christ Jesus our Lord" (Rom. 8:38–39). We are in Christ, safe and secure from all alarm. Jesus has saved us from God's wrath. He saved us from the power and pollution of sin, and he will save us even from the presence of sin. When he comes again, he will give us glorious bodies like unto his own glorious body. He is going to create a new heaven and new earth wherein dwells righteousness.

2. The Gospel Is Good News

Paul also says he is not ashamed because this gospel is God's good news. We live in a fallen world in which we hear only bad news from morning till evening. The gospel is the light of God in our world of pitch moral darkness.

When Adam sinned, all sinned in him. The whole world fell. Sinful man can only sin all the time. So man is fallen, miserable, wretched, and unrighteous, as Paul proves throughout Romans 1:18–3:20. For example, in Romans 3 he writes,

"There is no one righteous, not even one; there is no one who understands, no one who seeks God. All have turned away, they have together become worthless; there is no one who does good, not even one."

"Their throats are open graves; their tongues practice deceit."

"The poison of vipers is on their lips."

"Their mouths are full of cursing and bitterness."

"Their feet are swift to shed blood; ruin and misery mark their ways, and the way of peace they do not know."

"There is no fear of God before their eyes." (Rom. 3:10–18)

But then he gives the good news: "But now a righteousness from God, apart from law, has been made known" (Rom. 3:21). The gospel is the shaft of light that enters the pitch moral darkness of this miserable world—the light that makes us alive, enables us to see, and causes us to look to God and be saved. The gospel light pierces through the darkness of the miseries of the world. God says, "Let there be light!" into our souls.

Yes, man is a guilty sinner, under the wrath of God. Man must die; he cannot save himself. Man needs the divine, infinite, perfect righteousness of God so that he may stand before God. All of man's philosophy, religion, science, military power, medicine, technology, politics, and morality fail to save him. There is no gospel in this world. We need the gospel that comes only from heaven. So Paul says, "I am not ashamed of the gospel." This epistle speaks of the gospel of God, the gospel concerning his Son Jesus Christ, who was crucified, buried, risen, ascended, seated, and is reigning as Sovereign Lord of the universe.

This gospel was promised in Isaiah: "How beautiful on the mountains are the feet of those who bring good news, who proclaim peace, who bring good tidings, who proclaim salvation, who say to Zion, 'Your God reigns!' . . . The Spirit of the Sovereign LORD is on me, because the LORD has anointed me to preach good news to the poor" (Isa. 52:7; 61:1). This good news promised in the Law and the Prophets is now manifested in Jesus. Every time the gospel is preached, the righteousness of God is revealed to us.

God has brought good news for man from heaven, revealed in the person and work of Christ. Luke writes: "And there were shepherds living out in the fields nearby, keeping watch over their flocks at night. An angel of the Lord appeared to them, and the glory of the Lord shone around them, and they were terrified. But the angel said to them, 'Do not be afraid. I bring you [the gospel] good news of great joy that will be for all the people. Today in the town of David a Savior has been born to you; he is Christ the Lord" (Luke 2:8–11).

3. THE POWER OF GOD UNTO SALVATION

Another reason Paul is not ashamed of the gospel is that it is *"the power of God for the salvation of everyone who believes"* (v. 16). Every sinner is born drowning in the ocean of divine wrath. Not only is he alienated from God and from his neighbors, but he is divided and depressed in himself, all because of sin. Fearful man is always running away from God. He is banished from God and his blessings. Not only does he not love God and his fellow man, but he harbors enmity toward them. He hates his own brother enough to kill him.

Man needs to be saved from God's wrath and from his own sin and death. He needs to be brought back to God. He must deal with his sin problem that prevents him from coming into God's glorious presence, so that he can enjoy eternal life and everlasting communion with God. All religions except Christianity speak of a manmade salvation that cannot save anyone. God's salvation is revealed only in the gospel. God promises to save us and unleash his power toward us that it may save us. The gospel does not just make salvation possible; the gospel saves sinners.

We need to be saved from the wrath of God (Rom. 5:9), from hostility to God (Rom. 5:10), from alienation from God and man (Eph. 2:12), from sin (Matt. 1:21), from being lost (Luke 19:10), from the frustration and futility of our life (1 Pet. 1:18), from the yoke of slavery (Gal. 5:1), from demon possession (Luke 8:36), from sickness (Luke 8:48), from danger (Matt. 8:25–26), and from this corrupt generation (Acts 2:40).

Every sinner has especially two needs, which God's powerful salvation satisfies—the need for forgiveness and the need for righteousness. When God regenerates us and gives us a new nature, we are experiencing conversion. God justifies, adopts, sanctifies, and glorifies us. The Holy Spirit dwells in us to enlighten, teach, and empower us to live lives pleasing in his sight. Jesus came that we may have life and have it to the full. The gospel is speaking about abundant salvation—not a little bit, but fullness of salvation. It is far beyond forgiveness. It is speaking about having the blessing of communion with God. The gospel Paul proclaims is the gospel that saved us, saves us, and will save us. We were saved by Jesus in the past when we heard the gospel and trusted in him. Jesus is saving us now by sanctifying us. And in the future, Jesus is going to glorify us. This is full-orbed salvation. Our bodies and souls are saved, qualified, and fitted to stand in the presence of the glorious, all-holy God. God said, "Be ye holy as I am holy." It is he who makes us holy.

Later in this epistle Paul writes, "And we know that in all things God works for the good of those who love him, who have been called according to his purpose. For those God foreknew he also predestined to be conformed to the likeness of his Son, that he might be the firstborn among many brothers. And those he predestined, he also called; those he called, he also justified; those he justified, he also glorified" (Rom. 8:28–30). Jesus has become for us "righteousness, holiness and redemption," that is, glorification (1 Cor. 1:30).

4. THE POWER OF GOD

Paul is not ashamed of the gospel because it is "*the power of God*" (v. 16). The gospel is a manifestation of the mighty power of God. Elsewhere Paul says, "God did not give us a spirit of timidity, but a spirit of power" (2 Tim. 1:7). Jesus said, "You will receive power when the Holy Spirit comes on you; and you will be my witnesses in Jerusalem, and in all Judea and Samaria, and to the ends of the earth" (Acts 1:8). God empowers us to declare the gospel, which comes with power to save sinners. When told she would bear a child, the virgin Mary asked the angel, "How will this be, since I am a virgin?" He answered, "The Holy Spirit will come upon you, and the power of the Most High will overshadow you" (Luke 1:34–35). The power of the mighty God, who created and sustains the universe, would accomplish it.

Paul often spoke of the power of God. To the Ephesians he wrote: "I pray also that the eyes of your heart may be enlightened in order that you may know . . . his incomparably great power for us who believe. That power is like the working of his mighty strength, which he exerted in Christ when he raised him from the

dead and seated him at his right hand in the heavenly realms"
(Eph. 1:18–20; see also 2:5–6; 3:7, 20). If the Holy Spirit is in us,
then God's power is in us, and we are powerful people who are
able to resist the devil and cause him to flee. We do not need
to yield to temptation, but can put up a fight by the power of
the Holy Spirit.

Wherever the gospel is proclaimed, God's power is unleashed
and succeeds in saving his people. Paul writes, "For the message
of the cross is foolishness to those who are perishing, but to us
who are being saved it is the power of God. . . . To those whom
God has called, both Jews and Greeks, Christ [is] the power of
God and the wisdom of God" (1 Cor. 1:18, 24). The gospel is the
power of God because Christ is the power of God. Where the
gospel is preached, the power of Christ is present to save us. The
gospel is not *about* God's power; it *is* God's power.

Paul later declares, "Therefore, there is now no condemnation
for those who are in Christ Jesus, because through Christ Jesus
the law of the Spirit of life set me free from the law of sin and
death. For what the law was powerless to do in that it was
weakened by the sinful nature, God did by sending his own Son"
(Rom. 8:1–3). What our self-righteousness could not do, God did.
Whenever the gospel is proclaimed, the power of God saves and
strengthens God's people. The gospel is God's saving power. It
planned our redemption, accomplished that redemption in Jesus
on the cross, and applies that redemption to every elect sinner by
the operation of the Spirit of the living God.

Jesus himself spoke of this working of God's power: "No one
can come to me unless the Father who sent me draws him"
(John 6:44). As sinners, we have moral inability. On our own,
we cannot come to God; in fact, we run away from him. God
himself must draw us to him by his omnipotence. When he does
so, we will come and call upon the name of the Lord to be saved.
Jesus explains, "This is why I told you that no one can come to
me unless the Father has enabled him" (John 6:65). The power
of God must work in us. And not only does the Father draw
us, but the Son does so as well: "But I, when I am lifted up
from the earth, will draw all men to myself" (John 12:32). So the
Father draws, Christ draws, and the Holy Spirit draws. When that
happens, we come to be set free, forgiven, justified, and adopted.

May we meditate upon this power of God that can help us as we daily meet with temptation!

The Lord spoke through Isaiah about this power to save us by the proclamation of his word: "As the rain and the snow come down from heaven, and do not return to it without watering the earth and making it bud and flourish, so that it yields seed for the sower and bread for the eater, so is my word that goes out from my mouth: It will not return to me empty, but will accomplish what I desire and achieve the purpose for which I sent it" (Isa. 55:10–11). When the gospel is preached, God is sending it to save, heal, and strengthen us.

Listen to the language of Paul: "Our gospel came to you not simply with words, but also with power, with the Holy Spirit and with deep conviction. . . . And we also thank God continually because, when you received the word of God, which you heard from us, you accepted it not as the word of men, but as it actually is, the word of God, which is at work in you who believe" (1 Thess. 1:5; 2:13). The gospel is God's power directed to save us. I once knew an accomplished, highly educated atheist, who would listen to the preaching of the gospel, all the while fuming and breathing out fire, anger, and misery. But in time the gospel saved him. The gospel overcomes all our resistance and inabilities. It saves us, as it also saved Paul, the chief of sinners.

The gospel is the power of God to raise the dead. Jesus once was going to the village of Nain and saw a funeral procession for a young man. The dead man had no father and his poor widowed mother was grieving. But as they were taking this man out to bury him, Jesus came by and insisted, "Young man, I say to you, get up!" and he got up (Luke 7:11–15). John also tells us about Lazarus, the friend of Jesus, who died and was buried four days before Jesus came. But Jesus told Lazarus' sister, "I am the resurrection and the life." And when he came to the tomb where the body lay, Jesus cried out in a loud voice, "Lazarus, come forth!" The dead man came forth, still bound in the grave clothes (John 11:1–44).

God raises the dead—not just those who are physically dead, but us who are dead in sins and trespasses. In Ephesians 2:1–10, Paul speaks about spiritually dead people who are ruled by the evil spirit. They are disobedient objects of God's wrath, but God makes them alive and seats them in the heavenly places to rule with Christ. This is what the gospel of God can do to us. We do not have to continue in our misery and death.

Paul was not ashamed of the gospel, for it is the power of God. He was ready to go to Rome, this great city that was known for power. Rome, however, was a slave to sin, as we learn when we study its culture and the lives of its Caesars and senators.

The power of the gospel sets sinners free. It is the saving power of God that regenerates, justifies, sanctifies, glorifies, and restores us to God forever. If you have experienced this power, be proud of the gospel and boldly proclaim it. If you have not experienced its saving power, believe on the Lord Jesus Christ, who fulfilled all God's law in behalf of us by his life, death, and resurrection. He will save you fully and he will save you now.

> The vilest offender who truly believes,
> that moment from Jesus a pardon receives.

Christ will set you free of the shackles of sin, guilt, Satan, death, hell, and the world. Jesus calls, "Look unto me and live!" Do not look to yourself and be miserable. Look to Christ and live, and be not ashamed of the gospel.

5. FOR EVERYONE WHO BELIEVES

The next reason Paul gives for not being ashamed of the gospel is that it is *"for the salvation of everyone who believes"* (v. 16). Every son of Adam, whether Jew or Gentile, man or woman, wise or foolish, master or slave, rich or poor, civilized or uncivilized, is born a sinner and practices sin. Paul writes, "There is no one righteous, not even one; there is no one who understands, no one who seeks God. . . . All have sinned and fall short of the glory of God" (Rom. 3:10, 23). We all lack the righteousness that God demands, which is perfect obedience to God's law in its entirety all the time. Romans 1:18 tells us God's wrath is being revealed against all the ungodliness and unrighteousness of men. Self-help salvation cannot help us.

But God has given us his way of salvation, and it is for all the people of the world. The gospel does not discriminate. The children's song is true:

> Jesus loves the little children, all the children of the world—
> red and yellow, black and white—they are precious in his sight;
> Jesus loves the little children of the world.

In John 3 we read, "Just as Moses lifted up the snake in the desert, so the Son of Man must be lifted up, that everyone who believes in him may have eternal life. For God so loved the world that he gave his one and only Son, that whoever believes in him shall not perish but have eternal life" (John 3:14–16). Joel proclaims, "Everyone who calls on the name of the LORD will be saved" (Joel 2:32). The gospel invitation is for everyone: "Whoever is thirsty, let him come; and whoever wishes, let him take the free gift of the water of life" (Rev. 22:17). Jesus exhorts, "Come to me, all you who are weary and burdened, and I will give you rest" (Matt. 11:28).

> His blood can make the foulest clean,
> his blood availed for me.

The church is an international body of people. We all are brothers and sisters in Christ, no matter what our background is. The gospel does not discriminate. Paul writes, "Brothers, think of what you were when you were called. Not many of you were wise by human standards; not many were influential; not many were of noble birth. But God chose the foolish things of the world to shame the wise; God chose the weak things of the world to shame the strong. He chose the lowly things of this world and the despised things—and the things that are not—to nullify the things that are, so that no one may boast before him" (1 Cor. 1:26–29; see also Luke 6:20). In fact, publicans and prostitutes often enter into the kingdom of God before scribes and Pharisees.

The gospel is for everyone. No one is superior to another before God. Paul assured the Gentile believers in Ephesus that they were "no longer foreigners and aliens, but fellow citizens with God's people and members of God's household" (Eph. 2:19). Through the gospel, Gentiles are heirs together with Israel, members together of one body and sharers together in the promise in Christ Jesus. We are all brothers; there is no superiority or inferiority. "You are all sons of God through faith in Christ Jesus, for all of you who were baptized into Christ have clothed yourselves with Christ.

There is neither Jew nor Greek, slave nor free, male nor female, for you are all one in Christ Jesus" (Gal. 3:26–28).

This idea that the gospel is for everyone is the basis for world missions. Jesus told his disciples, "You will receive power when the Holy Spirit comes on you; and you will be my witnesses in Jerusalem, and in all Judea and Samaria, and to the ends of the earth" (Acts 1:8). Jesus also declared, "This gospel of the kingdom will be preached in the whole world as a testimony to all nations, and then the end will come. . . . Therefore go and make disciples of all nations, baptizing them in the name of the Father and of the Son and of the Holy Spirit, and teaching them to obey everything I have commanded you" (Matt. 24:14; 28:19–20).

6. THE RIGHTEOUSNESS OF GOD

The next reason Paul gives for not being ashamed gets to the very heart of the gospel: *"For in the gospel a righteousness from God is revealed"* (v. 17). God is righteous, but we are all unrighteous. God's wrath is being revealed against all ungodliness and unrighteousness of men (Rom. 1:18).

Many try to cover themselves with a pretension of self-righteousness, but their efforts are like covering nakedness with a fig-leaf apron. Human self-righteousness cannot stand up against the gaze of the righteous God. He is unimpressed by our pretended self-righteousness. It is a stench in God's nostrils (Isa. 64:6).

In fact, God condemns human self-righteousness. The prodigal who confessed his sins to his father received his father's best robe in place of his dirty rags (Luke 15:21–22). In the parable of the wedding banquet, the king noticed a poor beggar not wearing the freely provided wedding clothes. This beggar stands for a self-righteous man who says, "I did it my way." But he was tied hand and foot and thrown outside into the darkness of everlasting hell (Matt. 22:1–14).

Our own righteousness is utterly reprehensible before God. Paul writes, "Since they did not know the righteousness that comes from God and sought to establish their own, they did not submit to God's righteousness" (Rom. 10:3). But in the gospel a righteousness from God, the perfect righteousness demanded by God, the righteousness of Jesus Christ based on his perfect obedience to God's law, is revealed to meet our need. Away with our filthy fig-leaf aprons and stinking dung righteousness! Come to God in Jesus Christ and receive the gift of righteousness from God (Rom. 5:17). So Paul says, "For just as through the disobedience of the one man the many were made sinners, so also through the obedience of the one man the many will be made righteous" (Rom. 5:19). God's righteousness comes through the gospel as a gift to all naked, sinful, rotten people.

Paul, who understood the difference between his self-righteousness and God's righteousness, explains, "If anyone else thinks he has reasons to put confidence in the flesh, I have more." After listing all his reasons, he concludes that he was "as for legalistic righteousness, faultless" (Phil. 3:4–6). Paul thought he was righteous! But after having a revelation of God's Son on the road to Damascus, he writes, "Whatever was to my profit I now consider loss for the sake of Christ. What is more, I consider everything a loss compared to the surpassing greatness of knowing Christ Jesus my Lord, for whose sake I have lost all things. I consider them rubbish [dung], that I may gain Christ and be found in him, not having a righteousness of my own that comes from [my keeping] the law, but that which is through faith in Christ—the righteousness that comes from God and is by faith" (Phil. 3:7–9). Our need is righteousness, and the gospel contains this great gift that we need.

It is also the righteousness by which Abraham was justified. Paul asks, "What does the Scripture say? 'Abraham believed God, and it was credited to him as righteousness'" (Rom. 4:3). It is the righteousness by which David was justified: "David says the same thing when he speaks of the blessedness of the man to whom God credits righteousness apart from works: . . . 'Blessed is the man whose sin the Lord will never count against him'" (Rom. 4:6, 8). Our sin is not counted against us because it is counted against another—Jesus, our mediator, substitute, and representative. It is also the righteousness by which the Old Testament prophet Habakkuk lived: "The righteous will live by his faith" (Hab. 2:4), a verse Paul quoted in Romans 1:17. All Old Testament saints lived by this righteousness.

Luther first misunderstood this righteousness of God as revealed in Romans 1:17. He thought it was the righteous nature of God by which he justly punishes sinners, as we read in Romans 2:5: "But because of your stubbornness and your unrepentant heart, you are storing up wrath against yourself for the day of God's wrath, when his righteous judgment will be revealed." Luther did not see any good news in the gospel because of this misunderstanding. In fact, he hated Romans 1:17 because it blocked the way to paradise for him.

Yet as he studied the Habakkuk 2:4 quotation, Luther eventually saw Romans 1:17 as the gateway to paradise. He came to understand that it is speaking about a righteousness from God provided to us as a gift. So he writes, "For God does not want to save us by our own [righteousness] but by an extraneous righteousness, one that does not originate in ourselves but comes to us from beyond ourselves, which does not arise on earth but comes from heaven."[2] It is a *iustitia aliena*, an alien righteousness. It is the righteousness of Jesus Christ, who fully obeyed God's laws by his life and death. Jesus Christ lived for us, died for us, and lives for us. Paul says Christ died for our sins and was raised for our justification (Rom. 4:25). Jesus Christ is our righteousness, sanctification, and glorification (1 Cor. 1:30).

Paul writes about the double transaction between elect sinners and Christ: "God was reconciling the world to himself in Christ, not counting men's sins against them" (2 Cor. 5:19). This is what David said: "Blessed is the man whose sin the Lord does not count against him" (Ps. 32:2; Rom. 4:8). David understood his sins were not counted against him because of the bloody sacrifices offered at the temple. But for God to justify us justly, our sins must be punished, because God is righteous. Paul then reveals against whom God counts our sins: "God made him who had no sin to be sin for us, so that in him we might become the righteousness of God" (2 Cor. 5:21). Christ took our sins upon himself, not even that we might be righteous, but that we might become the righteousness of God. Here we see the double imputation. The totality of our guilt and its punishment was put on him and into his account, and his perfect righteousness is put into our account.

The Perfect Righteousness of Christ

Jesus is our atonement, and his perfect righteousness is ours. Because God's law can demand nothing more from Jesus, it

2   Quoted by Hendriksen, *Exposition of Romans*, 62.

can demand nothing more from us. Jesus lived a life of perfect obedience to God. He told the Jews, "The one who sent me is with me; he has not left me alone, for I always do what pleases him. . . . Can any of you prove me guilty of sin?" (John 8:29, 46). No one could. When he came to John for baptism, "John tried to deter him, saying, 'I need to be baptized by you, and do you come to me?' Jesus replied, 'Let it be so now; it is proper for us to do this to fulfill all righteousness'" (Matt. 3:14–15). He told his disciples, "Do not think that I have come to abolish the Law or the Prophets; I have not come to abolish them but to fulfill them" (Matt. 5:17).

Jesus came to do the will of his Father. When Christ came into the world, he declared, "Here I am—it is written about me in the scroll—I have come to do your will, O God" (Heb. 10:7). God's will was for Jesus to redeem his people through his death on the cross. Paul writes, "But when the time had fully come, God sent his Son, born of a woman, born under law, to redeem those under law, that we might receive the full rights of sons. . . . Christ redeemed us from the curse of the law by becoming a curse for us, for it is written: 'Cursed is everyone who is hung on a tree.' He redeemed us in order that the blessing given to Abraham might come to the Gentiles through Christ Jesus, so that by faith we might receive the promise of the Spirit" (Gal. 4:4–5; 3:13–14).

Not only did Christ keep the law, but he also redeemed us from being under the law of sin and death. God in Christ liberated us. Having died to sin and law, we are no longer subject to them. We can sing,

Jesus, thy blood and righteousness
my beauty are, my glorious dress.

Arrayed in this *iustitia aliena*, we now can come into God's presence. God demands a righteous standard, which he achieves for us through the atoning sacrifice of Jesus. As unrighteous people, we need a righteous standing before a righteous God, and God provides just that—an infinite, perfect, everlasting righteousness of Jesus Christ that God accepts. Jesus is our righteousness.

We find this illustrated in the Old Testament in Zechariah 3, where we find a court scene. God the Father is the judge and the high priest Joshua stands before him. On Joshua's right hand is

Satan, accusing him before God, saying, in essence, "This one is unfit to make sacrifices because he is filthy and clothed in filthy clothes. Joshua is sinful, unclean, unrighteous." Though Satan is the father of lies, in this case he is telling the truth. But there is someone else standing by Joshua—it is the angel of the Lord. I believe he is the pre-incarnate Son of God, our advocate before Satan.

Zechariah writes, "Now Joshua was dressed in filthy clothes as he stood before the angel. The angel said to those who were standing before him, 'Take off his filthy clothes.' Then he said to Joshua, 'See, I have taken away your sin, and I will put rich garments on you'" (Zech. 3:3–4). Here we see the double transaction. Joshua got rid of his filthy garments—all of his sin, guilt, punishment, and hell were taken off instantly. Then Joshua was clothed with clean, rich, glorious garments, which stand for the righteousness of God and right standing with him.

Then the angel said to Joshua: "Listen, O high priest Joshua and your associates seated before you, who are men symbolic of things to come: I am going to bring my servant, the Branch. . . . I will remove the sin of this land in a single day" (Zech. 3:8, 9). This Branch is God's Son, who arrived in Jerusalem on Palm Sunday. And in one single day Jesus Christ removed our sin by his death on the cross.

The Lord called Joshua a burning stick snatched from the fire of God's wrath (Zech. 3:2). God in Jesus Christ plucked us also out of the fire of his own wrath against us, took off our filthy clothes of sin, guilt, and hell, and dressed us in clean, rich, and glorious garments.

The Lord also spoke through Isaiah about this alien righteousness: "I am bringing my righteousness near, it is not far away; and my salvation will not be delayed" (Isa. 46:13). Without righteousness, there is no salvation. But whose righteousness and salvation are these? Look at the rest of the sentence: "I will grant salvation to Zion, my splendor to Israel." God grants his splendor, righteousness, and salvation to us *gratis*, and we have received it. And in Isaiah 62:1 he says, "For Zion's sake I will not keep silent, for Jerusalem's sake I will not remain quiet, till her righteousness shines out like the dawn, her salvation like a blazing torch." God's righteousness in Jesus Christ comes to Zion like a blazing torch. Paul also writes of this: "Husbands, love your wives, just as Christ loved the church and gave himself up for her to make her holy, cleansing her by the washing with water through the word, and to present her to himself as a radiant church, without stain or wrinkle or any other blemish, but holy and blameless" (Eph. 5:25–27). We are radiant, clothed in God's righteousness and salvation.

This is illustrated also in the account of the Pharisee and the publican in Luke 18. The publican is a very wicked sinner who is convicted of his sin, yet he comes to the temple. Refusing to look up, he beats his breast under conviction of sin, at the same time exercising faith in God's provision of propitiation. He cries out, "O God, be propitiatory to me. May my sins be atoned for by a substitutionary sacrifice." Jesus said he went home justified, clothed in an alien righteousness. But the Pharisee clung to his dung of self-righteousness and went home condemned.

Proud of the Gospel

Once we were proud of our fig-leaf aprons of self-righteousness with which we covered ourselves. Like Paul, we were proud of our own refuse. We gloried in it and paraded it before others, especially before the holy God. We even called ourselves perfect. But when God opened our eyes, we understood our own righteousness was like filthy rags and dung.

Now we are clothed with the garments of heavenly salvation. Should we be ashamed of the gospel? No, we are proud of the gospel that saves and changes us. We glory in it, live it, and proudly proclaim it. If we are ashamed of the gospel and not giving witness to Jesus Christ, either we are not saved by him or we consider the gospel inferior to what the world can give us.

If we have been saved by this gospel, it is time that we showed it. May we not glory in our bank account, our family, our job, or anything else, but in the gospel that saved us. Let us not be afraid of the world, but remember that the world is going to be destroyed. God told Cornelius to send for Simon Peter to come and declare the gospel to him and his family. God is not depending on angels. He depends on us to declare the gospel to the world. If we are saved, let us be proud of it and proclaim it.

4

The Wrath of God

[18]The wrath of God is being revealed from heaven against all the godlessness and wickedness of men who suppress the truth by their wickedness, [19]since what may be known about God is plain to them, because God has made it plain to them. [20]For since the creation of the world God's invisible qualities—his eternal power and divine nature—have been clearly seen, being understood from what has been made, so that men are without excuse.

Romans 1:18–20

One wonderful thing about studying through the Bible is that we cannot pick and choose: we must accept all God has given us. Romans 1:18–20 speaks about the holy wrath of God, which many people would prefer not to think about. Yet if we do not understand God's wrath, then we cannot appreciate God's salvation.

In our modern scientific, cultured, and multi-religious times, who believes in the wrath of God? Such disbelief is not new. Douglas Moo says, "Since the time of certain Greek philosophers the idea that God would inflict wrath on people has been rejected as incompatible with an enlightened understanding of the deity."[1] Moo adds that the heretic Marcion in the second century AD omitted "of God" from the phrase "the wrath of God" in Romans 1:18. This dislike of the wrath of God is an ancient problem.

According to Dr. Martyn Lloyd-Jones, the idea of a wrathful God is unthinkable to modern sophisticated Western man. To such

---

1   Moo, *Epistle to the Romans*, 99.

people, God is a God of love; a wrathful God is simply a projection of the idea of a stern Victorian father, or a relic of the bloodthirsty tribal Jehovah God of the Old Testament. He is certainly not the God of the chorus, "Sweet Jesus." Many evangelicals, on the other hand, affirm the wrath of God in theory, but they refuse to preach it for fear of alienating "cultured" churchgoers. Instead, they preach, "God loves you and has a wonderful plan for your life. Come to our church, where you will hear only great music and soothing messages."[2] Many twenty-first century preachers take polls to see what their people want to hear. People want to hear pastors preach about their felt needs: how to be happy; how to not worry; how to get rid of bad habits; how to lose weight; how to deal with loneliness, sexual frustrations, marital discord, co-dependency, and addictions to drugs, alcohol, sex, pornography, and credit card abuse. No one wants to hear about the wrath of God, the sinfulness of man, the atonement of Christ, the cross, repentance, saving faith, the fear of God, obedience to God's word, Satan, eternal judgment, or hell. They just want to be told that God loves them and will bless them, no matter what they do.

Paul, however, said he is a debtor to all the people of the world. He owed them the full gospel, including preaching about the wrath of God, and therefore he was eager to preach in Rome. Paul boldly declared that he was "not ashamed of the gospel, because it is the power of God for the salvation of everyone who believes: first for the Jew, then for the Gentile" (Rom. 1:16). The gospel of God reveals exactly what man needs—the righteousness of God.

Why does man lack the righteousness of God? We find the answer in Romans 1:18–20. God gave man knowledge of himself in the book of creation. So man knows the true God, yet he constantly suppresses that knowledge, refusing to worship and serve God. Therefore, the wrath of God is revealed against man—against his ungodliness and unrighteousness. The only deliverance from this wrath of God is for us to receive by faith the righteousness of God, which comes to us freely in the gospel.

---

2   Lloyd-Jones, Romans, vol. 1, Gospel of God, 328–29.

The Wrath of God

"The wrath of God is being revealed from heaven" (v. 18). Paul begins this passage speaking of the wrath of God. This wrath does not originate with man but with God. It is revealed from heaven (i.e., from God). Therefore, unlike human wrath or the devil's wrath, God's wrath is just, because it is of God.

The word "wrath" appears ten times in Romans; it is a controlling concept in this epistle. Yet many theologians do not like this idea of the personal wrath of God. They say that wrath results from an inevitable, impersonal process of cause and effect. They say that sin has consequences, but God has nothing to do with these consequences. The fact that "a man reaps what he sows" (Gal. 6:7) is merely an outworking of the laws of the universe.

The God of the Bible, however, is not passive but active. God is personally involved in the affairs of his world. And because he is holy, God must and does punish sinners. Yet because God is also love, he saves from his wrath certain sinners who repent and believe in his Son.

Surprisingly, the Bible speaks more about the wrath of God than the love of God. For example, the psalmist writes, "You alone are to be feared. Who can stand before you when you are angry? . . . Surely your wrath against men brings you praise, and the survivors of your wrath are restrained" (Ps. 76:7, 10). Hell brings praise to God. Elsewhere we are told, "We are consumed by your anger and terrified by your indignation. You have set our iniquities before you, our secret sins in the light of your presence. All our days pass away under your wrath; we finish our years with a moan" (Ps. 90:7–9). Paul explains, "But because of your stubbornness and your unrepentant heart, you are storing up wrath against yourself for the day of God's wrath, when his righteous judgment will be revealed" (Rom. 2:5).

God's wrath is his perfection, glory, and nature. It is his holy hostility toward all evil in sentient beings, both angels and humans. God's wrath expresses the settled and active opposition of his holy nature to everything that is evil. The God of the Bible is not both good and evil. John Murray says God's wrath is "the holy revulsion of God's being against that which is the contradiction of his holiness."[3]

To the Thessalonians Paul writes:

> God is just: He will pay back trouble to those who trouble you and give relief to you who are troubled, and to us as well. This will happen when the Lord Jesus is revealed from heaven in blazing fire with his powerful angels. He will punish those who do not know God and do not obey the gospel of our Lord Jesus. They will be punished with everlasting destruction and shut out from the presence of the Lord and from the majesty of his power. . . . They perish because they refused to love the truth and so be saved. For this reason God sends them a powerful delusion so that they will believe the lie and so that all will be condemned who have not believed the truth but have delighted in wickedness. (2 Thess. 1:6–9; 2:10–12)

Man knows the truth but he hates it, preferring evil and wickedness instead. Therefore the wrath of God is being revealed against him, as Jesus himself said (John 3:18–20). And because man hates truth, he hates the God of truth. The wrath of God is integral to authentic evangelism. If we evangelize without speaking of the wrath of God, we have not evangelized.

God's Wrath Is Revealed

Paul says this wrath of God "is being revealed." The Greek word is *apokaluptetai*, a present passive indicative. It denotes a continuous revelation of the wrath of God. Just as the righteousness of God is continually revealed in the preaching of the gospel, so the wrath of God is also being revealed continuously. These are two parallel yet antithetical revelations.

J. C. F. Schiller declares, "The history of the world is the judgment of the world."[4] The wrath of God is revealed first in our conscience. When we do wrong, we experience remorse, misery, and pain unless we have killed our conscience through ever-increasing sin. Second, we experience physical consequences. A lazy student becomes a poor student; a sexually promiscuous person reaps diseases and passes

---

3   Murray, *Epistle to the Romans*, 35.
4   Quoted by Bruce, *Letter of Paul to the Romans*, 79.

those diseases on to others; a drunkard ends up with poverty and destruction; an adulterer tears his or her family apart.

The fall of man introduced thorns, thistles, pests, pollution, pain, hard labor, restlessness, and universal death (Gen. 3). Because of Adam's sin, all are now subject to spiritual, physical, and eternal death. These are all consequences of the wrath of God against sinners.

The history of the world is full of examples of the wrath of God being revealed. Consider Noah's flood and the fire that destroyed Sodom and Gomorrah. Look at the history of the Canaanites. When their iniquity reached its fullness, God wiped them out (Gen. 15:16; Deut. 9:5). Look at the history of the children of Israel, who were exiled because of their sin. The history of the world is a history of divine judgment (Dan. 2). Yet man refuses to recognize God as the Lord of history.

What about personal health? Paul writes, "That is why many among you are weak and sick, and a number of you have fallen asleep" (1 Cor. 11:30). Paul gives instructions about the man who was living with his father's wife: "Hand this man over to Satan, so that the sinful nature may be destroyed and his spirit saved on the day of the Lord" (1 Cor. 5:5). Many people's physical sicknesses can result from sin.

Additionally, we experience moral degeneration (Rom. 1:24, 26, 28). Paul says that because of their rejection of God, some people are handed over by God to a depraved mind to do whatever they want to do. People do not always engage in continuous immorality on their own. Such behavior can be a judgment of God. He sometimes hands unrepentant sinners over to their evil desires.

We cannot understand the cross of Christ without first understanding the wrath of God, because the cross not only reveals the love of God but also the wrath of God against sin. On the cross, God's wrath against his elect sinners was poured out on the One who knew no sin.

God is revealing his wrath every day to every person, family, and nation: "God is a righteous judge, a God who expresses his wrath every day" (Ps. 7:11). The Bible says all sinners are by nature objects of God's wrath (Rom. 9:22; Eph. 2:3).

Another manifestation of God's wrath is the public administration of justice by the state. Paul writes of the governing authority, "For he is God's servant to do you good. But if you do wrong, be afraid, for he does not bear the sword for nothing. He is God's servant, an agent of wrath to bring punishment on the wrongdoer" (Rom. 13:4).

God's wrath will be demonstrated on the final day of judgment. The resurrection of Jesus Christ itself reveals the wrath of God: "In the past God overlooked such ignorance, but now he commands all people everywhere to repent. For he has set a day when he will judge the world with justice [to mete out his wrath] by the man he has appointed [Jesus Christ]. He has given proof of this to all men by raising him from the dead" (Acts 17:30–31). Every time we preach about Christ's resurrection, we are also declaring that one day God's wrath will be poured out by this same Jesus upon all who are unrepentant, arrogant, rebellious, and fearless toward God.

Against All Ungodliness and Wickedness

Paul says this wrath is being revealed "*against all the godlessness and wickedness of men*" (v. 18). God's wrath is revealed against all sinners and every sin we commit. Every sin is called to account; not even one is exempt from God's just and holy wrath. In Romans 1:18–3:20 we see God's history of human sinfulness, not man's history of man. This is God's true history by the inspiration of the Holy Spirit.

God sees man in Adam, a sinner. Man's greatest problem is his wicked heart that rejects God. Because of this innate evil, man engages in wickedness against God, others, and, ultimately, himself. Jesus clearly identified this problem of the human heart, which exists no matter how sophisticated, educated, or religious a person is:

> Don't you see that nothing that enters a man from the outside can make him "unclean"? For it doesn't go into his heart but into his stomach, and then out of his body. . . . What comes out of a man is what makes him "unclean." For from within, out of men's hearts, come evil thoughts, sexual immorality, theft, murder, adultery, greed, malice, deceit, lewdness, envy, slander, arrogance and folly. All these evils come from inside and make a man "unclean." (Mark 7:18–23)

God's wrath is revealed daily against this godlessness of man. "The fool says in his heart, 'There is no God'" (Ps. 14:1). A godless man is a fool who negates God. The word of man becomes his standard, so that he can be god and do whatever he pleases. The philosophical foundation of every sinner is a negation of God and his law. If God does not exist, we can do whatever we please.

Godlessness, therefore, comes before evil deeds. The essence of sin is godlessness, which is the mother of all wickedness. Without godliness, morality is impossible in the world. If we hate God, we will hate others and, ultimately, we will hate ourselves. Paul summarizes it this way: "There is no fear of God before their eyes" (Rom. 3:18). In other words, they lack the fear of God, which keeps them from sinning. They think, "If God is not, I am free to do whatever I want." But all sin is against God. David said: "Against you, you only, have I sinned" (Ps. 51:4). All sin is finally against God because sin is the violation of God's law. Everyone sins against God and his word. Godlessness is seen in idolatry, which in turn produces immorality.

All Men Know God

Paul then tells us that this fallen, godless, wicked man knows God (Rom. 1:19-20). Man cannot plead ignorance of God, for God himself gave man a revelation of himself. God reveals himself in creation and he created man with a capacity to know God in creation. Therefore fallen man knows God. *What may be known about God is plain to them, because God has made it plain to them* (v. 19). If God has made it plain, do you think anyone can say to God, "You failed in making it plain to me"? Even fallen man has the capacity to know God from God's works that surround us every moment. God has not failed in revealing this knowledge to man. This means that every human being, whether rich or poor, man or woman, young or old, slave or free, knows God. No one is ignorant of God, and everyone is accountable to him every day and on the last day.

We cannot see the invisible God; he is infinite spirit and we are fallen, finite creatures. Yet God has graciously revealed himself to us in creation. *For since the creation of the world God's invisible qualities—his eternal power and divine nature—have been clearly*

53

seen, *being understood from what has been made, so that men are without excuse*" (v. 20). Just as we can look at a painting and the painter's signature, and discern something about the painter, so all men can observe creation and perceive God in his creation.

The psalmist exclaims, "O Lord, our Lord, how majestic is your name in all the earth! ... When I consider your heavens, the work of your fingers, the moon and the stars, which you have set in place, what is man that you are mindful of him, the son of man that you care for him? ... O Lord, our Lord, how majestic is your name in all the earth!" (Ps. 8:1, 3–4, 9). Psalm 19 also makes clear that God reveals himself through his creation: "The heavens declare the glory of God; the skies proclaim the work of his hands. Day after day they pour forth speech; night after night they display knowledge. There is no speech or language where their voice is not heard" (Ps. 19:1–3). Creation proclaims that God is! God is the holy, majestic, wise, and almighty Creator.

Through phenomena man discovers God's noumenal qualities. The first quality known of God is that he is a person. How can we be persons and God not be a person, since we are created in his image? God is an eternal person of eternal power. God is creator and has infinite wisdom. He is self-existing and independent of all his creation, yet he is also the sustainer of creation. And this God is holy: "Although they know God's righteous decree that those who do such things deserve death, they not only continue to do these very things but also approve of those who practice them" (Rom. 1:32). Since all can discern that this God is holy, all creatures must worship and serve this God. There can be no atheists in God's universe; everyone knows God. Greg Bahnsen quotes Calvin, "They cannot be conscious of themselves ... except they be at the same time conscious of God as their creator."[5]

Not only is the revelation of God all around man, but it is also within his own constitution as his conscience. John Frame states: "Natural revelation informs us of the existence of God, 'his eternal power and divine nature' (Rom. 1:20), and his moral law, that is, his norms (Rom. 1:32)."[6] It is authoritative revelation by which men will be judged. God has taken initiative to reveal himself to

---

5   Greg L. Bahnsen, Van Til's *Apologetic: Readings and Analyses* (Phillipsburg, NJ: Presbyterian and Reformed Publishing Company, 1998), 456.

6   Frame, *Doctrine of God*, 754.

man and has succeeded. Every man knows God and is accountable to him. Man has evidence of God's existence and his fundamental qualities. Therefore, when man sins, he is sinning against the knowledge he has. Thus, man's problem is not intellectual but moral. He refuses to worship and serve God. James Boice comments, "There is enough evidence of God in a flower to lead a child as well as a scientist to worship him."[7] We do not need to use a microscope to study a cell, or a telescope to study stars, to get this knowledge of God from creation. The entire creation itself tells us to look beyond nature to nature's Creator.

This is general revelation, meaning something that anyone in the world can understand. It is natural revelation, meaning revelation through the natural order, not the supernatural revelation we receive in Jesus Christ. It is also continuous revelation; it has been ongoing *since the creation of the world.*

Suppressing the Truth of God

What do unbelievers do with this knowledge that is continuously coming to them? *"[They] suppress the truth by their wickedness"* (v. 18). Paul uses the term *tēn alētheian*, meaning *"the truth (of God)."* Man knows the truth of God's existence and his basic qualities, and is supposed to love that truth and do it. But here we discover that man continuously and actively suppresses God's truth by actively doing wicked deeds. Man uses increasingly wicked acts to smother and, if possible, put out the fire of the knowledge of God that wells up within him.

As Adam and Eve sinned, so all fallen men also sin against the knowledge of God. When truth asserts itself, man suppresses it by evil deeds. He resists truth by doing more evil. In Romans 1:23, 25, 26, and 28 we read that man exchanges the truth that God exists for the lie that God is not. He does this so that he can freely engage in evil. Later in this epistle Paul tells us that man is an enemy of God (Rom. 5:10; 8:7), even though he experiences God's common grace daily. God's sun rises and his rain comes upon the wicked also. So Paul asks, "Do you show contempt for the riches of his kindness, tolerance and patience, not realizing that God's

---

7   Boice, *Romans*, vol. 1, *Justification by Faith*, 143.

kindness leads you toward repentance?" (Rom. 2:4). Paul spoke to the citizens of Lystra about God's common grace and provision of food for all his people (Acts 14:15–17). Yet after having received God's grace, men are interested in destroying this God whose common grace they experience daily.

Paul concludes that man is therefore *"without excuse"* (v. 20). He has no defense. Later Paul writes, "Now we know that whatever the law says, it says to those who are under the law, so that every mouth may be silenced" (Rom. 3:19). Every mouth will be stopped. Man cannot say he did not know about God. He has no excuse either this day or on the last. It is not as if man does not try to come up with excuses. In fact, he writes books and manufactures religions to deny the truth. These are but vain attempts to come up with an excuse not to acknowledge the true God. Man can defend himself before men, but he cannot defend himself before God.

We have no excuse for impiety and depravity: God's just and holy wrath is being revealed against the impious and the depraved daily.

The Good News

So far we have only spoken bad news. The true state of mankind is filled with darkness and gloom. But there is a beam of light that penetrates and overcomes the darkness. It is the revelation of the righteousness of God in Jesus Christ from heaven.

Is there any hope for the wicked? The answer from heaven is a resounding "Yes!" Jesus Christ, God's only Son, gave himself up for sinners on Calvary's cross. His death was propitiatory, for it turned God's wrath away from us and moved God to be gracious toward us. God the Father poured out his just and holy wrath that was against us, not upon us but upon his own Son, that he may be just in justifying the ungodly. Our sins are counted against Jesus, and his righteousness is put into our account.

Before he went to the cross, Jesus prayed, "My Father, if it is possible, may this cup be taken from me." Then he prayed, "Yet not as I will, but as you will" (Matt. 26:39). Finally he cried out the cry of dereliction: "My God, my God, why have you forsaken me?" (Matt. 27:46). The answer is, because God loves elect sinners.

God's wrath is just, holy, and certain. It must fall either on Jesus or on every sinner who refuses to trust in Christ. "Therefore, there is now no condemnation for those who are in Christ Jesus" (Rom. 8:1). If we have trusted in Christ, there is no longer any condemnation or death for us, but only justification and life. "Since we have now been justified by his blood, how much more shall we be saved from God's wrath through him!" (Rom. 5:9).

May God help us to rejoice in this great salvation! And may he grant authentic repentance and saving faith to all who are outside of Christ, all who are still objects of his just and holy wrath. May such people trust in the Son who suffered God's wrath for every believer.

5

The Giant Slide Down

[18]The wrath of God is being revealed from heaven against all the godlessness and wickedness of men who suppress the truth by their wickedness, [19]since what may be known about God is plain to them, because God has made it plain to them. [20]For since the creation of the world God's invisible qualities—his eternal power and divine nature—have been clearly seen, being understood from what has been made, so that men are without excuse.

[21]For although they knew God, they neither glorified him as God nor gave thanks to him, but their thinking became futile and their foolish hearts were darkened. [22]Although they claimed to be wise, they became fools [23]and exchanged the glory of the immortal God for images made to look like mortal man and birds and animals and reptiles.

[24]Therefore God gave them over in the sinful desires of their hearts to sexual impurity for the degrading of their bodies with one another. [25]They exchanged the truth of God for a lie, and worshiped and served created things rather than the Creator—who is forever praised. Amen.

[26]Because of this, God gave them over to shameful lusts. Even their women exchanged natural relations for unnatural ones. [27]In the same way the men also abandoned natural relations with women and were inflamed with lust for one another. Men committed indecent acts with other men, and received in themselves the due penalty for their perversion.

[28]Furthermore, since they did not think it worthwhile to retain the knowledge of God, he gave them over to a depraved mind, to do what ought not to be done. [29]They have become filled with every kind of wickedness, evil, greed and depravity. They are full of envy, murder, strife, deceit and malice. They are gossips, [30]slanderers, God-haters, insolent, arrogant and boastful; they invent ways of doing evil; they disobey their parents; [31]they are senseless, faithless, heartless,

ruthless. ³²Although they know God's righteous decree that those who do such things deserve death, they not only continue to do these very things but also approve of those who practice them.

Romans 1:18–32

Romans 1:18–32 describes man's giant slide down. Elsewhere we read, "In due time their foot will slip; their day of disaster is near and their doom rushes upon them" (Deut. 32:35). All who refuse to believe in the true God and his revelation of truth will experience a giant slide down to hell.

When a man closes his eyes to the light of God's truth and rejects the Creator who gave him a conscience, then God rejects that man. If we reject him, he will reject us, and we will slide downward into hell itself. We will be like Jonah, who refused to obey God. Instead, he went down—down to Joppa, down inside the ship, and down into the ocean, where he was swallowed up by a great fish. We will be like the rich man who, having rejected God's revelation in the Law and Prophets, went down to hell (Luke 16:19–31).

Adam rejected the God of truth and experienced the big slide (what we call the Fall). Since Adam's fall, every person who exchanges God's truth for a lie is on a giant slide down to hell. Is there any hope for those who are on this downward slide? Yes. The gospel is the power of God unto salvation to everyone who believes. We cannot lift ourselves up, but Jesus Christ came from heaven to rescue us from our hell.

As we learned in the previous chapter, man is not without knowledge of God. God has revealed himself and his invisible attributes both in creation and conscience. But man deliberately closes his eyes to truth. In fact, he continually suppresses it. He knows the true God, yet he refuses to glorify him by worshiping and obeying him. He refuses to thank him for all his gracious provisions (Rom. 1:21), so he becomes vain and worthless in his reasoning. He is incompetent to reason correctly because he reasons without God. He is like the ten spies who came back after forty days of inspecting Canaan. Not taking God into account, they spoke about defeat and destruction of God's people. Only Joshua and Caleb reasoned and spoke correctly. They did so because they had God in their minds. (Num. 13–14).

A man who rejects God is unable to understand truth because his heart is darkened. Since the Fall, man has been in spiritual darkness. He thinks he is enlightened; in fact, people generally speak positively about the "Enlightenment" period. But the heart of the Enlightenment was the rejection of the God of the Scriptures. Thus, we could truthfully call that time the Endarkenment. Man's heart was darkened, yet he knows truth. He knows God but exchanges the glory of God for idolatry (Rom. 1:23). He exchanges the truth of God for the lie of worshiping and serving creation. He prides himself on being wise, yet bows down in worship to creeping things. He exchanges the natural use of sexuality for the unnatural. Though he knows full well that those who do evil will go to hell, he keeps on sinning and celebrates others who do so also.

Man's problem, therefore, is not ignorance of God, for God himself has revealed truth to man and in man. Because of this revelation, man is accountable to live for the glory of God. Yet he refuses to do so and slides down to hell itself as he sins more and more.

How does God react to man's rejection of him and his word? God judges him. Paul writes, *"Therefore God gave them over in the sinful desires of their hearts to sexual impurity. . . . Because of this, God gave them over to shameful lusts. . . . Furthermore, since they did not think it worthwhile to retain the knowledge of God, he gave them over to a depraved mind"* (vv. 24, 26, 28). As we said before, God daily reveals his wrath against all the godlessness of men and is justly angry at sinners every day (Ps. 7:11). In judgment, therefore, God hands men over to the power of their sinful passions, to shame and uncleanness, to dishonor and abuse their bodies. He hands them over to the control of unnatural burning passions, including lesbianism and sodomy. He hands them over to a depraved mind that can never interpret reality correctly. God hands unbelieving haters of truth over to the power of a worthless mind, one that is incapable of thinking straight and delights in delusions. This is God's active, judicial action against all who reject their knowledge of him. Such men become fools, then filthy, and, finally, fighters against God and others.

Man Becomes a Fool

When we reject God and his light of truth, we become fools. "The fool says in his heart, 'There is no God'" (Ps. 14:1). He negates the greatest reality because of his reprobate mind. Therefore he is incapable of reasoning correctly and misinterprets reality. If a person reasons correctly, he will worship, serve, and thank God. Any person who does not glorify the true God of revelation is a fool, though he may think he is wise.

When we reject God, we become futile, fruitless, and purposeless. When an orange tree brings forth oranges, it is doing what it is supposed to do. When a man worships the true God, he is also fruitful because he is doing what his Creator wants him to do. But a sinning man is worthless, useless, and empty. He is a bad tree that can produce only bad fruit. Instead of fellowshiping with God in eternal happiness, he slides into the agony of hell. He becomes wormwood and gall, a restless wretch. Vanity, fruitlessness, and misery characterize the life of every unbeliever who will not glorify and obey God.

Of such people the Lord declares: "But my people would not listen to me; Israel would not submit to me. So I gave them over to their stubborn hearts to follow their own devices" (Ps. 81:11–12). Those who reject God are given over by God to be controlled by their own depraved minds. Such people are too proud to worship God and be thankful for his provision. Instead, they worship and serve likenesses of created things. They have no problem worshiping creatures that are inferior to them.

"Although they claimed to be wise, they became fools and exchanged the glory of the immortal God for images made to look like mortal man and birds and animals and reptiles" (vv. 22–23). Professing to be wise, these God-rejecting people make themselves morons. Cut off from God's truth, man experiences a "delirium" of irrational imaginations.[1] The Bible says the infinite personal God is the cause of all created things, yet the irrational Darwinian evolutionary hypothesis is the ruling philosophy in almost all the world's universities today. Those who subscribe to this hypothesis have no problem with contradiction and irrationalism. In fact, they become angry when we say the infinite, personal God is the cause

---

1   Murray, *Epistle to the Romans*, 42.

of all creation. Man rejects the glory of the incorruptible God but has no problem worshiping a golden bull or a snake.

These "wise men" call those who believe in the God of creation fools, declaring that anyone who believes in the Bible is a moron. Yet God says they are the true fools, in spite of their majestic pretensions:

> For the message of the cross is foolishness to those who are perishing, but to us who are being saved it is the power of God. For it is written: "I will destroy the wisdom of the wise; the intelligence of the intelligent I will frustrate." Where is the wise man? Where is the scholar? Where is the philosopher of this age? Has not God made foolish the wisdom of the world? For since in the wisdom of God the world through its wisdom did not know him, God was pleased through the foolishness of what was preached to save those who believe. (1 Cor. 1:18–21)

Elsewhere Paul says, "The man without the Spirit does not accept the things that come from the Spirit of God, for they are foolishness to him, and he cannot understand them, because they are spiritually discerned" (1 Cor. 2:14). The god of this world has blinded natural man so that he cannot see reality until God speaks into the depths of his being, "Let there be light!" Only then will he be able to understand, repent, believe, and glorify God.

"Their foolish hearts were darkened" (v. 21). The heart is the center of human personality. It stands for our mind, will, and feelings. A darkened heart is twisted and has gone bad. It can only think, will, and love evil. This is God's judgment upon a man who hates God.

Paul says those who reject God are given over to a depraved mind, will, and affections. Such people glory in their depravity. How many modern students will sit at the edge of their seats and glory in the "wisdom" they are learning, which is a stench in God's nostrils! Yet they take pride in it and refuse to worship the true and living God. Their theology has become anthropology, zoology, and worship of Mother Earth and extreme environmentalism. They will not worship the true and living God, but they will worship a tree.

Such people, hating the true God, devise for themselves a tame God. They downsize God and come up with dummy gods. They want a God who permits every sin. These fools say, "Take away the glorious, incorruptible, Creator God of the Bible, and give us an image of a corruptible creature to worship." I would say they are really choosing to worship themselves.

So they worship created things—presidents, rock stars, movie stars, politicians, pets, children, and spouses. They put them on pedestals, bow down to them, and write books about them. They worship pornography, fashions, hollow philosophies, scientism, money, sex, power, beauty, and brilliance. All these things, as well as all false religions, are the fruits of rebellion against the true God.

Even Israel worshiped the golden calf instead of Yahweh: "They exchanged their Glory for an image of a bull, which eats grass" (Ps. 106:20). Jeremiah declares, "Has a nation ever changed its gods? (Yet they are not gods at all.) But my people have exchanged their Glory for worthless idols" (Jer. 2:11). Stephen explains, "That was the time they made an idol in the form of a calf. They brought sacrifices to it and held a celebration in honor of what their hands had made. But God turned away and gave them over to the worship of the heavenly bodies" (Acts 7:41–42).

Man is daily exchanging truth for a lie—the lies of idolatry and self-worship. Although he boasts about being wise, he worships creation. The Bible says those who do not worship the true God are, in reality, worshiping demons: "They worshiped their idols, which became a snare to them. They sacrificed their sons and their daughters to demons" (Ps. 106:36–37; see also 1 Cor. 10:18–21). John writes, "The rest of mankind that were not killed by these plagues still did not repent of the work of their hands; they did not stop worshiping demons, and idols of gold, silver, bronze, stone and wood—idols that cannot see or hear or walk" (Rev. 9:20).

A depraved mind says good is bad and bad is good. So those who reject God will say that the worship of the true God is bad but the worship of a bull, or of Mother Earth, is good; creationism is bad but Darwinism is good; virginity is bad but promiscuity is good. Bad thinking leads to wicked worship. "As a man thinketh in his heart, so is he" (Prov. 23:7, KJV). But "the wisdom of this world is foolishness in God's sight. . . . 'The Lord knows that the thoughts of the wise are futile'" (1 Cor. 3:19, 20).

A classic illustration is found in the life of Nebuchadnezzar, the great king of Babylon. God used Daniel to witness to him about the true God. Later, however, "Nebuchadnezzar made an image of gold, ninety feet high and nine feet wide, and set it up on the plain of Dura in the province of Babylon" (Dan. 3:1). He then summoned all people to worship this image, saying that they would be killed if they did not. The three Hebrew youths refused, and God rescued them from the fiery furnace, to the great amazement of Nebuchadnezzar. But in Daniel 4 we see the proud, unthankful, rebellious heart of this man. God had put Nebuchadnezzar in power, but listen to his words: "Twelve months later as the king was walking on the roof of the royal palace of Babylon, he said, 'Is not this the great Babylon I have built as the royal residence, by my mighty power and for the glory of my majesty?'" (Dan. 4:29–30).

God will not put up with idolatry, which is, fundamentally, self-worship and demon worship. Look at what happened to Nebuchadnezzar: "Immediately what had been said about Nebuchadnezzar was fulfilled. He was driven away from people and ate grass like cattle. His body was drenched with the dew of heaven until his hair grew like the feathers of an eagle and his nails like the claws of a bird" (Dan. 4:33). This proud king was turned over to a depraved mind. Now, we do not see the God-rejecting people of this world with long claws and unkempt hair, but essentially they are just like Nebuchadnezzar. They suffer from the delirium of their imaginations. God punished this man for seven years before showing mercy to him: "At the end of that time, I, Nebuchadnezzar, raised my eyes toward heaven, and my sanity was restored. Then I praised the Most High; I honored and glorified him who lives forever" (Dan. 4:34).

Man Becomes Foul

The second point in this giant slide down to hell is that we become foul. Not only does God-rejecting man become a fool, but his depraved mind also causes him to do that which makes him unclean and full of moral filth.

Jesus said that it is from man's wicked heart—that is, from his depraved mind, will, and feelings—that all manner of evil comes: "For from within, out of men's hearts, come evil thoughts, sexual immorality, theft, murder, adultery, greed, malice, deceit, lewdness, envy, slander, arrogance and folly. All these evils come from inside and make a man 'unclean'" (Mark 7:21–23).

"Wherefore God delivered them over unto uncleanness in the [power of the] wicked lusts of their hearts for the purpose that they may dishonor their bodies among themselves" (v. 24, author's translation). People glory in their wickedness as though they are exercising great freedom. But here God is saying they are handed over to do these things by divine action. In other words, it is a judgment that a person engages in fornication, commits adultery, feeds on pornography, or molests children. God hands them over to their beloved sin. It is as though he puts them in the prison of their own moral filth and they cannot get out.

Not only do men become fools, but they also dishonor and abuse their bodies and minds by becoming foul. Sin causes disease and many other problems. In the Greco-Roman culture, one could go to the temple, which was also a bank, take out money, and engage in ritual prostitution. This is the kind of filth Paul is speaking about. God judges such people so that they wallow like the worms that thrive in the sewer. In the same way, a sinner enjoys remaining in his sin. This is due to divine judgment.

"On account of [man's foolish rejection of God], God handed them over unto passions of dishonor" (v. 26, author's translation). There is nothing wrong with passion. It is good to be passionate when we worship and work. But here we read about "passions of dishonor," or "dishonorable passions." God handed these people over to the control of dishonorable passions. What did that handing over result in? *"Their women exchanged the natural use of sexuality unto [that which is] contrary to nature"* (v. 26, author's translation). The expression Paul uses here, "contrary to nature" (*eis tēn para phusin*), meant homosexuality in the Greek world. God handed these women over to unnatural, dishonorable, detestable passions. God abandoned them to reject his natural order of heterosexuality in marriage and engage in the unnatural perversion of lesbianism. This text says it is a judgment that God metes out and from which people cannot get out. It is like a prison: the door has been locked and the key thrown away.

"Likewise also the men, having left the natural use of the woman, were inflamed, set ablaze in their desire for one another, men in

men, *performing uncleanness, shame, and receiving the due wages of their error in themselves"* (v. 27, author's translation). Here we are told that men also deliberately abandoned God's natural order of heterosexuality in marriage in their strong burning desire for other men. They engaged in sodomy, as we read in Genesis 19. Elsewhere Paul says that what they do in secret is not proper to speak about (Eph. 5:12). Here Paul gives us a little window into the moral filth of God-hating men: *"they receive in themselves the due penalty of their perversion."* William Barclay calls this a "passionate desire for forbidden pleasure."[2] I would call it a burning desire for filth.

God judges these people, and they suffer from serious physical and psychological problems. They receive due penalty in themselves for their wandering from the truth. They become foul fools who wallow in moral filth and boast about it. They detest sexual purity before and after marriage. Their depraved minds joke about it. They are like stray dogs who eat dung.

Such people hate God's order. But those who do wickedness must experience God's divine judgment. Fools practice filth and go from bad to worse. Paul says of them, "Evil men and imposters will go from bad to worse, deceiving and being deceived" (2 Tim. 3:13). He tells Titus, "At one time we too were foolish, disobedient, deceived and enslaved by all kinds of passions and pleasures" (Titus 3:3). Paul also says, "Do you not know that the wicked will not inherit the kingdom of God? Do not be deceived: Neither the sexually immoral nor idolaters nor adulterers nor male prostitutes[3] nor homosexual offenders nor thieves nor the greedy nor drunkards nor slanderers nor swindlers will inherit the kingdom of God" (1 Cor. 6:9–10).

In the Greco-Roman world, there was a slogan: "Food for the stomach and the stomach for food." In other words, whenever a person felt an urge, he should do whatever he wanted to satisfy that urge, whether eating or drinking or engaging in sexual activity. But Paul says, "God will destroy them both" (1 Cor. 6:13). Then

---

2   William Barclay, *The Letter to the Romans*, The Daily Study Bible series (Edinburgh: Saint Andrews Press, 1969), 34.

3   "Male prostitutes" can also be translated "effeminates." The Greek word *malakoi* means "soft ones," designating those who are passive in the homosexual relationship. The next word is *arsenokoitai*, "homosexual offenders." They are the active ones.

he says, "The body is not meant for sexual immorality." Created by God, the human body has the sacred purpose of serving the Lord. The body is meant for the service of the Lord, that we may live in accordance with God's revelation. Then Paul adds, "And the Lord [is] for the body." When we serve the Lord with our bodies, he takes care of them, even to the point of raising them up on the last day.

Because God has saved us, Paul says, "Honor God with your body" (1 Cor. 6:20). Elsewhere he writes, "Do not be deceived: God cannot be mocked. A man reaps what he sows. The one who sows to please his sinful nature, from that nature will reap destruction; the one who sows to please the Spirit, from the Spirit will reap eternal life" (Gal. 6:7–8). No one gets away with sin. Sin always damages. What we sow in secret, we will reap.

Man Becomes a Fighter

The third point in man's giant slide to hell is that he becomes one who fights against God and his fellow man. Those who reject God's truth and refuse to worship and serve God make themselves fools and worship and serve creation. They practice filth and receive in their bodies the fitting wages of their perversion. And not only are they fools and filthy, but they also become ferocious, fighting, anti-social people.

These people fight constantly against God in their thoughts, words, and deeds. They fight against him in their writings and teachings. They fight in the universities and high schools. They are fighting against God and suppressing their knowledge of him. Such people also lose their capacity to love each another. If we are Christians, we will love one another because we love God with all our heart, mind, soul, and strength. But when we do not love God, how can we love others? When we hate God with all our heart, we will also hate our spouse, our children, and our neighbors. We become so demon-possessed and self-centered that we devour people like roaring lions.[4]

---

4   This is not to say that unbelievers do not demonstrate any affection for others. God's common grace restrains many people from manifesting these vices fully. But we cannot truly love as God does unless we ourselves experience God's love and love God (1 John 4:10, 19).

What does God do with such fighters? "*[God] gave them over to a depraved mind, to do what ought not to be done*" (v. 28). God hands those who hate him over to a reprobate mind to do things that are immoral and unfitting. Paul describes these things in what is the longest list of evil in the New Testament (Rom. 1:29–32). There are at least twenty-one vices listed here. These anti-social traits bring about conflicts, quarrels, wars, and tensions among people.

One of these vices is *theostugēs*, meaning "God-haters" (v. 30). Every unbeliever hates God and his revelation and order. Another trait is "disobedience to parents" (v. 30). We must not underestimate the seriousness of this sin. It results from God abandoning us, and is a root sin that will bring us into every other sin. Then we find the word *asunthetous*, "faithless" (v. 31), which actually means "covenant breakers." Such people will sign a mortgage paper but not send the money. They will marry and vow to stay together until death parts them, but then break their vows by walking out. They will join a church but later break their covenant. An unbeliever is a covenant breaker by nature and cannot be trusted. He stands in stark contrast to God, who never breaks covenant. Another word, *astorgous*, can be translated "without family affection" (v. 31). It is a terrible thing not to love people belonging to one's own family. Such people hate their fathers, mothers, and their own children. Western women, for the sake of pleasure, kill millions of their own babies in their wombs. Then we read they are "ruthless" (v. 31). The Greek word, *aneleēmonas*, means "without mercy." Another trait is *epheuretas kakōn*, "inventors of evil" (v. 30). The old evil is not good enough; these people are inflamed and set ablaze to think of new ways to do filth.

These are fighting words. These vices are destructive of marriages, families, communities, and nations. Fools who do filthy things are also fighting people because they are filled to the brim with evil, and out of their wicked hearts come wars and fighting.

Hope for Filthy, Fighting Fools

If we reject God and refuse to live by his truth, we will slide right down into hell, going through the sewer of moral filth in the process. We will become morally filthy fools who ferociously fight against God and other people. Paul concludes, "*Although they know God's righteous decree that those who do such things deserve death, they not only continue to do these very things but also approve of those who practice them*" (v. 32). Man is fully aware that the wages of sin is death, which means hell. Regardless, he persists in doing evil and promotes evil by recruiting others to do the same.

But there is good news! God holds out hope for his foolish, filthy, fighting enemies. We cannot lift ourselves up from hell. But God has given us the gospel, which tells us that Jesus Christ, the Son of God, came from heaven to lift us up from our hell. Ephesians 2:1–10 describes how God made us alive, raised us up, and seated us with Christ in the heavenly places. That is why we glory in the gospel. We were helpless sinners at enmity with God. But Christ died while we were yet ungodly sinners, and now we have hope. The gospel is the power of God unto salvation from God's wrath to all who believe.

Remember Paul's words: "Do you not know that the wicked will not inherit the kingdom of God? Do not be deceived: neither the sexually immoral nor idolaters nor adulterers nor male prostitutes nor homosexual offenders nor thieves nor the greedy nor drunkards nor slanderers nor swindlers will inherit the kingdom of God." But now comes the great truth: "And that is what some of you were. But you were washed, you were sanctified, you were justified in the name of the Lord Jesus Christ and by the Spirit of our God" (1 Cor. 6:9–11). We find the same idea in 1 Thessalonians 1:9: "You turned to God from idols to serve the living and true God." This is the reversal of our descent. God comes down, lifts us up, and seats us with him in the heavenly places in Christ Jesus. Therefore, repent and believe on the Lord Jesus Christ and you will be saved to serve with gladness the loving and true God forever and ever.

6

The Final, Eternal Judgment

¹You, therefore, have no excuse, you who pass judgment on someone else, for at whatever point you judge the other, you are condemning yourself, because you who pass judgment do the same things. ²Now we know that God's judgment against those who do such things is based on truth. ³So when you, a mere man, pass judgment on them and yet do the same things, do you think you will escape God's judgment? ⁴Or do you show contempt for the riches of his kindness, tolerance and patience, not realizing that God's kindness leads you toward repentance?

⁵But because of your stubbornness and your unrepentant heart, you are storing up wrath against yourself for the day of God's wrath, when his righteous judgment will be revealed. ⁶God "will give to each person according to what he has done." ⁷To those who by persistence in doing good seek glory, honor and immortality, he will give eternal life. ⁸But for those who are self-seeking and who reject the truth and follow evil, there will be wrath and anger. ⁹There will be trouble and distress for every human being who does evil: first for the Jew, then for the Gentile; ¹⁰but glory, honor and peace for everyone who does good: first for the Jew, then for the Gentile. ¹¹For God does not show favoritism.

¹²All who sin apart from the law will also perish apart from the law, and all who sin under the law will be judged by the law. ¹³For it is not those who hear the law who are righteous in God's sight, but it is those who obey the law who will be declared righteous. ¹⁴(Indeed, when Gentiles, who do not have the law, do by nature things required by the law, they are a law for themselves, even though they do not have the law, ¹⁵since they show that the requirements of the law are written on their hearts, their consciences also bearing witness, and their thoughts now accusing, now even defending them.) ¹⁶This will take place on the day when God will judge men's secrets through Jesus Christ, as my gospel declares.

Romans 2:1–16

The final, eternal judgment of God is the theme of Romans 2:1–16. Paul says judgment is part of his gospel (v. 16), and it is the last in the list of essential Christian doctrines in Hebrews 6:1–2. The word "judgment" or "judge" appears ten times in this passage. God the Judge shall surely judge, both in and beyond history.

Paul already wrote about temporal judgment, saying that God will abandon people to uncleanness, perversion, and a depraved mind to do unfit and immoral things (Rom. 1:18–32). But there is also a final, eternal judgment that will occur after the resurrection of the dead, at Christ's second coming. God created all people as moral beings who are accountable to him.

In Romans 1 Paul dealt primarily with God's judgment of the Gentiles. Now Paul addresses God's judgment of the Jews. The Jewish people readily agreed with Paul's treatment of the Gentiles, concurring that the Gentiles should be judged for the vile sins Paul mentions. But the Jews were startled when Paul began to speak about their own judgment. They might even have said, "We can understand God judging the Gentiles, because they are unclean 'dogs.' But we Jews are God's chosen people, Abraham's circumcised children, and possessors of the law." But God does not have a double standard—one for Gentiles and a different one for Jews. The holy God cannot overlook the sins of the Jews. As Paul wrote earlier, "The wrath of God is being revealed from heaven against *all* the godlessness and wickedness of men who suppress the truth by their wickedness" (Rom. 1:18, italics added). No one is immune to divine judgment.

We must also ask: If God judges the Gentiles and Jews, what about Christians? God will also judge every false Christian—those who profess Christ but do not obey him. God's judgment is based on the degree of revelation received by every human being. Let us, then, consider the nature of God's final, eternal judgment.

God Is the Judge

Several verses in this passage clearly declare that the Judge is God (vv. 2, 3, 4, 5, 11, 13, 16). Understanding this, Abraham rhetorically asked God in reference to the destruction of Sodom, "Will not the Judge of all the earth do right?" (Gen. 18:25).

Man also makes judgments, but Paul says the judgments that man makes are unrighteous (Rom. 2:1–3). Jesus explained how we see the speck in the eye of another, but fail to see the plank in our own (Matt. 7:3–5). The Jewish leaders judged Jesus to be the greatest sinner and handed him over to be crucified. This treating of the holy Son of God as a blasphemer was the most unrighteous judgment in history.

Paul says the Jews were self-condemned because, while they condemned others, they engaged in the same sins (Rom. 2:1). We all do this. Not only do we judge others while engaging in the same sins, but we also think we can escape God's judgment. We know we must die, but question what God can do to us and sometimes wonder if there even is a God. Let me assure you, there is a God, and he will raise up all sinners who died in their sins and mete out to them the final judgment of eternal, conscious existence in hell, far from all forms of God's grace.

Every sinner experiences God's grace now, but there is no grace in hell. Man will be without excuse at the final judgment. There will be no escape from the omniscient, omnipresent, almighty God. Jesus warned, "How will you escape being condemned to hell?" (Matt. 23:33). God says, "These things you have done and I kept silent; you thought I was altogether like you. But I will rebuke you and accuse you to your face. Consider this, you who forget God, or I will tear you to pieces, with none to rescue" (Ps. 50:21–22). Neither pagans nor unbelieving Jews nor false Christians can escape God's final, eternal judgment.

"Or do you show contempt for the riches of his kindness, tolerance and patience, not realizing that God's kindness leads you toward repentance?" (v. 4). All sinners experience God's abundant goodness and longsuffering. In other words, God created us and provides for our every need, and he bears with us when we sin. He does not punish us instantly for our sins, but waits to see whether we will repent and think differently about God, ourselves, and reality. He waits to see whether we will forsake all our sins and turn to serve him only with all delight in all of life. The purpose of God's common grace is to lead us to repentance.

God could have judged us long ago. Instead, he shows us the abundance of his kindness, restraint, and longsuffering. Yet we can be willfully ignorant of the purpose of God's goodness and refuse to repent. Peter tells us God is patient with us, "not wanting anyone to perish, but everyone to come to repentance" (2 Pet. 3:9). Jesus has not come back yet so that we may repent and be saved.

How many people abuse the goodness, forbearance, and longsuffering of God by stubbornly refusing to respond to him! But by so doing, they are hardening their hearts. Engaging in ever-increasing sin, they become more violent, wicked, and filthy, thus storing up for themselves God's wrath. The wrath of God against sinners increases as they persist in their unrepentant lives. Remember what God told Abraham about the iniquity of the Amorites. He said that Abraham and his family could not yet take possession of Canaan but had to go first to Egypt for four hundred years, "for the sin of the Amorites has not yet reached its full measure" (Gen. 15:16). Four hundred years later, when their sin reached full measure, Joshua destroyed the Amorites and brought Israel into Canaan.

Every sinner outside of Jesus Christ increases his measure of God's wrath every day he lives. This wrath will be poured out on him on the last day when he faces the final eternal judgment of God.

God's Judgment Is according to Truth

"Now we know that God's judgment against those who do such things is based on truth" (v. 2). This judgment is "according to truth" (kata tēn alētheian). Man's judgment is generally not according to truth, because he either does not have all the facts or misinterprets the facts he has or is in the habit of suppressing and exchanging the truth for a lie. God's judgment alone is according to truth because God is truth. The omniscient God needs no witness, nor does he have to discover facts. The writer to the Hebrews declares, "Nothing in all creation is hidden from God's sight. Everything is uncovered and laid bare before the eyes of him to whom we must give account" (Heb. 4:13).

By the revelation of Jesus Christ, John says that books will be opened on the day of judgment, along with the book of life (Rev. 20:12). God's judgment will be just and according to truth.

God's Judgment Is Righteous and Certain

God's judgment is a righteous judgment. *"But because of your stubbornness and your unrepentant heart, you are storing up wrath against yourself for the day of God's wrath, when his righteous judgment will be revealed"* (v. 5). All judgments of men, even those of the Supreme Court of the United States, are marred by error and evil. When Supreme Court justices can say that killing babies in the womb is perfectly acceptable, we know how bad human judges can be. God's judgment alone is righteous, for God is righteous. It will be just and according to all facts correctly interpreted. All people will experience such judgment.

God's judgment is so certain that God has fixed a day for it. *"This will take place on the day when God will judge men's secrets through Jesus Christ, as my gospel declares"* (v. 16).

Every unbeliever knows in his heart about this final judgment and its outcome. Paul writes, "They know God's righteous decree that those who do such things deserve death" (Rom. 1:32). Elsewhere we read, "Man is destined to die once, and after that to face judgment" (Heb. 9:27). On that day, men will cry out to the rocks and mountains, "Fall on us and hide us from the face of him who sits on the throne and from the wrath of the Lamb! For the great day of their wrath has come, and who can stand?" (Rev. 6:16–17).

This judgment is appointed, certain, fixed, and coming soon. Paul says, "For we must all appear before the judgment seat of Christ, that each one may receive what is due him for the things done while in the body, whether good or bad" (2 Cor. 5:10). Elsewhere he says, "God is just: He will pay back trouble to those who trouble you and give relief to you who are troubled, and to us as well. This will happen when the Lord Jesus is revealed from heaven in blazing fire with his powerful angels" (2 Thess. 1:6–7).

God's Judgment Is Universal and Personal

"God 'will give to each person according to what he has done'" (v. 6). God is not simply going to judge nations, tribes, and families as corporate entities. Every individual everywhere who ever lived

shall be judged for what he has done while in the body. Every man is to obey his Creator and worship him only, and he will be judged for his actions. Did he conform to God's truth, or did he exchange the truth for a lie? Did he suppress the truth to practice godlessness and wickedness?

Notice, we will be judged according to what we ourselves have done, not according to what our parents or our political leaders have done. How many people blame their parents, their society, their government for their actions? But Paul is saying that each of us will be judged for what we have done. *"There will be trouble and distress for every human being who does evil"* (v. 9).

God's Judgment Is according to Works

"God 'will give to each person according to what he has done'" (v. 6). In the Greek it is "according to the works." Either we produce good works, evidencing our justification by faith, or we produce dead works, demonstrating our unbelief, stubbornness, unrepentance, and enmity against God. Those who are saved by grace through faith are to produce good works: "We are God's workmanship, created in Christ Jesus to do good works, which God prepared in advance for us to do" (Eph. 2:10).

Good works are God's works, the fruit that we as branches bring forth due to our union with Christ the vine. If we produce no fruit of obedience, we have no vital connection with Christ. We must produce good works. It is true that we are not saved by works, but by faith alone; but the faith that saves us is not alone. Saving faith will always issue in obedience to God. Paul writes, "[Christ] gave himself for us to redeem us from all wickedness and to purify for himself a people that are his very own, eager to do what is good" (Titus 2:14). A Christian delights in doing good works.

Jesus declares, "For the Son of Man is going to come in his Father's glory with his angels, and then he will reward each person according to what he has done" (Matt. 16:27). Elsewhere he teaches about the eternal destiny of people, based on their obedience:

> When the Son of Man comes in his glory, and all the angels with him, he will sit on his throne in heavenly glory. All the nations will be gathered before him, and he will separate the people one

from another as a shepherd separates the sheep from the goats. He will put the sheep on his right and the goats on his left. Then the King will say to those on his right, "Come, you who are blessed by my Father; take your inheritance, the kingdom prepared for you since the creation of the world. For I was hungry and you gave me something to eat, I was thirsty and you gave me something to drink, I was a stranger and you invited me in, I needed clothes and you clothed me, I was sick and you looked after me, I was in prison and you came to visit me." Then the righteous will answer him, "Lord, when did we see you hungry and feed you, or thirsty and give you something to drink?" . . . The King will reply, "I tell you the truth, whatever you did for one of the least of these brothers of mine, you did for me." Then he will say to those on his left, "Depart from me, you who are cursed, into the eternal fire prepared for the devil and his angels.". . . Then they will go away to eternal punishment, but the righteous to eternal life. (Matt. 25:31–37, 40–41, 46)

John Stott says, "The presence or absence of saving faith in our hearts will be disclosed by the presence or absence of good works of love in our lives."[1]

John tells us, "Then I heard a voice from heaven say, 'Write: Blessed are the dead who die in the Lord from now on.' 'Yes,' says the Spirit, 'they will rest from their labor, for their deeds will follow them'" (Rev. 14:13). The wicked are known for their dead works, which are the sins they commit daily in unbelief. These manifest their enmity toward God. Dead works are the works of those who are dead in trespasses and sins. They are works performed in obedience to the devil, the god of this world.

By good works we please God and by dead works the unbeliever pleases his master the devil every day. We shall be judged according to our works, good or bad. Our works will reveal who our master is.

God's Judgment Is without Respect of Persons

"For God does not show favoritism" (v. 11). God has no favorites, nor does he have any grandchildren. He does not look at man's outward appearance but desires truth in the inward parts (Ps. 51:6). He is called *kardiognōstēs*, the heart-knower. Jesus said,

---

1   23. Stott, *Romans: God's Good News*, 84.

"Stop judging by mere appearances, and make a right judgment" (John 7:24). Elsewhere he declares, "What is highly valued among men is detestable in God's sight" (Luke 16:15).

God is not impressed with the self-image we so carefully cultivate. Paul is teaching that the Jews would not experience immunity from this judgment as they had expected. Nor will there be immunity for antinomians who put asunder what God has joined together by separating justification from sanctification. Dr. Martyn Lloyd-Jones says, "The New Testament Scriptures teach us everywhere that no greater danger confronts anyone who makes a profession of the Christian faith, than what is called antinomianism."[2] Yet the antinomian (lawless) life is practiced by many evangelicals today. They think they can just receive Jesus and not have to obey him. Those who steal can continue to steal every day and still be saved. The one who continues in lying and fornication will be in heaven. But there is no favoritism with God. There is no immunity for either Jews or lawless Christians from judgment.

God's Judgment Is according to Knowledge Received

God is not going to judge by the law the Gentiles who did not have the law, nor will he judge by the gospel the Jews who did not have the gospel. We are judged according to the knowledge we have received (Rom. 2:12, 14–15).

Both Jews and Gentiles know the God of glory and his eternal power through creation. Beyond that, God has created every person with a sense of Deity, a built-in knowledge of God: *The requirements of the law are written on their hearts*" (v. 15). God himself wrote it there. Every man also has a conscience, a moral consciousness as to what is right and wrong. Therefore, every man knows the difference between good and evil. When man sins, he sins against this knowledge of God, for God wrote his will in his heart. Thus, every man is without excuse for his sin. He cannot plead ignorance on the day of the final, eternal judgment.

---

2   Lloyd-Jones, *Romans*, vol. 2, *Righteous Judgment of God*, 97.

But not only were the Jews given knowledge of God through creation and through the law written on their hearts, they were also given a revelation of God in the law of Moses. So the Jews possessed greater revelation than the Gentiles and will be judged in accordance with this greater knowledge of God.

What about Christians? They have maximum knowledge of God—knowledge from creation, knowledge from the work of the law written by God in their hearts, knowledge from the Old Testament, and, finally, knowledge of Jesus Christ from the New Testament. The judgment of Christians will be in accordance with this maximum light they have received. Therefore, false Christians will be punished with many stripes (Luke 12:47). For them the bottom of hell is reserved. To such people, who take pride in their prophecies, miracles, and ability to cast out demons, Jesus will proclaim, "I never knew you. Away from me, you evildoers!" (Matt. 7:23).

True Christians will look not just to creation or conscience but to the whole Bible to discover the will of God. Conscience is not an infallible guide, because it can be dead or defiled. A good conscience is one that is continually being adjusted by the word of God.

Sin is transgression of God's standard. Gentiles and Jews sin against the standards that have been given to them. But Christians sin against the highest possible standard.

God Will Judge Men's Secrets

"This will take place on the day when God will judge men's secrets through Jesus Christ, as my gospel declares" (v. 16). Before the omniscient God we stand naked, as Adam and Eve did after they sinned, and our fig-leaf shall not cover us. John tells about the Jewish leaders bringing a woman caught in the act of adultery to Jesus. Jesus challenged them, "If any one of you is without sin, let him be the first to throw a stone at her." No one took up the challenge, and eventually they all left (John 8:2–11). As he waited, Jesus was writing on the ground with his finger. Perhaps he was writing a list of their sins.

God knows all of our secret sins. He knows every idle word we spoke and every secret thing we did when no one was watching. He knows our every thought, word, and deed. Jesus said to the

Pharisees, "You clean the outside of the cup and dish, but inside [you] are full of greed and self-indulgence" (Matt. 23:25). How many people take secrets to their graves! Maybe they killed someone and never told anyone. Maybe they stole something, or had a secret affair. But God knows all our sins—our adultery, fornication, greed, abortion, and every form of wickedness about which no one else knows. On the day of judgment, he will open the books and judge the secrets of men.

Judgment Is through Jesus Christ

God judges through the agency of his Son: "*This will take place on the day when God will judge men's secrets through Jesus Christ*" (v. 16). The Jewish people believed that God himself would judge, not the Messiah. But here Paul declares that God will judge through Jesus Christ, whom they rejected, mocked, and refused to trust in. We will meet the incarnate Son as Judge. All who hate God will meet this King of kings who kept the law and lived a holy life, saying, "Thy will be done." All who profess to be Christians yet continue in sin will meet this Lord of lords, who died on the cross for our sins and was raised on the third day according to his own prophecy.

Paul tells us that because of Christ's obedience, "God exalted him to the highest place and gave him the name that is above every name, that at the name of Jesus every knee should bow, in heaven and on earth and under the earth, and every tongue confess that Jesus Christ is Lord, to the glory of God the Father" (Phil. 2:9–11). It is the Father's will that his Son be honored, obeyed, and worshiped. Paul also spoke about this to the mockers of Athens: "In the past God overlooked such ignorance, but now he commands all people everywhere to repent. For he has set a day when he will judge the world with justice by the man he has appointed. He has given proof of this to all men by raising him from the dead" (Acts 17:30–31).

Jesus himself spoke about this ministry of judging: "Moreover, the Father judges no one, but has entrusted all judgment to the Son, that all may honor the Son just as they honor the Father. . . . And he has given him authority to judge because he is the Son of Man" (John 5:22–23, 27).

Throughout the Scriptures we see Christ judging. In reference to the judgment of false Christians he says, "Not everyone who says to me, 'Lord, Lord,' will enter the kingdom of heaven, but only he who does the will of my Father who is in heaven. Many will say to me on that day, 'Lord, Lord, did we not prophesy in your name, and in your name drive out demons and perform many miracles?' Then I will tell them plainly, 'I never knew you. Away from me, you evildoers!'" (Matt. 7:21–23). He says the same thing in Matthew 25: "When the Son of Man comes in his glory and all the angels with him, he will sit on his throne in heavenly glory. All the nations will be gathered before him, and he will separate the people one from another. . . . Then [the wicked] will go away to eternal punishment, but the righteous to eternal life" (Matt. 25:31–32, 46).

Christianity is not an irrelevant appendix and adornment to life: it is life itself. In his last letter, Paul writes, "In the presence of God and of Christ Jesus, who will judge the living and the dead, and in view of his appearing and his kingdom, I give you this charge" (2 Tim. 4:1). Elsewhere he says, "We must all appear before the judgment seat of Christ" (2 Cor. 5:10).

Judgment Is according to the Gospel

Paul says this judgment is *"according to my gospel"* (v. 16, author's translation). What does that expression mean? Is Paul saying that the gospel he preached was different from that of the other apostles? No, when Paul says, "my gospel," he means the gospel of God, the gospel of God's Son (Rom. 1:1, 9). There is only one gospel. To the Galatians Paul wrote, "But even if we or an angel from heaven should preach a gospel other than the one we preached to you, let him be eternally condemned!" (Gal. 1:8). Then he said, "As for those who seemed to be important—whatever they were makes no difference to me; God does not judge by external appearance—those men added nothing to my message" (Gal. 2:6). The apostles agreed with Paul.

What is the gospel? Paul writes, "Now, brothers, I want to remind you of the gospel I preached to you, which you received and on which you have taken your stand. By this gospel you are saved, if you hold firmly to the word I preached to you. Otherwise, you have believed in vain. For what I received I passed on to you as of first importance: that Christ died for our sins according to the Scriptures, that he was buried, that he was raised on the third day according to the Scriptures" (1 Cor. 15:1–4).

What Paul is saying by the term "according to my gospel" is that this judicial outpouring of God's wrath is part of the gospel, and any preaching of the gospel devoid of this judgment aspect is deficient. It is a false, synthetic gospel that downsizes God. Such a gospel separates God's love from God's holiness and promotes the evil of antinomianism.

Modern people do not like anyone telling them what to do. We demand absolute freedom so that we can have "fun." Autonomy is a particular problem of Americans and Europeans. We do not want any restraint. Such an attitude is contrary to God's gospel.

The Verdict of God's Judgment

What is the final verdict of God's judgment? "God 'will give to each person according to what he has done.' To those who by persistence in doing good seek glory, honor and immortality, he will give eternal life. But for those who are self-seeking and who reject the truth and follow evil, there will be wrath and anger. There will be trouble and distress for every human being who does evil: first for the Jew, then for the Gentile; but glory, honor and peace for everyone who does good: first for the Jew, then for the Gentile" (vv. 6–10).

Those who are righteous and justified through Christ, those who love God and persevere in doing good, will receive eternal life. Good works are the result and fruit of justification by faith. Faith without works is the devil's faith. It is a lie. A true believer does good works, not once in a while, but with perseverance. That is his nature. He brings forth fruit, more fruit, much fruit, for the Father's glory even in the midst of great trials and tribulations. He receives glory, honor, and immortality from God; that is, the resurrection of the body. We shall receive an imperishable, glorious body of honor that is engineered by the Spirit to exist in the presence of God. God himself will make us holy, glorious, and honorable.

What is the purpose of Christ's incarnation? The Hebrews writer speaks of "bringing many sons to glory" (Heb. 2:10). This tells us we did not have any glory. We were dishonorable, dying, restless people. But God sent his Son to bring us to glory. Paul declares, "Therefore, since we have been justified through faith, we have peace with God through our Lord Jesus Christ, through whom we have gained access by faith into this grace in which we now stand. And we rejoice in the hope of the glory of God" (Rom. 5:1–2). We rejoice in the hope of the second coming of Christ, at which time we shall be glorified. He later says, "Not only so, but we ourselves, who have the firstfruits of the Spirit, groan inwardly as we wait eagerly for our adoption as sons, the redemption of our bodies. . . . For those God foreknew he also predestined to be conformed to the likeness of his Son, that he might be the firstborn among many brothers. And those he predestined, he also called; those he called, he also justified; those he justified, he also glorified" (Rom. 8:23, 29–30). We have absolute certainty of our glory. Elsewhere Paul says, "Therefore we do not lose heart. Though outwardly we are wasting away, yet inwardly we are being renewed day by day. For our light and momentary troubles are achieving for us an eternal glory that far outweighs them all" (2 Cor. 4:16–17). We are destined for glory.

Jesus Christ destroyed our death and brought us immortality. Paul says, "But it has now been revealed through the appearing of our Savior, Christ Jesus, who has destroyed death and has brought life and immortality to light through the gospel" (2 Tim. 1:10). Now we can live every day for the glory of God, knowing that God will glorify us. In his presence there is fullness of joy and on his right hand are pleasures forevermore. That is the purpose for which God has created us.

What about those who suppress truth and exchange it for a lie? What about those who are stubborn and unrepentant? Even as they are sinning, they know they are going to receive death (Rom. 1:32). Here we are told they will receive wrath, anger, trouble, and distress. Those who live by enmity and selfish ambition, who disobey the truth while freely obeying wickedness, who abuse God's kindness, forbearance, and longsuffering, must die an eternal death and experience the full fury of God's wrath. Their lifetime cumulative sin will be taken into full account on the judgment day. The longer we live, the more sin, guilt, and punishment we accrue.

Judgment Begins at Death

The first phase of judgment begins at death. Have you ever thought at a funeral, "Where did this person go?" We have become so materialistic that most people never think to ask. If they do, they may be told the dead person is in purgatory or in heaven or that he or she has ceased to exist.

Have you ever thought about where your family and friends went at death, and where they exist at the present time? The Bible says that those who mocked God and his word are in hell. Jesus spoke about a rich man who died (Luke 16:19–31). This man ignored God's truth as revealed in creation, in conscience, and in the Law and the Prophets. He abused God's abundance of goodness, including the witness of poor Lazarus. Jesus says at death he went to hell and was in fire, torment, and agony. But that is just the first phase. Everyone who died in his sins will be raised up, judged, and thrown into the lake of fire (John 5:28–29). There is no annihilation of the dead. That is an invention of man. John writes:

> And the devil, who deceived them, was thrown into the lake of burning sulfur, where the beast and the false prophet had been thrown. They will be tormented day and night for ever and ever. Then I saw a great white throne and him who was seated on it. Earth and sky fled from his presence, and there was no place for them. And I saw the dead, great and small, standing before the throne, and books were opened. Another book was opened, which is the book of life. The dead were judged according to what they had done as recorded in the books. The sea gave up the dead that were in it, and death and Hades gave up the dead that were in them, and each person was judged according to what he had done. Then death and Hades were thrown into the lake of fire. The lake of fire is the second death. If anyone's name was not found written in the book of life, he was thrown into the lake of fire. (Rev. 20:10–15)

How to Escape Judgment

What can we do in the light of this sober truth of this final and eternal judgment? First, we must realize that the destiny of those who have already died is sealed. They can do nothing. But for those of us who are still living, there is great hope (Rom. 1:16–17). Repent and believe on the Lord Jesus, and you shall be saved. Jesus is the Judge, but he is also the Savior—the only Savior of the world. The cross reveals God's justice and wrath, but it also reveals his great love. The Father judged Jesus in our behalf, pouring out every drop of wrath on him so that no wrath remains for us. "Therefore, there is now no condemnation for those who are in Christ Jesus" (Rom. 8:1).

No man can escape the Judge or the judgment. Do not try to flee or hide *from* him; rather, hide *in* him. Seek Christ and eternal life. Seek glory, honor, and immortality. Seek peace with God through repentance and faith. There are only two peoples, believers and unbelievers; only two ways, the broad and the narrow; and only two destinies, eternal life and eternal death. Now is the opportune time. May we all flee to Christ and be saved forevermore.

> Only one life, 'twill soon be past;
> only what's done for Christ will last.

7

God Condemns Hypocrisy

¹⁷*Now you, if you call yourself a Jew; if you rely on the law and brag about your relationship to God;* ¹⁸*if you know his will and approve of what is superior because you are instructed by the law;* ¹⁹*if you are convinced that you are a guide for the blind, a light for those who are in the dark,* ²⁰*an instructor of the foolish, a teacher of infants, because you have in the law the embodiment of knowledge and truth—* ²¹*you, then, who teach others, do you not teach yourself? You who preach against stealing, do you steal?* ²²*You who say that people should not commit adultery, do you commit adultery? You who abhor idols, do you rob temples?* ²³*You who brag about the law, do you dishonor God by breaking the law?* ²⁴*As it is written: "God's name is blasphemed among the Gentiles because of you."*

²⁵*Circumcision has value if you observe the law, but if you break the law, you have become as though you had not been circumcised.* ²⁶*If those who are not circumcised keep the law's requirements, will they not be regarded as though they were circumcised?* ²⁷*The one who is not circumcised physically and yet obeys the law will condemn you who, even though you have the written code and circumcision, are a lawbreaker.*

²⁸*A man is not a Jew if he is only one outwardly, nor is circumcision merely outward and physical.* ²⁹*No, a man is a Jew if he is one inwardly; and circumcision is circumcision of the heart, by the Spirit, not by the written code. Such a man's praise is not from men, but from God.*

Romans 2:17–29

A hypocrite is an actor whose outward appearance does not match his inward condition. History is replete with famous hypocrites who practice the opposite of what they preach—

politicians who prosecute people, only to be caught in the same crimes; ministers who preach vigorously against certain sins, only to be secretly indulging in such sins themselves; or leaders who claim to stand with and for the poor, even though they themselves live lavishly in exclusive neighborhoods.

Fallen man is a sinner and a hypocrite. We all have varying degrees of hypocrisy in us. This sin of hypocrisy is particularly a problem for leaders—for politicians, judges, parents, and pastors. James warns, "Not many of you should presume to be teachers, my brothers, because you know that we who teach will be judged more strictly" (James 3:1). The self-righteous accusers of the woman caught in the act of adultery could not stone her to death because they were convicted by Jesus Christ of committing sin themselves (John 8:3–11). Paul declares, "You, therefore, have no excuse, you who pass judgment on someone else, for at whatever point you judge the other, you are condemning yourself, because you who pass judgment do the same things" (Rom. 2:1). Jesus Christ alone was righteous and without hypocrisy. He even challenged his enemies, asking, "Can any of you prove me guilty of sin?" (John 8:46).

In Romans 2:17–29 Paul destroys the false confidence of the Jews by exposing their hypocrisy. Jesus did the same, warning his disciples of the hypocrisy of the Pharisees: "The teachers of the law and the Pharisees sit in Moses' seat. So you must obey them and do everything they tell you. But do not do what they do, for they do not practice what they preach" (Matt. 23:2–3). The entire chapter of Matthew 23 is an exposé and denunciation of the hypocrisy of the Jewish leaders. For example, Jesus exclaimed, "Woe to you, teachers of the law and Pharisees, you hypocrites! You are like whitewashed tombs, which look beautiful on the outside but on the inside are full of dead men's bones and everything unclean. In the same way, on the outside you appear to people as righteous but on the inside you are full of hypocrisy and wickedness" (Matt. 23:27–28).

The situation is the same today. In fact, every time we see the word "Jew" in Romans 2, we can substitute the word "Christian," because Paul's words also apply to us. In this television age, we may think that perception is all that matters, but God desires truth in our inner parts. May God's Holy Spirit expose our

Christian hypocrisy, that we may dispose of it by the blood of Jesus Christ.

From this passage we want to examine the image the Jews had of themselves, the contradiction between their profession and their actions, and the reality of new birth.

The Image of the Jews (vv. 17–20)

In Romans 2:17–20 Paul uses eight verbs to describe the privileges, status, and blessings of the Jewish people.[1]

1. *"Now you, if you call yourself a Jew"* (v. 17). Paul was addressing those who called themselves Jews. The word "Jew" means "praise to God." A Jew was a child of Abraham, one with whom God chose to enter into a covenant. The Bible says salvation was of the Jews, which was true, for Jesus himself was a Jew. The Jews looked down on the Gentiles, whom they called dogs. A Jew was pleased with himself, thinking he was superior to the Gentiles simply by being born a Jew.

Yet Jesus disagreed with this smug self-analysis of the Jews. To the church of Smyrna he declared, "I know your afflictions and your poverty—yet you are rich! I know the slander of those who say they are Jews and are not, but are a synagogue of Satan" (Rev. 2:9).

2. *"If you rely on the law"* (v. 17). The Jew rested in the law (i.e., the Old Testament). He thought possession of the word of God would exempt him from the judgment and wrath of God. He would say, "Only Gentiles are under the wrath of God; Jews are not, because we Jews possess superior knowledge. Have we not been given the special revelation of God's law?" But listen to the prophet Micah's condemnation of Israel's leaders: "Her leaders judge for a bribe, her priests teach for a price, and her prophets tell fortunes for money. Yet they lean upon the LORD and say, 'Is not the LORD among us? No disaster will come upon us.' Therefore because of you, Zion will be plowed like a field, Jerusalem will become a heap of rubble, the temple hill a mound overgrown with thickets" (Mic. 3:11–12). Their security was proven to be

---

1   These verbs are enumerated by John Stott in *Romans: God's Good News*, 90–91.

false in 586 BC, when the Babylonian armies burned the temple to the ground. Paul also writes, "For it is not those who hear the law who are righteous in God's sight, but it is those who obey the law who will be declared righteous" (Rom. 2:13). Hypocrites shall be condemned.

3. *"If you . . . brag about your relationship to God"* (v. 17). The Jews correctly boasted that the God of Israel was the true God, while the Gentiles worshiped idols. Their God was a national asset. To glory in God, as John Murray says, is the greatest act of piety.[2] Isaiah says that we are created for God's glory (Isa. 43:7). Paul declares, "Let him who boasts boast in the Lord" (1 Cor. 1:31). But when a hypocrite boasts in God, he is really boasting in himself.

4. *"If you know his will"* (v. 18). The Jew took great delight in arguing about the will of God. He knew God's will and could quote the Bible. He condemned the Gentiles' view of God. However, although he knew that God's will is revealed in the Bible, his was only an intellectual knowledge. He was thoroughly orthodox, but so is the devil. Orthodoxy without orthopraxy cannot save anyone. This is not just a Jewish problem. Today it is a specifically Christian problem, even among those who pride themselves on being evangelicals. Such people correctly say they know God's will, but they refuse to submit to it in practice. Many modern evangelicals have abandoned obedience and holiness in favor of lawlessness. To such the Lord will say on that day, "Depart from me, you workers of lawlessness (*anomia*)."

5. *"If you know his will and approve of what is superior"* (v. 18). Not only did the Jew know God's will, but he approved it as well. The Jews were able to discern what was excellent, moral, and right. They had a moral consciousness that was based not on conscience but on God's special revelation. They approved the Ten Commandments in theory but not in practice.

6. *"If . . . you are instructed by the law"* (v. 18). As God's people, the Jews were catechized in the word of God. Each Jewish father had the responsibility to teach his children God's law. A Jewish home was a place of Bible study. The Jews also went to the local church, called the synagogue, which was not only a place of worship but also a school where God's law was taught. It was Jesus' custom to

---

2   Murray, *Epistle to the Romans*, 82.

go to the synagogue every Sabbath, where he studied God's word (Luke 4:16). God's law was also taught in the temple in Jerusalem; so we see Jesus discussing the Scriptures with the doctors of the law in the temple (Luke 2:46–47).

7. *"If you are convinced that you are . . ."* The Jew was convinced he had certain responsibilities to the Gentile world in view of the entrustment of this special revelation of God to the Jews:

- A *guide for the blind* (v. 19). Because the Gentiles were blind to the truth of the Scriptures, it was the Jews' responsibility to guide them into the truth. Ironically, these hypocrites were total failures in this task, as Jesus pointed out: "They are blind guides. If a blind man leads a blind man, both will fall into a pit" (Matt. 15:14; see also Matt. 23).
- A *light for those who are in the dark* (v. 19). Israel's mission was to be a light to the world of Gentiles (Isa. 9:2; 42:6–7; 49:6).
- An *instructor of the foolish* (v. 20). With his knowledge of God's word, the Jew was to correct, rebuke, and counsel the Gentiles.
- A *teacher of infants* (v. 20). The Jew was responsible for teaching those who knew nothing of the word of God.

The Jews were convinced of their obligations to the world of Gentiles. But note Jesus' analysis of their carrying out of these responsibilities: "Woe to you, teachers of the law and Pharisees, you hypocrites! You travel over land and sea to win a single convert, and when he becomes one, you make him twice as much a son of hell as you are" (Matt. 23:15).

8. *"Because you have in the law the embodiment of knowledge and truth"* (v. 20). The Jew possessed the very word of God, God's revelation of knowledge and truth. No such truth can be found anywhere else—not in pagan wisdom and philosophy, which Paul calls "hollow and deceptive philosophy" (Col. 2:8). True truth is found in the Bible, which was the inheritance of the Jewish people.

The Internal Contradiction of the Jew (vv. 21–24)

The Jewish leaders failed not in their preaching of the truth but in their practice of it. In verses 21 through 24, Paul asks five diagnostic questions[3] to expose the hypocrisy of these Jews who

---

3   Stott, *Romans: God's Good News*, 91–92.

were resting in a false security from divine judgment. We see such an insightful exposé also in the book of Revelation when Jesus speaks to the church of Laodicea. They said they were rich and had need of nothing. But Jesus discloses their true condition: "You do not realize that you are wretched, pitiful, poor, blind and naked" (Rev. 3:17). Our self-exaltation and self-praise mean nothing. All that matters is what God says about us.

1. *"You, then, who teach others, do you not teach yourself?"* (v. 21). The problem with the Jews was that they taught others God's law but failed to teach themselves and practice it. They saw the speck very clearly in other people's eyes but failed to see the plank sticking out of their own. This is especially a problem of parents, pastors, and teachers.

2. *"You who preach against stealing, do you steal?"* (v. 21). These Jews preached against stealing even while they were engaging in theft. In fact, they were worse than normal thieves because most thieves do not tell others not to steal. But these people were teaching that it is wrong to violate God's commandment even while they were stealing.

3. *"You who say that people should not commit adultery, do you commit adultery?"* (v. 22). Here again, these people were preaching against adultery even while they were practicing it.

4. *"You who abhor idols, do you rob temples?"* (v. 22). The Jews self-righteously opposed the idolatry of the pagan Gentiles, but they themselves were robbing temples, either to worship those idols or to sell the idols to make money.

5. *"You who brag about the law, do you dishonor God by breaking the law?"* (v. 23). These Jews took pride in their possession of God's law, but they dishonored God by breaking the law in their daily lives. As a result, Paul says, *"God's name is blasphemed among the Gentiles because of you"* (v. 24). The Gentiles learned about the God of the Jews by observing their conduct. The people of God always reflect God to the unbelieving world, even if the picture we give of God is false. Therefore, a lazy Christian is portraying a lazy God; a lying Christian reflects a lying God; an adulterous Christian reveals a God who condones adultery; and a defeated Christian is declaring a powerless God. God has created us for his glory, but if we are not obeying his law, we bring shame and dishonor to his name.

The glory of God, not of ourselves, is the greatest reality with which we must be concerned. All creation exists to proclaim God's glory, and he will not tolerate any diminution of that glory through violations of his law. In the same way, when our children do not obey us, they are dishonoring us. More than that, they are also dishonoring God.

How do we violate God's law? We violate it when we fail to worship God when and how we ought. We do so when we fail to work hard for our employers. We do so when we look lustfully at another, or when we fail to love our spouses or train our children in piety. Dr. James Boice comments, "We break [the first commandment] whenever we give some person or some object or some worldly aspiration the first place in our lives, a place that belongs to God alone. Often today the substitute god is ourselves or our image of ourselves."[4] In contrast, Dr. John Stott says that to keep the first commandment "[is] to see all things from [God's] point of view and do nothing without reference to him; to make his will our guide and his glory our goal; to put him first in thought, word and deed; in business and in leisure; in friendships and in career; in the use of our money, time and talents; at work and at home."[5] May God help us, whether we are pastors or parents or teachers, apply this truth to ourselves.

To the Jews who prided themselves in being keepers of God's law, Jesus said, "Do not think I will accuse you before the Father. Your accuser is Moses, on whom your hopes are set" (John 5:45). Jesus exposes our hypocrisy. He sees our image and contradictions, our outside and inside. To the foolish virgins who thought they were authentic Christians, Jesus declared, "I tell you the truth, I don't know you" (Matt. 25:12). To others who came to Jesus and exclaimed, "Did we not prophesy in your name, and in your name drive out demons and perform many miracles?" Jesus replied, "I never knew you. Away from me, you evildoers!" (Matt. 7:22–23). Why? These "Christians" were hypocrites.

God similarly exposed the hypocrisy of David. After David's grievous sins of adultery with Bathsheba and the murder of Uriah, the prophet Nathan came to David telling a story about

---

4   Boice, *Romans*, vol. 1, *Justification by Faith*, 255.
5   Quoted by Boice, 255.

a rich man who had many cattle and sheep. There was also a poor man who bought a ewe lamb and raised her in his house as a pet, letting her eat, drink, and even sleep with her owner. When a traveler came to the rich man, instead of using his own flocks, the rich man stole the poor man's ewe lamb, killed her, and made a feast for the visitor. "David burned with anger against the man and said to Nathan, 'As surely as the LORD lives, the man who did this deserves to die! He must pay for that lamb four times over, because he did such a thing and had no pity.' Then Nathan said to David, 'You are the man!'" (2 Sam. 12:5–7). How clearly we see other people's problems but not our own!

We all are in danger of falling into hypocrisy. If a preacher cannot manage himself and his own house, he cannot be an effective, God-approved minister of the gospel. Every time I preach, I must preach first to myself. We must keep in mind the words of Asaph: "But to the wicked God says: 'What right have you to recite my laws or take my covenant on your lips? You hate my instruction and cast my words behind you. When you see a thief, you join with him; you throw in your lot with adulterers. You use your mouth for evil and harness your tongue to deceit. You speak continually against your brother and slander your own mother's son. These things you have done and I kept silent; you thought I was altogether like you'" (Ps. 50:16–21).

The Reality of God (vv. 25–29)

"Circumcision has value if you observe the law, but if you break the law, you have become as though you had not been circumcised" (v. 25). To bring the Jews to the reality God is interested in, Paul turns to their final argument: that they were circumcised. Circumcision was older than the law. It was given to Abraham as a sign and seal of God's covenant of promise. The Jew was proud of his circumcision, for it set him apart from the unbelieving Gentiles.

But circumcision was only a sign to point us to the reality of a relational life to God in faithful obedience to him as the Lord of the covenant. To confuse the sign with reality is the epitome of hypocrisy. In the same way, some Christians glory in their Christian nationality, Christian family background, and Christian marriage. They take pride in their baptism, church membership, and Bible. But Christian hypocrites glory in outward things even while lacking the inner reality of a life of obedience. Paul tells us he received his apostleship "to call people from among all the Gentiles to the *obedience* that comes from faith" (Rom. 1:5, italics added). Not only does God condemn the Jewish hypocrite, but he also condemns all Christian hypocrites who glory in their image but whose hearts are corrupt. The sign of baptism can never take us to heaven. Karl Barth said, "The heroes of God without God may be compared to a traveller who remains standing under the signpost instead of moving in the direction to which it directs him. The signpost has become meaningless."[6] Baptism is profitable only if the inner reality of a new heart exists.

The only remedy for this problem of a wicked heart is being born again by the Holy Spirit. Baptism, like circumcision, is a sign and seal of the reality of that new birth. It points to the reality of a covenant relationship with God and a covenant life of delightful obedience. It is a sign and seal of the reality that we are a new creation, created in Christ Jesus unto good works. John Piper states that circumcision without obedience means a disobedient Jew is, in reality, a pagan. But uncircumcision plus obedience means an obedient Gentile has now become a true Jew.[7]

Therefore, physical circumcision, like physical baptism, can achieve nothing. We need a circumcision of our heart performed not by man but by God himself. The Bible often speaks about circumcising our hearts: "The LORD your God will circumcise your hearts and the hearts of your descendants, so that you may love him with all your heart and with all your soul, and live" (Deut. 30:6). Notice, the Lord himself promises to do it. Paul writes, "Finally, my brothers, rejoice in the Lord! It is no trouble for me to write the same things to you again, and it is a safeguard for you. Watch out for those dogs, those men who do evil, those mutilators of the flesh." These Jews gloried in their physical circumcision. Then

---

6   Quoted in *A New Testament Commentary: Based on the Revised Standard Version*, G. C. D. Howley, general editor, F. F. Bruce and H. L. Ellison, contributing editors (London: Pickering and Inglis, 1969), 346.

7   John Piper, "Who Is a True Jew? Part 2," sermon Feb. 28, 1999, http://www. desiringgod.org/resource-library/sermons/who-is-a-true-jew-part-2

he says, "For it is we who are the circumcision," meaning those who are circumcised in our hearts by the Spirit of God, "we who worship by the Spirit of God, who glory in Christ Jesus, and who put no confidence in the flesh" (Phil. 3:1–3).

Do not trust in baptism or circumcision, as the unbelieving Jews did. "Rabbi Menachem in his *Commentary on the Books of Moses* (fol. 43, col. 1) says, 'Our Rabbins have said that no circumcised man will see hell.' In the *Jalkut Rubeni* (num. 1) it is taught, 'Circumcision saves from hell.' In the *Medrasch Tillim* (fol. 7, col. 2) it is said, 'God swore to Abraham that no one who was circumcised should be sent to hell.' In the book of *Akedath Jizehak* (fol. 54, col. 2) it is taught that 'Abraham sits before the gate of hell, and does not allow that any circumcised Israelite should enter there.'"[8]

A ring is a sign of marriage. But if you do not love your wife and live with her under God's word, you have no real marriage. So do not boast in rings, signs, baptism, or circumcision. Boast in the Lord, for he has given you a new heart, circumcised by the Spirit. The law of God is not written on a stone or on a paper. We belong to the new covenant. The law is written in our hearts and is part of our new nature. Like the saints of old, we delight in the law of the Lord. Circumcision or baptism has no intrinsic value without the reality it points to (i.e., regeneration, repentance, faith, justification, adoption, sanctification, and glorification). Without holiness no one will see God. Blessed are the pure in heart, for they will see God.

The true church of God consists of all Jews and Gentiles who are circumcised by the Spirit and serve God without hypocrisy. Called the Israel of God, we all are on equal footing before God. The world hates the people of God, especially those who live by the gospel. But God praises us and will glorify us. He will commend us, saying, "Thou good and faithful servant, enter into the joy of the Lord."

God's wrath is revealed against all ungodliness and unrighteousness of men who suppress the truth in wickedness. Neither Gentiles nor Jews nor Christians are exempt. In fact, Christians will be most severely judged due to the greater light of the gospel they possess. Charles Hodges says, "Whenever true religion declines, the disposition to lay undue stress on external

---

8   Quoted by Boice, *Romans*, vol. 1, *Justification by Faith*, 259.

rites is increased. . . . The Christian Church, when it lost its spirituality, taught that water in baptism washed away sin. How large a part of nominal Christians rest all their hopes on the idea of the inherent efficacy of external rites!"[9]

There is only one way out of this problem. The gospel of God is mighty to save. Christ died for our sins and was raised for our justification. When we believe on the Lord Jesus Christ, we will be saved. So let us repent of all hypocrisy as the Holy Spirit directs our hearts. Let us not be like the hypocrite Saul, to whom Samuel said, "Does the Lord delight in burnt offerings and sacrifices as much as in obeying the voice of the Lord? To obey is better than sacrifice, and to heed is better than the fat of rams. For rebellion is like the sin of divination, and arrogance like the evil of idolatry" (1 Sam. 15:22–23). May God help us to expose our hypocrisy and be completely forgiven that we may serve him in all integrity, with all our heart, mind, soul, and strength.

---

9 Hodge, *Romans*, 68.

8

Our Rich Jewish-Christian Heritage

¹What advantage, then, is there in being a Jew, or what value is there in circumcision? ²Much in every way! First of all, they have been entrusted with the very words of God.

Romans 3:1–2

What is the most precious gift God has given us? It is his word, which reveals Jesus Christ, the author of our eternal salvation. Romans 3:1–2 speaks about the rich Jewish-Christian heritage we have in the sacred Scriptures. In this study we want to consider three things: the question asked by an unbelieving covenant man, the gracious answer of his covenant Lord, and our response to the Lord's answer.

The Question of Unbelieving Covenant Man

In Romans 2 Paul made several provocative statements about the unbelieving Jews. He told them, "Circumcision has value if you observe the law, but if you break the law, you have become as though you had not been circumcised" (Rom. 2:25). In other words, he was saying they were just like the Gentiles. He also said, "A man is not a Jew if he is only one outwardly, nor is circumcision merely outward and physical" (Rom. 2:28). Paul was saying that mere possession of the law and being circumcised do not save a Jew from the wrath of God.

In response to Paul's statements, we find a question in Romans 3:1. Notice, this is not the question of a Gentile, but of an unbelieving covenant man: *"What advantage, then, is there in being a Jew, or what value is there in circumcision?"* In other words, what is the Jewish advantage over a Gentile if both Jew and Gentile stand before God in judgment? We can ask similar questions of ourselves: What does it benefit to be born in a "Christian" country or to have Christian parents? What is the profit of being baptized? What is the advantage of attending Sunday school and church services weekly?

God's Answer

God, through Paul, answers these questions in verse 2: *"Much in every way!"* To be born as a Jew has great advantage. To be a member of the covenant community is not without profit. Then he cites the most important advantage that covenant, unbelieving Jews, as well as covenant, unbelieving Christians, have: *"First of all, they have been entrusted with the very words of God."*

The Jews were the custodians of the living oracles, the very words of God. Paul speaks more about this in Romans 9:4–5, where he lists eight advantages:

1. *The adoption as sons.* No other nation was chosen and adopted by the sovereign God.
2. *The divine glory.* The Jews possessed the divine glory of God's presence that appeared on Mount Sinai and in the Holy of Holies. God's presence was with his people.
3. *The covenants.* God graciously entered into covenants with Abraham, Moses, and David.
4. *The receiving of the law.* The word "law" sometimes connotes the whole Old Testament, but it especially refers here to the law that God revealed to Moses.
5. *The temple worship.* Paul was referring to the sacrificial system.
6. *The promises of God.* The Old Testament is filled with promises of a God who saves sinners.
7. *The patriarchs.* Abraham, Isaac, and Jacob belonged to the Jewish people.
8. *The human ancestry of Christ.* Jesus came from the Jewish people.

But all these advantages did not save the Jewish people. Mere possession of such advantages will not save a Jew or a Christian.

We must have faith—active, penitent, obedient, and persevering faith in Jesus Christ.

The chief advantage of being a Jew was that the Jews were depositories and stewards of "the oracles of God" (*logia tou theou*). This phrase appears only three places outside of this passage: in Acts 7:38, where Stephen says Moses received the living words from God to give us, and in Hebrews 5:12 and 1 Peter 4:11. The Jews were the custodians of God's utterances now embodied in the thirty-nine books of the Old Testament.

What implications were there for those who were entrusted with this great deposit of the divine treasure of God's own word? The Jews were to read it, believe it, and obey it fully. They were to defend God's word from all heretics and false prophets. They were to proclaim this word throughout the world and teach it to themselves, their children, and their nation. They were to translate it into other languages and interpret it correctly with divine illumination. They were not to add to or subtract from the very word of God.

Jesus was taught the word of God in his home, in the synagogue, and in the temple. In fact, his purpose in coming into the world was to know God's word and obey it fully. Timothy was also taught the word of God, especially by his mother and grandmother. So Paul writes, "From infancy you have known the holy Scriptures, which are able to make you wise for salvation through faith in Christ Jesus" (2 Tim. 3:15). In the same way, we are to be taught. How many children in Christian churches have been entrusted with this precious word, yet have not trusted in Jesus Christ alone for their salvation!

There is no salvation for a Jew or a Christian outside of faith in the Messiah, Jesus Christ. But this faith comes only through the holy Scriptures. Therefore, we must cherish and teach the Scriptures. In the famous Shema passage Moses declares, "Hear, O Israel: The LORD our God, the Lord is one. Love the LORD your God with all your heart and with all your soul and with all your strength. These commandments that I give you today are to be upon your hearts. Impress them on your children. Talk about them when you sit at home and when you walk along the road, when you lie down and when you get up. Tie them as symbols on your hands and bind them on your foreheads. Write them on the doorframes of your houses and on your gates" (Deut. 6:4–9).

The Scriptures are full of divine authority and power. Joel Beeke and Ray Lanning say this: "Scripture is God speaking to us, as a father speaks to his children. In Scripture God gives us His Word as both a word of truth and a word of power. As a word of truth, we can trust in and rest our all upon Scripture for time and eternity. We can also look to Scripture as the source of transforming power used by the Spirit of God to renew our minds."[1]

The Jew was given this great entrustment of the divine treasure of Scripture. The Lord asks his people, "And what other nation is so great as to have such righteous decrees and laws as this body of laws I am setting before you today?" (Deut. 4:8). The psalmist declares, "He has revealed his word to Jacob, his laws and decrees to Israel. He has done this for no other nation; they do not know his laws. Praise the LORD" (Ps. 147:19–20).

The word that goes out from the mouth of God is powerful to accomplish God's purposes: "As the rain and the snow come down from heaven, and do not return to it without watering the earth and making it bud and flourish, so that it yields seed for the sower and bread for the eater, so is my word that goes out from my mouth: It will not return to me empty, but will accomplish what I desire and achieve the purpose for which I sent it" (Isa. 55:10–11).

This word comes upon our dried up, famished, lost souls as dew upon mown grass. Moses declares, "Listen, O heavens, and I will speak; hear, O earth, the words of my mouth. Let my teaching fall like rain and my words descend like dew, like showers on new grass, like abundant rain on tender plants" (Deut. 32:1–2). Imagine life without water! But the word of God has come down from heaven upon our souls to revive and refresh us.

What a blessing it is that God himself condescends to speak to us! If a famous man even glances at us, we are happy. But if he stops and speaks to us, we are excited and blessed. We go home and say, "This man stopped and even spoke to me." That is exactly what God has done. He himself has spoken to us, expressing his love for us. He speaks so that we may live, not by bread alone,

---

1   Joel R. Beeke and Ray B. Lanning, "The Transforming Power of Scripture" in *Sola Scriptura! The Protestant Position on the Bible*, Don Kistler, gen. ed. (Morgan, PA: Soli Deo Gloria Publications, 1995), 222.

but by every word that proceeds out of his mouth (Deut. 8:3). God has given us his word that we may eat it and live by the nourishment and direction it gives. We are blessed if we can hear God's word faithfully preached weekly.

Not only are we blessed when God speaks to us, but we are also in distress when he keeps silent. When God refuses to speak to us, we experience confusion and misery. Amos prophesies about an unusual famine: "'The days are coming,' declares the Sovereign LORD, 'when I will send a famine through the land—not a famine of food or a thirst for water, but a famine of hearing the words of the LORD. Men will stagger from sea to sea and wander from north to east, searching for the word of the LORD, but they will not find it" (Amos 8:11-12). After much longsuffering, God threw his people out; his word stopped coming to them. In 1 Samuel 3:1 we find a curious phrase: "The boy Samuel ministered before the LORD under Eli. In those days *the word of the LORD was rare*; there were not many visions" (italics added). God was refusing to speak to his own covenant people who had become wicked. We later read about Saul, to whom God spoke at first through Samuel. When Saul refused to live by God's word, we read, "[Saul] inquired of the LORD, but the LORD did not answer him" (1 Sam. 28:6). Saul then went to a witch to find out what would happen in the future. Elsewhere the prophet Azariah told King Asa, "For a long time Israel was without the true God, without a priest to teach and without the law. But in their distress they turned to the LORD, the God of Israel, and sought him, and he was found by them" (2 Chron. 15:3-4). What a great tragedy it is when we are not hearing the word of God! We may have a Bible in our home, but we do not understand it, because God refuses to speak to those who do not cherish his word.

What did the Jews do with the word of God? Most of them did not treasure it. Instead, they became like pagans and practiced idolatry. Those to whom God's word was entrusted treated that word as garbage, as something to be hated and discarded: "You hate my instruction and cast my words behind you" (Ps. 50:17). Additionally, such people developed a hatred for his agents who spoke his word—pastors, parents, teachers, and friends. But Isaiah tells us what happens to those who throw away God's word: "Therefore, as tongues of fire lick up straw and as dry grass sinks down in the flames, so their roots will decay and their flowers blow away like dust; for they have rejected the law of the LORD Almighty and spurned the word of the Holy One of Israel" (Isa. 5:24). And Jeremiah asks, "To whom can I speak and give warning? Who will listen to me? Their ears are closed so they cannot hear. The word of the LORD is offensive to them; they find no pleasure in it" (Jer. 6:10).

In the history of Israel there was a time when the Bible was lost. After many years, it was found and brought to the good King Josiah. When Josiah heard the words of the law, he trembled, repented, and brought about serious reforms both in his life and in the life of the nation (2 Chron. 34). But his wicked son Jehoiakim had the opposite reaction. As his secretary was reading the word of God to him from a scroll, King Jehoiakim "cut [the columns he had just read] off with a scribe's knife and threw them into the firepot, until the entire scroll was burned in the fire" (Jer. 36:23). This king showed such contempt to God and his grace, love, and care by burning God's word.

Moses warned the people of Israel to treasure the word of God: "When Moses finished reciting all these words to all Israel, he said to them, 'Take to heart all the words I have solemnly declared to you this day, so that you may command your children to obey carefully all the words of this law. They are not just idle words for you—they are your life. By them you will live long in the land you are crossing the Jordan to possess'" (Deut. 32:45–47).

The rich heritage of God's word is our life, and we ignore it to our eternal peril. Jesus spoke of a rich man who lived in great luxury. He was dressed in purple and feasted every day. This man had the Scripture, but he paid no attention to it. After he died, he was in the fire, torment, and agony of hell. Not wanting his brothers to join him there, he asked if God could send Lazarus back to tell them to repent and believe in the word. God said no because they already had the law and the prophets (Luke 16:19–31).

There is nothing of greater value in the world than the word of God. It is our life. David says in Psalm 19 that it revives the soul, makes wise the simple, and gives joy to the heart and light to the eyes. God's word endures forever, is more precious than gold, is sweeter than the best honey, and acts as an early warning system to keep us from sin. There is great reward for those who keep God's word. It is not the general revelation of God found in creation, but the special revelation that tells us the truth about who God is, who man is, and how a sinner can be saved.

Psalm 119, the great celebration of God's word, discloses many aspects of God's wonderful word:

- It is the ultimate standard for us to live by (v. 1).
- It tells us how to live a holy life (v. 9).
- It warns us of sin and keeps us from sinning (v. 11).
- Unbelievers cannot understand it; we need God to open our eyes through regeneration (v. 18).
- When enemies or problems arise, the word of God gives us strength (v. 23).
- It acts like a multitude of counselors whose wisdom gives us safety as we seek direction (v. 24).
- We must choose the way of God's word (v. 30).
- It is pure delight to a believer (v. 35).
- It gives comfort in all suffering (v. 50).
- It leads us to repentance (v. 59).
- It is most precious (v. 72).
- It is eternal because it is the word of the eternal God (v. 89).
- It is the love of our heart (v. 97).
- It is most sweet (v. 103).
- It gives us guidance (v. 105).
- It is our treasure (v. 127).
- It gives us knowledge (v. 144).
- It gives us the fear of God (v. 161).
- It gives us great peace—the peace of God that transcends all human understanding (v. 165).
- It is strength to our soul (v. 175).

God speaks to us in the Scripture; it is the living word of God. All Scripture is God-spoken (2 Tim. 3:16). Yes, it came through men whom God directed so that they wrote exactly what God wanted them to write. But the emphasis here is that it proceeds out of the mouth of God and is charged with absolute authority and divine power, to be heard and obeyed. Paul says it is "useful for teaching, rebuking, correcting and training in righteousness, so that the man of God may be thoroughly equipped for every good work" (2 Tim. 3:16–17). Peter tells us the source of the Scriptures is God, who guided human beings by the Holy Spirit (2 Pet. 1:19–21). And not only are the Old Testament books the very word of God, but so also are the New Testament books (see 2 Peter 3:15–16, where the writings of Paul are called Scriptures).

In this great treasure of Scripture, the Lord is speaking to his servants. Man is created to obey God. In redemption the Sovereign God reasserts his lordship; no one is saved without confessing Jesus as Lord. This Lord Yahweh makes absolute demands in the holy Scriptures. We cannot question him, even when he says, as he did to Abraham, "Take your son, your only son, Isaac, whom you love, and go to the region of Moriah. Sacrifice him there as a burnt offering on one of the mountains I will tell you about" (Gen. 22:2). That is exactly what Abraham did (Heb 11:17–19) because loyalty to the Lord God transcends all other loyalties.

Like Abraham, we cannot have any other gods nor can we serve two masters. We must hate our father and mother, our wife and children, and our own life, and follow Christ (Luke 14:25–27). The word of this Lord must govern all areas of our lives. Professor John Frame points out how throughout the Old Testament we see God's word regulating worship, diet, sexual life, economic life, family life, travel, and calendar. Frame then observes that this lordship is even more comprehensive in the New Testament, embodied in the words of Paul: "So whether you eat or drink or whatever you do, do it all for the glory of God" (1 Cor. 10:31).[2]

Our Response to God's Word

We have heard God's word—through the preaching, through our parents, through our private and family devotions, through our Sunday school teachers. What should be our response to God's entrusting to us his very word? Do we value this privilege, this precious treasure that is more precious than gaining the whole world? As Dr. James Boice says, it is this word that gives life to the spiritually dead, that convicts and cleanses us of our sins, and that teaches us the will of God and how we should live.[3]

---

2   John M. Frame, "Scripture Speaks for Itself," in *God's Inerrant Word: An International Symposium on the Trustworthiness of Scripture*, ed. John Warwick Montgomery (Minneapolis: Bethany Fellowship, 1974), 182–83.

3   Boice, *Romans*, vol. 1, *Justification by Faith*, 280.

There are several reactions to the Scriptures among those who claim to be Christians.

1. To theological liberals, the Scripture is only man's word, without any absolute authority. Therefore, they reject God and miracles.
2. Adherents of neo-orthodoxy say that God is so transcendent that he does not actually speak in human words, but reveals himself in ways we cannot talk about. To them the Bible is man's very weak witness to God's nonverbal revelation and a document with no binding authority.
3. Postmodernists say the Bible has no meaning in itself. Therefore, we can make it say whatever we want it to say, but it has no authority in our lives.
4. Many evangelicals today maintain that the Bible contains both God's word and man's word, resulting in truth and errors, which must be sorted out by critical scholars. They would say we must check with professionals to know what to believe and what not to believe.
5. Orthodox evangelicals, however, assert that the Bible is the word of God from beginning to end. It is entirely truthful because God is truthful.

There was one Jew, Jesus Christ, who came into the world and treasured the word of God as no one else ever has. It was he who told the devil that man shall not live by bread alone but by every word that proceeds out of the mouth of God. He said, "Do not think that I have come to abolish the Law or the Prophets; I have not come to abolish them but to fulfill them" (Matt. 5:17). He told his disciples that the whole Bible—the Law, the Prophets, the Writings, and the Psalms—all spoke of him, that "the Christ will suffer and rise from the dead on the third day, and repentance and forgiveness of sins will be preached in his name to all nations, beginning at Jerusalem" (Luke 24:46–47).

What about You?

The unbelieving Jews asked, "What is the advantage of being born a Jew? If Jews and Gentiles will both be judged by God, what advantage do we have over the Gentiles?" The answer is that they had the advantage of possessing the great treasure of God's word. But they had to believe it, as Abraham did, to be saved.

Even so, many of us were born in Christian families, educated in Sunday school, and have heard the word of God preached for many years. Many were dedicated and baptized in the church. What is our advantage over non-Christians? Much in every way! To us God has entrusted his very precious word that reveals the way of salvation through Jesus Christ crucified and risen. Have we examined the Scriptures and listened to the claims of Christ? The Jews did. They were like builders as they carefully examined this stone, Jesus Christ. In the end, however, he was not acceptable to them, so they rejected and crucified him. But God raised him up, and Christ has now become the capstone and the very precious cornerstone. All who trust in him will never be put to shame.

Jesus asked, "Who do you say that I am—the Sovereign Lord, or a blasphemer; a precious cornerstone, or a worthless stone to be cast away?" We must choose today. Either we will receive him as Lord or reject him as a fraud, but then face him on the day of judgment.

John Wesley, the great Methodist preacher, wrote:

> I am a creature of a day, passing through life as an arrow through the air. I am a spirit come from God and returning to God; just hovering over the great gulf, till a few moments hence I am no more seen—I drop into an unchangeable eternity! I want to know one thing, the way to heaven—how to land safe on that happy shore. God himself has condescended to teach the way: for this very end he came from heaven. He hath written it down in a book. O give me that book! At any price give me the Book of God! I have it. Here is knowledge enough for me. Let me be *homo unius libri* [a man of one book]. Here then I am, far from the busy ways of men. I sit down alone: only God is here. In his presence I open, I read his Book; for this end, to find the way to heaven. Is there a doubt concerning the meaning of what I read? Does anything appear dark or intricate? I lift up my heart to the Father of lights: "Lord, is it not thy word, 'If any man lacks wisdom, let him ask of God'? Thou hast said, 'If any be willing to do thy will, he shall know.' I am willing to do; let me know thy will."[4]

In the Scriptures, God offers us his Son. I urge you to receive him as Savior and Lord today. Paul says we do not have to go to

---

4   Quoted by Boice, *Romans,* vol. 1, *Justification by Faith,* 279–80.

heaven to get the word of God or to hell to bring it up. "'The word is near you; it is in your mouth and in your heart,' that is, the word of faith we are proclaiming: That if you confess with your mouth, 'Jesus is Lord,' and believe in your heart that God raised him from the dead, you will be saved" (Rom. 10:8–9).

9

Divine Diagnosis of Man's Heart

[3]What if some did not have faith? Will their lack of faith nullify God's faithfulness? [4]Not at all! Let God be true, and every man a liar. As it is written:

"So that you may be proved right when you speak and prevail when you judge."

[5]But if our unrighteousness brings out God's righteousness more clearly, what shall we say? That God is unjust in bringing his wrath on us? (I am using a human argument.) [6]Certainly not! If that were so, how could God judge the world? [7]Someone might argue, "If my falsehood enhances God's truthfulness and so increases his glory, why am I still condemned as a sinner?" [8]Why not say—as we are being slanderously reported as saying and as some claim that we say—"Let us do evil that good may result"? Their condemnation is deserved.

[9]What shall we conclude then? Are we any better? Not at all! We have already made the charge that Jews and Gentiles alike are all under sin. [10]As it is written:

"There is no one righteous, not even one; [11]there is no one who understands, no one who seeks God. [12]All have turned away, they have together become worthless; there is no one who does good, not even one."

[13]"Their throats are open graves; their tongues practice deceit." "The poison of vipers is on their lips."

[14]"Their mouths are full of cursing and bitterness."

[15]"Their feet are swift to shed blood; [16]ruin and misery mark their ways, [17]and the way of peace they do not know."

[18]"There is no fear of God before their eyes."

[19]Now we know that whatever the law says, it says to those who are under the law, so that every mouth may be silenced and the whole world held accountable to God. [20]Therefore no one will be declared righteous in his sight by observing the law; rather, through the law we become conscious of sin.

Romans 3:3–20

One Sunday afternoon a man with a small leather bag was taking a walk in Scotland. A couple of teenagers thought he had a camera in his bag and so asked him to take a picture of them. The man said he already had a picture of them. He then took his Bible from the bag and began reading to them Romans 3, which speaks about their sinful condition and need of a Savior.

The Bible is a mirror that reveals our sinful nature. It shows our need for the Lamb of God, who takes away the sin of the world. The chief advantage of the Jews was that they were entrusted with the very words of God in the Old Testament. But many of them failed to believe in God's covenant promises; therefore, they failed to believe in the promised Messiah in the person of Jesus Christ.

In Romans 3:3–20 we are given a divine diagnosis of the sinful heart of every man, both Jew and Gentile. From this passage we want to speak about our sinful condition, our sinful conduct, the cause of this conduct, and the conclusion.

Our Sinful Condition

All fallen men, whether educated or not, have knowledge of God and his will from creation as well as from their own hearts. Yet they refuse to live according to that knowledge and exchange truth for a lie. Paul writes, "Furthermore, since they did not think it worthwhile to retain the knowledge of God, he gave them over to a depraved mind, to do what ought not to be done" (Rom. 1:28). In judgment God gives people over to a twisted mind. Such people always prefer lies and wickedness to truth and righteousness. They live by the philosophy of atheism: "The fool says in his heart, 'There is no God'" (Ps. 14:1). The wrath of God, therefore, is being revealed against such men and their ungodliness and unrighteousness.

Sinful men are filled with evil. Paul tells us, "They have become filled with every kind of wickedness, evil, greed and depravity. They are full of envy, murder, strife, deceit and malice" (Rom. 1:29). In Romans 3:3-8 we see how the twisted, sinful minds of the Jews worked. Paul examines several questions that were no doubt put to him by Jewish hecklers whenever he preached the gospel.

A. Questions of the Hecklers

1. DOES OUR LACK OF FAITH NULLIFY GOD'S FAITHFULNESS?

The first question had to do with the Jews' unfaithfulness to the covenant God made with them: "What if some did not have faith? Will their lack of faith nullify God's faithfulness?" (v. 3). The Jews were entrusted with the word of God. But they refused to believe it and embrace the Messiah, Jesus Christ. Paul poses the question: Does the unfaithfulness of the Jewish people negate God's covenant with them? His resounding answer: "Not at all!"

Man's failure can never frustrate God's eternal purposes. God's fidelity is not measured by human fidelity, because God's faithfulness is ultimately to his own person and promises. God's ultimate concern is for his own glory and not even for our blessings. Paul declares, "Let God be true, and every man a liar" (v. 4). God is always faithful and reliable. He can always be trusted, in spite of all the sin and unfaithfulness of all the peoples of the world. Paul cites Psalm 51:4 to prove this point. When David was sinning against Bathsheba and her husband, he was also sinning against God. God judged David, and David acknowledged that God was right in his judgment against him: "So that you may be proved right when you speak and prevail when you judge" (v. 4). Though God punished David, he did not fail to keep his covenant with David.

David asked, "Is not my house right with God? Has he not made with me an everlasting covenant, arranged and secured in every part? Will he not bring to fruition my salvation and grant me my every desire?" (2 Sam. 23:5). David's salvation depended on God's keeping the covenant with him by sending the Messiah. David's wickedness did not make God to be unfaithful; rather, it brought out God's faithfulness in greater glory. David's unfaithfulness proved and established God's faithfulness.

2. IF MY UNRIGHTEOUSNESS MAGNIFIES GOD'S RIGHTEOUSNESS, IS GOD UNJUST IN PUNISHING SINNERS?

The second question these hecklers asked was a challenge to God's justice: *"But if our unrighteousness brings out God's righteousness more clearly, what shall we say? That God is unjust in bringing his wrath on us? . . . Certainly not! If that were so, how could God judge the world?"* (vv. 5–6). In other words, these people were saying, "If, as you say, God's glory shines brighter in the dark background of our sin, then when we sin, we are really doing God a favor by providing the dark background to make his glory shine more brightly. Therefore, God should not punish us but really thank us. Our sin brings more glory to God." See the depravity of the human mind!

These antinomian hecklers were arguing that the end justifies the means. But Paul replies, "If your argument is right, then God cannot judge the world, because every man's sin is merely bringing God's glory into greater luster." Here Paul is echoing a fundamental Jewish belief that regarded Yahweh as the eschatological Judge of the whole world. Every Jew believed that God would judge the world, but when they said, "the world," they really meant Gentiles. They believed themselves exempt from this final judgment.

Yet if human sin brings glory to God, Paul argues, then how can God judge even the Gentiles? The holy God must judge every sinner, both Jew and Gentile. The assumption of the hecklers was invalid; the end does not justify the means.

3. IF MY SIN INCREASES GOD'S GLORY, WHY AM I CONDEMNED AS A SINNER?

The third question follows: *"Someone might argue, 'If my falsehood enhances God's truthfulness and so increases his glory, why am I still condemned as a sinner?'"* (v. 7). Paul takes it further: *"Why not say—as we are being slanderously reported as saying and as some claim that we say—'Let us do evil that good may result'?"* (v. 8). Paul refuses to answer this question except to affirm that God's condemnation of us is just.

B. Biblical Proof of Man's Condition

We cannot understand reality unless we believe in the Genesis account of creation, fall, and redemption. Because of the Fall, man has by nature a depraved mind. This condition explains the antinomian questions of the hecklers.

Paul concludes that all people are under sin (Rom. 3:9). Paul is speaking of the universality of sin. He first proved that Gentiles were sinners (Rom. 1:18-32). Then he proved that Jews also are sinners (Rom. 2:1-3:8). There is no difference. Every man is under sin, meaning "under the power of sin." Sin is personified as the master, and man is enslaved to sin. We cannot get out from under the dominion of sin on our own.

In Genesis we read, "The LORD saw how great man's wickedness on earth had become, and that every inclination of the thoughts of his heart was only evil all the time" (Gen. 6:5). This speaks about three aspects of sin: it is internal, pervasive, and continuous. This describes the total depravity of man. Jeremiah declares, "The heart is deceitful above all things and beyond cure. Who can understand it?" (Jer. 17:9). The answer is that only God can.

This is God's diagnosis of the human heart. Jesus says sin and uncleanness are not external, but internal; they are problems of our hearts: "For from within, out of men's hearts, come evil thoughts, sexual immorality, theft, murder, adultery, greed, malice, deceit, lewdness, envy, slander, arrogance and folly. All these evils come from inside and make a man 'unclean'" (Mark 7:21-23). Paul also tells us that we are by nature dead in trespasses and sins, and under the rule of Satan (Eph. 2:1-3).

All people are sinners; there is no exception. That is why the Bible is relevant to everyone. In seminary I was told that when I preach the gospel, all manner of people will be listening to me—educated or uneducated, rich or poor—but I must not worry. They all are sinners who must hear the gospel so that they may be saved. God's word does not show favoritism. It levels everyone.

Paul gives ample proof from the Scriptures to prove the truth of our depravity, citing multiple scriptures from the Old Testament. He only needs to cite the scriptures, for the Jews understood that the Scriptures are the final authority.

1. *"There is no one righteous, not even one"* (v. 10; Eccl. 7:20). God demands perfect conformity to his law. But since the Fall, all have become twisted in their minds; there is no one who is upright in thought and life. J. B. Phillips says, "No man can justify himself before God by a perfect performance of the Law's demands—indeed, the Law is the straight-edge that shows us how crooked we are" (Rom. 3:20, Phillips translation).[1]

This is the reason many people do not want to read the Bible. Every theologian and higher critic who criticizes the Bible is revealing what the Bible affirms, that we are sinners who cannot tolerate what the Bible has to speak about us. And if we ourselves are not reading the Bible, it is for the same reason: we do not want to be confronted with our sin. Either this Book will keep us from sin, or sin will keep us from this Book. Because we are sinners, we tend to hate the Bible because it exposes our wickedness. Yet that is the very reason we should read it! It is like going to a doctor to have our problem diagnosed so that we can be healed. In the same way, we must read the Bible to know exactly what our problem is. And not only does the Bible tell us our problem, but it also tells how we can be saved.

So Paul says no man is righteous. Martyn Lloyd-Jones says, "The best man, the noblest, the most learned, the most philanthropic, the greatest idealist, the greatest thinker, say what you like about him—there has never been a man who can stand up to the test of the law. Drop your plumb-line, and he is not true to it."[2] This is why we should read the Bible from beginning to end.

2. *"There is no one who understands"* (v. 11; Ps. 14:2). How often do we tell others how much we understand! Only God knows all things, and he has here revealed his truth about man's condition: "No one understands." This is a universal condition; there is no exception. Because of the noetic effect of sin, no one understands God, man, or creation. Without knowing God first, we cannot understand even the simplest thing. In fact, most people see truth as lie and lie as truth, and deny the infinite, personal God. They do so because they lack spiritual understanding. They believe in a closed system where God is not permitted. They are like

---

1   http://www.ccel.org/bible/phillips/CP06Romans.htm
2   Lloyd-Jones, *Romans*, vol. 2, *Righteous Judgment of God*, 198.

the Sadducees, who denied the resurrection, angels, evil spirits, heaven, hell, and eternal judgment. Irrational materialists believe in evolution but not creation. Paul says that the natural man does not understand things that are spiritual; they are foolishness to him (1 Cor. 2:14). Spiritual things make him fume and fight.

Natural man is not wise, because he does not fear God. The fear of God is the beginning of wisdom. Paul says about the unbeliever's mind: "You must no longer live as the Gentiles do, in the futility of their thinking. They are darkened in their understanding and separated from the life of God because of the ignorance that is in them due to the hardening of their hearts. Having lost all sensitivity, they have given themselves over to sensuality so as to indulge in every kind of impurity, with a continual lust for more" (Eph. 4:17–19). Elsewhere Paul says, "The god of this age has blinded the minds of unbelievers, so that they cannot see the light of the gospel of the glory of Christ, who is the image of God" (2 Cor. 4:4). People hate the Bible and Jesus Christ because they are darkened in their understanding.

3. *"No one who seeks God"* (v. 11; Ps. 14:2). Not only is man's mind twisted, but his will is also twisted. He will not seek the true God—the Father, Son, and Holy Spirit—the God of the Scriptures. That does not mean he is not religious. In fact, he is a connoisseur of the false religions of idolatry, the demon-inspired religions that God abhors. He will worship creation, demons, trees, snakes, bulls, birds, and man. But he will not worship the true and living God. Natural man is an enemy of God (Rom. 5:10; 8:7).

4. *"All have turned away"* (v. 12; Ps. 14:3). Again, notice, there is no exception. All have turned away from God's path, the way of truth, to the broad way of the lie. Every man is on the way to hell: "The way of the wicked will perish" (Ps. 1:6). The Greek says all have turned away deliberately. In our depravity we say, "I do not want truth or light. I do not want to know what my problems are. I hate God's way!" Isaiah says, "We all, like sheep, have gone astray, each of us has turned to his own way" (Isa. 53:6).

5. *"They have together become worthless"* (v. 12; Ps. 14:3). This, again, is universal. Every person has become worthless and useless to God. They have become like milk that has gone sour, or like meat that has become rotten. Such people are useless to God and everyone else. Through God's common grace, man can still do

civic good, like discovering new medicines, but he is worthless in things that matter ultimately.

The Conduct of Sinful Man

Having described the condition of man, Paul continues his scriptural proofs as he examines the conduct of sinful man.

6. *"There is no one who does good, not even one"* (v. 12; Ps. 14:3). People like to parade their self-righteousness, but Isaiah said all human righteousness is like filthy rags (Isa. 64:6). Paul likened it to dung (Phil. 3:8). All works done by a sinner before he trusts in God are dead works, done for man's own glory, not for the glory of God. A good work is done by a believer for God's glory.

First Samuel 15 describes how Saul fought the Amalekites. When he returned from the battle, he got up early and went to build a monument. This monument, however, was not to the Lord but to Saul himself. Unbelievers perform works for their own glory, not God's. But Jesus says, "What is highly valued among men is detestable in God's sight" (Luke 16:15).

7. *"Their throats are open graves"* (v. 13; Ps. 5:9). The throat of a sinner is like a grave that is opened up: a stench comes out of it (cf. John 11:39). This expression can also mean they will eat or bury people. Jesus declares, "Out of the overflow of the heart the mouth speaks" (Matt. 12:34). Such people emit a stench from within them that destroys people.

8. *"Their tongues practice deceit"* (v. 13; Ps. 5:9). This simply means sinners lie continuously and use flattery to get their way. We have heard parents, philosophers, politicians, professors, pastors, advertisers, and many others lie. We have heard the lies of evolution, the innate goodness of man, and the equality of all religions. Sinners are not only deceived but they also deceive others, especially through words. Think of preachers who preach salvation without repentance. They will say, "Our God is nice. I know you do not like repentance, so I will just preach salvation without repentance, justification without sanctification, faith without faithfulness, a God who is love but not holy, and a Jesus who is Savior but not Lord." Such lying preachers are even more dangerous than lying professors or philosophers.

9. *"The poison of vipers is on their lips"* (v. 13; Ps. 140:3). Think of the counsel Job's wife gave her husband: "Curse God and die!" (Job 2:9). That is real poison, aimed to kill a person. How many people use their tongues to deceive others! They may use flattery and speak many nice words, but their intent is to destroy. Lloyd-Jones writes about this analogy:

> This is a very fine description in a zoological sense. The adder, or viper, which is so harmful and so poisonous, has the poison concealed in a little bag at the root of the lips. This little bag is under the upper jaw of the adder close to some fangs which lie in a horizontal position. When the adder is about to pounce upon a victim he puts back his head and as he does so, these teeth or fangs drop down and he bites the victim. As he is biting with the fangs one of them presses the bag that is full of poison and into the wound is injected this venom, this poison that is going to kill the victim! So the Bible gives an exact scientific description of how the adder kills by means of his poison.[3]

10. *"Their mouths are full of cursing and bitterness"* (v. 14; Ps. 10:7). The cursing and bitterness overflow from their cursed and bitter hearts.

11. *"Their feet are swift to shed blood"* (v. 15; Isa. 59:7). The history of the world is a history of killing and murder. The devil is behind all murder. Jesus said, "You belong to your father, the devil, and you want to carry out your father's desire. He was a murderer from the beginning, not holding to the truth, for there is no truth in him. When he lies, he speaks his native language, for he is a liar and the father of lies" (John 8:44). Elsewhere he explained, "The thief comes only to steal and kill and destroy; I have come that they may have life, and have it to the full" (John 10:10).

12. *"Ruin and misery mark their ways"* (v. 16; Isa. 59:7). The wicked are like tsunamis, hurricanes, cyclones, and earthquakes. We see them coming and going, leaving destruction and misery behind. The history of kingdoms and civilizations is a history of ruin and misery.

13. *"The way of peace they do not know"* (v. 17; Isa. 59:8). "'There is no peace,' says my God, 'for the wicked'" (Isa. 57:21). Jesus Christ is the Prince of peace. A man outside of Jesus is a man without peace. He is restless like the waves of the sea.

---

3   Lloyd-Jones, *Romans*, vol. 2, *Righteous Judgment of God*, 211.

The Cause of Man's Miserable Condition

What is the cause of all this misery, sin, and wickedness? Again, Paul quotes from the Scriptures: *"There is no fear of God before their eyes"* (v. 18; Ps. 36:1).[4] Jesus spoke about a judge "who neither feared God nor cared about men" (Luke 18:2).

As David declares, "The fool says in his heart, 'There is no God'" (Ps. 14:1). All the deeds of wicked men are done without any God-consciousness. It is fear of God that keeps us from sinning (Ex. 20:20). He who fears God shuns evil, as Joseph did, saying, "How then could I do such a wicked thing and sin against God?" (Gen. 39:9). The fear of God kept him from sinning. Daniel also refused to sin out of fear of God, as did his three friends, who would not worship the golden image.

Above all, Jesus Christ always feared God, even when tempted most severely. Isaiah said the Spirit of the fear of the Lord would be upon him (Isa. 11:2). The Holy Spirit also causes us to fear the Lord. David said, "I have set the LORD always before me. Because he is at my right hand, I will not be shaken" (Ps. 16:8). He is speaking about a God-conscious life, saying, "I have deliberately set the Lord before me so that he governs my thoughts, words, and deeds."

When Paul says there is no fear of God before their eyes, this does not mean every sinner is as bad as he could possibly be. Rather, it means that no action of a sinner can ever receive divine approbation. Even the best actions of a sinner are done for his own glory most of all. Can we ever come to God and say, "I did this or that; therefore, you should justify me"? Absolutely not! Jesus understood this and called such people "a wicked and adulterous generation" (Matt. 12:39; 16:4).

The Conclusion

Paul concludes this section, *"Now we know that whatever the law says, it says to those who are under the law,"* that is, "in the sphere of the law" (v. 19). If you have a Bible, it is speaking to you. The Jews were given the Old Testament, so they were in the

---

4   Ironically, when we do not fear God, we fear everything.

sphere of the law. The Gentiles were as well, for they were given the revelation of God through creation and the works of the law were written in their hearts. Every man, therefore, is under God's law and knows God; yet he refuses to glorify God and give thanks to him. Instead, he exchanges truth for a lie and worships creation. But the word of God is living. God is speaking to us; are we listening?

What is the purpose of the law? Paul continues, *"so that every mouth may be silenced"* (v. 19). The picture is that of being in the courtroom of God. God is the judge and we are the defendants. We are given time to speak but we cannot: our mouths are shut. We know we are guilty as charged; therefore, we cannot speak, because we have no defense. That is what will happen when we face God.

The second reason Paul gives is *"so that . . . the whole world [may be] held accountable to God"* (v. 19). Every man is under divine judgment and is without excuse. Elsewhere Paul writes especially about the Gentiles, "For since the creation of the world God's invisible qualities—his eternal power and divine nature—have been clearly seen, being understood from what has been made, so that men are without excuse" (Rom. 1:20). He said to the Jews, "You, therefore, have no excuse" (Rom. 2:1). Every mouth, therefore, is stopped and the whole world is under divine judgment. We all stand guilty before God.

This is the divine diagnosis. No one can be declared righteous in God's sight by observing the law. The reason is that no man can observe the law as God demands because every man is a sinner. Jesus spoke of a Pharisee who prayed to himself, parading his self-righteousness. He was saying, "I have no use for Jesus Christ or the cross. I can save myself." But he went home condemned (Luke 18:9–14). Paul also paraded his righteousness, saying, "As for legalistic righteousness, [I was] faultless" (Phil. 3:6). But when God apprehended him, Paul found out his righteousness was dung.

The law condemns us. Jesus said to those who were relying on their own works, "Away from me, you evildoers!" (Matt. 7:23). The psalmist says, "No one living is righteous before you" (Ps. 143:2). It is impossible to save ourselves.

What, then, is the purpose of the law? It is through the law that we receive knowledge of sin. God's law is the mirror for our lives. That is why we must read it all the time. It shows our sins. The law does not forgive our sins or justify us. In fact, the law makes sin worse by revealing, condemning, and aggravating our sin. A mirror shows dirt on our faces, but it cannot wash our faces clean. We need Christ to make us clean, and the law points to Christ, the Savior of the world. In other words, the law is the straight-edge that shows how crooked we are. Jesus alone can make us straight.

This, then, is the divine diagnosis of our heart: its condition, its conduct, its cause, and the conclusion. Knowing no one can save himself, is there any hope for a sinful man? Is there any effective medicine for a sinner? Can I obtain a new heart?

The answer is yes. Not only does the Bible reveal our problem, but it also gives us the remedy. In the next passage, Romans 3:21–26, Paul gives us the prescription that will heal us. As Paul declares, "I am not ashamed of the gospel, because it is the power of God for the salvation of everyone who believes: first for the Jew, then for the Gentile. For in the gospel a righteousness from God is revealed, a righteousness that is by faith from first to last, just as it is written: 'The righteous will live by faith'" (Rom. 1:16–17).

The publican simply said, "God, have mercy on me, a sinner," and he went home justified (Luke 18:13–14). The thief from the cross said, "Jesus, remember me when you come into your kingdom," and Jesus responded, "Today you will be with me in paradise" (Luke 23:42–43). Jesus came to seek and save lost sinners like us.

> Amazing grace, how sweet the sound
> that saved a wretch like me!

If Jesus Christ has taken us out of the dominion, power, and mastery of sin and placed us under the power of grace and the lordship of Christ, we can all go out justified, walking and leaping and praising God.

10

Justification by Grace

²¹But now a righteousness from God, apart from law, has been made known, to which the Law and the Prophets testify. ²²This righteousness from God comes through faith in Jesus Christ to all who believe. There is no difference, ²³for all have sinned and fall short of the glory of God, ²⁴and are justified freely by his grace through the redemption that came by Christ Jesus. ²⁵God presented him as a sacrifice of atonement, through faith in his blood. He did this to demonstrate his justice, because in his forbearance he had left the sins committed beforehand unpunished— ²⁶he did it to demonstrate his justice at the present time, so as to be just and the one who justifies those who have faith in Jesus.

Romans 3:21–26

Leon Morris regards Romans 3:21–26 as possibly the most important single paragraph ever written.[1] Luther calls it the chief point of the whole Bible. This passage speaks about three aspects of salvation: justification, redemption, and propitiation. This chapter will focus on justification by grace.

Increasingly, self-identified "Bible-believing" people report that they believe that there are many ways to eternal life. This directly contradicts the biblical view that salvation is found in Jesus Christ alone. Jesus himself proclaims, "I am the way and the truth and the life. No one comes to the Father except through me" (John 14:6). Peter also declares, "Salvation is found in no one else, for there is no other name under heaven given to men by which we must be saved" (Acts 4:12). Dr. John Stott says, "No

---

1   Morris, *Epistle to the Romans*, 173.

other system, ideology or religion proclaims a free forgiveness and a new life to those who have done nothing to deserve it but a lot to deserve judgment instead."[2] Let us examine this great passage that opens for us knowledge of the way of eternal salvation.

A New Era

Paul begins, *"But now . . ."* (v. 21). This "now" is contrasted with the former times of divine salvation. Earlier Paul spoke of the wrath of God being revealed against all godlessness and wickedness of men who suppress the truth in wicked deeds. He proved that all have sinned and are under God's wrath, that there is none righteous, none who seek God or do good, and that there is no fear of God before the eyes of man (Rom. 1:18–3:20). Later in this epistle he explains that man is a powerless, ungodly sinner. Man is an enemy of God, for the very heart of sin is enmity toward God. His mind is hostile to God, and he cannot please God. Guilty and hell-bound, man cannot save himself by his own good works.

So Paul writes, "Therefore, no one will be declared righteous in his sight by observing the law" (v. 20). We must be saved by another. The mighty God, against whom all men have sinned, must save us because there is no other savior. But, thank God, a new era has begun. In the fullness of time, the era of grace and divine salvation came in Jesus Christ. Paul declares, "But when the time had fully come, God sent his Son, born of a woman, born under law, to redeem those under law, that we might receive the full rights of sons" (Gal. 4:4–5). He also proclaimed to the Athenians, "In the past God overlooked such ignorance, but now he commands all people everywhere to repent" (Acts 17:30).

A new era of grace has come—the era of the Messiah. The Hebrews writer says, "Now [Christ] has appeared once for all at the end of the ages to do away with sin by the sacrifice of himself" (Heb. 9:26). We are living in this "now," when we sinners can call upon the name of Jesus and be set free from slavery to sin, guilt, condemnation, Satan, death, and hell. Paul writes, "Now is the time of God's favor, now is the day of salvation" (2 Cor. 6:2). Today

---

2   Stott, *Romans: God's Good News*, 118.

is the day of fulfillment of God's promise of a Savior—a promise first made in Genesis 3:15 and now fulfilled in Jesus Christ.

A Righteousness from God

Paul then explains what is happening in this new era: *"But now a righteousness from God, apart from law, has been made known"* (v. 21). This righteousness was revealed once for all in the life, death, and resurrection of Christ. Jesus died for our sins and was raised for our justification (Rom. 4:25). As Moses lifted up the brazen serpent in the wilderness for the healing of all who had been bitten by poisonous serpents, so Christ was lifted up on the cross to manifest a righteousness from God that alone can meet our need. The gospel reveals this righteousness from God.

This righteousness of God is apart from the law-works of man. The Jews of Jesus' day misunderstood the way of salvation. They taught that people could earn salvation by meritorious good works done in obedience to the Mosaic law. Jesus gave an example of such thinking: "To some who were confident of their own righteousness and looked down on everybody else, Jesus told this parable: 'Two men went up to the temple to pray, one a Pharisee and the other a tax collector. The Pharisee stood up and prayed about himself: "God, I thank you that I am not like other men—robbers, evildoers, adulterers—or even like this tax collector. I fast twice a week and give a tenth of all I get"'" (Luke 18:9–12).

Judaism taught salvation by self, not by the Messiah. The Messiah came to his own people but they rejected him, thinking they did not need a Savior. This is still true today. But the Mosaic law was never intended to save anyone. Paul writes, "Therefore no one will be declared righteous in his sight by observing the law; rather, through the law we become conscious of sin" (Rom. 3:20). To those who want to glory in their self-righteousness and human merit, he says, "Law brings wrath" (Rom. 4:15). In other words, the wrath of God shall be poured out on the one who depends on the law. The law aggravates and increases sin: "The law was added so that the trespass might increase" (Rom. 5:20).

Man, who is a slave of sin, cannot keep God's law perfectly. Paul writes in Romans 3:9 and 7:14 that we are "under sin," meaning we are so much under the control and power of sin that we cannot deliver ourselves from its grip. God himself had to deliver us through his Son. The angel told Joseph, "You are to give him the name Jesus, because he will save his people from their sins" (Matt. 1:21). Jesus Christ saves us, not *in* our sins, but *from* our sins—from their power and dominion over us. "If the Son sets you free, you will be free indeed" (John 8:36). That is why we must come to Jesus without any claim of merit. Jesus saves only those who know they are sinners and cannot save themselves. Any merit-based plea will condemn us.

Paul describes God as one who justifies the ungodly (Rom. 4:5). Are you ungodly? Are you a sinner? Are you loaded down with guilt? Then come to Jesus. He will do what is humanly impossible and save you. With God all things are possible.

Not a New Salvation

Look again at verse 21: "*But now a righteousness from God, apart from law, has been made known, to which the Law and the Prophets testify.*" The entire Old Testament spoke about a salvation by grace through faith. Abraham, David, and all other Old Testament saints were justified by grace through faith, as Paul discusses in Romans 4 and as we read in the book of Hebrews. Habakkuk said the just shall live by faith (Hab. 2:4). Paul later quotes David, "Blessed are they whose transgressions are forgiven, whose sins are covered. Blessed is the man whose sin the Lord will never count against him" (Rom. 4:7–8; Ps. 32:1–2). The idea here is that our sin will be counted against another. The Old Testament sacrificial system pointed to justification by grace through faith. Jesus himself spoke of this: "'Did not the Christ have to suffer these things and then enter his glory?' And beginning with Moses and all the Prophets, he explained to them what was said in all the Scriptures concerning himself. . . . He told them, 'This is what is written: The Christ will suffer and rise from the dead on the third day, and repentance and forgiveness of sins will be preached in his name to all nations'" (Luke 24:26–27, 46–47).

There is continuity in the way of salvation between the Old and the New Testament; the entire Old Testament speaks of this righteousness of God apart from the law. This way of justification is not a new idea; God saves sinners by grace through faith in all dispensations. The Bible never teaches a merit-based self-salvation. The Pharisee who prided in his works of the law went home condemned (Luke 18:14).

Justified Freely by His Grace

Sinners who believe in Christ "are justified freely by his grace" (v. 24). The words "righteousness," "justify," and "just" appear seven times in this passage. The righteousness of God is a justifying, divine, God-given righteousness that God demands of us. This objective righteousness of Christ meets our need. In the Greek it is "being justified," meaning one sinner at a time is given the righteousness of God that we read about in verse 21. God gives us his righteousness, we receive it, and we are justified.

Question 70 of the Westminster Larger Catechism asks, "What is justification?" The answer: "Justification is an act of God's free grace unto sinners, in which he pardoneth all their sins, accepteth and accounteth their persons righteous in his sight; not for anything wrought in them, or done by them, but only for the perfect obedience and full satisfaction of Christ, by God imputed to them, and received by faith alone."

Imagine a condemned criminal waiting to be executed for his crime being told he is free to go home to his wife, children, and friends. He can do so because an innocent person who loved the criminal has agreed to be executed for his crime in his stead. This is justification. Barabbas went home, while Jesus was crucified.

Justification is the language of the heavenly courtroom. Deuteronomy 25:1 says, "When men have a dispute, they are to take it to court and the judges will decide the case, acquitting the innocent and condemning the guilty." Yet in Romans 4:5 Paul speaks of "God who justifies the wicked." This seems to be a contradiction, for how can God justify the wicked? A judge should declare the innocent as innocent and the guilty as guilty. His business is not to make people innocent or guilty. We are guilty, ungodly, wicked enemies of God, yet God pronounces us just.

First, we must realize that when God justifies us, he is *declaring* us to be righteous, not *making* us righteous within. Justification is not sanctification. Dr. Stott says, "[God] is pronouncing [sinners] legally righteous, free from any liability to the broken law, because he himself in his Son has borne the penalty for their law-breaking."[3]

Justification is God's legal declaration that our sins are forgiven and that God's righteousness is ours. God gives us a new legal standing. God's legal declaration is irrevocable and irreversible. Who can challenge what the Supreme Judge of the universe has pronounced?

The justified are not automatically changed within, but God, who declares us to be legally righteous forever, will also see to it that we are changed within. In fact, if we do not change, we are not justified. Dr. Boice says, "Actual [or experimental] righteousness does follow on justification—so closely that we are correct in saying that if it does not, the one involved is not justified."[4] In other words, if the justified person is not being sanctified, as evidenced in obedience and godliness, then he is not justified. Justification necessarily leads to sanctification; we are made righteous progressively within. Our good works prove our prior justification.

Roman Catholics confuse justification and sanctification, and imputed and imparted righteousness. They teach that justification makes us righteous within, but that righteousness is based partly on God's works and partly on ours. Such theology cannot give us assurance of salvation because our justification would then rest partly on our own works.

God justifies the ungodly on the basis of Christ's work. By the sanctification of the Spirit, God makes the ungodly godly and the disobedient obedient. Therefore Paul says we *"are justified freely by his grace"* (v. 24). He uses a present passive participle, meaning we are not justifying ourselves; we are justified through the actions of another. God the Father declares us righteous in Jesus Christ.

The Source of Justification: Grace

The source of our justification is the grace of God. Paul says we are *"justified freely by his grace through the redemption that came by Christ Jesus"* (v. 24). Paul already proved that there is no one who

---

3   Quoted by Boice in *Romans*, vol. 1, *Justification by Faith*, 384.
4   Ibid., 383.

is righteous, that all have sinned, and that the wages of sin is death. We are totally depraved and completely powerless. By grace alone can we be justified, and this grace comes to us as a gift.

Grace costs us nothing, yet it is very costly. Because God did not spare his own Son from judgment, we are spared. Think of Abraham's joy when God provided a ram in Isaac's place, and Isaac could go home with his father (Gen. 22). That ram is Jesus Christ. Grace cost the Father the death of his Son, who cried out from the cross, "My God, my God, why hast thou forsaken me?" This high cost magnifies God's grace. Away with all cheap grace! Only the costly grace of God can justify us.

God's grace gives justification to those who merited condemnation, heaven to those who merited hell, and eternal life to those who merited everlasting death. This abounding grace is greater than all our sins. Paul writes, "For if, by the trespass of the one man, death reigned through that one man, how much more will those who receive God's abundant provision of grace and of the gift of righteousness reign in life through the one man, Jesus Christ. . . . The law was added so that the trespass might increase. But where sin increased, grace increased all the more" (Rom. 5:17, 20). This grace makes us able and more than able to do what God wants us to do. Paul says, "And God is able to make all grace abound to you, so that in all things at all times, having all that you need, you will abound in every good work" (2 Cor. 9:8). Additionally, this grace causes us to rejoice. In Greek, the word "grace" speaks about that which gives us great joy.

Although grace is a very costly gift, as we said, it costs us nothing. And because we cannot buy grace, salvation is free. Only those who have no merit of their own can receive it. So the Lord invites us: "Come, all you who are thirsty, come to the waters; and you who have no money, come, buy and eat! Come, buy wine and milk without money and without cost" (Isa. 55:1). We receive grace for nothing, yet it is the most expensive gift we can possess.

John speaks of this costly gift of grace: "[The risen Lord] said to me: 'It is done. I am the Alpha and the Omega, the Beginning and the End. To him who is thirsty I will give to drink without cost from the spring of the water of life'" (Rev. 21:6). Again, John says, "The Spirit and the bride say, 'Come!' And let him who hears say,

'Come!' Whoever is thirsty, let him come; and whoever wishes, let him take the free gift of the water of life" (Rev. 22:17). Those who are thirsty must acknowledge they are sinners who cannot be saved without God helping them. They see their need, as did the psalmist, who declared, "As the deer pants for streams of water, so my soul pants for you, O God. My soul thirsts for God, for the living God. When can I go and meet with God?" (Ps. 42:1–2).

Jesus spoke of a king who prepared a great feast (Matt. 22:1–14). The guests were asked to come, but they all refused, saying, "I have no need of this feast. I have bought land," or "I have bought oxen," or "I am married." So the king brought in the poor, the crippled, and the blind to enjoy the feast. God's abounding grace that makes us competent is not for the rich, famous, and arrogant, but for the poor, crippled, and blind. Great salvation is for each prostitute and publican who cries out, "Have mercy on me, the sinner." Great salvation is for the thief on the cross who with his last breath entreated Jesus, "Remember me when you come into your kingdom." To such people God opens the gates of paradise and they shall feast with Christ, both now and forever.

There is no grace for proud Herods, Pilates, high priests, Pharisees, and Sadducees. Jesus saves only sinners by his amazing and abounding grace. John Stott says, "Grace is God loving, God stooping, God coming to the rescue, God giving himself generously in and through Jesus Christ."[5]

The Ground of Justification

The ground of our justification is the work of Christ—his life, death, and resurrection. Justification is not amnesty, which is pardon without principle. It is not seeing bad people as good people. Justification is based on God's justice demonstrated in the life and death of Christ. The wrath of God against elect sinners was poured out on God's innocent Son, the spotless Lamb of God. Without the cross, the justification of the unjust would be unjustified, immoral, and impossible. But Christ died for and in place of the wicked.

Paul earlier says the wrath of God is revealed against all the ungodly (Rom. 1:18). Yet he later writes, "When we were still

---

5   Stott, *Romans: God's Good News,* 112.

powerless, Christ died for the ungodly" (Rom. 5:6). Therefore, we can now understand the statement in Romans 4:5: "God . . . justifies the ungodly." God does so because Christ died for the ungodly.

Jesus died as our substitute. He is our Passover Lamb. John the Baptist declared, "Look, the Lamb of God, who takes away the sin of the world!" (John 1:29). In Hebrews 9:14 we read, "How much more, then, will the blood of Christ, who through the eternal Spirit offered himself unblemished to God, cleanse our consciences from acts that lead to death, so that we may serve the living God!" Peter writes, "For you know that it was not with perishable things such as silver or gold that you were redeemed from the empty way of life handed down to you from your forefathers, but with the precious blood of Christ, a lamb without blemish or defect. . . . For Christ died for sins once for all, the righteous for the unrighteous, to bring you to God" (1 Pet. 1:18–19; 3:18). In our behalf Jesus satisfied the demands of all God's holy laws.

When God justifies us freely by his grace, he forgives all our sins. That is why Paul could say, "Blessed is the man whose sin the Lord will never count against him" (Rom. 4:8). Our sins are counted against Jesus Christ.

He also gives us the free gift of the righteousness of God, even the righteousness of Christ. Paul says, "For just as through the disobedience of the one man the many were made sinners, so also through the obedience of the one man the many will be made righteous" (Rom. 5:19). No longer are we under God's wrath and sin's dominion. No longer is Satan our master. We are now under God's blessing, which justification brings to us. On the basis of Christ's substitutionary work in our behalf, we are righteous and have righteousness; we have forgiveness, eternal life, and glory; we have peace with God and experience the peace of God. As adopted children of God, we are united with Christ. All he has is ours. We have fellowship with the Father and the Son.

Paul writes of this double transaction: "God was reconciling the world to himself in Christ, not counting men's sins against them. . . . God made him who had no sin to be sin for us, so that in him we might become the righteousness of God" (2 Cor. 5:19, 21). All our sins were taken from our head and put upon Jesus, who knew no sin. Our sin became his and he atoned for it, and his righteousness is now ours.

Elsewhere Paul says, "It is because of him that you are in Christ Jesus, who has become for us wisdom from God—that is, our righteousness, holiness and redemption" (1 Cor. 1:30). Christ is our righteousness, sanctification, and redemption. Christ is not divided. If we are justified, we will be sanctified and glorified.

No longer do we try to hide under our filthy rags of self-righteousness, nor do we boast of the dung of our human merit. Covered by the blood of Christ, we are now righteous and the righteousness of God. We are in Christ. The divine judgment was hanging over us, ready to fall and execute us. But, thank God, it fell not on us, but on the One on the cross of Calvary. Now this righteousness of God has been made manifest. May we look to him and be saved!

11

Redemption in Christ

[21]But now a righteousness from God, apart from law, has been made known, to which the Law and the Prophets testify. [22]This righteousness from God comes through faith in Jesus Christ to all who believe. There is no difference, [23]for all have sinned and fall short of the glory of God, [24]and are justified freely by his grace through the redemption that came by Christ Jesus. [25]God presented him as a sacrifice of atonement, through faith in his blood. He did this to demonstrate his justice, because in his forbearance he had left the sins committed beforehand unpunished— [26]he did it to demonstrate his justice at the present time, so as to be just and the one who justifies those who have faith in Jesus.

Romans 3:21–26

There are three sides to the triangle of salvation, described in three theological terms: justification, redemption, and propitiation. Paul speaks of being *"justified freely by his grace through the redemption that came by Christ Jesus"* (v. 24). In the last chapter, we looked at justification. In this study we will examine redemption, the second side of this triangle.

The Vocabulary of Redemption

When we study the words associated with redemption (redeem, redeemer, ransom), we find that many of them are constructed on the Greek verbal stem *lu*, which means "to loose, to set free, to liberate, to deliver from bondage to freedom." Thus we have *apoluō*, which means "to set free." Simeon used this word in reference to himself in Luke 2:29: "Sovereign Lord, as you have promised, you now *dismiss* your servant in peace." The word *lutroō* means "to set at liberty upon payment of a ransom." *Lutron* means "a ransom, the payment one makes to set someone free." *Lutrōsis* means "redemption" (see Luke 1:68). *Apolutrōsis*, which appears in Romans 3:24, means "to set a slave free upon payment of ransom, away from his former wretched condition and situation to a new situation, to a new owner, to new freedom." *Lutrōtēs*, used in reference to Moses in Acts 7:35, means "deliverer, redeemer."

Other words speak about redemption from the agora, the Greek marketplace. So we have *agorazō*, which means "to buy someone or something for oneself from the marketplace" (see 1 Cor. 6:19–20) and *exagorazō*, which means "to buy out of the marketplace, never to return to the former condition again" (see Gal. 3:13).

Slaves, prisoners of war, and captives condemned to death could be set free by another paying a ransom for them. Redemption, therefore, is releasing someone from the bondage of an alien power by paying a ransom. This ransom has to be paid by another because the captive is powerless to secure his own liberty. Captives condemned to die will surely die unless they are redeemed by another through a ransom payment.

The Scripture says we are redeemed by Jesus Christ from the alien power of Satan, from captivity to sin, from the curse of the law, from the guilt and power of sin, and from death eternal. We are redeemed to belong to our Redeemer, Jesus Christ, never again to return to our former owner and miserable situation.

Christ's redemption of us is not temporal but eternal. Speaking of the excellency and beauty of these words "redeemer" and "redemption," Everett F. Harrison declares, "No word in the Christian vocabulary deserves to be held more precious than Redeemer, for even more than Saviour it reminds the child of God that his salvation has been purchased at a great and personal cost, for the Lord has given himself for our sins in order to deliver us from them."[1] B. B. Warfield says that Redeemer "is the name specifically of the Christ of the cross. Whenever we pronounce it, the cross is placarded before our eyes and our hearts are filled with

---

1   Everett F. Harrison, Geoffrey W. Bromiley, and Carl F. H. Henry, eds., *Baker's Dictionary of Theology* (Grand Rapids: Baker Book House, 1982), 439.

loving remembrance not only that Christ has given us salvation but that he paid a mighty price for it."[2] Jesus himself stated, "The Son of Man did not come to be served, but to serve, and to give his life as a ransom for many" (Matt. 20:28).

Our Inability to Redeem Ourselves

Can a man redeem himself? The Bible clearly says no. The psalmist declares, "No man can redeem the life of another or give to God a ransom for him—the ransom for a life is costly, no payment is ever enough—that he should live on forever and not see decay" (Ps. 49:7–9). We read elsewhere, "If you, O LORD, kept a record of sins, O Lord, who could stand? . . . [The LORD] himself will redeem Israel from all their sins" (Ps. 130:3, 8).

Those who are not born again are in bondage to sin. "To the Jews who had believed him, Jesus said, 'If you hold to my teaching, you are really my disciples. Then you will know the truth, and the truth will set you free.' They answered him, 'We are Abraham's descendants and have never been slaves of anyone. How can you say that we shall be set free?' Jesus replied, 'I tell you the truth, everyone who sins is a slave to sin. Now a slave has no permanent place in the family, but a son belongs to it forever. So if the Son sets you free, you will be free indeed'" (John 8:31–36).

Paul makes the charge that "Jews and Gentiles alike are all under sin" (Rom. 3:9). By nature we are under the authority of master Sin and cannot free ourselves. Then Paul asserts, "*All have sinned and fall short of the glory of God*" (Rom. 3:23). Sin is the master of everyone not redeemed by Jesus Christ. Paul also comments, "We know that the law is spiritual; but I am unspiritual, sold as a slave to sin" (Rom. 7:14).

Moreover, "The wages of sin is death" (Rom. 6:23), and "The soul who sins is the one who will die" (Ezek. 18:20). We cannot get out of sin by ourselves. This is what we call total depravity.

We Need a Redeemer

We need a redeemer to set us free by payment of a ransom. In the Old Testament close relatives had certain rights: they could

---

2   Quoted by Boice, *Romans*, vol. 1, *Justification by Faith*, 363.

avenge the murder of a family member or buy back for the family any property that was sold to pay a debt. They also had the right to redeem with a ransom any family member who had sold himself as a slave or one who was under the sentence of death where such redemption was possible.[3]

Close relatives also had the right to marry the widows of their brothers so that the name of the dead brother would continue through the first son of the new marriage. Such a person is called a gōʾēl, a kinsman-redeemer. The book of Ruth is a beautiful love story that dramatizes the gracious redemption that Boaz, as kinsman-redeemer, accomplishes in buying up the property of his relative Elimelech and marrying Ruth, through whom came Christ, our great Redeemer.

We need a gōʾēl, a very close relative, to redeem us miserable sinners who are slaves to sin, Satan, and death. Not only must this person have the ability to pay our ransom, but he must also be willing to do so. Praise God, we have such a relative: our Lord Jesus Christ. Now we can understand more fully the importance of the incarnation of Christ.

Why did the Son of God become man? The writer to the Hebrews says, "In bringing many sons to glory, it was fitting that God, for whom and through whom everything exists, should make the author of their salvation perfect through suffering. . . . Since the children have flesh and blood, he too shared in their humanity so that by his death he might destroy him who holds the power of death—that is, the devil—and free those who all their lives were held in slavery by their fear of death" (Heb. 2:10, 14–15). We have a close relative in Jesus Christ, and he alone is able to pay the ransom to secure our freedom because he is God-man, the sinless One. Paul writes, "[Christ Jesus], being in very nature God, did not consider equality with God something to be grasped, but made himself nothing, taking the very nature of a servant, being made in human likeness. And being found in appearance as a man, he humbled himself and became obedient to death— even death on a cross!" (Phil. 2:6–8). God became incarnate as a

---

3   For example, Exodus 21 speaks about an ox that was in the habit of goring. If the owner did not take care of it, and the ox gored and killed someone, the ox must be killed. The owner also must be killed unless someone wanted to redeem him by paying whatever price was asked.

servant to die the shameful death of the cross so that we might be redeemed.

But is Jesus willing to redeem us? Consider the account of a leper: "When [Jesus] came down from the mountainside, large crowds followed him. A man with leprosy came and knelt before him and said, 'Lord, if you are willing, you can make me clean.' Jesus reached out his hand and touched the man. 'I am willing,' he said. 'Be clean!'" (Matt. 8:1-3). How much more willing is Jesus to redeem us from our slavery to sin!

The Old Testament speaks much of such a redeemer. In the midst of his suffering, Job declared, "I know that my Redeemer lives, and that in the end he will stand upon the earth" (Job 19:25). This was fulfilled in Jesus Christ: "The Word became flesh and made his dwelling among us. We have seen his glory, the glory of the One and Only, who came from the Father, full of grace and truth" (John 1:14).

Isaiah also spoke much about this great Redeemer's coming: "Sing for joy, O heavens, for the LORD has done this; shout aloud, O earth beneath. Burst into song, you mountains, you forests and all your trees, for the LORD has redeemed Jacob, he displays his glory in Israel" (Isa. 44:23); "Leave Babylon, flee from the Babylonians! Announce this with shouts of joy and proclaim it. Send it out to the ends of the earth; say, 'The LORD has redeemed his servant Jacob'" (Isa. 48:20); "This is what the LORD says—the Redeemer and Holy One of Israel" (Isa. 49:7); "Burst into songs of joy together, you ruins of Jerusalem, for the LORD has comforted his people, he has redeemed Jerusalem" (Isa. 52:9).

Who Is the Promised Redeemer?

This redeemer promised in the Old Testament is none other than Jesus Christ. He is our $g\bar{o}'\bar{e}l$, our kinsman-redeemer. The angel told Joseph, "You are to give him the name Jesus, because he will save his people from their sins" (Matt. 1:21). Zechariah prophesied about the redemption Christ would bring: "Praise be to the Lord, the God of Israel, because he has come and has redeemed his people" (Luke 1:68). Anna spoke similarly to the parents of the infant Jesus: "Coming up to them at that very moment, she gave thanks to God and spoke about the child to all who were looking forward to the redemption of Jerusalem" (Luke 2:38). Paul remarks, "In him we have redemption through his blood, the forgiveness of sins" (Eph. 1:7). Elsewhere he writes, "For he has rescued us from the dominion of darkness and brought us into the kingdom of the Son he loves, in whom we have redemption, the forgiveness of sins" (Col. 1:13–14).

In Hebrews 7:22, Jesus is called our "sponsor," which means he is responsible for all our obligations. Jesus guarantees our total and final salvation because of his person and permanent priesthood. There is no redemption outside of the person of Jesus Christ. There is no salvation in any other name. Jesus Christ alone is our Redeemer.

The High Cost of Redemption

Not only is Jesus our Redeemer, but he is also the ransom price paid for our redemption. All creation came into being by a command of God, but redemption was achieved by the incarnation and death of God's Son. This great price shows how much God loves us.

Paul spoke of this high cost of redemption to the Ephesian elders: "Keep watch over yourselves and all the flock of which the Holy Spirit has made you overseers. Be shepherds of the church of God, which he bought with his own blood" (Acts 20:28). Jesus himself spoke of this price: "I am the good shepherd. The good shepherd lays down his life for the sheep" (John 10:11). Peter declares, "For you know that it was not with perishable things such as silver or gold that you were redeemed from the empty way of life handed down to you from your forefathers, but with the precious blood of Christ, a lamb without blemish or defect" (1 Pet. 1:18–19). We see the same idea in 1 Corinthians 6:19–20: "Do you not know that your body is a temple of the Holy Spirit, who is in you, whom you have received from God? You are not your own; you were bought at a price. Therefore honor God with your body."

The Hebrews writer tells us, "Without the shedding of blood there is no forgiveness" (Heb. 9:22). The blood of bulls and goats cannot forgive our sins. Only the blood of God's Son can redeem us. But Jesus did not give his life to ransom every sinner. Jesus died to redeem only his elect sinners whose names are written in the Lamb's book of life. So Paul writes, "For he chose us in him before the creation of the world to be holy and blameless in his sight" (Eph. 1:4). If everyone was chosen, then choosing would have no meaning. In his high priestly prayer, Jesus says of his disciples, "I pray for them. I am not praying for the world, but for those you have given me, for they are yours" (John 17:9). There is a distinction. The church is an inner circle; the outer circle is the world. We are the Father's donation to the Son, that he may redeem us at the high price of his own death.

Jesus said to the unbelieving Jews, "You do not believe me because you are not my sheep. My sheep listen to my voice; I know them, and they follow me. I give them eternal life, and they shall never perish; no one can snatch them out of my hand" (John 10:26–28). J. I. Packer says, "The death of Christ actually put away the sins of all God's elect and ensured that they would be brought to faith through regeneration and kept in faith for glory."[4]

There are three views of how many people Christ died for. First, there is actual universalism, which says Christ died for everyone without exception, so everyone without exception will be saved. Adherents of this view say the death of Christ has unlimited extent and unlimited efficacy. Second, there is hypothetical universalism, which says Christ's death has unlimited extent but limited efficacy. Third, there is particular redemption, which says Christ's death has unlimited efficacy but limited extent—limited to the salvation of God's elect. We agree with this last view: Jesus Christ died for everyone who will repent and believe in him.

Present and Future Redemption

We experience the blessing of God's redemption in two stages. The first stage is the present time, and the second stage is in the coming age. Paul writes, "In him we have redemption through his blood, the forgiveness of sins" (Eph. 1:7). We presently experience forgiveness of all our sins. That is what it means to be justified. Paul says elsewhere: "For he has rescued us from the dominion of

---

4   J. I. Packer, *Concise Theology* (Wheaton, IL: Tyndale House Publishers, 1993), 137.

darkness and brought us into the kingdom of the Son he loves, in whom we have redemption, the forgiveness of sins" (Col. 1:13–14). Even now we are experiencing the kingdom of God, which is "righteousness, peace and joy in the Holy Spirit" (Rom. 14:17).

Paul writes that Jesus "gave himself for us to redeem us from all wickedness [lawlessness] and to purify for himself a people that are his very own, eager to do what is good" (Titus 2:14). What a blessing it is to be redeemed from lawlessness! We find the same word for lawlessness (*anomia*) in Matthew 7, where Jesus says many will come to him, saying, "Lord, Lord." And he will tell them, "Depart from me, you workers of lawlessness" (Matt. 7:22–23, author's translation). The problem of many evangelical churches today is that they speak of justification but practice lawlessness. But God has redeemed us from all lawlessness and is purifying us to be his own holy people, zealous to do what is good.

In 1 Corinthians 6:18–20, Paul exhorts us to flee from sexual immorality. Some modern evangelicals not only say we do not have to flee sexual immorality, but also teach that Christians can indulge in it and still be saved! But that is not what the Bible teaches. "Flee from sexual immorality. All other sins a man commits are outside his body, but he who sins sexually sins against his own body. Do you not know that your body is a temple of the Holy Spirit, who is in you, whom you have received from God?" The Holy Spirit is in us; this is a present blessing. Paul continues, "You are not your own; you were bought at a price." Many who sinned against their bodies have lived to regret it. True Christians will not boast of how much immorality they committed; rather, they will be ashamed, because sin is injurious to both body and soul. But now our ownership has been changed from Satan to Jesus Christ. Paul concludes, "Therefore honor God with your body." These are all present experiences of redemption.

What is going to happen in the future? Paul writes, "We know that the whole creation has been groaning as in the pains of childbirth right up to the present time. Not only so, but we ourselves, who have the firstfruits of the Spirit, groan inwardly as we wait eagerly for our adoption as sons, the redemption of our bodies" (Rom. 8:22–23). In our future installment of redemption, we will receive a glorified, sinless, Spirit-engineered physical body with which to live with God.

We are all going to die. God has decided to give us the fullness of the blessings of redemption in two installments. We may want it in one, but that is not God's plan. So we must die, but we will die in faith and in the sure hope that we will be with Christ in paradise.

Paul writes, "And you also were included in Christ when you heard the word of truth, the gospel of your salvation. Having believed, you were marked in him with a seal, the promised Holy Spirit" (Eph. 1:13). The Holy Spirit is the seal that signifies, first, ownership, that we belong to Christ; and, second, security, that we are secure in Christ. The Holy Spirit "is a deposit guaranteeing our inheritance until the redemption of those who are God's possession—to the praise of his glory" (Eph. 1:14). Here redemption is seen as future: Paul is speaking about the glorification of our bodies. In the same epistle he says, "Do not grieve the Holy Spirit of God, with whom you were sealed for the day of redemption" (Eph. 4:30).

The Blessings of Redemption

What blessings do we receive from this aspect of salvation called redemption?

1. *We enjoy freedom.* "It is for freedom that Christ has set us free. Stand firm, then, and do not let yourselves be burdened again by a yoke of slavery" (Gal. 5:1). As redeemed people of God, we enjoy freedom from sin, guilt, condemnation, death, and hell. We enjoy freedom to say no to sin and yes to righteousness. What glorious freedom—we do not have to sin! When Jesus was tempted, he said no to sin and yes to God. We have the same freedom.

How many people in today's churches think that because they are justified, they can do whatever they want! Such people say that repentance is not necessary and that Christians do not have to produce even one fruit of the Spirit. But Paul says, "You, my brothers, were called to be free. But do not use your freedom to indulge the sinful nature; rather, serve one another in love" (Gal. 5:13).

Jesus said, "I tell you the truth, everyone who sins is a slave to sin. Now a slave has no permanent place in the family, but a son belongs to it forever. So if the Son sets you free, you will be free indeed" (John 8:34–36). If we are sons of God, we must stand fast in the freedom Christ has given us.

2. *We have a new master.* In Ephesians 1:13–14 Paul writes that we are sealed with the Holy Spirit, demonstrating that we belong to our new master, Jesus Christ, to serve and love him. This change of ownership is what makes us Christians: "If you confess with your mouth, 'Jesus is Lord,' and believe in your heart that God raised him from the dead, you will be saved" (Rom. 10:9). Jesus tells us, "Come to me, all you who are weary and burdened, and I will give you rest. Take my yoke upon you and learn from me, for I am gentle and humble in heart, and you will find rest for your souls. For my yoke is easy and my burden is light" (Matt. 11:28–30). Christianity is an ongoing relational life with our new master, Jesus. There is no such thing as absolute freedom. All people serve either Satan or Christ.

3. *We experience forgiveness of all sins.* "In him we have redemption through his blood, the forgiveness of sins" (Eph. 1:7).

4. *We enjoy the redemption of our bodies.* Jesus was sent to bring many sons to glory, and God will glorify us in body and soul, saving us not only from the penalty and power of sin but also from the presence of sin. Today sin is present in us, but there is coming a day when our bodies will be like unto Christ's glorious body. "We shall be like him, for we shall see him as he is" (1 John 3:2).

5. *Sin has no dominion over us.* This may sound strange to us, but it is true, even in this life. Paul writes, "For sin shall not be your master" (Rom. 6:14). Our new master is the Lord Jesus Christ; we need no longer obey sin.

6. *We are not under law.* "But when the time had fully come, God sent his Son, born of a woman, born under law, to redeem those under law" (Gal. 4:4–5). We can now stand before God, not because we kept the law perfectly but because Jesus Christ did. We are not under law but under grace. This grace enables us to fulfill the law: to love our spouses, to go to work, to tell the truth, to stop stealing and work with our hands that we may have something to give, to honor our father and mother. God's moral laws are still applicable to us, but we as sinners can never keep them perfectly and stand before God in our own righteousness. Paul says, "In the same way, count yourselves dead to sin but alive to God in Christ Jesus" (Rom. 6:11). In his great love and rich mercy, God made us alive that we might serve him. This is spiritual resurrection. In our souls we possess the life of God, by

which we can resist the devil and enjoy the freedom to say no to sin. What we read about in Ephesians 2:1–3 has been reversed. Now we are alive toward God and dead toward sin—not dead *in* sin, but *toward* sin.

7. *Satan cannot harm us.* John admonishes, "We know that anyone born of God does not continue to sin; the one who was born of God keeps him safe, and the evil one cannot harm him" (1 John 5:18). Jesus declares, "I give them eternal life, and they shall never perish; no one can snatch them out of my hand" (John 10:28). Satan can never harm God's people. James exhorts, "Resist the devil, and he will flee from you" (James 4:7). The devil is a superhuman, angelic being. Yet we can resist him in the name of Jesus Christ and he will run.

Peter speaks of this: "Your enemy the devil prowls around like a roaring lion looking for someone to devour. Resist him, standing firm in the faith" (1 Pet. 5:8–9). We do not have to sin. We sin because we are arrogant, and pride goes before a fall. If you are not listening when the word is preached, be careful. You may soon fall. The devil's purpose is to keep us from God's word because it is the divine medicine that will heal us if we take it. Those who are humble, who listen to and fear God, can resist the devil in the name of Jesus by obeying Christ. That is what standing firm in the faith means. When we do so, he will flee. John writes, "They overcame [the devil] by the blood of the Lamb and by the word of their testimony" (Rev. 12:11).

8. *Redemption brings sonship.* "But when the time had fully come, God sent his Son, born of a woman, born under law, to redeem those under law, that we might receive the full rights of sons" (Gal. 4:4–5). We now belong to the family of God, and our status brings us inheritance. As sons, we are heirs of God and joint-heirs with Christ.

Sonship also brings the Spirit of God's Son into our hearts. How do we know that the Holy Spirit is in us? We will have a continuous cry: "*Abba,* Father." Children cry when they are born. In fact, we look for that cry as a sign of life; otherwise, it may be a stillbirth. We are to cry out continuously to our heavenly Father. It is automatic for a redeemed child of God to do so. We have been brought into the family of God and given the right of sons to cry out to our Father, who promises to hear us.

I pray that each of us will make certain that we belong to the company of the redeemed. When God saves us, he delivers us from all bondages and brings us into the glorious liberty of the children of God. Make sure, therefore, that you belong to Jesus Christ, the Redeemer, who loved us so much he laid down his own life for our redemption—a redemption that is just as irreversible and irrevocable as justification. And having been redeemed out of our former sphere of sin, guilt, and misery, we now belong to the family of God. We now can enjoy a life of freedom—freedom not to sin and freedom to obey God.

12

Salvation as Propitiation

21But now a righteousness from God, apart from law, has been made known, to which the Law and the Prophets testify. 22This righteousness from God comes through faith in Jesus Christ to all who believe. There is no difference, 23for all have sinned and fall short of the glory of God, 24and are justified freely by his grace through the redemption that came by Christ Jesus. 25God presented him as a sacrifice of atonement, through faith in his blood. He did this to demonstrate his justice, because in his forbearance he had left the sins committed beforehand unpunished— 26he did it to demonstrate his justice at the present time, so as to be just and the one who justifies those who have faith in Jesus.

Romans 3:21–26

In Romans 3:21–26, salvation is seen from three perspectives: justification, redemption, and propitiation. The last doctrine, propitiation, speaks about the Christ of the cross. It is a forgotten doctrine greatly detested by theological liberals who do not believe in the authority of the Bible, the deity of Christ, miracles, heaven and hell, or the fall of man. This distinction becomes important when we consider words like "propitiation." Liberal versions of the Bible translate the Greek word *hilasterion* in Romans 3:25 as "expiation" instead of "propitiation." But "propitiation" is correctly used by the King James Version, the English Standard Version, and the New American Standard Version. First, then, we must explore the meaning of this word propitiation.

Definition of Propitiation

Propitiation has to do with offering a sacrifice to appease an angry God so that he may be favorably disposed, or propitious, to the one making an offering. In contrast, expiation has no Godward reference. It speaks about cancellation of sins, but only in reference to man. In other words, expiation eliminates a God who is angry against human sin.

The word "propitiation" is taken from the world of ancient religion, just as justification comes from the legal world, and redemption comes from the marketplace. We see illustrations of propitiation in the religious world even today. Years ago, I visited a country where people would leave offerings such as flowers, food, cigarettes, and other commodities for their gods. These worshipers were trying to appease the wrath of their gods so that they in turn would be gracious to them.

In many churches today, the God of the Bible is not seen as angry or wrathful, but as an indulgent grandfather, a jolly Santa Claus who approves everything we do. Propitiation is not necessary with such a God. Additionally, liberal theologians have declared that propitiation is not a biblical idea. But the Bible speaks of a wrathful God on nearly every page. In the Old Testament, there are twenty different Hebrew words used some 580 times to express God's wrath against the sin of his people. And in Romans 1:18–3:20, Paul speaks clearly of the wrath of God being revealed against all ungodliness and unrighteousness of men. He concludes that passage stating that all have sinned against God's law and are under his wrath.

When Paul speaks of propitiation, he is not speaking of the capricious wrath of pagan deities; he is speaking of the stern and settled reaction of the holy God against the evil of man. Leon Morris states: "Certainly we must retain the idea of the wrath of God, for, as Edwyn Bevan has pointed out, the idea that God cannot be angry is neither Hebrew nor Christian, but something borrowed from Greek philosophy."[1] Ancient Greek philosophers spoke of a god who was without feelings and therefore could not

---

1   Leon Morris, *The Apostolic Preaching of the Cross* (Grand Rapids: Eerdmans, 1965), 212.

become angry. But such an apathetic God also cannot be loving. Theological liberals who speak about a non-wrathful God who is love and always forgives fail to deduce that if God is not wrathful, his love and forgiveness are meaningless.

The Scriptures teach about the wrath of God because it highlights the seriousness of sin. God hates sin with a perfect hatred (Ps. 11:5). Jesus himself often spoke of the eternal, un-quenchable fires of hell. The writer to the Hebrews speaks about God as a consuming fire (Heb. 12:29). It is only through God's own propitiation that his wrath can be averted and we can be brought into a new relationship with him.

Seeing how God's people were destroyed by the Babylonians, Jeremiah wrote, "We have sinned and rebelled and you have not forgiven. You have covered yourself with anger and pursued us; you have slain without pity. You have covered yourself with a cloud so that no prayer can get through. You have made us scum and refuse among the nations. All our enemies have opened their mouths wide against us" (Lam. 3:42–46). The entire book of Lamentations reveals a God who was angry with his people.

The psalmist says, "You are not a God who takes pleasure in evil; with you the wicked cannot dwell. The arrogant cannot stand in your presence; you hate all who do wrong. You destroy those who tell lies; bloodthirsty and deceitful men the LORD abhors" (Ps. 5:4–6). Jesus can also become angry (Mark 3:5). John speaks of the wrath of the Lamb (Rev. 6:16; 19:15; see also 2 Thess. 1:7–9). Therefore, we do not believe in an apathetic god of Greek philosophy, who neither becomes angry nor loves. We believe in the holy God of the Scriptures, who hates sin and punishes sinners.

Then we must ask: If God hates sin and punishes sinners, and all men are under God's wrath because all have sinned, how can anyone be saved from God's wrath? The answer is found in this passage: *"There is no difference, for all have sinned and fall short of the glory of God, and are justified freely by his grace through the redemption which is in Christ Jesus, whom God displayed publicly as a propitiation [a sacrifice of atonement] through faith in his blood"* (vv. 23–25, author's translation).

147

God Initiated Propitiation

Sinful man did not come up with a sacrifice to appease God's wrath. God himself took the initiative to provide us with a sufficient propitiation to deal with all our sins. In pagan religions, man brings an offering to appease the wrath of his god, but in Christianity man is not propitiating God. In one sense, it is not even Jesus Christ who propitiates God's wrath. God the Father took the initiative according to his own predeterminate counsel to appease his own wrath that he may be gracious to us and forgive our sins. Jehovah Jireh, the God who provides, especially provides for our salvation. So Paul writes, *"God presented him as propitiation"* (v. 25), or *"whom God publicly displayed as propitiation."* In this God-initiated propitiation, God's holy wrath and his love for sinners meet on the cross. God is holy; therefore, he must punish sinners. Yet God is also love and does not want to punish sinners. Thus, he punished a substitute in our stead—his own sinless Son. The entire Old Testament pointed to this substitutionary propitiation in the sacrificial system.

In Leviticus 17:11 we read, "For the life of a creature is in the blood, and I have given it to you to make atonement for yourselves on the altar; it is the blood that makes atonement for one's life." John writes, "For God so loved the world that he gave his one and only Son" (John 3:16). God gave his Son in sacrificial death to make atonement for our sins. Paul says, "He was delivered over to death for our sins and was raised to life for our justification." He later affirms, "But God demonstrates his own love for us in this: While we were still sinners, Christ died for us" (Rom. 4:25; 5:8). John declares, "This is love: not that we loved God, but that he loved us and sent his Son as propitiation for our sins" (1 John 4:10, author's translation). The NIV translates *hilasmos* as "an atoning sacrifice" for our sins.

God Publicly Displayed His Son

On the cross, God presented his Son as propitiation (Rom. 3:25). He put him forward, exhibiting him before the entire world to look at and ask why this innocent Son of God was being crucified.

148

Paul writes of this public declaration: *"But now a righteousness from God, apart from law, has been made known"* (v. 21). This is speaking about the cross on Calvary's hill.

Because of the sinful murmuring of his people in the desert, God sent poisonous serpents to bite them (Num. 21). After many people died, the rest acknowledged their sin. Then God instructed Moses to make a brazen serpent and lift it up so that all who looked at it would be healed. Jesus Christ spoke often of this idea in connection with his own crucifixion: "Just as Moses lifted up the snake in the desert, so the Son of Man must be lifted up" (John 3:14); "When you have lifted up the Son of Man, then you will know that I am the one that I claim to be, and that I do nothing on my own but speak just what the Father has taught me" (John 8:28); "But I, when I am lifted up from the earth, will draw all men to myself" (John 12:32).

Christ was displayed publicly in the midst of the universe in time and space on Calvary's hill for all intelligent beings, both human and angelic, to consider and ask why. Think about this action God the Father took. All people of the world must think about the crucified Christ. Peter tells us, "This man was handed over to you by God's set purpose and foreknowledge" (Acts 2:23). God delivered his Son over and publicly displayed him on the cross for his own glory, that his righteousness be displayed in this exhibition. God is declaring that he hates and punishes sin instead of passing over it.

God was glorified when he punished our sin in his Son. This was also the Son's prayer: "'Now my heart is troubled, and what shall I say? "Father, save me from this hour"? No, it was for this very reason I came to this hour. Father, glorify your name!' Then a voice came from heaven, 'I have glorified it, and will glorify it again'" (John 12:27–28).

The public display of God's Son on the cross brings glory to God's name. The Father displayed him for the world as a sacrifice of atonement. Unless a God-given sinless substitute dies in our stead, we must die, for we must suffer the fullness of God's wrath against our sin. The whole sacrificial system, therefore, teaches propitiation: the removal of God's wrath by a sacrifice so that God may be propitious to us, forgive all our sins, and restore us to favor and fellowship. "Without the shedding of blood there is no forgiveness" (Heb. 9:22). But whose blood is to be shed? Whose death ensures the appeasing of God's wrath?

Propitiation through the Blood of the Lamb

The writer to the Hebrews clearly states, "It is impossible for the blood of bulls and goats to take away sins" (Heb. 10:4). All the sacrificial animal blood that was shed throughout the Old Testament era pointed to the blood of the Lamb of God who alone can take away the sin of the world (John 1:29). The apostle writes, "[Christ] is the atoning sacrifice for our sins, and not only for ours but also for the sins of the whole world" (1 John 2:2).

Leviticus 16 describes the Day of Atonement, when sin offerings were offered for the sin of Aaron and his family, and also for the sins of all Israel. On that day, the high priest, properly washed and dressed, would go into the Holy of Holies carrying incense and the blood of the bull and goat sin offerings. He could enter this Most Holy Place only on the Day of Atonement.

Inside the Most Holy Place was an ark with a golden cover, on either end of which stood cherubim, whose wings overshadowed this golden lid, called the mercy seat. The mercy seat was the place of propitiation. It covered the ark, which contained tablets of God's commandments that man has broken. Man is guilty and God is angry, and God is seen as enthroned above this golden cover. When the high priest came in, he sprinkled blood from the sacrificed animals on the mercy seat and in front of it. The idea was that God would look down on the blood-sprinkled cover of the ark and see the blood. The guilt of man's sin was therefore removed by the death of the God-given substitute, and the wrath of God was averted. God could now be gracious to forgive and restore man into favor and fellowship. Thus, the sins of Aaron and the people of Israel were forgiven (Lev. 16:34).

Who is the God-given substitute whose death averts God's wrath against us? Whose death removes our sins from God's sight? It is Jesus Christ, whom God publicly displayed upon the cross as our propitiation. He is our mercy seat, as well as our sinless and eternal high priest. He is the God-provided victim who offered himself on the altar of the cross to appease God's wrath against us.

Hebrews 2:14 speaks about our kinsman-redeemer, Jesus Christ, who became incarnate that he may redeem us. The word "to propitiate" is found in Hebrews 2:17: "For this reason he had to be made like his brothers in every way, in order that he might become a merciful and faithful high priest in service to God [in dealing with things pertaining to God in behalf of us], and that he might make atonement [propitiate] for the sins of the people." And in Hebrews 2:9 we read, "But we see Jesus, who was made a little lower than the angels, now crowned with glory and honor because he suffered death, so that by the grace of God he might taste death for everyone." He is the propitiation, the sacrifice of atonement, who tasted death in behalf of us.

God presented Christ as a propitiation through faith in his blood (Rom. 3:25). Paul tells us that this propitiation was objectively achieved by Christ's blood poured out in his sacrificial death. Christ's shed blood is the means by which God's wrath is propitiated. The blood defines that in which the propitiatory sacrifice consisted, for the outpoured blood proves death has occurred. In John 10, Jesus declares five times that he will lay down his life for his sheep. In the same gospel, John describes how all the blood was drained out of this final sacrificial victim on the cross (John 19:34).

The Hebrews writer says, "Therefore, brothers, . . . we have confidence to enter the Most Holy Place by the blood of Jesus" (Heb. 10:19). Peter declares, "For you know that it was not with perishable things such as silver or gold that you were redeemed from the empty way of life handed down to you from your forefathers, but with the precious blood of Christ, a lamb without blemish or defect" (1 Pet. 1:18-19). Propitiation was achieved, not by our blood, but by the blood of the Lord Jesus Christ, our God-given substitute.

Jesus Is Our Substitute

Jesus Christ is our propitiation. Isaiah 53 tells us that he is our substitute, the Lamb of God who takes away the sin of the world. Paul writes, "For Christ's love compels us, because we are convinced that one died for all, and therefore all died. . . . God was reconciling the world to himself in Christ, not counting men's sins against them. . . . God made him who had no sin to be sin for us, so that in him we might become the righteousness of God" (2 Cor. 5:14, 19, 21). Peter tells us, "He himself bore our sins in his body on the tree, so that we might die to sins and live for righteousness; by his wounds you have been healed. . . . For Christ died for sins once for all, the righteous for the unrighteous, to bring you to God. He was put to death in the body but made alive by the Spirit" (1 Pet. 2:24; 3:18). In Christ, the wrath of God against sinners vanishes because the wrath of God in its fullness descended on this God-given substitute who cried out from the cross, "My God, my God, why hast thou forsaken me?" (Matt. 27:46, KJV).

For many years, John Bunyan was anxious about his salvation. Then God gave him this idea: "Sinner, thou thinkest that because of thy sins and infirmities I cannot save thy soul, but behold, my Son is by me, and upon him I look, and not on thee, and will deal with thee according as I am pleased with him."[2]

Christ died in our place and for our sins; we are accepted in the Beloved. When God sees the blood of his Son, he passes over our sins because they are punished fully in him. Jesus is our Passover and propitiation.

This propitiation has four aspects: first, the offense, or the sin to be taken away; second, the offended party (God), who must be pacified and reconciled; third, the offending person, who must be pardoned and received by God; and, fourth, a sacrifice that must be offered to make atonement. When Christ died, our sin was cancelled, God's wrath was appeased and taken away, and now we are forgiven and restored. Paul writes, "But now in Christ Jesus you who once were far away have been brought near" (Eph. 2:13). We have been brought into God's kingdom and into God's family—nearer we cannot be. We are in God and God is in us. God demanded propitiation and, thank God, he provided it.

No wonder Paul gloried in the cross! He reveled in preaching Christ as our atonement and propitiation: "We preach Christ crucified: a stumbling block to Jews and foolishness to Gentiles, but to those whom God has called, both Jews and Greeks, Christ

---

2   John Bunyan, *Grace Abounding to the Chief of Sinners* as found in *The Works of John Bunyan*, vol. 1 (Edinburgh: Banner of Truth, 1991), 39.

the power of God and the wisdom of God. . . . For I resolved to know nothing while I was with you except Jesus Christ and him crucified" (1 Cor. 1:23–24; 2:2). That is why Paul rebuked the Galatians for considering abandoning their faith: "You foolish Galatians! Who has bewitched you? Before your very eyes Jesus Christ was clearly portrayed [placarded] as crucified" (Gal. 3:1). Then he declares, "May I never boast except in the cross of our Lord Jesus Christ" (Gal. 6:14).

Propitiation Proves God's Righteousness

What is the purpose of Christ's propitiation in our behalf? It proves that God is righteous and just when he justifies a wicked person who believes in Jesus. In his forbearance, God passed over sins committed by the saints of the Old Testament. In other words, he did not punish the sins of the saints of the old covenant. Yet they were fully forgiven of their sins, for they trusted in the Messiah who was to come through the God-given sacrificial system. The saints of the Old Testament looked forward to the cross and their sins were forgiven; we look backward to the cross for the forgiveness of our sins.

Because God passed over the sins committed formerly without punishing them, one could argue that God is indifferent to the claims of divine justice. For example, King David committed adultery and murdered a believer, and Leviticus 20:10 and 24:17 call for the death penalty for such sins. But look at the language used by Nathan the prophet when David confesses his sin: "Then David said to Nathan, 'I have sinned against the LORD.' Nathan replied, 'The LORD has taken away your sin. You are not going to die'" (2 Sam. 12:13). What about God and his justice? How can God do this when his own word says to kill those like David who commit such sins? This passage in Romans tells us that God passed over the sins of God's people in the Old Testament in his forbearance because he was going to propitiate them in Christ. The cross, then, proves the righteous character of God because all the sins of the saints of the Old Testament were punished in Jesus Christ on the cross, as well as all the sins of believers who live after Christ.

We must understand that the sins of all the people of the world were not punished in Christ when he died on the cross, but only those of God's people, past, present, and future. All have sinned, and the wages of sin is death—not just physical and spiritual death, but eternal death—being eternally removed from God's presence. That is what Jesus experienced on the cross. He went to hell in our place.

Propitiation, therefore, upholds God's justice. Because God hates sin, he graciously punishes all our sin in his Son. God pronounces wicked sinners to be legally righteous because God himself, in his Son, bore the penalty for our law-breaking. Isaiah speaks about this: "But he was pierced for our transgressions, he was crushed for our iniquities; the punishment that brought us peace was upon him, and by his wounds we are healed. We all, like sheep, have gone astray, each of us has turned to his own way; and the LORD has laid on him the iniquity of us all" (Isa. 53:5–6).

Therefore, the propitiation of Christ's death on the cross proves, first, that God is righteous in his nature; second, that God punishes every sin of his elect; third, that God is just when he justifies sinners who believe in Jesus; and, fourth, that God will punish justly every sinner who refuses to trust in Jesus for every sin he committed.

Effects of Propitiation

What are the effects of this sacrifice of atonement?

1. *God forgives all our sins.* The Bible speaks of God blotting out our sins and remembering them no more, of removing them to the farthest extent of the universe, and of burying them in the very depths of the ocean. All these metaphors tell us that when God forgives our sins, he removes all our sin, guilt, death, hell, and wrath. Imagine the joy of Isaac and his father when God told Abraham to stop sacrificing Isaac and then provided a ram to be sacrificed in the place of Isaac. What relief! What inexpressible joy of both the father and the son! We can imagine the great excitement of Abraham and Isaac as they rejoined the servants and went home to tell Sarah what had happened. That is salvation. Our sins are forgiven and our guilt is taken away.

2. *We gain access to God.* As rebellious sinners, we were far from God. But now we have access to God. What happened at the moment Christ died? "When Jesus had cried out again in a loud voice, he gave up his spirit. At that moment the curtain of the temple was torn in two from top to bottom" (Matt. 27:50–51). There was a thick curtain that prevented not only ordinary Israelites and the priests but even the high priest from entering into the presence of God. Any who came in would experience death. Fire from the Most Holy Place would kill them, as it did Nadab and Abihu (Lev. 10). But now the curtain has been torn by God from top to bottom, and a new way is opened up so that we can go into the very presence of God in the name of Jesus Christ. Paul writes, "Therefore, since we have been justified through faith, we have peace with God through our Lord Jesus Christ, through whom we have gained access by faith into this grace in which we now stand. And we rejoice in the hope of the glory of God" (Rom. 5:1–2).

In Ephesians 2 Paul gives us an understanding of who we were and what Christ has done for us: "Therefore, remember that formerly you who are Gentiles by birth and called 'uncircumcised' by those who call themselves 'the circumcision' (that done in the body by the hands of men)—remember that at that time you were separate from Christ, excluded from citizenship in Israel and foreigners to the covenants of the promise, without hope and without God in the world. But now in Christ Jesus you who once were far away have been brought near through the blood of Christ" (Eph. 2:11–13). All hindrances have been removed.

The writer to the Hebrews exhorts, "Therefore, brothers, since we have confidence to enter the Most Holy Place by the blood of Jesus, by a new and living way opened for us through the curtain, that is, his body, and since we have a great priest over the house of God, let us draw near to God with a sincere heart in full assurance of faith, having our hearts sprinkled to cleanse us from a guilty conscience and having our bodies washed with pure water" (Heb. 10:19–22). Before, we did not have confidence. We were depressed because of the guilt of our sin. Our guilt was like an iron girder that sat on us and pushed us down. Our faces were downcast and we could not rejoice. But through Christ, our guilt is gone and we have confidence to come into God's presence. We can come to God to pray and enjoy the sunshine of his glorious presence.

Through the propitiatory sacrifice of Christ, we now can come to God. The Hebrews writer says, "But you have come to Mount Zion, to the heavenly Jerusalem, the city of the living God. You have come to thousands upon thousands of angels in joyful assembly, to the church of the firstborn, whose names are written in heaven. You have come to God, the judge of all men, to the spirits of righteous men made perfect, to Jesus the mediator of a new covenant, and to the sprinkled blood that speaks a better word than the blood of Abel" (Heb. 12:22–24). The better word of the blood of Christ is a word of forgiveness, grace, and acceptance. Christ's sprinkled blood is our passport to heaven.

3. *We now experience no condemnation.* Paul writes, "Therefore, there is now no condemnation for those who are in Christ Jesus" (Rom. 8:1). We are no longer condemned because we are justified. After her accusers left, Jesus asked the woman caught in adultery: "'Woman, where are they? Has no one condemned you?' 'No one, sir,' she said. 'Then neither do I condemn you,' Jesus declared. 'Go now and leave your life of sin'" (John 8:10–11).

In Luke 18 we see a terrible sinner, a publican, coming to the temple: "But the tax collector stood at a distance. He would not even look up to heaven, but beat his breast and said, 'God, have mercy on me, a sinner'" (v. 13). In the Greek it is, "God, be propitiated with reference to me, the sinner," that is, on the basis of the sprinkled blood on the mercy seat. This publican understood something about propitiation. We read that he went home justified, while the Pharisee went home condemned.

Our Need for Propitiation

We need God's propitiation for our sins. Because we are sinners, God's wrath is resting upon us (Rom. 1:18). The wages of sin is death; therefore, we must die. Being sinners, we cannot initiate or effect propitiation ourselves. We cannot bring a chicken or a cigarette or some flowers to God and expect him to turn away his wrath and be gracious to us. As sinners, all we do is sinful; therefore, we cannot propitiate our sins. We need a substitute, a kinsman-redeemer, an advocate, a mediator who is able to propitiate in behalf of us.

God has displayed Jesus Christ publicly as our propitiation, our sacrifice of atonement, on the cross. Our job is to confess our sins and believe in the Lord Jesus Christ, and God's gracious job is to remove the guilt of our sin. When we believe on him, God's wrath disappears. We are saved and shall live forever in God's presence.

But if we do not believe in Christ, the cross demonstrates that God must punish to the fullest extent anyone who refuses to trust in Jesus. John writes, "Whoever believes in the Son has eternal life, but whoever rejects the Son will not see life, for God's wrath remains on him" (John 3:36). Those who do not trust in Christ must find their own atonement, which is impossible to do. Propitiation is found only in Jesus Christ.

This is not mythology or false threatening. John writes, "Once more Jesus said to them, 'I am going away, and you will look for me, and you will die in your sin. Where I go, you cannot come.' This made the Jews ask, 'Will he kill himself? Is that why he says, "Where I go, you cannot come"?' But he continued, 'You are from below; I am from above. You are of this world; I am not of this world. I told you that you would die in your sins; if you do not believe that I am the one I claim to be, you will indeed die in your sins'" (John 8:21–24).

God must deal with those who do not trust in his Son. Paul writes, "God is just: He will pay back trouble to those who trouble you and give relief to you who are troubled, and to us as well. This will happen when the Lord Jesus is revealed from heaven in blazing fire with his powerful angels. He will punish those who do not know God and do not obey the gospel of our Lord Jesus. They will be punished with everlasting destruction and shut out from the presence of the Lord and from the majesty of his power on the day he comes to be glorified in his holy people and to be marveled at among all those who have believed" (2 Thess. 1:6–10).

Thank God that he regenerated us and gave us the gift of repentance and faith! God enabled us to lift up our empty beggar-hands to receive this great salvation as a free gift. Christ opened up the way to the Father and now we can come with confidence and full assurance that he will receive us. Thank God for the propitiatory death of Christ on our behalf!

13

Sola Fide

21But now a righteousness from God, apart from law, has been made known, to which the Law and the Prophets testify. 22This righteousness from God comes through faith in Jesus Christ to all who believe. There is no difference, 23for all have sinned and fall short of the glory of God, 24and are justified freely by his grace through the redemption that came by Christ Jesus. 25God presented him as a sacrifice of atonement, through faith in his blood. He did this to demonstrate his justice, because in his forbearance he had left the sins committed beforehand unpunished— 26he did it to demonstrate his justice at the present time, so as to be just and the one who justifies those who have faith in Jesus.

27Where, then, is boasting? It is excluded. On what principle? On that of observing the law? No, but on that of faith. 28For we maintain that a man is justified by faith apart from observing the law. 29Is God the God of Jews only? Is he not the God of Gentiles too? Yes, of Gentiles too, 30since there is only one God, who will justify the circumcised by faith and the uncircumcised through that same faith. 31Do we, then, nullify the law by this faith? Not at all! Rather, we uphold the law.

Romans 3:21–31

Paul argues in Romans that all have sinned and are therefore under the wrath of God and the curse of death. Yet God has in his grace accomplished salvation for sinners through the substitutionary death of his Son. In Jesus Christ there is righteousness, redemption, propitiation, and reconciliation for us. Salvation is accomplished by Christ's own self-offering. But how can we receive this full and free salvation? We have total moral inability and can do nothing to merit salvation. We are dying sinners, wilting under God's wrath. How, then, can we be saved? We are saved by faith in Jesus Christ. *Sola fide* means that we are saved by faith alone, without any works of our own.

What Is Faith?

The word "faith" (*pistis*) appears eight times in this passage and the related verb "believe" (*pisteuō*) appears once. For the first time in this epistle, Paul is telling us in whom we must trust. Romans 3:22 says we must have faith "in Jesus Christ." John often speaks of believing "*into* Jesus Christ." So faith speaks of moving out of ourselves and laying hold of the object of our faith, Jesus Christ. To this purpose John wrote his gospel: "These are written that you may believe that Jesus is the Christ, the Son of God, and that by believing you may have life in his name" (John 20:31).

Faith is self-renouncing and Jesus-trusting. When the Bible says Abraham believed God, it means Abraham put the entire weight of his life—his past, present, and future—upon a firm foundation that will never crumble or give way. Abraham believed in God's promises because God is truth and cannot lie. He trusted in the One who raises the dead and calls into existence things that do not exist.

The words for "believe" in the Old Testament speak of stability, security, and taking refuge in God from all our troubles. We can be secure in God even in the face of death itself. The God we trust in is life and light. The Bible, therefore, speaks about faith that knows, believes, and obeys truth. Such faith rests in God's promises, thanks God for his grace, and works for God's glory. Faith is trust.

Faith can also mean the body of truth that we must believe in (see Gal. 1:23; 1 Tim. 4:1, 6; Jude 3). We believe that Jesus Christ is the eternal Son of God who became incarnate and lived a sinless life. We believe that he created the universe, died for our sins, and was raised for our justification. We believe that Jesus alone is Lord, that he intercedes for us as our great sympathizing high priest, and that he will come again to judge the living and the dead. We believe the gospel as articulated by Paul (1 Cor. 15:1–8).

Our faith rests on the gospel, not on a self-authenticating, mystical experience or dream. God can give us dreams to guide us, but they will not save us. We either receive God's testimony concerning his Son, or we reject it through unbelief. John writes, "The man who has accepted [the testimony of God] has certified that God is truthful" (John 3:33). When we believe the gospel, we are certifying the truthful nature of God. But what happens when we reject the gospel? "Anyone who believes in the Son of God has this testimony in his heart. Anyone who does not believe God has made him out to be a liar, because he has not believed the testimony God has given about his Son" (1 John 5:10).

The fundamental ingredient of saving faith is orthodoxy; we must believe the gospel. Therefore, churches that do not preach the gospel are not true churches, but entertainment centers that entertain people into damnation. They are, in reality, synagogues of Satan, and what they preach cannot save anyone. The gospel alone points to the person and work of Jesus Christ, our great God and Savior. The object of our faith is God's eternal Son, whom the Father delivered over to death to save his people from their sins. It is Jesus, who is the way and the truth and the life, in whom alone the salvation of the whole world is found, and in whom is redemption (Rom. 3:24).

In What Does Our Faith Rest?

According to the Bible, our faith must rest in God (Mark 11:22), in Christ (Rom. 3:22), in the name of Jesus (Acts 3:16), in Christ's blood (Rom. 3:25), and in the gospel (Phil. 1:27).

Faith Is the Instrumental Cause

Our faith is not the foundation, or basis, of our salvation. In other words, it is not the efficient cause of justification, redemption, propitiation, and reconciliation. The ground of our salvation is the sacrificial death of Jesus Christ. What, then, is faith? Faith is the instrumental cause only. It is the means by which we receive salvation from God as a free gift.

This faith we exercise in Jesus Christ is non-meritorious. John Stott remarks, "Faith is the eye that looks to him, the hand that receives his free gift, the mouth that drinks the living water."[1] B. B. Warfield wrote: "It is not faith that saves, but faith in Jesus Christ. . . . It is not, strictly speaking, even faith in Christ that saves, but Christ that saves through faith."[2] This faith that trusts is the faith of an infant who trusts his mother and sucks her milk freely.

We are saved, not by looking within ourselves or looking to the world around us, but by looking up to Jesus Christ, the object of our faith. Faith is coming to the crucified Christ because he invites us to come. Faith is receiving Christ and calling on his name. It is not resting on anything done in us or by us, but on what is done for us by Jesus Christ. Faith is not our contribution to our own salvation.

Faith Is a Gift

We cannot manufacture saving faith; it is a gift granted to us by God. We must believe to be saved, yet this faith is a supernatural gift that does not originate in ourselves.

How can we who are dead in trespasses and sins believe? God must regenerate us and raise us up spiritually. When God saves us, we experience a spiritual resurrection that produces faith. Natural man is incapable of believing the gospel. Faith is a gift of God (Eph. 2:8; Phil. 1:29).

When God sent Paul to Philippi, he preached to a number of women gathered at the river. God opened the heart of Lydia to respond to the gospel, which she did by putting faith in the preached word (Acts 16:14).

Faith Trusts without Doubt

Saving faith trusts in Christ without wavering. Because God is truth, and his promises are true, we can fully trust in him. The psalmist says, "I have trusted in the LORD without wavering" (Ps. 26:1). Faith trusts without doubt. Paul writes,

---

1   Stott, *Romans: God's Good News*, 117.
2   Quoted by Murray, *Collected Writings*, vol. 2, *Systematic Theology*, 260.

162

Therefore, the promise comes by faith, so that it may be by grace and may be guaranteed to all Abraham's offspring—not only to those who are of the law but also to those who are of the faith of Abraham. . . . He is our father in the sight of God, in whom he believed—the God who gives life to the dead and calls things that are not as though they were. Against all hope, Abraham in hope believed and so became the father of many nations, just as it had been said to him, "So shall your offspring be." Without weakening in his faith, he faced the fact that his body was as good as dead—since he was about a hundred years old—and that Sarah's womb was also dead. Yet he did not waver through unbelief regarding the promise of God, but was strengthened in his faith and gave glory to God, being fully persuaded that God had power to do what he had promised. (Rom. 4:16–21)

Proverbs 3:5 reads, "Trust in the LORD with all your heart and lean not on your own understanding." We trust in God, not in our own native powers. Sarah trusted in her own mind, and the result was Ishmael and much subsequent trouble. That is what happens when we trust in our own understanding.

Faith Is Essential for Salvation

Faith is the *sine qua non* of salvation. All must believe in Jesus Christ to be saved. Like us, the Old Testament saints were saved by faith. The Hebrews writer remarks, "Without faith it is impossible to please God, because anyone who comes to him must believe that he exists and that he rewards those who earnestly seek him" (Heb. 11:6).

What role does work have in our salvation? Jesus says, "The work of God is this: to believe in the one he has sent" (John 6:29). To the Athenians Paul declared, "[God] commands all people everywhere to repent" (Acts 17:30). There is no faith without repentance and no repentance without saving faith.

Where there is genuine faith, there shall also be authentic, godly repentance, which is characterized by deep sorrow for having offended God and a full and free confession of sins. The truly penitent man detests and forsakes his sins. He will make restitution when needed and possible, and he will aim to glorify God by doing what God wants him to do.

163

Faith Is Directed to Christ

This faith is directed to Christ's person and work. His name is Jesus, "because he will save his people from their sins" (Matt. 1:21). There is no salvation in anyone else (Acts 4:12). Paul writes, "Here is a trustworthy saying that deserves full acceptance: Christ Jesus came into the world to save sinners—of whom I am the worst" (1 Tim. 1:15). Our faith is directed to Christ and his finished work of atonement as well as to his continuing work as our high priest who always makes intercession for us. Paul asks, "Who is he that condemns? Christ Jesus, who died—more than that, who was raised to life—is at the right hand of God and is also interceding for us" (Rom. 8:34).

Faith is directed to Jesus Christ our Savior who, in the offer of the gospel, is not simply making salvation possible but is offering salvation itself, full and free, to be received by faith. He saves every elect sinner.

A Universal Offer of Salvation

This salvation Christ accomplished by his death is offered to all. A universal invitation is given to Jews and Gentiles, rich and poor, male and female. There is no respect of persons; all have sinned and must hear the gospel call.

Paul declares, *"This righteousness from God comes through faith in Jesus Christ to all who believe"* (v. 22). Elsewhere he writes, "I am not ashamed of the gospel, because it is the power of God for the salvation of everyone who believes: first for the Jew, then for the Gentile" (Rom. 1:16). The Lord himself invites us to believe in him: "Turn to me and be saved, all you ends of the earth; for I am God, and there is no other. . . . Come, all you who are thirsty, come to the waters; and you who have no money, come, buy and eat! Come, buy wine and milk without money and without cost" (Isa. 45:22; 55:1).

Jesus told his disciples to go into all the world and preach the gospel. God also commands all people everywhere to repent. Christ shall come again when the gospel is preached to all nations.

164

Faith and God's Word

Our faith is born, defined, nourished, and sustained by God's word. God created faith in Lydia through the preached word. Paul tells us, "Faith comes from hearing the message, and the message is heard through the word of Christ" (Rom. 10:17). In other words, faith comes by hearing the gospel preached with all courage and clarity.

Faith is sustained by God's word. As Paul bade farewell to the Ephesian elders, he said, "Now I commit you to God and to the word of his grace, which can build you up and give you an inheritance among all those who are sanctified" (Acts 20:32). The word of God is able to build us up. That is why the devil tries to distract people when the gospel is preached.

No true faith can exist, in other words, without the preaching of the gospel. Thus, true faith does not exist in churches where the word is not preached. Faith in Christ is faith in the word. Without the word, we cannot have even little faith.

Since faith comes by hearing of the word, our faith will grow as we grow in our knowledge of God's word. Therefore, we must be part of a church that declares the gospel and preaches through the entire Bible. We must listen carefully to the preached word and read the Bible daily so that we may have great faith. Older Christians should have stronger faith in Jesus Christ, and younger Christians should consult them, that they may also grow in faith.

Faith Produces Good Works

We are saved by faith in Jesus Christ alone. We believe in Christ so that he may save us, and he saves us apart from any merit of our own, as Paul states: *"But now a righteousness from God, apart from law, has been made known"* (v. 21). We are saved by grace through faith plus nothing.

Yet this faith that saves us also enables us to do good works as evidence of our salvation. Paul writes, "A man is not justified by observing the law, but by faith in Jesus Christ. . . . For in Christ Jesus neither circumcision nor uncircumcision has any value. The only thing that counts is faith expressing itself through love" (Gal. 2:16; 5:6).

Faith without works is a corpse. It is not true saving faith; rather, it is the faith of demons (James 2:19). Demons believe, yet their end will be the lake of fire. Theirs is a dead faith, like the faith of the second and third soil–hearers of the gospel (Matt. 13). It is the faith of Achan, King Saul, Judas, Ananias and Sapphira, Simon Magus, and Demas. True faith results in active obedience to God's word. Paul declares, "Through [Christ] and for his name's sake, we received grace and apostleship to call people from among all the Gentiles to the obedience that comes from faith" (Rom. 1:5).

Our good works prove that our salvation is by faith alone apart from works. They are the evidence that we are true people of God. For example, notice the language Paul uses to Timothy on the issue of a man's responsibility for his family: "If anyone does not provide for his relatives, and especially for his immediate family, he has denied the faith and is worse than an unbeliever" (1 Tim. 5:8). This is also true of a man who does not love his wife. His faith is false. Paul says we are created in Christ Jesus unto good works, which God has foreordained that we should walk in them (Eph. 2:10). Jesus himself said, "By their fruit you will recognize them" (Matt. 7:20).

We are saved by faith and must live by faith. We do not come to Jesus by faith first and then abandon our faith to live by sight. We must always live by faith in God. Faith unites us to Christ, and by faith we abide in Christ, who is wisdom, righteousness, sanctification, and redemption.

Elements of Faith

Saving faith has three constitutive elements: knowledge (*notitia*), agreement (*assensus*), and trust (*fiducia*). Knowledge of the gospel leads us to conviction (i.e., active agreement with the truth), and such conviction leads us to personal trust in Jesus Christ.

The first element of faith is knowledge. Christian faith is not pious ignorance. Nor is it trusting in oneself, trusting in one's positive thinking, or trusting in one's church. True faith is trusting in Jesus Christ to be saved. Therefore we need knowledge of the gospel of Christ. Without knowledge we cannot have true faith,

ROMANS 3:21-31

because true faith is born, defined, and nourished by the word of God. Faith comes by hearing the gospel facts preached by one commissioned and sent by Christ.

Roman Catholics claim that biblical knowledge is not necessary, as long as one trusts implicitly in the Roman church. Such people would say, "You trust the church and the church will relate to Christ on your behalf." But we say, "We must trust in Christ directly." James M. Boice relates a story:

> A man was being interviewed by a group of church officers before being taken into membership. They asked him what he believed about salvation, and he replied that he believed what the church believed.
>
> "But what does the church believe?" they probed.
>
> "The church believes what I believe," he answered.
>
> They tried again: "Just what do you and the church believe?"
>
> The man thought this over for a moment and then replied, "We believe the same thing."[3]

Christianity is a reasonable faith based on knowledge. It is not a leap into the darkness of irrationality. We must base our faith on information. Churches, therefore, must give knowledge of the gospel that will lead people to faith. Our faith is based on God's revelation of what he has done in Jesus Christ.

We can liken these elements of faith to stages of courtship. When a woman begins to date a person, she wants to collect information. Who is this person? Who are his parents? What type of job history does he have? Does he have money in the bank? Does he have any spiritual character? Dating is the time for the primacy of the intellect. She is merely gathering information.

The second element is agreement, *assensus*. Our knowledge of the facts of the gospel now moves us to conviction, which means we agree that the gospel is true—that Jesus Christ is Savior and Lord, that he died for our sins, and that we can be saved by trusting in him. This is similar to the second stage in dating; it is a movement of the heart. At this point a girl will agree that this man is handsome, intelligent, of excellent character, healthy, and hardworking. She comes to the conclusion that this person can

---

3   Boice, *Romans*, vol. 1, *Justification by Faith*, 389.

167

be an excellent husband for her, and she can live with him all of her life in great joy.

But *assensus* is not trust. Conviction must move to trust—*fiducia*. Otherwise, it is dead faith, the faith of Judas, the devil's faith. As we said, the devil is orthodox. He believes in the Scriptures, has knowledge of God, and even agrees with this knowledge. That is why the third aspect of faith is so important. Faith in its essence is commitment to Christ that we may be saved. We must trust in Jesus Christ alone for our salvation, entrusting ourselves to him now and forever. We do not trust in ourselves or in any human or angelic resources, but in Jesus Christ alone as Savior and submit to him as Lord, that we may be saved. We trust in Jesus as an infant trusts in his mother. We declare, "Jesus is my Savior, my Lord, my Shepherd, my Healer." This speaks of the third stage in dating: making a lifetime commitment to one's spouse in marriage. Jesus is our bridegroom and we are his beloved bride (Rev. 19:6–9). By faith we are united with him. All his assets are ours; all our liabilities are his.

Do You Live by Faith Alone?

God has accomplished salvation by the sacrifice of his Son. A great feast has been made ready for all dying sinners. All the fitness God requires is for us to see our need of Christ, for Jesus saves only sinners. We must come by faith; no merit is required.

Heed the words of John Owen:

> This is somewhat of the word which he now speaks unto you: Why will ye die? why will ye perish? why will ye not have compassion on your own souls? Can your hearts endure, or can your hands be strong, in the day of wrath that is approaching? . . . Look unto me, and be saved; come unto me, and I will ease you of all sins, sorrows, fears, burdens, and give rest to your souls. Come, I entreat you; lay aside all procrastinations, all delays; put me off no more; eternity lies at the door . . . do not so hate me as that you would rather perish than accept of deliverance by me.

> These and the like things doth the Lord Christ continually declare, proclaim, plead and urge on the souls of sinners. . . . He doth it in the preaching of the word, as if he were present with you, stood amongst you, and spake personally to every one of

you. . . . He hath appointed the ministers of the gospel to appear before you, and to deal with you in his stead, avowing as his own the invitations that are given you in his name.[4]

What must we do to be saved? Believe on the Lord Jesus Christ and you will be saved.

---

4   Quoted by Wayne Grudem, *Systematic Theology* (Grand Rapids: Zondervan Publishing House, 1994), 712.

14

Soli Deo Gloria

²⁷*Where, then, is boasting? It is excluded. On what principle?*
On that of observing the law? No, but on that of faith. ²⁸*For we*
maintain that a man is justified by faith apart from observing the
law. ²⁹*Is God the God of Jews only? Is he not the God of Gentiles too?*
Yes, of Gentiles too, ³⁰*since there is only one God, who will justify*
the circumcised by faith and the uncircumcised through that same
faith. ³¹*Do we, then, nullify the law by this faith? Not at all! Rather,*
we uphold the law.

Romans 3:27–31

In Romans 3:21–26, Paul spoke about God's plan of salvation
through faith in Christ alone. Now he makes the logical
connection: If salvation for sinners is by grace alone (*sola gratia*)
through faith in Christ alone (*sola fide*), then the saved sinner
must give glory to God alone (*soli Deo gloria*). A dying beggar
who has been given a feast by a gracious king cannot boast that
he deserved this royal feast. He must give all the glory to the
king. In the same way, the saved saints shall praise God forever,
proclaiming: "Salvation belongs to our God, who sits on the
throne, and to the Lamb" (Rev. 7:10).

Consider who we were when we met Jesus Christ. First, we
were impotent to save ourselves. No man can save himself,
even though all other religions speak in terms of self-salvation.
Second, we were sinners who transgressed God's holy laws and
thus dishonored him. Third, we were ungodly and therefore
unrighteous fools who said in our hearts that there is no God.
Fourth, we were enemies of God, for sin is essentially enmity

toward God. Yet we were loved by the Father, who sent his Son to die for us. Away with all human pride! Instead, let us praise God in all humility.

The proper response to our eternal salvation is not boasting but rather praising the triune God who saved us. In Romans 3:27–31, Paul teaches us that salvation by grace through faith in Jesus Christ excludes three things: boasting, discrimination, and lawlessness.

Justification Excludes Boasting

Justification by grace through faith excludes all boasting: *"Where, then, is boasting? It is excluded. On what principle? On that of observing the law? No, but on that of faith"* (v. 27).

Pride is the sin that made Lucifer the devil: "How you have fallen from heaven, O morning star, son of the dawn! You have been cast down to the earth, you who once laid low the nations! You said in your heart, 'I will ascend to heaven; I will raise my throne above the stars of God; I will sit enthroned on the mount of assembly, on the utmost heights of the sacred mountain. I will ascend above the tops of the clouds; I will make myself like the Most High'" (Isa. 14:12–14). The essence of arrogance is for man to dethrone God and establish himself as God. But God declares to such usurpers: "I will rise up against them. . . . I will cut off from Babylon her name and survivors, her offspring and descendants. . . . I will turn her into a place for owls and into swampland; I will sweep her with the broom of destruction" (Isa. 14:22–23). The Lord will not tolerate human arrogance.

C. S. Lewis, in *Mere Christianity*, speaks about pride:

> There is one vice of which no man in the world is free; which every one in the world loathes when he sees it in someone else; and of which hardly any people, except Christians, ever imagine that they are guilty themselves. I have heard people admit that they are bad-tempered, or that they cannot keep their heads about girls or drink, or even that they are cowards. I do not think I have ever heard anyone who was not a Christian accuse himself of this vice. And at the same time I have very seldom met anyone, who was not a Christian, who showed the slightest mercy to it in others. There is no fault which makes a man more unpopular, and no fault which we are more unconscious of in ourselves.

> And the more we have it in ourselves, the more we dislike it
> in others. The vice I am talking of is Pride.[1]

The Jews were boasters who constantly bragged about their race and religious privileges. They considered themselves holy and looked down on others, calling them unclean dogs. Paul speaks about their bragging: "Now you, if you call yourself a Jew; if you rely on the law and brag about your relationship to God . . . You who brag about the law, do you dishonor God by breaking the law? . . . If, in fact, Abraham was justified by works, he had something to boast about—but not before God" (Rom. 2:17, 23; 4:2). Elsewhere he lists the privileges the Jews boasted about: "Theirs is the adoption as sons; theirs the divine glory, the covenants, the receiving of the law, the temple worship and the promises. Theirs are the patriarchs, and from them is traced the human ancestry of Christ, who is God over all, forever praised! Amen" (Rom. 9:4–5). John the Baptist rebuked such boasters: "Do not think you can say to yourselves, 'We have Abraham as our father.' I tell you that out of these stones God can raise up children for Abraham" (Matt. 3:9).

Jesus spoke of the boastful pride of a Pharisee: "To some who were confident of their own righteousness and looked down on everybody else, Jesus told this parable: 'Two men went up to the temple to pray, one a Pharisee and the other a tax collector. The Pharisee stood up and prayed about himself: "God, I thank you that I am not like other men—robbers, evildoers, adulterers—or even like this tax collector. I fast twice a week and give a tenth of all I get"'" (Luke 18:9–12). And consider the words of another Pharisee, who became a battle-scarred veteran of the cross: "If anyone else thinks he has reasons to put confidence in the flesh, I have more: circumcised on the eighth day, of the people of Israel, of the tribe of Benjamin, a Hebrew of Hebrews; in regard to the law, a Pharisee; as for zeal, persecuting the church; as for legalistic righteousness, faultless" (Phil. 3:4–6).

Such bragging, however, was not only the business of the Jews; Gentiles boasted also. Paul writes of the Gentiles, "Although they claimed to be wise, they became fools. . . . They exchanged the truth of God for a lie, and worshiped and served created things rather than the

---

1   C. S. Lewis, *Mere Christianity* (New York: Macmillan Company, 1971), 108–9.

Creator. . . . Furthermore, since they did not think it worthwhile to retain the knowledge of God, he gave them over to a depraved mind. . . . [They are] slanderers, God-haters, insolent, arrogant and boastful" (Rom. 1:22, 25, 28, 30). Paul elsewhere remarks,

> For the message of the cross is foolishness to those who are perishing, but to us who are being saved it is the power of God. For it is written: 'I will destroy the wisdom of the wise; the intelligence of the intelligent I will frustrate.' Where is the wise man? Where is the scholar? Where is the philosopher of this age? Has not God made foolish the wisdom of the world? . . . Brothers, think of what you were when you were called. Not many of you were wise by human standards; not many were influential; not many were of noble birth. But God chose the foolish things of the world to shame the wise; God chose the weak things of the world to shame the strong. He chose the lowly things of this world and the despised things—and the things that are not—to nullify the things that are, so that no one may boast before him. . . . Therefore, as it is written: "Let him who boasts boast in the Lord." (1 Cor. 1:18–20, 26–29, 31)

Though Jews and Gentiles may boast, the Bible clearly teaches that sinful man is not justified by any human merit, but only by the merit of Jesus Christ. As Paul writes, "Therefore no one will be declared righteous in his sight by observing the law. . . . But now a righteousness from God apart from the law has been made known. . . . For we maintain that a man is justified by faith apart from observing the law" (Rom. 3:20, 21, 28). Our own works only can condemn us to hell; the work of Christ alone saves us.

Paul gives the reason God sent his Son to be a propitiation for our sins: "He did it to demonstrate his justice at the present time, so as to be just and the one who justifies those who have faith in Jesus" (Rom. 3:26). The efficient cause of justification *by works* is what man does, while the efficient cause of justification *by faith* is what Christ does. Our faith is extraspective (looking always to Christ alone), not introspective (looking to ourselves). Paul thus declares, "We live by faith, not by sight" (2 Cor. 5:7).

Even Abraham, the father of all believers, had no cause to boast in himself, but believed in God and was justified (Rom. 4:1–3). Salvation by Christ's death excludes all human boasting. The cross has done it all.

Jesus paid it all; all to him we owe.

and

Amazing grace, how sweet the sound,
that saved a wretch like me.

What about our good works of obedience to God? All our good works are the effect of God's grace. Jesus taught that a branch can do nothing unless it is united to the vine and lives by its life: "Because I live, you also will live" (John 14:19). Paul also argues this point: "God is able to make all grace abound to you, so that in all things at all times, having all that you need, you will abound in every good work" (2 Cor. 9:8). We are God's workmanship, "created in Christ Jesus unto good works, which God has foreordained that we should walk in them" (Eph. 2:10, KJV), but we do all these works by grace. And if they are by grace, where is our boasting?

Yet the saints of God can boast, both here and in heaven. We boast in God and give him all the glory, as Paul did: "Therefore, as it is written: 'Let him who boasts boast in the Lord'" (1 Cor. 1:31). Jeremiah speaks of this: "This is what the LORD says: 'Let not the wise man boast of his wisdom or the strong man boast of his strength or the rich man boast of his riches, but let him who boasts boast about this: that he understands and knows me, that I am the LORD, who exercises kindness, justice and righteousness on earth, for in these I delight,' declares the LORD" (Jer. 9:23–24).

If you still want to boast, consider these words of Paul: "For who makes you different from anyone else? What do you have that you did not receive? And if you did receive it, why do you boast as though you did not?" (1 Cor. 4:7). Therefore, let us pour contempt upon all our pride and sing praise to our gracious God.

Justification Excludes Discrimination

The second thing that justification by grace through faith excludes is all sinful discrimination. We can make rules against discrimination, but it resides deep within every human heart. But there is no such discrimination with God; all have sinned and fall short of his glory, and all need to be saved by Christ.

"For we maintain that a man is justified by faith apart from observing the law" (v. 28). The Greek text uses *anthrōpos* as the word for "man," meaning *every* man, both Jew and Gentile. The only way of salvation for all people is through faith in Jesus Christ. In other words, man is justified by faith, not by his works. Either one tries to save himself by his good works, which is true of all other religions, or he is saved by faith in the work of Jesus on the cross.

Then Paul adduces the argument that God is one, and that this one God is the God of both Jews and Gentiles: *"Is God the God of Jews only? Is he not the God of Gentiles too? Yes, of Gentiles too, since there is only one God, who will justify the circumcised by faith and the uncircumcised through that same faith"* (vv. 29–30). Paul is using the monotheistic doctrine of the Jews to defeat their arrogance and exclusivism.

This idea that God is one is found throughout the Scriptures. Moses declared, "Hear, O Israel: The LORD our God, the LORD is one" (Deut. 6:4; see also Isa. 43:11; 45:5, 21–22). The psalmist exhorts: "Sing to the LORD a new song; sing to the LORD, all the earth" (Ps. 96:1). Abraham asks the Lord, "Will not the Judge of all the earth do right?" (Gen. 18:25). If God is one, then he is God of all people, and there can therefore be only one way of salvation. There is one God and one Savior.

Man is always creating differences, whether based on race, income, gender, or rank. But Paul declares in Romans 3:22–23, "There is no difference, for all have sinned and come short of the glory of God." Just as there are not many gods, so there are also not many ways of salvation—one way for the Jews and another way for the Gentiles. There is no discrimination in the way sinners are saved. That is why Paul so boldly proclaims, "I am not ashamed of the gospel, because it is the power of God for the salvation of everyone who believes: first for the Jew, then for the Gentile" (Rom. 1:16).

This way of salvation was God's plan from all eternity. The Lord told Abraham, "I will bless those who bless you, and whoever curses you I will curse; and all peoples on earth will be blessed through you" (Gen. 12:3). We also read, "And through your offspring [meaning Jesus Christ] all nations on earth will be blessed, because you have obeyed me" (Gen. 22:18). Jesus confirmed this to his disciples: "This is what is written: The

Christ will suffer and rise from the dead on the third day, and repentance and forgiveness of sins will be preached in his name to all nations, beginning at Jerusalem" (Luke 24:46-47). Paul also speaks of this plan: "Consider Abraham: 'He believed God, and it was credited to him as righteousness.' Understand, then, that those who believe are children of Abraham. The Scripture foresaw that God would justify the Gentiles by faith, and announced the gospel in advance to Abraham: 'All nations will be blessed through you.' So those who have faith are blessed along with Abraham, the man of faith" (Gal. 3:6-9).

There is one God, one people, and one way of salvation through faith in the one Savior, Jesus Christ. Jesus said, "I am the way and the truth and the life" (John 14:6). Peter declares that there is salvation in no other (Acts 4:12). Paul explains that God is one and is God of all, and this one God has one way of salvation (1 Tim. 2:5-6). At the foot of the cross, we are all equal. There is no difference, whether in sin, condemnation, or salvation. God pardons the sins of Jews and Gentiles alike, making them all saints and sons of God. All other ways of salvation are false because they refuse to recognize Jesus as the Son of God.

Sinful discrimination in the church, therefore, should be outlawed. How many churches are organized by ethnicity? I read of a situation in which a black family visited a predominantly white church and the pastor later visited the black family and suggested that they would be more comfortable in a black church several miles away. But a church that discriminates in such a way is not a church of Christ. Paul insists that the people of God consist of believing Jews and Gentiles. Both circumcised and uncircumcised are saved by faith in Christ. The church is an international body of believers from all tribes and languages and nations, all colors in the spectrum.

Jesus Christ destroys sinful discrimination. Paul speaks of this:

> Therefore, remember that formerly you who are Gentiles by birth and called 'uncircumcised' by those who call themselves 'the circumcision' . . . remember that at that time you were separate from Christ, excluded from citizenship in Israel and foreigners to the covenants of the promise, without hope and without God in the world. But now in Christ Jesus you who once were far away have been brought near through the blood of Christ.

For he himself is our peace, who has made the two one and has destroyed the barrier, the dividing wall of hostility, by abolishing in his flesh the law with its commandments and regulations. His purpose was to create in himself one new man out of the two, thus making peace, and in this one body to reconcile both of them to God through the cross, by which he put to death their hostility. He came and preached peace to you who were far away and peace to those who were near. For through him we both have access to the Father by one Spirit.

Consequently, you are no longer foreigners and aliens, but fellow citizens with God's people and members of God's household, built on the foundation of the apostles and prophets, with Christ Jesus himself as the chief cornerstone. In him the whole building is joined together and rises to become a holy temple in the Lord. And in him you too are being built together to become a dwelling in which God lives by his Spirit. (Eph. 2:11–22; see also Eph. 3:6; 4:4–6)

Elsewhere he writes, "You are all sons of God through faith in Christ Jesus, for all of you who were baptized into Christ have clothed yourselves with Christ. There is neither Jew nor Greek, slave nor free, male nor female, for you are all one in Christ Jesus. If you belong to Christ, then you are Abraham's seed, and heirs according to the promise" (Gal. 3:26–29).

I was born into an upper-caste Syrian Orthodox church, and my family did not associate with anyone of a lower caste. But when the Holy Spirit was poured out in that area, God destroyed all such human barriers. I remember going as a young boy with my father and our pastor to visit an untouchable who had come to know Christ. We sat on the ground in this pariah's hut, ate what he gave us, and experienced true biblical fellowship. When the Holy Spirit was poured out, our deeply embedded distinctions were abolished.

We all belong to one family—we have one heavenly Father, and are brothers and sisters in Jesus Christ. We all are saints of God and can all approach God in the name of Jesus. John Stott says: "All who believe in Jesus belong to the same family and should be eating at the same table. That is what Paul's doctrine of justification by faith is all about."[2] Yet we must always fight against the sinful impulse to discriminate. Even Peter, who was

---

2 Stott, *Romans: God's Good News*, 120.

taught this lesson of oneness in Christ in Acts 10, failed to practice it later in the church at Antioch. Paul had to rebuke him publicly for his discriminatory actions (Gal. 2:11ff).

Justification Excludes Lawlessness

The third thing that justification by grace through faith excludes is lawlessness, or antinomianism. Far too many evangelicals today consider law and grace to be antithetical. In fact, they proudly assert that they are living by grace because they do not obey God's law.

Paul deals with this in the last verse of our text: *"Do we, then, nullify the law by this faith? Not at all! Rather, we uphold the law"* (v. 31). The argument goes like this: If justification is not by the works of the law but by faith in Jesus Christ, then what is the use of the law? Is the law worthless? Does the faith principle nullify the law? The answer is, "By no means!" We do not annul the law; instead, we uphold the law. The law is never antithetical to grace. Let us look at certain reasons:

1. The law reveals the character of God, especially his holiness. The law was given by God; therefore, it is holy, righteous, good, and spiritual (Rom. 7:12).
2. The law reveals our character. Like a mirror, it shows our moral filth (Rom. 3:20; 7:7).
3. The law itself testifies to salvation by grace (Rom. 3:21).
4. The goal of the law is Jesus Christ (Rom. 10:4).
5. Jesus came to fulfill the law in behalf of us (see Matt. 3:15; 5:17-18; Gal. 4:4-6; Heb. 5:8). Salvation is by the works of Christ's obedience to God's law, so salvation for us can be found through faith in Christ, who obeyed the law. Martyn Lloyd-Jones says, "What the Apostle maintains here is that God's way of declaring those who believe in Christ to be righteous honours and establishes the Law."[3]
6. God did not give the law to impart life to us (Gal. 3:21).
7. The law condemns us, yet it also points us to Jesus for salvation. It acts like John the Baptist, who said, "Look, the Lamb of God, who takes away the sin of the world!" (John 1:29). The law leads us to Christ (Gal. 3:23-25).
8. Grace enables us to keep the moral law of God. Jesus said, "If you love me, you will obey what I command" (John 14:15). Paul

---

3 Lloyd-Jones, *Romans*, vol. 3, *Atonement and Justification*, 144.

writes, "Let no debt remain outstanding, except the continuing debt to love one another, for he who loves his fellowman has fulfilled the law. The commandments, 'Do not commit adultery,' 'Do not murder,' 'Do not steal,' 'Do not covet,' and whatever other commandment there may be, are summed up in this one rule: 'Love your neighbor as yourself.' Love does no harm to its neighbor. Therefore love is the fulfillment of the law" (Rom. 13:8–10). Jesus said the first commandment is, "Love the Lord your God with all your heart and with all your soul and with all your mind." The second is this: "Love your neighbor as yourself." All the Law and the Prophets hang on these two commandments (Matt. 22:37–40). Those who are justified by faith will keep God's commandments by God's enabling grace.

9. The law pronounces judgment on all violators of God's law. "The wrath of God is being revealed from heaven against all the godlessness and wickedness of men" (Rom. 1:18; see also Rom. 6:23; Ezek. 18:20).

Conclusion

If you have not trusted in Jesus Christ alone and have not been redeemed by Christ's death, then the law of God condemns you. If you are not justified by the Father on the basis of the righteousness of Christ alone, then God's wrath is abiding on you. Soon you shall die in your sins and enter into God's eternal judgment. I pray that you will recognize the seriousness of this danger and repent of your sins, believe in Jesus Christ who fully obeyed the law for you, and be saved forever.

To those who are justified by faith: Let us be humble and not boast in anything except in the cross of Christ. Let us worship God all of life and live for his glory. Let us not discriminate, but let us love one another, knowing that we are equally sinners, saints, and sons of God in God's only Son. Let us lay down our lives for our brothers.

Finally, let us uphold the law of God by his grace. Away with all Christian antinomianism, autonomy, and cheap grace! God has made us who were his enemies into lovers of God, and love fulfills God's law. Let us prove daily that we are God's children by obeying our heavenly Father exactly, immediately, and with great joy as the Holy Spirit enables us.

15

The Blessed Man

¹What then shall we say that Abraham, our forefather, discovered in this matter? ²If, in fact, Abraham was justified by works, he had something to boast about—but not before God. ³What does the Scripture say? "Abraham believed God, and it was credited to him as righteousness."

⁴Now when a man works, his wages are not credited to him as a gift, but as an obligation. ⁵However, to the man who does not work but trusts God who justifies the wicked, his faith is credited as righteousness. ⁶David says the same thing when he speaks of the blessedness of the man to whom God credits righteousness apart from works:

⁷"Blessed are they whose transgressions are forgiven, whose sins are covered.

⁸Blessed is the man whose sin the Lord will never count against him."

Romans 4:1–8

Who is a blessed man? Is it the man who is the world's greatest athlete, the world's most wealthy person, or the one holding the most political power? Is it the healthiest man, the wisest man, or the most-admired man? Not according to the Bible. The most blessed man is the man who is right with God, who has been acquitted in God's court and whose sins have been forgiven. The blessed man is the man who is justified on the basis of Christ's redemption and propitiatory sacrifice and is declared righteous through his faith in Christ. Such a man has no boasting in himself, but praises God all his life and gives God all the glory. He is the blessed man in the biblical sense.

The Testimony of Abraham (Rom. 4:1–2)

"What then shall we say that Abraham, our forefather, discovered in this matter? If, in fact, Abraham was justified by works, he had something to boast about—but not before God" (vv. 1–2). Judaism boasted that Abraham, the progenitor of Israel, was justified by his own works and not by faith. The Book of Jubilees states that Abraham was perfect in all his deeds with the Lord and well-pleasing in righteousness all the days of his life. Rabbis cited Genesis 15:6 as proof that Abraham was justified by his works and not by faith, and stated, "No one has been found like Abraham in glory. Abraham had obeyed the law perfectly even before it had been given" (Sirach 44:19). But concerning the righteousness of God, Paul states, "Where, then, is boasting? It is excluded" (Rom. 3:27). The Jews were claiming that Abraham was justified by his works, but the Scriptures make it clear that Abraham was not. Paul does not see Abraham as an exception to the doctrine of justification by grace through faith alone.

The proud Pharisee of Luke 18 represents the Jews of Paul's day. According to them, Abraham worked for his salvation and God owed him his justification. But Abraham was an ungodly sinner like everyone else. Joshua said Abraham was an idol worshiper before the God of glory called him (Josh. 24:2).

No one can be saved by his works. From eternity there has been only one God and only one way of salvation—salvation by grace through faith. All the people of God, from Genesis through Revelation, are saved by grace. We cannot earn salvation; we receive it as a free gift. Noah found grace in the sight of God (Gen. 6:8), as did Abraham, and as does every elect child of God.

Abraham believed in the promised Messiah and was saved by grace alone. Jesus spoke of this to the Jews: "Abraham rejoiced at the thought of seeing my day; he saw it and was glad." This puzzled the Jews, who exclaimed, "You are not yet fifty years old and you have seen Abraham!" He replied, "Before Abraham was born, I am!" (John 8:56–58). Jesus was declaring to them, "I am the Messiah; I am the Lord; I am God. Abraham saw me and was saved by his faith."

Paul writes, "The Scripture foresaw that God would justify the Gentiles by faith, and announced the gospel in advance to Abraham: 'All nations will be blessed through you'" (Gal. 3:8). This was speaking about Abraham's offspring, Jesus Christ. He continues, "For if the inheritance depends on the law, then it no longer depends on a promise; but God in his grace gave it to Abraham through a promise" (Gal. 3:18). So Paul is telling his Jewish adversaries who believed in salvation by good works that they were wrong; Abraham was no exception to the principle of justification by faith that Paul articulated. Even Abraham had nothing to boast about before God.

The Testimony of Scripture (Rom. 4:3)

Paul goes on to a second point, which is the testimony of the Scripture itself. He asks, "What does the Scripture say?" (v. 3). He then quotes Genesis 15:6: "Abraham believed God, and it was credited to him as righteousness."

Paul appealed to the Scripture on this matter of Abraham's justification because the Scripture is God-breathed and useful for teaching (2 Tim. 3:16). The term "Scripture" refers to the written word of God, whether it be in part or the whole. Though written many centuries ago by different people, it is the word of God and it always speaks to those who read it with faith. God himself speaks authoritatively in the Scripture; therefore, the Scripture is the basis for all teachings and the standard for our doctrine and life. Ever-settled in heaven, the Scripture is the final authority. The Scripture is flawless and perfect.

Therefore Paul poses the question, "What does the Scripture say?" Judaism had cited Genesis 15:6 to prove that Abraham was justified by works; now Paul uses the same scripture to prove the opposite, that Abraham was justified by faith.

Abraham trusted in a personal God, not in an undefined entity. Our trust and confidence should also be in the infinite, personal God. We rest in him, putting our entire weight on him. When we do so, we discover he is able to bear all our concerns, whether past, present, or future.

Abraham's faith was also propositional, meaning he believed in the promise that God made to him concerning a vast multitude of descendants. But his faith rested not on that vast multitude but in one descendant—the Messiah—who would save him and every elect of God.

Abraham believed God by trusting in his promises to give this aged man a multitude of children, one of whom would be the Messiah, the Savior of Abraham and of the world. *"Abraham believed God, and it was reckoned to him as righteousness."* This word "reckon" (*logizomai*) appears five times in verses 3 through 8. It is an accounting term that deals with reality. Paul uses it here to assure us that what we did not possess has been put into our account by another. It is like having no money and then receiving a million dollars, put into our account by someone else. It is not wages we earned; it is purely a gift. God puts into our account his righteousness and does not count our unrighteousness against us.

Notice, God is not reckoning our faith as righteousness. He is not considering our faith in lieu of righteousness. God's own righteousness is put into our account through the channel of our faith, which itself is a gift of God to us.

Of Abraham Paul writes, "And he received the sign of circumcision, a seal of the righteousness that he had by faith while he was still uncircumcised. So then, he is the father of all who believe but have not been circumcised, in order that righteousness might be credited to them" (Rom. 4:11). We are unrighteous and in need of righteousness. God puts into our account his own righteousness to deal with all our unrighteousness. It is imputed to us in place of our unrighteousness, in view of our faith. Faith is the instrumental, not efficient, cause of our salvation. The efficient cause is grace, what God has done in Jesus Christ. Our faith is a gift of God. It is likened to a beggar's hand lifted up to receive the gift of grace.

Paul also uses *logizomai* in Philemon 18–19 in speaking about Onesimus the slave and his debt: "If he has done you any wrong or owes you anything, charge it to me. I, Paul, am writing this with my own hand. I will pay it back." In the same way, Jesus is saying to the Father, "If my people owe you anything, charge it to my account and I will pay it back." Our debt is put into Christ's account and his infinite riches are put into ours.

So Abraham believed God and his promise. In time, God sent his Son, the Savior of the world, the seed of the woman, the seed of Abraham, who saves all elect sinners.

God Who Justifies the Ungodly (Rom. 4:4–5)

"Now when a man works, his wages are not credited to him as a gift, but as an obligation. However, to the man who does not work but trusts God who justifies the wicked, his faith is credited as righteousness" (vv. 4–5). Justification by faith is a gracious act of God. The one who works receives wages, not grace. If we could work for our salvation, then God would owe it to us and we could boast that we saved ourselves by our good works. Such salvation would not be by grace. Whenever a Christian boasts, he is behaving like the Pharisee of Luke 18, who boasted in his work righteousness and looked down on everyone else.

All human boasting, therefore, is excluded. And Paul explains that the one who does not work for his salvation but trusts in the one who justifies the ungodly—to such a one God credits his faith for righteousness, even the righteousness of God, apart from any work that we do.

Some might argue that believing is working, but Paul dispels that myth: *"To the man who does not work but trusts God who justifies the wicked, his faith is credited as righteousness"* (v. 5). Trusting is the opposite of working. In other words, believing is not a meritorious work.

Romans 4:5 includes a surprising and shocking phrase: *"God who justifies the wicked."* When God comes to save us, we are ungodly, unrighteous, wicked, sinful enemies of God. It is not that we can wash ourselves a little and make ourselves slightly more acceptable to God. The truth is, all have sinned and are ungodly, enemies of God. But God justifies the ungodly.

There seems to be a paradox. The Bible says we must not justify the guilty. How can God contradict the Scripture? The answer is found in Romans 3, where we learn that God can justify sinners justly because our sin problem is dealt with in the life and death of another, Jesus Christ. God himself justifies the ungodly through the death of his eternal Son. As we meditate on this great truth, we will discover the munificence of God's grace unleashed toward us. God pursued, found, saved, and justified us. He never justifies the godly. He always justifies the ungodly.

Why do you think people do not want to believe in Jesus Christ? Because they maintain that they are righteous on their own terms. They measure themselves by their own perceived standard. But God in Jesus Christ justifies the ungodly on the basis of Christ's redemptive and atoning work on the cross. If we come to Christ as ungodly, we will go home as godly. If we come weary of the burden of our real guilt, we can go in heavenly peace. The publican cried out, "Have mercy upon me, a sinner," and he went home justified. The thief on the cross cried out to Christ, and Jesus said, "Today you will be with me in paradise."

Romans 4:5 is music in the sinner's ears. William Temple famously stated: "The only thing of my very own which I can contribute to my own redemption is the sin from which I need to be redeemed." Let us come to God as one who is without strength and at enmity with him. God who justifies the ungodly will redeem us from all our sins. This justification is a divine verdict. He can justify us this moment if we cry out to him.

> The vilest offender who truly believes,
> That moment from Jesus a pardon receives.

God justifies only the ungodly and condemns the self-righteous. If we do not want to trust in Christ, we will die in our sins, because all people die either in the Lord or in their sins. We must come believing in the One who died for our sins. God will grant us this faith as a gift right now. The faith God requires is not based on mathematical probability—it is supernatural faith, which God must give us, and he does. John Stott says, "Christ became sin with our sins, in order that we might become righteous with God's righteousness."[1]

The Testimony of David (Rom. 4:6–8)

What did David say about his salvation? "*David says the same thing when he speaks of the blessedness of the man to whom God credits righteousness apart from works*" (v. 6). Here again Paul speaks

---

1   Stott, *Romans: God's Good News*, 127.

of the idea of crediting faith as righteousness. God credits divine righteousness "apart from works." Then Paul quotes Psalm 32:1–2 as proof from the Scripture.

David was a great sinner. He had a copy of the Bible and knew God's law. He was supposed to live according to it, to counsel others from it, and to mete out justice in Israel in conformity with it. Yet he violated God's law through adultery, murder, and deception. How could such an ungodly man be justified by works?

David did have in his account an infinite amount of unrighteousness. We all do, because any sin we commit is infinite because it is against an infinite God. But God blotted out David's unrighteousness forever and in its place put divine righteousness. This is the fullness of blessing! So David celebrates his salvation by grace: *"Blessed are they whose transgressions are forgiven, whose sins are covered. Blessed is the man whose sin the Lord will never count against him"* (Rom. 4:7–8). David speaks of the inexpressible and glorious joy of the man to whom God credits righteousness apart from works.

Blessed with all spiritual blessings in heavenly places in Christ are those whose iniquities are forgiven, whose sins are covered! "Iniquity" speaks about having a boundary and crossing over it into sin. "Covered" means the Lord will never count our sins against us. "Sin" is falling short of the standard which God has given us in his word. Blessed are those whose sin the Lord does not ever count against them. This is what it means to be a blessed man.

Let us now look more closely at what this blessing entails:

1. BLESSED ARE THOSE WHOSE INIQUITIES ARE FORGIVEN

The word "forgiven" (*aphiēmi*) is also used in Matthew 13:36: "Having sent away the crowd." The idea is that God sent our sins far away from us. We may look for them, but they cannot be found. It speaks about the Day of Atonement, when the high priest confessed upon the scapegoat all the sins of Israel and sent the scapegoat away into the wilderness. It speaks of the mission of Jesus Christ: "Look, the Lamb of God, who takes away the sin of the world!" (John 1:29).

Our sins are forever separated from us! Our guilt, condemnation, punishment, and hell are separated from us forever. Isaiah 53 gives us more light on how this separation came to be, as does Peter: "[Jesus Christ] himself bore our sins in his body on the tree" (1 Pet. 2:24).

2. BLESSED ARE THOSE WHOSE SINS ARE COVERED UP

The Greek word *epikaluptō* means fully and permanently covered up. Even God will not uncover them. Satan will try to accuse and uncover, but we must overcome him by the blood of the Lamb and the word of God's testimony.

The picture is of the high priest going into the Holy of Holies and sprinkling the blood on the mercy seat. By doing so, he was covering the sins of Israel through the blood of an innocent substitute. Even so, the blood of Christ has fully covered the guilt of our sins. If this does not cause us to praise the Lord, we may not have experienced this wonderful, radical separation from our iniquities, sins, and guilt.

Many use every possible means to cover up their sins, but that is exactly what we should not do. "He who conceals his sins does not prosper" (Prov. 28:13). Our business is to confess and expose our sins. If we are concealing them, we will be miserable and may experience all sorts of problems in our bodies. We will have no joy of the Lord. Paul writes to those who sinned in the church: "That is why many among you are weak and sick, and a number of you have fallen asleep" (1 Cor. 11:30). But there is hope. Proverbs 28:13 continues: "but whoever confesses and renounces them finds mercy." God already knows our sins. From whom, then, are we covering and concealing? We may try to hide them from our spouse or parents or pastors or other authorities. But if we confess and renounce our sins, we shall find mercy. John says, "If we confess our sins, [God] is faithful and just and will forgive us our sins and purify us from all unrighteousness" (1 John 1:9). It is our job to reveal our sins; it is God's job to cover them permanently by the blood of Christ.

Zechariah gives an illustration of such covering: "Then he showed me Joshua the high priest standing before the angel of the LORD, and Satan standing at his right side to accuse him. The LORD said to Satan, 'The LORD rebuke you, Satan! The LORD, who has chosen Jerusalem, rebuke you! Is not this man a burning stick snatched from the fire?' Now Joshua was dressed in filthy clothes as he stood before the angel." In other words, it was true that Joshua was a sinner. Satan does not always lie. Joshua was filthy, and he represents all God's people. Zechariah continues, "The angel said to those who were standing before him, 'Take off his filthy clothes.'" This is speaking about the forgiveness of sins. But there is more: "Then he said to Joshua, 'See, I have taken away your sin, and I will put rich garments on you'" (Zech. 3:1–4). Justification is more than forgiveness; God clothes us with his righteousness and receives us as his sons. He loves us, embraces us, and fellowships with us. He is not saying, "I forgave your sins; now go away." He qualifies us to be with him now and forever.

Let us look more closely at Psalm 32. If we find ourselves in David's miserable situation, here is the solution. David says, "When I kept silent . . ." (v. 3). David refused to confess his sins because of arrogance. But God has a way of dealing with us. David continues, "My bones wasted away through my groaning all day long." David had great wealth and held many great celebrations with feasting and music. David had everything, but he was not a blessed person. He had everything but joy. "For day and night your hand was heavy upon me; my strength was sapped as in the heat of summer" (v. 4). David was experiencing great pressure, pain, and depression. Pain can be God's messenger. It has one message: Repent and confess. Here is David's solution: "Then I acknowledged my sin to you and did not cover up my iniquity. I said, 'I will confess my transgressions to the LORD'—and you forgave the guilt of my sin" (v. 5). Weeks and months had gone by for David as he groaned in misery day and night. He went without sleep, was terrified, experienced bad dreams, and his bones wasted away. But finally he confessed his sins, and God forgave him.

If we are miserable as Christians, it may be because we have failed to identify, confess, and forsake our sins. When we do so, the joy of the Lord will fill our hearts once again. So David sings: "You are my hiding place; you will protect me from trouble and surround me with songs of deliverance" (v. 7). Joy is not something outside of David; it is within. God the Rock has a hiding place for us. He surrounds us with songs of deliverance; we are in the center of the circle called deliverance. David continues, "Many are the woes of the wicked, but the LORD's unfailing love surrounds the man who trusts in him" (v. 10).

3. BLESSED IS THE MAN WHOSE SIN THE LORD WILL NEVER COUNT AGAINST HIM

In the Greek, the idea of Romans 4:8 is that our sin is never again counted against us. Sin, guilt, death, and hell are gone from us forever, and God is with us forever. He will never leave us nor forsake us, whether in life or in death. The blessed man is the one whose iniquities are forgiven, whose sins are covered up by God, the one to whom the Lord does not count sin.

The Old Testament is filled with wonderful promises of God that he will put our sins away. Consider these verses:

1. "As far as the east is from the west, so far has he removed our transgressions from us" (Ps. 103:12);
2. "You have put all my sins behind your back" (Isa. 38:17);
3. "I, even I, am he who blots out your transgressions, for my own sake, and remembers your sins no more" (Isa. 43:25);
4. "I have swept away your offenses like a cloud, your sins like the morning mist" (Isa. 44:22);
5. "I will forgive their wickedness and will remember their sins no more" (Jer. 31:34);
6. "'In those days, at that time,' declares the LORD, 'search will be made for Israel's guilt, but there will be none, and for the sins of Judah, but none will be found, for I will forgive the remnant I spare'" (Jer. 50:20);
7. "Who is a God like you, who pardons sin and forgives the transgression of the remnant of his inheritance? You do not stay angry forever but delight to show mercy. You will again have compassion on us; you will tread our sins underfoot and hurl all our iniquities into the depths of the sea" (Mic. 7:18–19).

God did not spare his own Son, but he spares us and forgives all our sins—past, present, and future. This illustrates the potency of the atoning blood of Christ. Sin prevented us from having fellowship with God, but God in Christ has removed our sins. Now clothed in God's righteousness, we enjoy everlasting fellowship with God. The joy of the Lord is our strength and all is well with our souls. This is true blessing.

Before he confessed his sins, David was miserable, although he was king. Guilt rested on him like a heavy iron girder. He was not a blessed man. But when he confessed, God forgave his iniquities and did not count his sins against him. Clothed in the perfect righteousness of Christ, his Lord and Son, David began to sing.

Psalms 32 and 51 are the songs of this forgiven saint, this blessed man. Only a true Christian can be blessed in this way. And justification by faith does not merely mean forgiveness of sins; God also gives us his perfect righteousness and embraces us, accepts us as sons, and invites us to come into his presence, where there is fullness of joy and on his right hand pleasures forevermore.

John Piper says that this blessedness is a condition in which we are deeply secure and content and happy in God.[2] We are blessed in life and in death, in prison, when stoned, when beaten, when beheaded, when slandered, and when disease eats us up. Nothing can terrify the blessed man—he is with God and God is with him. He is surrounded with songs of deliverance and covenant love.

How does God justify the ungodly? Paul says that "God was reconciling the world to himself in Christ, not counting men's sins against them" (2 Cor. 5:19). How can he do that? "God made him who had no sin to be sin for us, so that in him we might become the righteousness of God" (2 Cor. 5:21). Elsewhere he says, "It is because of [God] that you are in Christ Jesus, who has become for us wisdom from God—that is, our righteousness, holiness and redemption" (1 Cor. 1:30). Christ is our life and our hope; we are united with him by faith. He will never leave us nor forsake us. All others may desert us or fall away, but the Lord will receive us. Let us rejoice in the truth that God justifies the ungodly.

James Boice speaks about a sixty-year-old woman who once came to an evangelist and confessed a murder she had committed when she was twenty years old. A boarder had raped her, so she went into his room, turned on the gas, and he died. She had carried this very heavy load of guilt for forty years. But when she trusted in Christ, the burden was instantly lifted from her. Her sins were separated from her and her iniquities sent away. God justified this ungodly woman and she became blessed instantly.[3]

Are you weary of the guilt of your sins? Come to the one who calls, "Come to me, all you who are weary and burdened, and I

---

2   John Piper, "When the Lord Does Not Take Account of Sin," sermon Aug. 15, 1999, http://www.desiringgod.org/resource-library/sermons/when-the-lord-does-not-take-account-of-sin

3   Boice, *Romans*, vol. 1, *Justification by Faith*, 447–48.

will give you rest" (Matt. 11:28). If you do, you will be blessed. Only Jesus can and will remove your burden.

16

Abraham Our Father

⁹Is this blessedness only for the circumcised, or also for the uncircumcised? We have been saying that Abraham's faith was credited to him as righteousness. ¹⁰Under what circumstances was it credited? Was it after he was circumcised, or before? It was not after, but before! ¹¹And he received the sign of circumcision, a seal of the righteousness that he had by faith while he was still uncircumcised. So then, he is the father of all who believe but have not been circumcised, in order that righteousness might be credited to them. ¹²And he is also the father of the circumcised who not only are circumcised but who also walk in the footsteps of the faith that our father Abraham had before he was circumcised.

Romans 4:9–12

The Jews placed great value on circumcision as a sign of their covenant relationship with God. Yet the gospel knows no discrimination between those who are circumcised and those who are not. In this passage, Paul asserts that everyone who believes in Jesus, the son of David, the son of Abraham, whether Jew or Gentile, whether circumcised or uncircumcised, is a true child of God and a son of Abraham. We want to examine three points: that circumcision, which stands for any sacrament, does not save anyone; the true meaning of circumcision; and the divine purpose of circumcision.

Circumcision Does Not Save

The Jews maintained that Abraham was their father only and not the father of the Gentiles. In fact, this was a point of great pride for the Jews. Therefore, Paul's statement in this passage that Abraham was the father of all believers, Jew or Gentile, was startling to them. Earlier in this epistle Paul said, "I am not ashamed of the gospel, because it is the power of God for the salvation of everyone who believes: first for the Jew, then for the Gentile" (Rom. 1:16). Paul now argues that the blessedness of David and Abraham that he spoke about is not only for the circumcised Jews but also for the uncircumcised Gentile believers. This gospel of universal salvation that Paul preached was aimed at destroying Jewish pride.

Christianity knows no discrimination. Man tries to create differences all the time, in every society and nation. Such differences enable groups or individuals to look down upon others. But in fact "there is no difference, for all have sinned and fall short of the glory of God" (Rom. 3:23). God levels everyone by this statement of the universality of sin. God in Jesus Christ saves all who truly believe.

Before God, one people group is not superior to another. There is only one God, one people of God, and one way of salvation. Earlier Paul established that justification is by faith in Jesus Christ apart from works of the law. Now he anticipates another argument of Jewish unbelief: What about the God-ordained rite of circumcision? What relevance does circumcision have with reference to this salvation by faith that Paul was speaking about? The Jews were asking, "Can we not say that salvation is by faith plus circumcision?" Here Paul responds that circumcision has no material or essential bearing on one's salvation.

To bolster his argument, Paul comes up with an example from history: Was Abraham justified by faith before or after he was circumcised? Paul answers, *"It was not after, but before!"* (v. 10). Abraham was declared righteous (Gen. 15) some fourteen years before he was circumcised (Gen. 17). He was justified while he was a Gentile and did not earn his salvation by any works of obedience, especially not through the work of being circumcised. The Jews maintained that their circumcision was not only a mark on their bodies, but also the means of their salvation. But Paul argues from Scripture that circumcision was not the cause or ground of Abraham's salvation.

The Jews looked down upon the Gentiles, calling them "uncircumcised" and "defiled" (Isa. 52:1; Acts 11:3). The Jews were proud of their circumcision. It was their passport to heaven, for they believed no circumcised person would go to hell. They believed the Gentiles should first become Jews by conversion and circumcision before they could be saved. To them, circumcision was a necessary condition for salvation.

But Paul put no confidence in circumcision for his salvation. He was circumcised on the eighth day and considered himself perfect concerning the righteousness of the law. He was proud of these things, but he was not saved until he put his faith in Jesus Christ.

Jeremiah says, "'But let him who boasts boast about this: that he understands and knows me, that I am the LORD, who exercises kindness, justice and righteousness on earth, for in these I delight,' declares the LORD. 'The days are coming,' declares the LORD, 'when I will punish all who are circumcised only in the flesh. . . . For all these nations are really uncircumcised, and even the whole house of Israel is uncircumcised in heart'" (Jer. 9:24–26). This applies also to the sacraments of baptism and the Lord's Supper. Paul writes: "A man is not a Jew if he is only one outwardly, nor is circumcision merely outward and physical. No, a man is a Jew if he is one inwardly; and circumcision is circumcision of the heart, by the Spirit" (Rom. 2:28–29).

This issue of circumcision was settled by the early church by the Council of Jerusalem in light of what happened in Cornelius' house when Peter ministered to them. "Some men came down from Judea to Antioch and were teaching the brothers: 'Unless you are circumcised, according to the custom taught by Moses, you cannot be saved'" (Acts 15:1). Paul and Barnabas were sent by the church of Antioch to Jerusalem to ask the elders about this question. After the council discussed this, Peter said of the Jews and Gentiles, "[God] made no distinction between us and them, for he purified their hearts by faith. . . . We believe it is through the grace of our Lord Jesus that we are saved, just as they are" (Acts 15:9, 11).

Let us stop glorying in external things. Paul writes, "Mark my words! I, Paul, tell you that if you let yourselves be circumcised, Christ will be of no value to you at all. . . . For in Christ Jesus neither circumcision nor uncircumcision has any value. The only thing that counts is faith expressing itself through love" (Gal. 5:2, 6). He further explains, "Those who want to make a good impression outwardly are trying to compel you to be circumcised. The only reason they do this is to avoid being persecuted for the cross of Christ. Not even those who are circumcised obey the law, yet they want you to be circumcised that they may boast about your flesh. May I never boast except in the cross of our Lord Jesus Christ, through which the world has been crucified to me, and I to the world. Neither circumcision nor uncircumcision means anything; what counts is a new creation" (Gal. 6:12–15).

Paul himself was circumcised on the eighth day, but that did not save him. He became a new creation by the mighty miracle of regeneration by the Holy Spirit. If salvation is only by grace through faith and not by works, and not even by the particular God-ordained work of circumcision, why did God decree that Abraham and his descendants be circumcised? We must examine what true circumcision is. It is a command of God and a blessing, when its true divine significance is understood.

The Meaning of Circumcision

"[Abraham] received the sign of circumcision, a seal of the righteousness that he had by faith while he was still uncircumcised" (v. 11). God gave circumcision to Abraham as a sign and seal of the righteousness God had given to him through faith. It was a sign of the covenant of God's salvation relationship with Abraham, which he ratified in Genesis 15.

A sign is not the reality; it is something external and visible that points to a greater reality. Charles Hodge points out, "What answers well as a sign, is a miserable substitute for the thing signified."[1] A sign we may see on the freeway that advertises a restaurant is not a restaurant. We cannot go to the sign and get food and drink. We must drive ten miles to arrive at the reality to which the sign pointed.

Likewise, a wedding ring is not what brings about a marriage relationship. A wedding ring points to a prior reality and reminds us of our ongoing responsibility to one another. Even

---

1   Hodge, *Romans*, 125.

so, Abraham's circumcision when he was ninety-nine years old pointed to his prior justification. So circumcision, Paul argues, is not the ground or the necessary condition of our salvation.

Not only was circumcision a sign, but it was also a seal of the righteousness Abraham had by faith. A seal is that by which something is confirmed, authenticated, or guaranteed. It confirms the truth or reality of something else. The mark of circumcision Abraham received in his body confirmed to him the righteous status God had conferred on him fourteen years earlier. Circumcision has no independent value. It is not a passport to heaven, as the Jews maintained. It is confirming and comforting because it assures us of the reality of our justification by faith, but it is not productive of our salvation. It is like the seal and stamp on my passport. It does not make me a citizen of my country, but it confirms and assures me that I am. The seal presupposes the existence of the thing sealed.

Baptism is also a seal of the prior reality. James Boice speaks about the doubts that plagued the great reformer Martin Luther in his final days. He questioned the value of the Reformation, his own faith, and even the work of Jesus Christ. But when such doubts came to him one after another, he would write, "*Baptizatus sum!*" which means, "I have been baptized." His baptism was a sign and a seal of the reality of his salvation in Christ. Luther was telling himself, "I have been baptized. I belong to Jesus Christ." The thought of his baptism confirmed and assured him of his prior salvation by grace through faith alone.[2]

The Purpose of Circumcision

Why did God give the sign and seal of circumcision to Abraham in particular? Paul discloses the divine purpose in verses 11–12. The first reason was that Abraham might be the father of all Gentiles who believe and are saved, though uncircumcised. That is why I can proudly say that I, a Gentile, am truly a child of Abraham. There is not one way of salvation for the Jews and another for the Gentiles. There is only one way of salvation for all sinners—the way of faith in Jesus Christ.

---

2   Boice, *Romans*, vol. 1, *Justification by Faith*, 457.

Why was Abraham justified before he was circumcised? Paul reveals that it was to demonstrate that we do not need to be circumcised to be justified by grace through faith. Abraham was uncircumcised when God justified him by faith. In the same way, God can justify all Gentiles without them being circumcised. Abraham, therefore, is the father of all believers who are not circumcised. Most Christians today were Gentiles by birth, not circumcised in the biblical sense. But we believed in Jesus Christ and are therefore children of Abraham. There is no discrimination. As God credited Abraham with the righteousness of God in view of his faith, so also God reckons the righteousness of God to a believing Gentile through his faith, though he is uncircumcised. So Abraham truly is the father of all believers. God told Abraham that all the nations would be blessed through his offspring (Gen. 18:18), and Abraham's blessing comes through his Seed, Jesus Christ.

"And he is also the father of the circumcised who not only are circumcised but who also walk in the footsteps of the faith that our father Abraham had before he was circumcised" (v. 12). The second reason is that Abraham also is the father of all believing Jews, though they are circumcised. Abraham was circumcised, though after his justification. So he is the father of the Jews, not because they are circumcised, but because they believe as Abraham did. They walk in the steps of the faith of their father Abraham. At age seventy-five, while he was in idolatry, he was called by God to follow him. Abraham lived another one hundred years, walking in faith until he died. Abraham, therefore, is also the father of all Jewish people who follow in his faith.

Whether Gentile or Jew, we must walk in faith in the footprints of our father Abraham. We must walk single file behind him, not abreast, following in the footprints of his faith life. We must become disciples of Abraham, who himself was a disciple of Jesus the Messiah. Jesus said, "Abraham rejoiced at the thought of seeing my day; he saw it and was glad" (John 8:56). All along Abraham believed in the Messiah promised to him by God the Father. This Messiah calls us to deny ourselves, take up the cross daily, and follow him through death unto life everlasting. Paul exhorts, "Follow my example, as I follow the example of Christ" (1 Cor. 11:1). We walk by faith, not by sight—by faith in God and in the holy Scriptures.

Paul is telling all believers to imitate Abraham's faith, not his circumcision. He uses the word "follow in step with" elsewhere: "Since we live by the Spirit, let us keep in step with the Spirit" (Gal. 5:25). We must follow in the Spirit's footprints. We must follow in Jesus' footprints, not creating our own way.

The Jews claimed they were Abraham's descendants, yet only a few believed in Jesus. Paul addresses this issue with great sorrow: "It is not as though God's word had failed. For not all who are descended from Israel are Israel" (Rom. 9:6). In the same way, not all who claim to be Christians are Christians. There is the larger circle of professing Christians, and a smaller circle inside of those who are true Christians. There is a large circle of Jews, but a smaller one who are true believers. Yet they are not Abraham's children through natural means. Paul clarifies this point: "Nor because they are his descendants are they all Abraham's children. On the contrary, 'It is through Isaac that your offspring will be reckoned.' In other words, it is not the natural children who are God's children, but it is the children of the promise who are regarded as Abraham's offspring. For this was how the promise was stated: 'At the appointed time I will return, and Sarah will have a son'" (Rom. 9:7–9).

They claimed they were Abraham's descendants, just as many today claim to be Christians. They boasted in their circumcision and that they were physically descended from Abraham. They claimed that as children of Abraham they were heirs of eternal salvation. But Jesus told them, "Your father is not Abraham, for he believed in me, but you do not. Your father is the devil" (see John 8:31–59). There are also professing Christians whose father is the devil, though they may be baptized and have joined a church. All these things can mean nothing. The devil is the father of every unbeliever until God in his rich mercy makes us his children. Paul speaks of this great transformation:

> As for you, you were dead in your transgressions and sins, in which you used to live when you followed the ways of this world and of the ruler of the kingdom of the air, the spirit who is now at work in those who are disobedient. All of us also lived among them at one time, gratifying the cravings of our sinful nature and following its desires and thoughts. Like the rest, we were by nature objects of wrath. But because of his great love for us, God, who is rich in mercy, made us alive with Christ. (Eph. 2:1–5)

Abraham is the father of all who are characterized by faith in God. What does "father" mean? We find some understanding in Genesis 4:20–21: "Adah gave birth to Jabal; he was the father of those who live in tents and raise livestock. His brother's name was Jubal; he was the father of all who play the harp and flute." Here, the idea of fatherhood is linked with character. The descendants of Jabal lived in tents and raised livestock because their father did so, while Jubal's descendants were noted for playing the harp and flute because of their father.

Likewise, the believer Abraham is the father of all who believe in Jesus Christ and are justified by grace through faith alone. In other words, faith is the determining criterion, not circumcision. In fact, circumcision divides, but faith in Christ unites us. Without discrimination, Jesus receives all sinners, both Gentiles and Jews. If we believe, we belong to the Seed of Abraham and are heirs of God, heirs together with Abraham, and joint-heirs with Christ. We are saved by faith alone, not faith plus circumcision or baptism or anything else. All believers are children of Abraham; all unbelievers are children of the devil.

Paul explains, "Therefore, the promise comes by faith, so that it may be by grace and may be guaranteed to all Abraham's offspring—not only to those who are of the law but also to those who are of the faith of Abraham. He is the father of us all" (Rom. 4:16). Elsewhere he writes, "Understand, then, that those who believe are children of Abraham" (Gal. 3:7).

Are You a Child of Abraham?

Those who believe in Christ are children of Abraham, whether they are Jew or Gentile, black or white, rich or poor, master or slave, male or female. What about you? Do you have faith in Jesus Christ? Do you walk in the footsteps of the faith of Abraham before he was circumcised? Do not boast that you are a citizen of a Christian country; or that you were born into a Christian family; or that you were baptized and are a member of a Bible-believing church; or that you take holy communion weekly, give to the church, serve in the church; or that you are a missionary, or even a pastor, bishop, or pope. All these things mean nothing.

Neither circumcision nor baptism can save anyone. Baptismal regeneration is a falsehood; baptism cannot produce spiritual life. Only the Holy Spirit raises people from the dead and gives them life in Jesus Christ. Only Jesus Christ can save us from our sins. What must we do to be saved? Only believe. When Christ died on the cross, the veil of the temple was torn from top to bottom. There is now nothing to prevent us from coming to God through Jesus. Not only did Christ's death destroy the barrier between man and God, but it also destroyed the dividing wall of hostility between Jew and Gentile, man and man. We are all one in the Spirit, one in the Lord, and one in the faith. We are the one body of Christ.

There are no superior Christians, whether Jew or Gentile. Paul says, "This mystery is that through the gospel the Gentiles are heirs together with Israel, members together of one body, and sharers together in the promise in Christ Jesus" (Eph. 3:6). Then he states, "For this reason I kneel before the Father, from whom his whole family in heaven and on earth derives its name" (Eph. 3:14–15). Jew and Gentile are brothers and sisters in the one family of God.

We are all sons of God, and so we are all sons of Abraham. We are all spiritual Israel of God. We are blessed with the fullness of the blessing of the gospel of Jesus Christ. What, then, is circumcision? What is baptism? What is the Lord's Supper? They are all signs that point to the greater reality of Christ and our identification with him. They seal to us the blessings we received when we trusted in Christ. They declare to us that God is our Father, Abraham is our father, and we are the one people of God. They comfort us and confirm to us our acceptance by God, our fullness of salvation in Christ. They authenticate and assure us that we have passed from death to life, from hell to heaven, from darkness to light, from fear to eternal confidence, from hopelessness to the hope of the glory of God.

I recently celebrated Holy Communion with a sister in Christ who is dying of cancer. This sacrament is a sign and seal to her that she is a child of God and has eternal life. It is a sign pointing to heaven, a seal that assures her she has a share in Jesus and is on her way to seeing him face to face. It was a brief service, for she could not sit up long. But before she lay down, she said six words: "Life is short; live for Christ."

May God have mercy on those who are outside of Christ, and may they believe in him and be saved. There is no other Savior. No one else died and rose again for our salvation. And may God help us who are already in Christ to realize the brevity of life and that we must live each day for the glory of God.

17

Heirs of the World

[13]It was not through law that Abraham and his offspring received the promise that he would be heir of the world, but through the righteousness that comes by faith. [14]For if those who live by law are heirs, faith has no value and the promise is worthless, [15]because law brings wrath. And where there is no law there is no transgression.

[16]Therefore, the promise comes by faith, so that it may be by grace and may be guaranteed to all Abraham's offspring—not only to those who are of the law but also to those who are of the faith of Abraham. He is the father of us all. [17]As it is written: "I have made you a father of many nations." He is our father in the sight of God, in whom he believed—the God who gives life to the dead and calls things that are not as though they were.

Romans 4:13–17

In Romans 4:13–17, God promises that we are heirs of the world. Paul is saying in this passage, "Rejoice, you saints of God. You are heirs of God and joint-heirs with Christ." Every believer in Christ owns all the riches that Jesus, the seed of Abraham, possesses. We are blessed with all spiritual and material blessings in Christ forever.

Context

Paul previously established the truth that we are justified not by works but by faith in Jesus Christ, refuting the arguments of the unbelieving Jews. Then he set forth another argument of the Jews: "Was not Abraham justified by circumcision?" Paul disproved this by the historical argument that Abraham was justified fourteen years before he was circumcised and, therefore, his circumcision had nothing to do with his justification. The application to us is that we are not saved by any sacraments such as baptism. The saved are baptized, but the baptized are not saved because they are baptized.

Now Paul anticipates another argument of the unbelieving Jews: "What about the Mosaic law that tells us how to live and makes demands upon our conduct?" Unbelief always comes up with yet another argument why we should not believe in Jesus Christ. Unbelief is like a child who does not want to obey the father because he wants to play. The child comes up with many arguments designed to delay, deny, or entirely alter what the father has said.

Here Paul answers the anticipated argument about the Mosaic law. We want to look at four points: the law; the promise; grace and faith; and the character of the God of promise.

The Law

Contrary to what the rabbis said, God's promise did not come to Abraham and his seed through the law. Some rabbis maintained that Abraham was justified by keeping the law, not by grace through faith. They wrote that, long before the law was given, Abraham had a thorough knowledge of the law and obeyed it in all its details. This pure fabrication misses the bull's-eye regarding the Messiah. Paul refutes this with a historical argument that Abraham was not justified by keeping the Mosaic law, because the Mosaic law came 430 years after the promise was given to Abraham (Gal. 3:17). The idea that salvation could be obtained by keeping the law was an utter misunderstanding by the Jewish people. There is only one God, one people, and one plan of salvation, which is by faith in God's promise.

What, then, is the purpose and nature of the law? Through the law we come to know sin (Rom. 3:20). In fact, the law tends to increase our sin (Rom. 5:20). The law produces the wrath of God (Rom. 4:15) and indirectly produces death in us (Rom. 7:13).

The law is powerless to save us (Rom. 8:3). In fact, it was given not to save us but to show us our utter impotence so that we may be led to Jesus Christ, who alone is able to save us (Gal. 3:24).

So if anyone relies on law-keeping to become righteous, he is negating and nullifying the gospel (Gal. 2:21). All who rely on the law to save them are under a curse (Gal. 3:10).

Yet all religions except orthodox Christianity teach self-salvation. Man is ever-trying to save himself so he can boast. But justification by grace through faith excludes all boasting. Paul argues, then, that the promise to Abraham and all his seed was not given through the law.

The Promise

What is the promise given to Abraham, to his seed Jesus Christ, and to all believers? In Romans 4:13 the promise is defined: that Abraham and all his seed may become heirs of the whole creation (see also Rom. 8:17; Gal. 3:29; 4:7). As heirs of God and joint-heirs with Christ, the saints of God are truly rich. We have no need to run after the things of this world (Matt. 6:32). Christians who do so are fools because they do not realize how rich they already are in Christ.

Elsewhere Paul writes, "Praise be to the God and Father of our Lord Jesus Christ, who has blessed us in the heavenly realms with every spiritual blessing in Christ. For he chose us in him before the creation of the world to be holy and blameless in his sight. In love he predestined us to be adopted as his sons through Jesus Christ" (Eph. 1:3–5). We are sons, joint-heirs with Christ, and heirs of all creation, who enjoy all Spirit-given blessings in Christ.

The Hebrews writer says God appointed Christ the heir of all things (Heb. 1:2). In Jesus we share that heritage. God promised Abraham: "I will surely bless you and make your descendants as numerous as the stars in the sky and as the sand on the seashore. Your descendants will take possession of the cities of their enemies, and through your offspring all nations on earth will be blessed, because you have obeyed me" (Gen. 22:17–18). Offspring here refers especially to the person of Christ.

Matthew 4 tells how Jesus refused to worship the devil, who promised to give him all the kingdoms of the world and their glory. He defeated the devil by following the way of obedience, even to death on the cross, and God gave him the world and exalted him to the highest place. Jesus is Lord, whether we acknowledge it or not. Whether we have faith in him or not makes no difference—he is Lord, because God made him Lord. Every knee shall bow down to him, every tongue shall confess him. He is the one of whom the psalmist wrote:

> I will proclaim the decree of the LORD: He said to me, "You are my Son; today I have become your Father. Ask of me, and I will make the nations your inheritance, the ends of the earth your possession. You will rule them with an iron scepter; you will dash them to pieces like pottery." Therefore, you kings, be wise; be warned, you rulers of the earth. Serve the LORD with fear and rejoice with trembling. Kiss the Son, lest he be angry and you be destroyed in your way, for his wrath can flare up in a moment. Blessed are all who take refuge in him. (Ps. 2:7–12)

Jesus said, "Blessed are the meek, for they will inherit the earth" (Matt. 5:5). He was speaking of Psalm 37, where this idea of our inheriting the world appears several times. John tells us, "The kingdom of the world has become the kingdom of our Lord and of his Christ, and he will reign for ever and ever" (Rev. 11:15). Paul also speaks of this: "So then, no more boasting about men! All things are yours, whether Paul or Apollos or Cephas or the world or life or death or the present or the future—all are yours, and you are of Christ, and Christ is of God" (1 Cor. 3:21–23). Elsewhere he says, "Do you not know that the saints will judge the world? And if you are to judge the world, are you not competent to judge trivial cases? Do you not know that we will judge angels?" (1 Cor. 6:2–3).

God promised worldwide dominion to Abraham. It belongs to his seed, Jesus Christ, and to us who are in Christ. We are destined to rule the world and possess the cosmos. The risen Lord says, "To him who overcomes and does my will to the end, I will give authority over the nations—'He will rule them with an iron scepter; he will dash them to pieces like pottery'—just as I have received authority from my Father. I will also give him the morning star" (Rev. 2:26–28). Jesus is Lord of all and is seated on the right hand of the Father as King of kings and Lord of lords. As King, he will deal ever so severely with all who do not come to him by the way of faith.

Yet his rule is invisible to the world at this time, so atheists mock him and his saints. But soon he will return to earth in all his glory and splendor to rule visibly on this earth with his saints. At his coming, all believers who died in Christ shall rise, and all believers shall be transformed. We all shall receive immortal glorious bodies and reign with Christ here on earth. This is the millennial reign of which the Bible speaks (e.g., Ps. 72:8-14; Isa. 11:6-9; 65:20; Zech. 14:4-21; 1 Cor. 15:23-28; Rev. 20:1-6).

Daniel spoke of this rule of Christ: "Then the sovereignty, power and greatness of the kingdoms under the whole heaven will be handed over to the saints, the people of the Most High. His kingdom will be an everlasting kingdom, and all rulers will worship and obey him" (Dan. 7:27). Matthew also declares it: "Then the King will say to those on his right, 'Come, you who are blessed by my Father; take your inheritance, the kingdom prepared for you since the creation of the world'" (Matt. 25:34).

Christ will rule over all the earth and we will reign with him. Satan will be fully bound during this time. All nations will be subject to David's greater Son. Every tongue will be forced to confess him as Lord. This millennial reign will end in a final manifestation of unbelief and a final demonstration of Christ's victorious power. Then the final judgment will take place and the eternal state shall be ushered in—a new heaven and a new earth, wherein God dwells with his people in righteousness.

The promise to Abraham was that he and his seed would inherit the world. Christ is his seed. He is the heir of the world and in him we all, even now, are heirs of the world. Ours is not a small salvation; it is full and complete.

God's Way of Salvation by Grace through Faith

Our receiving this promise of inheritance is not based on law but on faith alone. *"It was not through law that Abraham and his offspring received the promise that he would be heir of the world, but through the righteousness that comes by faith"* (v. 13). Law means our works, our self-righteousness, and our merit. Then he says, *"For if those who live by law are heirs, faith has no value and the promise is worthless"* (v. 14). The principle of law negates grace, faith, and any praise to God. Salvation by law is ever-opposed to salvation by grace through faith alone. The law divides, but faith unites all people, both Jew and Gentile. The law empties faith and nullifies God's promise of salvation. The law says, "You shall"; the promise says, "I will."

If one desires to be saved by law-keeping, God's promise can never be fulfilled, because it will be dependent on us. By keeping the law no one can be saved or become an heir of the whole creation. In fact, Paul then explains that the law produces wrath (v. 15).

There are only two destinies for the people of the world—either we become heirs of the world in Christ or we are subject to God's wrath, which means we will experience hell. *"[The] law brings wrath."* Therefore, it is sheer arrogance for a person to depend on law-keeping for his salvation. God's wrath is revealed against all who refuse to acknowledge that they are sinners by nature and practice. Such people refuse to acknowledge they are impotent to keep the law and are dead in their sin. Paul already proved that "there is no one righteous, not even one; there is no one who understands, no one who seeks God. All have turned away, they have together become worthless; there is no one who does good, not even one" (Rom. 3:10–12). The law guarantees God's wrath. Sin is transgression of the law, and God must punish all sinners. If through faith you depend on God's grace in Jesus Christ, you will go to heaven; but if you depend on the law, you must go to hell.

If you have not trusted in Christ, I urge you to forsake all self-salvation by keeping the law and run to Christ the Savior. Seek the way of faith and trust in God. He who depends on law is cursed. The law imposes penalties on those who fail to keep it. Salvation is not merit-based but mercy-based. It is based on grace to be received by faith alone.

Jesus revealed the principle of law and grace in the story of the Pharisee and the publican (Luke 18:9–14). The Pharisee depended on his own keeping of the law; therefore, he thought he did not need the mercy and grace that comes from Jesus Christ. This was also the case of Paul. Yet Paul confessed that all his righteousness was loss, dung, and filthy rags. It could not save him (Phil. 3:4–9). Paul went the way of grace through faith and was saved. Likewise, the publican cried out, "Have mercy on me, a sinner," and went home justified.

There is no salvation through keeping the law. As long as we depend on our own merit and good works, including circumcision or baptism, there is one thing we can count on: the wrath of God will abide on us. Trusting in keeping the law takes people to hell. Legalists are hell-bound frauds. Salvation is of faith. Where law fails, faith succeeds.

Away with all boasting of law, merit, and works! Let us glory in grace and faith, a faith that is also God's gift to us. We merited death and hell, but grace gives us life and heaven, which we receive by faith. Grace also gives us a kingdom, a crown, and a throne which we receive by faith. Grace overrides all our demerits, inadequacies, and failures.

Why does Paul insist on grace and faith? Why does he so vigorously oppose the law principle? There are a number of answers.

1. The way of faith alone establishes grace. What grace gives freely, faith receives humbly. The free gift of the fullness of salvation cannot come to the arrogant and self-righteous but only to the beggar who lifts up his hand of faith to receive it in humility. An unbeliever, therefore, cannot become an heir of the world.
2. The way of faith alone guarantees all glory to God. Salvation by works, sacraments, or law promotes human boasting. Only salvation by grace through faith promotes worship of God. Grace and faith exclude all human boasting.
3. The way of faith and grace alone ensures the salvation of all God's elect, whether Jews or Gentiles, circumcised or uncircumcised. "The point is, we can come into this salvation irrespective of our antecedents," declares Dr. Martyn Lloyd-Jones.[1] Faith and grace remove all human distinctions. All are sinners and all are welcome to come to Jesus.
4. The way of faith and grace guarantees full salvation to all God's elect. God chose this way of salvation because to the degree any human merit is constitutive of our salvation, we cannot have any certainty of salvation. Faith plus our works can only guarantee total anxiety and uncertainty, especially at the point of death. Those who trust in Christ alone will not rely on their own merit but will cry out, "Lord, have mercy upon me, a sinner."[2]

Salvation is all of God, all of grace, and therefore all of faith. We rely on nothing in ourselves while depending on God for everything. Salvation from beginning to end depends on him.

---

1   Lloyd-Jones, *Romans*, vol. 3, *Atonement and Justification*, 200.
2   These points are from Boice, *Romans*, vol. 1, *Justification by Faith*, 474–75.

Paul speaks of this: "[I am] confident of this, that he who began a good work in you will carry it on to completion until the day of Christ Jesus" (Phil. 1:6). He saved us, he is saving us, and he will save us to the very end.

We find this glorious guarantee throughout the Bible. Paul writes, "And we know that in all things God works for the good of those who love him, who have been called according to his purpose. For those God foreknew he also predestined to be conformed to the likeness of his Son, that he might be the firstborn among many brothers. And those he predestined, he also called; those he called, he also justified; those he justified, he also glorified" (Rom. 8:28–30). The same group of people are foreknown, predestinated, called, justified, and glorified by God himself.

Jesus said, "I give them eternal life, and they shall never perish; no one can snatch them out of my hand. My Father, who has given them to me, is greater than all; no one can snatch them out of my Father's hand. I and the Father are one" (John 10:28–30). Neither the devil nor demons nor even ourselves can extricate us from the hand of Christ; it will never happen. So Paul exclaims, "No, in all these things we are more than conquerors through him who loved us. For I am convinced that neither death nor life, neither angels nor demons, neither the present nor the future, nor any powers, neither height nor depth, nor anything else in all creation, will be able to separate us from the love of God that is in Christ Jesus our Lord" (Rom. 8:37–39). Notice, he puts death first. Unbelievers live in fear of death. Every believer can be certain of his or her eternal salvation. This is the doctrine of eternal security.

> My hope is built on nothing less
> than Jesus' blood and righteousness.

The Character of the God of Promise

We should believe the promise because of the character of God. Our hope of being the heirs of the world and possessing and ruling the whole cosmos with Christ the King is based on God's character.

What do we know about the character of God? First, we know that he is reliable. God alone can be trusted wholly, for he is truth and cannot lie. "God is not a man, that he should lie, nor a son of man, that he should change his mind. Does he speak and then not act? Does he promise and not fulfill?" (Num. 23:19). God fulfills every promise he makes. God promised a Messiah, and in the fullness of time the Messiah came and accomplished our salvation by defeating the devil and his works. He was raised from the dead as he prophesied and now rules on the right hand of the Father. Soon he shall come again and we shall reign with him on this earth.

Second, we know that God is able. Death does not confuse him. He is the resurrection and the life who gives life to the dead. He is the conqueror of death; he holds the keys of death and hell. He goes out conquering and to conquer. Our God gave life to the dying Abraham and Sarah so that they could have a son. He raised Abraham's Son, Jesus Christ, from the dead, and he has also raised us spiritually. We were dead in trespasses and sins, but God raised us up spiritually, and he shall physically raise up all those who die in Christ. Death has been swallowed up in victory through our Lord Jesus Christ!

Not only is God powerful enough to raise the dead, but he is also the Creator. He creates out of nothing things that did not exist. God said, "Let there be light," and there was light. Abraham did not exist and God called him into existence. Isaac did not exist and God called him into existence. We all are called into existence by God. Yet by nature we were dead in sins and trespasses, so he also effectually called us by the gospel, and we became believers in Christ. He said, "I will build my church, and the gates of hell shall not prevail against it" (Matt. 16:18, KJV). We are invincible and indestructible. God calls the church into existence that we may live with him forever.

Abraham saw God and heard his promise. He trusted in him, knowing that this reliable and powerful God could raise the dead and call into existence things that are not as though they are. He trusted in the God of glory and was justified by faith. If we have trusted in the God of Abraham, Isaac, and Jacob, the God and Father of our Lord Jesus Christ, we also will surely inherit the promise, the fullness of salvation. In Christ we are heirs of the whole cosmos. We are heirs of God, joint-heirs with Christ. All God has is ours, and all Christ has is ours.

There are only two destinies. We will either inherit the cosmos and rule with Christ or go to hell and suffer the wrath of God. Do not depend on the law to save you. Run to Christ, trust in him, and be saved, that you may be enriched by every spiritual blessing in heavenly places in him.

18

The Nature of Saving Faith

[18]Against all hope, Abraham in hope believed and so became the father of many nations, just as it had been said to him, "So shall your offspring be." [19]Without weakening in his faith, he faced the fact that his body was as good as dead—since he was about a hundred years old—and that Sarah's womb was also dead. [20]Yet he did not waver through unbelief regarding the promise of God, but was strengthened in his faith and gave glory to God, [21]being fully persuaded that God had power to do what he had promised. [22]This is why "it was credited to him as righteousness."

Romans 4:18–22

Romans 4:18–22 speaks about the faith of Abraham. Our faith in God is identical to that faith by which Abraham believed God and was justified. Many atheists think that belief in the holy Scriptures is dangerously irrational. But studies show that atheists are more superstitious and irrational than Bible-believing Christians, and that true Christian belief is antithetical to pseudo-science, occultism, superstition, paranormal phenomena, and irrationalism. They confirm what G. K. Chesterton said about all atheists, secularists, humanists, and rationalists being susceptible to superstition: "It's the first effect of not believing in God that you lose your common sense, and can't see things as they are."[1]

It is most rational to believe in the infinite, personal God of the Scriptures, who created the universe out of nothing. It is

---

1   Quoted by Molly Ziegler Hemingway, "Look Who's Irrational Now," *Wall Street Journal*, September 19, 2008, http://online.wsj.com/ article/ SB122178219865054585.html.

utter irrationalism to believe that the universe evolved by itself out of nothing. Abraham believed the God of glory, and it was credited to him as righteousness. Because Abraham was justified by faith alone and is the father of all believers, we want to look at the nature of his saving faith.

As Dr. Martyn Lloyd-Jones says, saving faith is not based on mathematical probability, nor is it natural faith.[2] It is Spirit-created, supernatural faith that believes in the word of God. Saving faith believes in what is humanly impossible, but possible to God. We want to consider several aspects of saving faith that we learn from this passage.

Saving Faith Goes against Naturalism

"Against all hope, Abraham in hope believed" (v. 18). Saving faith goes against naturalism and human hope. Saving faith drives out unbelief as light drives out darkness. It acts in defiance of all human expectations, calculations, and abilities. When the devil or our disease-filled body or any other obstacle says, "No," saving faith cries out, "Yes!" by the power of God. Saving faith puts its trust in God and his promises against everything else.

Saving faith goes beyond fallen human reason and fallen common sense, because human reason does not take into account the omnipotent God. The people of this world are described by Paul as being without God and without hope (Eph. 2:12). Atheists, therefore, are hopeless.

But saving faith puts hope in God, who is unseen, rather than in what is seen. In 2 Kings 6 we read about Elisha's servant, who was afraid of all the horses and chariots of the Arameans surrounding him. That was all he could see. But Elisha told his servant, "Don't be afraid. Those who are with us are more than those who are with them" (2 Kings 6:16). Then he prayed for him, and the Lord opened the eyes of the servant so that he could see the horses and chariots of fire God had put around them for protection.

Just as God was around Elisha and his servant, so he is around his church and his people. Saving faith, therefore, is not a leap

---

2   Lloyd-Jones, *Romans*, vol. 3, *Atonement and Justification*, 232.

in the dark. It is a leap from the evidence of our senses into the security of God's ability to perform his promises.

Abraham believed that God could produce nations through him, though it was humanly impossible for him to father a child at his advanced age and for Sarah to conceive and bear one. Their situation was as impossible as that of Lazarus, who died and had been buried for four days when Jesus came. It was humanly impossible to raise him back to life. But Jesus asked Martha, "Did I not tell you that if you believed, you would see the glory of God?" (John 11:40). Jesus is the resurrection and the life, and he did raise Lazarus from the dead. So also we hope against all natural human hope, knowing that God is able to do what he has promised. He who is in us is greater than he who is in the world.

The object of our faith, therefore, is not ourselves and our weaknesses, but God and his promises. Saving faith rests completely in God's promises; hope expects the fulfillment of those promises. So Paul writes that Abraham against hope believed on the basis of his hope in God to fulfill his promises. Saving faith looks away from ourselves and our circumstances and fixes its eyes on God alone.

Certainly, we can imagine that doubts assailed Abraham like fiery darts at times. Yet he always sprang back to faith and hope. Unbelief was not his permanent condition; Abraham was characterized by faith. So he did not waver through unbelief but steadily moved forward in faith and hope to see God fulfill his promises.

Saving Faith Believes God's Promises

"Abraham in hope believed" (v. 18). Saving faith believes God's promise. The noun "promise" appears several times in this chapter (vv. 13, 14, 16, 20) and the verb appears once (v. 21). The promise was that Abraham was going to be the father of many nations (Gen. 15, 17). God promised to give Abraham descendants as numerous as the stars in the sky and the sand on the seashore. Many nations who would believe in God were to come from him. Additionally, from Abraham would come the Messiah, who would save Abraham and all God's people from their sins. Jesus said, "Abraham rejoiced at the thought of seeing my day; he saw it and was glad" (John 8:56). Abraham and all God's people were to become the heirs of the world in and through the Savior-Messiah. Abraham saw God, heard his promises, and put his faith in them long before he had a son.

We do not now see the God of glory as Abraham did, but we believe in him through his written word. The Bible is the very word of God. It is inerrant, infallible, and full of power. Paul tells us, "For everything that was written in the past was written to teach us, so that through endurance and the encouragement of the Scriptures we might have hope" (Rom. 15:4). Elsewhere he says, "These things happened to them as examples and were written down as warnings for us, on whom the fulfillment of the ages has come" (1 Cor. 10:11).

What God promises, he fulfills. In Joshua we read, "Not one of all the LORD's good promises to the house of Israel failed; every one was fulfilled" (Josh. 21:45). Joshua himself testified, "Now I am about to go the way of all the earth. You know with all your heart and soul that not one of all the good promises the LORD your God gave you has failed. Every promise has been fulfilled; not one has failed" (Josh. 23:14). God promises and fulfills because he is mighty and reliable. So Paul writes, "For no matter how many promises God has made, they are 'Yes' in Christ. And so through him the 'Amen' is spoken by us to the glory of God" (2 Cor. 1:20).

Since we have seen the fulfillment of these promises, we have greater historical reason to believe God's promises than Abraham had. We know that Abraham did become the father of many nations. We also know that in time the Messiah came as Abraham's offspring, died and rose again, and is the Savior of the world. We know that Abraham's true descendants now exist as a vast multitude of people who believe in the God of Abraham, Isaac, and Jacob.

The past fulfillment of these promises guarantees our future, complete salvation. Paul makes this argument from the lesser to the greater, citing God's past faithfulness: "Since we have now been justified by his blood, how much more shall we be saved from God's wrath through him! For if, when we were God's enemies, we were reconciled to him through the death of his Son, how much more, having been reconciled, shall we be saved through his life! . . . He who did not spare his own Son, but gave him up for us all—how will he not also, along with him, graciously give us all things?" (Rom. 5:9–10; 8:32).

Let us, then, believe the word of God with its humanly impossible promises, which only God can make and only God can fulfill. God tells us in his word, "Believe in the Lord Jesus, and you will be saved—you and your household" (Acts 16:31). That is what it says, and that is what we must do. Let us be like Naaman, the leprous Gentile general who came to Elisha the prophet for help. Elisha directed him to go to the Jordan River, dip himself seven times, and he would be healed. Naaman was angry at his counsel and almost went home in unbelief. But God gave him repentance, and when he went to the Jordan and dipped himself seven times, Naaman emerged completely healed (2 Kings 5). This is the power of God's promise—we must believe and be saved.

The Bible is full of God's good and precious promises. As we believe them and act upon them daily, we will be blessed.

Saving Faith Believes in God

Paul says Abraham was *"fully persuaded that God had power to do what he had promised"* (v. 21). In other words, God is mighty to fulfill his promises. Saving faith believes in the God who raises the dead and calls into existence things that are not.

This God in whom Abraham believed was not an idol from his former pagan life, but the God of glory who appeared to him. He is the eternal, infinite, personal, living, and true God. He is the righteous, omnipotent, omniscient, independent, unchanging God of truth, who cannot lie or die. He is majestic and transcendent, yet ever-present. Of him Jeremiah exclaims, "Ah, Sovereign LORD, you have made the heavens and the earth by your great power and outstretched arm. Nothing is too hard for you" (Jer. 32:17). The Lord himself asked Abraham, "Is anything too hard for the LORD?" (Gen. 18:14). In other words, he was saying, "Don't you believe me, Abraham? Nothing is too difficult for me. I am the God who raises the dead." The bodies of Abraham and Sarah were sexually dead. Sarah had never been able to conceive and bear children, and now she was ninety years old, long past childbearing age. Abraham had fathered Ishmael when he was eighty-six, but at ninety-nine he was also incapable of begetting the son of promise.

But the deadness of Abraham and Sarah was not a problem for God. In fact, God waited until they both were in this state to demonstrate his great power. God alone can raise the dead. In God's time, this couple experienced resurrection in their bodies, and Isaac the son of promise was conceived and born to them. God raises the dead and calls into being things that do not exist. God called Isaac into existence. By his power, God has called into existence a vast multitude of believers who did not exist before. We believe in the true and living God who creates out of nothing, conquers death by life, and has power to fulfill his great and humanly impossible promises.

Behind all promises lies the character of the one who makes them. We cannot trust in man, for man can lie, die, change his mind, or lose his ability to help. As Jeremiah says, "Cursed is the one who trusts in man, who depends on flesh for his strength" (Jer. 17:5). But look at the character of God. Our God can be trusted, because he is reliable and able.

Jesus says, "With God all things are possible" (Matt. 19:26). Elsewhere he says, "What is impossible with men is possible with God" (Luke 18:27). The Lord told Abraham, "Is anything too hard for the LORD? I will return to you at the appointed time next year and Sarah will have a son" (Gen. 18:14). God's promise was fulfilled.

God is able to do what he promises. Paul writes, "God is able to make all grace abound to you, so that in all things at all times, having all that you need, you will abound in every good work" (2 Cor. 9:8). The Hebrews writer recounts, "By faith Abraham, even though he was past age—and Sarah herself was barren—was enabled to become a father because he considered him faithful who had made the promise" (Heb. 11:11). And in response to a later test of Abraham's faith we read, "Abraham reasoned that God could raise the dead, and figuratively speaking, he did receive Isaac back from death" (Heb. 11:19).

Therefore, do not focus on yourself and your disease or your poverty or your misery or your children's rebellion. Do not look at your circumstances; look to God alone. Fix your eyes on Jesus, the author and finisher of our faith, as Peter did during a storm on the Sea of Galilee. Peter saw Jesus walking on the waves toward the boat and said, "Lord, if it's you, tell me to come to you on the water." Jesus beckoned him to come, and Peter started walking on the water toward Jesus (Matt. 14:22–31). Let us look away from our own problems and look to Jesus, so that we may walk on the waves of our problems through Jesus Christ.

Let us also meditate on God's past faithfulness to us. God appeared to Abraham in Mesopotamia and brought him to Canaan. He defended him from every enemy, protected him in Egypt, and blessed him with great wealth. He appeared to encourage him several times. This same God has helped us in the past, and he will continue to help us in the present and the future. God is called Faithful and True (Rev. 19:11).

Let us trust not in ourselves or in men or in princes or in the god of this world or in silver and gold, but in God alone. A. W. Pink writes, "Everything about God is great, vast, incomparable. He never forgets, never fails, never falters, never forfeits his word. To every declaration of promise or prophecy the Lord has exactly adhered, every engagement or covenant or threatening he will make good, for 'God is not a man, that he should lie; neither the son of man, that he should repent: hath he said and shall he not do it? or hath he spoken, and shall he not make it good?' (Num. 23:19)."[3] It is God's nature to be faithful. In Deuteronomy we read, "Know therefore that the LORD your God is God; he is the faithful God, keeping his covenant of love to a thousand generations of those who love him and keep his commands" (Deut. 7:9). Paul declares, "If we are faithless, he will remain faithful, for he cannot disown himself" (2 Tim. 2:13).

If a person is outside of Christ, it is because of unbelief. The greatest insult we can give to God is to not believe in him and his promises. When people do not believe God, they have to believe in other things. That is why unbelievers trust in pseudo-science, occultism, cults, and paranormal phenomena. The antidote to all fear, misery, anxiety, confusion, and complaining is to trust in the true and living God of Abraham.

Saving Faith Grows

"Without weakening in his faith, [Abraham] faced the fact that his body was as good as dead—since he was about a hundred years

---

3   Quoted by Boice in *Romans*, vol. 1, *Justification by Faith*, 489.

old—and that Sarah's womb was also dead. Yet he did not waver through unbelief regarding the promise of God, but was strengthened in his faith and gave glory to God" (vv. 19–20). Unbelievers are characterized by unbelief. But God's people have supernatural faith, which may start out small but grows into great faith, like an infant grows into an adult. There are degrees of faith: little faith, growing faith, and great faith. Our faith grows in strength as we grow in the knowledge of God and obedience to his will.

Doubts about God and his promises can weaken saving faith. Doubts make us anxious, fearful, complaining, and confused. But in view of the great promise of God, Abraham did not stagger due to unbelief, but was strengthened by God because of his saving faith. God gives everyone who believes in him strength to do mighty things. Unbelief weakens, but faith strengthens.

We can imagine how Abraham grew strong. While he was a worshiper of the mute idols of Mesopotamia, the God of glory appeared to him and spoke to him. Abraham began to meditate on God's majesty and eternity, contemplating God's holiness, righteousness, omnipotence, omniscience, omnipresence, goodness, wisdom, love, and immutability. His faith in God grew as he came to know God and his attributes in increasing measure.

Unlike Abraham, we meet God today in his word. Therefore, the more we read and meditate on the Scriptures, the stronger we will grow in God. The more we make use of the means of grace, the stronger we will grow in faith. The more we pray and hear the word preached, the more we worship and fellowship, the more we partake of the Lord's Supper, the more we give and serve, the more we witness and obey—the more we will grow, until we have gone from little faith to great faith.

We also must put our faith to work. Once when he was at the Sea of Galilee, Jesus told his disciples, "Let us go over to the other side" (Mark 4:35). While they were still in the boat, a storm arose and Jesus asked his fearful disciples, "Why are you so afraid? Do you still have no faith?" (v. 40). These disciples needed to put their faith into practice. Jesus had told them to go to the other side. That is what they needed to do, despite any storms or other obstacles.

If you have faith, apply it in your daily life. Do not operate on the basis of fear or defeat. Jesus tells us to go forward through the storm, river, or mountain. As we apply faith in our lives, we will grow strong, because obedience builds faith. When we believe God and his word, we shall be victorious. Nothing in all creation can separate us from the love of God. If God is for us, who can be against us?

Do not be like unbelievers, who regard our holy God as a liar. John writes, "Anyone who believes in the Son of God has this testimony in his heart. Anyone who does not believe God has made him out to be a liar, because he has not believed the testimony God has given about his Son" (1 John 5:10). Every unbeliever treats God with utter contempt. But Jesus exhorts us, "Now that you know these things, you will be blessed if you do them" (John 13:17).

Saving Faith Faces Facts

"[Abraham] faced the fact that his body was as good as dead—since he was about a hundred years old—and that Sarah's womb was also dead" (v. 19). Faith faces the challenges and adversities of reality. Abraham faced the facts of the deadness of his body and Sarah's womb, but he did not weaken in his faith. Instead, he looked to God and his mighty promises. Abraham and Sarah's sexual deadness ruled out any confidence in themselves. They had to trust fully in God their Creator to raise them up and enable them to become parents of the son of promise.

Faith is not self-delusion, positive thinking, or repetition of a mantra. Faith proclaims, "I can do all things through Jesus Christ who strengthens me" (Phil. 4:13, author's paraphrase). Faith declares, "By the grace of God I am what I am" (1 Cor. 15:10). Faith asserts, "I can do nothing, but God can do all things through me" (John 15:5 and others). Satan blinds the eyes of unbelievers; but God opens our eyes to see the reality of our deadness and incompetence, and the reality of God who raises the dead and fulfills all his purposes concerning us.

Abraham and Sarah had no previous historical evidence of a very old, sexually dead couple becoming parents. But they believed the clear word of God without seeking additional proof. They believed God could do the humanly impossible, and he did.

Saving Faith Gives Glory to God

"[Abraham] gave glory to God" (v. 20). Faith gives glory to God even before the fulfillment of promise, because if God makes a promise, it is as good as done. So we can thank God before the fulfillment comes as well as after the promise is fulfilled. As Abraham grew in faith, God strengthened him, and he gave glory to God.

It is the habit of unbelievers not to thank God. Paul writes, "For although they knew God, they neither glorified him as God nor gave thanks to him" (Rom. 1:21). In fact, it is their nature to exchange the glory of God for idols (Rom. 1:23). But believers are always glorifying God. Salvation by grace through faith alone excludes all human boasting. Therefore, believers give all glory to God. In fact, that is the purpose for which we are created and redeemed (see Isa. 44:23; 49:3; 60:21; 61:3; Jer. 13:11; 1 Pet. 2:9). God delivered us from darkness, death, corruption, and hell itself that we may declare the praises of him who brought us out of darkness into his marvelous light. We glorify God when we believe him, worship him, and do his will.

We should emulate the three Hebrew children who were about to be thrown into a fiery furnace because they worshiped the true and living God. They were determined to glorify God, whether by life or death: "Shadrach, Meshach and Abednego replied to the king, 'O Nebuchadnezzar, we do not need to defend ourselves before you in this matter. If we are thrown into the blazing furnace, the God we serve is able to save us from it, and he will rescue us from your hand, O king. But even if he does not, we want you to know, O king, that we will not serve your gods or worship the image of gold you have set up'" (Dan. 3:16–18).

What does it mean to give glory to God? It means to reckon God to be what he is and rely upon his power and faithfulness. Thomas Watson says, "Faith is a grace that takes a man off himself, and gives all the honour to Christ and free grace."[4]

---

4   Thomas Watson, A Body of Divinity (Edinburgh: Banner of Truth Trust, 2000), 218.

Saving Faith Enjoys Full Assurance

"*[Abraham was] fully persuaded that God had power to do what he had promised*" (v. 21). God filled Abraham with full assurance that God would fulfill his promise. There was no more doubt, for Abraham knew God fulfills all his promises. The Hebrews writer says, "Now faith is being sure of what we hope for and certain of what we do not see" (Heb. 11:1). Faith substantiates what we hope for, giving full assurance of things we do not yet see: "All these people were still living by faith when they died. They did not receive the things promised; they only saw them and welcomed them from a distance" (Heb. 11:13).

Jesus told Thomas, "Because you have seen me, you have believed; blessed are those who have not seen and yet have believed" (John 20:29). On the basis of the historical work of Christ and the written Scriptures, we hear, we believe, and we are given certainty of our salvation. Peter writes, "Though you have not seen him, you love him; and even though you do not see him now, you believe in him and are filled with an inexpressible and glorious joy, for you are receiving the goal of your faith, the salvation of your souls" (1 Pet. 1:8–9). As God's people, we are filled with certitude that we are on our way to heaven because of the promises God has given us in his word.

Suppose a father is in a pool and his little son is standing at the edge. The father tells his son to jump and promises to catch him. The son not only believes the father, but he is also fully assured he will keep his promise. So he jumps, and his able, loving father catches him. We too can be fully assured of our final salvation because Jesus said we are in his and the Father's hands, and nothing can snatch us out of them. Underneath us are the everlasting arms of God.

Saving faith is not mental assent without any feeling. It is not merely saying, "Jesus is Lord," and thinking that is all there is to Christianity. Such mental gymnastics are historically attributed to Sandemanianism. Mere mental assent has no conviction, trust, feeling, or life. Saving faith is full assurance given by God to those who believe in him. Assurance of faith is a blessing every saint can enjoy.

Saving Faith Works

Saving faith obeys God gladly and constantly; faith that does not obey God does not save anyone. Abraham's faith manifested itself in obedient acts.

1. When the God of glory came to Abram in Mesopotamia and said, "Leave your country, your kindred, your father's house, and your gods," by faith Abram left in obedience "even though he did now know where he was going" (Heb. 11:8).
2. By faith Abram settled in Canaan and worshiped the true God of glory by building an altar and sacrificing to God instead of worshiping the gods of Canaan.
3. By faith Abram gave Lot first choice of the land. Lot chose the Jordan Valley and pitched his tent toward the secular city of Sodom, while Abram chose the hill country of Canaan, which God had promised him.
4. By faith Abram waged war against four powerful kings and rescued Lot.
5. By faith Abram refused to receive his due of the spoils from the king of Sodom, for he trusted in God to bless him materially.
6. God appeared to Abram when he was ninety-nine years old and told him that he and every male in his household must be circumcised. By faith Abram obeyed what God commanded and became a man of the covenant.
7. God came to Abram and said, "I am going to change your name from Abram, which means 'exalted father,' to Abraham, meaning 'father of many nations.'" God also changed the name of Sarai to Sarah, indicating that she would be the mother of many nations. Though the son of promise had not yet been born, Abram believed and obeyed God. By faith he told people to start calling him Abraham and to call his wife Sarah. Abraham relied on God to fulfill his promise of offspring.
8. By faith Abraham sacrificed Isaac. This was the most difficult act of obedience of his life. God commanded Abraham to sacrifice the son of promise from whom the Messiah himself was to come. It is likely Abraham reasoned in this way: "Isaac is not married and has no son. Yet the God of glory wants me to kill him and burn him up in worship. How can God ask me to do this? How can God's other promises be fulfilled through Isaac? There is a paradox here, two ideas colliding, both from God. How can this be resolved?" Abraham exercised his mind, reasoning that God cannot lie and always fulfills what he promises. He concluded that the God who raises the dead and creates out of nothing would have to raise Isaac from his own ashes. Abraham believed this God who is the resurrection and the life, and

"figuratively speaking, [Abraham] did receive Isaac back from death" (Heb. 11:19).

Do You Have Saving Faith?

What about you? If you do not believe the true God of the Bible, you are dishonoring him and calling him a liar. You are without God and without hope. But God will come to judge all his enemies. Therefore, I urge you to believe on the Lord and be saved. The Messiah has come, and in him all God's promises are "Yes."

What if you have already trusted in Christ? I counsel you to grow in faith. Get to know God more through his word. Then you will have strength to believe and love God. And as you serve and obey God, your faith will grow until you become fully assured of your salvation and will be able to give glory to God, even at the moment of your death. I pray that all of us will live in faith that we may die in faith and in sure hope of dwelling in God's presence forever.

19

Justified unto Peace with God

¹Therefore, since we have been justified through faith, we have peace with God through our Lord Jesus Christ, ²through whom we have gained access by faith into this grace in which we now stand. And we rejoice in the hope of the glory of God.

Romans 5:1–2

In Romans 1:18–4:25, Paul gave us an exposition of the doctrine of justification by faith. How can a sinner be right with God? How can a sinner under the wrath of God be declared righteous? How can his sins be forgiven forever? Now, in Romans 5–8, Paul teaches us concerning the complete certainty of our final salvation. The justified shall surely be glorified.

"Therefore, having been justified by faith . . ." (v. 1). "Therefore" points to logic. The Christian faith is logical and reasonable. "Therefore" means in the light of what Paul has told us in the previous section. "Therefore" means in the light of a once-for-all action of justification by God. "Therefore" refers to our justification by grace through faith in the blood of Christ. By this divine action, our final salvation will surely come to pass. In other words, as we read in Romans 8:30, the justified are glorified. Martin Luther says that "the Apostle [Paul] speaks as one who is extremely happy and full of joy."[1] That is how we ought to behave also. It is like seeing Canaan from Mount Pisgah. From here we see heaven, and soon we will experience glorification and be with God forever. We can be certain of it because God has declared us righteous.

---

1   Quoted by Moo, *Epistle to the Romans,* 297.

The goal of justification, therefore, is glorification. This truth ought to fill every believer with inexpressible and glorious joy. Have you been justified? Have you trusted in Jesus the Son of God, who was delivered over to death for our transgressions and raised from the dead for our justification? If we have so trusted in Christ, then we must rejoice in all circumstances. Because we have been justified, we shall be glorified to live with God eternally. From the shame of our sin, guilt, and death, God in Christ has brought us to eternal glory. Therefore, rejoice and be exceedingly glad.

Certain blessings flow abundantly to us on the basis of our justification by faith. Three of them are recorded in Romans 5:1–2: peace, presence, and triumphant praise. In this chapter we will look at the blessing of peace with God.

Justification Leads to Peace

St. Augustine correctly said, "Our hearts are restless until they find rest in God." Nothing in this world can give true peace to the ungodly. Before God saved and justified us, we were helpless (Rom. 5:6), ungodly (Rom. 5:6), sinners (Rom. 5:8), and enemies of God (Rom. 5:10). The sinful mind is at enmity against God (Rom. 8:7).

But the Supreme Court of heaven declared us just on the basis of the propitiatory, bloody sacrifice of Christ on the cross. Paul writes, "[We] are justified freely by his grace through the redemption that came by Christ Jesus. God presented him as a sacrifice of atonement, through faith in his blood. He did this to demonstrate his justice, because in his forbearance he had left the sins committed beforehand unpunished—he did it to demonstrate his justice at the present time, so as to be just and the one who justifies those who have faith in Jesus" (Rom. 3:24–26).

Jesus paid the penalty for all our sins by his death. "The soul who sins is the one who will die" (Ezek. 18:20). I sinned, but Christ died. Six times in this chapter Paul makes reference to the death of Jesus, because it is the basis for our justification (Rom. 5:6, 7, 8, 9, 10). Paul says he was the worst of sinners and a blasphemer, but Christ loved him and gave himself for him. I say to all believers, "Jesus died for your sins. You trusted in him and prayed the sinner's prayer. You are justified and saved forever. You now have a heavenly Father whom you can call, 'Abba.'" Because we are justified and clothed in the righteousness of Jesus, because our sins are all forgiven and we are saved by the death of Christ, we have peace with God.

Reconciliation with God

"Therefore, since we have been justified through faith, we have peace with God" (v. 1). Before, we could look forward only to wrath and anger, but now we have peace with God. Paul uses the present tense, meaning we continually have peace with God. God was our enemy and we were his. But Christ's death on the cross changed all that. Paul describes how Christ destroyed man's enmity toward God and man:

> For he himself is our peace, who has made the two one and has destroyed the barrier, the dividing wall of hostility, by abolishing in his flesh the law with its commandments and regulations. His purpose was to create in himself one new man out of the two, thus making peace, and in this one body to reconcile both of them to God through the cross, by which he put to death their hostility. He came and preached peace to you who were far away and peace to those who were near. (Eph. 2:14–17)

Elsewhere he writes, "Once you were alienated from God and were enemies in your minds because of your evil behavior. But now he has reconciled you by Christ's physical body through death to present you holy in his sight, without blemish and free from accusation" (Col. 1:21–22).

We were at war with God, our neighbors, our families, and ourselves. Now the enmity is gone forever. God is no longer our judge, and we are no longer under his wrath. We are free from the accusations of our conscience, the devil, and everyone else.

God Is Our Heavenly Father

"Therefore, since we have been justified through faith, we have peace with God through our Lord Jesus Christ" (v. 1). God has reconciled us to himself through Christ. Because he poured out his wrath on Christ, there is no more wrath against us. God is now our heavenly Father. We can call him "Abba," an Aramaic word that indicates great intimacy between a father and his children. It can be likened to our word "Daddy." This word appears three times in the New Testament, always in reference to God the Father. Jesus himself used it as he prayed in Gethsemane: "*Abba*, Father, everything is possible for you. Take this cup from me. Yet not what I will, but what you will" (Mark 14:36).

The heavenly Father has become our Daddy, and we are his children. Paul also speaks of this great truth: "For you did not receive a spirit that makes you a slave again to fear, but you received the Spirit of sonship. And by him we cry, 'Abba, Father'" (Rom. 8:15). There is a change of relationship. God is our Daddy, and we are his dear children. He has loved us from all eternity, loves us now, and will love us forever.

Because we have peace with God, we have peace with our neighbors, peace in our families, and peace in the depths of our beings. Jesus said, "I have called you friends" (John 15:15). God is our friend and Jesus is our older brother, our only mediator. God loves us and we love God. Having peace with God means we have a friendly relationship with him so that we commune with him. This peace does not just mean a cessation of hostilities. *Shalom* in Hebrew speaks of well-being, of blessings, of prosperity, and of enjoying a restored relationship. We now have fellowship with the Father and the Son in the Holy Spirit. We were prodigals, but the Father has invited us to come into his home and has given us all the privileges of sons.

We have peace with God, says Paul, "*through our Lord Jesus Christ.*" In Romans 5:1–11 Paul speaks five times of this peace coming through Christ (vv. 1, 2, 10, 11). This is an objective peace brought about only by Christ's propitiatory death. That means no one can be justified apart from Christ; no other religion can accomplish this. Jesus alone is the way, the truth, and the life (John 14:6). He is the only Savior of the world, both for Jews and Gentiles. Christ is the only mediator between God and men.

Jesus is the Prince of peace because he alone brought righteousness through his life and death, and from that righteousness comes peace. Jeremiah says the Lord is our righteousness (Jer. 23:6). Isaiah declares, "The fruit of righteousness will be peace; the effect of righteousness will be quietness and confidence forever. My people will live in peaceful dwelling places, in secure homes, in undisturbed places of rest" (Isa. 32:17–18). We experience such peace because the righteousness of Jesus Christ is imputed to us freely.

Paul says Jesus Christ is our wisdom, righteousness, sanctification, and glorification (1 Cor. 1:30). Only by being justified by faith can we have peace with God through our Lord Jesus Christ. Wealth, power, fame, brilliance, education, health, beauty, and mind-altering substances cannot give us peace.

Jesus wants us to experience this peace. He is ever calling to sinners: "Come to me, all you who are weary and burdened, and I will give you rest" (Matt. 11:28). Elsewhere he says, "The thief comes only to steal and kill and destroy; I have come that they may have life, and have it to the full" (John 10:10). The devil promises peace and pleasure, but his intent is to destroy us. But Jesus came to give us eternal life and peace. Christ invited us, the Holy Spirit drew us, and we came to him by faith. We were enemies, but God changed us inside and out by his effectual call. We are no longer enemies of God.

Jesus gives us peace. He says, "Peace I leave with you; my peace I give you. I do not give to you as the world gives. Do not let your hearts be troubled and do not be afraid" (John 14:27). Christ's peace is not a subjective feeling that changes; it is an objective peace. It is not the kind of peace the United Nations and other international bodies try to accomplish. This infinitely superior, divine peace of Christ comes to all who trust in him and call upon his name. It flows from him to us in abundance, filling our anxious hearts to overflowing. Jesus himself says, "I have told you these things, so that in me you may have peace. In this world you will have trouble. But take heart! I have overcome the world" (John 16:33). Because of this objective peace with God, we also enjoy a subjective peace in our hearts that passes all human understanding (Phil. 4:7).

This is the only peace that can steady us. What happens to us in this world may shake us to our very core. It is like a compass when it is hit. The needle may go back and forth, but soon it goes back to pointing to the north again. The peace of God guards our hearts and our minds and makes us stable even in the face of death.

Beware of False Peace

We must, however, beware of a false peace that comes through a false gospel and a false faith. Jeremiah speaks of those who use religion to make money and acquire power and political influence: "From the least to the greatest, all are greedy for gain; prophets and priests alike, all practice deceit. They dress the wound of my people as though it were not serious. 'Peace, peace,' they say, when there is no peace" (Jer. 6:13–14). That is why people crowd into churches that merely entertain and soothe but never speak about sin, the wrath of God, hell, justification, holiness, and obedience to God's moral law.

Paul speaks about this: "For if someone comes to you and preaches a Jesus other than the Jesus we preached, or if you receive a different spirit from the one you received, or a different gospel from the one you accepted, you put up with it easily enough. . . . Such men are false apostles, deceitful workmen, masquerading as apostles of Christ. And no wonder, for Satan himself masquerades as an angel of light. It is not surprising, then, if his servants masquerade as servants of righteousness. Their end will be what their actions deserve" (2 Cor. 11:4, 13–15). Of such people John writes, "They went out from us, but they did not really belong to us. For if they had belonged to us, they would have remained with us; but their going showed that none of them belonged to us" (1 John 2:19).

Examine yourselves and see whether you are in the faith. Make your calling and election sure.

Benefits Resulting from Justification by Faith

In his treatment of this passage, Martyn Lloyd-Jones highlights several benefits that result from justification by faith.[2]

1. *Our minds are at rest.* Due to this change of God's relation to us, and our God-caused change of relation to him, our minds are now at rest. God was our enemy and we were his. We deserved his wrath and deserved to die, but Christ died in our place. Now God is reconciled to us and we to him; now we have peace with

---

2   Lloyd-Jones, *Romans*, vol. 4, *Assurance*, 17–23.

God. Lloyd-Jones says that without intelligent understanding of this gospel, we cannot have peace with God because our reasonable minds will not be satisfied. Emotionally driven people can never have peace. The mind must understand what has happened. In the parable of the sower, the fourth soil people alone understood the gospel and were saved (Matt. 13:8, 23).

2. *God loves us in spite of our still being sinners.* Though we have been justified by faith, we may still sin. But all our sins have been paid for by Jesus Christ. No sin remains in our account. Our position is changed from being enemies of God to being sons of God. Yet when we sin, we will experience discipline from our heavenly Father. He disciplines us as sons for our benefit so that we may share in his holiness, because without holiness no one will see God.

3. *Our accusing consciences are silenced.* We agree with God that we are sinners. We have sinned in the past, we may sin in the present, and we may also sin in the future. But when we trusted in Christ, God justified us. The blood of Christ cleanses us from all our sins.

4. *The devil is silenced.* The devil comes to tempt us, trip us, and swallow us whole. But John tells us, "They overcame [the devil] by the blood of the Lamb and by the word of their testimony" (Rev. 12:11). This is objective reason: "the blood of the Lamb" stands for atonement, for a propitiatory sacrifice. In other words, it does not matter how we feel. When the devil tests us, we overcome him by pleading the blood of Jesus Christ and articulating this doctrine of justification by faith. Peter tells us, "Be self-controlled and alert. Your enemy the devil prowls around like a roaring lion looking for someone to devour. Resist him, standing firm in the faith" (1 Pet. 5:8–9). James says the same thing: "Submit yourselves, then, to God. Resist the devil, and he will flee from you" (James 4:7). John assures us, "The one who is in you is greater than the one who is in the world" (1 John 4:4). Then he writes, "Everyone born of God overcomes the world. This is the victory that has overcome the world, even our faith" (1 John 5:4). Our articulation of the gospel overcomes the world and the devil.

5. *Death itself is silenced.* The sacrifice of God's Son delivered us from the fear of death to which we were enslaved. Paul writes, "'Death has been swallowed up in victory.' 'Where, O death, is your victory? Where, O death, is your sting?' The sting of death is sin, and the power of sin is the law. But thanks be to God! He gives us the victory through our Lord Jesus Christ" (1 Cor. 15:54–57; see also Heb. 2:14–15). Jesus said, "Whoever lives and believes in me will never die" (John 11:26). Elsewhere he says, "Whoever hears my word and believes him who sent me has eternal life and will not be condemned; he has crossed over from death to life" (John 5:24).

6. *We will not be condemned at the final judgment.* Paul writes, "Therefore, there is now no condemnation for those who are in Christ Jesus" (Rom. 8:1). He elaborates elsewhere, "What, then, shall we say in response to this? If God is for us, who can be against us? He who did not spare his own Son, but gave him up for us all—how will he not also, along with him, graciously give us all things? Who will bring any charge against those whom God has chosen? It is God who justifies. Who is he that condemns? Christ Jesus, who died—more than that, who was raised to life—is at the right hand of God and is also interceding for us" (Rom. 8:31–34). Then he asks: "Who shall separate us from the love of Christ?" The answer is given: "Neither death nor life . . . nor anything else in all creation, will be able to separate us from the love of God that is in Christ Jesus our Lord" (Rom. 8:35–39).

7. *Our justification is certain.* The final point Lloyd-Jones makes is that if we fall into sin, instead of questioning our salvation we must remember that we have been justified by faith. Our relationship with God is certain; we are justified. But we must not conceal our sin. We must repent, confess, forsake, and embrace chastisement, and then live a transformed life by faith. In other words, when Christians sin, we sin as sons, and our heavenly Father disciplines us for our own good. Paul writes, "That is why many among you are weak and sick, and a number of you have fallen asleep" (1 Cor. 11:30). That is discipline. But we must always keep in mind that we were not justified on the basis of any goodness in us, but only on the basis of the righteousness of Christ.

Do You Have Peace?

If you are a believer in Christ, you have been justified forever by the Supreme Court of heaven through the saving work of Christ alone. God justifies the ungodly; you are justified by faith in Jesus, not on the basis of any good works. And the goal of your justification is glorification. Your final and complete salvation is secure and sure and certain. The justified shall be glorified.

Therefore, you can enjoy peace and fellowship with God. As one hymnist wrote,

> There's a peace in my heart that the world never gave,
> a peace it cannot take away;
> though the trials of life may surround like a cloud,
> I've a peace that has come here to stay!

Another declared,

> When peace, like a river, attendeth my way,
> when sorrows like sea billows roll;
> whatever my lot, thou hast taught me to say,
> "It is well, it is well with my soul."
>
> My sin—O the bliss of that glorious thought!—
> my sin, not in part, but the whole,
> is nailed to the cross and I bear it no more;
> praise the Lord, praise the Lord, O my soul!

If you have not received by faith the salvation of Jesus Christ, you are insulting God and calling him a liar. The wrath of God is now abiding upon you (John 3:36) and you shall die in your sins. At the final judgment, you shall be condemned and experience the eternal fire of God's wrath. Heed this solemn warning of the Lord: "It is mine to avenge; I will repay. In due time their foot will slip; their day of disaster is near and their doom rushes upon them. . . . I lift my hand to heaven and declare: As surely as I live forever, when I sharpen my flashing sword and my hand grasps it in judgment, I will take vengeance on my adversaries and repay those who hate me" (Deut. 32:35, 40–41).

But if you are reading this, there is still hope. Paul writes, "Now is the time of God's favor, now is the day of salvation" (2 Cor. 6:2). Jesus calls you today to come to him. Come to Christ! Come as you are, as a sinner, with all your burdens and anxieties, and he will set you free. God will justify you forever and you will experience peace with God, the peace of God, peace with your neighbor, peace with your family, and peace within yourself.

20

Standing in God's Presence

¹Therefore, since we have been justified through faith, we have peace with God through our Lord Jesus Christ, ²through whom we have gained access by faith into this grace in which we now stand. And we rejoice in the hope of the glory of God.

Romans 5:1–2

Justification dealt with our sin problem once and for all. Romans 5:1–2 speaks about three blessings that result from our having been justified: peace with God, the presence of God, and triumphant praise. Our last chapter was about having peace with God and therefore experiencing the peace of God that passes all human understanding. In this chapter we will consider the second blessing: enjoying God's presence. When we learn to enjoy God's presence, all our troubles will be resolved.

Justification necessarily brings us into the presence of God, that we may enjoy fellowship with him. The ultimate goal of our salvation is to bring us home to our heavenly Father. This acceptance by the Father is "an implicate of justification"[1] by faith. John tells us, "We proclaim to you what we have seen and heard, so that you also may have fellowship with us. And our fellowship is with the Father and with his Son, Jesus Christ" (1 John 1:3). Peter says, "For Christ died for sins once for all, the righteous for the unrighteous, to bring you to God" (1 Pet. 3:18).

---

1   Murray, *Epistle to the Romans*, 161.

Jesus leads all his elect wandering sheep home and introduces them to the Father.

The Hebrews writer speaks of this ultimate purpose of our redemption: "In bringing many sons to glory, it was fitting that God, for whom and through whom everything exists, should make the author of their salvation perfect through suffering" (Heb. 2:10). Jesus brings those who have sinned, and have no glory, to God. We can go from shame to glory because Jesus dealt with our sin problem. Now we are without sin, as far as God is concerned, and fit to be in his presence. *Having been justified by faith, we have peace with God through our Lord Jesus Christ, through whom we have gained access by faith into this grace in which we now stand* (Rom. 5:1–2, author's translation).

Saints of God, realize this great truth. It does not matter who forsakes you in this world. You are in God's presence and he will never leave you. Through Jesus we have been admitted forever to the most exclusive club in heaven and on earth. To the praying thief Jesus said from the cross, "I tell you the truth, today you will be with me in paradise." We also have been brought to paradise to enjoy God's glorious presence forever.

Access through Our Lord Jesus Christ

All spiritual blessings flow to us *in* and *through* Jesus Christ. Paul uses the preposition "through" (*dia*) seven times in Romans 5:1–11 (vv. 1, 2, 5, 9, 10, 11). All blessings flow to us from the Father through the Son by the Holy Spirit. These blessings include peace with God, access to God, glory of God, love of God, future fullness of salvation, reconciliation with God and man, and joy in the Holy Spirit. There is no salvation apart from Christ. Jesus is not a minor god of a hill or country; he is the Sovereign Lord of the universe and salvation comes through him alone. Jesus proclaims, "I am the way and the truth and the life. No one comes to the Father except through me" (John 14:6). Peter understood this, declaring, "Salvation is found in no one else, for there is no other name under heaven given to men by which we must be saved" (Acts 4:12). This was the purpose of Christ's incarnation, as the angel told Joseph: "You are to give him the name Jesus, because he will save his people from their sins" (Matt. 1:21).

We have access to God only through Christ. This is the exclusivism of Christianity. Therefore, if someone is outside of Christ, he will not enjoy God's presence. Paul speaks of this truth throughout his epistles: "God our Savior . . . wants all men to be saved and to come to a knowledge of the truth. For there is one God and one mediator between God and men, the man Christ Jesus, who gave himself as a ransom for all men" (1 Tim. 2:3–6). Elsewhere he says, "Do not be ashamed to testify about our Lord, or ashamed of me his prisoner. But join with me in suffering for the gospel, by the power of God, who has saved us and called us to a holy life—not because of anything we have done but because of his own purpose and grace. This grace was given us in Christ Jesus before the beginning of time, but it has now been revealed through the appearing of our Savior, Christ Jesus, who has destroyed death and has brought life and immortality to light through the gospel" (2 Tim. 1:8–10). He also writes, "No one can lay any foundation other than the one already laid, which is Jesus Christ" (1 Cor. 3:11).

Paul says this access comes to us *"through our Lord Jesus Christ"* (v. 1). Jesus is Lord of all. We do not make him so; the Father did. In fact, it does not matter whether we believe in him or not: he *is* Lord. Paul says God the Father "raised [Christ] from the dead and seated him at his right hand in the heavenly realms, far above all rule and authority, power and dominion, and every title that can be given, not only in the present age but also in the one to come. And God placed all things under his feet and appointed him to be head over everything for the church, which is his body, the fullness of him who fills everything in every way" (Eph. 1:20–23). Paul declares that this Lord destroyed our enmity against God and his enmity against us by his death on the cross (Eph. 2:14, 16). Now God is favorably disposed to us and we have been made to love God.

Is Jesus your Lord, that you may enjoy this peace with God and access to his presence? Paul was a violent, blaspheming enemy of God. But after God confronted him and saved him, Paul called him Lord. Paul himself instructs us, "If you confess with your mouth, 'Jesus is Lord,' and believe in your heart that God raised him from the dead, you will be saved" (Rom. 10:9). If you surrender your life to Christ, you will live forever in God's presence.

Access to God's Presence

Many of us would be satisfied to obtain access to some famous or powerful person's presence. But through Christ we have been admitted to the most exclusive place, the presence of God. Through Christ, we have immediate, direct, and continual access to the Father. There is no difference: everyone who believes in Jesus, whether Jew or Gentile, rich or poor, master or slave, enjoys this great privilege. And having gained this blessed access, we shall never be thrown out. The Father planned our salvation from all eternity; the Son accomplished it by his death on the cross; and the Holy Spirit applies it effectually to every sinner.

If the Father is for us, who can be against us? More than that, the Son, our great high priest who lives eternally, intercedes for us in heaven. Additionally, the Holy Spirit dwells in us and intercedes for us with groans that words cannot express (Rom. 8:26). Since such intercession is effectual, our eternal salvation is assured.

We have this access to God's presence for all eternity. No matter what trouble we experience here, we have access to God. We are in the presence of "the Father of compassion and the God of all comfort, who comforts us in all our troubles" (2 Cor. 1:3–4). We cannot be miserable, anxious, or fearful in God's presence. God who is for us will even now fill our hearts with his eternal joy. We do not need the intercessions and merits of priests, the Virgin Mary, or saints. We do not need purgatory or indulgences. Jesus Christ our great high priest has brought us and introduced us to the Father, who loves us with an everlasting love (Jer. 31:3).

Our problem was that there had been a blockade to God's presence. Adam sinned, and in him we all sinned and became godless, lifeless, and hopeless. In Adam, we were cast outside of paradise and denied access to the tree of life. In fact, the entrance itself to paradise was blocked with cherubim with flaming swords. Who could open it and bring us back to paradise and into God's presence? Who could destroy our death and bring life and immortality to light? Who could rescue us from the dominion of darkness, of Satan, of death, and bring us into the kingdom of God's beloved Son, the kingdom of righteousness, peace, and joy in the Holy Spirit?

Exodus 19 and Hebrews 12 tell us that this blockade existed because of our sin. John also speaks of this wall of separation between people and God. First he says, "Blessed are those who wash their robes, that they may have the right to the tree of life and may go through the gates into the city." But then he declares, "Outside are the dogs, those who practice magic arts, the sexually immoral, the murderers, the idolaters and everyone who loves and practices falsehood" (Rev. 22:14–15). God's presence is a place of life, joy, and glory. But outside there is darkness, gloom, storm, death, sin, and the wrath of God. Outside is the physical Mount Sinai that cannot be touched, because it is burning with fire. Everyone is trembling, including Moses. There is a trumpet blast warning of no admittance to God's presence. The way to God is blocked for all guilty sinners, who deserve only punishment. Who will bring us out of Mount Sinai and into Mount Zion, the city of the living God?

The temple itself had a system of blockades that kept people from God's presence. When worshipers came to the temple, the first thing they would see was the court of the Gentiles, beyond which no Gentile could go, under penalty of death. Then there were the courts of Israelite women and Israelite men, respectively. They could not go further, into the court of the priests, and only the high priest could go through the thick veil into the Most Holy Place, where God was. Only once a year, on the Day of Atonement, could the high priest, with the blood of the sin offering and the incense cloud, come into God's presence for a brief moment. Who, then, is able to remove all these blockades and bring us sinners to God? Who can bring us from outside to inside, from death to life, from gloom to joy, from hell to heaven?

Our Lord Jesus Christ alone is the sinless Son of God, the God-man, our kinsman-redeemer, our only mediator and great high priest who sacrificed himself once for all for our sins. Because the Father accepted his propitiatory sacrifice, God's wrath has been averted, and God himself is now gracious to us. Now God is our heavenly Father and we are his adopted sons. Only Jesus our older brother can bring us to God, for he alone is without sin.

When Christ died on the cross, he declared, "It is finished." He was speaking of the work of redemption for which he had come. Matthew writes, "At that moment the curtain of the temple was torn in two from top to bottom" (Matt. 27:51). A new way was opened up for us to God through the body of Christ. The Hebrews writer explains,

> Therefore, brothers, since we have confidence to enter the Most Holy Place by the blood of Jesus, by a new and living way opened for us through the curtain, that is, his body, and since we have a great priest over the house of God, let us draw near to God with a sincere heart in full assurance of faith, having our hearts sprinkled to cleanse us from a guilty conscience and having our bodies washed with pure water. Let us hold unswervingly to the hope we profess, for he who promised is faithful. (Heb. 10:19–23)

Why do we have confidence? We have been sprinkled with the blood of Christ; our sin and guilt are gone. Now we are children of God and citizens of his kingdom; as such, we have boldness (*parrēsia*) to enter his presence. No longer are we timid and fearful, wondering whether God will accept us or not. We know that he delights to see us and that he exhorts us to draw near to him any time. We have come to the heavenly Jerusalem.

Elsewhere we read, "For surely it is not angels he helps, but Abraham's descendants" (Heb. 2:16). This idea of helping is that, just as a father runs to help his child, God is running to take hold of us and to help us, saying, "Be not afraid. Peace be with you." The writer continues, "Because he himself suffered when he was tempted, he is able to help those who are being tempted" (Heb. 2:18). The writer also declares, "Let us then approach the throne of grace with confidence, so that we may receive mercy and find grace to help us in our time of need" (Heb. 4:16). Our time of need is every moment. We are tempted every day. What should we do? We should approach the throne of grace with confidence, knowing that through justification we have been brought into God's very presence. When we do so, he will give us grace that is more than sufficient for our need. He gives us exceedingly and abundantly more than all we can ask or imagine.

God gives us grace and mercy to help us in our time of need. His mercies are new every morning. There is always manna coming down, and we are welcome to gather it. Therefore, let us approach the throne of grace with confidence, because our sin is gone and our consciences have been cleansed.

Where has God brought us? The Hebrews writer declares, "But you have come to Mount Zion, to the heavenly Jerusalem, the city of the living God." His use of the perfect tense means we have come and we will remain there forever. "You have come to thousands upon thousands of angels in joyful assembly, to the church of the firstborn, whose names are written in heaven." Sinai was a gloomy, miserable place; heaven is a joyful assembly. "You have come to God, the judge of all men, to the spirits of righteous men made perfect." The moment a believer dies, God perfects his spirit and takes him to heaven. Finally, he says we have come "to Jesus the mediator of a new covenant, and to the sprinkled blood that speaks a better word than the blood of Abel" (Heb. 12:22–24).

Through Christ we have come inside to God's presence. We do not belong outside any longer. We belong inside with our Father in our true home. We have gone from Mount Sinai to Mount Zion. We are not under the authority of law but under the rule of grace, and we can never go back. No more doom, trembling, and death for us. We have come into God's house and have gathered in his name to worship him. Knowing these things will stabilize us when trouble comes.

Notice, these blessings come to us through the triune God. Paul writes, "For through [Christ] we both have access to the Father by one Spirit" (Eph. 2:18). A person who does not believe in the Trinity cannot be a Christian. We believe in one God in three persons, co-equal and co-eternal. All the persons of the Trinity love us and work to bring about our salvation. That is why we are baptized in the name of the Father and of the Son and of the Holy Spirit. God's people are always under the care of the triune God. We are eternally secure; nothing can separate us from God or snatch us out of his hand. He neither sleeps nor slumbers. Notice, Paul says "we both" have access. There is no discrimination between Jewish and Gentile believers. And the verb he uses means we have continuous access to the Father. As children of God, we always live in our Father's presence with exceeding joy.

But this idea of living continuously in the presence of God brings up a question. The Bible says God is a holy, righteous

Father in whom there is no darkness. He is also a consuming fire. Isaiah asks, "The sinners in Zion are terrified; trembling grips the godless: 'Who of us can dwell with the consuming fire? Who of us can dwell with everlasting burning?'" (Isa. 33:14). Who can dwell with God who is fire? Only those who believe in Jesus Christ. The fire does not consume us because it consumed Christ, who bore our sins. Now we are declared righteous and can dwell with God.

God makes a beautiful promise in Jeremiah 50:20: "'In those days at that time,' declares the LORD, 'search will be made for Israel's guilt, but there will be none, and for the sins of Judah, but none will be found, for I will forgive the remnant I spare.'" I do not think God does the searching. The devil and our own conscience may search, but God forgives. We are the remnant that God spares. He who did not spare his own Son but gave him up for us all, spared us. That is why we are ushered by Christ into his presence. Does he bring us before God to convict us of our sins and judge us? No, we are already justified. We are brought to God to enjoy glorious fellowship with the Father and the Son. Jesus said, "This is eternal life: that they may know you, the only true God, and Jesus Christ, whom you have sent" (John 17:3). Knowing God means we love God and he loves us. This knowledge should calm all our fears.

Paul writes, "In him and through faith in him we may approach God" (Eph. 3:12). All blockades are lifted. The veil is torn from top to bottom. A new and living way has been established through the body of Christ for us to enter straight into the throne room of God. We can do so because our sin problem has been dealt with once for all. Because Christ died for our sins, we are reconciled to God and God to us. The door is opened; with freedom and confidence we can now draw near. Paul wrote his letter to the Ephesians while he was in prison, experiencing pain and misery, but he had this wonderful privilege of going into the presence of God and learned to be content despite his circumstances.

We all have problems in this world. Some have more, some less. But like Paul, we should learn the secret of being content. As we draw near to God, he will draw near to us. Paul told the Ephesians, "I ask you, therefore, not to be discouraged because of my sufferings for you, which are your glory" (Eph. 3:13). Note the plural: "sufferings." Then he continues, "For this reason I kneel before the Father" (Eph. 3:14). Because we are justified, we have peace with God, we can enter God's presence, and he will hear our prayers. Just like an earthly father hears his children's cries, even more so will our heavenly Father hear and answer our prayers and meet our every need by giving us more grace—grace that is greater than all our sin, sufferings, and misery.

In effect, Paul is saying, "Do not feel sorry for me. I enjoy God's presence in prison. I pray to him, have fellowship with him, and am comforted by him." Elsewhere he says, "Praise be to the God and Father of our Lord Jesus Christ, the Father of [mercies] and the God of all comfort, who comforts us in all our troubles" (2 Cor. 1:3-4). God gives us an abundance of mercies and fills us with overflowing comfort so we can comfort others.

Yes, we were once God's enemies, but our status has changed: "Yet to all who received him, to those who believed in his name, he gave the right to become children of God" (John 1:12). God has become our heavenly Father; as children, it is now natural for us to speak to him about all kinds of things. We have a right, therefore, not only as citizens of God's kingdom but also as children of God, to come into his presence and pray in faith, knowing that our Father will hear our prayers and give us grace.

The king's children have free access to the king's presence, just like my grandchildren always have access to my presence. They run to my door and knock until I open it. I am happy to see them. If this is true of us, how much more is our heavenly Father interested in seeing us, whom he loves as he loves his own Son.

Access through Prayer

We have access to God through prayer. We pray to the heavenly Father in Jesus' name by the Holy Spirit. The greatest blessing on this side of heaven is to be able to pray to the infinite, all-wise, all-compassionate God. We should make use of this privilege at all times, not only when we have troubles. Paul says, "I bow my knees before the Father" (Eph. 3:14). Paul speaks of his prayers for the churches throughout his epistles.

Prayer by the Spirit is the sign that we are alive and have been brought into relationship with our heavenly Father. As God's children, we lack nothing. God will take care of us when we cry to him, just as young parents rush to care for their crying baby. Paul declares, "For you did not receive a spirit that makes you a slave again to fear, but you received the Spirit of sonship. And by him we cry, 'Abba, Father'" (Rom. 8:15).

As soon as a person is born of God, the Spirit of God comes in and causes that person to cry, "Abba, Father." We pray in the power of the Spirit and by his guidance, because we are heirs with God and joint-heirs with Christ. We exercise our right to come into God's presence and pray boldly. All believers, young or old, can pray. Those experiencing temptation can pray and be set free by God. We can rejoice in tribulations because we can pray and fellowship with God in the midst of all problems.

In another epistle written from prison, Paul revealed his secret that helped him transcend all his troubles: "Do not be anxious about anything, but in everything, by prayer and petition, with thanksgiving, present your requests to God. And the peace of God, which transcends all understanding, will guard your hearts and your minds in Christ Jesus" (Phil. 4:6–7). God's grace is greater than all our troubles.

We should pray boldly, because we stand firmly on the rock-solid foundation of God's free and unmerited favor. We are not under the government of law but under grace. Paul exhorts, "Now, brothers, I want to remind you of the gospel I preached to you, which you received and on which you have taken your stand" (1 Cor. 15:1). We stand in grace and in the promises of God. He remains true to his promises. Paul also admonishes, "Who are you to judge someone else's servant? To his own master he stands or falls. And he will stand, for the Lord is able to make him stand" (Rom. 14:4). We do not stand in our strength; God enables us to stand.

Our Master will see to it that we stand until the day we die. Jude writes, "To him who is able to keep you from falling and to present you before his glorious presence without fault and with great joy—to the only God our Savior be glory, majesty, power and authority, through Jesus Christ our Lord, before all ages, now and forevermore! Amen" (Jude 24–25). The psalmist declares, "Therefore the wicked will not stand in the judgment" (Ps. 1:5). This means the righteous will stand. Elsewhere he states: "The arrogant cannot stand in your presence" (Ps. 5:5). There is no greater judgment than not standing in God's presence. Those who proudly mock God and his word will not stand. God will see to it that they fall in due time.

Not only do we stand, but we are also seated with Christ in heavenly places (Eph. 2:6). Think of our condition when we were outside: we were helpless, ungodly enemies of God. But now we are inside: justified, in the company of the redeemed, children of the heavenly Father and heirs of God, rich and famous in the whole universe.

Pray boldly and often, because our heavenly Father delights in our prayers. Jesus says, "In that day you will no longer ask me anything. I tell you the truth, my Father will give you whatever you ask in my name. Until now you have not asked for anything in my name. Ask and you will receive, and your joy will be complete. . . . In that day you will ask in my name. I am not saying that I will ask the Father on your behalf. No, the Father himself loves you because you have loved me and have believed that I came from God" (John 16:23–27). Jesus also says, "I have given them the glory that you gave me, that they may be one as we are one: I in them and you in me. May they be brought to complete unity to let the world know that you sent me and have loved them even as you have loved me" (John 17:22–23). God loves us even as he loves his eternal Son. We must never doubt this, even when we sin.

Jesus introduces us to the Father, and we are given access to him. We stand before him on the foundation of grace abounding. We are secure forever and shall never fall. As children of God, we must exercise our right to have fellowship with God and pray prevailingly. Our God joyfully hears our prayers and answers them even as he answered the prayers of Jesus, for God loves us even as he loves Jesus.

Therefore, pray! Pray in faith. Pray in the will of God and in the power of the Holy Spirit. Pray wrestling, prevailing prayer as Jacob did, declaring, "I will not let you go until you bless me." Jacob had received a blessing from his father by cheating, but he received a blessing from God by confessing. Paul speaks about the Asian minister Epaphras, who was always wrestling in prayer (Col. 4:12). He did not just pray for two minutes and then run off. Pray until God answers your prayer and gives you grace to overcome all your troubles. Pray with fasting.

Martin Luther was a man who prevailed in prayer because he had so many problems. In 1540 Luther's dear friend and fellow soldier, Frederick Myconius, became ill and was dying. So he wrote a letter to Luther anticipating his imminent departure to God's presence. Immediately Luther wrote back: "Frederick, I earnestly admonish you to pray to dear God to preserve you the longer to profit the church and to defeat the devil. This shall be my petition. This is my desire and my will be done. Amen. For my will seeks the honor of the divine Name, not my own honor and pleasure. Farewell, dear Frederick, and may the Lord not let me hear that you have died but may God cause you to survive me." After the letter was read to Myconius, he revived, and lived six years and two months more, outliving Luther by two months.[2] When our will is the will of God, we will pray powerfully and prevail.

Are You Standing in God's Presence?

What about you? Are you still outside, or have you come to enjoy the blessing of being in God's presence? If you are outside, let me remind you of the prodigal son. This man hated God, his father, and everyone else. He went to a far place to sin. But finally his money ran out and he found himself without a job and without food. Luke writes,

> When he came to his senses, he said, "How many of my father's hired men have food to spare, and here I am starving to death! I will set out and go back to my father and say to him, 'Father, I have sinned against heaven and against you. I am no longer worthy to be called your son; make me like one of your hired men.'" So he got up and went to his father. But while he was still a long way off, his father saw him and was filled with compassion for him; he ran to his son, threw his arms around him and kissed him. The son said to him, "Father, I have sinned against heaven and against you. I am no longer worthy to be

---

2   James M. Boice, *The Sermon on the Mount: An Exposition* (Grand Rapids, MI: Zondervan, 1972), 218.

called your son." But the father said to his servants, "Quick! Bring the best robe and put it on him. Put a ring on his finger and sandals on his feet. Bring the fattened calf and kill it. Let's have a feast and celebrate. For this son of mine was dead and is alive again; he was lost and is found." So they began to celebrate. (Luke 15:17–24)

This is what happened to us. God's Son came and sought us, found us, and brought us to the very presence of the Father. Justification brings us to our heavenly Father, who is eagerly waiting to welcome us, bless us, kiss us, embrace us, and forgive us. We are received not as hired servants but as sons.

Thank God that, *"having been justified by faith, we have peace with God through our Lord Jesus Christ, through whom we have gained access by faith into this grace in which we now stand."* This means we will never go out of God's presence again. The prodigal was cured of all his wanderlust. He found out that the pasture was not greener elsewhere. We find everything in the house of the Father. God brought us home, as David did Mephibosheth (2 Sam. 9). This crippled son of Jonathan should have been killed, but David decided to show him kindness. He was brought to David, who said, "From now on you will eat with me as one of my sons." That is what God has done for us. He adopts us as sons and brings us into his presence, where we will be with him forever.

May God help us to grasp this message! Then, no matter what troubles we undergo, we will learn the secret of going into the presence of God to receive mercy and find grace for the time of our need.

21

The Saints' Triumphant Praise

¹Therefore, since we have been justified through faith, we have peace with God through our Lord Jesus Christ, ²through whom we have gained access by faith into this grace in which we now stand. And we rejoice in the hope of the glory of God. ³Not only so, but we also rejoice in our sufferings, because we know that suffering produces perseverance; ⁴perseverance, character; and character, hope. ⁵And hope does not disappoint us, because God has poured out his love into our hearts by the Holy Spirit, whom he has given us.

Romans 5:1–5

This passage teaches that because of justification we experience three blessings: the peace of God, access to God's presence, and the ability to rejoice in all things. In this chapter we will examine the third blessing of triumphant praise, looking at what it means to rejoice, what it means to rejoice in hope, and what it means to rejoice in the glory of God.

Only Christians can rejoice in all circumstances. When Paul was in chains in a Roman prison for the sake of the gospel, he exhorted the Philippians, "Rejoice in the Lord always. I will say it again: Rejoice!" (Phil. 4:4). It is the grace of God that enables us to rejoice always.

The joys of this world will eventually end. "For everything in the world—the cravings of sinful man, the lust of his eyes and the boasting of what he has and does—comes not from the Father but from the world. The world and its desires pass away, but the man who does the will of God lives forever" (1 John 2:16–17). The joy of salvation will never end; therefore, we can rejoice despite any trials we experience in this world.

We Rejoice

"Through our Lord Jesus Christ . . . we have gained access by faith into this grace in which we now stand. And we rejoice in the hope of the glory of God" (v. 2). The Greek word kauchōmetha (rejoice) means "to brag, boast, glory, exult, or triumphantly praise." The Bible speaks of rejoicing with exceeding joy. That implies a fuller jubilation than merely rejoicing. Paul uses the present tense, meaning that we are to praise God continually, not only when good things happen. Every believer can triumphantly praise always in view of the hope of the glory of God and the absolute certainty of our ultimate salvation.

The Jewish people used to rejoice about many things. Claiming to be justified by their own good works, they boasted constantly about their relationship to God, saying, "The Lord is our God. Gentile dogs are without God." Like the rich young ruler, they bragged that they kept the law (Rom. 2:23). They also took pride in their flesh, pointing out that their circumcision was proof that they were saved (Gal. 6:13). In the same way, people today glory in being baptized or going to church regularly. But Paul tells us that we are saved by grace, "not by works, so that no one can boast" (Eph. 2:9).

There is a type of negative boasting that is prohibited. Jesus spoke about a Pharisee who rejoiced in himself: "The Pharisee stood up and prayed about himself: 'God, I thank you that I am not like other men—robbers, evildoers, adulterers—or even like this tax collector. I fast twice a week and give a tenth of all I get'" (Luke 18:11–12). Paul, another Pharisee, wrote, "For it is we who are the circumcision, we who worship by the Spirit of God, who glory in Christ Jesus, and who put no confidence in the flesh— though I myself have reasons for such confidence. If anyone else thinks he has reasons to put confidence in the flesh, I have more: circumcised on the eighth day, of the people of Israel, of the tribe of Benjamin, a Hebrew of Hebrews; in regard to the law, a Pharisee; as for zeal, persecuting the church; as for legalistic righteousness, faultless" (Phil. 3:3–6). But Paul says such glorying is excluded before God (Rom. 3:27). He also declares, "What then shall we say that Abraham, our forefather, discovered in this matter? If, in fact, Abraham was justified by works, he had something to boast about—but not before God" (Rom. 4:1–2). He then proves that Abraham was justified by grace through faith.

In this passage, however, Paul speaks about a positive boasting. We are exhorted to boast, to brag, and to rejoice greatly in God and in what he has done for us. Paul cites Jeremiah 9:24: "Let him who boasts boast in the Lord" (1 Cor. 1:31). Elsewhere he declares, "May I never boast except in the cross of our Lord Jesus Christ" (Gal. 6:14). We are proud of the cross, because it tells us there is nothing good in us, and we stand solely in the grace of God.

Our salvation is all of grace so that God may be praised both now and throughout all eternity. Paul writes, "In love he predestined us to be adopted as his sons through Jesus Christ, in accordance with his pleasure and will—to the praise of his glorious grace" (Eph. 1:4–6). He repeats this theme throughout Ephesians 1: "In him we were also chosen . . . in order that we, who were the first to hope in Christ, might be for the praise of his glory" (vv. 11–12); "[The Holy Spirit] is a deposit guaranteeing our inheritance until the redemption of those who are God's possession—to the praise of his glory" (v. 14). We should brag, glory, and praise in this way because God has graciously given us great blessings in the gospel.

Incomparable and unsearchable riches come to us in the gospel. Paul declares, "In him we have redemption through his blood, the forgiveness of sins, in accordance with the riches of God's grace" (Eph. 1:7). Note the plural: "the riches of God's grace." Then he writes, "In order that in the coming ages he might show the incomparable riches of his grace. . . . Although I am less than the least of all God's people, this grace was given me: to preach to the Gentiles the unsearchable riches of Christ. . . . I pray that out of his glorious riches he may strengthen you" (Eph. 2:7; 3:8, 16). When we unpack the gospel package, we will glory in the riches that God has given us. But if we do not understand the gospel, we will remain timid, anxious, and sinful.

Paul exhorts, "Be joyful in hope," that is, in hope of the glory of God (Rom. 12:12). Elsewhere he says, "Therefore I glory in

Christ Jesus in my service to God" (Rom. 15:17). We are entitled to some boasting. We should triumphantly praise God in hope of his coming glory. We can rejoice even in tribulations, knowing that our ultimate salvation is so certain that not even death can prevent us from being glorified. Our salvation depends entirely on God, not on ourselves. Paul writes, "Not only is this so, but we also rejoice in God through our Lord Jesus Christ" (Rom. 5:11). Paul says that we rejoice *in God*—not in ourselves or anything else. Our salvation depends one hundred percent on God and zero percent on ourselves. Therefore, we can be absolutely certain of our salvation. If salvation depended on us in any way, then we could not be so certain.

Therefore, we glory, exult, and praise always. It is a shame for a Christian to go about downcast and miserable. We must seek to understand what God has done for us in Christ. And when we understand, if we are lying down, we will sit up; if we are sitting, we will stand; and if we are standing, we will jump up and down and praise God. We will agree with Paul, whose life of joy was expressed throughout his letter to the Philippians: "I thank my God every time I remember you. In all my prayers for all of you, I always pray with joy" (Phil. 1:3–4); "But what does it matter? The important thing is that in every way, whether from false motives or true, Christ is preached. And because of this I rejoice. Yes, and I will continue to rejoice" (Phil. 1:18); "Then make my joy complete" (Phil. 2:2); "But even if I am being poured out like a drink offering," that means, even if I die, "on the sacrifice and service coming from your faith, I am glad and rejoice with all of you. So you too should be glad and rejoice with me" (Phil. 2:17–18); "Therefore, my brothers, you whom I love and long for, my joy and my crown . . . I rejoice greatly in the Lord" (Phil. 4:1, 10). This great apostle continued to rejoice, though he was arrested, thrown into a cold Roman prison, chained, and deprived of many things.

When the disciples came back from their preaching tour, they told Jesus, "Even demons are subject to us in your name!" Jesus told them, "Do not rejoice that the spirits submit to you, but rejoice that your names are written in heaven" (Luke 10:20). Our names are also written in God's book of life from all eternity. God foreknew, predestinated, called, and justified us, and he will also glorify us. God does it all. We shall never fall from God's grace, for

God himself will keep us from falling. That is why we can brag in the Lord.

We Rejoice in Hope

The second point is that we rejoice "in hope." In modern usage, the word "hope" is full of contingencies and doubts. It usually connotes "hope so." In the New Testament, however, hope signifies absolute certainty. It is faith oriented to the future based on the promise of the good, almighty God, who does not change his mind. Hope, as Dr. Ernst Käsemann said, is not "the prospect of what might happen but the prospect of what is already guaranteed."[1] John Frame remarks, "Hope is not something radically different from faith, but it is a kind of faith: directed toward the future fulfillment of the promises of God."[2]

Paul writes, "Against all hope, Abraham in hope believed and so became the father of many nations" (Rom. 4:18). Against the reality of the deadness of the bodies of Abraham and Sarah, Abraham believed that God would fulfill his promise. His faith was based on his hope in God. He reasoned, "God promised me a son, and he is faithful. He creates out of nothing and raises the dead. Nothing is too hard for him. I believe in his promise of an heir." In the same way, we can rejoice in the absolute certainty of our final salvation. At the coming of our great God and Savior Jesus Christ, we will be transformed to be like God. This is our blessed hope for which we wait (Titus 2:13).

Hope means we wait because hope has to do with the future. Our hope is based on God's promise. Speaking of the redemption and glorification of our bodies, Paul explains, "For in this hope we were saved. But hope that is seen is no hope at all. Who hopes for what he already has? But if we hope for what we do not yet have, we wait for it patiently" (Rom. 8:24–25).

This hope *"does not disappoint us"* (Rom. 5:5). Its fulfillment is certain; therefore, we can hold on to it and patiently endure all troubles, knowing that we are destined for nothing less than glory. We cannot put our hope in this world. People will disappoint us,

---

1   Ernst Käsemann, *Commentary on Romans* (Grand Rapids: Eerdmans, 1980), 134.
2   Frame, *Salvation Belongs to the Lord*, 194.

whether our spouses, children, employers, or political leaders. We must, therefore, put our hope in God and in his gospel. When we do so, the Holy Spirit in us will guarantee our final salvation (Eph. 1:13–14). Having been marked and sealed, believers enjoy complete security.

Unbelievers are without God and therefore without hope (Eph. 2:12; 1 Thess. 4:13). Since their hope is only in this world, they run after the things of this world, which will pass away. But their joy shall come to an end and they will hear the terrible words: "The party is over for you." Such people dread to die.

But our hope is in the Lord. Paul speaks of "Christ in you, the hope of glory" and of "Christ Jesus our hope" (Col. 1:27; 1 Tim. 1:1). Ours is a living hope stored up in heaven, where Jesus is. Our life is hidden with Christ in God (Col. 3:3). It is the hope of an inheritance kept in heaven for us that does not perish, spoil, or fade. This hope is revealed to us in the gospel (Col. 1:23). It is like an anchor that stabilizes our souls when we face all sorts of tribulations. We can smile even in the midst of terrible sorrow.

By the enlightenment of the Holy Spirit we come to know this hope to which we are called, even our glorification. Paul says this abounding hope fills our hearts to overflowing (Rom. 15:13). That is why we must pay full attention when we worship and hear the gospel preached. The gospel alone can give us hope in the midst of all problems. This hope enables us to endure persecutions; in fact, trials only make it stronger. It also enables us to live a holy life (1 John 3:3).

On what are you basing your hope? Are you taking pride in your family, your children, your education, your work, your beauty, your friends, your wealth, your power, your fame, or your country? All these things will surely disappoint us. But if we hope in Christ, we shall never be ashamed. Believe in the Lord Jesus and you shall be saved into this living hope.

We Rejoice in the Glory of God

Not only do we rejoice in hope, but we also rejoice "in . . . the glory of God" (v. 2). "The glory of God" means either the glory God has or the glory God gives us so that we receive glory. Both are true here.

God alone is eternally glorious and lives in unapproachable light. He is light; in him there is no darkness. Adam was created with glory to behold this God of glory. But because of his sin, he lost his God-likeness. In Adam, we also sinned and lost our glory. Paul writes, "Although they claimed to be wise, they became fools and exchanged the glory of the immortal God for images made to look like mortal man and birds and animals and reptiles" (Rom. 1:22–23). Man exchanges truth for a lie, and then he glories in his shame.

The wages of sin is death, but God devised a plan that will restore us to glory. This was the mission of Jesus. The Son of God became incarnate, and through his death and resurrection we are brought back from our shame, death, and corruption. The author of Hebrews declares, "In bringing many sons to glory, it was fitting that God, for whom and through whom everything exists, should make the author of their salvation perfect through suffering" (Heb. 2:10). Paul also speaks of this: "He called you to this through our gospel, that you might share in the glory of our Lord Jesus Christ" (2 Thess. 2:14). Peter writes, "To the elders among you, I appeal as a fellow elder, a witness of Christ's sufferings and one who also will share in the glory to be revealed. . . . When the Chief Shepherd appears, you will receive the crown of glory that will never fade away" (1 Pet. 5:1, 4).

Why should we run after the pleasures of sin? To do so is to be like a hobo rummaging through the trash. If we are believers, we will share in Christ's glory and receive a crown of glory when he comes. Paul says, "I consider that our present sufferings are not worth comparing with the glory that will be revealed in us. . . . The creation itself will be liberated from its bondage to decay and brought into the glorious freedom of the children of God. . . . Not only so, but we ourselves, who have the firstfruits of the Spirit, groan inwardly as we wait eagerly for our adoption as sons, the redemption of our bodies" (Rom. 8:18, 21, 23). This is speaking about our glorification. Elsewhere he says about the body that dies: "It is sown in dishonor, it is raised in glory; it is sown in weakness, it is raised in power" (1 Cor. 15:43).

Jesus tells us that, in one sense, God's glory has already been given to us. He prayed, "I have given them the glory that you gave me" (John 17:22). But we are also being changed from glory to glory. Paul writes, "And we, who with unveiled faces all reflect the Lord's glory, are being transformed into his likeness with ever-increasing glory, which comes from the Lord, who is the Spirit" (2 Cor. 3:18). As we behold the Lord in the Scriptures, we are being changed from one degree of glory to another. This is sanctification.

Paul speaks with certainty about our future glorification: "But our citizenship is in heaven. And we eagerly await a Savior from there, the Lord Jesus Christ, who, by the power that enables him to bring everything under his control, will transform our lowly bodies so that they will be like his glorious body" (Phil. 3:20–21). It is with that glorious body that we shall see God face to face.

God is glorious. As sons of God, we are re-created in God's image and likeness that we might reflect his glory. But when Christ comes again in great glory and power, he will transform our lowly bodies so that they will be like his glorious body. Moses was permitted to see only the back part of God. But when Christ glorifies us, we shall see him face to face because we will be without sin. Then the hope shall be reality. We shall possess glory that we may dwell with God forever.

Why do you seek trash when you are destined for glory? A glorious people shall dwell with the God of glory in a glorious universe in which there will be no more sin and death. Then the hope of our calling shall be realized fully.

We can receive great comfort and hope from the words of Paul: "He did this to make the riches of his glory known to the objects of his mercy, whom he prepared in advance for glory" (Rom. 9:23). This is God's purpose for us. Before the creation of the world, we were prepared for radiant, immortal, sinless perfection. Glory is our destiny and destination.

Paul also says: "We speak of God's secret wisdom, a wisdom that has been hidden and that God destined for our glory before time began. None of the rulers of this age understood it, for if they had, they would not have crucified the Lord of glory. However, as it is written: 'No eye has seen, no ear has heard, no mind has conceived what God has prepared for those who love him'" (1 Cor. 2:7–9). God prepared us for glory.

God has a wonderful plan for all who believe in Jesus Christ. It is not to make us rich, famous, or powerful. God's plan is more transcendent than that: "'For I know the plans I have for you,' declares the LORD, 'plans to prosper you and not to harm you, plans to give you hope and a future" (Jer. 29:11). God's plan is for our glory!

What Are You Choosing?

What are you choosing—trash or glory? Years ago in India, I noticed a number of young people from the West who were raised with knowledge of the gospel going after other religions and philosophies with great zeal. I exhorted these youths, "You are looking for a grain of wheat in the midst of a large cow-dung pie. You rejected the bread of life that you heard growing up. You are seeking trash because you rejected the God of glory and the gospel that promised you glory."

The rich fool chose trash (Luke 12), as did the rich man (Luke 16) and the rich young ruler (Matt. 19). But another young man made a different choice: "By faith Moses, when he had grown up, refused to be known as the son of Pharaoh's daughter. He chose to be mistreated along with the people of God rather than to enjoy the pleasures of sin for a short time. He regarded disgrace for the sake of Christ as of greater value than the treasures of Egypt, because he was looking ahead to his reward" (Heb. 11:24–26). David writes, "One thing I ask of the LORD, this is what I seek: that I may dwell in the house of the LORD all the days of my life, to gaze upon the beauty of the LORD and to seek him in his temple" (Ps. 27:4). Jesus told Martha, "Only one thing is needed. Mary has chosen what is better" (Luke 10:42).

Have you chosen that one thing needful, the source of all things: the inexhaustible, incomparable riches of God's grace? Have you chosen Jesus Christ, in whom alone is life and hope? Trust in Christ, not for health, wealth, power, or fame, but for eternal life and glory. After showing Jesus all the kingdoms of this world and their glory, the devil said, "All this I will give you if you will bow down and worship me." Jesus refused, saying, "Away from me, Satan! For it is written: 'Worship the Lord your God, and serve him only'" (Matt. 4:9–10). May God help us to choose his glory, as Jesus did, and rejoice in the hope of the glory of God.

22

Why Do Good People Suffer?

¹Therefore, since we have been justified through faith, we have peace with God through our Lord Jesus Christ, ²through whom we have gained access by faith into this grace in which we now stand. And we rejoice in the hope of the glory of God. ³Not only so, but we also rejoice in our sufferings, because we know that suffering produces perseverance; ⁴perseverance, character; and character, hope. ⁵And hope does not disappoint us, because God has poured out his love into our hearts by the Holy Spirit, whom he has given us.

Romans 5:1-5

Why do true believers in Jesus Christ suffer afflictions and persecution? Are they not exempt from all sufferings because of their salvation? Such questions have perplexed believers throughout the ages, and Romans 5:1-5 gives us the answers.

Chapters 5-8 of Romans teach about the full assurance of our ultimate salvation, which is our glorification (i.e., the redemption of our bodies). It is absolutely certain that those who are justified will be glorified. This is our sure hope. Paul writes in Romans 5 that, having been justified by faith, we have peace with God. Then he says that we are in God's presence and triumphantly praise God. We now can rejoice in hope of the glory of God. This hope of our glorification is the dominant theme in Romans 5:1-11.

Rejoicing Greatly in Suffering

"*And we rejoice in the hope of the glory of God. Not only so, but we also rejoice in our sufferings*" (vv. 2–3). As believers, we rejoice in God, who creates out of nothing, raises the dead, and keeps every one of his promises. Paul writes, "And those he predestined, he also called; those he called, he also justified; those he justified, he also glorified" (Rom. 8:30). It is certain that the justified shall be glorified; therefore, we can rejoice in the hope of our coming glory, even in the midst of any tribulations we experience in this life.

Christ's mission is to bring many sons to glory. God chose us in his Son before the creation of the world to be holy and blameless in his sight. God's election was not intended to make us rich, healthy, and famous in this life, as some fraudulent ministers assert. Rather, in this life we are sure to suffer.

Paul tells us that those who are justified will rejoice, and the Greek expression tells us it is a continuous rejoicing, even during trials. We can rejoice even in suffering because our God has guaranteed to make us glorious. Thus we not only triumphantly praise, but we also rejoice greatly in our present sufferings.

The Greek word for affliction or tribulation is *thlipsis*, which has to do with applying pressure on our soul and body—the type of pressure that is applied to grapes to extract juice or olives to extract oil. Gethsemane means "olive press"; it was so-named because there was a press in the garden to squeeze olives for their oil. But it also was the place where Jesus experienced intense pressure on his soul.

As Christians, we experience all forms of suffering. But we especially suffer for the sake of our Christian faith, as millions of believers throughout the world experience every day. These sufferings include slander, broken relationships, divorce, enmity of children, enmity of fellow workers, loss of jobs, confiscation of properties, torture, and martyrdom.

Jesus himself told us to expect such sufferings: "Blessed are those who are persecuted because of righteousness, for theirs is the kingdom of heaven. Blessed are you when people insult you, persecute you and falsely say all kinds of evil against you because of me. Rejoice and be glad, because great is your reward in heaven, for in the same way they persecuted the prophets who were before you" (Matt. 5:10–12). However, in a similar passage, he warns, "Woe to you when all men speak well of you, for that is how their fathers treated the false prophets" (Luke 6:26). Such a reaction could indicate one is a false prophet; ministers who are popular are often also frauds. Jesus elsewhere encouraged his disciples: "I have told you these things, so that in me you may have peace. In this world you will have trouble. But take heart! I have overcome the world" (John 16:33). At the end of their first missionary journey, Paul and Barnabas visited some of the cities they had gone to earlier, "strengthening the disciples and encouraging them to remain true to the faith. 'We must go through many hardships to enter the kingdom of God,' they said" (Acts 14:22).

Paul often speaks about suffering in his epistles: "It has been granted to you on behalf of Christ not only to believe on him, but also to suffer for him" (Phil. 1:29). These Philippians had received two gifts: the gift of believing in Christ and the gift of suffering for him. Paul told the Thessalonian believers not to be unsettled by trials: "You know quite well that we were destined for them" (1 Thess. 3:3). After recounting his trials to Timothy he wrote, "In fact, everyone who wants to live a godly life in Christ Jesus will be persecuted" (2 Tim. 3:12). True Christians are destined to real suffering in this life. Yet because this idea is not popular in America, most ministers will not preach what Paul and Jesus are teaching us.

When we speak of tribulations, we are not speaking about minor inconveniences like a headache or traffic problems, but about serious issues. Paul alludes to such severe trials: "Who shall separate us from the love of Christ? Shall trouble or hardship or persecution or famine or nakedness or danger or sword? As it is written: 'For your sake we face death all day long; we are considered as sheep to be slaughtered'" (Rom. 8:35–36). Elsewhere he lists some of the problems he personally faced:

> Are they servants of Christ? (I am out of my mind to talk like this.) I am more. I have worked much harder, been in prison more frequently, been flogged more severely, and been exposed to death again and again. Five times I received from the Jews the forty lashes minus one. Three times I was beaten with rods, once I was stoned, three times I was shipwrecked, I spent a night and a day in the open sea, I have been constantly on the move.

> I have been in danger from rivers, in danger from bandits, in danger from my own countrymen, in danger from Gentiles; in danger in the city, in danger in the country, in danger at sea; and in danger from false brothers. I have labored and toiled and have often gone without sleep; I have known hunger and thirst and have often gone without food; I have been cold and naked. Besides everything else, I face daily the pressure of my concern for all the churches. (2 Cor. 11:23–28)

Compared to Paul, what have we suffered? Yet it is Paul who says "we also rejoice in our sufferings." Those who preach, "Receive Jesus and all your problems will disappear," are false witnesses of the gospel and manifest the characteristics of a cult. The true gospel declares that true believers will suffer trials and severe pressures in this life. Yet Paul asserts that we can rejoice exultantly and triumphantly praise God in our tribulations.

Notice seven things about our rejoicing in tribulations:

1. We should not *murmur* during tribulations, as the Israelites did.
2. We are not to *suffer stoically*, always maintaining a stiff upper lip.
3. We are not to fall into *commiseration and self-pity*, calling attention to our misery.
4. We are not rejoicing *in spite of suffering*.
5. We are not rejoicing *because we enjoy suffering*, as masochists do.
6. We are not rejoicing *in the midst of tribulations*.
7. Paul is saying that we rejoice greatly *because of sufferings*. To rejoice because of sufferings appointed and governed by the Father is an entirely different idea. Though these sufferings are bad, God brings good out of them.

In the same epistle Paul writes, "And we know that in all things God works for the good of those who love him, who have been called according to his purpose" (Rom. 8:28). Our sufferings prove that we are children of God. Only the righteous experience this kind of suffering, because the world, the devil, and the false church all hate the true people of God.

"We also rejoice in our sufferings." Note the use of the plural. If we are true believers, we will face many tribulations in our lives. One after another, sufferings came for Job. Paul uses the present tense, meaning we are continually rejoicing. Finally, note the word "we." Not only the apostle, who received special spiritual endowments, but also all true believers ought to rejoice in tribulations.

Do not misunderstand; I do not naturally welcome suffering. I understand, however, that only legitimate children will experience the loving discipline of the heavenly Father to remove evil from their hearts. Such discipline is not pleasant at the time but painful, but it later produces a harvest of righteousness and peace for those who have been trained by it. Having gone through it, we will share in the holiness of God, without which no one shall see God (see Heb. 12:4–14). As we recognize the value of discipline, we will be able to embrace it and even rejoice greatly in it.

Because We Know

Paul gives us several reasons we can rejoice in tribulations. The first is knowledge: *"Not only so, but we also rejoice in our sufferings, knowing . . ."* (v. 3). The Greek word is *eidotes*, "knowing and continually knowing." Christians are educated people. They are students of the Bible, which reveals to us God's purpose and holy will. Christian ministers, therefore, are to preach and teach the Bible, not psychology, politics, science, or sociology. They are to preach the word and equip believers to know God's good purpose in the sufferings they face.

In the parable of the sower, the stony soil represents foolish people who refuse to spend time understanding the gospel. They are defined by their feelings, not by using their minds. Such people receive the word with joy, but they are rootless. When trouble or persecution comes because of the gospel, they quickly fall away. They do not persevere to the end because they do not know God's word nor do they want to. It is too much for these false Christians to spend five minutes in the Bible. But true Christians, like the good soil people, will know the gospel and God's will, design, and purpose for them from daily reading God's infallible word. "The one who received the seed that fell on good soil is the man who hears the word and understands it. He produces a crop, yielding a hundred, sixty or thirty times what was sown" (Matt. 13:23).

Murmuring Christians are foolish and mindless. They refuse to exercise their minds to know the Scripture and do not rise early to spend time in the word of God. When trouble comes, they cannot resist temptation and say, "It is written."

True Christians, however, know that through tribulations God works for our eternal good. They know that tribulations initiate a process that results in our sanctification—the beautification of our heart, which is a prerequisite to glorification.

Like a silversmith who purifies silver by heating it in a crucible, God refines us through fiery trials to make us holy, blameless, and fit for heaven. God declares, "In the whole land . . . two-thirds will be struck down and perish; yet one-third will be left in it. This third I will bring into the fire; I will refine them like silver and test them like gold. They will call on my name and I will answer them; I will say, 'They are my people,' and they will say, 'The LORD is our God'" (Zech. 13:8–9).

The psalmist also speaks of God's use of affliction in our lives. In Psalm 119 he writes, "Before I was afflicted I went astray, but now I obey your word" (v. 67); "It was good for me to be afflicted so that I might learn your decrees" (v. 71); "I know, O LORD, that your laws are righteous, and in faithfulness you have afflicted me" (v. 75); "If your law had not been my delight, I would have perished in my affliction" (v. 92). In the midst of his affliction, this man was reading God's word and delighting in it and receiving its comfort.

Paul next gives more reasons why we can rejoice in our sufferings: suffering produces endurance, endurance produces proof of character, proof of character produces hope, and hope does not disappoint *"because God has poured out his love into our hearts by the Holy Spirit."*

Suffering Produces Endurance

We can rejoice in suffering because we know the pressure of tribulation produces endurance. Tribulations reveal our impatience and produce patience. Nothing else can produce in us the ability to endure pressure. Nothing else can develop our spiritual muscle power.

Tribulations destroy human self-confidence and pride, causing us to rely on God and say, "I can do everything through him who gives me strength" (Phil. 4:13). Paul writes, "Indeed, in our hearts we felt the sentence of death. But this happened that we might not rely on ourselves but on God, who raises the dead" (2 Cor. 1:9).

Suppose we are not reading the Bible or praying regularly. If we start to experience troubles, we will read the word more often, pray more frequently, seek Christian fellowship more earnestly, worship more regularly, and witness continually. Tribulations produce constancy in our Christian walk. We experience a kind of stress test that we pass by God's grace. That is why Peter, in chains, could sleep in jail; why Stephen, while being stoned, could pray for his killers as he saw the Lord; why the three Hebrew young men could walk with the Lord in the fiery furnace; why Daniel could sleep with the hungry lions; and why Paul, beaten and chained in prison, could sing, pray, and write epistles exhorting the saints to joyfully endure hardship like a good soldier.

If we sing and pray when we are going through tribulations, we know we are getting stronger. Endurance produced by tribulations helps us to know we are true saints.

We may testify that we are Christians, but God tests our testimony as he tested Abraham. He was asked to sacrifice his son Isaac, his beloved son of promise, and he passed the test. God said to him, "Do not lay a hand on the boy. . . . Do not do anything to him. Now I know that you fear God, because you have not withheld from me your son, your only son" (Gen. 22:12).

Endurance Produces Proof of Character

Another reason to rejoice is that endurance produces godliness, or proof of character. Endurance produces the state of being qualified. Paul writes about God-accredited, God-certified servants (1 Thess. 2:4). Endurance produces proof that we are of good character. It produces godliness that we may share in God's holiness (Heb. 12:10). We have a harvest of righteousness and peace as we endure God's discipline.

James says, "Consider it pure joy, my brothers, whenever you face trials of many kinds, because you know that the testing of your faith develops perseverance. Perseverance must finish its work so that you may be mature and complete, not lacking anything" (James 1:2–4). The testing of our faith develops endurance, but it takes time. God's work in us through trials is finished when we sing, pray, and rejoice even when experiencing tribulations. His purpose is that we may be mature; God does not want immaturity.

We may want to remain infants to be fed, washed, and taken care of. But God wants his children to reflect his image by having his holy character. James continues, "Blessed is the man who perseveres under trial, because when he has stood the test, he will receive the crown of life that God has promised to those who love him" (James 1:12). Sanctification even through tribulations is the necessary prerequisite and prelude to our glorification.

Proof of Character Produces Hope

In our natural thought, we would expect that sufferings would destroy our hope of being glorified. But tribulations, in fact, strengthen our hope by weaning us from focusing on ourselves and the world, and turning us to God. Tribulations make us heaven-focused. They cure our worldliness—the lust of the flesh, the lust of the eyes, and the boasting of what we possess in this world—so that, instead of boasting about possessions and ourselves, we boast in God. The things of this world become strangely dim through the ministry of God-ordained sufferings.

In the pitch darkness of tribulations, true Christians see the glory star in the heavens very clearly. This guides us to the third heaven, to paradise, to Abraham's bosom, to God, even as the star guided the three wise men to Bethlehem to Jesus to worship him.

Romans 4 taught us that Abraham believed against hope and on the basis of hope that God was able to perform what he had promised. Proven character brought about by tribulations and endurance produces a strong hope of our future glorification, not a hope of getting rich and famous here and now.

Paul explains, "Now if we are children, then we are heirs—heirs of God and co-heirs with Christ, if indeed we share in his sufferings in order that we may also share in his glory. I consider that our present sufferings are not worth comparing with the glory that will be revealed in us" (Rom. 8:17–18). Those who are being sanctified through sufferings enjoy a greater hope of their coming glory. Peter states, "In this you greatly rejoice, though now for a little while you may have had to suffer grief in all kinds of trials. These have come so that your faith—of greater worth than gold, which perishes even though refined by fire—may be proved genuine and may result in praise, glory and honor when Jesus Christ is revealed" (1 Pet. 1:6–7).

Hope Does Not Disappoint

Another reason we can rejoice is that the certain hope of our coming glorification will not disappoint us, for it is not an illusion. It does not shame us even in this life. That is why Paul declares, "I am not ashamed of the gospel, because it is the power of God for the salvation of everyone who believes: first for the Jew, then for the Gentile" (Rom. 1:16). Paul wrote to Timothy from prison, "So do not be ashamed to testify about our Lord, or ashamed of me his prisoner. But join with me in suffering for the gospel, by the power of God, who has saved us and called us to a holy life" (2 Tim. 1:8–9).

Do you expect any modern preacher to say, "Join with me in suffering"? Yet that is what Paul is telling Timothy. He continues: "That is why I am suffering as I am. Yet I am not ashamed, because I know whom I have believed, and am convinced that he is able to guard what I have entrusted to him for that day" (v. 12). We must acknowledge that the reason we do not witness to Jesus Christ is that we are ashamed of him, of the Bible, of miracles, and of heaven. We have accepted the unbelieving world's thesis that intelligent people will not believe in God. Paul goes on: "May the Lord show mercy to the household of Onesiphorus, because he often refreshed me and was not ashamed of my chains" (v. 16).

Isaiah spoke about the certainty of this hope: "So this is what the Sovereign LORD says: 'See, I lay a stone in Zion, a tested stone, a precious cornerstone for a sure foundation; the one who trusts will never be dismayed'" (Isa. 28:16). That stone is Jesus Christ (1 Pet. 2:4–6). Hope in people, in a country, or in a politician regularly disappoints us. But the one who trusts in God and his promises will never be ashamed.

Paul therefore writes, "And we, who with unveiled faces all reflect the Lord's glory, are being transformed into his likeness with ever-increasing glory, which comes from the Lord, who is the Spirit" (2 Cor. 3:18). As we behold the Lord, especially in the Scriptures, a transforming work is done in us, and we are progressively transformed into his likeness. In other words, even now through the process of sanctification we are being glorified as we await our final glorification.

Elsewhere Paul says, "For our light and momentary troubles are achieving for us an eternal glory that far outweighs them all. So we fix our eyes not on what is seen, but on what is unseen. For what is seen is temporary, but what is unseen is eternal" (2 Cor. 4:17–18). We must not misunderstand Paul's words. He speaks of "light" troubles, which can include martyrdom, which he ultimately experienced. "Momentary" does not necessarily mean brief—our trials can last our entire lifetime. But compared to eternity, anything we suffer here is momentary, and compared to glory it is light. That is why our hope in God does not disappoint us. God ordains troubles, pain, disease, and broken relationships to wean us away from trusting in this world, that we may focus on our eternal home.

God Has Poured Out His Love

We can also rejoice in tribulations because *"God has poured out his love into our hearts"* (v. 5). This is not speaking about our love for God, but God's love for us. God's pouring out his love into our hearts is not a theoretical action. The love of God is poured out into our hearts once for all in a mighty effusion that fills our whole being, affecting our mind, will, and emotions. This outpouring of God's love into our hearts creates a responsive love in us for God and his people.

We glory in tribulations because God's love fills our hearts now and functions as God's signature guarantee that we will be glorified. Not only does the Father love us (Rom. 5:5, 8; 8:39), but the Son also loves us. Paul asks, "Who shall separate us from the love of Christ?" (Rom. 8:35). The implied answer is, "No one." This love of Christ powerfully motivates and compels us (2 Cor. 5:14).

Moreover, the Holy Spirit also loves us: "I urge you, brothers, by our Lord Jesus Christ and by the love of the Spirit, to join me in my struggle by praying to God for me" (Rom. 15:30). Paul exhorted young, timid Timothy, "For God did not give us a spirit of timidity, but a spirit of power, of love and of self-discipline" (2 Tim. 1:7). He is speaking about the Holy Spirit.

Christians are baptized in the name of the Father, the Son, and the Holy Spirit. All three persons of the Godhead love us, and this love registers in our hearts. We know this love experientially and existentially. It is not theoretical. So we rejoice in tribulations.

This love guarantees our ultimate and final salvation, which is our glorification. This love of God to us is the spring of our love to God. "We love because he first loved us" (1 John 4:19). This love controls, captivates, and capacitates us. It empowers us to rejoice in tribulations, even to the point of cheerfully enduring martyrdom. By this mighty effusion of God's love into our hearts, we are being hugged by the Father, the Son, and the Holy Spirit. We are being kissed and caressed as dearly loved children, and we hear words of love spoken to our hearts. God's love in abundance is poured out into us, and from us it flows out to others. As God's love flows into us, it must flow out, bearing witness to the world about Jesus Christ and his saving work in behalf of us. As Jesus said concerning the baptism in the Holy Spirit, "If anyone is thirsty, let him come to me and drink. Whoever believes in me, as the Scripture has said, streams of living water will flow from within him" (John 7:37–38).

As God works in us, we work out our salvation with fear and trembling (Phil. 2:12–13). His love does not trickle into our hearts drop by drop; it comes in as a flood upon the dry, parched land of our heart. It is poured out lavishly and in profusion even as the Holy Spirit was poured out on the Day of Pentecost: "'In the last days,' God says, 'I will pour out my Spirit on all people'" (Acts 2:17). *Ekcheō* means "outpouring in abundance." We see this idea also in Acts 2:33: "Exalted to the right hand of God, [Jesus] has received from the Father the promised Holy Spirit and has poured out what you now see and hear." And not only was the Holy Spirit poured out on the Jewish people, but he was also poured out upon the Gentiles: "The circumcised believers who had come with Peter were astonished that the gift of the Holy Spirit had been poured out even on the Gentiles" (Acts 10:45). The word is used again in Titus 3:5–6: "He saved us through the washing of rebirth and renewal by the Holy Spirit, whom he poured out on us generously through Jesus Christ our Savior" (see also Luke 11:13). I hope we will seek the Holy Spirit. When God pours out his Holy Spirit upon us, the Spirit takes control of our mind, will, and emotions, that we may live a joyful and triumphant life.

This love is not theoretical, based on study of theology or the history of Christ's death on the cross, though these things are important to study. This outpouring of love is an experience every true Christian can have in his being now. Dr. Martyn Lloyd-Jones says it is a direct activity of God, not merely a deduction that God loves us.[1] It is experiential. It is the highest form of assurance that we are children of God. And so we shall be like him when we shall see him.

Poured Out by the Holy Spirit

This love of God which is shed abroad in our hearts, which can never be taken away from us, which fills our hearts to overflowing and creates in us a responsive love to God and his people, is distributed to us by the Holy Spirit. It is what happens when a believer is baptized in the Holy Spirit. This is what happened on the Day of Pentecost: "All of them were filled with the Holy Spirit and began to speak in other tongues as the Spirit enabled them" (Acts 2:4).

This filling is not just the privilege of the one hundred and twenty; every believer can experience it. On the Day of Pentecost the crowd asked the disciples, "Brothers, what shall we do?" Peter answered, "Repent and be baptized, every one of you, in the name of Jesus Christ for the forgiveness of your sins. And you will receive the gift of the Holy Spirit" (Acts 2:37–38). Paul speaks of this as well: "And you also were included in Christ when you heard the word of truth, the gospel of your salvation. Having believed, you were marked in him with a seal, the promised Holy Spirit, who is a deposit guaranteeing our inheritance until the redemption of those who are God's possession—to the praise of his glory" (Eph. 1:13–14).

In Acts 19 we find a historical example of how it happened. When Paul came to Ephesus, he found twelve disciples whom he thought were Christians but were not. They had only heard of John's baptism.

> So Paul asked, "Then what baptism did you receive?" "John's baptism," they replied. Paul said, "John's baptism was a baptism of repentance. He told the people to believe in the one coming after him, that is, in Jesus." On hearing this, they were baptized

1   Lloyd-Jones, Romans, vol. 4, Assurance, 80–88.

into the name of the Lord Jesus. When Paul placed his hands on them, the Holy Spirit came on them, and they spoke in tongues and prophesied. (Acts 19:3–6)

First these disciples heard the true gospel from Paul and were baptized; subsequently they were baptized in the Holy Spirit.

When a believer is baptized in the Holy Spirit, sealed with the Holy Spirit, and given the deposit and firstfruits of the Holy Spirit once-for-all, his final salvation is guaranteed. Paul writes, "Now it is God who makes both us and you stand firm in Christ. He anointed us, set his seal of ownership on us, and put his Spirit in our hearts as a deposit, guaranteeing what is to come" (2 Cor. 1:21–22). Our glorification is guaranteed. We can make the same connection from Romans 8:23: "Not only so, but we ourselves, who have the firstfruits of the Spirit, groan inwardly as we wait eagerly for our adoption as sons, the redemption of our bodies."

We have many reasons to rejoice in tribulations. This Holy Spirit is the guarantee that we shall be saved, come what may. People can arrest or kill us for preaching what the Bible says. But we can rejoice, knowing that we have the Holy Spirit, who is the guarantee that we shall enjoy our final salvation, that we shall be glorified, that we shall be like Christ, and that we shall be blessed with the ultimate blessing of the beatific vision of God.

Christianity is not merely theoretical. As we go through the sufferings, the Spirit of God ministers to us in our hearts, thus we sing in the midst of troubles. Jesus says, "Whoever has my commands and obeys them, he is the one who loves me. He who loves me will be loved by my Father, and I too will love him and show myself to him" (John 14:21). What a revelation! What a manifestation of God into our inner being that completely satisfies us and makes us happy! The person who cannot be made happy by Jesus is not a true Christian. It is God's business to make us happy. Our hearts are restless until they find rest in God. Jesus tells us, "If anyone loves me, he will obey my teaching. My Father will love him, and we will come to him and make our home with him" (John 14:23). This glorious truth should cheer us up. Again, Paul writes, "You became imitators of us and of the Lord; in spite of severe suffering, you welcomed the message with the joy given by the Holy Spirit" (1 Thess. 1:6). This Holy Spirit releases love and joy to our hearts. He distributes to our hearts every grace we need, including "love, joy, peace, patience, kindness, goodness, faithfulness, gentleness and self-control" (Gal. 5:22–23).

If you are murmuring in your troubles, let me encourage you from God's word: "Now, brothers, we want you to know about the grace that God has given the Macedonian churches. Out of the most severe trial, their overflowing joy and their extreme poverty welled up in rich generosity" (2 Cor. 8:1–2). When the Holy Spirit dwells in us, he grants us grace to do everything God wants us to do. Paul asserts, "And God is able to make all grace abound to you, so that in all things at all times, having all that you need, you will abound in every good work" (2 Cor. 9:8). Elsewhere Paul writes, "But he said to me, 'My grace is sufficient for you, for my power is made perfect in weakness.' Therefore I will boast all the more gladly about my weaknesses, so that Christ's power may rest on me. That is why, for Christ's sake, I delight in weaknesses, in insults, in hardships, in persecutions, in difficulties. For when I am weak, then I am strong" (2 Cor. 12:9–10). Tribulations make us weak so that we will look to God.

What if we are not experiencing this great love, joy, and peace? It may be because of sin in our lives. Paul warns, "Do not grieve the Holy Spirit of God, with whom you were sealed for the day of redemption" (Eph. 4:30). When Christ sets us free through the gospel, we are enabled to love God and keep his commandments. But we are also free to sin. When we sin and continue to sin, we will not experience these graces of love, joy, and peace. If the Holy Spirit is grieved, how can we be happy? Read Psalms 32 and 51, where we find David's own testimony of the misery he was in before he confessed and forsook his sins.

The kingdom of God is like the house of the confessing prodigal: there is singing, dancing, and feasting. It is righteousness, peace, and joy in the Holy Spirit. But a sinning prodigal cannot enjoy it until he repents and comes home. Then he will be greeted, embraced, kissed, hugged, and received back as a son. So let us repent and come home to our heavenly Father. Let us rejoice as children of God, even in tribulations that produce our sanctification. Let us rejoice, because we know the Father's will and purpose. Suffering produces sanctification, which is the beauty of holiness.

Without pain, we will not gain endurance; without endurance, we cannot grow in godliness; without godliness, we have no hope. Therefore, although I do not pray for sufferings, when they come, I will embrace them. I will even try to rejoice because of them, knowing God's purpose in sending them. And God has also sent the Holy Spirit, who distributes his unchanging, infinite love to us, that we may endure to the end. He who endures to the end will be saved.

23

Proof of the Father's Love

⁶You see, at just the right time, when we were still powerless, Christ died for the ungodly. ⁷Very rarely will anyone die for a righteous man, though for a good man someone might possibly dare to die. ⁸But God demonstrates his own love for us in this: While we were still sinners, Christ died for us.

Romans 5:6–8

People are always making promises. A young man may promise a young woman that he loves her and wants to marry her, but if she has any sense, she may say, "Prove that you love me."

I have heard many promises, agreements, and confessions that later proved to be meaningless. But Romans 5:6–8 declares that God the Father is not just making a promise when he says he loves us; he has proved his love for us beyond disputation: *"But God demonstrates his own love for us in this: While we were still sinners, Christ died for us"* (v. 8).

Definition of God's Love

There are four words for love in the Greek language. *Storgē* speaks of affection within the family between parents and children. *Philia* means love between friends. *Eros* refers to sexual love. *Agapē* describes the highest form of love. It is very rarely used in classical Greek but is commonly found in the New Testament. *Agapē* speaks especially of the holy, gracious, everlasting, sacrificial love of God to sinful man. It is the type of love Paul is speaking about in Romans 5. Elsewhere he states, "Christ loved the church and gave himself up for her" (Eph. 5:25); "The Son of God . . . loved me and gave himself for me" (Gal. 2:20). John also speaks about this *agapē* love: "For God so loved the world that he gave his one and only Son" (John 3:16).

Agapē love gives, serves, sacrifices, and dies for another. It is the type of love Jacob demonstrated when he worked seven years as a shepherd for Laban to gain Rachel as his wife (Gen. 29:30). Othniel similarly proved his love for Achsah by conquering Debir (Judg. 1:12–13). David proved his love for Michal, King Saul's daughter, by killing two hundred Philistines (1 Sam. 18:20–27). But the greatest demonstration of *agapē* love is that of God the Father, who showed his love by giving his only Son to die on the cross to secure our salvation. Christ's death on the cross is the proof of God's everlasting love, a love so great that it is beyond human comprehension, a love that even our death cannot destroy. It is this love of the Father that has enabled saints of God throughout history to suffer cruel persecution and death at the hands of their enemies.

Have you experienced this love of God the Father? Paul states that the love of God is poured out in abundance in our hearts by the Holy Spirit, who is given to us (Rom. 5:5). Every true Christian can experience it. When we do, we will know it with our minds, feel it with our emotions, and be motivated to love God and obey his commands with joy. This love compels us to boldly share the good news of salvation with others and enables us to rejoice even in tribulations. Let us consider three proofs of God's love for us from this passage.

God's Love Seen in the Love of the Father

The first proof is the Father's own love for us. God loves us with a love that goes beyond the love God has for the rest of his creation. Under his common grace, the Father shows love even to those who hate him. Jesus instructs, "Love your enemies and pray for those who persecute you, that you may be sons of your Father in heaven. He causes his sun to rise on the evil and the good, and sends rain on the righteous and the unrighteous" (Matt. 5:44–45). Paul also speaks of God's common grace: "He has shown kindness by giving you rain from heaven and crops in their seasons; he provides you with plenty of food and fills your hearts with joy" (Acts 14:17).

God gives food and shelter to all his creatures. He feeds the birds and clothes the lilies of the field (Matt. 6:26–30). James says, "Every good and perfect gift is from above, coming down from the Father of the heavenly lights, who does not change like shifting shadows" (James 1:17).

But God loves his elect with his special love that saves them from their sins and makes them beloved saints. The Father gave his only Son to die in behalf of them only. Isaiah tells us, "'Come now, let us reason together,' says the LORD. 'Though your sins are like scarlet, they shall be as white as snow; though they are red as crimson, they shall be like wool'" (Isa. 1:18). Isaiah also declares, "We all, like sheep, have gone astray, each of us has turned to his own way; and the LORD has laid on him the iniquity of us all" (Isa. 53:6). In light of this great love of God, Daniel prayed in Babylon:

> Now, our God, hear the prayers and petitions of your servant. For your sake, O Lord, look with favor on your desolate sanctuary. Give ear, O God, and hear; open your eyes and see the desolation of the city that bears your Name. We do not make requests of you because we are righteous, but because of your great mercy. O Lord, listen! O Lord, forgive! O Lord, hear and act! For your sake, O my God, do not delay, because your city and your people bear your Name. (Dan. 9:17–19)

In response to God's love, we are to love God with all our heart, mind, soul, and strength. And God may test our love for him as he tested Abraham's. At the last moment God spared Isaac from being sacrificed, declaring: "Do not lay a hand on the boy. Do not do anything to him. Now I know that you fear God, because you have not withheld from me your son, your only son" (Gen. 22:12). But herein we also see the great love of the Father for us: he did not spare his only Son, but handed him over to wicked men to be crucified. So Paul says, "He who did not spare his own Son, but gave him up for us all—how will he not also, along with him, graciously give us all things?" (Rom. 8:32). God's love shed abroad in our hearts is the love manifested on the cross.

Paul delights in expounding on this love: "Praise be to the God and Father of our Lord Jesus Christ, who has blessed us in the heavenly realms with every spiritual blessing in Christ. For he chose us in him before the creation of the world to be holy and blameless in his sight. In love he predestined us to be adopted as his sons through Jesus Christ, in accordance with his pleasure and will—to the praise of his glorious grace, which he has freely given us in the One he loves" (Eph. 1:3–6). He also says, "For those God foreknew [foreloved] he also predestined to be conformed to the likeness of his Son" (Rom. 8:29). Again, Paul declares, "'No eye has seen, no ear has heard, no mind has conceived what God has prepared for those who love him'—but God has revealed it to us by his Spirit" (1 Cor. 2:9–10). Of this great demonstration of God's love, Peter declares, "This man was handed over to you by God's set purpose and foreknowledge; and you, with the help of wicked men, put him to death by nailing him to the cross" (Acts 2:23).

The height and depth and length and width of God's love for us is beyond human comprehension (Eph. 3:18–19). Yet we can in a measure understand it through Christ's sacrifice on our behalf. John says, "This is how God showed his love among us: He sent his one and only Son into the world that we might live through him. This is love: not that we loved God, but that he loved us and sent his Son as an atoning sacrifice for our sins" (1 John 4:9–10).

The day is coming when God will pour out his wrath in his righteous judgment. Even now, Paul says, "The wrath of God is being revealed from heaven against all the godlessness and wickedness of men who suppress the truth by their wickedness" (Rom. 1:18). But not only is the wrath of God being revealed, the love of God is also being revealed. That is what Paul is declaring in Romans 5:8. Through the cross of Christ, God the Father is revealing and clearly proving to all thinking beings of the universe his unique love for sinners. Paul writes that the Father presented Jesus Christ "as a sacrifice of atonement" (Rom. 3:25). Let us, therefore, survey the wondrous cross, and be amazed and impressed, not only by the Father's promise of love, but also by his proof of it.

"God demonstrates his own love for us in this: While we were still sinners, Christ died for us" (v. 8). Paul's use of the present tense (*sunistēsin*) highlights that the cross is constantly unveiling and placarding the love of the Father for us, that we may look to it

and be saved. The Lord exhorts us, "Turn to me and be saved, all you ends of the earth; for I am God, and there is no other" (Isa. 45:22). Jesus tells us, "Just as Moses lifted up the snake in the desert, so the Son of Man must be lifted up, that everyone who believes in him may have eternal life" (John 3:14–15). When Paul came to Corinth, he determined not to know anything but Jesus Christ and him crucified (1 Cor. 2:2). To the Galatians he said, "Before your very eyes Jesus Christ was clearly portrayed as crucified" (Gal. 3:1). The charge of every preacher is to declare to all the Father's love for sinners, which he demonstrated by sacrificing his own Son on their behalf.

Salvation is not a joint venture in which we have fifty percent interest and God has fifty percent. It is not even a matter of us having one percent and God ninety-nine. Salvation is all by grace from first to last. This salvation is of the Father. Hell-deserving people are given heaven; death-deserving people are given eternal life. And because our salvation is all of grace, it is totally secure. If the Father loved us because we loved him, he would only love us as long as we loved him. There is no security in such an arrangement. But our salvation depends not on our loveliness or holiness. It depends on the constancy of the love of the Father. God is not *promising* to love us; he has *proven* in history that he loves us. The greatest love is the Father's love for his enemies, revealed in Christ's death on the cross.

Paul prays, "May the Lord direct your hearts into God's love" (2 Thess. 3:5). I hope we will pray this when we are discouraged: "Lord, direct my heart into your eternal, sovereign, unchanging, constant love for me." Elsewhere Paul encourages us: "For I am convinced that neither death nor life, neither angels nor demons, neither the present nor the future, nor any powers, neither height nor depth, nor anything else in all creation, will be able to separate us from the love of God that is in Christ Jesus our Lord" (Rom. 8:38–39).

God's Love Seen in Christ's Death

The second proof of the love of God is the death of his Son. Paul writes, "For if, when we were God's enemies, we were reconciled to him through the death of his Son, how much more, having been reconciled, shall we be saved through his life!" (Rom. 5:10). First of all, this verse tells us that Jesus is God's Son. He is not just a prophet or an angel, but the one and only beloved Son of God. Jesus was not a mere sinner dying on behalf of another sinner to spare him temporarily from physical death. No, the Son of God died for sinners to give them eternal life. He is the sinless God-man, the eternal Deity who became mortal. God sent his Son in the likeness of sinful flesh to die our eternal death for our infinite sin. Four times Paul uses the word "huper" (in behalf of) in Romans 5:6–8, stressing the point that while someone may dare to die in behalf of a good man, Christ died *huper asebôn*, in behalf of the ungodly.

The emphasis in this passage is not on Christ's life, teaching, or miracles, but on his death. The Bible teaches that all have sinned and must die. We all became sinners through Adam's one sin. Every human being is conceived in sin, born a sinner, practices sin daily, and must die eternal death and go to hell unless God intervenes. But God did intervene, and now we are spared because the sinless Son of God died for our benefit, in our interest, as our substitute. We sinned, but Christ died. He did not die as a martyr, nor did he die for his own sins, for he was sinless. He died so that we will not die eternally. And because of his death, those who believe in him have crossed from death to life (John 5:24). Jesus promises, "Whoever lives and believes in me will never die" (John 11:26).

Jesus spoke about laying down his life for his sheep, meaning his people: "The reason my Father loves me is that I lay down my life—only to take it up again. No one takes it from me, but I lay it down of my own accord. I have authority to lay it down and authority to take it up again. This command I received from my Father" (John 10:17–18; see also vv. 11 and 15). Because he loved us, the Father gave the Son the assignment of laying down his life in our behalf. In the death of Jesus Christ, therefore, we see the love of the Father.

These are not just promises without fulfillment. When John saw Jesus, he declared, "Look, the Lamb of God, who takes away the sin of the world!" (John 1:29). When Karl Barth came to the United States, he was asked, "What is the greatest thought that ever went through your mind?" He simply said, "Jesus loves me, this I know, for the Bible tells me so."[1] The entire Old Testament sacrificial system pointed to Christ's substitutionary death. The Son of God became incarnate to taste death for every man (Heb. 2:9).

Paul says, "For Christ's love compels us, because we are convinced that one died for [huper] all, and therefore all died." There is the idea that Christ's death is in place of the death of another. "And he died for [huper] all, that those who live should no longer live for themselves but for him who died for [huper] them and was raised again" (2 Cor. 5:14–15). Compelled by the love of God, we henceforth live for him who died for us.

The love of the Father is seen in the death of his Son. That is clear proof that God loves us. And we are told that Christ died *kata kairon* (at the right time). It was God's plan that his Son take on human flesh in his appointed time and die for the sins of those the Father foreloved and predestinated. When all human efforts for self-salvation failed, whether false religions or human philosophies or social action, Christ came. "'The time has come,' [Jesus] said. 'The kingdom of God is near. Repent and believe the good news!'" (Mark 1:15). Paul says, "But when the time had fully come, God sent his Son, born of a woman, born under law, to redeem those under law" (Gal. 4:4–5).

Christ died and went to hell on the cross in our place for our salvation. Therefore, we will not die but will live with God forever in heaven. We are blessed with all spiritual blessings in Jesus Christ in heavenly places before the creation of the world.

God's Love Seen in the Salvation of Sinners

The third proof that God loves us is that he saves wicked people. Christ did not die for the righteous. No one dies for a Pharisee like Saul of Tarsus, who said that he was perfect as far as legalistic righteousness was concerned.

Christ also did not die for good people who move beyond legalism. Such people may be benefactors and show kindness to others. Paul says some people perhaps may dare to die for good people.

Neither did Christ die for nice people. What the Holy Spirit is saying in Romans 5:6–8 is that Christ died for wicked sinners.

---

1   Quoted by Boice, *Romans*, vol. 2, *Reign of Grace*, 539.

Such an act of love never happened in history until Jesus came, and it has not happened since. A man may die for his family or friends, but not for wicked people.

So God proved his love for us because his Son died for us when we were helpless, ungodly, sinful, and at enmity with him. Paul calls us "helpless ones": *"You see, at just the right time, when we were still powerless, Christ died for the ungodly"* (v. 6). Suffering from total moral inability, we could do nothing to please God; we could only do dead works. We were not well or merely sick; we were *dead* in trespasses and sins and thoroughly regulated by the devil. We were sons of disobedience (Eph. 2:1–3). Yet although it was impossible for us to save ourselves, we did not understand that truth because unregenerate, powerless people cannot understand spiritual things. We could not see or enter the kingdom of God, nor did we seek God. So God himself provided a solution: "But because of his great love for us, God, who is rich in mercy, made us alive with Christ" (Eph. 2:4–5).

Not only were we helpless, but we were also ungodly. By nature man is ungodly, and the wrath of God is justly directed against him. As a fool, he says in his heart, "There is no God" (Ps. 14:1). He is godless, lawless, and refuses to worship and serve God. In fact, he only does the opposite of God's will. Yet in this we see the love of the Father: God sent his Son to die for the ungodly, pouring out his wrath not on us but on his own Son.

Not only were we ungodly and helpless, but we were also sinners. Paul declares, "All have sinned and fall short of the glory of God" (Rom. 3:23). Sinners relish in challenging God's sovereignty and violating his laws. A sinner actively opposes God's attributes—his wisdom, sovereignty, holiness, and power. How can God love such unlovely sinners? If he were but a man, he could not, for human love is based on the attractiveness of the object of love. But God demonstrates his special heavenly love by loving terrible sinners like us.

Finally, we were at enmity with God (Rom. 5:10). Not only were we helpless, ungodly sinners, but we were also God's sworn enemies. We declared war against God, and God declared war against us. "The sinful mind is hostile to God" (Rom. 8:7). As God's enemies, we wanted to kill him. In fact, the essence of sin is enmity against God. That is why Jesus was crucified. Yet Christ's death was part of God's plan. The Father handed his Son over to be crucified. The wrath of God that was due us was poured out upon his own Son. He did not spare him that he may spare us from eternal damnation.

How much more proof could you ask for that the Father loves us! Therefore, survey the wondrous cross. Study the Bible carefully. Fill your mind with God's word, and your heart will be filled to overflowing with the love of God, so much so that you will be able to rejoice in tribulations and will live to please God. This love of God the Father and Christ his Son will motivate you to proclaim daily the good news of the gospel by the power of the Holy Spirit.

The Roman Christians were like us—helpless, ungodly, sinful, enemies of God. Yet because of the love of the Father and the Son applied to them by the Holy Spirit, Paul addresses them in Romans 1:7 as "beloved," "effectually called," and "saints." And not only were they beloved of the Father, the Son, and the Holy Spirit, but we are too. We were helpless, ungodly, sinners, enemies of God—but no longer so. We have been justified and redeemed. Now we are called effectually to be God's beloved children.

This is good news. The Father loved us, he loves us, and he will love us throughout all eternity. Even when we falter and fall, he will come and pick us up. He may discipline us, but he will never stop loving us. This love of the Father is everlasting and unchanging. Therefore, I urge you to believe it and live forever in joy unspeakable and full of glory.

And if you are not yet a believer in Christ, may you confess to God, "I am not righteous or good. I am a morally corrupt, ungodly sinner, and a sworn enemy of God. But I understand that you love sinners with an everlasting, unchanging love. I believe in your Son, Jesus Christ, who died in my place on the cross in history. Lord Jesus, save me, both now and forever." Jesus saves only sinners. Come to him as you are, and he will receive you and save you. Jesus justifies the ungodly.

24

Eternal Security

⁹Since we have now been justified by his blood, how much more shall we be saved from God's wrath through him! ¹⁰For if, when we were God's enemies, we were reconciled to him through the death of his Son, how much more, having been reconciled, shall we be saved through his life!

Romans 5:9–10

All of us are going to die one day unless Christ comes back first. But how can we be certain that we will be raised up with a glorious body to dwell with God forever after we die? How can we be sure that God will not pour out his wrath upon us on the day of judgment? Is it possible for us to face death with complete assurance of our final salvation? Romans 5:9–10 answers these questions.

Romans 5:1–11 speaks of God the Father's love for us, a love that guarantees not only our present salvation, but also our future glorification. Salvation (*sōzō*) is used in three tenses in the Bible: we have been saved (justified), we are being saved (sanctified), and we will be saved (glorified). These usages speak about salvation from the penalty, power, and presence of sin. In justification, the penalty of sin has been dealt with once for all. In sanctification, the power of sin is broken, and we are free to overcome sin. As Christians, we do not need to give in to our sinful urges. And in glorification, the very presence of sin will be removed from us.

From all eternity God planned a complete salvation for his people. God declares, "I have loved you with an everlasting love" (Jer. 31:3). God has loved us from all eternity with an everlasting love to achieve for us an everlasting salvation (Isa. 45:17). He has accomplished for us eternal redemption (Heb. 9:12) and appointed us to eternal life (Acts 13:48). Paul writes, "The wages of sin is death, but the gift of God is eternal life in Christ Jesus our Lord" (Rom. 6:23). This eternal life is for our eternal joy (Isa. 35:10). True Christians rejoice always, even in tribulations, because they enjoy the eternal security of their ultimate salvation.

Paul presents logical arguments for this eternal security in Romans 5:9–10. Dr. Lloyd-Jones remarks that these two verses present the most powerful argument found in the entirety of Scripture for our assurance of salvation.[1] We must apply the reasoning powers of our renewed minds to these great truths. It is spiritual to think logically and sinful not to. Only a logical Christian can enjoy the full assurance of his final salvation that God guarantees. If we do not like to study and think, we will be emotional, unsteady people. Our final argument should not be the tears we so easily shed. Our final argument should always be what God has spoken in his word.

The Logical Arguments of Paul

The first reason, then, for our eternal security is derived from the logical arguments Paul makes in this passage. There are two types of arguments in the Bible: from minor to major and from major to minor. For example, Jesus argues from minor to major: "Look at the birds of the air; they do not sow or reap or store away in barns, and yet your heavenly Father feeds them. Are you not much more valuable than they?" (Matt. 6:26). In other words, if God takes care of birds, then logically and necessarily he will certainly take care of his people. The same passage argues that if God takes care of the lilies of the field, he will surely take care of us as well. Another minor to major argument Jesus uses is: "If you, then, though you are evil, know how to give good gifts to your children, how much more will your Father in heaven give good gifts to those who ask him!" (Matt. 7:11).

Then there are the arguments from major to minor, the *a fortiori* ("how much more") arguments. Paul uses four of them in Romans

---

1   Lloyd-Jones, *Romans*, vol. 4, *Assurance*, 128.

5 (vv. 9, 10, 15, 17). For example, he says, *"Since we have now been justified by his blood, how much more shall we be saved from God's wrath through him!"* (v. 9). In justifying us by Christ's blood, God the Father accomplished the most difficult thing already at the highest possible cost to him. He did so for the benefit of the most undeserving people—helpless, ungodly enemies of God who did nothing to merit salvation, but did everything to merit eternal wrath. Therefore, we can be absolutely certain that he will also accomplish the less difficult work of giving us the final installment of our salvation.

"For if, when we were God's enemies, we were reconciled to him through the death of his Son, how much more, having been reconciled, shall we be saved through his life!" (v. 10). Again, this argument is from major to minor. The major issue is reconciliation of enemies to God. The argument is that if justification and reconciliation have been achieved by God through the death of his Son, how much more will God complete our salvation by giving us sinless, glorious bodies in the life of his Son! Knowing this powerful argument, we can die in complete assurance of our final salvation. If the more difficult thing is already accomplished, the less difficult thing will more readily be accomplished. Our resurrection is guaranteed; it is a logical necessity that we can count on, both now and in the hour of our death. No one would question the financial ability of a man who bought a million-dollar house to put up some nice curtains. In the same way, if God has already done the difficult work, can we not trust him to do the easy task of putting the finishing touches on our salvation?

If God reconciled us while we were his enemies, he will certainly glorify us after we have become his friends. If the greatest benefit has been bestowed, the less will not be withheld. Western man has become an irrational existentialist, a feeling-centered being. But because the Holy Spirit is logical, let us be logical also and enjoy the eternal security of our final salvation that we learn about from this passage. The death of God's Son secured our justification and reconciliation; therefore, the life of his Son will give us all things. Paul declares, "He who did not spare his own Son, but gave him up for us all— how will he not also, along with him, graciously give us all things?" (Rom. 8:32). This includes our glorification.

Yet we may wonder how we can be sure that we will not be lost in the end. After all, we are still living in an evil world, and sin still dwells in us. We also acknowledge that we are weak and fallible, and that sinless perfection is impossible in this life. We may therefore wonder if God will pour out his wrath on us on the last day instead of glorifying us. Paul assures us in this passage that God surely will not. He cannot, for he has already justified and reconciled us on the sure basis of the death of his Son. He has done the most difficult thing for us, his enemies, at the cost of his Son's death. Now we are his friends, and he will save us fully by the resurrection life of his Son. We can, therefore, be fully assured of our eternal security.

Let us now look more closely at how Paul applies this logic to justification in verse 9 and reconciliation in verse 10.

The Logic of Justification

The second reason for eternal security is the fact that we have been justified: *"Since we have now been justified by his blood, how much more shall we be saved from God's wrath through him!"* (v. 9). If we are Christians, God has already justified us. We were helpless sinners who merited his wrath, yet God pronounced us righteous because his Son, the sinless God-man, died in our place to satisfy God's justice.

We must always remember this if we need assurance, especially in the hour of our death. In Jesus Christ we not only kept every law of God perfectly but we also suffered for every infraction of God's law. So in Christ we are not under sin and law, but under grace. All our sins are forgiven, and we are clothed with the divine righteousness of Christ. Already we are at peace with God and enjoy his presence. Justification is a present possession of each child of God, achieved by Christ's bloody sacrifice for our sins. This justification is the act of God the Father, the head of the Supreme Court of heaven. Paul throws out the challenge: "Who will bring any charge against those whom God has chosen?" (Rom. 8:33). The answer is no one, because it is God himself who justifies.

Justification is the opposite of condemnation. For us there is now no condemnation because we are in Christ by faith

(Rom. 8:1). God justified the ungodly, not on the basis of our works, regeneration, faith, sanctification, new obedience, or even on the basis of the work of Christ in us, but on the basis of what God himself did in and through Christ's death on the cross. God, who by no means clears the guilty, justified us on the basis of the objective shed blood of his Son. Our righteousness does not enter into it.

By his Son's shed blood, God's wrath against us has been propitiated. No more wrath remains to be poured out on us on the last day. Let the devil, our enemies, and even our own conscience accuse us. It does not matter; we are saved forever and eternally secure.

The Logic of Reconciliation

The third reason for this eternal security is divine reconciliation: *"For if, when we were God's enemies, we were reconciled to him through the death of his Son, how much more, having been reconciled, shall we be saved through his life!"* (v. 10). God accomplished the most difficult task of reconciling us to himself when we were still his enemies. As atheists, we were trying to kill God. And not only were we God's sworn enemies, but God himself was our enemy. It is illogical to wage war against the almighty God, but foolish people do it all the time. Yet God brought about objective reconciliation for us, his enemies, by the death of his Son on the cross.

Paul declares, "All this is from God, who reconciled us to himself through Christ and gave us the ministry of reconciliation: that God was reconciling the world to himself in Christ, not counting men's sins against them. And he has committed to us the message of reconciliation" (2 Cor. 5:18-19). Though God is the offended party, he removes the offense from the offending party. Usually, the offending party must go to the offended party and remove the cause of enmity. But no man can effectually deal with the enmity between God and man. Only God can; therefore, moved by his everlasting love, God reconciled his sworn enemies to himself by removing the cause of enmity—our sin, guilt, condemnation, and eternal death. He did so in the death of his Son. Now we are no longer enemies of God; we are God's friends, and more than that, his children. We are beloved of God and called to be his saints (Rom. 1:7). And if God accomplished the most difficult task of reconciliation while we were enemies, now that we are God's beloved friends, children, and saints, he certainly will complete our salvation.

When we study verses 9 and 10, we see five passive verbs: "having been justified," "having been reconciled" (twice), and "we will be saved" (twice). These verbs tell us that God is the one doing the work, not us. He justifies us, reconciles us, and will save us in the future. We, as God's elect, are recipients of these actions. We receive justification and reconciliation by faith; we do not perform these actions.

We will be saved from God's wrath on the last day because we have been justified and reconciled. Only God can separate us from his wrath, and he did. The crushing iron girder of God's wrath abides upon every unbeliever, but for us the wrath has been removed forever by God himself.

Our past justification and reconciliation, therefore, guarantee our enjoyment of the final installment of our salvation. "For those God foreknew he also predestined to be conformed to the likeness of his Son, that he might be the firstborn among many brothers. And those he predestined, he also called; those he called, he also justified; those he justified, he also glorified" (Rom. 8:29–30). There is a specific number of people the Father loved from all eternity, and in time he called them effectually and justified them. In fact, Paul says they are also already glorified. That is full assurance.

What about you? Are you convinced of your eternal security? You cannot find true security in money, health, a spouse, or children. They will all disappear, and you have to die. You came into this world alone through your mother's womb, and eventually you will also have to go out alone. But if you are a believer in Christ, you need not worry. If God is for us, who can be against us? The same God who foreknew us, predestinated us, called us, justified us, and reconciled us, will also glorify us.

That is why Paul declares, "Not only is this so, but we also rejoice in God" (Rom. 5:11). A Christian can rejoice in God even when everything else is changing. The Greek philosopher Heraclitus said the only thing we can count on is change. But God never changes. What he has promised, he fulfills. He cannot lie. Suppose you go to the doctor and he says you have only a few months left to live. If you are a Christian, you may be a little shaken at first. But then you will say, "I rejoice in God because he does not change. In fact, I am going to him who came to me, and I have full assurance that he will glorify me." I pray that we will all be fully assured of our final salvation and rejoice, not in this world, but in God.

Christ Our Mediator

The next reason we have for assurance of our ultimate salvation is that this salvation comes to us through our Lord Jesus Christ. Paul writes, "For there is one God and mediator between God and men, the man Christ Jesus, who gave himself as a ransom for all" (1 Tim. 2:5–6). This mediator is Jesus, who died and lives for us. Justification and reconciliation are achieved through the death of God's Son. The Greek uses a preposition *dia* (through) to tell us that our salvation is accomplished *through* the work of Jesus Christ. Therefore, if one does not believe in Jesus Christ, one cannot be saved.

Through the frequent use of *dia*, Paul emphasizes in Romans 5 that God achieves salvation, not through ourselves nor through any man, but only through Jesus, who alone is a fit mediator between God and man. So he writes,

1. "We have peace with God *through* our Lord Jesus Christ" (Rom. 5:1). A person who has not trusted in Christ has no peace. He is without God and without hope in this world;
2. "*Through* our Lord Jesus Christ we have gained access by faith into this grace in which we now stand" (Rom. 5:2);
3. "We shall be saved from God's wrath *through* Jesus Christ" (Rom. 5:9);
4. "We are reconciled to God *through* the death of his Son . . . how much more shall we be saved *through* his life" (Rom. 5:10);
5. "We rejoice in God *through* our Lord Jesus Christ, *through* whom we have now received reconciliation" (Rom. 5:11);
6. "We shall reign in life *through* the one man, Jesus Christ" (Rom. 5:17);
7. "*Through* the obedience of the one man the many will be made righteous" (Rom. 5:19);
8. "Grace reigns *through* righteousness unto eternal life *through* Jesus Christ our Lord" (Rom. 5:21).

This shows the importance of trusting in Jesus Christ alone for our eternal salvation. Full salvation comes to us only through Christ's death in behalf of guilty sinners. Sin is the most horrible thing in the world. Because we are sinners, either we must die, or someone who is fit must die in our place. God warned, "You must not eat from the tree of the knowledge of good and evil, for when you eat of it you will surely die" (Gen. 2:17). Paul explains, "Although they know God's righteous decree that those who do such things deserve death, they not only continue to do these very things but also approve of those who practice them" (Rom. 1:32). In this chapter he writes, "Therefore, just as sin entered the world through one man, and death through sin . . . in this way death came to all men, because all sinned" (Rom. 5:12).

The wages of sin is eternal death. We sinned; therefore, we must die. But Jesus died in our place, and we died in him. If anyone does not believe in Jesus Christ, he cannot be justified or reconciled to God. Belief in monotheism is not enough. We must believe in one God existing in three persons—the Father, the Son, and the Holy Spirit. The sole ground of our justification and reconciliation is the death of God's incarnate Son in our place. Jesus himself said, "No one comes to the Father except through me" (John 14:6). And John writes, "He who has the Son has life; he who does not have the Son of God does not have life" (1 John 5:12). John the Baptist declared, "Whoever believes in the Son has eternal life, but whoever rejects the Son will not see life, for God's wrath remains on him" (John 3:36).

Union with Christ

The next reason we have for complete assurance is our union with Christ. "In Christ" is used frequently in the New Testament to speak about our unbreakable union with Christ. Paul asks,

> What shall we say, then? Shall we go on sinning so that grace may increase? By no means! We died to sin; how can we live in it any longer? Or don't you know that all of us who were baptized into Christ Jesus were baptized into his death? We were therefore buried with him through baptism into death in order that, just as Christ was raised from the dead through the glory of the Father, we too may live a new life. . . . Now if we

died with Christ, we believe that we will also live with him."
(Rom. 6:1–4, 8)

By faith we have been united to Jesus Christ forever. When
he died for our sins, we died with him; when he was buried,
we were buried with him; when he rose, we rose with him. We
were under sin, but we are not any longer (Rom. 3:9; 6:14–18).
We were under the dominion of sin and law, but now we are
under grace because of our vital union with Christ by faith. Paul
says, "For Christ's love compels us, because we are convinced
that one died for all, and therefore all died" (2 Cor. 5:14). Our
sin problem is dealt with. Because Christ lives, we also live. Our
salvation never depends upon anything that we have ever done
or ever will do.

Jesus will never die again. Therefore, we do not have to be
anxious about our salvation. Paul puts such fears to rest: "Now
if we died with Christ, we believe that we will also live with
him. For we know that since Christ was raised from the dead,
he cannot die again; death no longer has mastery over him"
(Rom. 6:8–9). We are raised with Christ, who cannot die again;
therefore, we also will live forever. Jesus himself said so: "Because
I live, you also will live" (John 14:19).

Jesus said, "I am the vine; you are the branches. If a man remains
in me and I in him, he will bear much fruit; apart from me you
can do nothing" (John 15:5). We are united with Jesus Christ. He
is life, and from his life, life flows to us and we live. Paul speaks
about this vital union with the risen Christ:

> But Christ has indeed been raised from the dead, the firstfruits
> of those who have fallen asleep. For since death came through
> a man, the resurrection of the dead comes also through a man.
> For as in Adam all die, so in Christ all will be made alive.
> But each in his own turn: Christ, the firstfruits; then, when he
> comes, those who belong to him. (1 Cor. 15:20–23)

Jesus Intercedes for Us

Another reason we can have absolute assurance of our salvation
is because Jesus Christ, the living One, intercedes for us as our

high priest. "Who is he that condemns? Christ Jesus, who died—more than that, who was raised to life—is at the right hand of God and is also interceding for us" (Rom. 8:34). His intercession is effectual. He already prayed for us when he was on earth: "I will remain in the world no longer, but they are still in the world, and I am coming to you. Holy Father, protect them by the power of your name. . . . Father, I want those you have given me to be with me where I am, and to see my glory" (John 17:11, 24). We cannot see God's glory unless we are glorified, but we can be certain that the Father heard Christ's petition. Therefore, we can be certain that we will be glorified and able to see Christ's glory.

The Hebrews writer speaks also of this certainty: "Now there have been many of those priests, since death prevented them from continuing in office; but because Jesus lives forever, he has a permanent priesthood. Therefore he is able to save completely those who come to God through him, because he always lives to intercede for them" (Heb. 7:23–25). Because Christ is interceding for us, we can be assured of our eternal salvation.

Not only does the Lord Jesus intercede for us, but the Holy Spirit does also. "And he who searches our hearts knows the mind of the Spirit, because the Spirit intercedes for the saints in accordance with God's will" (Rom. 8:27). The Holy Spirit is now interceding in our behalf, and his prayer to God the Father is effectual. And not only does he intercede, but he also lives in us: "And if the Spirit of him who raised Jesus from the dead is living in you, he who raised Christ from the dead will also give life to your mortal bodies through his Spirit, who lives in you" (Rom. 8:11). In the Greek, the word translated "if" does not denote contingency or doubt; it is a statement of fact. In other words, Paul is saying this will happen because the Holy Spirit is dwelling in us. The indwelling Spirit of the living God guarantees our glorification.

The Father's Love

Not only are Jesus and the Holy Spirit interested in us, but God the Father is also interested in us. Paul writes, "And hope does not disappoint us, because God has poured out his love into our hearts by the Holy Spirit, whom he has given us" (Rom. 5:5).

Assurance comes to us not only by logical deduction, but also on the basis of an existential outpouring of God's love into our hearts. This is the most direct, immediate, and highest form of assurance we can experience. We feel and know that God loves us. It does not matter who else loves us; our heavenly Father does. Let everyone forsake us; our God will receive and take care of us.

Paul also says, "But God demonstrates his own love for us in this: While we were still sinners, Christ died for us" (Rom. 5:8). Elsewhere he states, "For I am convinced that neither death nor life, neither angels nor demons, neither the present nor the future, nor any powers, neither height nor depth, nor anything else in all creation, will be able to separate us from the love of God that is in Christ Jesus our Lord" (Rom. 8:38–39). Hold on to this certainty. When dark days come, when the storm rages, when the thunder rumbles and the lightning flashes, when the rain falls, when the political situation and economic life changes, and when all the foundations of man crumble, we need not worry: God loves us. Nothing can separate us from the love of our heavenly Father.

Jesus Christ Is Able

The next reason we have for assurance is the ability of Christ to save us. The Hebrews writer declares, "Therefore he is able to save completely those who come to God through him" (Heb. 7:25). Jesus is able to save us because he has an indestructible life, and we are linked to him. Additionally, the Hebrews author says, "Because he himself suffered when he was tempted, he is able to help those who are being tempted" (Heb. 2:18). Are you being tempted? Are you facing trouble? I offer you a Savior who is able to help you and bring you out of temptation, misery, and failure.

Paul says, "And God placed all things under his feet and appointed him to be head over everything for the church" (Eph. 1:22). Paul also writes, "Now to him who is able to do immeasurably more than all we ask or imagine, according to his power that is at work within us . . ." (Eph. 3:20). Jude exclaims, "To him who is able to keep you from falling and to present you before his glorious presence without fault and with great joy . . ." (Jude 24). And Jesus himself said, "I give them eternal life, and they shall never perish; no one can snatch them out of my hand" (John 10:28).

> He is able, he is able,
> I know my Lord is able.
> I know my Lord is able
> to carry me through.

God Finishes What He Starts

The final reason for assurance of eternal security is that God always finishes what he begins. Jesus spoke about man's tendency not to complete what he starts: "Suppose one of you wants to build a tower. Will he not first sit down and estimate the cost to see if he has enough money to complete it? For if he lays the foundation and is not able to finish it, everyone who sees it will ridicule him, saying, 'This fellow began to build and was not able to finish'" (Luke 14:28–30). But about God Paul writes, "He who began a good work in you will carry it on to completion until the day of Christ Jesus" (Phil. 1:6). God planned our salvation before the creation of the world. In the fullness of time he sent his Son, who lived, died, and was raised up; who ascended into the heavens; who is seated on the throne; and who is coming again to finish his work.

We Can Have Great Assurance

In view of this great assurance of our final salvation, we can rejoice always in our immutable God, who is truth. We can count on God's word and rest on his promises. No matter what happens, we can know that God has justified and reconciled us to himself. And having accomplished these most difficult parts of our salvation, God will surely put the finishing touches on us by glorifying us. So we rejoice in God himself—not in his gifts, but in the Giver. If we possess God, we possess everything. He loved us when we were his enemies, he loves us now as his friends and beloved sons, and he will love us forever.

Now we can say with the psalmist, "Whom have I in heaven but you? And earth has nothing I desire besides you. My flesh and my heart may fail, but God is the strength of my heart and my portion forever" (Ps. 73:25–26). We can echo the words of the prophet Habakkuk: "Though the fig tree does not bud and there are no grapes on the vines, though the olive crop fails and the fields produce no food, though there are no sheep in the pen and no cattle in the stalls, yet I will rejoice in the LORD, I will be joyful in God my Savior. The Sovereign LORD is my strength; he makes my feet like the feet of a deer, he enables me to go on the heights" (Hab. 3:17–19).

What about you? Have you been justified by the Supreme Judge of the universe and reconciled to him? Have you trusted in Christ alone, whose death is the basis of our justification and reconciliation? If so, you need not fear. On the last day, you will stand justified before God and no wrath will be poured out on you. You will be saved to enjoy eternal life. Because Christ died, we also died to sin and to law; because he lives, we will live forever. Nothing can separate us from the love of God or snatch us from God's mighty hand. He is able to keep us from falling.

But if you have not trusted in Christ, his wrath will surely be poured out on you on the last day. Just as his salvation is sure, so also his judgment on the unrepentant and unbelieving is sure. Paul speaks of this:

> God is just: He will pay back trouble to those who trouble you and give relief to you who are troubled, and to us as well. This will happen when the Lord Jesus is revealed from heaven in blazing fire with his powerful angels. He will punish those who do not know God and do not obey the gospel of our Lord Jesus. They will be punished with everlasting destruction and shut out from the presence of the Lord and from the majesty of his power on the day he comes to be glorified in his holy people and to be marveled at among all those who have believed. This includes you, because you believed our testimony to you. (2 Thess. 1:6–10)

I urge you to trust in Christ today so that you too may enjoy this great assurance of ultimate salvation.

25

The Reign of Original Sin

¹²Therefore, just as sin entered the world through one man, and death through sin, and in this way death came to all men, because all sinned— ¹³for before the law was given, sin was in the world. But sin is not taken into account when there is no law. ¹⁴Nevertheless, death reigned from the time of Adam to the time of Moses, even over those who did not sin by breaking a command, as did Adam, who was a pattern of the one to come.

Romans 5:12–14

Why are there wars, plagues, and times of economic chaos? Why do people murder, abort, steal, commit adultery, and rape? In Romans 5:12–14, Paul gives us the key to unlock the meaning of human history and to understand the human problem. This passage speaks about the reign of sin and therefore the reign of death, because death is punishment for sin. In other words, Paul here describes the universality of sin and death.

In Romans 5:12–21, all human history is described through the histories of two men: Adam and Jesus Christ. All the people of the world are represented by one or the other. The problems of sin, condemnation, and death came through the first Adam, the first man; the solution of righteousness, justification, and eternal life came through the last Adam, also called the second man, Jesus Christ.

Swedish theologian Anders Nygren refers to Romans 5:12–21 as the high point and key of the epistle to the Romans.[1] Dr. Lloyd-Jones says he agrees with Nygren in that this passage is

---

1   Nygren, *Commentary on Romans*, 209.

undoubtedly the most important section, in a sense, in the whole of this wonderful epistle.[2] I would say this section is the key to interpreting all Scripture and all human history. If we want to know why people are bad and do bad things, or why a sinner cannot save himself, we should read this passage. If we want to understand why human salvation is by grace alone through faith alone in Jesus Christ alone, we should read this passage. If we want to comprehend the doctrine of union with Christ and be fully assured of our ultimate salvation, we must read this passage. In this study we will consider Romans 5:12–14, which deals with the universal reign of sin and therefore the universal reign of death.

Therefore . . .

This section begins with "Therefore . . ." (v. 12). Paul is citing all he said prior as the reason for his next point. His "therefore" is especially linked to Romans 5:10–11 concerning our ultimate salvation: "For if, when we were God's enemies, we were reconciled to him through the death of his Son, how much more, having been reconciled, shall we be saved through his life!" (v. 10). It is crucial to grasp Paul's reasoning if we want to enjoy full assurance of our ultimate salvation, both now and in the hour of our death.

Christians are in Jesus Christ and are inseparably united with him. Because he lives and will never die again, we shall also live forever in him. Such full salvation can be found in the life of Christ.

Our problem is that we were united with Adam, who sinned against God's specific command. God dealt with Adam not just as an individual, but as the federal head of all mankind, as one representing us. The biblical logic, therefore, is that when Adam sinned, was condemned, and died, we also sinned, were condemned, and died. "The wrath of God is being revealed from heaven against all the godlessness and wickedness of men" (Rom. 1:18).

But now that we are in Christ, we are no longer in Adam. We have been transferred from the kingdom of darkness and death into the kingdom of light and life. We are in the sphere

---

2   Lloyd-Jones, Romans, vol. 4, Assurance, 176, 183.

of life forever and ever. Not only are we forgiven, justified, and reconciled, but we are also inseparably united to Christ, who is our life. Jesus himself taught this: "I am the vine; you are the branches" (John 15:5). In his high priestly prayer he also spoke about this union and communion we enjoy with him: "[I pray] that all of them may be one, Father, just as you are in me and I am in you. May they also be in us" (John 17:21).

In Romans 5:12, Paul begins a comparison, an "as/even so" pattern. He does not complete the comparison, though had he done so, it would read this way: "As through one man, Adam, sin entered the world, and death through sin, and in this way death spread through all men whom he represented because all sinned in him, even so righteousness entered the world through one man, Jesus Christ, and life through righteousness. In this way life spread to all men whom Christ represented. For all obeyed in Jesus Christ." That is the implied comparison.

Principles of Representation and Imputation

We see here the principles of representation and imputation in these two men representing two classes of people. The effect of each man's response to God, whether disobedience or obedience, is imputed to all whom each represents. Romans 5:12-14 reveals the representation of Adam, and his response of disobedience to God's specific word. The effect of that disobedience is sin, condemnation, and death.

These effects are imputed to all descendants of Adam—to all people, from every race and every nation. Every human being is descended from Adam. All sinned in Adam, all are condemned in Adam, and all died in Adam. Then, at the end of verse 14, we are told that Adam is a type (*tupos*), a pattern, of the last Adam. It is through this coming One's obedience that righteousness, justification, and eternal life will come to all his offspring.

In Romans 5:12-21, the word "one" (*hen*) appears twelve times, in reference to one man Adam and one man Jesus Christ, one sin of Adam and one act of Christ's obedience. Adam and Christ are the responsible parties. Notice that though Eve sinned first, she is not mentioned here. This is because she was not the responsible party. Adam was the head, not Eve.

Adam and Christ are historical people. Many people today do not believe in the historicity of Genesis 1–3. They choose to understand the passage mythologically, not literally. But if Adam was not historical, then there would be no fall, no sin, no need for redemption, and no need for Jesus to come and die for our sins.

We are in good company when we assert the historicity of Adam. Paul believed Adam was historical; there is no other way to understand this passage. Jesus himself believed Adam was historical, for he opposed divorce by stating, "At the beginning the Creator 'made them male and female,' and said, 'For this reason a man will leave his father and mother and be united to his wife, and the two will become one flesh'" (Matt. 19:4–5). He was speaking about the historical Adam and Eve. The whole Christian position collapses if we reject the literal, historical Adam. That is why we deny the validity of Darwinian evolution.

Through one historical man named Adam, sin invaded the world, coming to all people. In the Greek text, sin is personified ("*the* sin invaded"), which means sin is a mighty force. In verse 21, sin is pictured as a king who rules and makes all people its slaves. Note also that Romans 5:12 is not speaking about the origin of sin, but about the origin of human sin. Sin came into existence through the devil, before Adam sinned.

Romans 5:12 gives sin as the true diagnosis of the world's problem. It is not lack of education or money. If we reject this diagnosis, we will not truly understand the problem of the world, the problem of our families, the problem of our churches, and the problem of our nation. We will also have no understanding of true salvation.

In Romans 5 Paul is referring to Genesis 3. Sin came in from the outside through the door of Adam. God himself said that the world he had created was very good. Now it has been spoiled by this invasion of sin. And through sin, death also entered the world. Death is penal, a punishment for sin. Death is also personified in this passage. This mighty force is depicted as a king in verses 14 and 17. Death comes to all sinners, whether rich or poor, doctors or patients, educated or ignorant. Death is no respecter of persons.

Just as sin is king, so also death is king. Just as sin appears unconquerable, so also does death. Death is comprehensive—spiritual, physical, and eternal. It is, in its ultimate sense, separation from God in hell. God warned Adam about this punishment: "But you must not eat from the tree of the knowledge of good and evil, for when you eat from it, dying you will die" (Gen 2:17; author's translation). The New International Version translates, "You will surely die." Paul declares, "The wages of sin is death" (Rom. 6:23). Master Sin pays his wages without fail to all his slaves in the currency of death.

Yet we must remember that both death and sin are not natural, but are intruders into this world. Many people say death is natural. Lloyd-Jones comments that many unbelievers say that "death leads to life by liberating the nitrogen that is needed to form the molecules of new life. Death is just part of the cycle of life."[3] But this verse affirms not only the universality of sin but also the universality of death. So Lloyd-Jones concludes, "The world is a place of cemeteries."[4]

Human sin began with Adam, and so human death began with Adam. In Genesis 5, the Hebrew word *wiamoth* ("and he died") is repeated throughout the account of Adam and his descendants: "Altogether, Adam lived 930 years, and then he died" (v. 5; see also vv. 8, 11, 14, 17, 20, 27, 31). Through Adam, therefore, death spread to all men, and now all people everywhere die. Man is born to die. God determines the very number of breaths we will take. We come into the world breathing and after we deplete our number of breaths, we die. Two dates mark every man and woman—birth and death.

Who, then, can conquer King Death and stop him from killing people? Through sin, Adam became mortal. People today try to become immortal, but they shall fail unless they are united to the heaven-sent conqueror of sin and death, Jesus Christ.

"Because All Sinned"

Then Paul explains why death spread to all men: *"because all sinned"* (v. 12). What does this phrase mean? One may say that all people personally sin, which is true (excepting infants). Or some may say that all have a corrupt sin nature, which is true (including infants), or that all were in the loins of Adam, which is also true.

---

3   Lloyd-Jones, *Romans*, vol. 4, *Assurance*, 192.
4   Ibid., 261.

But what Paul means here is that all sinned based on this principle of representation. Adam was the representative of all his descendants. God appointed him as our federal head; therefore, the effect of his response to God's specific direct word is imputed to us. When he sinned, we sinned. Notice, "all *sinned*." It does not say "all *sin*." It refers to something that happened in history past, as recorded in Genesis 3. All descendants of Adam sinned when Adam sinned, based on this representative principle that God uses, whether we like it or not. That means Adam's sin is our sin, his guilt is our guilt, his condemnation is our condemnation, and his death as sin's punishment is our death.

Paul says elsewhere, "In Adam all die" (1 Cor. 15:22). Why do all die? The answer is given here: "For in Adam all sinned." We all sinned *in* Adam, not we all sinned *like* Adam. There is a difference. Likewise, we are righteous *in* Christ, not *like* Christ, who obeyed God fully and perfectly. In the one sin of one man Adam, we all sinned. Who are we to argue with God, who operates on the basis of his own principles?

All sinned in the past in Adam. Paul writes, "The result of one trespass was condemnation for all men . . . Through the disobedience of the one man the many were [constituted] sinners" (Rom. 5:18–19). Notice, in 5:12, when Paul says, "because all sinned," he is not dealing with our many sins. He will touch on that in verses 16 and 20, but not here. Here he is dealing with the one sin of the one man Adam, our God-appointed representative, in whose sin we sinned. He is speaking of our original sin, for which we are all condemned and must die.

In his *The Imputation of Adam's Sin*, John Murray notes the important conjunctions here:

1. "The immediate conjunction of the sin of Adam and the death of all";[5]
2. "The immediate conjunction of the sin of Adam and the condemnation of all";[6]
3. "The immediate conjunction of the sin of Adam and the sin of all."[7]

---

5   Murray, *Imputation of Adam's Sin*, 65.

6   Ibid., 67.

7   Ibid., 68.

This tells us that the sin of Adam is responsible for the sin, condemnation, and death of those whom he represented.

A Jew may argue there was no law until Moses, and where there is no law, there cannot be any transgression of the law. Thus he would say that sin cannot be put into the account of anyone. He may say that only Adam had a specific command that he violated; therefore, his sin should affect only himself. But Paul argues that the external written law is not necessary to prove the universality of sin. In other words, sin was in the world even before the law was given. Sin worked from Adam to Moses to us, and it is still working. Sin and death are in the world, whether there is law or no law, and death reigns over all people. Why do all people die? They have all sinned. We can prove they all sinned because they die, for death is punishment for sin.

Why do both Jews, who have the law, and Gentiles, who never had an external written law, die? Paul says they die because they are descended from Adam and sinned in Adam. Even infants, who may not sin personally, die because they sinned in Adam. Adam should have understood the terrible implications of his disobedience. We sin because we do not care about anyone. We sin only for our own pleasure.

This principle of representation is illustrated in the story of Achan, who took and hid several items that were forbidden by God. Not only was Achan killed for his sin, but his sons and daughters were also destroyed (Josh. 7).

William Barclay says this about Romans 5:12:

1. Adam sinned because he broke a direct commandment of God—the commandment not to eat of the fruit of the forbidden tree—and because Adam sinned, Adam, who was meant to be immortal, died.
2. The law did not come until the time of Moses; now, if there is no law, there can be no breach of the law; that is to say, if there is no law and no commandment, there can be no sin. Therefore, the men who lived between Adam and Moses did in fact sin, but it was not reckoned against them because there was as yet no law, and they could not be condemned for breaking a law which did not exist.
3. But, in spite of the fact that sin could not be reckoned to them, they still died. Death reigned over them although they could not be accused of breaking a non-existent law.

4. Why, then, did they die? They died because they had sinned in Adam. It was their involvement in the sin of Adam that caused their deaths, although there was no law for them to break. That, in fact, is Paul's proof that all men did sin in Adam.[8]

There is no other correct way to explain it. There is a divinely instituted solidarity under the headship of Adam and Christ. God deals with men in terms of this solidarity principle. We were in solidarity with Adam; but now, thank God, we are in solidarity with Christ. Adam was our head; now Christ is our head. As we were condemned on account of what Adam did as our representative, so we are justified on account of what Christ did as our representative. In Romans 5:15 Paul introduces Jesus, the last Adam, who brings us righteousness, justification, and life through his one act of obedience, specifically his atoning death. The first Adam is a type of the coming One promised in the Old Testament, the Messiah, who reversed forever what the first Adam did. Paul says, "For as in Adam all die, so in Christ all will be made alive" (1 Cor. 15:22). All who belong to Jesus by faith are now receiving the abundance of grace and the gift of righteousness through the one man, Jesus Christ, who came to reverse what Adam did. In Adam we died; in Christ we live. Adam has his descendants; Christ has his. Now we are Christ's offspring, his children, and his brothers.

The Mystery of God's Mercy

One may say, "I do not understand this solidarity principle, this principle of representation and imputation." I say, "Neither do I." I also do not understand an infinite, personal God who created the universe out of nothing. I do not understand the Trinity—one God in three persons. I do not understand the two natures in the one person of Christ. I do not understand the virgin birth. I do not understand God-man dying on the cross. I do not understand the mystery of iniquity. I do not understand grace. I do not understand heaven or hell.

---

8   William Barclay, *The Letter to the Romans*, The Daily Study Bible series (Edinburgh: Saint Andrews Press, 1969), 80.

One may ask, "Is it fair to put the sin of Adam to my account?" I would ask: "Is it fair to put the righteousness of Christ into my account? Is it fair for God to justify the ungodly and reconcile his enemies?" I do not understand all of these things perfectly, but I do rejoice that once I was in Adam—in his sin and condemnation and death; but now I am in Christ—in his righteousness, justification, and eternal life. My salvation is totally secure. I do not understand it all, but I am rejoicing all the way to heaven!

If you are also in Christ, rejoice with me all the way to heaven! When we arrive there, then we can ask him all these questions. But if you are still in Adam, I beseech you to repent and receive the abundance of grace he offers you so that you also may be transferred from the sphere of Adam to the sphere of Christ. As you are justified and receive eternal life, you also will join in singing the praises of God.

26

Grace Abounding to Miserable Sinners

[15]But the gift is not like the trespass. For if the many died by the trespass of the one man, how much more did God's grace and the gift that came by the grace of the one man, Jesus Christ, overflow to the many! [16]Again, the gift of God is not like the result of the one man's sin: The judgment followed one sin and brought condemnation, but the gift followed many trespasses and brought justification. [17]For if, by the trespass of the one man, death reigned through that one man, how much more will those who receive God's abundant provision of grace and of the gift of righteousness reign in life through the one man, Jesus Christ.

Romans 5:15–17

Romans 5:15–17 speaks about God's abounding grace to miserable sinners. Infinite grace came to the hell of God's enemies, lifted them up, transported them to the heavenly realms, and seated them with Jesus Christ. About this passage Karl Barth said, "Though the sentence of death was not pronounced at any moment in time, yet, like the sword of Damocles, it is suspended over our heads at every moment."[1] I disagree with two aspects of this famous theologian's statement. First, the sentence of death was pronounced in time: "And the Lord God commanded [Adam], 'You are free to eat from any tree in the garden; but you must not eat from the tree of the knowledge of good and evil, for when you eat of it you will surely die'" (Gen. 2:16–17). Second, although

---

1   Quoted by Morris, *Epistle to the Romans*, 237.

it is true that the sentence of physical death hangs over each of Adam's descendants, Adam also died spiritually the moment he ate the forbidden fruit. So Adam experienced separation from life with God long before he physically died at age 930.

The Two Heads of Humanity

In Romans 5:12–21, Paul speaks of the history of humanity under the headship of two men—Adam and Jesus Christ. Paul calls them the first man and the second man. When we compare the person and work of Adam with that of Jesus Christ, we first see that both were men, though Jesus Christ was God-man, and both were appointed by God to be heads of a humanity. Both were to keep a covenant before God, and what each did affected all whom they represented. Because of the one sin of the one man Adam, all his descendants became sinners and so were condemned to death. Because of the obedience of Jesus Christ, all who belong to him are forgiven of all their sins, justified forever, and given the gift of righteousness and eternal life. So Adam brought to the world sin, condemnation, and death, but this text tells us that God is not defeated by Adam's sin, condemnation, and death. God's action in Christ Jesus reversed these deadly effects of Adam's work and achieved for God's people the infinitely greater blessings of grace.

Through his one sin, Adam became a mass murderer, bringing death to all his descendants. But Jesus Christ, who is eternal life, makes alive all who are his. That was why he came from heaven into this world. Jesus said, "The thief comes only to steal and kill and destroy; I have come that they may have life, and have it to the full. . . . I give them eternal life, and they shall never perish" (John 10:10, 28).

God created Adam innocent and righteous, but his was a defectible righteousness. It was possible for him to sin (*posse peccare*) and he did so, thereby plunging all his descendants into the abyss of sin and death. But thanks be to God for Jesus Christ, the second man, the last Adam. As a result of his covenant-keeping, he came to our hell and transported us, not back to the defectible innocence of Adam, but to heaven itself. Having justified us of all sins, he seated us with him in the heavenly realms. He clothed us with his own divine, indefectible righteousness so that we may

312

receive the gift of eternal life. Jesus did all this by his death and resurrection for his people.

What about you? Are you one of his people? Are you his offspring? Are you united with Christ through faith? We must make certain that we trust in Jesus Christ alone. We are God's people if we have entrusted ourselves to Christ now and forevermore. Paul asserts, "I know whom I have believed, and am convinced that he is able to guard what I have entrusted to him for that day" (2 Tim. 1:12). We do not depend on ourselves or on anything else; we depend on the Lord Jesus Christ to transport us into heaven, where we are already seated with Christ.

Romans 5:15–17 particularly emphasizes the contrast between Adam the sinner and Jesus Christ the righteous one. No matter what our problems are, Jesus is mighty to solve them all. Trust in King Jesus, who through the cross defeated King Sin, King Death, and King Satan. Jesus declared, "When a strong man, fully armed, guards his own house, his possessions are safe. But when someone stronger attacks and overpowers him, he takes away the armor in which the man trusted and divides up the spoils" (Luke 11:21–22). A stronger one has come in the person of Jesus Christ to deliver us from the powerful control of death, the devil, and the world. This passage informs us about our liabilities in Adam and our riches in Christ.

Our Liabilities in Adam

1. SIN

The first liability we have in Adam is sin. The "one sin of the one man" is speaking about Adam's deliberate eating of the forbidden fruit (Gen. 3:6). In verses 15 and 18 Paul describes how Adam fell from the state of righteousness and innocence and brought us all down into the pit. Then he says, "Through the disobedience of the one man . . ." (v. 19). Because Adam disobeyed, we do too. That is why we spurn God's commands. When a parent speaks, rebellious children ask, "Who are you to tell me what to do?"

"But the gift followed many trespasses and brought justification" (v. 16). Although one sin of Adam brought us into this miserable condition of condemnation and death, Adam's one sin is not our only problem. We have also personally committed many

trespasses. "All have sinned and fall short of the glory of God. . . . He was delivered over to death for our sins" (Rom. 3:23; 4:25). Paul says elsewhere, "Christ died for our sins" (1 Cor. 15:3). Notice the plural. Adam's one sin has produced a multitude of sins in our lives.

Not only have we and Adam sinned, but Paul declares, "Sin reigned" (Rom. 5:21). Sin is pictured here as king. By nature, all are under the dominion and control of sin. When we continue in sin, we must conclude that we are under the control of King Sin. Elsewhere Paul says, "Because all sinned" (Rom. 5:12b). Every human being, except Jesus Christ, has therefore sinned unconsciously in the one sin of Adam our representative, as well as committing personally a multitude of sins. This is our serious liability of sin.

2. Condemnation

Another liability we have in Adam is condemnation. *"Again, the gift of God is not like the result of the one man's sin: The judgment followed one sin and brought condemnation"* (v. 16). For one sin of one man, God has judged all men, according to his own strict justice. God had clearly told Adam, "The day you eat thereof, you will die." The judgment Adam reaped for his disobedience is condemnation for him and his descendants.

God judged us in the one sin of Adam and declared us to be unrighteous. Therefore, all who are outside of Christ are judged and condemned, not by any court of this world, but by God. "For just as through the disobedience of the one man, the many were constituted sinners" (v. 19, author's translation). We are declared to be sinners by God himself and are therefore condemned.

But about those who have believed in Christ, Paul writes, "Therefore, there is now no condemnation for those who are in Christ Jesus" (Rom. 8:1). He also writes, "Who is he that condemns? Christ Jesus, who died—more than that, who was raised to life—is at the right hand of God and is also interceding for us" (Rom. 8:34). The opposite of condemnation is justification. *"But the gift followed many trespasses and brought justification"* (v. 16). God declares his people righteous in spite of the fact that we have sinned both in the one sin of Adam and by committing many sins ourselves in thought, word, and deed.

3. DEATH

The third liability is death. *"For if, by the trespass of the one man, death reigned through that one man . . ."* (v. 17). The wages of sin is spiritual, physical, and eternal separation from the life of God. Paul says, "Therefore, just as sin entered the world through one man, and death through sin, and in this way death came to all men, because all sinned . . . Nevertheless, death reigned" (Rom. 5:12, 14). Death is pictured as a mighty, universal king. No one is able to oppose King Death as he marches on from village to village, from mansion to little hut.

Whenever someone dies, we must remember that death came through that first man who rebelled against God. This makes Adam a mass murderer. Sin reigns through death (Rom. 5:21). All who hate Christ are under the mighty power of sin and death, which are God's judgments on rebels.

"Many died . . ." (v. 15). We see from verse 12 that "many" here means all: "Death came to all men, because all sinned." Why do people die? They are all sinners under the dominion of sin and death. "It is appointed for man once to die and then comes the judgment" (Heb. 9:27, author's translation). No sinner can escape death on his own. Moses writes, "The length of our days is seventy years—or eighty, if we have the strength; yet their span is but trouble and sorrow, for they quickly pass, and we fly away" (Ps. 90:10). The wisest, wealthiest, or most powerful person cannot defeat death. *"For . . . by the trespass of the one man, death reigned"* (v. 17). Like sin and condemnation, death is a liability that has come to us through the one man, Adam.

Our Riches in Christ

Having looked at the liabilities we have inherited from Adam, let us now examine the riches we have in Christ.

1. JESUS CHRIST

The first treasure we have is Jesus Christ himself. Only those who have trusted in Christ by saving faith can be rich and free from all liability. After telling us of the misery of sin and death that Adam brought, Paul introduces the one who will deal with these things: "Nevertheless, death reigned from the time of Adam to the time of Moses, even over those who did not sin by breaking a command, as did Adam, who was a pattern of the one to come" (Rom. 5:14). Paul explains that Adam was a type, a pattern of the promised one—the seed of the woman who would come to crush the head of the serpent. The promised Messiah, the second Adam, came to undo the works of Adam and destroy the work of the devil. Paul proclaims, "And having disarmed the powers and authorities, [Christ] made a public spectacle of them, triumphing over them by the cross" (Col. 2:15).

The writer to the Hebrews tells us, "Since the children have flesh and blood, he too shared in their humanity so that by his death he might destroy him who holds the power of death—that is, the devil—and free those who all their lives were held in slavery by their fear of death" (Heb. 2:14–15). Let us praise Jesus Christ for delivering us from the fear of death.

2. THE GRACE OF GOD

The second treasure we have in Christ is abounding, infinite, logic-defying grace. The words "grace" and "gift" appear ten times in Romans 5:15–21. Many trespasses call for much condemnation, but God gives grace. He gives grace to helpless sinners who merit death and hell, grace to those who are enemies of God, grace to the objects of divine wrath, and grace to those who have committed multitudes of sins. "Where sin abounded, grace superabounded" (v. 20, author's translation). Grace means eternal life. Heaven is given to us who merited eternal death and hell.

In heaven we are for the praise of his glorious grace. Paul says, "In order that in the coming ages he might show the incomparable riches of his grace, expressed in his kindness to us in Christ Jesus" (Eph. 2:7). Elsewhere he declares, "Although I am less than the least of all God's people, this grace was given me: to preach to the Gentiles the unsearchable riches of Christ" (Eph. 3:8). This bank-busting, overflowing grace swept away all our sins, condemnation, and death, and gave us super-abounding life.

In Romans 5:15–16 we read about *charisma*, which means a gift bestowed by grace. Another word used several times is *dōrea*, which means a free gift that comes from God the Father. *Dōrea* is used only with respect to the blessings and gifts God gives to men, as we read in James 1:17: "Every good and perfect gift is from above, coming down from the Father of the heavenly lights." This grace cost the Father his Son, but it is offered to us free of cost: "Come, all you who are thirsty, come to the waters; and you who have no money, come, buy and eat! Come, buy wine and milk without money and without cost" (Isa. 55:1). Grace is a free gift. Isaiah continues: "Why spend money on what is not bread, and your labor on what does not satisfy?" This makes good sense. Why should we waste our lives in pursuit of that which will not satisfy us, when what we really need is offered free of charge?

C. E. B. Cranfield comments about this wonderful treasure of grace coming to us through Christ: "That one single misdeed should be answered by judgment, this is perfectly understandable; that the accumulated sins and guilt of all the ages should be answered by God's free gift, this is the miracle of miracles, utterly beyond human comprehension."[2] Because of the truth of particular redemption, this grace is for all the sins of all God's elect of all the ages.

Adam's one sin plus the mountains of all our sins are answered by God's abounding grace. The saving work of Jesus is "much more," a phrase we see in verses 15 and 17. It is always much more, exceeding and abundantly above all that we ask or imagine. When Christ fed the five thousand people, there was much more than needed. His grace exceeds and is more than sufficient for our needs. The grace of Christ not only reverses the effect of Adam's sin, but it also reaches down to our hell, and makes us holy and blameless children of God. It takes us to heaven to be seated with Christ on the right hand of God. The grace of God in Christ makes us the bride of Christ. It makes us heirs of God and joint-heirs with Christ.

It is abounding grace. *"But the gift is not like the trespass. For if the many died by the trespass of the one man, how much more did God's grace and the gift that came by the grace of the one man, Jesus Christ, overflow to the many!"* (v. 15). God's grace abounds to the many. Elsewhere Paul says, "God is able to make all grace abound to you, so that in all things at all times, having all that you need, you will abound in every good work" (2 Cor. 9:8). If we are not obedient to God in doing good works, it is because we do not

---

2   Cranfield, *Romans*, 118.

have grace. God gives grace, but he does so only to the humble who pray and confess that they need his grace.

"For if, by the trespass of the one man, death reigned through that one man, how much more will those who receive God's abundant provision of grace and of the gift of righteousness reign in life through the one man, Jesus Christ" (v. 17). We also read of this abundant grace in verse 20: "The law was added so that the trespass might increase. But where sin increased, grace increased all the more," or "grace super-abounded." We have no excuse for being lazy and not doing God's work. We cannot say, "I did not have grace." God gives abounding, more-than-sufficient grace to all who come and ask for it.

Jesus said he came that we might have abundant life. Paul says, "Hope does not disappoint us, because God has poured out his love into our hearts by the Holy Spirit, whom he has given us" (Rom. 5:5). The idea is that God's love is poured out in a mighty effusion. Therefore, let us stop complaining and making excuses. Instead, let us pray and receive grace that we may work hard and accomplish even greater things for God. As branches are connected to the vine, so we are united with Christ. From him a mighty stream of grace flows into every true believer.

3. JUSTIFICATION

As a result of Adam's sin, we received condemnation, but in Christ we receive the treasure of justification based on his one righteous act (v. 18). Based on Christ's obedient death on the cross, God has given us the alien righteousness of Christ. We were sinners, but God constituted us righteous; therefore, we are righteous forever. The basis of this justification is the obedience of Christ. Therefore, the condemnation we inherited from Adam is overcome by Christ's righteousness. Justification has come to us in Jesus Christ.

Our sin in Adam justly called for our condemnation, and our many sins called for many condemnations. But grace does the opposite. Abounding grace justifies the ungodly. Those who committed many sins are declared righteous by the Supreme Judge of the universe.

4. BENEFICIARIES OF CHRIST'S OBEDIENCE

The fourth treasure is that we are beneficiaries of Christ's obedience. The effect of the obedience of Christ flows into all who belong to him. "Consequently, just as the result of one trespass was condemnation for all men, so also the result of one act of righteousness was justification that brings life for all men" (Rom. 5:18). Universalists say this means all people are going to be saved. Others say this means that the majority of Adam's descendants are going to be saved. Both views are not true, based on Christ's own words. Many are traveling on the broad way of destruction, but only a few shall walk in the narrow way of life (Matt. 7:13–14).

What, then, does "all" in verse 18 mean? Paul gives us a clue: "For as in Adam all die, so in Christ all will be made alive. But each in his own turn: Christ, the firstfruits; then, when he comes, those who belong to him" (1 Cor. 15:22–23). Only those who belong to Christ will receive the life-flow from Christ. And who belongs to him? Isaiah proclaims, "And who can speak of his descendants? . . . Yet it was the LORD's will to crush him and cause him to suffer, and though the LORD makes his life a guilt offering, he will see his offspring and prolong his days" (Isa. 53:8, 10). Those who belong to Christ are his spiritual children. Isaiah also says, "Here am I, and the children the LORD has given me" (Isa. 8:18). We are Christ's descendants, his offspring.

5. RECIPIENTS OF GRACE AND RIGHTEOUSNESS

The fifth treasure is receiving grace and righteousness. How can we know that we belong to Christ? We will receive God's abundant provision of grace and the gift of righteousness. *"For if, by the trespass of the one man, death reigned through that one man, how much more those who are receiving abundant provision of grace and the gift of righteousness shall reign in life through the one man, Jesus Christ"* (v. 17, author's translation). "Receiving" is in the present tense, meaning this abundant provision is coming to us continually, even as we read and hear the word of God. Grace comes to us through the proclamation of the gospel through God-called and God-commissioned human beings. If we receive the gospel of God's grace when it is proclaimed, we can know that we belong to Christ. If we treat God's grace and gift of righteousness with contempt, we are not saved. We will pay for our despising of God's word on that day when we face him.

How do we receive the abundance of grace and the gift of righteousness that is coming to us? Paul writes, "This righteousness from God comes through faith in Jesus Christ to all who believe" (Rom. 3:22). Therefore, to "receive" means to believe in Jesus Christ. Paul also says, "If you confess with your mouth, 'Jesus is Lord,' and believe in your heart that God raised him from the dead, you will be saved" (Rom. 10:9). To receive means to confess. Finally, he says, "Everyone who calls on the name of the Lord will be saved" (Rom. 10:13). To receive means to call upon the name of God, like blind Bartimaeus called out, "Jesus, Son of David, have mercy upon me." We must feel our need for God, for life eternal, and for the forgiveness of all our sins. We must feel our need to be clothed with the perfect righteousness of Christ.

If we are chosen by God from all eternity, we will experience the effectual call of God in our soul when the gospel message comes, and we will call upon the name of the Lord. Paul explains this process: "For those God foreknew he also predestined to be conformed to the likeness of his Son. . . . And those he predestined, he also called; those he called, he also justified; those he justified, he also glorified" (Rom. 8:29–30). We will confess, believe, receive, and be thankful for this great salvation. Our souls will be drawn to the triune God: "All that the Father gives me will come to me, and whoever comes to me I will never drive away. . . . No one can come to me unless the Father who sent me draws him, and I will raise him up at the last day" (John 6:37, 44).

Are you Christ's offspring? Do you belong to him? Jesus proclaims, "I am the good shepherd; I know my sheep and my sheep know me" (John 10:14). In other words, he loves his sheep and they love him. Jesus also said, "I am the gate; whoever enters through me will be saved" (John 10:9). If we are Christ's, we will be drawn to him. We will call upon the name of the Lord and we will know that we are saved.

I pray that we would receive the abundance of grace and the free gift of righteousness God offers to us. Luke 18:9–14 speaks about a Pharisee who rested in his self-righteousness and went home condemned. But the publican received the righteousness of God and went home justified.

"For in the gospel a righteousness from God is revealed" (Rom. 1:17). The Bible reveals a righteousness from God, which we need. "But now a righteousness from God, apart from law, has been made known, to which the Law and the Prophets testify. This righteousness from God comes through faith in Jesus Christ" (Rom. 3:21–22). The moment we believe in Christ, this righteousness is given to us freely. If we are outside of Christ, we are naked and ashamed. But in Christ, God covers our nakedness: "God made him who had no sin to be sin for us, so that in him we might become the righteousness of God" (2 Cor. 5:21).

6. WE ARE MADE RIGHTEOUS

The next treasure is found in verse 19, which says we are constituted righteous through the obedience of Christ. Who made us righteous? God did so. He made us righteous and declares that it is so. Because of this, we can resist the devil and he shall flee from us. Those who receive the abundance of grace and the free gift of righteousness are constituted righteous by God. Who can then condemn us?

In Christ we are forgiven of all our sins; they are blotted out, swept away, buried in the bottom of the ocean, and God remembers them no more. We can search as far and as long as we want, but they cannot be found.

7. REIGNING IN LIFE

Finally, we have the treasure of reigning in life through Christ: *"How much more those who are receiving the abundance of grace and gift of righteousness shall reign in life through the one man, Jesus Christ"* (v. 17, author's translation). Oh, what riches we have in Jesus Christ! Those who were slaves of sin and death have been made kings by God! We died with Christ, were buried with Christ, and were raised with Christ to live a new life.

Paul writes, "For if, when we were God's enemies, we were reconciled to him through the death of his Son, how much more, having been reconciled, shall we be saved through his life!" (Rom. 5:10). Now we live the life of Christ in the sphere of everlasting, indestructible life. For Christ "brought life and immortality to light" by his death and resurrection (2 Tim. 1:10).

We reign in life because we were made alive by the life of Christ. Christ came to stinking Lazarus's tomb. He said, "Lazarus, come forth!" and he came forth. The dead are raised up by the life of Christ. Having been taken out of Adam and the kingdom of death and darkness, we are now in the sphere of life. Death no longer rules over us, as it does over those who are outside of Christ. In Christ we have defeated sin, death, and the devil, for Christ by his death has triumphed over them all. In Christ we can say that death for us is not loss but gain. Now we can resist the devil by the blood of the Lamb and the word of God, and he shall flee from us. This is what it means to reign in life.

"As many as received him, to them he gave authority to become children of God" (John 1:12, author's translation). Because we have been given authority by the one to whom all authority in heaven and earth is given, we rule as kings both now and forever. "God raised us up with Christ and seated us with him in the heavenly realms in Christ Jesus" (Eph. 2:6). Seated with Christ, we are now ruling with him.

Paul says, "Do you not know that the saints will judge the world? ... Do you not know that we will judge angels," who are superior to us? (1 Cor. 6:2–3). Angels are ministering spirits to us, but we judge them. Peter declares, "But you are a chosen people, a royal priesthood" (1 Pet. 2:9). We are priests and kings. John states, "[Jesus] has made us to be a kingdom and priests to serve his God and Father—to him be glory and power for ever and ever! ... You have made them to be a kingdom and priests" (Rev. 1:6; 5:10).

Because we know what God says about us, we do not care what our enemies say. We are kings who reign in life with Christ. Speaking about heaven, John says, "There will be no more night. They will not need the light of a lamp or the light of the sun, for the Lord God will give them light. And they will reign for ever and ever" (Rev. 22:5). We have begun reigning now, and we will continue to reign. The moment we believed in the Lord Jesus, confessed him, and called upon his name, we began to rule for God.

Saints of God, are you reigning with Christ? Are you reigning over sin, death, the world, and the devil? If not, they are ruling over you. They are able to do so because you are a rebel who does not want to believe in the gospel. I urge you to believe in Christ and reign as victorious kings with him.

In Christ we reign in all circumstances. We reign in prison and when we are stoned, slandered, and beheaded. We reign when we are persecuted, cursed, naked, and hungry. We can do so because we have the life of God in us, and God himself is with us. We live with Christ, and he lives in us. Read what Paul says about this reigning, victorious life:

> Are they servants of Christ? (I am out of my mind to talk like this.) I am more. I have worked much harder, been in prison more frequently, been flogged more severely, and been exposed to death again and again. Five times I received from the Jews the forty lashes minus one. Three times I was beaten with rods, once I was stoned, three times I was shipwrecked, I spent a night and a day in the open sea, I have been constantly on the move. I have been in danger from rivers, in danger from bandits, in danger from my own countrymen, in danger from Gentiles; in danger in the city, in danger in the country, in danger at sea; and in danger from false brothers. I have labored and toiled and have often gone without sleep; I have known hunger and thirst and have often gone without food; I have been cold and naked. (2 Cor. 11:23–27)

We will face troubles and hardships as Paul did, but we can rule and reign in all circumstances because God is in us and we are in God. We are invincible kings; no devil can harm us. All these blessings are ours through Jesus Christ.

Conclusion

Friends, does it make any sense to remain in Adam, from whom flows the muck and mire of sin, condemnation, and death? Thank God for the second Adam, Jesus Christ! By his atonement he reversed the deleterious effects of our father, the mass murderer Adam. The stronger one, Jesus Christ, bound the devil and is setting his people free from their bondage in Adam. Jesus sets us free from sin and death. For the first time in our lives we are free to live, and we shall reign in life with Christ. For us Christ has become "wisdom from God—that is, our righteousness, holiness and redemption" (1 Cor. 1:30). Yes, death flowed from Adam, but life eternal flows to us from Christ. May we receive him by faith and be set free, that we may also receive God's abounding grace and his free gift of righteousness.

27

The Triumph of Grace

¹⁸*Consequently, just as the result of one trespass was condemnation for all men, so also the result of one act of righteousness was justification that brings life for all men.* ¹⁹*For just as through the disobedience of the one man the many were made sinners, so also through the obedience of the one man the many will be made righteous.*

²⁰*The law was added so that the trespass might increase. But where sin increased, grace increased all the more,* ²¹*so that, just as sin reigned in death, so also grace might reign through righteousness to bring eternal life through Jesus Christ our Lord.*

Romans 5:18–21

What can a huge elephant do to save itself if it falls into a fifty-foot deep pit? The answer is absolutely nothing. It cannot save itself, and eventually it will die. When Adam committed his first sin of disobeying God by eating of the fruit of the forbidden tree, he fell into hell itself, and with him all his descendants. God says that we all sinned in that one sin of Adam and were condemned to spiritual, physical, and eternal death.

Just as the fallen elephant cannot save itself, so also fallen man cannot save himself. Man must die unless God in grace chooses to save him. No fallen devil or man can defeat the purposes of the sovereign God. He alone triumphs by his grace and by his wrath. God triumphs by pouring out his wrath upon wicked sinners who refuse to receive his abounding grace and the free gift of righteousness.

Nothing can defeat God, whether man's sin or the devil or the unbelieving, God-hating world. Our God is a warrior who fights and wins. He is stronger than all devils. Jesus himself said that he binds the strong one, the devil, and sets free his elect sinners.

By both his grace and wrath our God fights and wins. Paul declares, "For in the gospel a righteousness from God is revealed, a righteousness that is by faith from first to last, just as it is written: 'The righteous will live by faith.' The wrath of God is being revealed from heaven against all the godlessness and wickedness of men who suppress the truth by their wickedness" (Rom. 1:17–18).

We cannot win if we are against God. Adam was the first to learn this truth: "And the LORD God commanded the man, 'You are free to eat from any tree in the garden; but you must not eat from the tree of the knowledge of good and evil, for when you eat it you will surely die'" (Gen. 2:16–17). There is no escape from God. Yet even now we have an opportunity to surrender our lives to Jesus Christ and be saved.

In Romans 5:18–21 Paul summarizes his argument and celebrates the triumph of grace. Paul completes here what he did not finish earlier in this chapter. According to John Murray, had Paul completed verse 12, it would have read: "Therefore, as through one man sin entered into the world and death through sin, and so death passed on to all men, in that all sinned, even so through one man righteousness entered into the world and life through righteousness, and so life passed on to all men, in that all men were accounted righteous."[1] This "just as/so also" balance is now found in verses 18, 19, and 21.

What Adam did affected all his descendants and created a huge, cosmic problem. But, thank God, through Jesus Christ the problem is solved.

The Great Cosmic Problem

The three aspects of our great cosmic problem are sin, death, and condemnation. Our cosmic problem began with the fall of Adam. God commanded Adam not to eat of a particular tree, but Adam responded, in essence, "I am going to do what is

---

1   Murray, *Epistle to the Romans*, 199.

forbidden. What are you going to do about it?" Adam sinned against God deliberately. "When the woman saw that the fruit of the tree was good for food and pleasing to the eye, and also desirable for gaining wisdom, she took some and ate it. She also gave some to her husband, who was with her, and he ate it" (Gen. 3:6). Through Adam's first disobedience, sin entered the world and death through sin, because all sinned in that one sin of Adam.

After Adam's fall, sin became a mighty king with laws, power, subjects, and a kingdom. Sin still reigns by death among those who are the descendants of Adam, whether Jews or Gentiles (Rom. 5:21). The whole world is under the power, rule, and authority of sin (Rom. 3:9). Moreover, like that elephant, we cannot free ourselves from sin's bondage, because sin is a king who enslaves his people. No one is able to get out from the grip of King Sin. Man under sin is not able not to sin (*non posse non peccare*).

Fallen man serves King Sin as a slave. Jesus said, "I tell you the truth, everyone who sins is a slave to sin" (John 8:34). And Paul says, "For we know that our old self was crucified with him so that the body of sin might be done away with, that we should no longer be slaves to sin. . . . Don't you know that when you offer yourselves to someone to obey him as slaves, you are slaves to the one whom you obey—whether you are slaves to sin, which leads to death, or to obedience, which leads to righteousness?" (Rom. 6:6, 16).

"*Through the disobedience of the one man the many were made [constituted] sinners*" (Rom. 5:19). All the descendants of Adam are legally classified as sinners on the basis of the disobedience of one man. The basis is not our own many sins, but the first sin of the first man. This sin, and its accompanying guilt, is imputed to all Adam's descendants. Yes, we are sinners ourselves because of our sin nature, but the ground of our classification as sinners is the first sin of the first man, Adam. In other words, in Adam all men stand before God judicially as sinners.

Another aspect of the big cosmic problem is condemnation. Verse 18 says, "*Consequently, just as the result of one trespass was condemnation . . .*" We saw earlier that "the judgment followed one sin and brought condemnation" (Rom. 5:16). God has

327

condemned Adam and all his descendants. Since Adam's one sin made all his descendants sinners, God judged and condemned them all. Every descendant of Adam, old or young, man or woman, slave or free, Jew or Gentile, is judged and condemned by God in Adam's one sin. All are born as condemned slaves of sin. We must believe this, for if we do not, we cannot believe what the Bible says the solution is.

Death is the third aspect of our great cosmic problem. We are born dead, with the sentence of death on us. Sin reigns by death (Rom. 5:21). Where King Sin goes, there goes also King Death. When sin entered the world, death also entered. We are told that death is a king (vv. 14, 17) who has a kingdom with laws and mighty power. Every sinner is his subject. None can escape his icy grip. All are under the sentence of death. Every day people live in the fear of death—not just physical death but also eternal death, to which every sinner is condemned.

God has decreed that every sinner must die and stand before him in judgment. Man cannot live forever. His lifespan is but a handbreath. He lives seventy, or by reason of strength eighty, years; then he must die. Death is the wages he earned because of his sin, and death is paid to him without fail. "The wages of sin is death" (Rom. 6:23).

The words of God in Genesis 2:17 are still valid when people die: "Dying, you will surely die." Every sinner knows that he is worthy of death, yet he keeps on sinning. Paul says, "Although they know God's righteous decree that those who do such things deserve death, they not only continue to do these very things but also approve of those who practice them" (Rom. 1:32). He later asks, "What benefit did you reap at that time from the things you are now ashamed of? Those things result in death!" (Rom. 6:21).

The Law as Solution?

Paul's readers in Rome, especially those of Jewish background, would ask at this point: "Is the law God has given us the solution that will save us?" The Jews were proud of the ceremonial, civil, and moral law of Moses. They treasured the law as God's gift to man. The Jews viewed the Gentiles as unclean dogs, but themselves as clean because they possessed the law. They declared themselves righteous because they tried to keep the law of God.

The Pharisee of Luke 18 was very proud of his standing before God. Saul of Tarsus once declared himself to be perfect in regard to the righteousness of the law (Phil. 3:6). The question Paul faced from Christian Jews is this: "What then is the purpose of the law if it cannot save and if it is not necessary even to condemn us?"

"The law was added so that the trespass might increase" (v. 20). The law came in beside sin so that sin might increase. The law incites us to sin more; it works as a catalyst, not a reagent. This is one of a number of other purposes for the law. Paul makes a number of points throughout his epistles about what the law can and cannot do:

1. The law does not justify (Rom. 3:20; Gal. 2:16);
2. The law cannot justify (Rom. 8:3);
3. The law is not necessary for God to condemn us (Rom. 5:14);
4. The law cannot impart life (Gal. 3:21);
5. The law was given to define sin and make it a legal offense (Gal. 3:19);
6. The law increases our knowledge of sin (Rom. 3:20; 7:7);
7. The law brings the wrath of God (Rom. 4:15);
8. The law produces death (Rom. 7:13);
9. The law reveals the utter vileness, horribleness, and sinfulness of sin (Rom. 7:13);
10. The law reveals the deceitfulness of sin (Rom. 7:11);
11. The law reveals sin's mighty and enslaving power (Rom. 6:14).

The Holy Spirit uses the preaching of the law to bring deep conviction and knowledge of our sin. Our sin is the most serious problem we have, and yet we have no idea of its extent. That is why we must go to churches where our sin is revealed through the preaching of the law.

By convicting us of our sin, the law leads us to Christ. Paul says, "The law was put in charge to lead us to Christ that we might be justified by faith" (Gal. 3:24). Elsewhere he writes, "Christ is the end of the law so that there may be righteousness for everyone who believes" (Rom. 10:4).

Paul declares to the Jewish Christians that the law will not save anyone. But that is not the end of the story. Grace solves our problem.

The Greater, Divine Solution

1. GRACE

If law cannot save us from the rule of sin and death, what can? Grace alone can save sinners who are fallen into the pit of hell with their father Adam. The grace of God reaches out from heaven in Jesus Christ to ungodly, helpless, sinful objects of God's wrath.

Sin is king (Rom. 5:21) and death is king (Rom. 5:14, 17), but grace is also king. Grace is not just equal in power to sin and death. There is no equal ultimacy of evil and good. Grace, being infinitely greater, reigns over sin and death. The grace of God in Jesus Christ comes to our hell and takes us to heaven itself. This is the power of grace.

Grace comes to our hell to take us, not to where Adam was before his fall, but to sit at the right hand of Christ himself. Grace is king and reigns forever. It is the grace of God (v. 15); the grace of our Lord Jesus Christ (v. 15); abounding grace (v. 17); and even super-abounding grace (v. 20). This super-abounding grace of God takes the initiative to seek us, find us, save us from our hell, and take us to heaven. This amazing grace is triumphant and full of glorious, incomparable, and unsearchable riches (Eph. 2:5–8).

This grace gives us the free gift of righteousness, which is our greatest need. This grace flows to us through the Seed of the woman, who crushed the ancient serpent's head. Peter speaks of this grace flowing from eternity: "[Christ] was chosen before the creation of the world, but was revealed in these last times for your sake" (1 Pet. 1:20). Paul likewise says that Jesus "saved us and called us to a holy life—not because of anything we have done but because of his own purpose and grace. This grace was given us in Christ Jesus before the beginning of time, but it has now been revealed through the appearing of our Savior, Christ Jesus, who has destroyed death and has brought life and immortality to light through the gospel" (2 Tim. 1:9–10).

This grace is irresistible. It fights even with God's own people and wins. This grace defeats our rebellion, stubbornness, and wickedness. In fact, if grace is not winning, it means we are not God's sheep and do not belong to the elect. This irresistible grace saves the most wicked of sinners, like the wicked king Manasseh. It saved Saul of Tarsus, the self-righteous Pharisee, the "chief of sinners" who went out to destroy Christianity like a beast breathing out slaughter and threatenings. The mighty grace of God conquered him and transformed him into an apostle and slave of Christ and a battle-scarred veteran of the cross.

Paul spoke of this work of grace in his life: "I too was convinced that I ought to do all that was possible to oppose the name of Jesus of Nazareth. And that is just what I did in Jerusalem. On the authority of the chief priests I put many of the saints in prison, and when they were put to death, I cast my vote against them. Many a time I went from one synagogue to another to have them punished, and I tried to force them to blaspheme. In my obsession against them, I even went to foreign cities to persecute them" (Acts 26:9–11). But grace won.

This grace redeemed the one with the legion of demons who wandered about restless, breaking his chains, naked, and crazy. Grace sought him and found him, and we read of him being clothed and sitting down in his right mind. Grace also redeemed the thief on the cross, the prodigal, and the publican.

Grace redeems every elect sinner. When our heavenly Father draws, the sinner will come humbly, believingly, and with deep sorrow of repentance. Jesus declares, "All that the Father gives me will come to me, and whoever comes to me I will never drive away. . . . No one can come to me unless the Father who sent me draws him, and I will raise him up at the last day" (John 6:37, 44).

I used to fish when I was a boy. Once a fish is hooked, it can struggle as long as it wants, but it eventually comes. It is true that some fish get away, but no one gets away from God. Jesus said, "I, when I am lifted up from the earth, will draw all men to myself" (John 12:32). What grace begins, it completes. Grace never fails.

Grace is necessarily irresistible. If it were not, no one would ever be saved. Grace elects, predestinates, effectually calls, regenerates, and enables us to repent and believe. Grace adopts us into God's family, makes us heirs with God and joint-heirs with Christ. It justifies, sanctifies, and glorifies us, making us super-conquerors in Christ.

2. RIGHTEOUSNESS

From Adam we received sin; in Jesus Christ we receive righteousness. As sinners, we were naked and had no righteousness of our own. Where could we get a righteousness that is unlike Adam's defectible righteousness? We needed an alien, indefectible righteousness. We needed the righteousness of God.

Thank God that such a divine righteousness has been revealed to us in the gospel of Christ! Paul proclaims, "For in the gospel a righteousness from God [and of God] is revealed, a righteousness that is by faith from first to last" (Rom. 1:17). This righteousness is a gift received by faith. Paul also states, "But now a righteousness from God, apart from law, has been made known, to which the Law and the Prophets testify. This righteousness from God comes through faith in Jesus Christ to all who believe" (Rom. 3:21–22).

This righteousness is a free gift of grace (vv. 15, 17). It is based on one righteous deed done in obedience by Jesus Christ (vv. 18–19). That "one obedience" refers to the death of the obedient Son. Jesus came to fulfill all righteousness. He told John the Baptist, "It is proper for us to do this to fulfill all righteousness" (Matt. 3:15). Elsewhere he said, "Do not think that I have come to abolish the Law or the Prophets; I have not come to abolish them but to fulfill them" (Matt. 5:17). Paul tells us, "But when the time had fully come, God sent his Son, born of a woman, born under law, to redeem those under law, that we might receive the full rights of sons" (Gal. 4:4–5). Paul uses the phrase *hupo nomon* to describe being born "under the rule or authority of the law." Jesus came to fulfill all the law perfectly in our place.

We were under the law, which demanded that we obey every law and always do so perfectly. This is utterly impossible for children of Adam to do, but Jesus Christ did it. Peter tells us, "You were redeemed ... with the precious blood of Christ, a lamb without blemish or defect" (1 Pet. 1:18–19). The innocent, obedient Son died.

We must understand and glory in this, that "God [reconciled] the world to himself in Christ, not counting men's sins against them" (2 Cor. 5:19). How can God not count our sins against us? On whose head did he put all our sins? The answer is that "God made him who had no sin to be sin for us, so that in him we might become the righteousness of God" (2 Cor. 5:21). The free gift of righteousness, therefore, has no basis in our good works, but is based entirely on the one act of righteousness of Jesus Christ alone (Rom. 5:18). It is based solely on the obedience of Christ in our behalf.

3. Justification

Adam gave the inheritance of condemnation to all his descendants. But Romans 5:18 tells us that through Christ we receive justification: *"The result of one act of righteousness was justification that brings life for all men."* Those who receive this grace-gift of Christ's righteousness are justified and their condemnation is canceled forever. Their sin and condemnation in Adam is effaced because of Christ's obedience and righteousness, and all other sins are forgiven and blotted out as well. This is God's work of justification.

Paul tells us, "Therefore, there is now no condemnation for those who are in Christ Jesus" (Rom. 8:1). What is the ground of this justification? *"For just as through the disobedience of the one man the many were made [constituted] sinners, so also through the obedience of the one man the many will be [constituted] righteous"* (Rom. 5:19). On the basis of one man's obedience, the court of heaven classifies us no longer as sinners but as righteous. We are righteous solely on the ground of the righteousness of Christ, not on the basis of any of our works, whether done on earth or in heaven. We have been taken out of the category of sinners and placed in the category of the righteous—out of the kingdom of darkness, death, and the devil, and into the kingdom of light and life in Christ. We are constituted righteous by the imputation of Christ's righteousness and declared righteous by God himself. Therefore, we truly are righteous. This is not speculation or fantasy. We are righteous, now and forever.

4. Life Eternal

Additionally, in place of eternal death, he has given us life eternal: *"So that, just as sin reigned in death, so also grace might reign through righteousness to bring eternal life through Jesus Christ our Lord"* (v. 21). In Adam we received sin, condemnation, and death; in the second Adam, Jesus Christ, we receive righteousness, justification, and eternal life. The righteousness of Christ leads to justification, and justification leads to eternal life. This eternal life is not merely the extension of the sinner's life in this world. Eternal life is a quality of life; it is living for God by God's life. If we have received eternal life, we will live for God.

We have this eternal life through Jesus Christ. The only way to heaven is through Jesus Christ, God's Son, the only mediator, our propitiation and righteousness. The Hebrews writer tells us, "Since the children have flesh and blood, he too shared in their humanity so that by his death he might destroy him who holds the power of death—that is, the devil—and free those who all their lives were held in slavery by their fear of death" (Heb. 2:14–15).

Jesus Christ "has destroyed death and has brought life and immortality to light through the gospel" (2 Tim. 1:10). It is tragic to see people running after everything in the world but not seeking God. Through Jesus Christ we find freedom from the devil and from death. Paul also says, "The last enemy to be destroyed is death. . . . When the perishable has been clothed with the imperishable, and the mortal with immortality, then the saying that is written will come true: 'Death has been swallowed up in victory.' 'Where, O death, is your victory? Where, O death, is your sting?' The sting of death is sin, and the power of sin is the law. But thanks be to God! He gives us the victory through our Lord Jesus Christ" (1 Cor. 15:26, 54–57).

Grace Has Triumphed!

Sin is no longer king for us. "Therefore do not let sin reign in your mortal body so that you obey its evil desires" (Rom. 6:12). And not only is sin not our king, but death also is not. For us, grace reigns *"through righteousness [unto] eternal life through Jesus Christ our Lord"* (v. 21).

Jesus is our King and Lord. He is King of kings and Lord of lords, and he has made us kings. "For if, by the trespass of the one man, death reigned through that one man, how much more will those who receive God's abundant provision of grace and of the gift of righteousness reign in life through the one man, Jesus Christ" (Rom. 5:17). We who have received the abundance of grace and the gift of Christ's righteousness are made kings by God; therefore, let us stop behaving like slaves of sin and start acting with dignity like the kings we are in Christ!

334

By the triumph of the grace of God, we who were slaves of sin and death have been made kings. In place of death we are given eternal life. We now live and reign in the sphere of life eternal over sin, death, the devil, the world, and angels. All things are ours in Jesus Christ.

Paul asks, "Who shall separate us from the love of Christ? Shall trouble or hardship or persecution or famine or nakedness or danger or sword? As it is written: 'For your sake we face death all day long; we are considered as sheep to be slaughtered.' No, in all these things we are more than conquerors through him who loved us. For I am convinced that neither death nor life, neither angels nor demons, neither the present nor the future, nor any powers, neither height nor depth, nor anything else in all creation, will be able to separate us from the love of God that is in Christ Jesus our Lord" (Rom. 8:35–39). We face and conquer all enemies and obstacles. Let us, therefore, stop all our murmuring, faultfinding, and envy! Let us instead wage battle as the kings we are and win.

Grace has triumphed! The elephant that fell into the fifty-foot-deep pit has been raised to live. We who fell with Adam into the pit of sin, condemnation, and death have been raised to righteousness, justification, life eternal, and to heaven itself, where we are seated with Christ. All this comes to us by the mighty operation of grace.

28

Union with Christ: The Key to Holiness

¹What shall we say, then? Shall we go on sinning so that grace may increase? ²By no means! We died to sin; how can we live in it any longer? ³Or don't you know that all of us who were baptized into Christ Jesus were baptized into his death? ⁴We were therefore buried with him through baptism into death in order that, just as Christ was raised from the dead through the glory of the Father, we too may live a new life.

⁵If we have been united with him like this in his death, we will certainly also be united with him in his resurrection. ⁶For we know that our old self was crucified with him so that the body of sin might be done away with, that we should no longer be slaves to sin—⁷because anyone who has died has been freed from sin.

⁸Now if we died with Christ, we believe that we will also live with him. ⁹For we know that since Christ was raised from the dead, he cannot die again; death no longer has mastery over him. ¹⁰The death he died, he died to sin once for all; but the life he lives, he lives to God.

Romans 6:1–10

There are more verses in the Bible calling us to live holy lives in this world than there are teaching the foundational doctrine of justification. This shows the importance of holiness in the life of a Christian. In Romans 6, Paul speaks about why believers should live holy lives and how they can do so in Christ. Holiness is the key to happiness.

The only basis of our salvation is the death and resurrection of our Lord Jesus Christ, the great event that took place in the midpoint of time. Our union with Adam brought us sin, condemnation, and death; but our union by faith with Jesus Christ canceled all that and brought us righteousness, justification, and eternal life.

When Paul said, "Where sin abounded, grace superabounded" (Rom. 5:20), he knew this doctrine of abounding grace could be misinterpreted, and it was. Throughout the history of Christianity, this misinterpretation has produced antinomianism, a perversion that is prominent in many churches today. The slogan of an antinomian is, "Only believe, and live as you please. Sin all you want, because more sin means more grace, which means more forgiveness and more glory to God." Paul vigorously opposed this heresy, as did Jude in his epistle and Peter in his second letter.

Antinomianism

First, Paul warns of the antinomianism that teaching about grace may produce. He begins Romans 6 by asking, *"Shall we go on sinning so that grace may increase?"* (v. 1). In other words, "Shall we continue on in the sphere of sin, that we may obtain more grace?"

In this chapter alone, "sin" appears in the singular fifteen times. And throughout this epistle, sin is personified: as a king (5:21; 6:12), a slavemaster (6:6), and a world ruler (3:9). The whole world is under the authority of sin and death, and behind sin and death is the personal devil, the god of this world. Every unbeliever is a slave ruled by King Sin, King Death, and King Satan; but through his death on the cross, Jesus Christ sets us free from this most heinous and tyrannical slavery.

The gospel declares that believers are taken out of the sphere of sin, death, and Satan, and brought into the sphere of righteousness, peace, and joy in the Holy Spirit. We have been brought from sin to righteousness, from condemnation to justification, from death to life, from darkness to light, from Satan to Christ, from the tyrannical slavery to sin to the glorious liberty of the children of God in and through Jesus Christ. Paul exclaims, "For he has rescued us from the dominion of darkness and brought us into the kingdom of the Son he loves, in whom we have redemption, the forgiveness of sins" (Col. 1:13).

Once we were united with Adam, but through faith we are now and forever united with Jesus Christ. Paul elsewhere states,

"It is because of [God the Father] that you are in Christ Jesus, who has become for us wisdom from God—that is, our righteousness, holiness and redemption" (1 Cor. 1:30). In this spiritual union with Christ we are justified, sanctified, and glorified, for Christ himself is our justification, sanctification, and glorification. Those who have been justified are being sanctified and shall surely be glorified. Therefore, it is utterly impossible for a person to be justified and not be sanctified. We cannot come under the almighty kingship of grace and still live under the control of sin as our slavemaster.

Grace has defeated King Sin, King Death, and King Satan! All believers are under grace and Christ, and those ruled by grace cannot be ruled by sin at the same time. Grace and sin are opposites, just as Christ and the devil are opposites. Christ came to vanquish the devil and his work: "Since the children have flesh and blood, he too shared in their humanity so that by his death he might destroy him who holds the power of death—that is, the devil—and free those who all their lives were held in slavery by their fear of death" (Heb. 2:14–15). John tells us, "He who does what is sinful is of the devil, because the devil has been sinning from the beginning. The reason the Son of God appeared was to destroy the devil's work" (1 John 3:8).

Therefore, a believer cannot go on sinning that grace may abound. In verse 2 Paul emphatically exclaims, "By no means!" (*Mē genoito!*). It is blasphemy to say that a Christian can continue in the realm of sin once he has been delivered from it. Having been taken out of Satan's dominion, he has been brought into the kingdom of God to live under the rule of Christ and grace; he cannot stay on in Egypt. Therefore, a person who claims to be a believer yet continues to serve King Sin is a liar. He is not saved. To such people Christ will say on that day, "Depart from me, you workers of *anomia!*"

The Key to Holiness

How, then, can a believer live a holy life? The key to holiness is our union with Jesus Christ in his death, burial, and resurrection. The key to holiness is to know the truth that we died with respect to sin once for all in the death of

Christ. Sin did not die; we died to sin, our former master. Sin has no claim upon a slave who just died. He who died is free with respect to sin.

The emphasis in this first section of Romans 6 is on death. We find the words death, dead, die, and crucify many times in the first thirteen verses: "We died to sin" (v. 2); "were baptized into his death" (v. 3); "buried with him through baptism into death" (v. 4); "we have been united with him like this in his death" (v. 5); "we know that our old self was crucified with him" (v. 6); "because anyone who has died" (v. 7); "if we died with Christ" (v. 8); "we know that since Christ was raised from the dead, he cannot die again; death no longer has mastery over him" (v. 9); "the death he died, he died to sin once for all" (v. 10); "count yourselves dead to sin" (v. 11); "Do not offer the parts of your body to sin, as instruments of wickedness, but rather offer yourselves to God, as those who have been brought from death to life" (v. 13). This idea of the death of the believer to sin in the death of Christ is the key to our understanding of holiness.

We died to sin (v. 2). We died with respect to sin. It does not say we are dying to sin or we will die to sin. We died; it is past history. Sin was our master, but we have been taken out of his kingdom. We are no longer there to be ruled and tyrannized by sin. King Sin lost a subject, and King Grace gained one. The wages of sin is death, but Christ died for our sins. In his death we died, and we have no further obligation to sin anymore. Jesus paid our penalty of death. We have been set free.

Before we were dead in sins, but now we are dead to sin. Paul speaks of this: "All of us also lived among them at one time, gratifying the cravings of our sinful nature and following its desires and thoughts. Like the rest, we were by nature objects of wrath. But because of his great love for us, God, who is rich in mercy, made us alive with Christ even when we were dead in transgressions—it is by grace you have been saved. And God raised us up with Christ and seated us with him in the heavenly realms in Christ Jesus" (Eph. 2:3–6). We are united with Christ in his death, burial, resurrection, and session. Paul elsewhere exhorts, "Since, then, you have been raised with Christ, set your hearts on things above, where Christ is seated at the right hand of God. Set your minds on things above, not on earthly things. For you died, and your life is now hidden with Christ in God" (Col. 3:1–3).

Paul speaks later in Romans 6 about our being freed from sin: "But thanks be to God that, though you used to be slaves to sin, you wholeheartedly obeyed the form of teaching to which you were entrusted. You have been set free from sin and have become slaves to righteousness. . . . But now that you have been set free from sin and have become slaves to God, the benefit you reap leads to holiness, and the result is eternal life" (vv. 17–18, 22). We have been set free by the Father, the Son, and the Holy Spirit.

When did we die to sin? We did so in our baptism: *"Don't you know that all of us who were baptized into Christ Jesus were baptized into his death? We were therefore buried with him through baptism into death in order that, just as Christ was raised from the dead through the glory of the Father, we too may live a new life"* (vv. 3–4). In other words, Paul was asking the Roman Christians, "Don't you know the meaning of your baptism?" He made this appeal because every believer in the apostolic church was baptized in water and knew that his or her baptism symbolized death. Water baptism was not optional.

The New Testament mode of baptism is immersion. In apostolic times, baptism followed immediately upon confession of faith in Jesus Christ. Water baptism dramatically signifies our death in the death of Christ. It represents our union with Christ in all phases of his mediatorial work: we died, were buried, and have been raised with Christ. Therefore, immersion (going into the water) points to our death with Christ, submersion (being underwater) points to our burial, and emersion (coming out of the water) points to our resurrection with Christ. Paul writes elsewhere, "[You were] buried with him in baptism and raised with him through your faith in the power of God, who raised him from the dead" (Col. 2:12).

"The death he died, he died to sin once for all" (Rom. 6:10). Jesus Christ died to sin once for all, and in his death we also died to sin once for all. Therefore, Paul exhorts, "Count yourselves dead to sin but alive to God" (v. 11). From now on we are living our resurrection life to serve God.

Jesus came once to die. He was raised by the power of the Father and returned to heaven, where he lives forever. Though he was without sin, he came under the dominion of sin and death when he took our sin and its penalty upon himself. Yet death could not keep him in the grave, because he was without sin; and he will never have to die again, because his death for our sins was completely effectual.

In Christ's death we died spiritually; in his burial we were buried spiritually; in his resurrection we are raised in our spirits; and at his second coming, we shall also be raised up physically. He "will transform our lowly bodies so that they will be like his glorious body" (Phil. 3:21). We are, therefore, no longer united with Adam in his sin, condemnation, and death. We have a new representative. We have been taken out of Adam and united to Christ by faith. Our baptism indicates that we are united to Christ in his death, burial, and resurrection. And since Jesus will never die again, we who are in him will also never die again. Jesus says, "He who believes in me will live, even though he dies; and whoever lives and believes in me will never die" (John 11:25–26). Death can only send us to the very presence of God.

We are vitally united with Christ as branches are united to the vine. His life, his death, and his victory over sin, death, and the devil are ours. Christ is King, and we who receive God's abundant provision of grace as a result of our vital union with Christ are also kings (Rom. 5:17). We are seated with Christ and our life is hidden with Christ in God. As kings, we live victorious Christian lives. We not only declare war against sin, death, and the devil, but we also rule over these enemies. We resist the devil by the gospel, and he flees from us because he knows Christ defeated him by his death, and he knows we know that. Knowing that we are united with Christ, the devil runs from us as we exercise faith in the gospel.

As Christians we have the power of the Holy Spirit. Jesus told his disciples, "You will receive power when the Holy Spirit comes on you" (Acts 1:8). We are not weaklings. The life of God in us gives us supernatural power. The power of God flows into us and makes us able to do what is right. We do not have to live in sin any longer; we have the power of God. John writes, "We know that anyone born of God does not continue to sin; the one who was born of God keeps him safe, and the evil one cannot harm him" (1 John 5:18). If we are held by God, the evil one cannot touch us. He who is in us is greater than he who is in the world. We are held by the hand of Christ and the hand of the Father. Nothing in the whole world can defeat us and separate us from the life and love of God.

Living the Resurrection Life

Above all, may we remember Christ's resurrection, which is the ultimate proof of the total defeat of all powers opposed to God. Because of our union with Christ, we are now on the other side of the grave. Sin, death, and the devil have no further claim on us. We have been set free from these things to serve God in the resurrection life.

We must not focus on ourselves and our weakness and misery. Instead, let us look to the risen Christ. His death and resurrection have been credited to our account, becoming effectual to us when we believed and were baptized.

This union with Christ is the mother of all doctrines. It speaks of what is true of us in Christ. This is not mere imagination. The purpose of this union with Christ is that we live the resurrection life. That is why it is impossible for true believers to continue in sin. We died to sin; sin is no longer our master.

Risen with Christ, we now live by Christ's resurrection life. Jesus came to give us this life. An unbeliever is dead even as he lives. He may accomplish many things in the world, but he remains under the wrath of God. He is a dead man walking. But we walk in the newness of eternal life. We cook, clean, work at our jobs, make decisions, worship, and proclaim the gospel in the power of the resurrection life. We may even suffer and be killed in this resurrection power of the Holy Spirit.

We must think about this truth when we are tempted to murmur and complain. The death and resurrection of Christ matters in our everyday lives. It is not some fantastic idea that has no relevance to the present. Our old man is dead; our old sinful humanity does not exist anymore. Paul says, "I have been crucified with Christ and I no longer live, but Christ lives in me. The life I live in the body, I live by faith in the Son of God, who loved me and gave himself for me" (Gal. 2:20).

Paul also writes, "For Christ's love compels us, because we are convinced that one died for all, and therefore all died [to sin]. And he died for all, that those who live should no longer live for themselves but for him who died for them and was raised again" (2 Cor. 5:14–15). Elsewhere he says, "For to be sure, he was crucified in weakness, yet he lives by God's power. Likewise, we are weak in him, yet by God's power we will live with him to serve you" (2 Cor. 13:4). We live the Christian life by God's power. Peter tells us, "Therefore, since Christ suffered in his body, arm yourselves also with the same attitude, because he who has suffered in his body [i.e., died in his body] is done with sin. As a result, he does not live the rest of his earthly life for evil human desires, but rather for the will of God" (1 Pet. 4:1–2).

Freedom in Christ

In Christ, we are done with the reign of sin. Now we are in heaven on earth, for God dwells in us and we in him. Our body of sin has been disabled and does not rule us anymore; rather, we rule it. Paul says, "I beat my body and make it my slave" (1 Cor. 9:27). We have been bought at a price, so we honor God with our bodies, which are the temple of the Holy Spirit.

Thanks be to God for our new identity! God has made us alive with Christ; now we are a new creation with a new nature. We have the resurrection power of the Holy Spirit. We are God's handiwork, created in Christ Jesus to obey the will of God. Before, we were obedient to the devil and disobedient to God. Now we are disobedient to the devil and gladly obey God. We are free at last!

Shall we, therefore, go on sinning so that grace may abound? Unthinkable! How can we trade life for death, freedom for slavery, joy for misery? There has been an emancipation proclamation from heaven. All slaves of sin who believe in Jesus are set free. Our shackles are loosed and our prison doors opened. Now we are free to rise up and go out into the sunlight, into the glorious liberty of the children of God. The stronger one, Jesus Christ, has come and bound Satan to set us free. Let us, therefore, go forth walking and leaping and praising God.

Once we could only sin—we were *non posse non peccare*. Now we have freedom to resist sin and live for God in righteousness (*posse non peccare*). We have freedom from both the guilt and power of sin. And at Christ's second coming, we shall be glorified and brought into a state in which we will not sin at all (*non posse peccare*), a state superior to the state of Adam in his innocence, which was *posse peccare*.

Sin still desires to reassert its authority in our lives. We are tempted, but we resist. We are no longer the old slaves of sin. Empowered by Christ, we rule and fight as kings. We wield the sword of the Spirit, the word of God, and the devil and his demons flee. In God we leap over walls and are able to live a victorious life.

Live in the Truth of God's Word

The key to holiness is to know this great truth of being united to Christ. If we do not know it in our minds, we will go astray. Christianity demands, not the sacrifice of our intellect, but the maximum use of our renewed minds. We must know the gospel facts.

Paul asks, *"Don't you know?"* (v. 3) The Greek is, "Are you ignorant?" What would our answer be? *"For we know"* (vv. 6, 9). We must exercise our minds. Look at verse 11. Paul writes, "In the same way, count yourselves dead to sin." We must not live as though we are still under the dominion of sin. We have been emancipated. We are no longer under sin's authority. Now that we are united to Christ, we are under the authority and power of grace, and we shall never again be under sin. Knowing this truth is the key to a triumphant, happy life of holiness.

29

Steps to Holiness

11In the same way, count yourselves dead to sin but alive to God in Christ Jesus. 12Therefore do not let sin reign in your mortal body so that you obey its evil desires. 13Do not offer the parts of your body to sin, as instruments of wickedness, but rather offer yourselves to God, as those who have been brought from death to life; and offer the parts of your body to him as instruments of righteousness. 14For sin shall not be your master, because you are not under law, but under grace.

Romans 6:11–14

Too many Christians today maintain that sanctification is not mandatory but optional. Christian antinomianism has become normal. They deem justification by grace through faith is all that is necessary to get to heaven. But what does the Bible say?

Paul states, "It is God's will that you should be sanctified" (1 Thess. 4:3), and he exhorts, "Train yourself to be godly. For physical training is of some value, but godliness has value for all things, holding promise for both the present life and the life to come" (1 Tim. 4:7–8). The writer to the Hebrews tells us, "Without holiness no one will see the Lord" (Heb. 12:14). John says, "Everyone who has this hope in him purifies himself, just as he is pure" (1 John 3:3). Jesus Christ declares in the Sermon on the Mount, "Blessed are the pure in heart, for they will see God" (Matt. 5:8).

Holiness is mandatory for every true believer. The man who lives in sin is not saved at all, for the grace that saves is at the same time opposed to sin. He who sins habitually will hear from the Lord on the last day, "Depart from me, you who practice lawlessness."

Romans 6:1–10 taught us that the basis of a godly life is our union with Christ in his death, burial, and resurrection. Jesus died once for all to sin, and in him we also died to sin. Jesus rose from the dead and we also rose with him. Our old man, our in-Adam man, has been crucified with Christ on the cross (v. 6). This body of sin is rendered powerless so that we may not serve sin but serve God. Paul declares, "I am crucified with Christ: nevertheless I live; yet not I, but Christ liveth in me" (Gal. 2:20, KJV). The in-Christ man is a new creation. He is a free man who is capable of saying "No" to sin and obeying Christ.

The new man is not passive; he is active. He fights against the devil and sin, and he wins, because Jesus defeated all our enemies by his death. Sin is not dead, but it is defeated. So the in-Christ man can resist the devil and the devil will flee from him. The in-Christ man is a super-conqueror, like David, who by faith killed the giant Goliath. As those who are new creations in Christ, let us consider the steps of holiness taught in Romans 6:11–14.

Step 1: Consider

Paul begins, "*In the same way, [consider] yourselves dead to sin but alive to God in Christ Jesus*" (v. 11). This is the first of several exhortations in the book of Romans. In justification, God declares us just on the basis of our faith in what Jesus Christ alone has done. In sanctification, we work out what God works in us. He works in us both to will and to do his good pleasure.

He who justifies also sanctifies. Jesus is not only righteousness; he is also holiness. He imparts that holiness to us, but unlike in justification, in sanctification the believer has a part to play. Sanctification is not an experience or a gift to be received; instead, it is a life of obedience lived out in the power of God. In sanctification we are active, not passive. "We are his workmanship, created in Christ Jesus unto good works [i.e., unto obedience], which God hath foreordained that we should walk in them" (Eph. 2:10, KJV).

So the first step in holiness is to consider ourselves dead with respect to sin and alive to God in Christ Jesus. The Greek word used (*logizethe*) speaks of logical thinking. We must keep on considering, thinking, realizing, remembering, meditating, accounting, calculating, reasoning, and keeping before our minds the reality of our union with Christ in his death, burial, and resurrection.

The imperative is based on the indicative of our union with Christ. Paul calls us to count as true what is in fact true. It is like my telling an adult, "Do not behave as a baby; you are a grown-up," or saying to a married man, "Do not act like a single person; you are now married." We must consider what is objectively true.

The truth is, we are dead to sin and alive to God forever. For us, the regime of sin is over, and the eternal regime of God has begun. We have been rescued from the kingdom of sin and are brought now into the kingdom of life. Therefore, do not just emote—think! We must know who we are, where we are, and who our new King is. Keep on accounting the truth. We are dead to sin.

Dr. James Boice points out what Paul does not mean when he says we are dead to sin.[1] It is not that our duty is to die to sin. No, we died to sin. It is not a command to die to sin. We are already dead. It is not to reckon sin as a force in us to be dead. Sin is still a force in us, but it is not dominant. It is not that sin in us has been eradicated. Sin is still in our dying bodies as a power that desires to reassert its former authority, but it has been defeated. It is not that we are dead to sin as long as we gain victory over sin. It is not that reckoning ourselves dead to sin makes us dead to sin. We must consider this: In the death of Christ, we died to sin both now and forevermore, just as in Christ's resurrection we rose again and now live to God forever.

This reckoning is not cooking the books or wishful thinking. It is not an ugly person reckoning himself to be very beautiful or a pauper accounting himself to have great wealth. It is knowing and thinking truth, as Abraham did: "By faith Abraham, when God tested him, offered Isaac as a sacrifice. He who had received the promise was about to sacrifice his one and only son, even though God had said to him, 'It is through Isaac that your offspring will be reckoned.' Abraham reasoned that God could raise the dead,

---

1   Dr. Boice summarizes these thoughts of Dr. Martyn Lloyd-Jones in *Romans*, vol. 2, *Reign of Grace*, 676–77.

and figuratively speaking, he did receive Isaac back from death" (Heb. 11:17–19).

Look at the use of the verb "reckon" in the Bible. God reckons our sins to Jesus Christ, meaning he puts our sins upon him. And God reckons Christ's perfect righteousness to us. This is not fantasy; it is the truth. We are clothed with the righteousness of Jesus Christ.

Positively, we must recognize that in Jesus we are alive to live for God. All of these things are true when we are in union with Christ. The phrases "in Christ," "in Jesus," and "in him" appear 164 times in Paul's writings, but this is the first time they appear in this epistle.

We are in Jesus Christ. No enemy can touch us, destroy us, or take us away from Christ. We are in him. Consider yourselves, in your whole being, dead to sin and alive to God in union with Jesus Christ. No devil can take us back as his slaves again.

We have been set free from sin and now are privileged to be God's slaves. "But now that you have been set free from sin and have become slaves to God, the benefit you reap leads to holiness, and the result is eternal life" (Rom. 6:22).

Knowledge of this is so important! We read in Hosea 4:6, "My people are destroyed from lack of knowledge. Because you have rejected knowledge, I also reject you as my priests; because you have ignored the law of your God, I also will ignore your children." God declares in Isaiah 1:2–3: "I reared children and brought them up, but they have rebelled against me. The ox knows his master, the donkey his owner's manger, but Israel does not know, my people do not understand."

We must know this truth of being in Christ and live by it daily. No longer are we obligated to sin. We are obligated to God alone; therefore, we live for the praise of his glorious grace.

Step 2: Do Not Let Sin Reign

"Do not let sin reign in your mortal body so that you obey its evil desires" (v. 12). This is the second step to holiness. Being united with Christ Jesus, we died with him and are risen with him. Because Jesus paid all our debts and we have no obligation to sin, we must not let the old master Sin exercise dominion in

our dying bodies. In other words, we must not let sin rule us again. As believers in Christ, we have freedom to resist our former defeated king and stop him in his tracks by disobeying sin, which desires to reassert its dominion over us. We who were slaves have been set free, but our old master does not want us to know this fact. That is why we must know that we have been set free and are no longer obliged to that master.

During our pre-regenerate days, we were obedient slaves of sin and disobedient to God: "As for you, you were dead in your transgressions and sins, in which you used to live when you followed the ways of this world and of the ruler of the kingdom of the air, the spirit who is now at work in those who are disobedient. All of us also lived among them at one time, gratifying the cravings of our sinful nature and following its desires and thoughts. Like the rest, we were by nature objects of wrath" (Eph. 2:1-3).

Now we are regenerated and have been given a new, divine nature. We have a new dynamic—the resurrection power within us. In us dwells the Holy Spirit, who now leads us. We serve God in the newness of life in the Holy Spirit, exercising our freedom to disobey sin and obey God.

Grace is now our king. Jesus Christ received all authority in heaven and on earth. He is the King of kings, and we have been made kings with him.

We have been seated with Christ and now we reign in life. Paul writes, "For if, by the trespass of the one man, death reigned through that one man, how much more will those who receive God's abundant provision of grace and of the gift of righteousness reign in life through the one man, Jesus Christ" (Rom. 5:17). We exercise authority and dominion over sin, the devil, the world, and the flesh. Paul teaches, "For the grace of God that brings salvation has appeared to all men. It teaches us to say 'No' to ungodliness and worldly passions, and to live self-controlled, upright and godly lives in this present age, while we wait for the blessed hope—the glorious appearing of our great God and Savior, Jesus Christ, who gave himself for us to redeem us from all wickedness and to purify for himself a people that are his very own, eager to do what is good" (Titus 2:11-14). Paul told us that we, along with the whole world, were under sin's authority

(Rom. 3:9). Moreover, we were also under a law that commanded and condemned us. But in the death of Jesus Christ, we died to sin and we died to the law that condemned us.

Yes, sin is still in our mortal bodies. It twists and perverts the good instincts of the body and makes them sinful. For example, hunger is good, but sin twists it into gluttony, bulimia, and anorexia. Thirst is also good, but sin perverts it into alcoholism and caffeine addiction. Sexuality is good, but sin turns it into pornography, fornication, adultery, bestiality, homosexuality, and incest. Rest and sleep are good, but sin twists them into sloth and laziness. The tongue is a good member of our body, but sin twists it for slander and gossip.

"Do not let sin reign in your mortal bodies, that you may be obedient to its lusts" (v. 12, author's translation). Do not say you sinned again. You did not have to do it. Though we are not entirely free from sin, we are free from its dominion. We must reckon ourselves dead to sin and alive to God. So flex your spiritual muscle. No longer are you a servant of sin; you are a servant of Christ. Be a good soldier and fight the good fight. Be strong in the Lord and in the power of his might. Put on the full armor of God and wrestle against all enemies of godliness.

Christus victor means Christ is victor. Christ has defeated all our enemies; now we can resist sin and the devil, who shall and must flee from believers who stand with Christ and fight. Joseph victoriously resolved, "How then could I do such a wicked thing and sin against God?" (Gen. 39:9). Daniel resolved not to defile his body with non-kosher food, and he was victorious. But David the great warrior did not fight temptation when he saw Bathsheba, and he experienced a terrible defeat.

Fight! We can do all things through Jesus Christ who makes us strong. We know sin has no claim on us. Now in Christ we rule sin. We control our bodies and decide how much we eat, drink, or sleep. We control our minds and take every impure thought captive to make it obedient to Christ. We know our position and our rights. We believe in the Bible. We study it to know who we are and what our rights are. We overcome by the blood of the Lamb and the word of our testimony.

We do not fight without purpose; we fight to win. We know from the Scriptures that we are in Christ and the Holy Spirit is in us. We are not spiritually ignorant. We declare with conviction to the devil: "It is written." We live by the Spirit and use the sword of the Spirit. God's grace abounds to us, and we abound in every good work.

Listen to what Paul says: "For Christ's love compels us, because we are convinced that one died for all, and therefore all died. And he died for all, that those who live should no longer live for themselves but for him who died for them and was raised again" (2 Cor. 5:14–15). That is the purpose of our Christian life. Listen to Peter: "Therefore, since Christ suffered in his body, arm yourselves also with the same attitude, because he who has suffered in his body is done with sin. As a result, he does not live the rest of his earthly life for evil human desires, but rather for the will of God" (1 Pet. 4:1–2).

Be a fighter. Listen to the violent language Paul uses: "For if you live according to the sinful nature, you will die; but if by the Spirit you put to death the misdeeds [sins] of the body, you will live" (Rom. 8:13). Elsewhere Paul says, "Put to death, therefore, whatever belongs to your earthly nature: sexual immorality, impurity, lust, evil desires and greed, which is idolatry" (Col. 3:5). Put them to death! See how Paul uses his freedom: "I beat my body and make it my slave so that after I have preached to others, I myself will not be disqualified for the prize" (1 Cor. 9:27). We rule our bodies; they do not rule us. As God's free men and women, we beat our bodies and make them our slaves to obey Jesus Christ. We have no obligation to the flesh. We put to death the misdeeds of the body by the Holy Spirit. We are led by the Spirit and filled with the Spirit. Sin shall not win. In Christ, having done all, we will stand.

We are set free and are able to put to death whatever belongs to our earthly nature. We have a new nature and are filled with the Holy Spirit. And having been redeemed from sin, our bodies are the temple of the Holy Spirit, so we honor God with our bodies. We are no longer like slaves in Egypt who must obey Pharaoh. As citizens of heaven, we are now obligated to obey God. Now we work out our salvation with fear and trembling, for it is God who works in us to will and to do his good pleasure (Phil. 2:12). We follow in the footsteps of Jesus Christ. He commanded us to deny ourselves, take up the cross daily, and follow him.

We surely face temptation daily, but what does the Scripture say? "No temptation has seized you except what is common to man. And God is faithful; he will not let you be tempted beyond what you can bear. But when you are tempted, he will also provide a way out so that you can stand up under it" (1 Cor. 10:13). God is faithful. He will make certain that you are shown a way so that you will win.

Peter says, "Dear friends, I urge you, as aliens and strangers in the world, to abstain from sinful desires, which war against your soul. Live such good lives among the pagans that, though they accuse you of doing wrong, they may see your good deeds and glorify God on the day he visits us" (1 Pet. 2:11–12). Paul guarantees that we do not have to sin at all: "So I say, live by the Spirit, and you will not gratify the desires of the sinful nature [the flesh]. For the sinful nature desires what is contrary to the Spirit, and the Spirit what is contrary to the sinful nature. They are in conflict with each other, so that you do not do what you want. But if you are led by the Spirit, you are not under law" (Gal. 5:16–18). "In conflict" means the Holy Spirit is against the flesh, and the flesh is against the Holy Spirit. As long as we are led by the Holy Spirit, the Holy Spirit will win through us.

Do not let King Sin, our defeated former boss, reassert his kingship in your mortal body. Exercise your freedom and power. Resist him and be an overcomer. Become what you are! Reckon daily that you are dead to sin and alive to serve God. Know that he who is in you is greater than he who is in the world.

Sin no longer is our master. It used to be. But something wonderful happened to us. God made us alive in Christ! We have been regenerated, given a new nature, and are indwelt by the Holy Spirit. We have a renewed mind, with which we now delight in God's law. The love of God is shed abroad in our hearts, so we love God and obey his commands. We hate sin and love righteousness. We love Jesus Christ, who loved us and gave himself for us. We are no longer hell-bound objects of God's wrath. We belong to God's family as his sons and daughters. We have joined the holy church, which is on her way to heaven. As we fight the devil and the remaining sin in our bodies, we will win and sing praise to God. Super-abounding grace is king. Since we daily receive this super-abounding grace, we too are kings. We exercise our kingship and power in our war against our enemies and live our daily lives for God's glory.

God delivered us out of Egypt. God is with us, and he will guide us. God fights against the Amalekites in our lives, and we fight also. And because God always wins, so will we. He goes before us and leads us through Jordan to the city of the living God. He is the way, the truth, and the life.

There is a day coming when all wars will cease and all enemies will be disposed of. There shall be peace forevermore under the Prince of peace. So Isaiah says:

> A shoot will come up from the stump of Jesse; from his roots a Branch will bear fruit. The Spirit of the LORD will rest on him—the Spirit of wisdom and of understanding, the Spirit of counsel and of power, the Spirit of knowledge and of the fear of the LORD—and he will delight in the fear of the LORD. He will not judge by what he sees with his eyes, or decide by what he hears with his ears; but with righteousness he will judge the needy, with justice he will give decisions for the poor of the earth. He will strike the earth with the rod of his mouth; with the breath of his lips he will slay the wicked. Righteousness will be his belt and faithfulness the sash around his waist. The wolf will live with the lamb, the leopard will lie down with the goat, the calf and the lion and the yearling together; and a little child will lead them. The cow will feed with the bear, their young will lie down together, and the lion will eat straw like the ox. The infant will play near the hole of the cobra, and the young child put his hand into the viper's nest. They will neither harm nor destroy on all my holy mountain, for the earth will be full of the knowledge of the LORD as the waters cover the sea. (Isa. 11:1-9)

We look forward to that day of great peace in the new heaven and on the new earth. But in the meantime, we are to fight in the power of the mighty Holy Spirit.

The Believer's Union with Christ

From Romans 6:13-14 we will consider the third and fourth steps to holiness. First, though, we need to mention that these divine imperatives are based on the indicative of our vital union with Christ in our faith baptism (Rom. 6:3-4). We are *in Christ*

Jesus. Having died to King Sin, we now live forever to serve only the living and true God. In the death and resurrection of Jesus, we died and rose again. Paul writes, "The death he died, he died to sin once for all; but the life he lives, he lives to God" (Rom. 6:10).

What is true of Jesus is true of every true believer. Jesus will not die again. Instead, he declares, "I am the Living One; I was dead, and behold I am alive for ever and ever! And I hold the keys of death and Hades" (Rev. 1:18). He also assured his disciples, "Because I live, you also will live" (John 14:19).

We live by the resurrection power of Jesus Christ, walking in the newness of life, which is the life of Christ, serving God in the newness of the Spirit (Rom. 7:6). As soldiers of the King of kings and Lord of lords, we are triumphant in Christ. Jesus declared, "I have overcome the world" (John 16:33). John writes, "This is the victory that has overcome the world, even our faith" (1 John 5:4). Jesus said, "To him who overcomes and does my will to the end, I will give authority over the nations. . . . He who overcomes will inherit all this, and I will be his God and he will be my son" (Rev. 2:26; 21:7).

We are more than conquerors (Rom. 8:37). We are not lying down as doormats, asking the world to step on us. We are people of God and soldiers of Christ, living holy lives in this world. We are not monks in a monastery or patients lying in a hospital. We are soldiers engaged in a good fight for truth, wrestling in the power of the Holy Spirit against all evil. We kill the sin that still dwells in us. Though we experience hardship, we obey and please our commanding officer, who has received all authority in heaven and on earth.

Step 3: Do Not Present Your Members to Sin

The third step to holiness is a negative command: *"Do not offer the parts of your body to sin, as instruments of wickedness"* (v. 13a). This is the third imperative in this epistle in which Paul applies the doctrine of our union with Christ.

"Present" (*parestemi*) means to offer, yield, put at the disposal of another's use, sacrifice, or devote. Jesus uses this word in Matthew 26:53: "Do you think I cannot call on my Father, and he will at once put at my disposal more than twelve legions of

356

angels?" We find it also in Luke 2:22: "Joseph and Mary took [Jesus] to Jerusalem to present him to the Lord." We must not put at the disposal of our old slave master Sin our faculties and the members of our bodies. We died in our relation to sin; now the triune God is our master, not sin. "Jesus paid it all; all to him we owe." We owe nothing to sin, the devil, the world, or our flesh.

"Do not present the parts of your body . . ." The members of our body include all our powers as well as our eyes, ears, hands, feet, sex organs, tongues, minds, emotions, and money. In other words, all that we are and all that we have is to be put at God's disposal. Therefore, we must not look at a woman lustfully or view pornography. We should not listen to evil music or read books that corrupt us. We must not watch corrupting television shows and movies, or abuse alcohol, drugs, or food. We must not gossip, lie, or slander. We should not fold our hands in laziness, but must work with our hands. We should use money not for evil purposes but for God. We must not emulate Eve, Esau, Achan, David, and Judas, who put the members of their bodies at the disposal of sin. They saw, they coveted, and they took, thus committing evil with their bodies.

As believers, we are not helpless in our fight against sin. Rather, we have been raised from the dead and given a divine nature. Having repented of our sins and trusted in Christ, we have been justified, adopted, and inseparably united with Christ. Now the Holy Spirit dwells in us to teach and empower us. As soldiers in the army of God, we are fully equipped to fight against evil and win.

It would be sheer cruelty to ask a slave in chains to behave as a free man. But it is love to tell one who has been set free by King Jesus to behave as a free man because he is a free man. Therefore, when sin and the devil try to reassert their authority over us, we must resist, fight, and wrestle them down.

So Paul says, "Do not yield your members as weapons of wickedness" (author's translation). The word *hopla* is best translated as "weapons," not "instruments," "implements," or "tools." Everywhere else in the New Testament it is translated as "weapons" (e.g., John 18:3; 2 Cor. 6:7, 10:4). The idea is that every man and woman is a soldier either in the army of Satan and sin or in the army of Christ. All of our resources are utilized in the extension either of the kingdom of God or the kingdom of the devil. As Christians, we have been empowered and enlisted in the army of God to fight and kill sin. May we use our abilities to expand the kingdom of God! May we join with all other soldiers who are serving in the kingdom of God and oppose the expansion of Satan's kingdom.

To those who continue to serve in the kingdom of the evil one, Jesus will say, "I never knew you. Away from me, you evildoers!" (Matt. 7:23). Such people work hard for the expansion of the kingdom of Satan, using all their resources.

Non-Christians can only sin, because they are not set free. But if we died to sin and have been set free, even if sin might command us, we do not have to obey. We must know our doctrine: sin is not our lord. We have been delivered out of the iron-smelting furnace of Egypt to be the holy people of God.

Step 4: Present Your Members to Righteousness

The fourth step to holiness is a positive command: *"But rather offer yourselves to God, as those who have been brought from death to life; and offer the parts of your body to him as instruments of righteousness"* (v. 13b). In the Greek, the "but" that begins this verse is a strong adversative, denoting a sharp contrast. Before we served sin, but now as believers in Jesus Christ we serve the interests of the kingdom of God in our whole personality and through all we possess.

"But rather offer yourselves." Paul uses *parestemi* again, this time as an aorist imperative, which means we are to present ourselves to God wholly once for all. This is total dedication in the service of Christ our king. We are voluntarily putting our entire being at the disposal of God once for all. In Romans 12:1 Paul says, "Offer your bodies as living sacrifices."

Throughout the Old Testament we read about animal sacrifices. These animals did not offer themselves freely. Yet now, as God's people, we freely put ourselves at the disposal of God. We find the same idea in Romans 6:19: "Just as you used to offer the parts of your body in slavery to impurity and to ever-increasing wickedness, so now offer them in slavery to righteousness leading to holiness."

As slaves of Christ, we delight in worshiping and serving him. Several times in Exodus 10 we read that the reason the Lord was delivering his people from Egypt was so that they could worship and serve him. We are rescued from Satan's dominion so that we can serve God exclusively.

How do we serve God with our minds? Once, we used our minds to think and imagine evil. Now, as Paul states, we are to let the word of Christ dwell in us richly as we use our minds to teach and admonish one another (Col. 3:16). Elsewhere he exhorts, "Finally, brothers, whatever is true, whatever is noble, whatever is right, whatever is pure, whatever is lovely, whatever is admirable—if anything is excellent or praiseworthy—think about such things" (Phil. 4:8). "For as [a man] thinketh in his heart, so is he" (Prov. 23:7, KJV). Jesus taught, "The good man brings good things out of the good stored up in his heart" (Luke 6:45). Let us use our minds to think God's thoughts after him. Blessed is the man whose "delight is in the law of the LORD, and on his law he meditates day and night" (Ps. 1:2).

We are not our own; we have been redeemed by the precious blood of Christ. Paul explains, "Do you not know that your body is a temple of the Holy Spirit, who is in you, whom you have received from God? You are not your own; you were bought at a price. Therefore honor God with your body" (1 Cor. 6:19–20). Paul also states, "For Christ's love compels us, because we are convinced that one died for all, and therefore all died. And he died for all, that those who live should no longer live for themselves but for him who died for them and was raised again" (2 Cor. 5:14–15). There is no such thing as independence. Our only choice is to serve either Satan or Christ.

But we now belong to Jesus Christ! Paul writes, "So, my brothers, you also died to the law through the body of Christ, that you might belong to another, to him who was raised from the dead, in order that we might bear fruit to God" (Rom. 7:4). No longer are we under the power and authority of sin. The triune God is now our Lord, and we are under his rule. "Those who are led by the Spirit of God are sons of God" (Rom. 8:14).

John Frame speaks about three aspects of the absolute demands of our Lord Jesus Christ.[2] First, he says, his commands "cannot be

---

2   John M. Frame, "Scripture Speaks for Itself," in *God's Inerrant Word: An International Symposium on the Trustworthiness of Scripture*, ed. John Warwick Montgomery (Minneapolis: Bethany Fellowship, 1974), 183.

questioned." When the Lord told Abraham to sacrifice his son, his only son, the son whom he loved, Abraham did so without wavering. To waver or disobey would have been sin. Nobody can question Christ's absolute demands.

Second, Frame says that God's demand "transcends all other loyalties." The Lord declares, "You shall have no other gods before me" (Exod. 20:3). When a potential disciple requested permission to go bury his father, Jesus told him, "Follow me, and let the dead bury their own dead" (Matt. 8:21–22). In other words, he was saying, "Don't you know who is calling you? I am the Lord. So don't tell me about your father and mother or spouse or boss. When I call, you must follow." To the rich young man, Jesus said, "If you want to be perfect, go, sell your possessions and give to the poor, and you will have treasure in heaven. Then come, follow me" (Matt. 19:21).

Third, Frame says that God's demand for obedience is comprehensive and unlimited: "It governs all areas of life." This includes our worship as well as "diet, political life, sex life, economic life, family life, travel, and calendar." I would add recreational life and thought life to Frame's list. This is what the confession "Jesus is Lord" means. Jesus affirmed, "Anyone who loves his father or mother more than me is not worthy of me; anyone who loves his son or daughter more than me is not worthy of me" (Matt. 10:37). Anyone who loves anything in this world more than Christ is not worthy of him.

Romans 6:17 illustrates the comprehensiveness of the lordship of Christ in the life of every believer: "But thanks be to God that, though you used to be slaves to sin, you wholeheartedly obeyed the form of teaching to which you were entrusted." "Teaching" means mind; "obeyed" means will; "wholeheartedly" means emotions. That is what happens to us when God saves us.

Paul insists, "So whether you eat or drink or whatever you do, do it all for the glory of God" (1 Cor. 10:31). This is absolute, yet delightful, slavery. He also states, "Whatever you do, whether in word or deed, do it all in the name of the Lord Jesus, giving thanks to God the Father through him" (Col. 3:17).

God gives us both the responsibility and the ability to "demolish arguments and every pretension that sets itself up against the knowledge of God." We are to "take captive every thought to make it obedient to Christ" (2 Cor. 10:5). We are to demolish arguments that arise from our own desires and thoughts that

Satan puts into our minds. We can do so because the weapons of our warfare are empowered by the Holy Spirit. We can order every thought to obey Christ, just as Jesus did in the desert when he resisted Satan by stating, "It is written."

We are to offer ourselves to God *"as from the dead living"* (v. 13, author's translation). Unbelievers are spiritually dead, going and coming like dead men walking. But God came and said, "Live," and we lived by the power of the Spirit of God. He made us alive with Christ. We are regenerated, justified, adopted, and indwelt by the Holy Spirit. Now we have freedom to rebel against Satan and obey God. Therefore, let us offer the parts of our bodies as weapons, not for wickedness, but for righteousness.

Jesus commissions us to go into all the world and preach the gospel. We are to make disciples and teach them to obey all of God's commands (Matt. 28:19–20). Our life goal should be the extension of God's kingdom, for that is what we have been set apart to do. In Leviticus 14:14–18 we read that blood was put on the right ear lobe and the right thumb and the right big toe of the person to be cleansed. In the same way, we have been sprinkled with the blood of Christ. Then oil was put in the same places, symbolizing the Spirit's work in our lives. We are totally cleansed and consecrated to serve God with our whole heart, mind, soul, and strength.

If we belong to the family of Jesus, we will do the will of his Father. When his mother and siblings came to Jesus, he asked, "Who is my mother, and who are my brothers?" He replied, "Whoever does the will of my Father in heaven is my brother and sister and mother" (Matt. 12:48–50).

As regenerate people, we live for God's glory, not for our own. The Lord speaks of "everyone who is called by my name, whom I created for my glory" (Isa. 43:7). Peter declares, "You are a chosen people, a royal priesthood, a holy nation, a people belonging to God, that you may declare the praises of him who called you out of darkness into his wonderful light" (1 Pet. 2:9).

A Word of Encouragement

Paul concludes this section with a word of encouragement: *"For sin shall not be your master, because you are not under law, but under grace*" (v. 14). Because we are now under grace, we will not present the members of our bodies to wickedness; we will present ourselves and the members of our bodies as those raised from the dead to righteousness.

This word of encouragement is founded upon three indicatives. First, we can say "No" to sin and "Yes" to Jesus because sin is not our master. We died to sin; it has no power over us. God the Father, the Son, and the Holy Spirit is our master. Formerly we fought in the army of Satan; now we fight against sin and Satan in the army of God.

Second, we can present our members to do righteousness because we are not under law. That is another indicative. "But when the time had fully come, God sent his Son, born of a woman, born under law, to redeem those under law, that we might receive the full rights of sons" (Gal. 4:4–5). We have been taken out from being under the law.

The law condemns and demands. It only brings the wrath of God; it cannot impart life. Yet all Pharisees and other self-righteous people depend on their own law-keeping. All unbelievers are under the law and its condemnation. If we speak to them about their sin, they get upset and declare, "I am not a sinner. I have always done what is right." Such people are hypocrites. Otherwise, they would bow down before Christ and confess, "Lord, have mercy upon me, a sinner." Jesus has redeemed us from being under law by his perfect lawkeeping.

Third, we can walk in holiness because we are under grace. We have received God's unmerited favor. We merited wrath and death, but God in Christ gave us love and life eternal. The love of God has been shed abroad in our hearts, a love that enables us to keep God's commandments. Grace reigns in us, and we reign in life. Our reign is evidenced by our doing God's will gladly because his will is now written in our hearts. It is now our nature to keep God's law.

By grace we delight in knowing and doing God's law, and grace is mighty to help us: "And God is able to make all grace abound to you, so that in all things at all times, having all that you need, you will abound in every good work" (2 Cor 9:8). Praise God for grace! When people speak evil of us, or when our spouses die, or when we find ourselves staring at death itself, God's grace will come to us. Paul declared, "But by the grace of God I am what I am, and his grace to me was not without effect" (1 Cor. 15:10). Let us live under grace, knowing that God's grace has great effect in our lives.

James says that God gives more grace to the humble (James 4:6). The Hebrews writer tells us, "Let us then approach the throne of grace with confidence, so that we may receive mercy and find grace to help us in our time of need" (Heb. 4:16). We need grace every moment of every day. We need grace for everything. I can do all things through Jesus Christ who gives me strength (Phil. 4:13).

Thank God, we are now under grace—under God the Father, under his Christ, under the Holy Spirit, under the word, and under God's delegated authorities. We now hate sin and delight in righteousness. Justified by Christ's righteousness, we demonstrate our justification by our holiness. Being under grace, we make use of all the means of grace to grow in grace: the word of God, prayer, breaking of bread, and fellowship. By grace we live and by grace we die. By grace we are more than conquerors, and by grace we shall shine as stars in this fallen universe. Let us, therefore, march to Zion as soldiers of Christ and happy slaves of Jesus.

30

Slaves to Righteousness

[15]What then? Shall we sin because we are not under law but under grace? By no means! [16]Don't you know that when you offer yourselves to someone to obey him as slaves, you are slaves to the one whom you obey—whether you are slaves to sin, which leads to death, or to obedience, which leads to righteousness? [17]But thanks be to God that, though you used to be slaves to sin, you wholeheartedly obeyed the form of teaching to which you were entrusted. [18]You have been set free from sin and have become slaves to righteousness.

Romans 6:15–18

A few years ago a man in Los Angeles wore a sandwich board sign that read on the front: "I am a slave of Jesus Christ." On the back it asked: "Whose slave are you?" Theologian Anders Nygren stated, "The idea that man could be free, in the sense that he can be lord of his own life, is nothing but a chimera [a monstrosity]."[1]

According to Romans 6, everyone is a slave of someone. No one is a self-determining, independent being. At the end of one's life, no one can say, "I did it my way." It is an illusion to think we can live however we want. We are either slaves of sin and Satan, or slaves of Jesus Christ. Either way, we all offer strict obedience to the lord we serve.

We Are under Grace

In Romans 6:14 Paul declared that sin was no longer the master of the believer because he is now under grace, not law. Now he

---

1   Nygren, *Commentary on Romans*, 254.

asks, *"Shall we sin because we are not under law but under grace?"* (v. 15). Paul is dealing with a question of an opponent, as he did in Romans 6:1. This time it may be a legalist who is asking, "What will happen to our ethical lives if we are not under law? Can we transgress the law with impunity?" This was a big question for first-century Jewish Christians.

The truth is, believers are no longer under law. Therefore, they are no longer trying to establish their own righteousness and justification. The law can only demand, curse, and pronounce death. It can never justify a sinner, and no fallen man can keep it. But the sinless Son of God was born under law to redeem those under law from being under law. He took us out from being under the condemnation and curse of the law and brought us into his kingdom of righteousness, peace, and joy in the Holy Spirit.

The Pharisees attempted to justify themselves through keeping the law. Even today, orthodox Jews depend on their own righteousness to save them. They do not see their need for a redeemer. This was also true in the New Testament times. The Pharisee in Luke 18, unlike the publican, went home unjustified because he gloried in being under law. Paul describes how he himself gloried in his legalistic righteousness before coming to know Christ: "If anyone else thinks he has reasons to put confidence in the flesh, I have more: circumcised on the eighth day, of the people of Israel, of the tribe of Benjamin, . . . as for legalistic righteousness, faultless" (Phil. 3:4–6). Elsewhere Paul says, "I do not set aside the grace of God, for if righteousness could be gained through the law, Christ died for nothing!" (Gal. 2:21).

Those who are justified by the righteousness of Christ are members of the new covenant. The wonderful thing about the new covenant is that the law of God is now written in our hearts and we take delight in it. It is not merely external; it has become internal. Even the Old Testament speaks about God's people delighting in the law of God (e.g., Psalms 1, 19, and 119).

The law, therefore, which expresses the very nature of God, has become the very nature of God's people. If a person despises God's law, his claim to be a Christian is false. To despise God's law is to despise God himself. Paul says in Romans 7 that the law is holy, righteous, spiritual, and good. True Christians honor

God's law. The Lord declares, "I will put my law in their minds and write it on their hearts. I will be their God, and they will be my people" (Jer. 31:33). The people of God delight in God's law and do it by new capacities given to them—divine nature and the Holy Spirit. Believers eagerly obey the law of God, not to accomplish their justification, but as evidence of it. Therefore, it is abominable to ask, "Shall we deliberately sin because we are not under law but under grace?" As in Romans 6:2, Paul answers emphatically, "God forbid!"

A Christian is not under sin and law; rather, he is under grace. Being "under grace" means to be under the authority, power, and rule of grace. Grace reigns through righteousness (Rom. 5:21). To be under grace means to be under our Lord Jesus Christ. We love Jesus our Redeemer, who exhorts, "If ye love me, keep my commandments" (John 14:15, KJV). We have love-power that enables us to keep his commandments. Paul says that the love of God compels, motivates, impels, pushes us forward (2 Cor. 5:14). The most powerful force in the whole world is the love of God. And we have the Holy Spirit, who sheds abroad in our hearts this love, so that we overflow with love.

Therefore, under-grace people are not lawless and careless; they are holy and obedient. The grace of God will never lead anyone to sin. On the contrary, the grace of God always leads us to honor God's law by obeying it. Those touched by this superpower of God's grace will love God's law.

It is sheer foolishness to ask: "Why not sin, since we are not under law but under grace?" Justification by Christ's perfect righteousness guarantees our sanctification and glorification. In other words, our justification guarantees our holy living. Jesus Christ is "our righteousness, holiness and redemption" (1 Cor. 1:30). He is not just our righteousness; he makes us righteous. That is why one who continues in sin is not justified, despite his claims, for "without holiness no one will see the Lord" (Heb. 12:14).

Romans 6:1–14 argued that we should not continue in sin because we died to sin through our union with Christ in his death and resurrection. In Romans 6:15–23, Paul argues that we are not to sin, because we are slaves of God. Everyone is a slave, either to master Sin or to God, the great Master. Paul reasons elsewhere, "But if you are led by the Spirit, you are not under law" (Gal. 5:18). That is why we must not say, "Since I am under grace and not under law, I can sin." "Under grace" means we are under the control of the Holy Spirit of God.

Not being under law for the purpose of justification does not mean we are free to do what we want. You are under God the Holy Spirit, who commands and enables you to honor God's law. Emil Brunner remarks, "Freedom from the Law does not mean freedom from God but freedom for God."[2] Similarly, Robert Haldane comments, "The freedom from the moral law which the believer enjoys, is the freedom from an obligation to fulfill it in his own person for his justification."[3] Freedom from the law means freedom from trying to justify ourselves by keeping the law. Thank God, we are set free from that! Haldane also says, "If a man voluntarily sins, on the pretext that he is not under the law, but under grace, it is a proof that the grace of God is not in him."[4]

Romans 6:16 is a self-evident truth. A slave will obey his master implicitly and always. His will is the master's will. Owned by the master, he has no independence. In this world there are only two masters and two opposing results of their slavery. Slavery to master Sin reaps death, while slavery to master God results in experimental righteousness, holiness, and eternal life. We must ask ourselves whom we are obeying.

The cruel master Sin deceives and gives death through temporal pleasure. He is like a dope pusher whose only purpose is to fry your brain. Sin says, "Feel good and die." Sin pushes his slavery on people by telling them to eat the forbidden fruit and be free from God and all his delegated authorities. Sin says, "Don't study; have fun. Have an abortion and be free. Divorce and be happy. Don't work but eat well. Eat too much and lose weight. Borrow much and feel great. Don't read the Bible; view pornography instead." But sin leads only to eternal death. Adam and Eve believed Satan's lie and disobeyed God's word. Jesus believed the word of God, obeyed it, and saved us from sin's lie.

---

2   Quoted by Morris, *Epistle to the Romans*, 261.
3   Haldane, *Exposition of Romans*, 259.
4   Ibid., 258.

We Are under the Word of God

Not only are we under grace, but we are also under the word of God: *"But thanks be to God that, though you used to be slaves to sin, you wholeheartedly obeyed the form of teaching to which you were entrusted"* (v. 17). This is a doxology: "Thanks be to God!" Paul is praising God for saving the Roman Christians. "Thanks be to God that, though you used to be slaves to sin . . ." That is our past history, not our present reality. We were slaves. Paul continues, "You wholeheartedly obeyed the form of teaching . . ." We expected Paul to say that we "believed" or "received" the form of teaching. But that is not what he wrote: "You wholeheartedly obeyed the form of teaching to which you were entrusted." The point is that we obey God because we are under his word. Scripture is over us. God handed us over to this doctrine. We are under grace, but we are also under the Bible.

We were sons of disobedience. But something supernatural and miraculous happened to us; a great change took place in our lives and God delivered us from our slavery to sin.

David speaks of having "escaped like a bird out of the fowler's snare" (Ps. 124:7). God broke the snare and we came out, flying like a bird. Paul writes, "Those who oppose him he must gently instruct, in the hope that God will grant them repentance leading them to a knowledge of the truth, and that they will come to their senses and escape from the trap of the devil, who has taken them captive to do his will" (2 Tim. 2:25–26). Those who are not Christians must understand their trapped condition. They are enslaved to do the will of their captor, Satan.

But we have been freed from our slavery to sin and Satan. At the midpoint of time, someone stronger came from heaven, born of a woman, born under the law, and redeemed us from our slavery to sin and Satan by his perfect obedience to God's law. He opened our prison doors, broke our chains, and set us free.

Our help is in the name of the Lord, who kept the law. He paid the highest price of his own precious blood. We have been born again, justified, and adopted into God's family. What a change! Before we hated God's law; now we love the law that God himself has written into our hearts. Ezekiel describes this glorious transformation: "I will give them an undivided heart and put a new spirit in them; I will remove from them their heart of stone and give them a heart of flesh. Then they will follow my decrees and be careful to keep my laws. They will be my people, and I will be their God" (Ezek. 11:19–20). Elsewhere he says, "I will sprinkle clean water on you [i.e., preaching the word of God], and you will be clean; I will cleanse you from all your impurities and from all your idols. I will give you a new heart and put a new spirit in you; I will remove from you your heart of stone and give you a heart of flesh. And I will put my Spirit in you and move you to follow my decrees and be careful to keep my laws. . . . You will be my people, and I will be your God" (Ezek. 36:25–28).

Obedience to God is our new lifestyle: *"You obeyed from your heart the form of teaching to which you were handed over"* (Rom. 6:17, author's translation). Christians obey the gospel. "They devoted themselves to the apostles' teaching" (Acts 2:42). Paul told Timothy, "What you heard from me, keep as the pattern of sound teaching" (2 Tim. 1:13). He also exhorted him, "Until I come, devote yourself to the public reading of Scripture, to preaching and to teaching" (1 Tim. 4:13). God has put us under sound doctrine, under the gospel, under the Bible, the very word of God.

The Roman Christians heard the gospel preached, exercised their intellects, and understood it. A Christian must exercise his intellect, his will, and his holy affections toward God. Christianity is not for intellectually lazy people. It is for intelligent people who have received a new heart, a new mind, a new will, and new affections through regeneration. "Obeyed from the heart" means they exercised their wills in obeying God's law and took delight in doing so.

When we understand and love the word of God, we will obey it. Earlier in this epistle Paul stated, "Through him and for his name's sake, we received grace and apostleship to call people from among all the Gentiles to the obedience that comes from faith" (Rom 1:5). Later, he tells these Roman Christians, "I will not venture to speak of anything except what Christ has accomplished through me in leading the Gentiles to obey God by what I have said and done" (Rom. 15:18). Some people attempt to separate faith and obedience, but we cannot separate what God has joined together. Jesus said, "Go and make disciples of all nations, baptizing them in the name of the Father and of the Son and of the Holy Spirit, and teaching them to obey everything I have commanded you" (Matt. 28:19–20).

> Trust and obey, there is no other way
> To be happy in Jesus, but to trust and obey.

The essence of sin is disobedience, but salvation leads to obedience to God. Even many Christians think obedience is a shame. It is deemed shameful to obey one's parents or one's employer or any other authority immediately. But immediate obedience is the nature of God's people. Christian doctrine always leads to Christian ethics. James Boice said, "Obedience is the very essence of believing. It is what belief is all about."[5]

People take medicine because they believe it will help them. They do not say, "I will just believe in the medicine, but I won't take it." Such non-active faith would not do them any good. Yet belief without obedience is the demonic doctrine that prevails in many churches today.

We were born slaves of sin and Satan; now we have been born again as slaves to righteousness, to Jesus Christ our Savior. We became Christians by divine action alone. God has set us free and handed us over to the gospel. So the Bible teaches us, rebukes us, corrects us, and trains us to do the will of God. We are being trained to godliness. We want to hear and do, not hear, argue, and not do.

Through obedience to the gospel, we are being transformed and conformed to the character of Christ. The gospel puts its own imprint on us. We are under the custody of the gospel. It leads us, and we follow. Therefore, we must diligently and prayerfully study the word of God. We must meditate upon it and do what it says. We must honor the Bible because it is the very word of God.

Jesus Christ is speaking to us through the word of God. God's word renews our minds that we may worship and serve him acceptably. Calvin said, "Obedience is the mother of true knowledge of God."[6]

---

5 Boice, *Romans*, vol. 2, *Reign of Grace*, 695.
6 Quoted by Moo, *Epistle to the Romans*, 399.

We Are Slaves to Righteousness

Now Paul declares, *"You have been set free from sin and have become slaves to righteousness"* (Rom. 6:18). It should read, "Having been set free from sin, you have been enslaved to righteousness." We have been enslaved to our new master. We obey God because we are under the authority of righteousness.

Who enslaved us to righteousness? God. After setting us free from sin, he then enslaved us to righteousness. It is not possible for anyone to be independent; we serve either sin or righteousness. Paul is saying that we have been set free from our former master, Sin. In this verse he personifies sin and righteousness, just as he personified obedience in verse 16.

The great miracle is that God has enabled us to get out of the pit of slavery to sin. Elsewhere Paul reminds us how bad our condition was when we were slaves to sin and Satan: "As for you, you were dead in your transgressions and sins, in which you used to live when you followed the ways of this world and of the ruler of the kingdom of the air, the spirit who is now at work in those who are disobedient.[7] All of us also lived among them at one time, gratifying the cravings of our sinful nature and following its desires and thoughts" (Eph. 2:1–3). Sin is totalitarian; it controls every aspect of an unbeliever's life. There is not even one small part wherein an unbeliever exercises autonomy. He has no freedom or ability to disobey the thoughts and desires of his sinful nature.

But we have been set free from sin through the gospel by the Holy Spirit! Being set free from sin does not mean that we have achieved sinless perfection or that we are free from sin's continuing influence and its temptation. It does not mean Christians may not sin through carelessness. But it means that sin no longer is our master. We have been permanently removed from the sphere of sin, and the Lord Jesus will keep us from ever going back into this slavery.

Positively, we have been enslaved to a power called righteousness. This is speaking about our new obligation. We no longer have an

---

7   In the Greek it is "sons of disobedience." Our father's name was Disobedience.

obligation to serve the flesh (Rom. 8:12); now we are obligated to serve God. We have been set free from sin so that we can now devote ourselves to righteousness. We have been made good trees; therefore, we bear good fruit. The purpose of our lives is to glorify God.

We are to obey God always, not occasionally. We are enslaved to righteousness—and what glorious slavery this is! This slavery is the maximum freedom that God intends his creatures to enjoy. It was never God's intention that man should be independent of God. Man enjoys his life to the utmost when he is utterly dependent on God. Obedience to God is sheer happiness.

Paul declares, "Through Christ Jesus the law of the Spirit of life set me free from the law of sin and death" (Rom. 8:2). The Lord appeared to Moses and told him, "I will be with you. And this will be the sign to you that it is I who have sent you: When you have brought the people out of Egypt, you will serve God on this mountain" (Exod. 3:12, author's translation). In other words, they were being set free from Pharaoh's slavery to serve the covenant Lord. This was confirmed later: "When the king of Egypt was told that the people had fled, Pharaoh and his officials changed their minds about them and said, 'What have we done? We have let the Israelites go and have lost their services!'" (Exod. 14:5). He lost their services because they were now servants of the Lord.

God's purpose for our lives is that we serve him. In Romans 6 we have read about being slaves of God, slaves of the gospel, and slaves of obedience. But here Paul says we are "slaves to righteousness." Righteousness is "doing what is right."[8] We are made slaves to the will of God, which we find in the Bible— "the form of teaching to which [we] were entrusted." We study the Bible to find out the will of God, and we oppose cultural standards that go against the Bible. Therefore, we oppose Darwinism, divorce, radical feminism, and abortion because the Bible opposes them. We say children should obey their parents and that one should provide for his own family because that is what the Bible teaches.

---

8 Paul is speaking here about experimental righteousness, not the gift of righteousness imputed to us. This imparted righteousness is practical obedience to the will of God.

The gospels speak of a man possessed by a legion of demons. This man was naked, restless, and miserable, wandering alone from cemetery to cemetery (Mark 5:1–20). His mind was gone, taken over by demons. That is the picture of an unbeliever. Then he was set free by Jesus, and for the first time in a long time, he was clothed and sitting down, and "in his right mind" (Mark 5:15). And, finally, this man wanted to follow Jesus. Jesus gives us a sound mind that can be put to the right use of thinking God's thoughts after him.

As slaves of righteousness, we have no right to do whatever we want with our bodies. Paul inquires, "Do you not know that your body is a temple of the Holy Spirit, who is in you, whom you have received from God? You are not your own; you were bought at a price. Therefore honor God with your body" (1 Cor. 6:19–20). Again Paul declares, "You were bought at a price" (1 Cor. 7:23). We have been redeemed from the slave market by Jesus Christ by his own precious blood.

How then shall we live? Paul instructs, "So whether you eat or drink or whatever you so, do it all for the glory of God" (1 Cor. 10:31). We are enslaved to righteousness, to the will of God. Paul states, "We demolish arguments and every pretension that sets itself up against the knowledge of God, and we take captive every thought to make it obedient to Christ" (2 Cor. 10:5).

If we are Christians, we will love the totalitarian lordship of Jesus Christ. As John Frame said, Christ's demand is absolute and transcends all other loyalties. To the man who wanted to bury his father, Jesus said, "Follow me, and let the dead bury their own dead" (Matt. 8:22). If a husband does not want his Christian wife to go to church, she still must go to church. A husband's authority is delegated by God, but the authority of the Lord Jesus transcends all other authorities.[9]

As children of God, we have no right to think evil thoughts. We must bring every thought to obey Christ. If God has justified us by the righteousness of Christ, then we are enslaved to Christ to obey him and his delegated authorities. This obedience is our practical, experimental righteousness,

---

9   John M. Frame, "Scripture Speaks for Itself," in *God's Inerrant Word: An International Symposium on the Trustworthiness of Scripture*, ed. John Warwick Montgomery (Minneapolis: Bethany Fellowship, 1974), 183.

proving we are justified by grace alone. "And if we are careful to obey all this law before the LORD our God, as he has commanded us, that will be our righteousness" (Deut. 6:25). And John writes, "The wedding of the Lamb has come, and his bride has made herself ready. Fine linen, bright and clean, was given her to wear. (Fine linen stands for the righteous acts of the saints.)" (Rev. 19:7–8).

Remember, we do not obey to be justified, but we obey because we are justified. When we obey, we are working out what God has already worked in us. So we obey by grace alone. Douglas Moo remarks, "The freedom of the Christian is not freedom to do what one wants, but freedom to obey God—willingly, joyfully, and naturally."[10] We can obey God because, as children of God, we have been given divine nature.

Jesus Christ came to the slave market of this world seeking us when we were slaves of the cruel masters Sin and Satan. He redeemed us, brought us out of their control by his precious blood, and now we are his glad bondslaves. He loves us forever, and we love him by obeying him. We deny ourselves, take up the cross daily, and are following him to the Celestial City. We were dead before; now we live forever. We are not sinlessly perfect, but we have freedom to serve God. We are given grace and are made able to put to death the misdeeds of the body by the power of the Holy Spirit.

What happens if we are caught in a sin and wander from the narrow path of God's will? Paul exhorts, "Brothers, if someone is caught in a sin, you who are spiritual should restore him gently" (Gal. 6:1). Leaders, other Christians, our spouses, and even our children can be used to bring us back to a holy walk. James writes, "My brothers, if one of you should wander from the truth and someone should bring him back, remember this: Whoever turns a sinner from the error of his way will save him from death and cover over a multitude of sins" (James 5:19–20). When someone comes to you in this way, do not deny, debate, or argue with that person. God is sending that brother or sister to you to bring to your attention your sin. You should thank God, repent, and receive forgiveness.

---

10   Moo, *Epistle to the Romans*, 399.

We all have a choice. We can serve sin, Satan, uncleanness, lawlessness, and reap eternal death; or we can by grace serve God, the gospel, righteousness, and enjoy the gift of eternal life. Today I set before you life and death. May God help you to choose life!

31

Free from Sin

19I put this in human terms because you are weak in your natural selves. Just as you used to offer the parts of your body in slavery to impurity and to ever-increasing wickedness, so now offer them in slavery to righteousness leading to holiness. 20When you were slaves to sin, you were free from the control of righteousness. 21What benefit did you reap at that time from the things you are now ashamed of? Those things result in death! 22But now that you have been set free from sin and have become slaves to God, the benefit you reap leads to holiness, and the result is eternal life. 23For the wages of sin is death, but the gift of God is eternal life in Christ Jesus our Lord.

Romans 6:19–23

Have you heard the story of John, the poor Scottish fisherman? He had a wife and many children, but the family lived in extreme poverty because John spent all the money getting drunk. Then one day Jesus found John, and he transformed this miserable bad tree into a good tree. Old John became new John. He stopped drinking and gave all the money he earned to his wife. There was now enough for food and even for new clothing. John's wife said, "If you are going to behave like this, let's move into a better apartment."

John agreed and told the landlord that he wanted to move into a better apartment.

The landlord asked, "Why would I allow an old drunk like you to move into a new place?"

John replied. "I am not the old John; I am the new John, and here is the money." His family moved into their new apartment.

Those who are in Christ Jesus experience this kind of drastic, fundamental change in belief and in behavior. They are "a new creation; the old has gone, the new has come!" (2 Cor. 5:17). They now bear new fruit for the glory of God. Paul says, "He who has been stealing must steal no longer, but must work, doing something useful with his own hands, that he may have something to share with those in need" (Eph. 4:28). This is true Christianity.

Our lives are like a field. The question is, what kind of harvest will we produce in the end? In Romans 6:19–23, Paul speaks of only two kinds of fruit: eternal death or eternal life. Our lives will produce either shame or glory.

We all must give an account to God on the last day. What have you done with your life? Did you please God, or did you please yourself? Are you a bad tree producing an abundance of bitter, bad fruit, or a good tree producing much sweet, good fruit? God controls the span of our lives; he numbers all our days. When our time is up, we must depart from this world. John the Baptist warned: "The ax is already at the root of the trees" (Matt. 3:10). Jesus himself stated, "Every tree that does not bear good fruit is cut down and thrown into the fire" (Matt. 7:19). In the story of the fruitless fig tree, the word had already gone out from the owner: "Cut it down! Why should it use up the soil?" Yet in God's mercy and longsuffering, one more year was granted (Luke 13:6–9). We also must repent and produce good fruit, more fruit, and much fruit—the fruit of righteousness leading to holiness unto eternal life.

Like the life of John, a converted drunkard, a Christian's life of limited years is divided into two segments—his past shameful life (the old John) and his present life that is pleasing to God (the new John). We will first examine the fruit of our past life—the old John.

The Old John

In the past, we were slaves of our former master called Sin. We had no choice but to obey him implicitly. Yet we liked this slavery and gloried in our life of sin. We were bad trees, always producing bad fruit. We were living illustrations of the words of Jesus: "For from within, out of men's hearts, come evil thoughts, sexual immorality, theft, murder, adultery, greed, malice, deceit, lewdness, envy, slander, arrogance and folly" (Mark 7:21–22).

What a variety of bad fruits we produced as we freely offered our minds, our wills, our affections, and the parts of our bodies to sin! While praising sin and sinners, we mocked God, his saints, and his truth. We daily gratified the cravings of our flesh and dutifully obeyed its desires and thoughts. Paul says of such people, "Their destiny is destruction, their god is their stomach, and their glory is in their shame" (Phil. 3:19).

Those who serve sin know God, but they refuse to glorify him by doing his holy will. Therefore, their thinking becomes futile and their foolish hearts hard. Because they exchange the glory of God for the shame of idolatry, God gives them over to shameful lusts and a depraved mind, to do what ought not to be done. Their lives are ever spiraling downward into the depths of the sewer. Describing such people, Paul says, "They have become filled with every kind of wickedness, evil, greed and depravity. They are full of envy, murder, strife, deceit and malice. They are gossips, slanderers, God-haters, insolent, arrogant and boastful; they invent ways of doing evil; they disobey their parents; they are senseless, faithless, heartless, ruthless. Although they know God's righteous decree that those who do such things deserve death, they not only continue to do these very things but also approve of those who practice them" (Rom. 1:29-32).

In Romans 6, Paul reminds these Roman Christians of their sinful, shameful past: *"Just as you used to offer the parts of your body in slavery to impurity and to ever-increasing wickedness . . ."* (v. 19). As sinners, these people worked hard, day and night, toiling and sweating in the service of sin and Satan. They offered their bodies and souls, minds and monies, to the service of Master Sin for temporal, glandular excitement. Slaves of uncleanness, they were filthy and prided themselves in doing filth. They were like people today who abort their own children for the temporal pleasures of sin.

Not only were they slaves of uncleanness, but they were also slaves of lawlessness. They hated God's law. They mocked God and his holy, spiritual, righteous and good law by violating it. Their lives spiraled downward from uncleanness to lawlessness.

This describes our life as the old John. When we were slaves of sin, we had absolutely nothing to do with God and his righteousness. Our total commitment was to sin and to sin alone. We were a stench to God. We served sin with great demonic power. Like the man who was possessed of a legion of demons, we worked very hard in the service of sin and self-destruction. Everyone who refuses to confess Jesus Christ as Savior and Lord is a slave of sin. He is not free or autonomous. A sinner serves Satan by sinning.

The psalmist declares, "Those who make [idols] will be like them, and so will all who trust in them" (Ps. 135:18). So a sinner ultimately becomes like Satan—uncouth and miserable. All unbelievers change from one degree of wretchedness to another until they become like the devil.

Paul then asks the probing question, "What benefit did you reap at that time from the things you are now ashamed of?" (Rom. 6:21). Paul is addressing our consciences. Let us look back ten, twenty, or thirty years. When we lived in sin, what fruit did we produce before we repented and believed in Jesus Christ? Then we gloried in our sin, but now we are ashamed. We were so proud of our adultery, idolatry, disobedience, and atheism, and we encouraged others to do the same: "Although they know God's righteous decree that those who do such things deserve death, they not only continue to do these very things but also approve of those who practice them" (Rom. 1:32).

We are now ashamed because we are the new John. By God's grace we now see the reality that our pre-regenerate life was wasteful and shameful, destructive of ourselves and of those around us. It was a life of loss, sorrow, guilt, depression, and restlessness.

We are living at a time when perversion is popular. It is no longer in the closet; it is in the living room, on display for all to see. Yet even this lack of shame is not new. The prophet Jeremiah asks, "Are they ashamed of their loathsome conduct? No, they have no shame at all; they do not even know how to blush. So they will fall among the fallen; they will be brought down when they are punished, says the LORD" (Jer. 8:12).

What was the final outcome of our serving sin? What did it profit us? The harvest of living sinful lives is shame, uncleanness, lawlessness, wickedness, disease, destruction, depression, divorce, destitution, and death. Paul states, "For when we were controlled by the sinful nature, the sinful passions aroused by the law were at work in our bodies, so that we bore fruit for death" (Rom. 7:5). Our sin produces the fruit of physical, spiritual, and eternal death. "The wages of sin is death" (Rom. 6:23).

380

The Bible speaks of the second death: "Then death and Hades were thrown into the lake of fire. The lake of fire is the second death" (Rev. 20:14). Those who remain in their sins will die, but he who lives forever will raise them up and throw them into the lake of fire. The risen Lord declares: "But the cowardly, the unbelieving, the vile, the murderers, the sexually immoral, those who practice magic arts, the idolaters and all liars—their place will be in the fiery lake of burning sulfur. This is the second death" (Rev. 21:8).

Paul wants us to pause, think, and reflect on the bad, bitter fruit that we produced as sinners. Jesus asked, "What shall it profit a man, if he shall gain the whole world, and lose his own soul?" (Mark 8:36, KJV). We may live seventy or eighty years—what will we have to show for it? Only waste, loss, death, and shame, if we are outside of Christ.

Moses warns us about the fruit of doing evil in Deuteronomy 28:15–68. For example, he says, "The LORD will send on you curses, confusion and rebuke" (v. 20); "The LORD will afflict you with madness, blindness and confusion of mind" (v. 28); "Among those nations you will find no repose, no resting place for the sole of your foot. There the LORD will give you an anxious mind, eyes weary with longing, and a despairing heart. You will live in constant suspense, filled with dread both night and day, never sure of your life. In the morning you will say, 'If only it were evening!' and in the evening, 'If only it were morning!'—because of the terror that will fill your hearts and the sights that your eyes will see" (vv. 65–67). What fruit do sinners produce? Uncleanness, lawlessness, wickedness, and death.

The New John

But now the old John is gone; the new John has come! Thanks be to God for the great change that happened to us. Thank God for his saving action in Jesus Christ. Thank God for the Spirit's regenerating work in us making us good people. Now we bear good fruit by doing good works. Now we serve our master in righteousness and obey from the heart the gospel to which we have been delivered. Now, by God's grace, we enjoy everlasting life.

Let us now examine the fruit of our present Christian life. By the miracle of God we are born again into the family of God. We are justified, adopted, and permanently set free from sin and Satan. We are kept by the Father and the Son in the Holy Spirit. We are indwelt and empowered by the Spirit of God. By God's grace we are now able not to sin and able to love God and keep his commandments. We are children of God with free access to our Father. We now worship God and read his word with a voracious appetite. We pray to God in the name of Christ, and God truly answers our prayers. God gives us sufficient grace to abound in every good work.

Before, we were dead in sins; now we are dead to sin and living for God. Before, we had nothing to do with righteousness; now we are joyful slaves of righteousness. Before, we were sons of disobedience; now we are children of obedience. Before, we were working hard in the service of sin; now we work hard in the service of righteousness. Before, we were ashamed; now we are truly proud of our new status as slaves of our Savior. We boast in God, who came to our hell and transported us to heaven. He destroyed our death by his death on the cross and gave us eternal life. To obey God is now a joy for us, for in our new nature we delight in God's law.

We are proud of being given the great dignity of being enslaved to God himself. We had no glory, but now we are given glory as slaves of Christ. Paul himself gloried in this slavery, and so he introduced himself to the Romans as "Paul, a slave of Christ Jesus, called apostle, set apart unto the gospel of God" (Rom. 1:1, author's translation).

Thank God for the amazing change in our lives. Thank God for the past and present division in our lives. We were sinners, but now we are saints of God. Paul addresses the Roman believers as those "called to be saints" (Rom. 1:7). Let the people of this world slander us, lie about us, or mock us—God calls us saints. He also calls us friends and brothers. He calls us sons of God, for we have received the Spirit of adoption by whom we cry, "*Abba*, Father."

Thank God for Jesus' incarnation. The "But now" of Romans 3:21 introduces this gospel age—the messianic age, the age of salvation, the age of the cross. Jesus Christ has come to redeem us from sin. Look at Romans 6:19: "*Just as you used to offer the parts of your body in slavery to impurity and to ever-increasing wickedness, so now . . .*" Or look at verse 22: *"But now that you have been set free from sin . . ."*

Thank God for the cross. Christ died for our sins and was raised for our justification. In this messianic age, there is now regeneration, redemption, freedom, justification, and sanctification. In this age of the Spirit, the Spirit dwells in us and teaches us the will of God. This same Spirit empowers us to work out with fear and trembling our salvation, which God himself is working into us. We are set free from sin and enslaved to God. We are not fruitless trees; we are branches united to the vine, and so we bear fruit. And we are being constantly pruned by God's grace to bear more fruit and much fruit to our Father's glory.

We are enabled to do all things for the glory of God. Justification leads to an obedient life. If it does not lead to holy living, we are not saved. If we are not sanctified, we are not justified. We are the same old drunk, lying, lazy, wicked John, committed to uncleanness and glorying in filth.

But we have been saved, we are being saved, and we will be saved. Jesus is our righteousness, sanctification, and glorification. We are new creations in Christ. What is the purpose of this new life? Paul writes, "We are God's workmanship, created in Christ Jesus to do good works, which God prepared in advance for us to do" (Eph. 2:10).

If sin is lawlessness, then obedience is lawfulness. As God's obedient children, we do good works and walk in the paths of righteousness for his name's sake. We are not set free from the bondage of sin to roam aimlessly, doing our own will. We have heard the call of Christ: "Deny yourself, take up your cross daily, and follow me to death and resurrection." Paul assures us we have the fruit of holiness: *"But now that you have been set free from sin and have become slaves to God, the benefit you reap leads to holiness, and the result is eternal life"* (v. 22). We are producing the fruit of holiness by divine energy.

Examine yourself. Do you have fruit? If not, you are not saved, because no Christian can go to heaven without fruit. The fruit of sanctification is the proof of our salvation. "Without holiness no one will see the Lord" (Heb. 12:14). Jesus came to save us *from* our sins (Matt. 1:21).

If we are in Christ, we will bear fruit that abides, fruit that lasts to eternity. Our lives will be fruitful—not a waste or loss. Paul writes, "And we pray this in order that you may live a life worthy of the Lord and may please him in every way: bearing fruit in every good work" (Col. 1:10). We have a good harvest coming, a harvest of righteousness. We are good people because God who is good has made us good, and we in turn do good and influence others for good.

As God's children, we are disciplined and trained by our Father to do good. Paul speaks about such training: "You were taught . . . to put on the new self, created to be like God in true righteousness and holiness" (Eph. 4:22, 24). Those who believe the gospel will have righteousness and holiness. Paul describes us as being "filled with the fruit of righteousness that comes through Jesus Christ—to the glory and praise of God" (Phil. 1:11). The writer to the Hebrews also speaks about this divine chastisement: "No discipline seems pleasant at the time, but painful. Later on, however, it produces a harvest of righteousness and peace for those who have been trained by it" (Heb. 12:11).

We are called to live as Jesus lived (1 John 2:6). Paul writes, "For he chose us in him before the creation of the world to be holy and blameless in his sight" (Eph. 1:4). That is God's plan and purpose for our lives. Elsewhere Paul exhorts, "Husbands, love your wives, just as Christ loved the church and gave himself up for her to make her holy, cleansing her by the washing with water through the word, and to present her to himself as a radiant church, without stain or wrinkle or any other blemish, but holy and blameless" (Eph. 5:25–27). Not only did God choose us to be holy and blameless, but he will also make us so.

The one who serves Satan becomes like Satan; the one who serves Jesus Christ becomes like Jesus Christ. From glory to glory God is changing us (2 Cor. 3:18). Even now we bear fruit unto holiness, resulting in eternal life. The end of a sinner is death eternal; our end is life eternal. Death for sinners begins here, to be experienced in its fullness in hell. Eternal life also begins for us here, to be experienced in its fullness in communion with God in the new heaven and the new earth. John writes about this glorious final state: "And I heard a loud voice from the throne saying, 'Now the dwelling of God is with men, and he will live with them. They will be his people, and God himself will be with them and be their God. He will wipe every tear from their eyes. There will be no more death or mourning or crying or pain, for the old order of things has passed away'" (Rev. 21:3–4).

How, then, can an old John become a new John? How can we be set free from the bondage of sin and Satan? We cannot save ourselves, nor can any religion, philosophy, politician, or scientist save us. Only Jesus can set us free: "If the Son sets you free, you will be free indeed" (John 8:36). Jesus declares, "I am the bread of life. He who comes to me will never go hungry, and he who believes in me will never be thirsty" (John 6:35).

Come to Jesus! When the Father draws you, come. When the Spirit draws you, come. When Christ draws you, come, and prove yourself to be an elect of God. Receive the bread of life, that you may never hunger or thirst, and then start producing fruit unto holiness leading to the fullness of joy in God's presence. All those who are justified by grace through faith alone will follow Jesus in the way of righteousness. They will be led by the Spirit to obey the Scripture taught faithfully by God's holy church, and will ultimately produce a harvest of righteousness.

Thank God, we came when he drew us. We ate the bread of life, we drank the water of life, and we were made alive. The old John is dead, buried, and gone. I am a new John. May we all believe in this truth and be transformed by it, even this day.

32

What Will Your End Be?

For the wages of sin is death, but the gift of God is eternal life in
Christ Jesus our Lord.

Romans 6:23

The end of all things is near, the Bible says (1 Pet. 4:7). This
world will pass away, and we also will pass away. All descendants
of Adam must die because the wages of sin is death. Ezekiel
tells us, "The soul who sins is the one who will die" (Ezek. 18:4).
Though Methuselah lived 969 years, he finally died (Gen. 5:27).
Moses said, "The length of our days is seventy years—or eighty, if
we have the strength; yet their span is but trouble and sorrow, for
they quickly pass, and we fly away" (Ps. 90:10).

The last verse of Romans 6 speaks about the two possible
destinies of all people on earth: eternal death or eternal life. The
purpose of our brief life is not to amass wealth, fame, and power;
rather, it is to receive eternal life. The vast majority of the people
in the world will earn eternal death; only a small remnant will
enjoy the gift of eternal life.

Romans 6:23 is a one-verse summary of the gospel in which
Paul sets before us death and life. To experience the destiny
of eternal death, we need not do anything. Though we are
active and move about in this world, as descendants of Adam
we are all born dead in our sins. To enjoy the gift of eternal
life, we must be united to Jesus Christ, who declares, "I am
the resurrection and the life. He who believes in me will
live, even though he dies" (John 11:25). Christ came into this

world that we might have abundant life. Eternal life is found in Jesus Christ alone.

We are told in the Bible that the end of all unbelievers is destruction, burning, and death, while the end of all believers is salvation and eternal life. What will your end be? We must all think seriously about it before our own death, which is coming soon. There is a day fixed by God when we will die. It is decreed how many days we will live, and we will not live one day more.

Let us then examine three things from Romans 6:23: two masters, two slaveries, and two destinies.

Two Masters

There are only two masters: the living God and Satan (or sin). All people must serve one of these masters. There is no independence.

Through Satan, sin entered the world, a situation which God permitted for his own eternal glory. In Genesis 3 we read how the serpent beguiled Eve and how Adam sinned deliberately. In Revelation 12:9 John declares, "The great dragon was hurled down—that ancient serpent called the devil, or Satan, who leads the whole world astray." Then he says, "And the devil, who deceived them, was thrown into the lake of burning sulfur, where the beast and the false prophet had been thrown. They will be tormented day and night for ever and ever" (Rev. 20:10).

The devil, the god of this world, is the ruler of all who do not believe in Jesus Christ. In other words, the master of every unbeliever is Satan, or sin, because everyone sins through the direction of Satan. The word "sin" (*hamartia*) appears in the singular twenty-two times in Romans 5:12–6:23. Sin is personified as a great king, who reigns and rains down death (Rom. 5:21).

An unbeliever thinks he is free to serve himself and do his own thing, but this is mere delusion. It is spiritual deception, for a sinner is always working for his master, Satan. Having been conceived in sin, the wicked are born sinners and practice sin every day of their lives. Satan, sin, and death reign over all unbelievers.

But we who have believed in Jesus Christ no longer serve sin and Satan; we serve the living God! So Paul exhorts, "Do not offer the parts of your body to sin, as instruments of wickedness, but rather offer yourselves to God, as those who have been brought from death to life; and offer the parts of your body to him as instruments of righteousness" (Rom. 6:13). We are now God's slaves. Paul declares, "You have been set free from sin and have become slaves to God" (Rom. 6:22). The triune God is our new master; now we obey from the heart the form of doctrine to which he has entrusted us (Rom. 6:17).

Notice the emphasis on the Lordship of Christ: "But the gift of God is eternal life in Jesus Christ *our Lord*" (v. 23). Paul later says, "If you confess with your mouth, 'Jesus is Lord,' and believe in your heart that God raised him from the dead, you will be saved" (Rom. 10:9). Jesus said, "I am the gate; whoever enters through me will be saved" (John 10:9). In the introduction to this epistle, Paul calls himself a slave of Jesus Christ. Our new master is Christ, who gave himself for our eternal redemption.

Two Slaveries

All people are slaves. We serve either God or sin in complete obedience. Paul explains, "Don't you know that when you offer yourselves to someone to obey him as slaves, you are slaves to the one whom you obey—whether you are slaves to sin, which leads to death. . . . But thanks be to God that, though you used to be slaves to sin . . . you have been set free from sin. . . . What benefit did you reap at that time from the things you are now ashamed of? Those things result in death!" (Rom. 6:16, 17, 18, 21).

If we are walking in sin, the first thing we lose is our minds. Paul writes, "Furthermore, since they did not think it worthwhile to retain the knowledge of God, he gave them over to a depraved mind, to do what ought not to be done." As we lose the ability to understand and analyze reality, we misunderstand and misjudge it. This losing of the mind precedes many other sins. Paul continues, "They have become filled with every kind of wickedness, evil, greed and depravity. They are full of envy, murder, strife, deceit and malice. They are gossips, slanderers, God-haters, insolent, arrogant and boastful; they invent ways of doing evil" (Rom. 1:28–30).

Serving sin and Satan is extremely hard work, but many people do it. We read about this slavery throughout the New Testament:

1. *Ephesians 2:1–3:* "As for you, you were dead in your transgressions and sins, in which you used to live when you followed the ways of this world and of the ruler of the kingdom of the air, the spirit who is now at work in those who are disobedient. All of us also lived among them at one time, gratifying the cravings of our sinful nature and following its desires and thoughts. Like the rest, we were by nature objects of wrath."

2. *Titus 3:3:* "At one time we too were foolish, disobedient, deceived and enslaved by all kinds of passions and pleasures. We lived in malice and envy, being hated and hating one another."

3. *Galatians 5:19–21:* "The acts of the sinful nature are obvious: sexual immorality, impurity and debauchery; idolatry and witchcraft; hatred, discord, jealousy, fits of rage, selfish ambition, dissensions, factions and envy; drunkenness, orgies, and the like. I warn you, as I did before, that those who live like this will not inherit the kingdom of God."

4. *1 Corinthians 6:9–10:* "Do you not know that the wicked will not inherit the kingdom of God? Do not be deceived: Neither the sexually immoral nor idolaters nor adulterers nor male prostitutes nor homosexual offenders nor thieves nor the greedy nor drunkards nor slanderers nor swindlers will inherit the kingdom of God."

5. *2 Thessalonians 1:6–10:* "God is just: He will pay back trouble to those who trouble you and give relief to you who are troubled, and to us as well. This will happen when the Lord Jesus is revealed from heaven in blazing fire with his powerful angels. He will punish those who do not know God and do not obey the gospel of our Lord Jesus. They will be punished with everlasting destruction and shut out from the presence of the Lord and from the majesty of his power on the day he comes to be glorified in his holy people."

6. *Ephesians 4:19:* "Having lost all sensitivity, they have given themselves over to sensuality so as to indulge in every kind of impurity, with a continual lust for more."

7. *1 Peter 4:1–5:* "Therefore, since Christ suffered in his body, arm yourselves also with the same attitude, because he who has suffered in his body is done with sin. As a result, he does not live the rest of his earthly life for evil human desires, but rather for the will of God. For you have spent enough time in the past doing what pagans choose to do—living in debauchery, lust, drunkenness, orgies, carousing and detestable idolatry. They think it strange that you do not plunge with them into the same flood of dissipation, and they heap abuse on you. But they will have to give account to him who is ready to judge the living and the dead."

8. *2 Thessalonians 2:10–12:* "They perish because they refused to love the truth and so be saved. For this reason God sends them a powerful delusion so that they will believe the lie and so that

all will be condemned who have not believed the truth but have delighted in wickedness." He is speaking about everyone who refuses to believe in Jesus Christ. It is hard labor and yet they do it with great delight, deceived by the pleasures of sin for a season.

Romans 8:4–14 contrasts those who live according to the flesh with those who live according to the Holy Spirit. Paul writes, "in order that the righteous requirements of the law might be fully met in us, who do not live according to the sinful nature but according to the Spirit" (v. 4).

We serve God only and obey his word (Rom. 6:13, 16–19, 22). We live according to the Spirit "because those who are led by the Spirit of God are sons of God" (Rom. 8:14). Led by the Spirit of God, we go where the Spirit of God sends us.

Paul exhorts, "So I say, live by the Spirit, and you will not gratify the desires of the sinful nature" (Gal. 5:16). That is a guarantee. "Since we live by the Spirit, let us keep in step with the Spirit. Let us not become conceited, provoking and envying each other" (Gal. 5:25–26). When we live by the Spirit, we will produce the fruit of the Spirit: "love, joy, peace, patience, kindness, goodness, faithfulness, gentleness and self-control" (Gal. 5:22).

Two Destinies: The Wages of Sin

Finally, let us look at the two destinies waiting for all people. *"For the wages of sin is death"* (Rom. 6:23). The destiny awaiting all who do not believe in Jesus Christ is eternal death. A child of Adam does not need to do anything to attain this destiny of death; it is the natural result of a life of sin. Just be autonomous and do your thing. Do not listen to the voice of the Lord or come to church. Do not listen to your parents or the Bible.

The idea Paul is conveying is of a commander, sin, paying wages for his soldiers. Elsewhere Paul asks, "Who serves as a soldier at his own expense?" (1 Cor. 9:7). The answer is, no one. The soldier of sin is paid daily for his services; his wages consist in death. He receives the first installment while he lives, for we are all dying even as we live. The second installment comes the moment he dies. He will get the third installment when Jesus Christ comes again, raises him up, judges him, and sends him to hell.

The wages of death that sin pays is the wrath of God, which Paul declares is already revealed against all ungodliness and unrighteousness of men (Rom. 1:18). In the same passage, Paul speaks of the downward spiral of sinners as they continue to reject God and serve sin: "Therefore God gave them over in the sinful desires of their hearts to sexual impurity for the degrading of their bodies with one another" (v. 24). Being given over means such people can only sin. "Because of this, God gave them over to shameful lusts," including lesbianism and homosexuality (v. 26). "Furthermore, since they did not think it worthwhile to retain the knowledge of God, he gave them over to a depraved mind" so that they could sin all the time (v. 28).

We all have experienced the daily wages of sin. We have received some payment for our sins in this life, if we think back. Some have experienced poverty, disease, demon possession, drug addiction, divorce, anxiety, loneliness, fear, prison, and being conformed to the devil himself in our nature. Paul alludes to this in Romans 6:19: "You used to offer the parts of your body in slavery to impurity and to ever-increasing wickedness." This is the downward spiral, descending into filthiness, lawlessness, ever-increasing wickedness, shame, and death. It is like a big truck, loaded with the wages of one's sin, arriving at the house to unload death.

The person may protest: "I never ordered this," but he did. If a person serves sin all his life, he must receive what is due him. A sinner will be paid in full.

The rich man of Luke 16 lived a life of sin. He dressed himself in purple and fine linen, lived in luxury, and considered himself blessed. He fully expected to go to Abraham's bosom when he died. But instead he went to hell and found himself in torment, agony, and the fire of divine wrath. Luke says he was thirsty, conscious, and very sober.

Do you say you do not want to believe the gospel? Wait until you die. Then you will become a believer, but it will be too late. The rich man desired to cross over from death to life. He desired that his brothers would consider their end and not go to hell as he did. He prayed for the first time from hell. But no one answered his prayer. And eventually he will be raised to experience the fullness of death, for which he worked while he was living.

The wages of sin is death. John calls it the second death, everlasting death: "And the devil, who deceived them, was thrown into the lake of burning sulfur, where the beast and the false prophet had been thrown. They will be tormented day and night for ever and ever. Then I saw a great white throne and him who was seated on it. Earth and sky fled from his presence, and there was no place for them. . . . Then death and Hades were thrown into the lake of fire. The lake of fire is the second death. If anyone's name was not found written in the book of life, he was thrown into the lake of fire" (Rev. 20:10–11; 14–15).

Paul writes, "[God] will punish those who do not know God and do not obey the gospel of our Lord Jesus. They will be punished with everlasting destruction and shut out from the presence of the Lord and from the majesty of his power" (2 Thess. 1:8–9). Jude says, "In a similar way, Sodom and Gomorrah and the surrounding towns gave themselves up to sexual immorality and perversion. They serve as an example of those who suffer the punishment of eternal fire" (Jude 7).

Sin and Satan promise a happy life but deliver a miserable death. Sin deceives; Satan lies. At the last judgment, all sinners who lived a lawless life will be told by Jesus, "'Depart from me, you who are cursed, into the eternal fire prepared for the devil and his angels.' . . . Then they will go away to eternal punishment, but the righteous to eternal life" (Matt. 25: 41, 46).

Jesus spoke more about hell and its eternal nature than anyone else in the Bible. In fact, he prepared it for the devil, his angels, and all humans who follow his devilish ways. Some imagine Jesus to be like a teddy bear that is nice, lovely, and huggable. But we must look at the Bible. When we do, we will discover the real Jesus, who is both Savior and Judge.

In Genesis 3:4 Satan told Eve, "You will not surely die." But she and Adam did die, and in Adam all have died. Who can get out from hell? It is an irreversible condition. Physical death seals our destiny and nothing more can be done. The fire of hell is the fire of the wrath of God, for our God is a consuming fire.

Yet no people go to hell unless they choose all their lives to do so. They earned it and receive justice from God. When sinners die, they discover hell is not a joke or a swear word. Hell exists, and it is prepared to receive hell-seeking sinners.

Two Destinies: The Gift of God

But there is one other destiny: *"The gift of God is eternal life in Jesus Christ our Lord"* (v. 23). If all in Adam are sinners and all are to die eternal death for their sins (Rom 5:12), then how can anyone be saved from God's wrath and merited hell?

The answer is found in Jesus Christ. The Son of God became sinless man, and this God-man died on the cross in the place of elect sinners. In him we died, were buried, and were raised to live a new life. That is the gospel. The Hebrews writer proclaims, "But we see Jesus, who was made a little lower than the angels, now crowned with glory and honor because he suffered death, so that by the grace of God he might taste death for everyone" (Heb. 2:9). Then he says, "Since the children have flesh and blood, he too shared in their humanity so that by his death he might destroy him who holds the power of death—that is, the devil—and free those who all their lives were held in slavery by their fear of death" (Heb. 2:14–15).

Paul plainly states how Christ accomplished our salvation: "God [the Father] presented [Jesus Christ] as a sacrifice of atonement, through faith in his blood" (Rom. 3:25). He says later, "Since we have now been justified by his blood, how much more shall we be saved from God's wrath through him! For if, when we were God's enemies, we were reconciled to him through the death of his Son, how much more, having been reconciled, shall we be saved through his life!" (Rom. 5:9–10).

Eternal life is a gift from God, not wages for our obedience. Eternal life is a gratuitous bounty of God. It is a grace-gift *(charisma)*, based on the merit and righteousness of Jesus Christ our Redeemer. It is God's free, unmerited gift. To those who merited death, God gives the gift of life. He welcomes to his glorious heaven of eternal blessings those who merited fiery hell.

We experience this gift of eternal life also in three installments. First, in this life, the moment we trust in Jesus Christ, we receive eternal life: "For if, by the trespass of the one man, death reigned through that one man, how much more will those who receive

God's abundant provision of grace and of the gift of righteousness reign in life through the one man, Jesus Christ" (Rom. 5:17). The moment we trust in Jesus Christ, we are given eternal life and we begin to reign with Christ even here in this life.

The second installment comes to us the moment we die. In the parable of the rich man and Lazarus, we see Lazarus in Abraham's bosom. To the thief who believed in Jesus Christ, Jesus said, "Today you will be with me in paradise" (Luke 23:43). John heard the voice from heaven proclaim, "Blessed are the dead who die in the Lord" (Rev. 14:13). They are blessed because they are with God. Paul calls death gain (Phil. 1:21). At death, our spirits are perfected and received into the very presence of God. We read in Hebrews 12:22–23: "You have come to Mount Zion. . . . You have come to God. . . . [You have come] to the spirits of righteous men made perfect."

The third installment will come when Jesus returns. At that time, our perfected spirits will be united with glorious bodies like unto the body of Christ. In these bodies we will live with God forever in full enjoyment of eternal life.

What is eternal life? Jesus Christ gives us this definition: "Now this is eternal life: that they may know you, the only true God, and Jesus Christ, whom you have sent" (John 17:3). Eternal life is to know God through Jesus Christ, and to know God is to love him.

Eternal life has its own quality. It is intimate fellowship with God in the new garden of Eden, which is happiness par excellence. It also has quantity. Methuselah lived 969 years, but we will live forever because we are given eternal life. Eternal life is indestructible. Paul says, "[Christ] has destroyed death and has brought life and immortality to light through the gospel" (2 Tim. 1:10). Whenever the gospel is preached, we are declaring that in Jesus Christ we can receive immortality—eternal life.

By divine design from all eternity, only a few will enjoy this eternal life. Jesus asserts, "But small is the gate and narrow the road that leads to life, and only a few find it" (Matt. 7:14). About the twins, Esau and Jacob, God pronounced, "Jacob I loved, but Esau I hated" (Rom. 9:13). Seeing us all as sinners, God shows mercy to some but not to others. God could have saved all sinners to glorify his mercy, or he could have condemned and sent to hell all sinners to glorify his justice. But he chose to save some and not save others to glorify both his mercy and his justice.

Jesus declared, "Many are called, but few are chosen" (Matt. 22:14, KJV). Yet Jesus gives eternal life to all who come to him in true repentance and faith. And when he comes again, he will say to those who are his: "Well done, good and faithful servant! You have been faithful with a few things; I will put you in charge of many things. Come and share your master's happiness! . . . Come, you who are blessed by my Father; take your inheritance, the kingdom prepared for you since the creation of the world" (Matt. 25:21, 34).

Eternal life is the most precious gift God bestows upon his elect people. Jesus told his disciples, "Do not rejoice that [demons] submit to you, but rejoice that your names are written in heaven" (Luke 10:20). If our names are written in the Lamb's book of life, we will dwell with God in the new heaven and new earth. There shall be no more sin, curse, death, tears, pain, mourning, crying, separation, night, sickness, wars, or poverty. The old order of things has passed away and the new order has come (Rev. 21:4). The kingdom of God has truly come, and it is the fullness of righteousness, peace, and joy in the Holy Spirit.

This gift (charisma) of eternal life leads to joy (chara). God's purpose is that our joy be full, which will happen in the highest degree when we see God face to face. We shall see him as he is, for we shall be changed. We shall shine in glory and dwell in our Father's house forever.

Even now by faith we are in heaven, seated with Christ in heavenly places. The Hebrews writer declares, "But you have come to Mount Zion, to the heavenly Jerusalem, the city of the living God. You have come to thousands upon thousands of angels in joyful assembly, to the church of the firstborn, whose names are written in heaven. You have come to God, the judge of all men, to the spirits of righteous men made perfect, to Jesus the mediator of a new covenant, and to the sprinkled blood that speaks a better word than the blood of Abel" (Heb. 12:22–24).

Your Life's End

How will your life end? I set before you eternal life and eternal death. The vast majority of people have been working all their lives for eternal death. They will receive their just wages in due time. But God is offering us the gift of eternal life in Jesus Christ our Lord. Paul says, "Just as sin reigned in death, so also grace might reign through righteousness to bring eternal life through Jesus Christ our Lord" (Rom. 5:21). We cannot find eternal life outside of Jesus Christ. So the answer to the question of what we must do to be saved is truly, "Believe on the Lord Jesus Christ and you will be saved." Repent earnestly and trust savingly in Jesus Christ today, and receive eternal life. The Bible says, "Now is the time of God's favor, now is the day of salvation" (2 Cor. 6:2). We are saved only through Christ. Paul writes,

> I keep asking that the God of our Lord Jesus Christ, the glorious Father, may give you the Spirit of wisdom and revelation, so that you may know him better. I pray also that the eyes of your heart may be enlightened in order that you may know the hope to which he has called you, the riches of his glorious inheritance in the saints, and his incomparably great power for us who believe. That power is like the working of his mighty strength, which he exerted in Christ when he raised him from the dead and seated him at his right hand in the heavenly realms, far above all rule and authority, power and dominion, and every title that can be given, not only in the present age but also in the one to come. And God placed all things under his feet and appointed him to be head over everything for the church, which is his body, the fullness of him who fills everything in every way. (Eph. 1:17–23)

Jesus Christ is God and Lord. He is not a mere man who died. Therefore, eternal life is found only in Christ Jesus—not in Moses, Mohammed, or anyone else. "Salvation is found in no one else, for there is no other name under heaven given to men by which we must be saved" (Acts 4:12).

Paul concludes Romans 6 with this assertion: *"But the gift of God is eternal life in Christ Jesus our Lord."* Let me ask you: Is Jesus your Lord? You cannot have eternal life unless you confess with your mouth, "Jesus Christ is Lord," and believe in your heart that God raised him from the dead. May we serve the Lord Jesus Christ with fear and rejoice with trembling. "Kiss the Son, lest he be angry and you be destroyed in your way, for his wrath can flare up in a moment. Blessed are all who take refuge in him" (Ps. 2:12).

Yes, the wages of sin is eternal death, but thank God, the gift of God is eternal life through Jesus Christ our Lord. May we accept God's gracious gift of eternal life through his Son.

33

Married to Jesus Christ

¹Do you not know, brothers—for I am speaking to men who know the law—that the law has authority over a man only as long as he lives? ²For example, by law a married woman is bound to her husband as long as he is alive, but if her husband dies, she is released from the law of marriage. ³So then, if she marries another man while her husband is still alive, she is called an adulteress. But if her husband dies, she is released from that law and is not an adulteress, even though she marries another man.

⁴So, my brothers, you also died to the law through the body of Christ, that you might belong to another, to him who was raised from the dead, in order that we might bear fruit to God.

Romans 7:1-4

In the opening verses of Romans 7, Paul uses the illustration of marriage to describe a believer's relationship to Christ. The purpose of this marriage is to bring forth the fruit of holiness to God.

Antinomianism and Legalism

Paul's argument about the reign of grace in a believer's life leaves off in Romans 5:21 and resumes in Romans 8:1–5. Chapters 6 and 7 are, therefore, parenthetical. Chapter 6 dealt with the antinomianism that can result from a misunderstanding of Paul's statement, "But where sin increased, grace increased all the more" (Rom. 5:20). Paul addresses the error right away: "What shall we say, then? Shall we go on sinning so that grace may increase? By no means!" (Rom. 6:1–2). Antinomianism, which says we can sin as much as we please because grace will take us to heaven, is the curse of many modern churches.

Romans 7 deals with the contrasting issue of legalism—the idea that justification and sanctification are based on keeping God's law. Paul has already declared that we are not under law but under grace (Rom. 6:14). Yet the Jews of his day thought of the law as the bulwark against sin. The question then became whether or not Paul was dishonoring the law of God.

In this chapter Paul explains that salvation is not based on our lawkeeping, as the Pharisee of Luke 18 maintained, but on Christ's active and passive obedience to God's law. We must understand that all of Adam's children are under the power and control of both sin and the law. But the truth is, no one obeys the law perfectly. In fact, it can only incite and increase sin in unregenerate people.

Legalists say man's justification and sanctification are due to his ability to keep the law, while antinomians say justification and sanctification are by grace alone, so one can sin freely. In this section, Paul explains that true believers can rejoice in their freedom from the law for justification and sanctification, yet we can also rejoice in the freedom we have to obey God's law, by the Spirit's power, as evidence of our justification by grace alone through faith alone. True believers, in other words, walk in the newness of life. Living by the power of the Holy Spirit, we delight in God's holy law. We know that the letter kills, but the Spirit gives life.

Jesus came to fulfill the law perfectly as our representative head. In his death, his people also fully kept the law. Jesus was born under the law to obey and establish God's law and to redeem us from being under the law. Every unbeliever is under the power and rule of sin until he is saved by grace by the obedient Son of God. Paul states, "The sting of death is sin, and the power of sin is the law." Then he declares, "But thanks be to God! He gives us the victory through our Lord Jesus Christ" (1 Cor. 15:56–57). So also in Romans 7 Paul asks the question, "Who will rescue me from this body of death?" Then he says, "Thanks be to God—through Jesus Christ our Lord!" (vv. 24–25).

Romans 7 can be divided into three parts. The first division (vv. 1–6) speaks about our relationship to the law. We died to the law in the death of Christ. Having thus been set free from the law, we are now married to Christ. In the second division (vv. 7−13) Paul vindicates the law. The law did not die, but we died to the law. Paul explains that God's law is not the cause of sin and death; in fact, it is holy, good, just, and spiritual, revealing God's holy character to us. The last section (vv. 14−25) tells us that the law cannot justify or sanctify. This section is not describing the life of a Christian but that of an unregenerate unbeliever who is dead in trespasses and sins.

Free from the Power of Law

"Do you not know, brothers—for I am speaking to men who know the law—that the law has authority over a man only as long as he lives?" (v. 1). This speaks about the power of the law. Most people understand that a law rules over a man only as long as he lives. When a man dies, he is set free from that law's power and control. It is like owing a million dollars to the Internal Revenue Service. The moment we die, we are set free from that obligation. In the same way, Christ's death releases every believer from the power of the law and its demands on his or her life.

Sin exercises authority over every unbeliever's life (Rom. 5:21; 6:14). But when a believer dies with Christ, sin no longer exercises dominion over him (Rom. 6:8−14). A believer is dead to sin (Rom. 6:2). In the same way, Romans 7:1 tells us that every unbeliever is under the rule, control, and power of the law. But since the believer died with Christ, law has no power over him. He is under grace, not law. Since the believer died with Christ in his death on the cross, death no longer has power over him but is swallowed up in victory. A believer is under grace; King Grace rules over him. A believer is under Christ; King Jesus rules over him. The Holy Spirit has dominion over him. We who are believers, who receive an abundance of grace, rule as kings in triumph through Christ in this life (Rom. 5:17).

The death of a man releases him from the power and control of law. The legal principle here is that death annuls the law, severing one's bondage and obligation to it. Romans 7, therefore, parallels Romans 6. Paul argues in Romans 6 that we died to sin in the death of Christ, and he argues in Romans 7 that we died also to law in the death of Christ because Christ died in reference to sin and law.

Those who believe in Christ's death and resurrection are set free from the imperious authority of and bondage to sin, law, and death. We therefore are no longer under the dominion, control, and power of sin, law, and death. We are not under the wrath of God but under grace—a powerful grace that is greater than all our sins. That is why Paul exclaims later that nothing in all creation is "able to separate us from the love of God that is in Christ Jesus our Lord" (Rom. 8:39).

Illustration of Marriage

"By law a married woman is bound to her husband as long as he is alive" (v. 2). Paul here adduces a marriage illustration. If a married woman lives with another man while her husband is alive, she is called an adulteress. But if the husband dies and she marries another, she is not an adulteress. She is set free from the law that bound her to her first husband. Death severs the law of marriage and cancels one's obligation to the dead person. Such severance enables the living spouse to enter into a new marriage. Marriage is a lifelong relationship between God's people, and only death should break the marriage bond.

"Therefore, my brothers, you also were put to death to law through the body of Christ that you might be joined [married] to another, to the one raised from the dead, that we might bear fruit for God" (v. 4, author's translation). This is the key verse in this chapter because it applies the illustration of marriage, death, and remarriage to our Christian position. Paul is saying that when we were unbelievers, we were under sin, law, and death. We were married to the law, which declares, "The soul who sins is the one who will die" (Ezek. 18:4) and, "The wages of sin is death" (Rom. 6:23). Therefore, a sinner must die for having violated God's law. But thanks be to God! In God's plan, another could keep the law and die in our place. Paul writes, "But when the time had fully come, God sent his Son, born of a woman, born under law, to redeem those under law" (Gal. 4:4–5). This Son is "the Lamb of God, who takes away the sin of the world!" (John 1:29). He is the one who died, the just for the unjust. "God made him who had no sin to be sin for us, so that in him we might become the righteousness of God." (2 Cor. 5:21).

Jesus Christ honored and fulfilled the law in our place. So through Christ's keeping of the law we died to the law so that we might live for God (Gal. 2:19). We are not justified by observing the law but by faith in the death and resurrection of Jesus Christ. Paul states, "I have been crucified with Christ and I no longer live, but Christ lives in me" (Gal. 2:20). How can a sinner be released from his bondage to a law he cannot keep? The answer is by his death to the law in the death of Christ. Simply, it is by faith in the gospel.

The law cannot die because it is God's law, but we can die *to the law* in the death of Christ. Jesus, our representative head, met all the obligations of the law in our behalf. When Jesus, therefore, was put to death on the cross, we also were put to death in him. When the law demanded death, we died in Christ and now the law has no further claim upon us. Discharged from the law, we are now outside of its jurisdiction.

Not only did we die with Christ, but we have also been raised with him to live for God in this life. Our new husband, the Lord Jesus, replaced our old husband, the law. We are under Christ, submitting to him in everything. Christ's resurrection declares that God's law has been fully satisfied and God has no further legal claim on us. It was all taken care of when Jesus lived and died in our behalf.

Law no longer has a claim on us. We are not under law and sin; we are under the regime of God's enabling grace. We are married to the risen Christ who dies no more, and our marriage to him is eternal. He lives forever and so will we. There is no divorce or death for us.

Listen to Paul's language elsewhere about this marriage to Christ: "Husbands, love your wives, just as Christ loved the church and gave himself up for her to make her holy, cleansing her by the washing with water through the word, and to present her to himself as a radiant church, without stain or wrinkle or any other blemish, but holy and blameless. . . . After all, no one ever hated his own body, but he feeds and cares for it, just as Christ does the church. . . . This is a profound mystery—but I am talking about Christ and the church" (Eph. 5:25–27, 29, 32).

The Purpose of Salvation: Bearing Fruit for God

We are set free from law and are now married to Christ. When we were married to the law in Adam, we were barren and incapable of bearing fruit to God. But now, through the ability of our new husband, we can bear fruit to God, which is the ultimate purpose of this new marriage relationship. This fruit is the fruit of the Spirit, the fruit of holiness. Therefore, if a person is living in sin he is not a Christian, because the ultimate purpose of our union with Christ is to bear fruit consisting in holiness.

Let's look at some scriptures to demonstrate this truth that we must bear fruit to God.

1. *Romans 6:21–22:* "What [fruit] did you reap at that time from the things you are now ashamed of? Those things result in death! But now that you have been set free from sin and have become slaves to God, the [fruit] you reap leads to holiness, and the result is eternal life." When we were wicked, we bore the fruit of evil. But now we bear the fruit of holy living.
2. *Romans 8:29:* "For those God foreknew he also predestined to be conformed to the likeness of his Son, that he might be the firstborn among many brothers." Paul is speaking about holy brothers.
3. *Romans 13:8–10:* "Let no debt remain outstanding, except the continuing debt to love one another, for he who loves his fellowman has fulfilled the law. The commandments, 'Do not commit adultery,' 'Do not murder,' 'Do not steal,' 'Do not covet,' and whatever other commandment there may be, are summed up in this one rule: 'Love your neighbor as yourself.' Love does no harm to its neighbor. Therefore love is the fulfillment of the law."
4. *Ephesians 1:4:* "For he chose us in him before the creation of the world to be holy and blameless in his sight."
5. *Ephesians 2:4–6:* "But because of his great love for us, God, who is rich in mercy, made us alive with Christ even when we were dead in transgressions—it is by grace you have been saved. And God raised us up with Christ and seated us with him in the heavenly realms in Christ Jesus."
6. *Ephesians 2:10:* "For we are God's workmanship, created in Christ Jesus to do good works, which God prepared in advance for us to do."

7. *Ephesians 5:9:* "For the fruit of the light consists in all goodness, righteousness and truth."
8. *Jude 24-25:* "To him who is able to keep you from falling and to present you before his glorious presence without fault and with great joy—to the only God our Savior be glory, majesty, power and authority, through Jesus Christ our Lord, before all ages, now and forevermore! Amen."
9. *Revelation 19:7-8:* "'Let us rejoice and be glad and give him glory! For the wedding of the Lamb has come, and his bride has made herself ready. Fine linen, bright and clean, was given her to wear.' (Fine linen stands for the righteous acts of the saints.)"
10. *Psalm 45:11, 13-14:* "The king is enthralled by your beauty; honor him, for he is your lord. . . . All glorious is the princess within her chamber; her gown is interwoven with gold. In embroidered garments she is led to the king; her virgin companions follow her and are brought to you."

Are you holy and blameless, or are you wallowing in the mud while pretending to be a Christian? How can we know that we died to law and sin and are married to Jesus Christ? The proof of our marriage is the fruit of holiness. We are married to Jesus, the Mighty One, who enables us to keep the law as evidence of our salvation.

Justification is evidenced by sanctification of the Spirit. Arrayed in beautiful garments, we who are the bride of Christ obey God's law that is now written not on a stone but in our hearts. We delight in God's law. It has become our nature to love our Lord and keep his commandments. We are the new covenant people of God. Our God is in us, and we know and love God. Our sins are forgiven, and now we have a new heart of flesh, a new spirit, and the Holy Spirit of God dwelling in us, teaching and empowering us. We have new life, a new relationship with Christ, a new purpose of bearing fruit to God, and new power to do God's will.

Jesus proclaims, "Apart from me you can do nothing" (John 15:5). Paul declares, "I can do everything through him who gives me strength" (Phil. 4:13).

The Benefits of Marriage to Christ

What a blessed life it is to be married to Christ! We were nothing. But we married up as we married into Christ. As a result, we have great privileges.

1. WE BEAR HIS NAME

Our old name is gone now. We have the name of our royal bridegroom, the name that is above every name.

2. WE HAVE A NEW STANDING

Ruth was a nobody, but she married up to Boaz, who was described as a man of standing. Like Boaz, our Lord Jesus Christ is a man of great standing. We had no status, but now we are seated with Christ in the heavenly places.

3. WE HAVE ACCESS TO GOD THE FATHER

We could not approach God before because of our sin. Now in Christ we can come into his presence with confidence to pray, worship, and enjoy wonderful sweet communion with the Father.

4. WE HAVE PROVISION

We are heirs of God and joint heirs with Christ. Paul says, "My God will meet all your needs according to his glorious riches in Christ Jesus" (Phil. 4:19). He also says, "[God] is able to do immeasurably more than all we ask or imagine, according to his power that is at work within us" (Eph. 3:20). This is abundant provision. "So then, no more boasting about men! All things are yours, whether Paul or Apollos or Cephas or the world or life or death or the present or the future—all are yours, and you are of Christ, and Christ is of God" (1 Cor. 3:21–23).

5. WE HAVE PROTECTION

Jesus promises, "Surely I am with you always, to the very end of the age" (Matt. 28:20). Elsewhere he declares, "I give them eternal life, and they shall never perish; no one can snatch them out of my hand. My Father, who has given them to me, is greater than all; no one can snatch them out of my Father's hand" (John 10:28–29). Do you need protection? Come to Christ!

6. WE HAVE THE SERVICE OF ANGELS

Angels serve believers as they served Jesus Christ. "Are not all angels ministering spirits sent to serve those who will inherit salvation?" (Heb. 1:14). See how they took care of Lazarus: "The time came when the beggar died and the angels carried him to Abraham's side" (Luke 16:22).

7. WE REIGN WITH CHRIST

Paul inquires, "Do you not know that the saints will judge the world? And if you are to judge the world, are you not competent to judge trivial cases? Do you not know that we will judge angels? How much more the things of this life!" (1 Cor. 6:2–3).

8. WE ENJOY THE VERY PRESENCE OF GOD

How many people miss out on this fellowship when they do not spend time in Bible reading and prayer! As we read the Song of Solomon, we notice that above all else the beloved desires the presence of her lover. In daily fellowship with our heavenly husband, we enjoy special communication of his love to us. Dr. Martyn Lloyd-Jones speaks of this great joy:

> Do you give Him an opportunity to tell you [of his love]? Do you put everything on one side in order to look into His face and listen to Him? Or is it that, when He comes to you, you are busy with other things? Or, like the bride depicted in the 5th chapter of the Song of Solomon, have you gone to bed and put off your clothes, and when you hear Him at the door, you say to Him: "I have put off my coat; how shall I put it on? I have washed my feet, how shall I defile them?" Then you suddenly realize how foolish you have been, and you get up and you open the door. But He has gone and you have nothing left but a smell of the myrrh that has been dropping from His fingers. And you do not know what to do with yourself; and you seek Him. If you would know the love of Jesus "what it is," give Him opportunities of telling you. He will meet you in the Scriptures, and He will tell you. Give time, give place, give opportunity. Set other things aside, and say to other people, "I cannot do what you ask me to do; I have another appointment, I know He is coming and I am waiting for Him." Do you look for Him, are you expecting Him, do you allow Him, do you give Him opportunities to speak to you, and to let you know His love to you? We are married to Him.[1]

As Christians, we are entirely outside of the jurisdiction of the law because Christ received the just and full penalty demanded

---

1   Lloyd-Jones, *Romans*, vol. 6, *The Law*, 62.

by the law. Jesus paid all our debts. Therefore, we are no longer afraid of the law with its condemnation, death, and judgment. We are in Christ, married to him.

This freedom from the law is not secured by the abolition of the law, but rather through Christ's vicarious fulfillment of all the law's demands. The law exacts penalty for sin, which is death. This penalty was fully paid by Christ by his death. It is to this Christ we are now married, and it is by his love and power we bear fruit of holiness by fulfilling his will. Paul said the love of Christ impelled him. May the love of Christ also impel us to fulfill God's law and be holy.

34

Life in the Spirit

⁵For when we were in the flesh, the passions of sins which through the law were powerfully and effectually working in our members brought forth fruit to death. ⁶But now we have been discharged, set free, released from the law, having died in that which was holding us under as prisoners, and we serve God in the newness of the Spirit and not in the oldness of the written code.

Romans 7:5-6, author's translation

The subject of these verses is a Christian's life—our past life in the flesh (v. 5) and our present life in the Holy Spirit (v. 6).

In one sense, the unregenerate live by a spirit, as we read in Ephesians 2:1-3. But it is the evil spirit, and they live in complete obedience to it. Unbelievers are called sons of disobedience, but in reality they live in complete obedience to the evil spirit.

All unbelieving sons of Adam are under sin and law. When we say "under," it means under the rule, authority, dominion, and power of these entities. So every unbeliever is under the power and dominion of sin and under the curse and condemnation of the law. Therefore, an unbeliever can only sin. He is like the happy worm in the sewer. He can only live a life of lawlessness.

But believers have been taken out of Adam and are now united to Jesus Christ. We are in Christ. We have been delivered from the power and rule of sin. We died to sin and law through the atoning death of Christ on the cross. Christians are dead to sin and alive to God in Christ Jesus. We are raised with Christ to live new, resurrection lives. Sin shall not have dominion over us. Or to use the analogy of marriage, Christians have died to the law, our former husband. We have been set free from the law that we may be married to another, even Jesus Christ, to produce fruit for God. This fruit consists of holiness, obedience, and good works.

As believers, therefore, we are not under the rule of sin or law but under the rule and kingship of grace, the greatest power in the universe. Sin reigned in death, but grace reigns now in our lives through righteousness unto eternal life through Jesus Christ our Lord. Super-abounding and all-conquering grace reigns in us. Praise God for the triumph of grace!

Having been delivered from our bondage to sin and law, we are now married to our husband, Jesus. The proof of our celestial marriage is a life of holiness. Christians have absolutely nothing to do with lawlessness. In fact, God disciplines his sons for their good so that they may share in his holiness (Heb. 12:7–11). Because God is holy, his children must necessarily be holy. If we are not holy, we are not children of God.

Our Past Life in the Flesh

"For when we were in the flesh . . ." (v. 5). This verse explains verse 4, which said that we are now married to Jesus Christ in order to bear fruit for God. When we were in the flesh (i.e., under the power of sin and the condemnation of the law), we were barren of fruit pleasing to God. We could only sin. Paul says we were slaves to sin (Rom. 6:17). Sin is personified as the greatest power in the world except for the grace of God. So Paul says in the past we were slaves of King Sin, free from the control of righteousness (Rom. 6:20). We could not please God.

Yes, we bore fruit, but it was the fruit of shame. Paul declares, "What benefit did you reap at that time from the things you are now ashamed of? Those things result in death!" (Rom. 6:21). Elsewhere he writes, "For it is shameful even to mention what the disobedient do in secret" (Eph. 5:12).

We were "in the flesh." In the Bible, "flesh" has different meanings. It can mean the soft part of the body without the bone, or the whole body, or all of mankind. But here Paul uses it in an ethically depreciatory sense of sin-controlled human life (see Rom. 7:18, 24; 8:3–5, 8, 9, 12, 13).

410

"Flesh" speaks of our unregenerate pre-conversion existence, when we were under law, sin, Satan, and death. It refers to our in-Adam existence, which Paul writes about in Romans 8:5–8. The minds of those who are in the flesh are at enmity with God. Such people hate God, God's word, and all who bring God's word to them. They do not and cannot submit to God's law. They cannot please God.

Every unbeliever is in the flesh in this ethically depreciatory sense. Such people are like the self-righteous Pharisees, who put confidence in their flesh. They are graceless, lifeless, hopeless, miserable wretches. Lacking the Holy Spirit, they engage in self-service, which is really service to sin, Satan, and death.

There are only two classes of people: those who are in the flesh and those who are in the Holy Spirit. We can also call them "in-Adam" and "in-Christ" people. "In-Adam" people are hardworking and always active, but the fruit they bear is unto death. Paul says that the sinful passions aroused, inflamed, and intensified by the law are powerfully and effectually at work in our members. Our bodies have natural desires and appetites, which, because they are given by God, are therefore good. But our sin nature twists and perverts these drives and passions, and the law aggravates and inflames them so that we sin more and more.

For example, eating is a wonderful blessing, and God gives us food to eat. But how many people easily fall into obesity or anorexia! Or look at greed. How many people think they must always work hard to have more. Yet they can destroy their marriage and family in their never-ending quest for wealth.

The law arouses sinful passions in unbelievers, functioning as a catalyst to promote more sin. Dr. Martyn Lloyd-Jones says, "The very law that prohibits [sins] encourages us to do them, because we are impure."[1] Suppose you see a sign: "Don't spit here." All of a sudden, you start to salivate and want to spit. Or you see another sign: "Don't walk on the lawn." Suddenly your chief desire is to walk on the lawn. Another example is that of sex education. Some educators have said we should teach it to first graders. Yet such sex education has only produced more immorality in this country, not less. The problem is not God's law; it is our sin

---

1   Lloyd-Jones, *Romans*, vol. 6, *The Law*, 80.

problem. The more the law forbids sin, the more unbelievers want to sin. That is one function of the law.

The cause of sinful acts lies in our sin nature, not in God's law. The law does not cause passions of sin but rather arouses and intensifies them due to sinners' enmity toward God's law. When the law tells sinners not to do something, our sinful nature rebels and we do evil with even more intensity. So the law increases rather than decreases immorality in the world. Paul warns, "Therefore do not let sin reign in your mortal body so that you obey its evil desires" (Rom. 6:12). Jesus himself said the problem is not in our environment but in our hearts: "What comes out of a man is what makes him 'unclean.' For from within, out of men's hearts, come evil thoughts, sexual immorality, theft, murder, adultery, greed, malice, deceit, lewdness, envy, slander, arrogance and folly. All these evils come from inside and make a man 'unclean'" (Mark 7:20–23).

Do you want to know what the works of the flesh are? Paul gives a long list of uncleanness in Romans 1:28–32. And elsewhere he writes, "The acts of the sinful nature are obvious: sexual immorality, impurity and debauchery; idolatry and witchcraft; hatred, discord, jealousy, fits of rage, selfish ambition, dissensions, factions and envy; drunkenness, orgies, and the like. I warn you, as I did before, that those who live like this will not inherit the kingdom of God" (Gal. 5:19–21).

In-the-flesh people are very busy, working very hard day and night. Paul exhorts, "Put to death, therefore, whatever belongs to your earthly nature: sexual immorality, impurity, lust, evil desires and greed, which is idolatry. Because of these, the wrath of God is coming. You used to walk in these ways, in the life you once lived. But now you must rid yourselves of all such things as these: anger, rage, malice, slander, and filthy language from your lips. Do not lie to each other, since you have taken off your old self with its practices and have put on the new self, which is being renewed in knowledge in the image of its Creator" (Col. 3:5–10). These sinful passions, aggravated and inflamed by law, were working powerfully and effectually in our members before we came to know Christ. Paul uses an imperfect tense to mean they were constantly, continually, powerfully, effectually working.

412

A sinner has great demonic energy. He serves self and Satan by continuous sinning. He is a slave of sin. Like a man with a legion of demons, he is powerful and restless. He sins always, by day and especially by night, in thought, word, and deed. Of such people Paul says, "As for you, you were dead in your transgressions and sins, in which you used to live when you followed the ways of this world and of the ruler of the kingdom of the air, the spirit who is now at work in those who are disobedient. All of us also lived among them at one time, gratifying the cravings of our sinful nature and following its desires and thoughts. Like the rest, we were by nature objects of wrath" (Eph. 2:1-3).

It is the evil spirit in these people that makes them powerful to do evil. So they use all their faculties—their minds, wills, affections, bodies, and monies—in the service of Satan. In Romans 6 we read about unrighteousness, uncleanness, lawlessness, wickedness, and shame. But these people have no shame. In fact, they parade it through the streets. Paul says, "Their destiny is destruction, their god is their stomach, and their glory is in their shame. Their mind is on earthly things" (Phil. 3:19).

Speaking of such in-flesh people, Peter writes, "Therefore, since Christ suffered in his body, arm yourselves also with the same attitude, because he who has suffered in his body is done with sin. As a result, he does not live the rest of his earthly life for evil human desires, but rather for the will of God. For you have spent enough time in the past doing what pagans choose to do—living in debauchery, lust, drunkenness, orgies, carousing and detestable idolatry. They think it strange that you do not plunge with them into the same flood of dissipation, and they heap abuse on you. But they will have to give account to him who is ready to judge the living and the dead" (1 Pet. 4:1-5).

Sinners produce the fruit of death. They daily render service to King Sin (Rom. 5:21) and King Death (Rom. 5:14, 21; 6:21-23). A life of sin, therefore, is a life of death. Sinners die daily in their minds and bodies. Such people waste away, and the first place we see decay is in their minds, so that they cannot understand the Bible. Each day's work produces more misery for them. As they work hard serving sin, they are dying spiritually, physically, prematurely, and eternally.

Romans 7:4 teaches that believers bring forth fruit of holiness to God, but Romans 7:5 teaches that sinners bear the fruit of sin unto death.

Our Present Life in the Spirit

"But now, by dying to what once bound us, we have been released from the law so that we serve in the new way of the Spirit, and not in the old way of the written code" (v. 6). This speaks of our present life in the Spirit. Notice the phrase: "But now," an expression also used in Romans 3:21 and 6:22. Paul is saying, "We were once . . . But now." What a great contrast between our sinful past life and our holy present life! Our past was pitch darkness; our present is bright light. Our past was death; our present is life eternal. Our past was condemnation; our present is justification, sanctification, and glorification. We were in the flesh, but now we are in the Spirit. We were under sin; now we are under grace. Before, we served Satan; now we serve our Lord Jesus Christ. Before, we were in Adam; now we are in Christ, and we are a new creation. Before, we were energized by Satan; now we are indwelt and empowered by the Holy Spirit.

Now we have been set free from what held us as prisoners: the law that condemned us and demanded our death. In the atoning death of our substitute head, we died to the power of sin and law. Therefore, law cannot make any further demands on us. By the death of Christ, we have been set free from sin, law, death, and the wrath of God forever. We will never go back to the dominion and power of sin, law, and death. We are secure eternally in Jesus Christ.

Not only are we set free, but we are also united to Jesus as his bride. We are set free from sin and enslaved to Christ (Rom. 6:18, 22). Oh, what a glorious and delightful slavery—enslaved to God and righteousness! What freedom and joy for those who have been set free from the regime of sin and law!

Paul writes, "But when the time had fully come, God sent his Son, born of a woman, born under law, to redeem those under law" (Gal. 4:4–5). We are redeemed from being under the law. Again, he says, "For through the law I died to the law so that I might live for God" (Gal. 2:19). It is all through Christ and his work. So Paul declares, "The sting of death is sin, and the power of sin is the law. But thanks be to God! He gives us the victory through our Lord Jesus Christ" (1 Cor. 15:56–57). And in this epistle he says, "What a wretched man I am! Who will rescue me from this body of death? Thanks be to God—through Jesus Christ our Lord!" (Rom. 7:24–25). By his atoning death and resurrection we are set free from all sinful bondages. Now we enjoy glorious bondage to Christ our liberator. No more obligation to sin, law, or death. Jesus paid all our bills in full:

> Jesus paid it all, all to him I owe;
> sin had left a crimson stain,
> he washed it white as snow.

As a result of Christ liberating us from all bondages, we now serve God continually and joyfully in the newness of the Spirit. Under the new covenant it is the will of God for us to live a holy life in the newness of the Spirit. "Without holiness no one will see the Lord" (Heb. 12:14). Christ's bride is not dirty and filthy; she is holy, clean, blameless and radiant, without spot or wrinkle or any other blemish. Therefore, if we are not living holy lives, we do not belong to Christ; we are still in the flesh, under the rule of sin and law.

God's people are being sanctified because they are justified. Therefore, they serve God in holiness, in the newness of the Spirit, not in the oldness of law written on a stone or a scroll. The law cannot justify, sanctify, or give life. Its function is to condemn, curse, define and aggravate sin, and to kill. But it also points us to Christ, that he may justify and sanctify us. The law says, "I cannot do it, but he will do it."

Thank God for Jesus Christ! The grace of our Lord made us new creations in whose hearts the Spirit has written the law of God. Now we delightfully obey God's law in the energy and power of the Spirit of the living God who is in us. We were once flesh, but we have been regenerated, born of the Spirit, and now we are spirit. Having received divine nature, we have a new mind to think God's thoughts, a new will to will God's will and do it, and new affections to hate what God hates and love what God loves. All of this is because of the Holy Spirit.

Isaiah foretold that the Spirit of the Lord would rest upon Christ (Isa. 11:2). The same Spirit shall also rest on every elect, dwelling in us and applying Christ's redemption to us. He gives us new wisdom, new knowledge, new counsel, new supernatural power, and a new fear of God in which we delight.

> 'Twas grace that taught my heart to fear,
> and grace my fears relieved.

As new covenant believers whose sins are forgiven, we know God and have been given a new heart. We have a new family (the holy church) and the Spirit-authored holy Scriptures, through which we can interpret all reality and to which we submit every thought. That is why we cannot believe every idea of the world, such as the evolutionary hypothesis and the medical model. If we believe these things, we cannot be Christians. We must accept the reality of God's moral universe.

We also have a new hope of the glory of God. We walk according to the Spirit in the light of God's word, pleasing God by serving and worshiping him. The Spirit profusely sheds abroad in our hearts the love of God, which motivates us to love God and keep his commandments. The great difference between an unbeliever and a Christian is that the Holy Spirit lives in the Christian: "You, however, are controlled not by the [flesh] but by the Spirit, if the Spirit of God lives in you. And if anyone does not have the Spirit of Christ, he does not belong to Christ. But if Christ is in you, your body is dead because of sin, yet your spirit is alive because of righteousness. And if the Spirit of him who raised Jesus from the dead is living in you, he who raised Christ from the dead will also give life to your mortal bodies through his Spirit, who lives in you" (Rom. 8:9–11).

If you have a sin problem, look at Romans 8:13: "For if you live according to the [flesh], you will die; but if by the Spirit you put to death the misdeeds of the body, you will live." We have the power to put to death the sin that still dwells in us. We do so, not by positive thinking, but by the power of the Holy Spirit.

The Spirit has made us good trees and so we produce good fruit. "The fruit of the Spirit is love, joy, peace, patience, kindness, goodness, faithfulness, gentleness and self-control. Against such things there is no law" (Gal. 5:22–23). Now we worship, work, and live in the Spirit. We were brittle, old wineskins, but now God has made us new wineskins and poured into us the new wine of the Spirit of God. Paul says, "Do not get drunk on wine, which leads to debauchery. Instead, be [being] filled with the Spirit. Speak to one another with psalms, hymns and spiritual songs. Sing and make music in your heart to the Lord, always giving thanks to God the Father for everything, in the name of our Lord Jesus Christ. Submit to one another out of reverence for Christ" (Eph. 5:18–21). Notice that the fulfillment of these commands is dependent upon being filled with the Spirit.

All of our Christian life is to be lived in the newness of the Spirit. When we serve God in this way, we will experience joy in serving Jesus. Christians are Spirit-created, Spirit-filled, Spirit-controlled, Spirit-satisfied, and therefore happy, people. We do not crave the world and its allurements; we desire the word of God and long for fellowship with our God. And as we hunger and thirst for God, we shall be filled.

The Holy Spirit creates new life, new vision, new purpose, and new ambition in us, filling us with power to do all of God's will. Dr. Lloyd-Jones said sin is the greatest power next to God. Thank God, it is not above God. "The one who is in you is greater than the one who is in the world" (1 John 4:4). We can do all the will of God through Jesus Christ who strengthens us by his indwelling Spirit. We were serving sin daily. But now, thank God, we continually serve God in the newness of the Spirit.

If you have experienced this freedom, this life in the Spirit, if you have been set free from sin and law and death and the wrath of God, if you have been married to Christ, regenerated and indwelt by the Spirit to serve God with celestial delight, give praise to God. And if you are still in the flesh, a slave to sin, I have good news for you also. Call upon the name of God and he will save you.

35

Can Mosaic Law Save Us?

7What shall we say, then? Is the law sin? Certainly not! Indeed I would not have known what sin was except through the law. For I would not have known what coveting really was if the law had not said, "Do not covet." 8But sin, seizing the opportunity afforded by the commandment, produced in me every kind of covetous desire. For apart from law, sin is dead. 9Once I was alive apart from law; but when the commandment came, sin sprang to life and I died. 10I found that the very commandment that was intended to bring life actually brought death. 11For sin, seizing the opportunity afforded by the commandment, deceived me, and through the commandment put me to death. 12So then, the law is holy, and the commandment is holy, righteous and good.

13Did that which is good, then, become death to me? By no means! But in order that sin might be recognized as sin, it produced death in me through what was good, so that through the commandment sin might become utterly sinful.

Romans 7:7–13

Have you ever noticed that unbelievers are happy as long as the Spirit is not convicting them through God's law? If you ask them how they are doing, they will earnestly assert that they are doing just fine. After all, their marriages are working out splendidly, and their children are studying at top universities. They are doing well at their jobs and their retirement funds are growing. They have no health problems and expect to live long and happy lives. But the truth is, such people are dead men walking. They are not concerned about their standing before a holy God.

The rich fool thought everything was going well for him. But God said to him, "You fool! This very night your life will be demanded from you" (Luke 12:20). There was a time when Saul of Tarsus lived such a carefree, happy life. The Holy Spirit was not convicting him of his sins by the application of God's law, so he felt fine. In fact, he said that he was perfect concerning the righteousness of the law, was advancing in Judaism beyond many Jews of his age, and was extremely zealous for the traditions of his fathers (Phil. 3:6; Gal. 1:14). But here he writes, *"Apart from law, sin is dead. Once I was alive apart from law; but when the commandment came, sin sprang to life and I died"* (vv. 8–9).

In Romans 7:7–13, Paul is vindicating the Mosaic law because up to this point in his epistle he has said many negative things about it. He declared the law cannot justify (Rom. 3:20, 28); the law cannot sanctify (Rom. 7:5); the law increases sin (Rom. 5:20); that believers are not under law but under grace (Rom. 6:14); that believers have died to law in the death of Christ (Rom. 7:4); and that through the law comes knowledge of sin (Rom. 3:20). The law cannot restrain or curb sin; in fact, it does just the opposite.

Such negative teaching about God's law could prompt a person, especially a first-century Jew, to ask, "What then are you saying? Is God's law sin?" to which Paul responds, "Certainly not!" Then he goes on to demonstrate the relationship of the law to sin and death. Here Paul the Christian is looking at his life before conversion. He is thinking back to the time when the Holy Spirit applied God's law to his heart after his encounter with the risen Lord on the road to Damascus. He may especially be thinking of the three days when, as a blind man, he fasted and prayed in Judas' house on Straight Street in the city of Damascus.

On the Damascus road Paul saw that he had totally misunderstood the design and purpose of God's law. He realized that it was a false way of salvation. He began to see that God designed the law so that through its application, sin might become so utterly sinful and foul that man might turn to Christ alone for salvation. The law was given to unmask sin so that it may be shown in its true color of utter deception, destruction, and foulness. When the Holy Spirit convicts a sinner of sin, that person cries out, "I am all unrighteousness. Have mercy upon me, a sinner! I am a wretch. I am blind. I am lost. I am dead." Leon Morris comments that God's law is not given to boost our self-esteem but to bust it.[1] So Paul is speaking from the standpoint of a convinced Christian, telling us from his own experience what happens to any sinner who is confronted with the law. Only in the light of God's law does one see sin as an offense against Almighty God himself.

The Nature and Function of God's Moral Law

Paul was aware of the fact of sin, but he was not aware of its real nature and power until the Holy Spirit convicted him through the law, cutting him to the heart especially by the tenth commandment: "Thou shalt not covet."

Most first-century Jews thought that only outward deeds like adultery and murder were sin, not inward attitudes like lust and anger. But the tenth commandment says lust itself is sin, as Jesus explained: "You have heard that it was said, 'Do not commit adultery.' But I tell you that anyone who looks at a woman lustfully has already committed adultery with her in his heart" (Matt. 5:27–28). What, then, is the nature and function of God's moral law?

1. THE LAW SHOWS THAT WE COMMIT SIN BY TRANSGRESSING GOD'S LAW

When we have an evil desire for things belonging to another, or for things that are evil, we are transgressing the tenth commandment. We are sinning in our heart against God, and God knows our heart. This evil lust shows that our rebellion is against God himself because it is revealing that we are not content with what God ordained for us. Rather, we want to grasp and possess what is not given to us. So we become greedy and self-focused, a perversion that is the opposite of love. Our lack of contentment in God is the very heart of worldliness. We think the things of the world will make us happier than God and his presence.

The tenth commandment destroyed Paul's self-righteousness. He had to admit that he lusted sinfully countless times, though he

---

1   Morris, *Epistle to the Romans*, 282.

never stole, murdered, or committed adultery. Once he thought he was blameless, but now he was convinced that he was blameful. The law revealed that he was a sinner who had committed a multitude of sins in his heart. Yet the law is not sin. It is a reagent that identifies the very presence of sin.

2. THE LAW PROVOKES SIN, FUNCTIONING AS A CATALYST SO THAT WE SIN MORE

So sin, through the law, creates a surge of rebellion in our hearts against God and his agents. Sin is enmity toward God; thus, a sinner is an enemy of God. Our sin nature twists God's law so that we sin more. In this sense, God's law stimulates sin.

When St. Augustine was sixteen years old, he and his friends went to his neighbor's field at night, shook a pear tree, and stole all the pears. Later on, he analyzed why he stole. He was not hungry and he had lots of pears at home. In fact, he threw the stolen pears to the pigs. He stole the neighbor's pears simply to enjoy the excitement and thrill of stealing, because God said, "Do not steal." The commandment "Do not steal" provokes stealing due to our sin nature. Sin twists God's law and uses it for evil purposes.

We have seen this in our children. We say, "Do not do it," and they immediately want to do the forbidden action. Then we direct them to do something, and they will not do it at all. Our sin nature is real and God's law stimulates us to sin.

3. THE LAW CONDEMNS SIN

"Once I was alive apart from law; but when the commandment came, sin sprang to life and I died" (v. 9). Coming into contact with God's law is like going to the doctor for a routine check-up when you feel very good and seem to have no problems. But all of a sudden the doctor turns to you and says in a serious tone, "You have terminal cancer." That is the idea here.

Paul was happy outside of the law. He thought he had no problem at all. He would say that he was doing just fine and was pleasing God with his "righteous" life. But then the Great Physician confronted him with the law and revealed his serious problem. So Paul says, "When the law came, sin revived and I died."

How many people are dead spiritually while they think they are fine! Yet God in his mercy tells us about our state through the gospel preaching. That is why many people will not go to a church where the whole Bible is preached, because God uses the preaching of the law to bring conviction of sin.

At one time Paul, like the Pharisee and the rich young ruler of Luke 18, thought he was "perfect" and living a righteous life. He had no need of a Savior or atonement. But the Holy Spirit through the law cut Paul's heart and convicted him of his sin. No longer alive in his self-esteem, self-righteousness, and self-approbation, he died and became all unrighteousness. Once he felt very righteous, though he was killing Christians. Now he realized what a wretched sinner he was.

When the Holy Spirit came upon Paul, he said of himself:

> I thank Christ Jesus our Lord, who has given me strength, that he considered me faithful, appointing me to his service. Even though I was once a blasphemer and a persecutor and a violent man, I was shown mercy because I acted in ignorance and unbelief. The grace of our Lord was poured out on me abundantly, along with the faith and love that are in Christ Jesus.

> Here is a trustworthy saying that deserves full acceptance: Christ Jesus came into the world to save sinners—of whom I am the worst. But for that very reason I was shown mercy so that in me, the worst of sinners, Christ Jesus might display his unlimited patience as an example for those who would believe on him and receive eternal life. (1 Tim. 1:12-16)

The law, therefore, is the straightedge that shows how crooked our hearts are. When Peter first preached at Pentecost, the people were cut to the heart and asked, "Brothers, what shall we do?" (Acts 2:37). Jesus himself declared, "When [the Holy Spirit] comes, he will convict the world of guilt in regard to sin and righteousness and judgment" (John 16:8). After being confronted by Nathan, David confessed, "I have sinned against the LORD" (2 Sam. 12:13).

When God is not working in our hearts through his law and convicting us, we can be happy. Paul once felt that way. But when he understood the law, he died because he realized the law condemned him. So he cried out, "Have mercy upon me, a sinner!" The law is God's way of bringing sin to a head before its power is broken by the stronger grace of God.

We must see how sinful we truly are. Once after Professor John Gerstner had preached, a sophisticated woman came up to him and showed him her index finger and thumb half an inch apart. She said, "You made me feel like this much." Dr. Gerstner responded, "That is much too much. It will take you to hell."

4. THE LAW STRENGTHENS SIN

Elsewhere Paul writes, "The sting of death is sin, and the power of sin is the law. But thanks be to God! He gives us the victory through our Lord Jesus Christ" (1 Cor. 15:56–57). The law cannot break the power of sin. A legalist who depends on the law to justify and sanctify him can only sin, because the law gives power for the sinner to sin. When he hears, "Do not fornicate," he wants to fornicate and does so. We need to be born of the Holy Spirit to break the power of sin. More dependence on law means more sin, which means more guilt and more condemnation. But thanks be to God who gives us the victory through Jesus our Lord by his death and resurrection! Through Christ, therefore, we die to sin and law. Set free from sin and law, we are united to Christ and saved forever by his life.

5. THE LAW POINTS US TO CHRIST

Paul says, "Christ is the end of the law so that there may be righteousness for everyone who believes" (Rom. 10:4). Elsewhere, he declares, "What, then, was the purpose of the law? It was added [to define] transgressions until the Seed to whom the promise referred had come. The law was put into effect through angels by a mediator" (Gal. 3:19). He adds, "So the law was put in charge to lead us to Christ that we might be justified by faith" (Gal. 3:24). The law only condemns and kills us. It destroys our self-esteem and self-righteousness, that we may look to Christ to justify, sanctify, and glorify us through his death and resurrection. The law kills so that Christ may raise us up from the dead.

6. FOR GOD'S PEOPLE, THE LAW REVEALS GOD'S WILL SO THAT WE MAY DO IT

Paul writes, "Let no debt remain outstanding, except the continuing debt to love one another, for he who loves his fellowman has fulfilled the law. The commandments, 'Do not commit adultery,'

424

'Do not murder,' 'Do not steal,' 'Do not covet,' and whatever other commandment there may be, are summed up in this one rule: 'Love your neighbor as yourself.' Love does no harm to its neighbor. Therefore love is the fulfillment of the law" (Rom. 13:8–10).

God does not use our subjectivism to define sin. We must measure ourselves in the light of the objective standard of God's law. For a believer, the law tells us what pleases God so that we may do it by the power of the Holy Spirit. A believer is given a new heart and a new nature, and is indwelt by the Holy Spirit. No longer hating God's law, he delights in meditating on it. He glorifies God by doing all things to the glory of God (1 Cor. 10:31).

Through the power of the love of God shed abroad in our hearts by the Holy Spirit, we fulfill the law. A sinner is lawless because sin is lawlessness, but a believer is lawful. He is not antinomian; he is pro-nomian. Love fulfills the law. Jesus said, "If you love me, you will obey what I command" (John 14:15).

7. THE LAW WAS NEVER INTENDED TO SAVE US

Paul refers to this common misunderstanding: *"I found that the very commandment that was intended to bring life actually brought death"* (v. 10). Note the phrase: "intended to bring life." Judaism taught that people could be justified through keeping the law. But it was never given to save us. So Paul says, "Therefore no one will be declared righteous in his sight by observing the law; rather, through the law we become conscious of sin" (Rom. 3:20). Then he says, "The law was added so that the trespass might increase" (Rom. 5:20). He writes, "For what the law was powerless to do in that it was weakened by the sinful nature, God did by sending his own Son in the likeness of sinful man to be a sin offering. And so he condemned sin in sinful man" (Rom. 8:3). Again he writes, "Is the law, therefore, opposed to the promises of God? Absolutely not! For if a law had been given that could impart life, then righteousness would certainly have come by the law" (Gal. 3:21). The truth is, the law was not given to impart life.

The Nature and Function of Sin

Having discussed the nature and function of the law, let us now look at the nature and function of sin. All children of Adam are born with a sin nature. We are born enemies of God; our very thoughts and imaginations are against God. Dead in trespasses and sins, we are ruled by Satan, the spirit who now works in the sons of disobedience. We can only sin every day of our lives.

When such a sinner is given law by parents, teachers, police, or pastors, the sin in him takes advantage of the law to produce many sins, even sins he had not thought about. The sin that is resident in us uses law as a base of military operation within our souls. So Paul sinned much against God, especially in terms of the commandment not to covet.

Sin is extremely powerful. Only the grace of God can defeat and conquer sin's great power. In this epistle Paul speaks of sin as a king with great power and authority. He writes, "So that, just as sin reigned in death, so also grace might reign through righteousness to bring eternal life through Jesus Christ our Lord" (Rom. 5:21). He also exhorts, "Therefore do not let sin reign in your mortal body so that you obey its evil desires. . . . For sin shall not be your master, because you are not under law, but under grace. . . . Don't you know that when you offer yourselves to someone to obey him as slaves, you are slaves to the one whom you obey—whether you are slaves to sin, which leads to death, or to obedience, which leads to righteousness? But thanks be to God that, though you used to be slaves to sin, you wholeheartedly obeyed the form of teaching to which you were entrusted" (Rom. 6:12, 14, 16–17).

We find this idea of the powerfulness of sin throughout the Bible. The Lord told Cain, "If you do what is right, will you not be accepted? But if you do not do what is right, sin is crouching at your door; it desires to have you, but you must master it" (Gen. 4:7). Jeremiah declares, "The heart is deceitful above all things and beyond cure. Who can understand it?" (Jer. 17:9). And Jesus taught, "What comes out of a man is what makes him 'unclean.' For from within, out of men's hearts, come evil thoughts, sexual immorality, theft, murder, adultery, greed, malice, deceit, lewdness, envy, slander, arrogance and folly. All these evils come from inside and make a man 'unclean'" (Mark 7:20–23).

Not only is sin powerful, but it is also ever-active. There is no Sabbath-rest for sin. It works hard day and night, from the time we are very young to when we are very old. Sin works hard even when we worship. Sin is active because the devil is active. He goes about as a roaring lion, seeking to devour God's elect, if possible. If you feel angry as you hear the gospel preached, sin is working in your heart. But if the Holy Spirit is working in your heart, you will say to the preacher, "Amen," meaning, "What you are saying is the truth."

Sin works in us through our own evil lust. Lust is the root; fornication is the fruit. Lust is the root; stealing is the fruit. Lust is the root; murder is the fruit. First there is attitude, then action. This is why we need a new heart and the Holy Spirit so we can love God and do his will. Eve lusted and ate the forbidden fruit. Achan lusted and stole. Ahab lusted and took Naboth's vineyard by killing him. David lusted and took Bathsheba. Amnon lusted and raped Tamar. Judas lusted and sold Jesus for thirty pieces of silver. Demas lusted and abandoned Paul and the gospel for this world. Lust is the root; the specific sin is the fruit.

Sin cannot be cured by education or by political, economic, or scientific progress. Yet think about how modern man hates the word "sin." He says that man is born good and is getting better all the time. But such highly educated and civilized men are responsible for killing millions of people in wars in this century alone. And in the United States alone, fifty million unborn children have been killed through abortion since 1973. Sophisticated, educated, rich people can be wicked murderers. They can violate every commandment because they hate the God of the Bible and anyone who preaches the Bible. Their anger against those who preach the gospel shows the hardness of their hearts. They do not like to hear about sin and how we should practice righteousness. Such nice, civilized people hate the moral model given in the Bible. Instead, they love the medical model that came out of evolutionary hypothesis and naturalism. So they will not call people sinners, but rather "patients." And above all, they hate Jesus Christ.

Sin is a good fisherman. It uses the bait of pleasure and thrill to catch its prey. Sin shows us pleasure but hides the death that results from it. There is pleasure in sin, and we sin because we want that pleasure. The Hebrews writer recognized this aspect of sin when he said Moses "chose to be mistreated along with the people of God rather than to enjoy the pleasures of sin for a short time" (Heb. 11:25). How many people have been deceived by the excitement of sin! Eventually they crash to the ground, having ruined their lives through sin.

Sin kills its victims. So Paul writes, "Sin reigned in death" (Rom. 5:21) and "The wages of sin is death" (Rom. 6:23). No one sends a person to hell; people work every day of their lives to go there, and they will go.

Sin totally deceives man. The serpent lied to the woman: "You will not surely die. . . . For God knows that when you eat of it your eyes will be opened, and you will be like God, knowing good and evil" (Gen. 3:4–5). How many have listened to such a lie and sinned! Look at verse 13: "Then the LORD God said to the woman, 'What is this you have done?' The woman said, 'The serpent deceived me, and I ate.'" Paul writes, "You were taught, with regard to your former way of life, to put off your old self, which is being corrupted by its deceitful desires" (Eph. 4:22). The Hebrews writer says, "But encourage one another daily, as long as it is called Today, so that none of you may be hardened by sin's deceitfulness" (Heb. 3:13). Paul also writes,

> For the secret power of lawlessness is already at work; but the one who now holds it back will continue to do so till he is taken out of the way. And then the lawless one will be revealed, whom the Lord Jesus will overthrow with the breath of his mouth and destroy by the splendor of his coming. The coming of the lawless one will be in accordance with the work of Satan displayed in all kinds of counterfeit miracles, signs and wonders, and in every sort of evil that deceives those who are perishing. They perish because they refused to love the truth and so be saved. (2 Thess. 2:7–10)

The antichrist is called the lawless one. Some people call themselves Christians, yet they live like the lawless one. Such people, deceived by sin and Satan, are not Christians.

Sin deceives us in many ways, including the following:[2]

1. Sin misuses the law. The law must be used lawfully. Paul says, "We know that the law is good if one uses it properly" (1 Tim. 1:8). The law cannot justify or sanctify us. It reveals sin to us, and if we are God's people, it reveals God's will so we can do it. But sin misuses the law by saying lust is permissible as long as one does not sin outwardly. It says that evil intentions are not sin and God does not judge evil desire.

2　Most of these points are listed by D. Martyn Lloyd-Jones in *Romans*, vol. 6, *The Law*, 155–60, and James M. Boice in *Romans*, vol. 2, *Reign of Grace*, 744–45.

2. Sin comes to us and says, "Because you sinned once and broke the law, you are hopeless. You might as well keep on sinning. More sins make no difference."

3. Sin encourages antinomianism, which says that we should not be troubled when we sin because we are saved by grace from first to last. It says, "Once saved, always saved, so it does not matter whether we sin or not. In fact, we can bring greater glory to God by sinning more because where sin abounds, grace super-abounds. More sin equals more grace equals more glory to God." This is the message of many modern evangelicals. People want pastors who champion antinomianism. Dr. Lloyd-Jones says, "Antinomianism is one of the most blinding curses that have ever afflicted the life of the Church."[3]

4. Sin deceives us by creating within us an antagonism to the law, saying God is against us. Sin says God does not want us to have fun; that is why he prohibits us from doing certain things. It says if God were for us, he would let us do what we want.

5. Sin says God's law is unreasonable, unjust, and impossible.

6. Sin deceives us into thinking very highly of ourselves.

7. Sin says God's law is oppressive, keeping us from developing into a god without needing law. God does not like competition.

8. Sin deceives about itself. Sin makes itself very attractive and pleasurable. Sin says, "If it feels good, do it. Express yourself."

9. Sin makes righteousness look drab and unattractive. It says an obedient son is a mere dullard, but a rebellious son is a lively and exciting person.

10. Sin deceives us into overlooking the terrible, eternal consequences it brings to our own bodies and souls and to those of our children and our children's children for generations to come. Do we think about such long-term effects when we sin? Sin results in terrible consequences, including the final consequence of hell itself. But sin says, "You shall not surely die."

11. Sin deceives us into thinking, "I have kept the law perfectly. I am perfect. My pastor, my parents, and others have no clue about my perfection. Why are they so upset about my behavior?"

12. Sin promises life but gives death. It promises happiness but gives misery. Sin promises divinity but makes us demons. Sin promises holiness but gives corruption.

Is the Law Sin?

So we must ask: Is God's law sin? In verse 12 Paul explains the true nature of God's law: *"The law is holy, and the commandment is holy, righteous and good."* God's law is holy. It is the absolute

---

3   Lloyd-Jones, *Romans*, vol. 6, *The Law*, 156.

antithesis of evil. God is holy, so his law is holy. It is also righteous. Sin accuses the law's demands as being unfair, but they are perfectly just. A criminal is put to death as a penalty for his crime, not because of an unjust law. Finally, God's law is good. The law tells us that God alone is good, and so his law is good and good for us. A good life is one lived in conformity with the law of God. The life of Jesus was *the* good life. So law is not evil. Sin, not law, is the cause of all misery and death.

What, then, is the divine design and intention of the law? Paul explains that God gave the law so that sin may be unmasked (Rom. 7:13). The nature of sin is deception, so God uses his law to expose sin that it may be recognized for what it is—utterly foul. Sin is stench in the nostrils of God. It is destructive and can only send us to hell.

The law reveals sin as utterly sinful so that we will hate sin with all our being. Jesus exposed Satan when he said, "The thief comes only to steal and kill and destroy" (John 10:10). The devil is a liar and the father of all lies.

Application

The law is not sin; rather, it reveals and unmasks sin. Therefore, we must preach the law so that the Holy Spirit may convict sinners of their sin that they may turn to Jesus. He saves only sinners who are convinced of their utter sinfulness.

Examine yourself. What is your reaction to a holy God who is the Judge? What is your reaction to the preaching of the cross? What is your reaction to the Lord Jesus Christ? What is your reaction to the Bible? Is it hatred, or is it delight?

This doctrine of sin and law is absolutely essential to understanding the gospel. That is why we must preach the whole Bible. We cannot merely say, "God forgives you" or "God saves you." What does he forgive? From what does he save us? When we preach God's law, the Holy Spirit convicts us of our sin that we may turn to Christ and be saved.

The law cannot justify or sanctify. We are saved from sin's penalty, power, and pollution only by the blood of Jesus applied to us by the Holy Spirit. Therefore, if you are looking for a church, choose one where God's entire word—law and gospel—is fully preached. Avoid churches that preach antinomian forgiveness; it will only encourage sin.

May God help us to welcome the brightness of the light of God's word. Once we were in darkness but now we are light in the Lord. May we live as children of light!

36

A Wretched Man
Becomes a Saint

[14]*We know that the law is spiritual; but I am unspiritual, sold as a slave to sin.* [15]*I do not understand what I do. For what I want to do I do not do, but what I hate I do.* [16]*And if I do what I do not want to do, I agree that the law is good.* [17]*As it is, it is no longer I myself who do it, but it is sin living in me.* [18]*I know that nothing good lives in me, that is, in my sinful nature. For I have the desire to do what is good, but I cannot carry it out.* [19]*For what I do is not the good I want to do; no, the evil I do not want to do—this I keep on doing.* [20]*Now if I do what I do not want to do, it is no longer I who do it, but it is sin living in me that does it.*

[21]*So I find this law at work: When I want to do good, evil is right there with me.* [22]*For in my inner being I delight in God's law;* [23]*but I see another law at work in the members of my body, waging war against the law of my mind and making me a prisoner of the law of sin at work within my members.* [24]*What a wretched man I am! Who will rescue me from this body of death?* [25]*Thanks be to God— through Jesus Christ our Lord!*

So then, I myself in my mind am a slave to God's law, but in the sinful nature a slave to the law of sin.

Romans 7:14–25

God never makes anyone his saint unless that person cries out, "*What a wretched man I am! Who will rescue me from this body of death?*" Whose experience is Paul describing in Romans 7:7–25? Is it his own experience as a Christian at the time he was writing the epistle to the Romans, or his experience before he was born again? Does it describe the normal Christian life, or the life of a sinner under conviction and not yet indwelt by the Holy Spirit?

In this exposition of Romans 7, we are in general agreement with the majority of the church fathers in the first three centuries of the Christian era and with modern scholars like Dr. Martyn Lloyd-Jones, Douglas Moo, and a number of others.

The Romans 7 Man

In Romans 7 we see a man who is aware of what is right and what is sinful, yet he always—not sometimes—ends up doing the wrong thing. This is a person to whom God's law has come home in its full meaning and power by the operation of the Spirit. Paul says that when the law came to him, "sin revived and I died" (Rom. 7:9). Romans 7:14–25 is speaking about this same person to whom the law came. He no longer thinks of himself as perfect concerning the righteousness of the law (Phil. 3:6). Those happy days are over for him. He now realizes he is a sinner. The law of God came home to him, condemned him, and he died. Yet we are not reading about a Christian who enjoys the freedom of *posse non peccare* (able not to sin), which is the freedom of a true believer. This passage describes a sinner who is under conviction of sin and has no freedom not to sin.

The Romans 7 man is a prisoner of sin. He is in the state of *non posse non peccare* (not able not to sin), meaning he can only sin all the time. The church fathers, especially in the first three centuries of the church, saw this man as unregenerate. But the Reformers, following Augustine's later views, generally thought this passage spoke of a Christian, even a Christian at his best. This latter view is partly responsible for the spirit of antinomianism that prevails in much of today's evangelical church. It also contributed to the dead orthodoxy of the seventeenth century, which the Pietists opposed.

In Romans 7:7–25 Paul speaks of what the law can and cannot do. The law can neither justify nor sanctify us. The law is weak because of our sin nature and cannot impart life. It cannot cause us to obey the law. It reveals our sin and condemns us as sinners. Law is powerless before the mighty power of sin.

Romans 7:14–25, therefore, cannot be an analysis of Paul at the time of writing this epistle or a description of a Christian at his best. Here Paul is describing himself under conviction of sin yet not born again. He is aware of his sin and his complete moral impotence and failure. He is aware of the great power of sin, yet he is not aware of the freedom of the gospel. It is probably describing his preconversion experience prior to his baptism by Ananias in Damascus. F. F. Bruce says, "Here is a picture of life under the law, without the aid of the Spirit, portrayed from the perspective of one who has now experienced the liberating power of life in the Spirit."[1] The *Spirit of the Reformation Bible* posits, "Paul was describing [in a dramatic fashion] a transitional experience, possibly his own, of one who has been awakened to his or her true spiritual need but who has not yet entered the full relief of justification by grace."[2] In Romans 7:7–24 we see no reference to grace, the Holy Spirit, or Christ.

The Key Verse

"*We know that the law is spiritual; but I am unspiritual, sold as a slave to sin*" (v. 14). This is the key verse in this section. Verses 7:15–25 simply explain verse 14, which itself gives reason for the previous verse. In the Greek, verse 14 starts with the word "for." Paul knows the law is holy, just, and good. But if the law is good, why did he die when it came to him? Why is it ministering death to him? So he asks, "Did that which is good, then, become death to me?" (v. 13). Not at all! Sin, not the law, is responsible for our death. But through the law, God unmasks sin and makes it appear in its true utterly corrupt and foul nature. Paul tells us not to blame God's holy, just, and good law. The law is spiritual because it is given by the Holy Spirit. The problem is not with the law but with us. We are sinful.

Then Paul explains, "*The law is spiritual; but I am unspiritual.*" The word is *sarkinos* (carnal). He is not partly carnal. He describes himself as all flesh in all its weakness, especially because of sin. He is controlled by sin and is an in-Adam, fallen man. In Romans 7:5 he said, "When we *were* in the flesh," meaning we are no longer

---

1   Bruce, *Letter of Paul to the Romans*, 143.
2   *New International Version Spirit of the Reformation Bible*, (Grand Rapids: Zondervan, 2003), 1821.

in the flesh. There he is speaking as a born-again, Spirit-indwelt man, one who is in the Spirit, able to bear fruit to God and serve him in the newness of the Spirit. But in Romans 7:14–25 he describes himself as one still in the flesh, incapable of bringing forth the fruit of obedience to God. We see this contrast also in Romans 6:17: "But thanks be to God that, though you used to be slaves to sin, you wholeheartedly obeyed the form of teaching to which you were entrusted." A regenerate person is no longer a slave to sin. Paul later makes this clear: "You, however, are controlled not by the sinful nature but by the Spirit, if the Spirit of God lives in you. And if anyone does not have the Spirit of Christ, he does not belong to Christ" (Rom. 8:9).

The third element of this verse is that this man is *"sold as a slave to sin."* We see this idea in Elijah's words to Ahab: "You have sold yourself to do evil in the eyes of the LORD" (1 Kings 21:20). Elsewhere we read that the Israelites sacrificed their sons and daughters in the fire and "practiced divination and sorcery and sold themselves to do evil in the eyes of the LORD, provoking him to anger" (2 Kings 17:17). Paul is saying, "I am in a state of slavery, and I cannot redeem myself. I need a redeemer who can buy me out of my slavery."

The fourth aspect of this verse is that Paul calls himself a slave *"to sin,"* meaning "under sin." Paul acknowledges that he is under the rule, authority, and power of sin. Yet earlier in this epistle he declared that a Christian is not under sin or law or death, but under grace, and that King Grace governs his life in righteousness: "Just as sin reigned in death, so also grace might reign through righteousness to bring eternal life through Jesus Christ our Lord" (Rom. 5:21). Yet here in Romans 7:14 Paul says he is sold under sin.

Finally, Paul implies that though the law is spiritual, he is carnal or unspiritual. Yet elsewhere he declares that a believer is spiritual: "The spiritual man makes judgments about all things, but he himself is not subject to any man's judgment" (1 Cor. 2:15). The believer is Spirit-born and has divine nature. He is Spirit-indwelt, Spirit-taught, Spirit-led, and Spirit-empowered to bring forth fruit to God through obedience. So Romans 7:7–25 is speaking, not about a spiritual man, a believer, but about a carnal man who is sold under sin.

436

Propositions from Verses 15–25

Let us then look at some propositions from verses 15–25, which explain verse 14.

"I do not understand what I do" (v. 15). In other words, he does not approve it. Then he says, *"For what I want to do, I do not do."* He is not speaking about occasional actions. He is saying, "I do not practice what I want to do at any time. I can only sin." Then he says, *"But what I hate, I do"* (v. 15). His actions are not occasional but constant. He is describing himself as a man who is not able not to sin (*non posse non peccare*): "I find myself always practicing not what I approve, but what I hate." This is strong language.

In verse 16 he says that he is doing what he does not purpose, desire, will, or want.[3] Therefore he deduces: "If I do what I don't desire, and I do what I hate, then it is not I but sin indwelling in me that is doing this evil" (see verse 17).

Paul is speaking about himself as a sin-possessed, sin-controlled person. He is saying that this indwelling sin is a permanent resident in him and defeats his purpose. This sin does what he does not will. He is its bondslave and cannot overcome it. He tells us this again in verse 20, essentially saying: "The sin is not outside of me, in the environment. It is inside, making me do its will instead of my own. The Holy Spirit is not dwelling in me. Sin, in all its power, is dwelling in me and controlling my life."

"I know that nothing good lives in me, that is, in my sinful nature [flesh]" (v. 18). Something good of greater power must dwell in us to oppose and conquer this indwelling sin. But he says that nothing good dwells in him. He is not born again, nor does he have a divine nature. The Holy Spirit does not dwell in him. This is not what he said earlier: "And hope does not disappoint us, because God has poured out his love into our hearts by the Holy Spirit, whom he has given us" (Rom. 5:5; see also 1 Cor. 6:19).

"For what I do is not the good I want to do; no, the evil I do not want to do—this I keep on doing" (v. 19). The reality is that the evil he does not will, he practices. And he does so not once in a while, as some theologians want to say, but always. And in verse 21 he says he discovered a law, a principle, in the light of his

---

3   He uses the present tense, showing continuous action.

experience, that when he wants to do that which is excellent (the law of God), evil is right there, poised to oppose, frustrate, and defeat him. And this evil wins every time.

"I see another law at work in the members of my body, waging war against the law of my mind and making me a prisoner of the law of sin at work within my members" (v. 23). This other law, which is different from and opposed to God's law, carries on a continuous campaign of warfare against God's law in his mind. It wins out all the time, defeating him and taking him captive (the Greek says it is like a prisoner taken at the point of a spear).

But this is not the language Paul uses in 2 Corinthians 10:4–5 to describe his Christian experience: "The weapons we fight with are not the weapons of the world [or "the flesh," *sarkika*]. On the contrary, they have divine power to demolish strongholds. We demolish arguments and every pretension that sets itself up against the knowledge of God, and we take captive every thought to make it obedient to Christ." Here Paul is speaking as a born-of-God, Spirit-empowered soldier of Christ who enjoys victory over sin.

"What a wretched man I am!" (v. 24). In other words, this man is saying, "I am weary and worn out. My hands are full of calluses." The word "wretched" (*talaipōros*) conveys the picture of a miserable man doing hard labor for sin. Satan wants to present the life of sin as a wonderful life of great joy and happiness. But Paul is proclaiming, "What a wretched man I am! I am a bondslave to sin and subject to death, which is the wages of sin. I cannot save myself. Who will save me from the law of sin and death?"

At this point, the Christian Paul surfaces. He breaks out in doxology and answers the heartrending question of this miserable, wretched man he has been describing. Man cannot save himself, and no man can save another, because every man in Adam is a weak, carnal sinner. But Paul triumphantly declares, *"Thanks be to God—through Jesus Christ our Lord!"* (v. 25)

A Man Convicted of Sin

God has a plan to save the miserable sons and daughters of Adam and make them into saints. He justifies, sanctifies, glorifies, and brings them to himself without sin. He has accomplished that eternal plan to make us holy and blameless in and through the one mediator, our Lord Jesus Christ.

Paul had already said of Christ that "he was delivered over to death for our sins and was raised to life for our justification" (Rom. 4:25). Now in Romans 7 he is summarizing the life of an unconverted sinner, who is under conviction of sin. When God's Spirit comes, he first convicts us of sin. When we see people calling themselves Christians who have no sense of sin, we can say they are not under the work of the Holy Spirit.

When the Holy Spirit comes, he will convict the world of guilt in regard to sin. After Peter preached on the Day of Pentecost, his listeners "were cut to the heart and said to Peter and the other apostles, 'Brothers, what shall we do?'" (Acts 2:37). In the middle of the night, the trembling Philippian jailer asked, "Sirs, what must I do to be saved?" (Acts 16:30).

It could be that Romans 7:7-25 is speaking about Paul's life before his baptism. Notice how Paul describes his own repentance and faith in Jesus Christ: "A man named Ananias came to see me. He was a devout observer of the law and highly respected by all the Jews living there. He stood beside me and said, 'Brother Saul, receive your sight!' And at that very moment I was able to see him. Then he said: 'The God of our fathers has chosen you to know his will and to see the Righteous One and to hear words from his mouth. You will be his witness to all men of what you have seen and heard. And now what are you waiting for? Get up, be baptized and wash your sins away, calling on his name'" (Acts 22:12-16). We are also told how Paul was filled with the Holy Spirit, his eyes were opened, and he was baptized (Acts 9:17-19).

When Paul said, "I myself with my mind serve the law of God" (v. 25, author's translation), we recognize that an outright pagan cannot serve God with his mind. But these words can be true of a man whom the Holy Spirit is convicting of his sin. His next statement— that with his flesh he is a slave of sin and sin wins out—indicates that the man of Romans 7:7-25 is a man to whom the law of God was coming with power and deep conviction. The man who once said he was perfectly righteous as a Pharisee now says, "Sin revived and I died. I am all unrighteousness and a bondslave of sin. I do not do what I will, and I do what I do not will. I do what I hate—yea, what is evil. Sin is dwelling in me as a permanent resident and is of greater power than my mind. No good thing dwells in me. From this slavery to sin, who will deliver me?"

So we must conclude that Romans 7:7–25 is not a description of normal Christian life or of Christian life at its best. Rather, it is the life of one who is convicted but not yet converted, the life of one who knows no victory in Jesus. He has not yet been indwelt by the Holy Spirit, who alone can triumphantly oppose the great yet finite power of sin and Satan.

In this passage, therefore, Paul says certain things only a man under conviction can say. He says the law is holy, just, good, and spiritual. He agrees that the law is good, and he wills to do what is good, but he cannot do it. Moreover, he rejoices over the law of God with his inner man (i.e., with his mind), and he says he serves God with his mind. But whatever he is doing, he is incompetent. He has no freedom and no divine ability to do the will of God. He must be saved through Christ.

The Difference between the Romans 7 Man and a True Believer

If Romans 7:7–25 describes normal Christian life or the life of a Christian at his best, then Paul is contradicting his own words elsewhere in Romans as well as in his other epistles. Just look at the following verses in which Paul describes the normal Christian life and compare them to the description of the Romans 7 man:

1. *Romans 5:1–2:* "Therefore, since we have been justified through faith, we have peace with God through our Lord Jesus Christ, through whom we have gained access by faith into this grace in which we now stand. And we rejoice in the hope of the glory of God." That is not what we see in Romans 7:7–25. There is no peace, no rejoicing.
2. *Romans 5:17:* "For if, by the trespass of the one man, death reigned through that one man, how much more will those who receive God's abundant provision of grace and of the gift of righteousness reign in life through the one man, Jesus Christ." Believers receive abundance of grace

and reign in life here and now. But that is not what we see in Romans 7.

3. *Romans 5:21b:* "So also grace might reign through righteousness to bring eternal life through Jesus Christ our Lord." Grace reigns through righteousness, not sin.

4. *Romans 6:1–2:* "Shall we go on sinning? . . . By no means! We died to sin; how can we live in it any longer?" The Romans 7 man continues to live in his sin.

5. *Romans 6:4:* "We were therefore buried with him through baptism into death in order that, just as Christ was raised from the dead through the glory of the Father, we too may live a new life." The life of Jesus Christ in us is the resurrection life. That is why we can get up in the morning and work for the Lord. We can do all things because God has given us a new nature, and the Spirit of God indwells us. We receive an abundance of grace to do mighty things.

6. *Romans 6:6–7:* "For we know that our old self was crucified with him so that the body of sin might be done away with, that we should no longer be slaves to sin—because anyone who has died has been freed from sin," meaning freed from the dominion, rule, authority, and power of sin.

7. *Romans 6:11:* "In the same way, count yourselves dead to sin but alive to God in Christ Jesus," that is, alive to serve God in Christ Jesus, not to serve sin.

8. *Romans 6:12:* "Therefore do not let sin reign in your mortal body so that you obey its evil desires." Christians enjoy freedom not to sin (*posse non peccare*). If you find yourself caught in sin, exercise your freedom and move out of Romans 7, because Romans 7 is not speaking about the normal Christian life. It is a life of defeat, bondage to sin, and misery.

9. *Romans 6:13:* "Do not offer the parts of your body to sin, as instruments of wickedness, but rather offer yourselves to God, as those who have been brought from death to life; and offer the parts of your body to him as instruments of righteousness." Every believer has the freedom to obey God and the freedom to disobey sin. We must not,

therefore, call ourselves Christians if we do not live by the power of the Holy Spirit and serve God in righteousness.

10. *Romans 6:14:* "For sin shall not be your master, because you are not under law, but under grace." We are no longer slaves to sin.

11. *Romans 6:17:* "But thanks be to God that, though you used to be slaves to sin, you wholeheartedly obeyed the form of teaching to which you were entrusted." Notice, the word is "obeyed," not "believed." Every true Christian is born of God and therefore has a new nature; and every Christian is indwelt by the Holy Spirit and therefore obeys from the heart the will of God as given to us in the word.

12. *Romans 6:18:* "You have been set free from sin and have become slaves to righteousness." We have been set free from the dominion, authority, and power of sin, and through the Spirit of the living God, we defeat sin.

13. *Romans 6:20:* "When you were slaves to sin, you were free from the control of righteousness." Now it is reversed. We are under the control of righteousness and set free from sin.

14. *Romans 6:22:* "But now that you have been set free from sin and have become slaves to God, the benefit you reap leads to holiness, and the result is eternal life." We are holy people.

15. *Romans 7:4:* "So, my brothers, you also died to the law through the body of Christ, that you might belong to another, to him who was raised from the dead, in order that we might bear fruit to God." We have a new husband to whom we belong, and he enables us to bear the fruit of obedience to God.

16. *Romans 7:6:* "But now, by dying to what once bound us, we have been released from the law so that we serve [God] in the new way of the Spirit [the new power of the Holy Spirit] and not in the old way of the written code."

17. *Romans 8:1–2:* "Therefore, there is now no condemnation for those who are in Christ Jesus, because through Christ Jesus the law of the Spirit of life set me free from the law of sin and death." We have been set free from the dominion of sin and Satan.

18. *Romans 8:9:* "You, however, are controlled not by the [flesh] but by the [Holy] Spirit, if the Spirit of God lives in you.

And if anyone does not have the Spirit of Christ, he does not belong to Christ." We can make any profession we want, but a true Christian is born of God and indwelt by the infinite person of the Spirit and his infinite power, which makes us able to do the will of God and be successful in this world and the world to come.

19. *Romans 8:11:* "And if the Spirit of him who raised Jesus from the dead is living in you, he who raised Christ from the dead will also give life to your mortal bodies through his Spirit, who lives in you." The convicted Romans 7 man cries, "Who will rescue me from this body of death?" Here is the answer: "Thanks be to God— through Jesus Christ our Lord!" The Holy Spirit has come and is dwelling in us. This same Spirit who raised Jesus from the dead will also raise our mortal bodies from the dead. The indwelling Holy Spirit guarantees our resurrection.

20. *Romans 8:37:* "No, in all these things we are more than conquerors through him who loved us." Believe, saints of God. If you are defeated, rise up and say, "From this day forward, by the energy of the mighty Spirit of God, I believe the truth that I am more than a conqueror through him who loved me. So neither death nor life, nor anything else in all creation is able to separate me from the love of God that is in Christ Jesus my Lord." Christians are powerful to live victorious lives in Jesus and overcome the temptations of this world.

21. *1 Corinthians 6:19-20:* "Do you not know that your body is a temple of the Holy Spirit, who is in you, whom you have received from God? You are not your own; you were bought at a price. Therefore honor God with your body." We should know that our bodies are no longer ours; they are the property of the Holy Spirit. We were bought with the blood of Jesus Christ. Therefore, we have no right to abuse or do whatever we want with them.

22. *1 Corinthians 9:27:* "No, I beat my body and make it my slave so that after I have preached to others, I myself will not be disqualified for the prize." Paul's practice was to make his body obey him, not to be enslaved to his body.

The Romans 7 man cannot do this. The Holy Spirit enables us to get up and do God's work.

23. *1 Corinthians 15:10*: "But by the grace of God I am what I am, and his grace to me was not without effect. No, I worked harder than all of them—yet not I, but the grace of God that was with me." All his success came to Paul by the grace of God. If we are Christians, we must evaluate our lives and begin to redeem the time and produce eternally significant works. God's grace is available if we avail ourselves of the means of grace, such as getting up early to read the Scriptures, listening with all attention when the word is preached, and praying with faith and passion, in accordance with the will of God.

24. *2 Corinthians 9:8*: "And God is able to make all grace abound to you, so that in all things at all times, having all that you need, you will abound in every good work." What a great promise! May we believe it, add faith to it, and receive grace to do all that God wants us to do. The grace we need is available to face all exigencies of life. A Christian is positive and confident, rather than pessimistic and retreating.

25. *2 Corinthians 12:9–10*: "But [the Lord] said to me, 'My grace is sufficient for you, for my power is made perfect in weakness.' Therefore I will boast all the more gladly about my weaknesses, so that Christ's power may rest on me. That is why, for Christ's sake, I delight in weaknesses, in insults, in hardships, in persecutions, in difficulties. For when I am weak, then I am strong." These are the words of a truly mature Christian.

26. *Galatians 2:20*: "I have been crucified with Christ and I no longer live, but Christ lives in me. The life I live in the body, I live by faith in the Son of God, who loved me and gave himself for me." These are not mythological statements; they are reality. As we add faith to these words, we will experience peace, comfort, victory, and success. If we have been born again, the infinite Holy Spirit dwells in us, always opposing finite sin and giving us victory.

27. *Galatians 5:16*: "So I say, live by the Spirit [by his teaching and by his power], and you will not gratify the desires

of the [flesh]." We are not saved from the flesh; sin is still in us. But there is a new reality. We are new creations in Christ and the Holy Spirit dwells in us, always opposing and defeating sin.

28. *Galatians 5:18:* "But if you are led by the Spirit, you are not under law." We are no longer under law, sin, and death.

29. *Ephesians 1:19:* Paul prayed that we may have spiritual assistance to know certain things to live a Christian life. We need to know "his incomparably great power for us who believe." When we sin, it is proof that we did not receive the grace and assistance of the Holy Spirit that would have come to us had we prayed and sought him. God offers his "incomparably great power" so that we might live by this resurrection power of Jesus Christ.

30. *Ephesians 2:10:* "For we are God's workmanship, created in Christ Jesus to do good works, which God prepared in advance for us to do." From all eternity it is God's will to have a holy and blameless people who obey him. If we do not obey God, we are not true Christians. We may be nominal Christians, but our profession is meaningless unless we live obedient, powerful, victorious lives.

31. *Ephesians 3:20:* "Now to him who is able to do immeasurably more than all we ask or imagine, according to his [infinite] power that is at work within us . . ." A Christian wife and mother can do all the work she should be doing. A Christian father and husband can do all the work he should be doing. All Christians can do all the work they should be doing because God's power is at work in them.

32. *Ephesians 4:28:* "He who has been stealing must steal no longer, but must work, doing something useful with his own hands, that he may have something to share with those in need." This is speaking about a thief who became a Christian. Before, he was stealing; now he is working hard. Why? God gave him a new nature and the Holy Spirit is indwelling him, so he is now eager to obey God's commandments. He pays his own bills and helps those in need. This is true Christianity.

33. *Ephesians 6:10, 13–14:* "Finally, be strong in the Lord and in his mighty power" and wage war against all evil, against

principalities and powers and heavenly wickedness. Resist the devil and he shall flee from you. "Therefore put on the full armor of God, so that when the day of evil comes, you may be able to stand your ground, and after you have done everything, to stand. Stand firm then, with the belt of truth buckled around your waist, with the breastplate of righteousness in place." I pray that especially husbands and fathers will believe what God is saying and go home to live such powerful lives that you inspire your wife and children to also live for God.

34. *Philippians 2:12-13:* "Therefore, my dear friends, as you have always obeyed—not only in my presence, but now much more in my absence—continue to work out your salvation with fear and trembling, for it is God who works in you to will and to act according to his good purpose." Josiah showed such fear and trembling when he discovered the Bible (2 Kings 22–23). If we are Christians, God works in us to will and to do his good pleasure. We do God's will because God makes us willing and able to do it. Even if we are steeped in sin, the Holy Spirit can deliver us instantly. The thief of Ephesians 4 is told to stop stealing immediately and start working with his hands. God works in him.

35. *Philippians 4:13:* "I can do everything through [Christ] who gives me strength." The Lord helps us all the time to do all that he wants us to do.

In light of all these scriptures,[4] we must say that if Romans 7:7–25 describes the normal Christian life, a mature Christian life, or the life of a Christian at his best, then Paul is contradicting himself everywhere else in his writings. Throughout all his epistles, Paul describes believers as those who live victorious Christian lives.

Conclusion

Have you noticed that most modern evangelical churches do not preach about sin anymore? They do not speak of repentance,

---

4   See also Lloyd-Jones, *Romans*, vol. 6, *The Law.*

judgment, hell, holiness, purity, separation from the world, saving faith, cross power, victorious Christian life, power of grace, power of the Holy Spirit, or the authority of the Scripture. Nominalism is the prevalent type of Christianity. People call themselves Christians but live pagan lives. They do so for the simple reason that they are still pagans. They have not experienced regeneration or the infilling and baptism of the Holy Spirit.

The view that Romans 7 describes the normal Christian life promotes such antinomianism. It says the more we sin, the more grace we can receive and the more God is glorified. Even Luther, by his statement, "*Simul iustus et peccator*" (simultaneously justified and still a sinner), may have inadvertently lent support to this antinomian Christianity in today's Protestant world. If Romans 7 speaks of normal Christian life, it also promotes the heresy of dualism, which says sin belongs to the body only. The dualist says that his body is sinning, but he is not. In fact, he can say, who cares what the body does? It is only going to die. Therefore, one can sin all he wants; he is saved forever.

People may not use the labels of "antinomianism" or "dualism," but this is the type of life many evangelicals are living today. This explains the lack of preaching of sin, repentance, holiness, judgment, and Holy Spirit power.

Jesus came to save his people *from* their sins, not *in* their sins. Yet this does not mean that Christians are sinlessly perfect. Christians sin, and it is very possible for a Christian to sin terribly and for a long time. That is why John writes, "If we confess our sins, [God] is faithful and just and will forgive us our sins and purify us from all unrighteousness" (1 John 1:9). But by the new nature and the dynamic of the indwelling Holy Spirit, those who are justified are also being sanctified to live victorious Christian lives. Once we were darkness; now we are light in the Lord. Let us therefore shine like stars in this dark world and bring glory to our heavenly Father.

37

God-Guaranteed Eternal Security

Therefore, there is now no condemnation for those who are in Christ Jesus.

Romans 8:1

The eighth chapter of Romans is described in many ways. Some people look at it as the highest peak in a range of mountains. Others say it is the most sparkling diamond in a ring of diamonds. Others call it "the holy of holies" of the Christian faith.

The theme of Romans 8 is God-guaranteed eternal security. A guarantee means nothing without knowing who is making the guarantee. In this chapter, God Triune is guaranteeing the ultimate salvation of his people.

Romans 8 sets forth the absolute certainty of the full and final salvation of all who are justified by faith and therefore live a holy life. Because of Christ's death on the cross, our salvation in all its aspects—justification, sanctification, and glorification—has been accomplished. God purposed from all eternity to bring many sons to glory, and he accomplishes that purpose.

This full salvation is being applied to every elect person by the Holy Spirit. This was the plan of our heavenly Father from all eternity when he chose a people to be made holy and blameless in his sight. The bride of Christ is a radiant church, without stain, wrinkle, or any other blemish. "It is because of [God the Father]

449

that you are in Christ Jesus, who has become for us wisdom from God—that is, our righteousness, holiness and redemption" (1 Cor. 1:30), or we could say, "our justification, sanctification, and glorification."

The Bible says Jesus saves his people *from* their sins, not *in* their sins. Those whom he justifies will also be sanctified and glorified. Such people will be admitted to his heaven.

God takes the objects of wrath and makes them objects of grace. He takes the sons of disobedience and makes them children of obedience. God justifies the ungodly and makes them godly. Saints of God, we are saved, we are being saved, and we will be saved on the last day by grace alone through faith alone in Christ alone. All praise be to God the Father, God the Son, and God the Holy Spirit, one God in three Persons!

We spoke of the miserable man of Romans 7:14–25 in our last study. That man was not justified or sanctified. He was a dying, defeated, hopeless wretch who was taken prisoner by the law of sin in his members. He was not free and was incapable of saving himself. So he cried out for a deliverer: "Who will rescue me from this body of death?" The answer came through the Christian Paul: "Thanks be to God—through Jesus Christ our Lord!" (Rom. 7:24–25). God saves us through Jesus Christ.

In this study we want to treat the first verse of Romans 8, which is a summary of the gospel. We will examine two points. First, Paul declares, *"Therefore, there is now no condemnation."* Second, "Therefore, there is now no condemnation *to those who are in Christ Jesus."*

No Condemnation

Paul begins this chapter with the word *"therefore."* Romans 8 is looking back on what has been stated about the gospel in the first seven chapters. Paul is saying, "In view of all I have said so far, here is the conclusion of the matter: Believers in Jesus Christ are secure beyond a shadow of doubt."

"Therefore there is *now* . . ." "Now" points to the gospel age, the time following the incarnation and atonement of God's eternal Son. "Now" is temporal, not logical. Paul is saying, "Now that Christ died, was buried, was raised, ascended, and is seated at

God's right hand as Sovereign Lord of the universe and Head of the church, there is no condemnation to those who are in Christ Jesus." Not only that, "now" also points to the time when we personally trusted in the gospel of God.

Then Paul says there is "no condemnation." The Greek word he uses for "no" (ouden) is not the simple word for "no" (ou). Paul is using a more powerful negation. He places this more powerful "no" at the beginning of the sentence, giving emphasis on the negation. When God saves wretched, dying sinners, he declares that there will never, ever be any condemnation for them. When we realize this truth that there is now no condemnation, the peace of God that passes all human understanding will come from heaven to fill our hearts to overflowing, guard our minds, and make us unshakable. So we can sing,

> Rolled away, rolled away, rolled away,
> Every burden of my heart is rolled away.

"Therefore there is now no *condemnation*." "Condemnation" points to a sentence of judgment and its punishment, which is death. We all deserve condemnation, because in Adam every man except Jesus Christ is a born sinner who practices sin daily. We are guilty before God and the wrath of God is being revealed against us. We are enemies of God, rebels who refuse to love truth and glorify God.

How can such rebels be given this glorious gospel sentence from heaven: "Therefore there is now no condemnation"? In place of the elect, sinful sons of the first Adam, the last Adam, Jesus Christ, fulfilled God's law in his life and death on the cross (see Rom. 5:12–21). Jesus Christ was condemned in our place. And not only was he condemned, but he was also executed in our place on Calvary's cross. So those who believe in Christ are not condemned. Instead, we are justified and seen by God as being without any sin.

"No condemnation," therefore, speaks of God's justification of us. Justification is a gift of grace from God, the gift of righteousness and eternal life (Rom. 5:15–17). Condemned people are given righteousness, an irreversible justification unto life. Once this sentence is pronounced, there is no longer any condemnation.

Our position cannot be reversed, because God himself will not reverse it. No angel, no devil, no man—nothing in all creation, including our sin—can reverse it. So Paul declares, "What, then, shall we say in response to this? If God is for us, who can be against us? He who did not spare his own Son, but gave him up for us all—how will he not also, along with him, graciously give us all things? Who will bring any charge against those whom God has chosen? It is God who justifies. Who is he that condemns? Christ Jesus, who died—more than that, who was raised to life—is at the right hand of God and is also interceding for us" (Rom. 8:31–34).

There is no condemnation and no separation from God for his people. No one can snatch us out of his omnipotent hands. What is the reason for this great security? Jesus solved our sin problem once for all. We have crossed over from death to life and we can never go back.

All our sins are gone. All God's wrath is gone. All our condemnation is gone. We are no longer under the rule, power, and authority of law, sin, death, wrath, or Satan. In Christ, not only are we righteous, but we are the righteousness of God. We have been transferred from the kingdom of darkness to the kingdom of God's beloved Son.

We are with God and in God. We are in Christ and Christ is in us. The Holy Spirit is in us. Notice, this is not our own testimony but God's own declaration. This is the great divine indicative: "Now no condemnation," says God in his word. God has pardoned all our sins, clothed us with Christ's divine righteousness, and given us the power of the Holy Spirit to live a life of victory. Through regeneration God has given us divine nature. No longer are we wretched, dying, hopeless prisoners of sin and Satan. We have been justified, pardoned, and given the righteousness of God.

God has made us super-conquerors in Jesus Christ (Rom. 8:37). We are not weaklings; we are mighty warriors who wage war against the powers of darkness. We have been empowered to triumph over sin. The world, the law, sin, Satan, and death no longer have dominion over us. As mighty men, women, and children of God, we are overcomers. With God we can fight and defeat Satan, sin, and the world.

There is now no punishment for us, because Christ died for our sins. There is no condemnation ever. It is utterly impossible for us to be unjustified.

To Those Who Are in Christ Jesus

"Therefore, there is now no condemnation *to those who are in Christ Jesus.*" "*Tois en Christō Iēsou*" means to those who are united with Christ, who are vitally linked to him, and who have been taken out of the first Adam and united with the last Adam, Jesus Christ. In him is life, light, hope, and everything else we need. Outside of him there is only curse, defeat, destruction, death, hell, and shame.

There are only two classes of people in the world: those who are in Adam (unbelievers) and those who are in Christ (believers). As sinners, those who are in Adam are condemned and waiting for their final execution. But those who are in Christ Jesus are justified forever by faith in Christ.

How can a wicked man be united to Christ? How can he believe? It calls for nothing less than a divine miracle. An elect sinner is made spiritually alive and given the gift of repentance and saving faith. He trusts in Christ alone—in his person and atonement—and he is thus justified. He is *in* Christ Jesus.

Paul writes of this miraculous change: "Don't you know that all of us who were baptized into Christ Jesus were baptized into his death? We were therefore buried with him through baptism into death in order that, just as Christ was raised from the dead through the glory of the Father, we too may live a new life" (Rom. 6:3–4). Having been raised up spiritually with Christ, we live a new life, the life of Christ. We are in the ark. We are in Christ.

We are the bride of Christ and he is our beloved husband. As a result of this union, all our liabilities become his and all his assets become ours. Oh, what a blessed union! Paul describes it in his letter to the Ephesians: "Husbands, love your wives, just as Christ loved the church and gave himself up for her to make her holy, cleansing her by the washing with water through the word, and to present her to himself as a radiant church, without stain or wrinkle or any other blemish, but holy and blameless" (Eph. 5:25–27). He is speaking about Christ and his bride.

453

We are "in Christ Jesus." Jesus himself said, "I am the vine; you are the branches. If a man remains in me and I in him, he will bear much fruit; apart from me you can do nothing" (John 15:5). He is the vine; we are the branches that are pruned to produce fruit, more fruit, and much fruit to the glory of God the Father. The life of the vine pulsating in us is the reason for all our fruitfulness. We live by grace. We are in Christ. What a vital union!

We see this idea of union also in the analogy of Jesus as the head and the church as his body: "And God placed all things under his feet and appointed him to be head over everything for the church, which is his body, the fullness of him who fills everything in every way" (Eph. 1:22–23). As our head, Christ directs us, provides for us, and protects us, and we serve him in the power of his resurrection life.

Not only that, he is also the foundation and we are the structure built upon him as living stones. We are "members of God's household, built on the foundation of the apostles and prophets, with Christ Jesus himself as the chief cornerstone. In him the whole building is joined together and rises to become a holy temple in the Lord. And in him you too are being built together to become a dwelling in which God lives by his Spirit" (Eph. 2:19–22).

As people of God, we are "in Christ Jesus." This phrase, and its equivalents (such as "in him"), is found 164 times in Paul's writings. What a blessing it is to be in Christ Jesus! Either we are in Christ or we are outside of him. In the ark we are safe; outside, we perish in the floodwaters. We are in Christ by saving faith. Outside are unbelievers, all who mock Christ. Outside are the unbelieving philosophers, scientists, and politicians; the rich, the beautiful, the powerful, the brilliant; and all religionists who reject Jesus Christ, the only God and Savior. Outside are the wretched, the hopeless, and the dying. John writes: "Outside are the dogs, those who practice magic arts, the sexually immoral, the murderers, the idolaters and everyone who loves and practices falsehood" (Rev. 22:15).

Are You in Christ?

Are you in Christ Jesus, or are you outside of him? Do not think that you are inside merely because you were born and brought up in a church, or that your parents are Christians. Such things mean nothing without personally trusting in Christ. The question is, are you in Christ Jesus? Can you say that there is now therefore no condemnation for you?

Jesus spoke about the destiny of those who are outside of Christ: "Then the king told the attendants, 'Tie him hand and foot, and throw him outside, into the darkness, where there will be weeping and gnashing of teeth'" (Matt. 22:13). If you are an unbeliever, live in maximum pleasure today, for the moment you die, you will descend into that far place away from God. God will say of you, "Throw that worthless servant outside, into the darkness, where there will be weeping and gnashing of teeth" (Matt. 25:30). To those who never truly served Christ as Lord, Jesus says, "Then I will tell them plainly, 'I never knew you. Away from me, you evildoers!'" (Matt. 7:23). And in the parable of the sheep and the goats, he describes the final destiny of two classes of people: "Then he will say to those on his left, 'Depart from me, you who are cursed, into the eternal fire prepared for the devil and his angels.' . . . Then they will go away to eternal punishment, but the righteous to eternal life" (Matt. 25:41, 46).

There is no condemnation only for those who by faith are in Christ Jesus. Awaiting such people on that day will be God's approbation, benediction, and eternal blessing. David said, "Blessed is he whose transgressions are forgiven, whose sins are covered. Blessed is the man whose sin the LORD does not count against him" (Ps. 32:1–2; cf. Rom. 4:7–8). Such people are blessed because all their sins were counted against Jesus Christ, our divine substitute.

Are you in Christ? God's beloved Son was sent into the world to deal with our sin problem. It is our sin that separates us from God. It is because of our sins that we are outside of Christ. Christ died for the sins of all who repent truly and trust in him savingly. Trust him, who was condemned and punished in our stead. He was crucified, not for his sins, but for ours.

If you are still outside, I urge you to come inside the ark and be saved. Outside is darkness, death, hopelessness, anxiety, misery, and condemnation. But inside is life, light, hope, peace, joy, and eternal security. Most importantly, inside is God himself.

Hear the call of Jesus to sinners who are outside: "Come to me, all you who are weary and burdened, and I will give you rest"

(Matt. 11:28). The Bible says, "Everyone who calls on the name of the Lord will be saved" (Rom. 10:13).

If you are in Christ Jesus, rejoice and be glad in him! If God is for us, who can be against us? It is God who justifies. So go and live courageously. Be a warrior, a super-conqueror for Christ. Live an overcoming life in the Spirit's power. Resist the devil, sin, temptation, and secularism. Live for God's Son, who died for us and lives for us, never to die again.

38

Freedom from Tyranny

Because through Christ Jesus the law of the Spirit of life set me free from the law of sin and death.

Romans 8:2

Who is a Christian? Some people think a Christian is one who was born in a so-called Christian land or someone born into a church. But these things do not make a person a Christian, according to the Bible. We need to think seriously about who is a true Christian.

In our last study we learned that a Christian is one who is united to Jesus Christ. Because we are in Christ, his life flows into us and we live in his life. A Christian is one concerning whom it can be said, "There is therefore now no condemnation" (Rom. 8:1). In this next verse we find a second blessing associated with being a Christian. A Christian is one who is liberated: *"For the law of the Spirit of life in Christ Jesus has set me free from the law of sin and death"* (author's translation). These two characteristics describe a Christian: there is no longer any condemnation for him, and he has been liberated from all evil.

There is no condemnation for those who are in Christ Jesus because the Holy Spirit liberated us from the tyranny of sin and death. Verse 3 tells us this liberation took place because of God's Son, sent by the Father from heaven to take care of our singular problem of sin. It was sin that kept us from heaven, from God, and from one another. But sin has been dealt a deathblow by Christ's effectual atonement on Calvary's cross.

457

Jesus declares, "Everyone who sins is a slave to sin" (John 8:34). Such slaves can be liberated, and if the Son sets us free, we will indeed be free. Only Christ can set us free; no one else can do so.

The man of Romans 7:7–25 was not a free man. He said, "When the law came, sin revived and I died" (v. 9). This wretched prisoner of sin cried out for deliverance from the law of sin and death. Only God through Jesus Christ can set him free forever.

Sin is a great power on the face of the earth. It is a terror that deceives people through the pleasure it gives. Sin promises power but delivers slavery. It promises eternal life but delivers eternal death. Jesus says, "The thief comes only to steal and kill and destroy" (John 10:10). Jesus came to give us life eternal by putting an end to our death by his death on the cross.

Before, we could only sin. Now, since we have been liberated, we have freedom not to sin—freedom to fight against sin and win. We have freedom to obey God because we have received in Christ not only pardon but also power. Not only the guilt of sin is dealt with, but also its dominion over our lives. Sin and death no longer rule over our lives as kings. As believers in Christ, we are in Christ. We have been set free forever from the power of sin, Satan, and death—free at last, and free forever. The wretched man, the slave of sin, the prisoner sold under sin, is now set free.

Why No Condemnation?

1. *"For* the law of the Spirit of life . . ."* Paul declared, "Therefore, there is now no condemnation" (Rom. 8:1), and in verse 2 Paul begins with the word "for" or "because," giving the reason why there is no condemnation. The Christian life is logical; therefore, we must think logically. We are speaking about biblical logic that begins with God.

There is no condemnation because the Holy Spirit accomplished our liberation. No condemnation means no sentence or execution awaits us. The reason is that the Spirit of God has set free all elect slaves of sin. The law of sin and death is no match for the infinite power of the Spirit of life.

The power of the Spirit is greater than Satan, greater than sin, and greater than the power of death. And this great power in the person of the Holy Spirit is in us, opposing all other powers that are intent on defeating us.

2. "For the *law* of the Spirit of life freed me from the law of sin and death." The word "law" occurs two times in this verse. What meaning should we give to this word in the phrase "the law of the Spirit of life"? In the New Testament, "law" is used to refer to the entire Old Testament, the Pentateuch, the Ten Commandments, or the Mosaic law. It can also mean the principle, the rule, or the governing authority. I take "the law of the Spirit of life" to mean the mighty ruling authority of the Holy Spirit.

3. "For the law of *the Spirit of life* freed me from the law of sin and death." "Spirit" here is the Holy Spirit, who applies Christ's redemption to every elect sinner. Paul mentioned the Holy Spirit four times earlier in this epistle, but in Romans 8 the Spirit is mentioned twenty times. There is no other chapter in the New Testament in which the Spirit is mentioned as frequently. The Holy Spirit is the agent of our liberation.

When the Holy Spirit opposes sin and death, the Spirit always wins. God the Father sent his Son to accomplish redemption, and the Father and the Son sent the Holy Spirit, the third Person of the Trinity, to apply this great redemption to us. Paul says, "But when the time had fully come, God sent his son, born of a woman, born under law, to redeem those under law, that we might receive the full rights of sons. Because you are sons, God sent the Spirit of his Son into our hearts, the Spirit who calls out, 'Abba, Father.' So you are no longer a slave, but a son; and since you are a son, God has made you also an heir" (Gal. 4:4–7).

The Holy Spirit is life and imparts life to the dead. He gives spiritual resurrection: "But because of his great love for us, God, who is rich in mercy, made us alive with Christ even when we were dead in transgressions—it is by grace you have been saved" (Eph. 2:4–5). He regenerates us. Jesus said, "You must be born again," that is, born of the Spirit (John 3:3–8). He is the life-giving Spirit of the new covenant: "a new covenant—not of the letter but of the Spirit; for the letter kills, but the Spirit gives life" (2 Cor. 3:6). God himself says, "I will put my Spirit in you and move you to follow my decrees and be careful to keep my laws" (Ezek. 36:27).

Not only does the Holy Spirit give us spiritual life, but he also raises us from the dead, granting us a glorious, physical, immortal, imperishable body. Paul writes, "And if the Spirit of him who raised Jesus from the dead is living in you, he who raised Christ from the dead will also give life to your mortal bodies through his Spirit, who lives in you" (Rom. 8:11). He is the Spirit of life, both spiritual and physical. Our need is life, and the Holy Spirit who is life gives us life. He resurrects our mortal bodies.

Paul also says, "Where the Spirit of the Lord is, there is freedom" (2 Cor. 3:17). Not only does the Holy Spirit give us eternal life, but he also gives us freedom to say no to sin and to resist the devil that he may flee from us. This Spirit who gives us new life also gives us new power. Before our conversion, sin permanently dwelt in us as king, ruling in power (see Rom. 7:17, 20). The Holy Spirit dwells in the man who is in Christ Jesus and opposes the defeated sin in that man. So Paul writes, "You, however, are controlled not by the [flesh] but by the Spirit, if the Spirit of God lives in you. And if anyone does not have the Spirit of Christ, he does not belong to Christ" (Rom. 8:9).

Elsewhere Paul declares, "Now it is God who makes both us and you stand firm in Christ. He anointed us, set his seal of ownership on us, and put his Spirit in our hearts as a deposit, guaranteeing what is to come" (2 Cor. 1:21–22). The fullness of salvation—our glorification—is guaranteed by the indwelling Holy Spirit. This ruling presence of the Holy Spirit is the distinguishing mark of a Christian. Yes, there is still sin in us, but the Holy Spirit also operates in us, making us overcomers. Thus, when Paul speaks of the law of the Spirit of life, he is speaking about the internal operation of the Holy Spirit in us.[1] Our problem is internal, and the Holy Spirit has come into us, making us taste victory in Christ.

This Holy Spirit unites us to Christ so that we enjoy Christ's life forever. We live in his life, which is eternal life. So we live in the newness of life and bear fruit for God. The law of the Spirit of life freed us from the law of sin and death.

4. "For the law of the Spirit of life freed me from the *law* of sin and death." What is the meaning of "law" in the phrase "law of sin and death"? This is a difficult question, but we have

---

1   Murray, *Epistle to the Romans*, 277.

the answer. It is the Mosaic law, as we see in verses 3, 4, and 7. But there is something else: It is the Mosaic law in its reaction, relation, and interaction with sin in the sinner. Though the law itself is holy, just, good, and spiritual, in its relationship with the flesh it aggravates sin and leads to sin and death. The law was never given to save or to impart life. This holy law provokes and stimulates sin, producing condemnation and death.

Paul speaks about this in Romans 7: "For when we were controlled by the sinful nature [flesh], the sinful passions aroused by the [Mosaic] law were at work in our bodies so that we bore fruit for death. . . . But sin, seizing the opportunity afforded by the commandment, produced in me every kind of covetous desire. For apart from law, sin is dead. Once I was alive apart from law; but when the commandment came, sin sprang to life and I died. . . . Did that which is good, then, become death to me? By no means! But in order that sin might be recognized as sin, it produced death in me through what was good, so that through the commandment sin might become utterly sinful" (vv. 5, 8–9, 13). Elsewhere he says, "The sting of death is sin, and the power of sin is the law" (1 Cor. 15:56). The good law produces sin and death. It does not weaken sin; it gives strength to it. That is why children who come from Christian homes may have more trouble unless they are born of God.

A believer who has experienced this liberation of the Holy Spirit is set free from law, sin, death, and Satan. He died to sin (Rom. 6:2) and law (Rom. 7:4). Therefore, he is not under the rule and authority of sin and the law. Paul declares, "But if you are led by the Spirit, you are not under law" (Gal. 5:18). The Christian is in Christ, united to him in his death, burial, and resurrection. Now he lives the resurrection life and enjoys the peace of God.

Christians live forevermore! The believer who is set free from the law of sin and death will live eternally in Christ because Christ will not die again. Jesus said, "I am the Living One; I was dead, and behold I am alive for ever and ever! And I hold the keys of death and Hades" (Rev. 1:18). As believers, we are liberated by the Spirit of life from the Mosaic law in its reaction, collaboration, and relation with the sin nature that produced sin and death. There is a connection with the Mosaic law and the law of sin (Rom. 7:23, 25). There is a connection with the Mosaic law and sin in our body. The man of Romans 7 was a prisoner who needed freedom. He was serving the law of sin, aggravated by the Mosaic law. Deliverance came for him in Christ Jesus by the law of the Spirit of life. Praise God, there is now no condemnation, but only liberation forever! We may speak about eating too much, drinking too much, smoking too much, or buying too much. All those behaviors are slavery. But Jesus Christ sets us free today. The truth will set us free!

The Mosaic law of God is, to fallen man, occasion of both sin and death.[2] The letter kills. Death is sin's natural concomitant. Paul writes, "Just as sin reigned in death [or through death], so also grace might reign through righteousness to bring eternal life through Jesus Christ our Lord" (Rom. 5:21). This death that is the wages of sin was destroyed by the death of Christ in our behalf. Christians, therefore, do not die; they sleep in Christ Jesus.

In Adam we received sin and death. In Christ we receive righteousness and eternal life. Praise God, we have been delivered from Adam and put in Christ by God.

5. "For the law of the Spirit of life *freed me* from the law of sin and death." Paul uses a technical term (*eleutheroō*) that speaks of bringing freedom to slaves. The Holy Spirit has freed us not only from the penalty of sin, but also from its reigning power. Before, Satan, sin, and death ruled us. We were their slaves. Now they have no more dominion over us. The cry, "Who shall rescue me from this body of death?" has been heard. We are no longer controlled by the flesh, but by the Spirit (Rom. 8:9).

We are in the Spirit and in Christ. Paul says, "[Jesus Christ] gave himself for our sins to rescue us from the present evil age. . . . For [God the Father] has rescued us from the dominion of darkness and brought us into the kingdom of the Son he loves" (Gal. 1:4; Col. 1:13). Friends, we are no longer in the realm of flesh, sin and death, or the law; we are now in the sphere of the Spirit. We have been taken out of Satan's dominion and are now in the kingdom of God, where there is life, righteousness, peace, and joy in the Holy Spirit. We have been taken out of Egypt and brought to the city of God, the heavenly Jerusalem. Our guilt is gone and we

---

2   Haldane, *Exposition of Romans*, 188.

have power to resist sin and Satan. Now Satan flees from us. In Christ we are warriors against sin by the Spirit. In Romans 8:13 we read that we can put to death the misdeeds of the body by the Holy Spirit.

It is true that we are not perfect. Sin has not been fully eradicated from a Christian. But sin has lost its dominion over us. Now we can fight against and defeat it. We enjoy freedom from sin and its tyranny. The gospel "is the power of God for the salvation of everyone who believes" (Rom. 1:16). The gospel liberates us from the terrible situation sin created. Christ was sent to deal with sin, and he defeated Satan and sin forever.

We have been freed! The verb is in the aorist tense, indicating a decisive act that took place in the past. Therefore, we are not being freed daily; we are freed once for all and freed forever. We will never go back to slavery or condemnation. We have crossed over in Christ from death to life. A great chasm has been fixed. The redeemed cannot go back to condemnation, the wrath of God, or the dominion of sin, death, and Satan. The stronger one, our Lord Jesus Christ, has attacked and defeated the strong one, the devil, and set his hostages free forever.

Romans 6:18 tells us we have been set free from the control of sin. Here *eleutheroō* is used in the aorist passive form, meaning God has set us free forever and he has done so in the past.

And not only have we been set free from sin, but God has also enslaved us to righteousness. Our freedom *from sin* is freedom *to serve righteousness*. We are slaves now to righteousness, to God. Before, as slaves of sin, we continually committed unclean, lawless, and wicked acts leading to death. Now we are slaves of righteousness, which leads to holiness: "But now that you have been set free from sin and have become slaves to God, the benefit you reap leads to holiness, and the result is eternal life" (Rom. 6:22). Sanctification is the evidence that God has saved us and justified us.

Many people complain about churches that exercise authority. They want freedom to sin, but true churches will oppose such "freedom." These people are really asking for autonomy and antinomianism. But God saved us from one slavery and brought us into another. There is no neutrality or autonomy for a Christian. We are still slaves, but now we serve a different master,

God Triune, who gives us justification for condemnation, power for weakness, life for death, and the ability to live a holy life rather than a life of uncleanness. He brought us out of hell and brought us into heaven. "It is for freedom that Christ has set us free," says Paul (Gal. 5:1). Use your freedom to serve God and one another in love.

How Should We Enjoy This Freedom of the Spirit?

How, then, shall we enjoy this freedom given to us by the Holy Spirit? T. W. Manson says, "Moses' law has right but not might; Sin's law has might but not right; the law of the Spirit has both right and might."[3] Paul speaks of living by the Spirit, meaning by his control, authority, and power: "So I say, live by the Spirit, and you will not gratify the lusts of the flesh" (Gal. 5:16). That is a guarantee. "Live by the Spirit" means "be led by the Spirit." The Holy Spirit is the Spirit of holiness, truth, power, and love. He leads us in the narrow way, the way of righteousness, the highway of holiness, the way of the word, of which he is the author. And the same Holy Spirit leads us into his holy church, where we have vital connectedness with God's people. Those who look for autonomy have not been delivered from the law of sin and death.

What do you want—tyranny or freedom, uncleanness or holiness, condemnation or justification, death or life, joy or misery? Thank God, there is therefore now no condemnation to those who are in Christ Jesus. Thank God there is liberation in Christ Jesus. Thank God we can be overcomers and live a victorious Christian life.

Jesus Christ sets us free, and no president, no Supreme Court, and no government can take this freedom away. Paul was God's free man, even when he was in chains in the Roman prison. Therefore he rejoiced in the Lord in all things. It is a great freedom.

Since we have been set free, let us enjoy this freedom to the fullest by serving Christ. Paul did so. That is why he identified himself as "Paul, a slave of Christ Jesus" (Rom. 1:1). Let us also call ourselves slaves of the only Sovereign, our Lord Jesus Christ, who himself was known as the suffering servant. There is no greater honor.

---

3   Quoted by Leon Morris, *Epistle to the Romans*, 301.

If you are not in Christ Jesus, you are outside and under condemnation. You are a slave of sin and death. May the truth of the gospel set you free today! If the Son sets you free, you will be free indeed. Repent of your sins and trust in Christ alone and his work of atonement. He breaks the iron yoke of slavery and sets every repenting sinner free.

39

The Center of Christianity

For what the law was powerless to do in that it was weakened by the sinful nature, God did by sending his own Son in the likeness of sinful man to be a sin offering. And so he condemned sin in sinful man.

Romans 8:3

In Romans 8:3 Paul deals with the center of Christianity, which is the person of Christ, God's incarnate Son, and his work of atonement, his death on the cross for our sins. This verse is our hope. This verse deals with our sin problem. No other religion can remedy the human problem of sin because no other religion has a savior to save his people from their sins.

The cross of Christ is the center of Christianity. Paul states, "For I resolved to know nothing while I was with you except Jesus Christ and him crucified" (1 Cor. 2:2). Elsewhere he declares, "Before your very eyes Jesus Christ was clearly portrayed as crucified" (Gal. 3:1). Jesus himself declared concerning his atoning work, "Just as Moses lifted up the snake in the desert, so the Son of Man must be lifted up, that everyone who believes in him may have eternal life" (John 3:14–15).

Before, sin and death ruled our lives. But now the eternal Son of God, in his human nature, defeated our enemies of sin and death. Now grace is king, and Jesus Christ is Lord. Now we ourselves are kings who receive the abundance of this grace. We can rejoice greatly because for us there is no condemnation but only liberation. All of this is because of God's saving work in the fullness of time through his incarnate Son.

God's work in Jesus Christ as described in verse 3 is the reason for our no longer being condemned (v. 1) and our liberation through the work of the Holy Spirit (v. 2). So Paul writes, *"For what the law was powerless to do in that it was weak through the flesh, God did by sending his own Son in the likeness of sinful flesh, and for sin condemned sin in the flesh"* (v. 3, author's translation).

The Weakness of the Law

The law could not do certain things. For example, the Mosaic law, when it interacted with our sin nature, failed to overcome sin and death. Sin instead defeated the law. The law could only pronounce judgment. Paul declares, "All who rely on observing the law are under a curse, for it is written: 'Cursed is everyone who does not continue to do everything written in the Book of the Law'" (Gal. 3:10). But it failed to defeat sin and punish sin in the flesh. It failed to justify, sanctify, or glorify us sinners. It failed to free us from sin's bondage and give us eternal life. It failed to help us to live the righteous life the Lord demands. The law failed to provide us the righteousness it demands. It could not conform us to the image of Jesus Christ. The law only empowers sin, so it is foolish to depend on it, as the Pharisee did to justify himself (Luke 18:9–14).

This weakness of divine law is not intrinsic to it. The law is holy, just, good, and spiritual. The problem is with our sin-dominated human nature. The law cannot give us divine nature, which we desperately need. For that we must look to the gospel.

The Father's Work of Salvation

What the law was unable to do, God did on his own initiative. Romans 8:3 teaches us that salvation is one hundred percent God's work and one hundred percent the work of grace. In the eternal council before the creation of the world, God the Father made a plan to save his chosen sinners. So Paul says, "Praise be to the God and Father of our Lord Jesus Christ, who has blessed us in the heavenly realms with every spiritual blessing in Christ. For [in love] he chose us in him before the creation of the world to be holy and blameless in his sight" (Eph. 1:3–4). Elsewhere we read, "All inhabitants of the earth will worship the beast—all whose names have not been written in the book of life belonging to the Lamb that was slain from the creation of the world" (Rev. 13:8); "This is how God showed his love among us: He sent his one and only Son into the world that we might live through him. This is love: not that we loved God, but that he loved us and sent his Son as an atoning sacrifice for our sins" (1 John 4:9–10; see also John 3:16 and Eph. 2:4–5).

What motivated the Father to save us from our sins and make us glorious? He was motivated by his own great love and rich mercy. God loved us because he loved us; there is no other reason. We were ungodly sinners with total moral inability to save ourselves, objects of divine wrath, sons of disobedience, without strength, and at enmity with God. Yet God loved us with an undeserving, everlasting love. We could not save ourselves, nor could Mosaic law save us. God the Father alone can save us.

Because salvation is a work of God, we can have full assurance of our final salvation. Not Adam but the triune God—the Father, Son, and Holy Spirit—is involved. God never fails; Jesus never fails; the Holy Spirit never fails. So we can be fully assured of our final salvation.

The Father sent his own Son in accordance with his eternal plan to crush the head of the ancient serpent. He sent him in the fullness of time, born of a woman, born under the law, to redeem us who were under the law. He did not send an earthly creature or an archangel. He did not send a new man, another Adam. No, he sent his own Son.

This sending was not an afterthought. It was in accordance with the eternal plan. God sent his eternal Son down to earth from heaven. From the bosom of the Father, he sent his one and only beloved Son. Notice, the Father planned our salvation; the Son accomplished it by his incarnation and atonement; and the Holy Spirit applies this salvation to us. This same Holy Spirit liberates us from the law of sin and death. Therefore, if God is for us, who can be against us? Sin and Satan cannot have the last word; God Triune does. God sent his Son to this earth to bring many sons to glory.

Adam was called a son of God. Angels are called sons of God. We are called sons of God by regeneration and adoption. But

Jesus Christ alone is eternal God, the one and only Son, the second Person of the Trinity, the uncreated Son who created all things and for whom all things exist.

The Arians thought Jesus Christ was a creature. Many people today believe this heresy. In fact, many theologians and ministers today are essentially Arians. But Paul says Jesus Christ is God's own Son. He is God, whom the Father sent to save us. There is no other Savior but Christ. "Salvation is found in no one else, for there is no other name under heaven given to men by which we must be saved" (Acts 4:12). No science, no human philosophy, no political leader, no material riches, no other religion, can save us. God sent his Son to save us. Believe in him who is co-eternal and co-equal with the Father, or perish.

The Son's Accomplishment of Salvation

Adam failed to obey God, but God's own Son did not. Our salvation is guaranteed by the triune God, into whose name we have been baptized. God sent his Son, whose existence in heaven as God preceded his human existence. Just as God spared Isaac, he also spared us. Yet he did not spare his Son but gave him up for us all.

The Father sent his own Son *"in the likeness of sinful flesh"* (v. 3, KJV). This is a unique expression not found anywhere else in the Bible. But we read about the incarnation in several scriptures: "The Word became flesh" (John 1:14); "born of a woman" (Gal. 4:4); "made in the likeness of man" (Phil. 2:7); "God was made manifest in the flesh" (1 Tim. 3:16); "He shared in our humanity of flesh and blood" (Heb. 2:14); "A body thou hast prepared for me" (Heb. 10:5); "of the seed of David according to the flesh" (Rom. 1:3); "A ghost does not have flesh and bones, as you see I have" (Luke 24:39).

Romans 8:3 does not say "in the likeness of flesh." If it did, Paul would be espousing the first-century heresy called Docetism, from the word *dokeō*, meaning "it seems." Docetism taught that Jesus seemed to have a body but his body was a phantom. Alternatively, it taught that "the Christ" came on a human Jesus at baptism and left at the cross. John deals with this heresy in his first epistle: "This is how you can recognize the

470

Spirit of God: Every spirit that acknowledges that Jesus Christ has come in the flesh is from God, but every spirit that does not acknowledge Jesus is not from God. This is the spirit of the antichrist, which you have heard is coming and even now is already in the world" (1 John 4:2–3).

Orthodox believers must confess that Christ came in the flesh, was crucified, died and was buried, and on the third day was raised from the dead. Doctrine is of fundamental importance. When you visit a church, listen to what the minister is teaching. If it is not biblical, have nothing to do with that church.

Romans 8:3 also does not say "in sinful flesh." Theologian Karl Barth thought the body of Jesus Christ was sinful. But a sinful Jesus cannot save us because he himself would need a savior. The Bible teaches that Jesus was sinless. The angel called him the holy one, the Son of God (Luke 1:35). Paul writes that Jesus knew no sin (2 Cor. 5:21). He was tempted like us in all things yet without sin (Heb. 4:15). He is called holy, blameless, pure, and separate from sinners (Heb. 7:26). He is unblemished and without spot (Heb. 9:14; 1 Pet. 1:19). It was impossible for death to keep its hold on him because he was sinless (Acts 2:24). The wages of sin is death, but he was sinless. Death did not have any power over our sinless Savior. He laid down his life freely for our sins, and on his own accord he took it up again (John 10:18).

The Son came "into the closest possible relation to sinful humanity without becoming himself sinful."[1] Incarnation was extreme humiliation for the Son of God, for he became subject to all human frailties except sin. Adam was without sin, yet he was tempted in paradise and fell. Jesus Christ came to this fallen world and was tempted in all points like us. He alone felt the greatest intensity and power of temptation, yet he did not sin. He suffered pain, sorrow, and disappointment and became mortal and weary, yet he did not fail. Jesus Christ was without sin.

Why did Jesus become incarnate? To honor God's law in his life and death, actively and passively. Adam failed to glorify God, but Jesus Christ glorified his Father by obeying God's law. He did so as our head and representative, perfectly fulfilling the law in our place.

---

1   Murray, *Epistle to the Romans*, 280.

Because of Christ's obedience, we are not condemned and enjoy full liberation. We can resist the devil by telling him: "Christ died for all my sin and obeyed in my place every law perfectly." We can do so because we died with Christ, were buried with him, and were raised with him to live a new life. Paul says, "For we know that our old self was crucified with him so that the body of sin might be [rendered powerless], that we should no longer be slaves to sin—because anyone who has died has been freed from sin" (Rom. 6:6–7).

"God sent his own Son in the likeness of sinful flesh." The Son possessed the necessary qualification to act as our substitute. What is true of Jesus is true of his people. So sin and death have no claim on us. He sent his own Son in the likeness of sinful flesh *"for sin,"* that is, to solve our sin problem once and forever. We cannot save ourselves; we needed a Savior. His name is Jesus, for he will save his people from their sins (Matt. 1:21).

Christ dealt with our sin problem that kept us from having fellowship with God. This sin problem, this Adamic nature, brought us under law, sin, death, and Satan. In the Septuagint the phrase "for sin" *(peri hamartias)* means "for a sin offering" (Isa. 53:10). Christ came to solve our sin problem by offering himself to God as a sin offering. He came to bear our guilt and be crucified, that he might remove in his death our spiritual and physical death. The whole sacrificial system pointed forward to him, because the blood of bulls and goats cannot cleanse our conscience from sin. God prepared for him a body in which he lived and died as our substitute.

God sent his own Son in human nature to suffer the wrath of God that was due us. He poured his wrath upon the Son that he may be just and the justifier of those who believe in the person and the atoning work of Jesus. Jesus offered himself as a sin offering so that we might receive the divine nature of Christ in place of our sinful nature. He tasted death in our place. The Hebrews writer says, "But we see Jesus, who was made a little lower than the angels, now crowned with glory and honor because he suffered death, so that by the grace of God he might taste death for everyone" (Heb. 2:9). We will not die; we will sleep in Jesus.

God condemned sin in the flesh of Jesus Christ. That is why there is now therefore no condemnation to those who are in

Christ Jesus. What the law could not do, God did in his Son. God punished our sin in the flesh of his Son. By Christ's death, the devil was condemned and driven out, our sins atoned for, and the law fulfilled. Now there is no condemnation for us but only liberation and victory. We overcome the devil by the blood of the Lamb and the word of our testimony. In fact, the devil, the super-powerful angelic creation, runs from us as we point our finger to the shed blood of Jesus Christ on the cross in our place.

God condemned Satan and sin in his court forever. By putting his Son to death, Satan and sin are defeated: "Since the children have flesh and blood, he too shared in their humanity so that by his death he might destroy him who holds the power of death—that is, the devil—and free those who all their lives were held in slavery by their fear of death" (Heb. 2:14–15).

John writes, "He who does what is sinful is of the devil, because the devil has been sinning from the beginning. The reason the Son of God appeared was to destroy the devil's work" (1 John 3:8). The cross of Christ solved our sin problem. From there he cried out, "My God, my God, why hast thou forsaken me?" The answer is, "To solve the sin problem of my elect sinners, that they may be justified, sanctified, and glorified." God broke the power of sin and Satan by his Son's death in order to bring many sons to glory. God accomplished his judicial action through the sacrifice of Christ. "He caused [his Son] to descend to hell for us, the hell climaxed at Calvary."[2]

What a glorious exchange! Christ took upon himself our sin and guilt that we may be given his perfect righteousness. He died our death, so we live his life forever. The psalmist says, "In the hand of the LORD is a cup full of foaming wine mixed with spices" (Ps. 75:8). It was our cup, but Jesus took it and drank it to the last drop, emptying the cup of God's wrath. And now the psalmist says, "I will lift up the cup of salvation and call on the name of the LORD" (Ps. 116:13). Our cup of salvation, our cup of rejoicing, runs over.

Now in Christ, we are under the rule of Jesus and King Grace. The guilt and power of sin are gone. We experience the benefit of Christ's redemption in three stages. First, we are made alive and

---

2   Hendriksen, *Exposition of Romans*, 247.

given eternal life, pardon, and power. We no longer live according to the flesh; we are in the Spirit, and in the Spirit we resist sin and win. Second, at death our spirit shall be perfected to dwell with God, which Paul says is a far better, blessed condition. Third, at Christ's coming, we will exchange our miserable bodies for an imperishable, immortal, glorious body.

> Listen, I tell you a mystery: We will not all sleep, but we will all be changed—in a flash, in the twinkling of an eye, at the last trumpet. For the trumpet will sound, the dead will be raised imperishable, and we will be changed. For the perishable must clothe itself with the imperishable, and the mortal with immortality. When the perishable has been clothed with the imperishable, and the mortal with immortality, then the saying that is written will come true: "Death has been swallowed up in victory." "Where, O death, is your victory? Where, O death, is your sting?" The sting of death is sin, and the power of sin is the law. But thanks be to God! He gives us the victory through our Lord Jesus Christ. (1 Cor. 15:51–57)

Jesus said, "Do not be anxious. Your heavenly Father knows what you need." What we needed was freedom from sin. From all eternity God has known our need, and in the fullness of time he took care of it by sending his own Son to hell on the cross. If Christ has redeemed us, we do not need to worry about anything. We can rejoice and serve God with great thanksgiving.

40

The Purpose of Redemption

And so he condemned sin in sinful man, ⁴in order that the righteous requirements of the law might be fully met in us, who do not live according to the sinful nature but according to the Spirit.

Romans 8:3b–4

Many churches in this country are "pop churches" that reflect popular culture. They teach that the purpose of our redemption is to promote an antinomian and unholy Christianity and a love that does not distinguish between truth and lie or righteousness and wickedness, but embraces all things. But consider the words of Jesus Christ about pop culture: "What is popular among men is an abomination in the sight of God" (Luke 16:15, author's translation).

What then is the purpose of redemption? What was the goal of the incarnation and atonement of Jesus Christ, which Paul spoke about in Romans 8:3? God's eternal purpose is to make us holy, and he will achieve it.

The Purpose of Redemption

Pop Christianity says that because Jesus Christ died for our sins, we can believe in him without repentance and continue to live the same old sinful life. The fact that salvation is by grace from first to last is taken to mean that salvation has nothing to do with how we live. If we believe in Jesus, we can be saved from hell once for all and yet live a life of sin here and now. No sacrifice or change is required of us. We can believe in Jesus as our Savior but need not serve him as Lord. We can be carnal Christians and not be spiritual Christians. Pop Christianity assures us that we are saved through faith in Jesus, though we may continue to be thieves, liars, adulterers, and drunkards. Pop churches teach that the more a person sins, the more grace is given to him for God's greater glory. Therefore, they would say, "Let us sin more that grace may abound to God's glory." Such a false gospel is not only popular in America but has also been popularized throughout the world.

The purpose of Christ's incarnation and atonement, however, is not that we continue to live a sinful life. *"What the law could not do in that it was weak through the flesh, God, having sent his own Son in the likeness of sinful flesh and to deal with sin, condemned sin in the flesh in order that the righteous requirement of the law might be fulfilled in us, who walk not after the flesh but after the Spirit"* (Rom. 8:3–4, author's translation). The purpose of God's condemning our sins in the flesh of Jesus Christ is that we may from now on live a holy life. In other words, the purpose of our justification is our sanctification.

Jesus told the woman who had committed adultery: "Neither do I condemn you." She was justified in view of his forthcoming sacrifice in her behalf. But that is not all he said. He also told her, "Go, and from now on, do not sin" (see John 8:11).

Where there is justification, there has to be sanctification. These two cannot be separated. Justification means we are not under the law or wrath of God, but under grace and the word of God. Justification means we have not only been set free from sin's mastery and bondage, but are also enslaved to righteousness. We died to sin and the law that we may be married to Jesus Christ and bring forth fruit of obedience to God. We have stopped serving sin and from now on serve God in the newness of the Holy Spirit.

Romans 8:4 clearly declares that a justified Christian lives a holy life in the power and direction of the Holy Spirit, who lives in him. Many commentators agree:

1. John Murray: "It is by the indwelling and direction of the Holy Spirit that the ordinance of the law comes to its fulfillment in the believer."[1]

---

1   Murray, *Epistle to the Romans*, 284.

476

2. Leon Morris: "Notice that Paul does not say 'we fulfill the law's righteous requirement', but that 'the righteous requirement of the law is fulfilled in us', surely pointing to the work of the Holy Spirit in the believer."[2]
3. William Hendriksen: "The purpose and result of Christ's work of redemption was that his people, by means of the operation of the Holy Spirit in their hearts and lives, should strive, are striving, to fulfill the law's righteous requirement. Out of gratitude for, and response to, the outpouring of God's love, they now love God and their neighbor."[3]
4. F. F. Bruce: "The law prescribed a life of holiness, but it was powerless to produce such a life. . . . All that the law required by way of conformity to the will of God is now realized in the lives of those who are controlled by the Holy Spirit and are released from their servitude to the old order. God's commands have become God's enablings."[4]
5. John Stott: "Holiness is the ultimate purpose of incarnation and atonement."[5]
6. John Frame: "And God saves us so that we may keep the law. . . . But the gracious work of the Spirit enables us to keep 'the righteous requirements of the law.'"[6]
7. St. Augustine: "Law was given that grace might be sought, grace was given that the law might be fulfilled."[7]

More importantly, the Lord says: "Be holy, because I am holy" (Lev. 11:44). Children of the heavenly Father are holy because they bear the lineaments of their Father. If children do not look like their father, there can be a question about who their father is. If a person is delighting in sin, God is not his Father. Jesus Christ declared to the lying Pharisees, "Your father is the devil. He was a liar and a murderer from the beginning" (see John 8:44). If this is true of you, I urge you to call upon the name of the Lord that you may be saved by the heavenly Father and start reflecting his holy character in your life.

In justification, Christ's righteousness is imputed to us (i.e., put into our account). In sanctification, this righteousness is imparted to us (i.e., by the Spirit we live out a righteous life).

2   Morris, *Epistle to the Romans*, 304.
3   Hendriksen, *Exposition of Romans*, 248.
4   Bruce, *Letter of Paul to the Romans*, 153.
5   Stott, *Romans: God's Good News*, 221.
6   John M. Frame, *The Doctrine of the Christian Life* (Phillipsburg, NJ: P&R, 2008), 291, 915.
7   Moo, *Epistle to the Romans*, 482.

We are being transformed and conformed to the image of Jesus Christ (see Rom. 8:29).

God justifies the ungodly to make them godly, not to keep them ungodly forever. An ungodly Christian is, in truth, an unsaved pagan. God in Christ condemned our sin on the cross, dealing with sin's guilt and punishment as well as its sovereign power. So even though sin was king before, now grace is king, Christ is king. And we are kings, we who receive the abundance of God's grace so that we can say no to ungodliness and yes to God's law.

Justified believers therefore will live a holy life, fulfilling the requirements of the law: "He who knew no sin became sin for us that in him we might become the righteousness of God" (2 Cor. 5:21). Jesus Christ is not divided. "It is because of [God the Father] that you are in Christ Jesus, who has become for us wisdom from God—that is, our righteousness, holiness and redemption" (1 Cor. 1:30), or "our justification, sanctification, and glorification." When we are united with Christ, we are destined to experience the fullness of salvation. We are not only justified, but we are also being sanctified, and will be glorified. Douglas Moo says, "Christ becomes what we are so that we might become what Christ is."[8]

The Requirement of Holiness

Holiness, therefore, is not optional for a true child of God. Rather, it is a necessary prerequisite to our eschatological salvation: "Without holiness no one will see the Lord" (Heb. 12:14). Jesus himself said, "Blessed are the pure in heart, for they will see God" (Matt. 5:8). He also said that our righteousness must exceed that of the Pharisees and teachers of the law (Matt. 5:20). So the purpose of God condemning our sin in his Son on the cross is that by the Spirit of holiness we can live a holy life before God who is holy.

Dr. James Boice states the following four important biblical truths concerning holiness:[9]

1. "Holiness is justification's goal."
2. "Holiness consists in fulfilling the law's just demands."

---

8   Moo, *Epistle to the Romans*, 483.
9   Boice, *Romans*, vol. 2, *Reign of Grace*, 800–802.

3. "Holiness is the work of the Holy Spirit." If we are regenerated by the Spirit of holiness, the Holy Spirit grieves in us when we sin, and we grieve too. A child of God can never be happy in sinning. If one is happy in sinning, that indicates he is still a pagan, though he may claim to be a Christian.
4. "Holiness is mandatory." What are *"the righteous requirements of the law"*? The law is holy, righteous, and good. The law's demands are just and spiritual, and the Holy Spirit brings about the fulfillment of that which is spiritual (i.e., God's law) in our lives. The Holy Spirit will never teach us to disobey Spirit-given law. The law reflects the will of God. In fact, the New Testament quotes the Ten Commandments in several places.

The law was weak because of our sin nature, so Christ condemned and defeated sin. Dr. Godet says, "What the law condemns was condemned in Christ, that henceforth through His Spirit the law might be fully carried out in us."[10]

Old Testament saints fulfilled the requirements of the law, as did New Testament believers. Both Zechariah and Elizabeth were said to be "upright in the sight of God, observing all the Lord's commandments and regulations blamelessly" (Luke 1:6). This was also true of Gentile believers: "If those who are not circumcised keep the law's requirements, will they not be regarded as though they were circumcised?" (Rom. 2:26). The moment we are saved, we are enabled to fulfill the righteous requirements of the law. If a thief comes to church and is truly saved, he will stop stealing right away. It is not that he just steals less and less. Paul writes, "He who has been stealing must steal no longer, but must work, doing something useful with his own hands, that he may have something to share with those in need" (Eph. 4:28). In the same way, drunkards who become Christians are to cease getting drunk on wine and be filled with the Spirit instead (Eph. 5:18).

Paul spoke about this transformation previously in Romans 6: "We were therefore buried with him through baptism into death in order that, just as Christ was raised from the dead through the glory of the Father, we too may live a new life" (v. 4). He continues in verses 6 and 7: "For we know that our old self was crucified with him so that the body of sin might be done away with, that we should no longer be slaves to sin—because anyone who has died has been freed from sin." Again in verses 17 and 18:

---

10   Godet, *Commentary on Romans*, vol. 2, 69.

"But thanks be to God that, though you used to be slaves to sin, you wholeheartedly obeyed the form of teaching to which you were entrusted. You have been set free from sin and have become slaves to righteousness." Or look at verse 22: "But now that you have been set free from sin and have become slaves to God, the benefit you reap leads to holiness, and the result is eternal life."

He continued this theme into Romans 7: "So, my brothers, you also died to the law through the body of Christ, that you might belong to another, to him who was raised from the dead, in order that we might bear fruit to God" (v. 4). We were bad trees, but now God has made us good trees to bear good fruit. "But now, by dying to what once bound us, we have been released from the law so that we serve in the new way of the Spirit" (v. 6). In the newness of the Spirit we serve God.

In fact, the gospel calls us to the obedience of faith: "Through him and for his name's sake, we received grace and apostleship to call people from among all the Gentiles to the obedience that comes from faith" (Rom. 1:5). True believers obey from the heart the form of teaching to which they have been entrusted (Rom. 6:17). If we are saved, we will obey God. Paul writes, "I will not venture to speak of anything except what Christ has accomplished through me in leading the Gentiles to obey God by what I have said and done" (Rom. 15:18). In Romans 16 he again commends the Roman believers for their obedience (v. 19) and remarks that God's purpose is "that all nations might believe and obey him" (v. 26).

There are many other verses that emphasize God's requirement for our obedience:

1. *Acts 5:32:* "We are witnesses of these things, and so is the Holy Spirit, whom God has given to those who obey him." The Holy Spirit is not given to us so that we can do wickedness. The Holy Spirit indwells us and is given to us to obey him.
2. *1 Corinthians 7:19:* "Circumcision is nothing and uncircumcision is nothing. Keeping God's commands is what counts" on the last day.
3. *2 Corinthians 5:15:* "And he died for all, that those who live should no longer live for themselves but for him who died for them and was raised again."
4. *1 Thessalonians 4:3-4, 7:* "It is God's will that you should be sanctified: that you should avoid sexual immorality; that each

of you should learn to control his own body in a way that is holy and honorable. . . . For God did not call us to be impure, but to live a holy life." When the Holy Spirit controls us, we will have self-control and will say no to sin and yes to the law of God.

5. *Titus 2:11–14:* "For the grace of God that brings salvation has appeared to all men. It teaches us to say 'No' to ungodliness and worldly passions, and to live self-controlled, upright and godly lives in this present age, while we wait for the blessed hope—the glorious appearing of our great God and Savior, Jesus Christ, who gave himself for us to redeem us from all wickedness and to purify for himself a people that are his very own, eager to do what is good." Grace teaches us to live holy lives here and now, not in heaven.

6. *Hebrews 5:8–9:* "Although he was a son, he learned obedience from what he suffered and, once made perfect, he became the source of eternal salvation for all who obey him."

7. *1 Peter 2:24:* "He himself bore our sins in his body on the tree, so that we might die to sins and live for righteousness; by his wounds you have been healed."

8. *1 Peter 4:2:* "As a result, he does not live the rest of his earthly life for evil human desires, but rather for the will of God," that is, the law of God.

9. *1 John 3:22:* "[We] receive from him anything we ask, because we obey his commands and do what pleases him."

This holy life is the new covenant life of which both Jeremiah and Ezekiel spoke. It is not that the law is abandoned and abrogated. The law was external, but in the new covenant the law is written in our new regenerate nature. The law is written in our hearts so that our earnest desire is to do God's law. Jesus said his food was to do the will of God and to finish it (John 4:34). We are given divine nature in Jesus Christ and delight in the law of the Lord. In this new nature, we love and do the divine will.

We read in Jeremiah 31:33: "'This is the covenant I will make with the house of Israel after that time,' declares the LORD. 'I will put my law in their minds and write it on their hearts. I will be their God, and they will be my people.'" The people of God meditate upon God's law and are eager to do it. This is covenant life. Look at Ezekiel 11:19–20: "I will give them an undivided heart and put a new spirit in them; I will remove from them their heart of stone and give them a heart of flesh.

Then they will follow my decrees and be careful to keep my laws. They will be my people, and I will be their God." The stubborn, rebellious heart of stone is taken out. Ezekiel 36:25–27 proclaims: "I will sprinkle clean water on you, and you will be clean; I will cleanse you from all your impurities and from all your idols. I will give you a new heart and put a new spirit in you; I will remove from you your heart of stone and give you a heart of flesh. And I will put my Spirit in you and move you to follow my decrees and be careful to keep my laws." Clean water is the gospel, the word of God. This is supernatural, spiritual heart surgery.

The Life of the Redeemed

We need power to live this new covenant life, and God graciously supplies all the power necessary.

1. THE HOLY SPIRIT

The first power is the Holy Spirit. We are not Christians unless the Holy Spirit indwells us. Sin still dwells in us, but if we are Christians, the infinite Holy Spirit also dwells in us as a resident boss who helps us wage war against the flesh. No Christian is alone. Four times in Romans 8:9–11 we read of Christ or the Holy Spirit living in us. Elsewhere Paul says, "Your body is a temple of the Holy Spirit" (1 Cor. 6:19). The Holy Spirit directs us and empowers us to fulfill the righteous requirements of the law, or to put it differently, to do the will of God.

2. DIVINE LOVE

The second power is the divine love that comes to us from the Holy Spirit. Divine love is very powerful. The love of God is shed abroad in our hearts by the Holy Spirit, who is given to us (Rom. 5:5). The moment we come to know Christ, the Holy Spirit comes into us and pours out divine love in great abundance. We are filled with love for God and his people.

Paul describes this inspiring love dynamic in his own life: "For Christ's love compels [impels, empowers, motivates] us" (2 Cor. 5:14). Love power was the reason he lived and died for the cause of Christ. "For in Christ Jesus neither circumcision nor uncircumcision has any value. The only thing that counts is faith expressing itself through love" (Gal. 5:6).

Reflect back to when you were first in love with your spouse. You would do anything and everything for that person. You would travel thousands of miles to see him or her. Or think about the love of a parent for a child. The story is told of a man who was afraid of driving on bridges. Then he was told his daughter had an accident on the other side of a bridge. He got into the car and drove across the bridge without any problem to help his child. Love motivates and empowers. Paul writes, "Serve one another in love. The entire law is summed up in a single command: 'Love your neighbor as yourself'" (Gal. 5:13–14).

Love is the first fruit of the Holy Spirit, and "against such things there is no law" (Gal. 5:22–23). The righteous requirement of the law is fulfilled in us by the love of God shed abroad in our hearts. "Let no debt remain outstanding, except the continuing debt to love one another, for he who loves his fellowman has fulfilled the law" (Rom. 13:8).

The charge Jesus Christ leveled against the church of Ephesus was that they had fallen from their first love (Rev. 2:4). This should cause us to examine our own lives. Have we fallen from our first love in our marriage? What about our relationship with God—have we fallen from our first love? If we have, may we remember from where we have fallen, repent, and do the first things (Rev. 2:5).

3. The Word of God

The third power is the word of God. The gospel is the power of God unto salvation (Rom. 1:16). Jesus said, "My word is spirit and my word is life" (see John 6:63). When we listen to the word of God, we should listen carefully so that the word may enter into us and perform its mighty work of transforming our lives. Those who listen carelessly receive nothing. "Hearing, they will not hear, seeing, they will not see." We must be very careful how we listen to the word of God preached. Paul refers to the word of God as the sword of the Spirit (Eph. 6:17). Jesus Christ overcame temptation by the use of the word of God. He told the devil, "It is written," and he spoke what he believed.

4. GOD THE FATHER

The last source of power is God the Father, who himself assists us. Paul writes, "Therefore, my dear friends, as you have always obeyed—not only in my presence, but now much more in my absence—continue to work out your salvation with fear and trembling, for it is God who works in you to will and to act according to his good purpose" (Phil. 2:12–13). We sin because we do not fear God. God's good purpose is that we be sanctified.

God the Father equips us and makes us competent to do the will of God: "May the God of peace, who through the blood of the eternal covenant brought back from the dead our Lord Jesus, that great Shepherd of the sheep, equip you with everything good for doing his will, and may he work in us what is pleasing to him, through Jesus Christ, to whom be glory for ever and ever. Amen" (Heb. 13:20–21). He works in us what is pleasing to him.

God's Eternal Purpose

God's eternal purpose is that the righteous requirements of the law be fulfilled in us. Our holiness is not an afterthought to God, and he will achieve his eternal purpose in our lives. Many Scriptures make this abundantly clear:

1. *Ephesians 1:4:* "For he chose us in him before the creation of the world to be holy and blameless in his sight"
2. *Ephesians 2:10,* KJV: "For we are God's workmanship, created in Christ Jesus unto good works, which God has foreordained that we should walk in them."
3. *Ephesians 5:25–27:* "Husbands, love your wives, just as Christ loved the church and gave himself up for her to make her holy, cleansing her by the washing with water through the word, and to present her to himself as a radiant church, without stain or wrinkle or any other blemish, but holy and blameless." He will have a bride who will be radiant, glorious, holy, and blameless. God himself takes ungodly people and makes us godly and glorious.
4. *2 Timothy 1:9:* "[God] has saved us and called us to a holy life." God has decreed from all eternity that we should be holy. He called us to a holy life.
5. *2 Timothy 2:19:* "Everyone who confesses the name of the Lord must turn away from wickedness." Holiness is not optional.
6. *1 Peter 1:15–16:* "But just as he who called you is holy, so be holy in all you do; for it is written: 'Be holy, because I am holy.'"

7. *Revelation 19:7–8:* "'Let us rejoice and be glad and give him glory! For the wedding of the Lamb has come, and his bride has made herself ready. Fine linen, bright and clean, was given her to wear.' (Fine linen stands for the righteous acts of the saints.)" Fine linen stands for our obedience to the will of God.

Fruit of Regeneration

When God makes a bad tree good, it will bear good fruit. If you are bearing bad fruit, call upon the name of the Lord, that God may perform the miracle of regeneration so that you may become a good tree. Jesus finds us as darkness, but he makes us light. Paul exhorts, "You were once darkness, but now you are light in the Lord. Live as children of light" (Eph. 5:8).

The Spirit of God in us wars against the flesh, or the sin, in us. In this conflict of Spirit against flesh, the Spirit, who is infinite God, wins every time. So Paul writes, "So I say, live by the Spirit, and you will not gratify the desires of the sinful nature [literally 'flesh']" (Gal. 5:16). It is a divine guarantee. If we live by the Spirit, we will not fulfill the desires of the flesh. Rather, we will fulfill the righteous requirement of God's law.

Sons of God are led by the Spirit of God. Paul states, "For if you live according to the [flesh], you will die; but if by the Spirit you put to death the misdeeds of the body, you will live, because those who are led by the Spirit of God are sons of God" (Rom. 8:13–14). The sons of God must put sin to death. There can be no negotiation. Kill it in the strength of the Spirit of God, as Paul did with the viper on his hand. He killed it by casting it into the fire (Acts 28:3–5).

The Holy Spirit in us leads us into the holy Scriptures because the Holy Spirit wrote the Scriptures. The Holy Spirit leads us into the holy Scriptures as they are preached and lived out in his holy church.

Walk according to the Spirit

The righteous requirements of the law are fulfilled only in those who walk not according to the flesh but according to the Spirit. Holy living is the proof of justification. We cannot live according to the flesh and claim to be true believers. It is a lie. The righteous requirement of the law is fulfilled by our walking according to the Holy Spirit, in the way of holiness prescribed in the word of God. That is why a Christian is always reading and studying the Bible to find out the will of God.

A Christian's walk is powered, controlled, and directed not by sin but by the Holy Spirit. What do we mean by "a Christian's walk"? It is the tenor, or bent, of his life. That tenor is toward God. A Christian is not in the flesh, not controlled by the flesh, not dominated by the flesh (Rom. 8:9). He is in the Spirit and the Spirit is in him. He walks in the opposite direction of his past sinful life. Those who were slaves to sin are now slaves to righteousness (Rom. 6:17; 7:5–6). There is change. The redeemed man walks according to the Spirit. The Spirit is his controller, director, and boss. He goes where the Spirit goes. The Spirit is the Spirit of holiness, truth, and love. The law is spiritual, Spirit-given, and the Spirit will never guide us to violate God's holy law.

God always enables us to fulfill God's law in our life. Paul clearly teaches this in Ephesians 2: "As for you, you were dead in your transgressions and sins, in which you used to live when you followed the ways of this world and of the ruler of the kingdom of the air, the spirit who is now at work in those who are disobedient" (vv. 1–2). We walked according to the values of this world in complete obedience to the devil. But now we are changed: "For we are God's workmanship, created in Christ Jesus to do good works, which God has decreed from eternity that we should walk in them" (v. 10, author's translation). We were going one way, and now we go the complete opposite direction, in the way of the word and the Holy Spirit. Believers walk after the Spirit every step of the way.

Many who make bad decisions will reap the fruit of their decisions for years to come. But a Christian lives one day at a time, making one decision at a time for the glory of God. Thus, he makes regular and steady progress in the direction of the city of God. He grows in grace and knowledge of the Lord Jesus Christ. He does not sit down and rest in worldly pleasures. He makes progress daily in holiness, reading God's word and praying daily. He works hard to provide for those in need, and worships and fellowships with God's holy people. He shines as light in this dark world. He is happy because he is holy. He is unafraid of death and even looks forward to it, because death has been defeated for him by Christ's death on the cross. For him death is gain, for it means he will be with God for all eternity.

True believers walk, not after the flesh, doing sin as before, but after the Spirit, doing the will of God. They do so because in Jesus Christ they are not in the flesh but in the Spirit. Christ is in them, the Holy Spirit is in them, and they submit to God's law. Their passion is to please God. By grace they are kings. They are soldiers who put sin to death by the sword of the Spirit, which is the word of God. They are overcomers and resisters. They say no to sin and Satan, and yes to righteousness and Jesus Christ.

God's people are pilgrims on a journey. This world is not their home. They do not travel on the world's highway of wickedness with wicked companions, but on God's highway of holiness that Isaiah spoke about: "And a highway will be there; it will be called the Way of Holiness. The unclean will not journey on it; it will be for those who walk in that Way; wicked fools will not go about on it. No lion will be there, nor will any ferocious beast get up on it; they will not be found there. But only the redeemed will walk there, and the ransomed of the LORD will return. They will enter Zion with singing; everlasting joy will crown their heads. Gladness and joy will overtake them, and sorrow and sighing will flee away" (Isa. 35:8–10).

Christians are not lone rangers in this journey to God's presence. They are joined by multitudes of people who are redeemed by the blood of the Lamb. They are vital members of Christ's holy church and travel together with them, clothed in the righteousness of Christ, singing songs of Zion.

Thank God, we in this church are traveling together. It is true that some who traveled with us went back to the City of Destruction, turning away from the highway of holiness. But a number have also already arrived ahead of us, reaching God's presence. Soon we too shall arrive.

If you are not journeying with us, if you are not a fellow pilgrim, I urge you to trust in Jesus Christ, who died on the cross for all the sins of his people. Repent and call upon the name of the

Lord. The Lord saves only sinners; therefore, if you are a repenting sinner, you qualify for Christ's free salvation. Come to Christ. He will justify you and liberate you from all the shackles of sin and Satan, from the law of sin and death. Then you too can join us in this happy journey home to God.

41

You Are What You Think

⁵Those who live according to the sinful nature have their minds set on what that nature desires; but those who live in accordance with the Spirit have their minds set on what the Spirit desires. ⁶The mind of sinful man is death, but the mind controlled by the Spirit is life and peace; ⁷the sinful mind is hostile to God. It does not submit to God's law, nor can it do so. ⁸Those controlled by the sinful nature cannot please God.

Romans 8:5–8

Romans 8 speaks about the absolute certainty of the final salvation of those in whom the righteous requirement of the law is fulfilled (i.e., those who live according to the Holy Spirit, not according to the flesh). This assurance of salvation belongs only to God's holy people. Only they shall see God.

In *The Great Divorce* C. S. Lewis says, "There are only two kinds of people in the end: those who say to God, 'Thy will be done,' and those to whom God says in the end, 'Thy will be done.'"[1] People either do the will of God gladly in response to God's great salvation, or they do their own will and go to hell. There is no other choice.

Romans 8:5–8 contrasts these two classes of people: the self-centered against the God-centered; flesh-directed people against Holy Spirit-controlled people; unbelievers versus believers; pagans

1   C. S. Lewis, *The Great Divorce* (New York: HarperCollins/Zondervan, 2001), 75.

versus Christians. No one is neutral. We either love God or hate him. There is radical difference between the two classes of people.

In this passage, Paul contrasts the mind of an unbeliever with the mind of a Christian. Examine yourself and see to which category you belong. It is my prayer that you belong in the class of God's holy people, those who have experienced a supernatural change in their lives. A bad tree must become a good tree to bear good fruit. Wolves must become sheep. Only God is able to change our natures. He does so by saving sinners and making them saints of God. If you determine that you are still an unbeliever, repent and believe on the Lord Jesus Christ. Surrender to Christ and be saved.

The Mind of an Unbeliever

We want to look at seven aspects of the mind of the unbeliever. When Paul uses the words "mind" or "think," he is not just talking about intellectual activity. Rather, he is speaking about the whole attitude of the heart. Such thinking involves not just the intellect but also the will and affections.

1. THE NATURE OF AN UNBELIEVER

The nature of unbelievers is described here as *kata sarka*, "according to the flesh" (v. 5). They follow the promptings of the flesh and surrender to its control.

What is flesh? It is human nature, under sin's total control, untouched by the mighty Holy Spirit. Unbelievers are slaves of sin. They live in sin. They are corrupted, directed, and controlled by sin and Satan. They are bad trees. They are wolves. They are dead toward God.

C. E. B. Cranfield says that flesh is "our fallen, egocentric human nature."[2] Unbelievers are in the sphere of the flesh, living according to the dictates of this fallen human nature. Therefore, they are against God and everything he is for—against their parents, against the church leaders, and against the Bible. Paul describes them as helpless, sinners, ungodly, and enemies of God (Rom. 5:6–10).

---

2   Quoted by Stott, *Romans: God's Good News*, 222.

2. He Thinks the Things of the Flesh

Second, unbelievers *think* the things of the flesh. The Greek word (*phronousin*) indicates that they do so continually (v. 5). Our mindset reveals our basic nature. What are we continually focused on, devoted to, striving for, and thinking about?

Unbelievers are engrossed with sin. They may come to church, but as they meet with people, their minds are thinking about with whom they can commit sexual immorality. Sexual predators come very nicely to church, but they have only one thing on their minds.

Unbelievers pursue the things of this world. They are taken up with buying and selling, planting and harvesting, building and acquiring, marrying and giving in marriage. They are like the people of Noah's day, who had no time to listen to God's warning about the coming destruction. They are like the people of Sodom. They hate God and do not think about their salvation. Their thinking is characterized by godlessness. They say, "Let us eat, drink, and fornicate, for tomorrow we die." They are narcissistic, atheistic, hedonistic, Satan-directed automatons.

They are what they think. "For as he thinketh in his heart, so is he" (Prov. 23:7, KJV). Our thinking defines who we are. "Out of the abundance of the heart the mouth speaketh" (Matt. 12:34, KJV). The unbeliever does not think of truth, God, eternal life, righteousness, love, everlasting joy, or eternal judgment. Like Mrs. Lot, he gives himself to worldliness.

The apostle John warns: "Do not love the world or anything in the world. If anyone loves the world, the love of the Father is not in him. For everything in the world—the lust of the flesh, the lust of the eyes, and the pride of life—comes not from the Father but from the world. The world and its lusts pass away, but the man who does the will of God lives forever" (1 John 2:15–17).

Thinking the things of the flesh means taking the side of Satan, not of righteousness. The unbeliever stands against God and is on the side of sin and Satan. He is single-minded in his devotion to sin and the service of Satan. He wholeheartedly seeks first the kingdom of Satan, sinning against God for his own illicit pleasure.

Unbelievers are idolaters who worship and serve creation and hate the Creator. They are materialistic and do not understand spiritual things (1 Cor. 2:14). They can be philosophers, politicians, preachers, scientists, and followers of various religions. They can be rich or poor, simple or sophisticated. They can be very moral people or even nominal Christians. They are enemies of the cross of Christ. "Their destiny is destruction, their god is their stomach, and their glory is in their shame. Their mind is on earthly things" (Phil. 3:19).

Their minds are focused only on the things of the flesh. With their minds, they exchange the truth for a lie (Rom. 1:21–32). Their minds are fixed on earthly things, on the works of the flesh. Paul lists these works: "Put to death, therefore, whatever belongs to your earthly nature: sexual immorality, impurity, lust, evil desires and greed, which is idolatry. Because of these, the wrath of God is coming. You used to walk in these ways, in the life you once lived. But now you must rid yourselves of all such things as these: anger, rage, malice, slander, and filthy language from your lips. . . . The acts of the sinful nature are obvious: sexual immorality, impurity and debauchery; idolatry and witchcraft; hatred, discord, jealousy, fits of rage, selfish ambition, dissensions, factions and envy; drunkenness, orgies, and the like. I warn you, as I did before, that those who live like this will not inherit the kingdom of God" (Col. 3:5–8; Gal. 5:19–21).

Unbelievers are like the fool of Luke 12, whose field brought such abundant crops. He boasted, "I will build a bigger barn and store everything in it. I will live for a long time." His mind was focused only on the things of this earth—a bigger house, a bigger barn, a bigger everything. They are like the rich man of Luke 16, who lived all his life in a sumptuous manner, dressed in purple. Never in his life did he think about God or heaven. When he wound up in hell, he finally thought about heaven. But it was too late.

What are you thinking? What are you devoted to? What is filling your heart? What are you planning? What are you spending your time, money, and energies on? We are what we think. Based on our thinking, we go either to heaven or to hell.

3. THE MIND OF THE FLESH IS DEATH

The unbeliever's mind is death (v. 6). It permeates his mentality, outlook, and philosophy. His last name is death. An unbeliever is death walking, death driving, death laughing, death eating, death working, death celebrating. It is a scary and sorry sight. If your parents, siblings, children, and friends are not true believers, they are death. The wages of sin is death. If you are a believer, and your spouse is an unbeliever, you are living with death. The dead person cannot make himself alive. He does not want to. He loves death, hell, and this world.

Look at the heart of the dead man: "For from within, out of men's hearts, come evil thoughts, sexual immorality, theft, murder, adultery, greed, malice, deceit, lewdness, envy, slander, arrogance and folly" (Mark 7:21–22). Jeremiah states, "The heart is deceitful above all things, and desperately wicked; who can know it?" (Jer. 17:9, KJV). Moses writes, "The LORD saw how great man's wickedness on the earth had become, and that every inclination of the thoughts of his heart was only evil all the time" (Gen. 6:5).

The unregenerate man is under sin, death, Satan, and condemnation. He is Mr. Death, looking forward to death eternal. He may dress nicely and do many things to impress people, but he is a dead man walking. No Bible-believer will be impressed by Death walking in a $5000 suit. It is just a shroud enveloping the dead.

When we speak to such a person about his soul, eternal life, Jesus Christ, and the Bible, he does not understand anything. He may come to church, but he will be bored to death. He will yawn and sleep, or he will be restless, looking this direction and that.

Paul tells us: "As for you, you were dead in your transgressions and sins, in which you used to live when you followed the ways of this world and of the ruler of the kingdom of the air, the spirit who is now at work in those who are disobedient. All of us also lived among them at one time, gratifying the cravings of our sinful nature and following its desires and thoughts. Like the rest, we were by nature objects of wrath" (Eph. 2:1–3). The unbeliever lives in the midst of death, looking forward to death eternal and the wrath of God. His entire life direction is death. Everything he does is against God. A fool, he says every day in his heart, "There is no God," and goes about sinning.

4. THE MIND OF THE FLESH IS ENMITY AGAINST GOD

"For the mind of the flesh is enmity against God" (v. 7, author's translation). An unbeliever is not neutral to God. He is an enemy of God. That kind, very moral person is without God and without hope. When you speak to him about his true condition

and declare that he must trust in Christ and his atonement, all of a sudden, such a nice, moral man begins to fume and reveal his true nature. He is an enemy of God and of the saints of God. All nominal Christians are enemies of God. They are against God and against those who preach the Bible. They are like those who stoned the prophets, killed the apostles, and crucified Christ. Religious people who are not true believers are the most dangerous people in the world.

Nominalists vehemently oppose those who preach the biblical way of life. They are like Ahab, who hated the prophet Micaiah because he never said anything good about him. They are like Jezebel, who hated Elijah. They are like those who stoned to death Stephen, the first martyr, because he spoke about the true God and his Son, Jesus Christ.

Paul says, "Once you were alienated from God and were enemies in your minds because of your evil behavior" (Col. 1:21). When we sin, we show our enmity to God by violating his holy laws. David confessed, "Against thee, thee only, have I sinned" (Ps. 51:4, KJV). The essence of sin is enmity against God, which reveals our total depravity. Therefore the wrath of God is revealed against all unrepentant sinners.

5. AN UNBELIEVER DOES NOT SUBMIT TO GOD'S LAW

The word *hupotassō* (submit) has to do with a soldier submitting to the orders of his commanding officer. The soldier is *under* the superior officer. A subordinate always salutes the person over him in the army. But a sinner refuses to acknowledge the rights of his Creator God. Being an enemy at heart, he daily transgresses God's law and receives great delight in doing so. When God says, "Thou shalt not," the sinner says, "I shall do what I want, when I want, how I want, and who are you to tell me how I should live?" He is under sin's control and enlisted in Satan's army. He refuses to take orders from God.

6. HE IS NOT ABLE TO SUBMIT TO GOD'S LAW

The unbeliever does not submit to God's law because he is not able (*ou dunatai*) to do so (v. 7). Total depravity produces total moral inability. They go hand in hand. As an enemy of God, the sinner does not obey God. He is unable to do so because he is

494

dead. All unbelievers, whether one's spouse or parents or children or friends, are wholly in the grip of sin, death, and Satan. They are slaves who can only sin.

7. HE CANNOT PLEASE GOD

An unbeliever cannot please God (v. 8). The purpose of human life is to please God. How do we please God? By knowing and doing God's will, which we discover by reading the Bible, the very word of God. The sinful man, the dead man, the enemy of God, the disobedient man, the morally incompetent man, cannot please God. He can only make God angry every day unless he has been set free by the Holy Spirit from the law of sin and death. The sinner remains at enmity with God, disobedient and morally powerless to please God. The sinner can only please himself by pleasing Satan, whose orders he perfectly obeys.

The Mind of a Christian

Now we want to examine seven aspects of the mind of a Christian, each of which stands in stark contrast to that of an unbeliever.

1. HIS NATURE IS "ACCORDING TO THE SPIRIT"

The nature of the believer is described as *kata pneuma*, "according to the Spirit" (v. 5). That means he is under the authority of the Holy Spirit, lives in the Spirit, and behaves according to the Holy Spirit's direction. His life is conditioned and patterned after the Holy Spirit. He is habitually dominated by the Holy Spirit. A believer is daily led by the Spirit because the law of the Spirit of life has set him free from the law of sin and death.

Before, he was in the flesh, walking *kata sarka*, dead and an enemy of God. He was disobedient and totally depraved. He was morally incompetent. But all that changed, as Paul describes:

> But because of his great love for us, God, who is rich in mercy, made us alive with Christ even when we were dead in transgressions—it is by grace you have been saved. And God raised us up with Christ and seated us with him in the heavenly realms in Christ Jesus, in order that in the coming ages he

might show the incomparable riches of his grace, expressed in his kindness to us in Christ Jesus. For it is by grace you have been saved, through faith—and this not from yourselves, it is the gift of God—not by works, so that no one can boast. For we are God's workmanship, created in Christ Jesus to do good works, which God prepared in advance for us to do. (Eph. 2:4–10)

Now he is regenerated. He is a new creation, indwelt, empowered, and taught by the Holy Spirit. This is true of every true Christian, not just a few super-Christians. A true Christian surrenders to the control of the Spirit, who resides in him as boss.

2. HE THINKS THE THINGS OF THE SPIRIT

The true Christian meditates on God's word, in which he delights. Like Jesus, his food is to do the will of God and to finish it (John 4:34). His eyes are fixed on Christ, his commanding officer. He walks in step with his Lord, who says to him, "Deny yourself, take up the cross daily, and follow me." He is a disciple of Jesus. He thinks the things of the Spirit, and the Holy Spirit reveals to him the glorious Christ in the pages of the Bible. Paul declares, "Let the word of Christ dwell in you richly as you teach and admonish one another with all wisdom, and as you sing psalms, hymns and spiritual songs with gratitude in your hearts to God" (Col. 3:16). He also says, "Finally, brothers, whatever is true, whatever is noble, whatever is right, whatever is pure, whatever is lovely, whatever is admirable—if anything is excellent or praiseworthy—think about such things" (Phil. 4:8).

The true Christian focuses his mind on Jesus Christ. Paul exhorts, "Your attitude should be the same as that of Christ Jesus" (Phil. 2:5). He deliberately and freely sets his mind on what the Holy Spirit desires, and sets his face like flint to do God's will. He sees the one thing needful and does it with an undivided heart. He follows Jesus, who was always minding the things of God, resisting the devil and obeying his Father. His authority is "what is written." The mind of Christ was focused on the mind of God, for he came to fulfill God's law and please him only. In the same way, our mind should be focused on the mind of God. We should be like the early believers, who devoted themselves daily to the apostles' doctrine (Acts 2:42).

What are you thinking? Your thinking defines you. Listen to what Paul says about his life: "Not that I have already obtained all this, or have already been made perfect, but I press on to take hold of that for which Christ Jesus took hold of me. Brothers, I do not consider myself yet to have taken hold of it. But one thing I do: Forgetting what is behind and straining toward what is ahead, I press on toward the goal to win the prize for which God has called me heavenward in Christ Jesus" (Phil. 3:12–14). Like Paul, our goal should be that Christ would fill our minds.

3. THE MIND OF THE SPIRIT IS LIFE AND PEACE

The mind of the Spirit is life and peace (v. 6). First, let us consider life. The majority of "Christians" are unregenerate, dead pagans. They are like plastic flowers that look good from a distance. These nominalists are good at simulation. But true Christians, born of the Spirit, enjoy eternal life, which is knowing God through Jesus Christ. We cannot receive eternal life and live apart from God. Eternal life is relational. It exists in union and communion with God. It is like love. We have to have at least one other person to practice love. God is love because the three Persons of the Godhead love one another. Eternal life cannot exist except in union and communion with God and his holy people. Adam killed us, but Christ gives us life eternal. He came to give us life, abundant life.

Moreover, the mind of the Spirit is peace. God in Christ forgives our sins and reconciles us to himself. We were his enemies, but now, having been justified by faith, we have peace with God. Forgiveness that does not lead to reconciliation and peace is a false forgiveness. Thank God, we have peace with God, and God is at peace with us. Therefore, we may come into his presence. The prodigal son was forgiven, so he did not remain outside as a hired hand but came inside as the father's son. He could do so because he was at peace with his father.

This peace is the antithesis of the misery that sin created in our life. No more hiding, no more fear, no more guilt, no more punishment. We have perfect peace with God. Isaiah compares the wicked to the restless sea: "But the wicked are like the tossing sea, which cannot rest, whose waves cast up mire and mud. 'There is no peace,' says my God, 'for the wicked'" (Isa. 57:20–21).

Now we can approach the throne of grace with boldness. Jesus Christ calls the restless, the weary, and the heavy-laden to himself.

497

He alone can give us rest. Dr. Lloyd-Jones remarks that at the center of a hurricane "there is a point of complete rest."[3] When we live in Christ, we experience a peace that passes all human reasoning, even when troubles of every kind rage against us. The doctor may say you have cancer and only one month remains. But in the center of this hurricane, the child of God can rest in Christ. So Paul says, "Do not be anxious about anything, but in everything, by prayer and petition, with thanksgiving, present your requests to God. And the peace of God, which transcends all understanding, will guard your hearts and your minds in Christ Jesus" (Phil. 4:6–7). Nothing in all creation, neither death nor life nor anything else, is able to separate us from the love of God that is in Christ Jesus our Lord (Rom. 8:38–39). Philip Doddridge writes:

> Now rest, my long-divided heart;
> fixed on this blissful center, rest;
> with ashes who would grudge to part,
> when called on angels' bread to feast?

We have peace with God and with God's people. Therefore we also enjoy great peace within. No division, no anxiety, no fear.

4. THE MIND OF THE SPIRIT LOVES GOD

If we are Christians, God is no longer our enemy and we are no longer his. God loved us and loves us. He proved his love when he spared us by not sparing his own Son but giving him over to the death of the cross on our behalf. Spirit-filled people will love God and his people.

5. HE SUBMITS TO GOD'S LAW

The man who says one can receive Jesus as Savior and not as Lord is from the pit. He has nothing to do with biblical understanding. Paul received apostleship to call the Gentiles to "the obedience that comes from faith" (Rom. 1:5), and he commended those believers who "wholeheartedly obeyed the form of teaching to which you were entrusted" (Rom. 6:17). Jesus said, "If you love me, you will obey what I command" (John 14:15). The proof of our

---

3   Lloyd-Jones, *Romans*, vol. 7, *Sons of God*, 48.

life and love is that we delight in God's law and eagerly obey it. If we do not obey God's moral law, we are pagans and enemies of God, our profession is false, and Jesus is not our Lord. In fact, he will say to us on the last day, "Depart; I do not know you. Depart, you lawless ones!" (see Matt. 7:23).

John proclaims, "Whoever claims to live in him must walk as Jesus did" (1 John 2:6). He later adds, "This is love for God: to obey his commands. And his commands are not burdensome" (1 John 5:3). For God's people, God's commandments are not grievous but a delight. We are to walk in Christ's path of obedience, as Peter declares: "To this you were called, because Christ suffered for you, leaving you an example, that you should follow in his steps" (1 Pet. 2:21).

If we willfully, deliberately disobey God's law, we are not Christians. John Gerstner told a story about an old woman in a hospital who refused to forgive someone, even though she was dying. She claimed to be a Christian, but Gerstner said she could not be. It is clearly God's will that we forgive any person who asks forgiveness of us. If we refuse, we are simply not Christians.

6. HE HAS MORAL ABILITY TO OBEY

Christians have moral ability to obey God's commandments because we have a new nature and a new power. The gospel is the power of God unto salvation. We are now good trees. We are no longer wolves but sheep.

7. HE PLEASES GOD

The passion and purpose of a true Christian is to please God. We do so by knowing and doing his will. The righteous requirement of the law is fulfilled in us because we walk after the Spirit (Rom. 8:4). Enoch walked with God and so pleased him.

How do we please God? We learn from Jesus, who obeyed God actively and passively. He knew the will of God and always did it; therefore, his Father said, "This is my beloved Son in whom I am well-pleased. Listen to him." When we fulfill the righteous requirements of the law, we too please and honor God. When a worker obeys his boss, he pleases not only the boss but also God. When a child obeys his parents, he pleases not only the parents but also God. So Paul writes, "Children, obey your parents in everything, for this pleases the Lord" (Col. 3:20).

Conclusion

We are what we think. No one can say he does not think. We are always thinking. Either we will think God's thoughts or the thoughts of Satan. Either we are dead or alive. Either we obey God or we sin. Either we are depraved and morally incompetent, or we are godly and morally able to obey God and please him. Our hearts are deceitful and wicked, and by nature dead toward God. But thank God, he raises the dead because of his great love and rich mercy for wicked sinners like us. May we therefore pray for a new outpouring of the Spirit, that he would raise the spiritually dead to think God's thoughts and delightfully do his holy will. The chief end of man is to glorify God and enjoy him forever.

42

The Radical Difference

⁹You, however, are controlled not by the sinful nature but by the Spirit, if the Spirit of God lives in you. And if anyone does not have the Spirit of Christ, he does not belong to Christ. ¹⁰But if Christ is in you, your body is dead because of sin, yet your spirit is alive because of righteousness. ¹¹And if the Spirit of him who raised Jesus from the dead is living in you, he who raised Christ from the dead will also give life to your mortal bodies through his Spirit, who lives in you.

Romans 8:9–11

In Romans 8:9–11 Paul shows us the radical difference between believers and unbelievers, the saved and the lost, those who are children of God and those whose father is the devil, those who live *kata pneuma* (according to the Spirit) and those who live *kata sarka* (according to the flesh).

What is this radical difference? It is the Holy Spirit. The saints of God are "in the Spirit," and the Spirit of God dwells in them. The Spirit is our home, and we are the home of God. We cannot fathom this mystery, but we enjoy its reality.

If you are not a believer and do not trust in Jesus Christ, either you do not know who he is, or you do not agree that he is the Son of God incarnate who died for the sins of the elect sinners of the world. Either way, you are not saved from God's wrath that is revealed against you. The greatest sin in the world is not murder or homosexuality; it is to not believe in God's only Son, who was sent for our salvation. Only the sin of unbelief will not be forgiven in this life or in the life to come.

Therefore, we must all examine ourselves to see whether we are really in the faith. We must test ourselves as we read this chapter, and make our calling and election sure. If we are not saved from the wrath of God to come, we must call upon the name of the Lord and be saved.

Paul speaks in Romans 8:9–11 concerning our past life, our present life, and our future life. In this chapter we will look at our past life and present life.

Our Past Life

Paul begins, "*But you are not in the flesh*" (v. 9). What type of life did we live before we trusted in Christ alone for our eternal salvation? We were "in the flesh" (*en sarki*). Those in the flesh are under God's wrath. "When we were in the flesh [controlled by the sinful nature], the sinful passions aroused by the law were at work in our bodies, so that we bore fruit to death" (Rom. 7:5). Sin deceived us and we were sold as slaves to sin. Sin was living in us (Rom. 7:11, 14, 17).

Every unbeliever is a son of Adam, whose one sin brought death to all his descendants: "Sin entered the world through one man, and death through sin, and in this way death came to all men, because all sinned" (Rom. 5:12). People do not understand original sin. We die because of the one sin our forefather Adam sinned one time. All of us are conceived in sin, born in sin, and can only sin; therefore, we must deny any idea of self-righteousness. "Every inclination of the thoughts of [man's] heart was only evil all the time. . . . Every inclination of his heart is evil from childhood" (Gen. 6:5; 8:21). The prophet Jeremiah said, "The heart is deceitful above all things, and desperately wicked" (Jer. 17:9, KJV).

All unbelievers are controlled by sin and directed by Satan himself. Jesus told Nicodemus that "flesh gives birth to flesh" (John 3:6). No man can know the wickedness of his own heart. Jesus said that from within, out of men's hearts, come evil thoughts and evil actions (Mark 7:21–22).

Earlier in this epistle, Paul declared, "There is no one righteous, not even one" (Rom. 3:10). Every unbeliever tries to negate that statement, saying, "I am righteous." But no unbeliever can be righteous. It is a universal negative. Paul continues, "There is no one who understands, no one who seeks God. All have turned away, they have together become worthless; there is no one who does good, not even one. . . . There is no fear of God before their eyes" (Rom. 3:11–12, 18). All unbelievers are dead in trespasses and sins. The evil spirit works in them, and they are slaves to Satan, the ruler of this world. In their thoughts and actions, they obey the devil.

In Romans 8:5–8 we see that an unbeliever lives according to the standard of evil. His mind is always thinking about how to sin. "The mind of those who are in the flesh [i.e., controlled by sin] is death" (v. 6, author's translation). His mind is at enmity against God. He violently opposes God's revealed truth and God's Son. He does so through philosophical lies, creating his own view of man and man's needs (creating his own anthropology). Such an unbelieving enemy of God is powerless to save himself (Rom. 5:6).

The unbeliever does not submit to God's moral law; in fact, he cannot (Rom. 8:7). Thus, he violates God's commandments daily because he has no moral ability in him to keep them. What explains this lack of moral ability? The sinner does not have the Holy Spirit. Paul states elsewhere, "The man without the Spirit does not accept the things that come from the Spirit of God, for they are foolishness to him, and he cannot understand them, because they are spiritually discerned" (1 Cor. 2:14). Jude agrees: "These are the men who divide you, who follow mere natural instincts and do not have the Spirit" (Jude 19). The Holy Spirit is the radical difference between a believer and an unbeliever.

Unbelievers are dominated by sin. They are under the thumb and control of sin. Paul writes, "We have already made the charge that Jews and Gentiles alike are all under sin" (Rom. 3:9). Every sinner is a bondslave of sin. Only God's Son and the truth of the gospel can set him free. A sinner is bound in chains by his own guilt. He is not only under sin but he is also under the wrath of God. This was our own condition. Thank God, it is in the past.

Our Present Life

So Paul continues, "*You are not in the flesh, but in the Spirit, if the Spirit of God dwells in you*" (v. 9). We are no longer under the dominion of sin and Satan; we have been set free! "But thanks be to God that, though you used to be slaves to sin, you wholeheartedly obeyed the form of teaching to which you were entrusted. You have been set free from sin and have become slaves to righteousness. . . . But now that you have been set free from sin and have become slaves to God, the benefit you reap leads to holiness, and the result is eternal life" (Rom. 6:17–18, 22).

Now we are "in Christ." That fact spells total salvation and total security. We are in Christ, and Christ is in us. Now we are in the Spirit, and the Holy Spirit is in us. What a glorious transfer—from flesh to Christ, from sin's control to the Spirit's control. Having been born of the Spirit, we now live in the sphere and realm of the Holy Spirit. Because our spirits have been made alive by the Spirit of God, we now can see and enter the kingdom of God, where we enjoy righteousness, peace, and joy in the Holy Spirit. We can enjoy eternal life even now, unlike the rich young ruler, who refused to believe in Jesus and went away sorrowful (Matt. 19:16–22). His is the condition of everyone who will not believe in Jesus Christ. He is miserable and restless, without God and without hope in the world.

But through the regenerating work of the Spirit, we have been taken out of the sphere of death and have been introduced to the sphere of life. We have been removed from the dominion of the flesh and brought into the dominion of God's Son. We confess by the Holy Spirit, "Jesus is Lord," and so we live according to the will of the Spirit (Rom. 8:4). We think the things of the Spirit (Rom. 8:5). We delight in reading the word of God and now enjoy life and peace because the mind of the Holy Spirit is life and peace (Rom. 8:6). We obey the law of God (Rom. 8:7). In fact, obedience to God's moral law is our joy, not pain. We are able to do so by the work of the Spirit in our lives. We now have moral ability.

We are now able to please God by doing his will. We glorify God and enjoy him forever in whatever we do, whether we eat or drink. Paul writes, "Finally, brothers, we instructed you how to live in order to please God, as in fact you are living" (1 Thess. 4:1).

As God's saved people, we are the temple of the Holy Spirit. The Spirit dwells in us permanently. He lives in us to rule, to empower, to direct, to provide, to protect, and to teach us. So Paul exhorts, "Do you not know that your body is a temple of the Holy Spirit, who is in you, whom you have received from God? You are not your own; you were bought at a price. Therefore honor God with your body" (1 Cor. 6:19-20). Jesus declares, "If anyone loves me, he will obey my teaching. My Father will love him, and we will come to him and make our home with him" (John 14:23). God is our home, and we are God's home.

The Holy Spirit never leaves us. What great security that gives us in this fallen world with all its troubles! No enemy can touch or harm us. We are in God and in God's hand. We are confident, not in ourselves, but in God. We are fearless. Once we were dead, but because of his great love for us, God, who is rich in mercy, made us alive with Christ. "Therefore, if anyone is in Christ, he is a new creation; the old has gone, the new has come!" (2 Cor. 5:17).

Because we possess the Spirit of Christ, we belong to Christ (Rom. 8:9). We are not our own; we belong to Jesus (1 Cor. 15:23). His seal of ownership is upon us, for we are baptized in the Holy Spirit: "And you also were included in Christ when you heard the word of truth, the gospel of your salvation. Having believed, you were marked in him with a seal, the promised Holy Spirit" (Eph. 1:13).

Because we belong to Christ, we are his responsibility. We can trust him, for he takes good care of us. He is the good shepherd who laid down his life for his sheep. He will not let a roaring lion devour us. He is the Lord of all, the Lion of Judah, under whose feet are all things, including his enemies. Even death itself was swallowed up in victory when Christ died and rose again. Jesus gives us eternal life, and we shall never perish.

This is true of all regenerate Christians. They are in the Spirit and the Spirit is in them as the Spirit of God, the Spirit of Christ, the Spirit of truth, the Spirit of promise, the Spirit of holiness, and our blessed Paraklete. Jesus promises, "I will not leave you as orphans," meaning without a father or mother, without brothers, without sisters, without a family, without a home, without any provision or security. We belong to the Father and the Son, who have come to dwell in us in his Holy Spirit. This is the radical difference between unbelievers and believers. Believers have the Holy Spirit.

The Work of the Holy Spirit

This Holy Spirit is our comforter, counselor, and advocate. He is the infinite third Person of the Trinity, co-equal with the Father and the Son. He gives witness to Jesus Christ and glorifies him. He tells us who Jesus is and what he has done in his life, death, and resurrection. As the Spirit of truth, he teaches us the truth of the gospel and opposes all Satan-inspired lies of philosophers and scientists in the world. The Holy Spirit makes us holy by applying Christ's salvation to us. He teaches us all things so that we may know God, which is eternal life. The Holy Spirit enables us to have fellowship with the holy God. This Spirit, who proceeds from the Father and the Son, never speaks of himself; he speaks of Christ our Savior. It is he who convicts sinners of their guilt. No sinner will repent on his own. Only when the Spirit convicts us can we truly repent and confess all our sins.

The Holy Spirit leads us and tells us how to live. He can do so because he is Lord. He enlightens us as we read the word of God. He opens our eyes and causes us to discover wondrous things out of God's word. He makes it bread to us that will strengthen our souls. He regenerates us and gives us faith to trust in Jesus Christ. He always guides us in the paths of righteousness and never leads us into sin. Isaiah declares that the Holy Spirit is the Spirit of the Lord, the Spirit of wisdom, the Spirit of understanding, the Spirit of counsel, the Spirit of power, the Spirit of knowledge, and the Spirit of the fear of the Lord (Isa. 11:2). Do you want wisdom and counsel? If we seek him for these things, he will give them to us. If we are weak, the Spirit of God will give us power. Jesus told his disciples, "You will receive power when the Holy Spirit comes on you" (Acts 1:8). When the Holy Spirit comes upon us, we will fear the Lord. Therefore, if a person is arrogant, he has nothing to do with the Holy Spirit.

Jesus baptizes every believer in the Holy Spirit and fire. The Spirit opens our closed minds to give us understanding in the Holy Scriptures. He gives us power to live a holy life in an evil world and enables us to boldly bear witness to our Savior. He brings to our minds what we should speak to the world. He abundantly distributes into our hearts the love of God with which we in turn love God and keep his commandments. With this love, we also love our brothers and sisters in Christ. And with this divine love, we also love sinners enough to proclaim to them the good news. We declare that Jesus alone can save sinners from God's wrath because he suffered that wrath in our place and for our salvation.

The Holy Spirit produces spiritual fruit in every true child of God. "The fruit of the Spirit is love, joy, peace, patience, kindness, goodness, faithfulness, gentleness and self-control (Gal. 5:22–23). Self-control is the Spirit's control realized in our lives. Every Christian will manifest this fruit in ever-increasing measure as he is led by the Spirit.

The Holy Spirit also distributes spiritual gifts just as he determines. We need spiritual gifts—the word of wisdom, the word of knowledge, faith, gifts of healing, miracles, prophecy, discerning of spirits, speaking in tongues, interpretation of tongues, gifts for helping, gifts of administration, gifts of teaching, and so on. We are to "eagerly desire" spiritual gifts (1 Cor. 12:31). If a person does not have such gifts, he or she did not desire them and pray for them. God gives the Holy Spirit to those who ask him (Luke 11:13). The Spirit distributes these gifts to equip the church to do her work.

The Spirit also works in us that we may work out God's will in the world. Our heavenly Father works, our Lord Jesus Christ works, and the Holy Spirit works. God's holy people, therefore, must work to please God, not themselves. Paul admonishes, "Therefore, my dear friends, as you have always obeyed—not only in my presence, but now much more in my absence—continue to work out your salvation with fear and trembling, for it is God [by the Spirit] who works in you to will and to act according to his good purpose" (Phil. 2:12–13).

The Spirit who dwells in us works in us as the agent of the Father and the Son. And as he works in us, so we will work out. A believer obeys God as a result of his saving faith in Christ. Paul told us that we are called to the obedience of faith (Rom. 1:5). Therefore, one who calls himself a Christian but does not obey God is a monstrosity, a liar, and a phony. He is like Judas, Demas, Achan, and Saul. The Holy

Spirit is not dwelling in him. He is an unregenerate person who suffers from moral inability to keep God's law. He cannot work out God's good purpose.

Such unbelievers exist with true believers in the church, as we read in the parable of the ten virgins (Matt. 25:1–13). All were invited. All belonged to the church. All professed that the bridegroom Christ was their Lord. All believed in the return of the bridegroom and were waiting for him. All fell asleep, and all woke up. But only five were admitted to the wedding feast. The other five—the foolish virgins—were rejected. The radical difference is that only five had the oil of the Holy Spirit with them. The foolish virgins had no oil; they did not have the Holy Spirit. So they heard the words of judgment: "Depart from me. I never knew you. You do not belong to me. I am not your bridegroom." What will you hear from Christ's lips on the last day: "Depart" or "Enter into the joy of the Lord"?

It is true that sin still dwells in us. But the radical difference is that the Holy Spirit now also dwells in us, enabling us not to sin. The power of the Holy Spirit is greater than the might of indwelling sin. Thus, because of the grace manifested in Christ, we can now say "No" to sin and "Yes" to righteousness and God's holy will. Paul says, "I beat my body and make it my slave" (1 Cor. 9:27). He was exercising discipline in his life. Elsewhere he writes, "So I say, live by the Spirit, and you will not gratify the [cravings of the flesh]" (Gal. 5:16). By the Spirit we can defeat sin and put to death the misdeeds of the body (Rom. 8:13). Through the Spirit we fight and win.

Be Different

I hope we will remember that we are children of God, born of God and indwelt by the Spirit of God. We are taught in the word of God and powered by the Holy Spirit. We are not our own; we are bought by the precious blood of Christ. So we honor God by obeying his holy will for his glory and for our eternal joy.

If you are a Christian, grieve not the Holy Spirit by whom you are sealed for the day of redemption. Do not resist or quench the Spirit, but yield to him. Discipline your body to obey the Spirit. God's Spirit dwells in his people permanently. He will not leave his temple, but will govern us, even through chastisement, if necessary, so that we will obey him. His will shall be done in us as it is in heaven. And finally he will take us to heaven to enjoy the presence of God, which is eternal life. The Holy Spirit is our resident boss. He rules us as Lord, and we obey him.

What is the will of our Lord? John explains, "Whoever claims to live in him must walk as Jesus did" (1 John 2:6). Peter says, "To this you were called, because Christ suffered for you, leaving you an example, that you should follow in his steps" (1 Pet. 2:21). Hear the call of Jesus himself: "Come to me, all you who are weary and burdened, and I will give you rest. Take my yoke upon you and learn from me, for I am gentle and humble in heart, and you will find rest for your souls." (Matt. 11:28–29). Jesus also said, "If anyone would come after me, he must deny himself and take up his cross and follow me" (Matt. 16:24). Denying ourselves means denying our will, our understanding, our opinion, our ambition, our philosophy, and everything else, and submitting ourselves totally to Christ.

Peter proclaimed, "Repent and be baptized, every one of you, in the name of Jesus Christ for the forgiveness of your sins. And you will receive the gift of the Holy Spirit." (Acts 2:38). Do not be like the rich young ruler. He was miserable, so he asked for eternal life. But he refused to pay the price and went away sorrowful.

If you are a sinner who has never trusted in Jesus Christ, you are miserable. But Jesus is calling you to make you happy by granting you salvation. The Holy Spirit is the radical difference. May you call upon the name of the Lord even today and be saved.

43

I Believe in the Resurrection of the Body

And if the Spirit of him who raised Jesus from the dead is living in you, he who raised Christ from the dead will also give life to your mortal bodies through his Spirit, who lives in you.

Romans 8:11

In our last study we examined the radical difference between Christians and non-Christians, and between our past life and our present life, if we are believers. In the present study we want to examine the glorious future life awaiting every true believer.

Romans 8:11 speaks about this key doctrine of Christianity: the resurrection of the body. The Apostles' Creed ends like this: "I believe . . . in the resurrection of the body, and the life everlasting." The fourth-century Nicene Creed makes a similar declaration: "We look for the resurrection of the dead, and the life of the world to come."

Salvation comes in installments. Now we are saved in our spirits, and our eyes are opened. We love and serve God. We delight in his word and in praying to God. But we do not yet have salvation in its fullness. There will be a time when we receive fullness of salvation accomplished by Christ through his death on the cross. The resurrection of the dead is our future salvation.

In Romans 8:9–11, Paul argues that the indwelling Holy Spirit is the essential difference between a pagan and a believer in Jesus Christ. In verses 9 and 10 Paul looked at the Christian's past sinful life and his present Spirit-controlled life. Now, in verse 11, Paul speaks about our future life of the fullness of salvation.

I Believe in the Resurrection

All orthodox Christians confess: "I believe in the resurrection of the body." This is our certain hope, a hope that will not make us ashamed. We therefore rejoice in the hope of the glory of God, though we experience sufferings in this life. "Our present sufferings," Paul says, "are not worth comparing with the glory that will be revealed in us" (Rom. 8:18).

The Platonists, Pythagoreans, Gnostics, and Sadducees did not believe in the resurrection of the body. To them, the physical body was a prison for the soul. They were only too glad to be set free from the body at death. But not so for Christians. We understand that matter was created by God, therefore matter is good. And we know that, although sin still dwells in our bodies, God has a glorious plan to resurrect and glorify our physical bodies.

Christians alone are saved from God's wrath. They alone are born of God and enjoy eternal life, which Jesus alone gives. So Christians alone can have hope as they live in this world. They enjoy freedom to think God's thoughts and do God's will. They alone can submit to God's law and please him.

Adam was once the head and representative of all men, but no longer. Jesus Christ is now the head and representative of those who trust in him. In Adam, we sinned and therefore we died. But now in Christ we are justified and therefore we live. We live spiritually now, and in the future we will live eternally in our glorious, physical bodies. The Holy Spirit dwelling in us guarantees our future bodily resurrection.

Consider this: God the Father, Jesus Christ, and the Holy Spirit are in us, and we are in the Father, the Son, and the Holy Spirit. Yet we are told that our bodies are mortal (Rom. 8:10–11). Our bodies must die because of sin (i.e., the sin of Adam). But our spirits are alive because of Christ's righteousness imputed to us.

In Adam, we experienced total death of spirit and body. In Christ, we experience total life of spirit and body. Yet we do not now experience our salvation in Christ in all its fullness. Our bodies must die, and they will. Yet when Christ returns, they will be made alive by the power of the triune God. Then our spirits will unite with our glorious resurrection bodies and we will enjoy the fullness of salvation in God's presence forever. Believers in Christ, who are alive in their spirits through the effectual work of the Holy Spirit, will experience the death of separation of their spirits from their bodies. Yet they do not die as unbelievers. They die in the hope of the glory of God. They "sleep in Christ" until they are awakened by the shout of Christ's command, the voice of the archangel, and the trumpet call of God. The dead in Christ will rise first, with a glorious resurrection body engineered by the Holy Spirit, to dwell in God's presence forever in a new heaven and a new earth.

Unbelievers fear death all their lives. But we are set free from this fear by Christ, who destroyed death by his death on the cross in our behalf. That is why we do not grieve as pagans do when our fellow believers die. We know they shall be raised together with us.

Death is not the last word for a Christian. Christ has defeated death; it has forever been swallowed up in victory.

The Guarantee of Resurrection

"*And if the Spirit of him who raised Jesus from the dead is living in you, he who raised Christ from the dead will also [make alive] your mortal bodies through his Spirit, who lives in you*" (v. 11). Here is the guarantee by God the Father that he will raise our mortal bodies. Our resurrection is sure because we are united with Jesus Christ by faith. Paul earlier stated, "This righteousness from God comes through faith in Jesus Christ to all who believe" (Rom. 3:22).

We have been united with Christ, who is life and who gives eternal life. This union is inseparable and everlasting. He is the vine, and we are the branches; he is the head, and we are members of his body; he is the foundation, and we are the building. So his life is our life, his righteousness is our righteousness, his authority is our authority, his victory is our victory, and his riches are ours. We are heirs of God and joint-heirs with Christ. And because of this vital union we have with Christ, his resurrection is also our resurrection. So we read phrases like: "We died with Christ"; "We are buried with Christ"; "We are raised with Christ"; "We are even now seated with Christ"; "Our life is hid with Christ in God" (see Rom. 6:4–5; Eph. 2:6; Col. 3:1–3).

Romans 8:11 declares that the Father raised Jesus from the dead. The Father will also make alive our mortal bodies through his Spirit, who dwells in us. Christ has been raised from the dead as our representative head, our second Adam; therefore, we will also be raised from the dead because we are in Christ and Christ is in us. The indwelling Spirit is our guarantee, whose work in our behalf is the application of the fullness of redemption to us. His presence in us is the proof that we belong to Christ and are his responsibility. He saves us from all the deleterious effects of sin.

In 1 Corinthians 1:30 Paul states that Christ is our righteousness (i.e., our justification), our holiness (i.e., our sanctification), and our redemption (i.e., our glorification). We are justified; we are being sanctified; and we shall be glorified. What God begins, he completes.

Divine Promises

Consider the following divine promises and bank on them:

1. *1 Corinthians 6:13–14:* "'Food for the stomach and the stomach for food'—but God will destroy them both. The body is not meant for sexual immorality, but for the Lord, and the Lord for the body. By his power God raised the Lord from the dead, and he will raise us also." Our bodies are not ours, to do with what we want. We are to honor the Lord with our bodies. "The Lord is for the body" means that the Lord will ensure the body's salvation, immortality, and glorification. By his power God the Father raised the Lord Jesus Christ from the dead. God will raise us up also because we are united with Christ.
2. *2 Corinthians 4:14:* "We know that the one who raised the Lord Jesus from the dead will also raise us with Jesus and present us with you in his presence." Note the linkage between the resurrection of Christ and the resurrection of his people. Since Christ rose from the dead, we can say, "I also will be raised from the dead." We can have this confidence because we are in Christ.
3. *1 Thessalonians 4:14* (author's translation): "For if we believe and continue to believe that Jesus died and rose again, even so we believe that God will bring with Jesus those who have fallen asleep in him." We are linked forever with Christ by faith. It is a fact of history that Jesus died and rose again. Therefore God the Father will also raise from the dead those believers who died in Christ. This is the sure hope of our resurrection. The Scripture cannot be broken. The God of truth cannot lie. He never changes;

therefore, we shall be raised up from the dead because Almighty God said so.

4. *1 Corinthians 15:20–23:* "But Christ has indeed been raised from the dead, the firstfruits of those who have fallen asleep. For since death came through a man, the resurrection of the dead comes also through a man. For as in Adam all die, so in Christ all will be made alive. But each in his own turn: Christ, the firstfruits; then, when he comes, those who belong to him." Christ has been raised from the dead as "the firstfruits of those who have fallen asleep." What does this mean? In the Old Testament, we read that people were to bring to the priest a sheaf of the first ripe grain from the field. They did so in thanksgiving to God, recognizing that the whole harvest belongs to him. Firstfruits are the harbinger of the coming great harvest. They also reveal that the whole harvest will be like them in nature and quality. Since Christ was the first to rise from the dead with a resurrection body, Paul says he is the firstfruit, pointing to the fact of the future harvest—our own resurrection. We too shall be raised from the dead with a body like his. "Christ, the firstfruits; then, when he comes, those who belong to him." This is speaking not about everyone but only about those who belong to Christ. We belong to Christ because we possess the Spirit of Christ (Rom. 8:9). His Spirit dwells in us, and so we shall be raised up from the dead when Christ comes. We are his and he belongs to us.

5. *Ephesians 1:13–14:* "And you also were included in Christ when you heard the word of truth, the gospel of your salvation. Having believed, you were marked in him with a seal, the promised Holy Spirit, who is a deposit guaranteeing our inheritance until the redemption of those who are God's possession—to the praise of his glory." We are marked with a seal, sealed with the Holy Spirit of promise. We are his property and responsibility. We are bought with the highest cost, the blood of Christ, and he takes good care of his property. We are secure forever. It is his responsibility to raise us up from the dead. The seal of the Spirit guarantees our full and final salvation.

Moreover, Paul uses the Greek word *arrabōn*, which is translated "deposit."[1] We read that God anointed us and "set his seal of ownership on us, and put his Spirit in our hearts as a deposit [arrabōn], guaranteeing what is to come" (2 Cor. 1:22; see also 2 Cor. 5:5 and Eph. 1:14). This word speaks of a deposit that guarantees the transaction; in this case, a deposit consisting in the Holy Spirit. God gives us the Holy Spirit as a deposit

---

1   *Arrabōn* is a transliteration of the Hebrew word translated as "pledge" in Genesis 38:17, 18, 20.

guaranteeing our final and full salvation, that is, our resurrection from the dead. God shall make alive our mortal bodies even as he raised Jesus from the dead.

The Intermediate State

What about the intermediate state, the time between a believer's death and resurrection? What happens when we die? Do our souls go to sleep? No, our souls do not go to sleep. Instead, we exist in conscious existence in God's presence. Do we then go to purgatory to suffer for our sins, thus making atonement so that our spirits will be purified and prepared to enter into God's holy heaven? No, we do not go to purgatory. Purgatory is not found in the canon of Scriptures. It comes from books like 2 Maccabees, which is not included in the canon (see Westminster Confession of Faith, chapter 1, section 2).

The Bible clearly teaches that at death we go to God and live with him in our spirit, awaiting our glorification: "[You have come] to the church of the firstborn, whose names are written in heaven. You have come to God, the judge of all men, to the spirits of righteous men made perfect" (Heb. 12:23). Our spirits are made perfect the moment we die and are brought into God's presence in the heavenly Jerusalem. Paul triumphantly writes, "For to me, to live is Christ and to die is gain" (Phil. 1:21). The believer is fearless in the face of death. Death is not a loss; it is gain. Paul continues, "I am torn between the two: I desire to depart and be with Christ, which is better by far" (Phil. 1:23). To be in the presence of Christ is better by far than even the most fruitful life on earth. Paul does not fear death; in fact, he prefers it. Elsewhere he comments, "We are confident, I say, and would prefer to be away from the body and at home with the Lord" (2 Cor. 5:8). Paul prefers death to earthly life because to die is to go home to the Lord. God is our home. We are only pilgrims here. This is not our home.

The psalmist says, "Precious in the sight of the LORD is the death of his saints" (Ps. 116:15), and a voice from heaven commanded the apostle John, "Write: Blessed are the dead who die in the Lord from now on" (Rev. 14:13). Blessed are those who die in the Lord, because blessing is found in God's presence. Jesus taught,

"He is not the God of the dead but of the living" (Matt. 22:32). All God's saints who have died now live in God's presence in their perfected spirits in great joy. Jesus said to the believing thief, "Today you will be with me in paradise" (Luke 23:43). We look forward to going home to paradise.

The Timing of Our Resurrection

The dead in Christ shall be raised up "at the last day" (John 6:40, 44, 54). On that day, those still living will also be given a glorious transformed body. When is that going to be? When Christ returns. Paul says, "For the Lord himself will come down from heaven, with a loud command, with the voice of the archangel and with the trumpet call of God, and the dead in Christ will rise first. After that, we who are still alive and are left will be caught up together with them in the clouds to meet the Lord in the air. And so we will be with the Lord forever. Therefore encourage [comfort] each other with these words" (1 Thess. 4:16–18). If we do not know the gospel, we may speak to grieving people about psychology or sociology, saying, "It's okay. Everything is all right." Such worldly reassurances do not give true comfort. We can comfort people only by the gospel.

When Christ returns, we will be glorified. He will return personally, publicly, visibly, and gloriously. Throughout history, foolish people have predicted dates for Christ's return, and some still do. But Jesus himself speaks differently: "No one knows about that day or hour, not even the angels in heaven, nor the Son, but only the Father" (Matt. 24:36). This is the word of God; anyone who contradicts it by pretending to know when Christ will return is a false prophet and a fool.

Paul declares, "But our citizenship is in heaven. And we eagerly await a Savior from there, the Lord Jesus Christ, who, by the power that enables him to bring everything under his control, will transform our lowly bodies so that they will be like his glorious body" (Phil. 3:20–21). Do you eagerly await your heavenly Savior? In 1 Corinthians 15:50–53 Paul speaks about the resurrection of Christ and then our resurrection. He begins, "I declare to you, brothers, that flesh and blood cannot inherit the kingdom of God." That means the body as it is now, marked by weakness and sin, cannot enter into the kingdom of God. Therefore, it must be raised up and transformed. Paul continues, "nor does the perishable inherit the imperishable. Listen, I tell you a mystery: We will not all sleep, but we will all be changed—in a flash, in the twinkling of an eye, at the last trumpet. For the trumpet will sound, the dead will be raised imperishable, and we will be changed. For the perishable must [by divine necessity] clothe itself with the imperishable, and the mortal with immortality."

Our mortal bodies cannot inherit the kingdom. Therefore God gives us bodies fit to dwell in God's presence. Our perishable bodies by divine decree must put on the imperishable, the immortal, the glorious, the powerful, and the spiritual. This transformation will happen in the twinkling of an eye, at the last trumpet call, when Christ comes to make us all new creations, not only in the spirit but also in the body. Our bodies will be exactly like that of Christ, dazzling and perfect. So Paul says, "Just as we have borne the likeness of the earthly man, so shall we bear the likeness of the man from heaven" (1 Cor. 15:49). John says, "Dear friends, now we are children of God, and what we will be has not yet been made known. But we know that when he appears, we shall be like him, for we shall see him as he is" (1 John 3:2).

Some think that Romans 8:11, which says that God will make alive our mortal bodies, is speaking about physical healing, because they say healing is in the atonement. But if healing is in the atonement, then why were the Thessalonians dying? If healing is in the atonement, then we must not die. Yes, salvation for the whole man is in the atonement: "By his stripes we are healed" refers to our full salvation. But salvation is applied to us in installments. We must die, and the triune God will raise us up from the dead and transform us. Only then shall we experience the fullness of salvation. Yet even now God heals us physically according to his sovereign will in response to our prayers.

Moreover, we do experience suffering now. In 2 Corinthians 5 Paul speaks twice about groaning (vv. 2, 4). In Romans 8 he says we are groaning (v. 23), creation is groaning (v. 22), and even the Holy Spirit is groaning (v. 26). We are burdened and our bodies are wasting away (2 Cor. 5:4; 4:16). The first breath we take is also one of our last. God has already determined how many breaths we will have. Our bodies are dying. Go to the hospitals and old people's homes. You can hear groaning.

Yet we wait in sure hope for the coming of Christ. Our resurrection must occur because it is God's decree. Jesus declared, "The Son of Man *must* be delivered into the hands of sinful men, be crucified and on the third day be raised again" (Luke 24:7). It was the divine decree. Again, listen to the words of Jesus: "Did not the Christ *have to* suffer these things and then enter his glory?" (Luke 24:26). Paul writes, "For the perishable *must* clothe itself with the imperishable, and the mortal with immortality" (1 Cor. 15:53). Because we are united with Christ, in one sense Jesus is not complete without us. We are his body and his bride.

So we must be raised from the dead. He who raised Jesus from the dead will raise us also because we are Christ's. Christ will have a glorious bride; he himself makes us glorious. Paul writes, "Husbands, love your wives, just as Christ loved the church and gave himself up for her to make her holy, cleansing her by the washing with water through the word, and to present her to himself as a radiant church, without stain or wrinkle or any other blemish, but holy and blameless" (Eph. 5:25–27). We are destined to shine in glory. Jesus said, "Then the righteous will shine like the sun in the kingdom of their Father" (Matt. 13:43).

Do You Believe?

We believe in the resurrection of the body, for the Bible tells us so. We must comfort our grieving fellow believers with this truth. As for ourselves, we must stand firm and be unshakable, always abounding in the work of the Lord because we know that our labor in the Lord is not in vain (1 Cor. 15:58).

If you are outside of Christ, you are without hope. I urge you to believe on the Lord Jesus Christ and be united with him. Only then will you have hope of the glory of God. You must do it now, while God is speaking to you. Repent of your sins and embrace Christ, who is the resurrection and the life. Even now cross from death to life. Do not be like the rich young ruler who refused to believe in Christ and went away sorrowful. Any moment death may descend upon you and you shall die, not in Christ, but in your sins, and you will descend into hell itself. There is no second chance after death; you must trust in Christ today.

If you profess to be in Christ, let me ask you some questions. Do you live to please God? Is God real to you? Is the Bible meaningful and nourishing to your soul? Do you pray in the Spirit? Do you bear witness to Christ without shame? Are you growing in grace and in the knowledge of the Lord? Are you eagerly awaiting the imminent second coming of Jesus? One who merely professes Christ but does not walk in his ways has no life of God in his soul. Being baptized and taking holy communion cannot save us. Church membership and singing in the choir cannot save us. Only Jesus Christ saves us. It is appointed for man once to die and then comes the judgment (Heb. 9:27). Let us examine ourselves today and make our calling and election sure, that we may live with God now and forever.

44

How to Defeat Sin

[12]Therefore, brothers, we have an obligation—but it is not to the sinful nature, to live according to it. [13]For if you live according to the sinful nature, you will die; but if by the Spirit you put to death the misdeeds of the body, you will live.

Romans 8:12–13

Romans 8:12–13 teaches about the progressive sanctification of a believer in Christ. John Murray speaks about another type of sanctification, called definitive sanctification, which means we are sanctified once for all when we put our trust in Christ. In his death, Jesus died to sin; therefore, in his death we have also died to sin and are raised with Christ to live for God (Rom. 6:2–4; 1 Cor. 1:2; 6:11).[1] While definitive sanctification is a once-for-all event, the progressive sanctification of a Christian continues until he dies. In definitive sanctification we are passive. But in progressive sanctification we are active in defeating sin by the power of the Holy Spirit.

Progressive sanctification teaches us how to put to death the sin that still dwells in us. According to Dr. Martyn Lloyd-Jones, "These two verses are perhaps the most important statement with regard to the practical aspect of the New Testament doctrine of sanctification in the whole of Scripture."[2] Paul here tells us how a believer can experience holiness and defeat sin.

---

1   Murray, *Collected Writings*, vol. 2, *Systematic Theology*, 277–293.
2   Lloyd-Jones, *Romans*, vol. 7, *Sons of God*, 92.

Wrong Ways of Defeating Sin

First, we must say that there are several wrong ways to defeat sin. We cannot become more holy through monasticism, by trying to isolate ourselves from the sinful world or by treating our bodies harshly. The reason this fails is that when a person enters a monastery, the world comes in with him, just as Egypt came with Israel when God's people came out of Egypt. This was demonstrated by Israel's continuous murmuring against God.

We also cannot experience sanctification through the legalism of enforcing on ourselves a code of ethics and trying to obey it through sheer self-effort. This is moralism.

We certainly cannot experience holiness by embracing the antinomian notion that Jesus can be our Savior without being our Lord. Yet this ideology pervades the evangelical church world today. Many preachers will teach that we are saved by grace alone and that any attempt to obey God's law adds "works" to grace. They also assert that if a believer sins, his sin only adds to God's glory; therefore, one can sin all he wants and yet praise God for his grace.

We also cannot be sanctified through a one-time spiritual experience. No single event can eradicate all the sin dwelling in us and lead us to sinless perfection in this life. The Bible teaches that believers must war against sin throughout their lives. How, then, are we to defeat sin and experience progressive sanctification?

Who We Are in Christ

In Romans 8:12–13, Paul moves from exposition to exhortation. He begins, "*Therefore, brothers,*" speaking of the logical consequence of what he has said so far in this epistle, especially in Romans 8:1–11. In light of what God has done for us, Paul exhorts us to do something: Let us put sin to death in the power of the Holy Spirit. Progressive sanctification is achieved, not by our passivity or even by our own activity, but by our actions in the might and direction of the Holy Spirit who lives in every believer.

In order to defeat sin and experience progressive sanctification, we must realize who we really are in Christ. Christianity is not Gnosticism or mysticism that bypasses logical thought and negates what God has done for us in Christ in history. Christianity is the most reasonable faith. As such, it demands that we have renewed minds. The atonement of Christ makes us his debtors, so that we think his thoughts and do his will by his power.

When Christ died and rose again, we died with Christ and were raised with him. Christ died to sin once for all; so also we died to sin once for all. Now we live no longer to serve sin but to serve God. Sin, Satan, the flesh, and the world system that is in rebellion against God have all been defeated by Christ and have no legal claim on us.

This truth is taught in Romans 6. We are no longer under sin, death, and the law. We no longer live in the flesh as slaves of sin. As those who are under grace, we are slaves to God and we reign in life by grace. We have been set free from sin by Christ. We are no longer obligated to serve Pharaoh, who defied Yahweh, asking, "Who is the Lord, that I should obey him?" (Exod. 5:2). Now we worship and serve Jesus Christ alone. We are slaves of Christ. So Paul exults, "The law of the Spirit of life set me free from the law of sin and death" (Rom. 8:2).

Now we walk according to the Spirit (kata pneuma), not according to our corrupt flesh (kata sarka). We think the things of the Spirit, delighting in the Holy Scriptures. The mind of the Spirit is life and peace. We submit to God's law. Our regenerate spirits are alive to God, and the indwelling Spirit assures us of the future resurrection of our bodies.

This indwelling Holy Spirit also promotes our holiness. Jesus is righteousness, holiness, and glorification for a believer (1 Cor. 1:30). Holiness is not optional but essential to our eternal fellowship with God. Because God is holy, we must become holy, so that we can enjoy holy communion with him. And it is our present delightful obedience (i.e., progressive sanctification) that proves our past justification and assures us of our future and final salvation. In mathematical terms, we can say that assurance of salvation is directly proportional to our present obedience to Christ.

We Are Debtors to God

Paul then says that "*we have an obligation,*" meaning we are debtors (v. 12). But to whom are we obligated? First, we must state that we owe nothing to the flesh, which stands for the powers of this age that are in total rebellion against God and his word. We owe nothing to sin, Satan, death, and the evil world system. We were slaves of these, but we have been set free forever and have been translated into the kingdom of God. We are in the Holy Spirit, and the Holy Spirit is in us, and we can never go back to the realm of sin and death. Now we are citizens of heaven, seated with Christ. The dominion of the flesh is past history; it is over. We do not owe anything to the flesh and its God-hating standard. Rather, we owe everything to our Savior.

Just as the slaves in this country were emancipated, so too we have been emancipated by Christ's salvation. Now we are sons of God, slaves of God, citizens of heaven, and the bride of Christ. We therefore reject all autonomy and antinomianism. We now love the triune God and his law. If our old master comes to assert authority over us, we must ask the question: What have sin, Satan, death, and the flesh done for us lately? Jesus reveals Satan's true motive: "The thief comes only to steal and kill and destroy" (John 10:10).

We were once dead *in sin,* but in Christ we are dead *to sin.* Do you see the difference? "Dead in sin" means we sin, but "dead to sin" means we say no to Master Sin. In Christ we are dead to sin and given the ability to defeat the sin that still dwells in us. Though sin still dwells in us, there is a greater reality—the Holy Spirit—who also dwells in us. As God, he is infinitely greater than all our sin. By his mighty power, we can fight against sin and win.

O to grace what great debtors we are! We are debtors to God Triune. God the Father planned our redemption from all eternity; God the Son accomplished it; and God the Holy Spirit applies that redemption to each one of us.

The Necessity of Defeating Sin

How do we defeat sin? We must put to death the evil deeds of the body. As believers in Jesus Christ, we now have real freedom not to sin. We can choose life and not death. We can love God and hate Satan. We can trust Christ and resist the devil. We can put sin to death and pursue righteousness. In the strength of Christ, we can wrestle against the devil and cause him to fall and flee, while we stand. Like David, we can kill Goliath by the stone of the Spirit and the sword of the word of God. In fact, we *must* kill Goliath, or he will kill us.

"Our obligation is . . . to the Spirit, to live according to his desires and dictates,"[3] says Dr. John Stott. We must kill Haman, who represents all the enemies of God, for he plans to kill God's people. A very tall gallows has already been constructed. But he can never succeed, for God is for us and with us and in us.

How do we know that we have been saved? A saved person will fight against sin, Satan, and the world by the life of God in the soul of man. If we do not fight against evil, our profession is false. It is our fighting against sin that reveals we have been made alive by the life of Christ. If we do not fight against sin, we are still dead in our sins. Our battle against sin begins at the moment of our new birth.

Paul tells us, "So I say, live by the Spirit, and you will not gratify the desires of the [flesh]. For the [flesh lusts after] what is contrary to the Spirit, and the Spirit what is contrary to the [flesh]. They are in conflict with each other" (Gal. 5:16–17). The Holy Spirit in us opposes sin. So if we stand with the Holy Spirit, we will win.

Peter says, "Dear friends, I urge you, as aliens and strangers in the world, to abstain from sinful desires, which war against your soul" (1 Pet. 2:11). There is a war going on. The moment we are born again, we are thrown out into the battlefield, not alone, but with God. So we have hope. John writes, "They overcame him by the blood of the Lamb and by the word of their testimony; they did not love their lives so much as to shrink from death" (Rev. 12:11). Fight to the death, and we will live forever.

Do not look for an easy, retiring life. We must fight! The Hebrews writer speaks of the struggles of past saints of God who "quenched the fury of the flames, and escaped the edge of the sword; whose weakness was turned to strength; and who became powerful in

---

3   Stott, Romans: *God's Good News*, 227.

battle and routed foreign armies" (Heb. 11:34). Paul told Timothy, "Fight the good fight of the faith. Take hold of the eternal life to which you were called when you made your good confession in the presence of many witnesses" (1 Tim. 6:12). And listen to what the veteran warrior Paul later said: "I have fought the good fight, I have finished the race, I have kept the faith" (2 Tim. 4:7).

Friends, we owe nothing to sin and Satan. Rather, we owe our life and allegiance to our Lord Jesus Christ, who paid our debt with his precious blood so that we will live and not die. Now we live to serve him all our lives, prompted by a huge debt of gratitude. And our gratitude toward God is expressed by our glad obedience to Christ. If anyone continues to live his same old sinful life, he is still unregenerate. He is a false professor who hates God and loves sin. His spirit has not been made alive.

A believer may sin, but he will not continue in it. He will repent truly and prove his repentance by godly sorrow and glad obedience. In contrast, the unregenerate false professor can only sin. He can only walk after the flesh, for he is without the Holy Spirit. If a professing Christian continues in sin, he will surely die, in spite of his Christian profession. Such a person will suffer God's wrath on the last day. Like the foolish virgins, he will not be admitted to the marriage supper of the Lamb.

Be not deceived, friends; God is not mocked. What we sow, that we shall reap (Gal. 6:7). Examine yourselves and see whether you are in the faith. Do you fight? Not against your brother and sister, mother and father, but against sin, the devil, and this world system. Do you wrestle? Do you put sin to death in your life? Are you being sanctified? Sanctification consists of two elements: mortification and conformation. Mortification means we put sin to death. Conformation means we are being conformed to the image of Jesus Christ. So Paul writes, "And we, who with unveiled faces all reflect the Lord's glory, are being transformed into his likeness with ever-increasing glory, which comes from the Lord, who is the Spirit" (2 Cor. 3:18), and, "Those God foreknew he also predestined to be conformed to the likeness of his Son, that he might be the firstborn among many brothers" (Rom. 8:29).

What should we put to death? Paul instructs us, "Put to death, therefore, whatever belongs to your earthly nature." Then he gives a list, though not comprehensive. He begins with sexual immorality. Some people would begin to argue with this first point, saying, "Pastor, don't you know that fornication is normal in today's church? You just don't understand." I do understand, because I understand the Bible. The Bible clearly tells us what to do with sexual immorality: Put it to death! So Paul writes, "Put to death . . . sexual immorality, impurity, lust, evil desires and greed, which is idolatry. Because of these, the wrath of God is coming. You used to walk in these ways, in the life you once lived. But now you must rid yourselves of all such things as these: anger, rage, malice, slander, and filthy language from your lips" (Col. 3:5–8).

Do you want to know what else we should put to death? Paul gives another list: "The acts of the sinful nature are obvious: sexual immorality, impurity and debauchery; idolatry and witchcraft; hatred, discord, jealousy, fits of rage, selfish ambition, dissensions, factions and envy; drunkenness, orgies, and the like. I warn you, as I did before, that those who live like this will not inherit the kingdom of God" (Gal. 5:19–21). The works of the flesh are not mysterious. They are obvious. We know what they are.

We must nip these things in the bud. We must deal with every sin at its very inception, at the thought level. We must not let ourselves be enticed by sin, as David was in the incident with Bathsheba. Rather than nursing, massaging, and feeding sin, be ruthless, angry, and violent in taking action against it. Foster enough hatred to slaughter sin. Keep in mind what Jesus said: "But I tell you that anyone who looks at a woman lustfully has already committed adultery with her in his heart. If your right eye causes you to sin, gouge it out and throw it away. It is better for you to lose one part of your body than for your whole body to be thrown into hell. And if your right hand causes you to sin, cut it off and throw it away. It is better for you to lose one part of your body than for your whole body to go into hell" (Matt. 5:28–30). Christ himself advocated violent actions against the evil in us: Gouge it out! Cut it off!

Never negotiate with sin. Sin only wants to kill us, so we must kill it first. Throw the viper into the fire and be finished with it. Understand the intentions of the viper so that you can produce the anger necessary to throw it into the fire. Sin wants to kill us and our children for generations to come.

Peter tells us to "abstain from sinful desires, which war against your soul" (1 Pet. 2:11). Paul says, "I beat my body and make it my slave" (1 Cor. 9:27). In other words, he is commanding his body to obey him. He also exhorts, "Flee [fornication] and pursue righteousness" (2 Tim. 2:22). Put sin to death! Kill it! Use the sword of the Spirit, which is the word of God.

We are no longer slaves of sin; we have been set free. Therefore, walk in freedom. We have the freedom to live a holy life. Be a soldier of Christ. Deny yourselves, take up the cross, and follow Christ the victor. He leads us in the way of righteousness, the narrow way of Christ's lordship, the highway of holiness. He leads us daily, triumphantly, from victory to victory. He leads us to heaven itself.

We must put sin to death, and the Greek word *thanatoute* means we are putting sin to death continuously. We are in a constant war. The devil, like a roaring lion, constantly prowls around, seeking to devour us. Do not negotiate with him! Resist him, and he will flee from you. Resist him in the name of Jesus Christ, who died on the cross for our sins, was buried, and was raised from the dead on the third day according to the Scriptures. And understand this: what God commands us to do, he will also enable us to do. Do not come up with excuses. We *must* put sin to death. We are the active ones in this war. We must put on the whole armor of God and fight daily until we experience peace, joy, and victory.

Killing Sin by the Spirit

How do we put to death the evil deeds of the body? Paul says we do so by the Spirit: *"If by the Spirit you put to death the misdeeds of the body, you will live"* (v. 13). The emphasis is on "by the Spirit."

Professor Douglas Moo says, "Human activity in the process of sanctification is clearly necessary; but that activity is never apart from, nor finally distinct from, the activity of God's Spirit."[4] He also states, "The same Spirit that 'set us free from the law of sin and death' has taken up residence within us, producing in us

---

4   Moo, *Epistle to the Romans*, 496.

528

that 'mind-set' which tends toward the doing of God's will and resists the ways of the flesh."[5]

We put to death. *We* are active. But we put to death *by the Holy Spirit*. The difference between a pagan and a Christian is that the Holy Spirit is dwelling in a Christian, enlightening him, guiding him, and empowering him to do the will of God.

Progressive sanctification, therefore, is a cooperative venture. Some people say, "Let God sanctify me." Yes, God will sanctify us, but he does so in cooperation with us. We work out exactly what God by his Spirit works in us, both to will and to do his good pleasure, and we do this work also by the power of the Spirit. We are Spirit-baptized, Spirit-filled, Spirit-indwelt people. Jesus told his disciples, "You will receive power when the Holy Spirit comes on you" (Acts 1:8). We must be continually filled with the Holy Spirit so that we can worship God and serve him in the world—in the home, in the workplace, or at school. We do all these things by the energy of the Spirit of the living God.

Without Christ, we can do nothing. But we can do all things through Christ, who continually makes us strong. We are vitally united to the vine. All that a branch does in its fruit-bearing activity is due to the energy it receives from the vine.

We must examine ourselves. If we find that we are stubborn or disobedient, we may not be Christians. It is a serious condition. The most important thing we must do in our lives is to make sure we are true Christians. If a person is not obedient, he is not a Christian. If a person is stubborn or arrogant, he is not a Christian. Christians are characterized by humility, and God gives grace to the humble.

Listen to Paul: "Now to him who is able to do immeasurably more than all we ask or imagine, according to his power that is at work within us . . ." (Eph. 3:20). By the power of the Holy Spirit, wives can be submissive to their husbands. By the Holy Spirit's power, husbands can love their wives and provide for their families. We do these things "according to his power that is continually at work within us." We are not talking about a Holy Spirit who is so transcendent we cannot reach him. God cannot be nearer to us: he is with us, in us, and for us. So Paul also

---

5   Ibid., 495.

writes, "To this end I labor, struggling with all his energy, which so powerfully works in me" (Col. 1:29). Labor means working hard and sweating. But such labor is not a problem. We can do all things God wants us to do because he makes us able. So Paul exhorts: "Finally, be strong in the Lord and in his mighty power" (Eph. 6:10).

The Bible tells us that our bodies belong to the Lord, and we have no right to put them in the service of ourselves or of the devil. "The body is . . . for the Lord, and the Lord for the body" (1 Cor. 6:13). The Lord will take care of our earthly bodies, even raising them from the dead in due time.

Our bodies are for the exclusive use of the Lord. They are not for immorality. Paul declares, "So whether you eat or drink or whatever you do, do it all for the glory of God" (1 Cor. 10:31). We must do everything, including mundane ordinary things like eating and drinking, for the glory of God. Again, he writes, "And whatever you do, whether in word or deed, do it all in the name of the Lord Jesus, giving thanks to God the Father through him" (Col. 3:17). Yes, we will face temptation. That is nothing new. We are tempted every day. But Paul writes, "No temptation has seized you except what is common to man. And God is faithful; he will not let you be tempted beyond what you can bear. But when you are tempted, he will also provide a way out so that you can stand up under it" (1 Cor. 10:13). Paul uses the word *exodus*, which means "exit" or "way out." God will show us a way out so that we do not have to sin. Do not come and say that you were tempted, so you sinned. Christians have the freedom not to sin (*posse non peccare*). We have a choice. And to further encourage us, Paul gives a guarantee: "So I say, live by the Spirit, and you will not gratify the desires of the [flesh]" (Gal. 5:16).

Some people may think sanctification is optional for a Christian. But the Bible clearly states, "It is God's will that you should be sanctified" (1 Thess. 4:3). There is no debate about it. It is God's will that we should be sanctified, that we should "avoid sexual immorality," and so on. And God himself will make us holy: "May God himself, the God of peace, sanctify you through and through. May your whole spirit, soul and body be kept blameless at the coming of our Lord Jesus Christ" (1 Thess. 5:23).

I pray that all of us will yield to the Holy Spirit even now. You may be stubborn, brittle, and hardhearted. Be encouraged; there is grace for you. Ask God to humble you and give you a soft heart. Walk after the direction of the Spirit, which is the way of the word of God.

How to Live

"If by the Spirit you put to death the [evil deeds] of the body, you will live" (v. 13). Paul is not directing these words to the pagans of the world or to sinning Christians. Those who are sinning do not live. Only Christians who put sin to death truly live and live eternally. There is a killing that is real living; there is a living that is real death. We can sin all we want and die eternal death; or kill sin and live. That is what the text is telling us.

How many people have been deceived by the temporary pleasures of sin! But we must put sin to death in order to live eternal life now and forever. The pleasures of sin are momentary. The Hebrews writer says that Moses rejected the temporary pleasures of sin and chose the eternal pleasures of God (Heb. 11:24–26). The psalmist also speaks of what true pleasure is: "You have made known to me the path of life; you will fill me with joy in your presence, with eternal pleasures at your right hand" (Ps. 16:11). The kingdom of God is righteousness, peace, and joy in the Holy Spirit. It is the citizens of the kingdom of God who really live, not those who are sinning morning, noon, and night. Such people are deceived and dying. Christians alone truly live.

What is the essence of this living? It is the approbation and benediction of God. It is the smile of God upon us. It is blessedness. It is the vision of God. The Bible says without holiness no one will see the Lord. God is holy, so only holy people may see him. Jesus said, "Blessed are the pure in heart, for they will see God" (Matt. 5:8).

Kill sin and pursue righteousness daily, and you shall live with God. John exclaims, "How great is the love the Father has lavished on us, that we should be called children of God! And that is what we are! The reason the world does not know us is that it did not know him. Dear friends, now we are children of God, and what we will be has not yet been made known. But we know that when he appears, we shall be like him, for we shall see him as he is. Everyone who has this hope in him purifies himself, just as he is pure" (1 John 3:1–3). Elsewhere he writes, "Then I saw a new heaven and a new earth, for the first heaven and the first earth had passed away, and there was no longer any sea. I saw the Holy City, the new Jerusalem, coming down out of heaven from God, prepared as a bride beautifully dressed for her husband. And I heard a loud voice from the throne saying, 'Now the dwelling of God is with men, and he will live with them. They will be his people, and God himself will be with them and be their God. He will wipe every tear from their eyes. There will be no more death or mourning or crying or pain, for the old order of things has passed away.' . . . They will see his face, and his name will be on their foreheads" (Rev. 21:1–4; 22:4). Even now, as we live a holy life, we have communion with God that fills our heart with celestial joy, a joy that no sin can give us.

"But if by the Spirit you put to death the misdeeds of the body, you will live." We began to live when God gave us new birth. So many people rely on extensive support systems of psychiatrists, psychologists, and other resources just to survive. But we are Spirit-filled, joy-filled, peace-filled, happy people. There is joy in serving Jesus.

Application

How can we put this teaching into practice?

1. By the power of the Spirit, believers must obey God's law, the Ten Commandments. When Jesus was asked, "Which is the greatest commandment?" he answered, "'Love the Lord your God with all your heart and with all your soul and with all your mind.' This is the first and greatest commandment. And the second is like it: 'Love your neighbor as yourself.' All the Law and the Prophets hang on these two commandments" (Matt. 22:36–40). There is no way to get away from the Ten Commandments. Jesus also said, "If you love me, you will obey what I command" (John 14:15). Paul instructs, "He who has been stealing must steal no longer, but must work, doing something useful with his own hands, that he may

have something to share with those in need" (Eph. 4:28). God has not abrogated the Ten Commandments, even though we may want him to do so.

2. As Christians, make no provision for the flesh (Rom. 13:14). In other words, starve your sinful nature to death. Emulate the Ephesians, who took all their sorcery materials and burned them up (Acts 19:17–20). We must vigorously destroy whatever things cause us to sin.

3. Recognize that sinning Christians do not evangelize. Such people cannot father spiritual children. The purpose of salvation is that we declare God's praises: "But you are a chosen people, a royal priesthood, a holy nation, a people belonging to God, that you may declare the praises of him who called you out of darkness into his wonderful light" (1 Pet. 2:9). But sinning Christians will never share their faith. If we are not sharing, it is because we are sinning.

4. Meditate on Scripture. Paul exhorts, "Set your minds on things above, not on earthly things" (Col. 3:2). The Hebrews writer says, "Let us fix our eyes on Jesus, the author and [finisher] of our faith" (Heb. 12:2). Doing so will help us to kill sin.

5. Pray for grace and receive it. We are encouraged, "Let us then approach the throne of grace with confidence, so that we may receive mercy and find grace to help us in our time of need" (Heb. 4:16). God promises to give grace to the humble (James 4:6), and Jesus said, "My grace is sufficient for you" (2 Cor. 12:9).

6. Use the sword of the Spirit, which is the word of God, to kill sin, as Jesus did when he was tempted, telling Satan, "It is written."

7. Be concerned not only about our own sanctification but also about the sanctification of others, because we are one body. If we see our brother sinning, we must rebuke him. We have a responsibility to our brothers and sisters. Jesus himself said, "As many as I love, I rebuke and chasten" (Rev. 3:19, KJV).

8. Daily train in godliness. Just as Olympic athletes train themselves for years, we also must train ourselves daily in godliness because, unlike physical training, training in godliness is profitable for this life and the life to come (1 Tim. 4:8). We train by doing the right thing for a long time until it becomes our habit. This includes rising early, praying, reading the Bible, and obeying God.

9. Keep in mind that the bride of Christ is holy, not a harlot, and live accordingly.

10. Remember that if God justifies us, he will also sanctify us, even if he has to kill us. I recently heard a Catholic priest say, "I would like to die because then I would not sin." That is true. If we remain stubborn after God has justified us, he will deal with us. Paul writes, "That is why many among you are weak and sick, and a number of you have fallen asleep" (1 Cor. 11:30).

The goal of our sanctification is the glory of God. A filthy bride brings no glory to her bridegroom. Paul writes, "Husbands, love your wives, just as Christ loved the church and gave himself up for her to make her holy, cleansing her by the washing with water through the word, and to present her to himself as a radiant church, without stain or wrinkle or any other blemish, but holy and blameless" (Eph. 5:25–27). Christ will have a holy bride. He is committed to sanctify us and he will succeed in doing it. May God use whatever measure he must to clean us up, so that we may enter his presence and live with him forever.

45

Proof of Sonship, Part 1

Those who are led by the Spirit of God are sons of God.

Romans 8:14

About two billion people in the world today call themselves Christians. Many do so because they are on the rolls of various Christian denominations or were born in "Christian" countries. Others do so because they frequently attend worship services and are baptized. But does God the Father of our Lord Jesus Christ acknowledge them as his sons? Are they true believers in Christ? Romans 8:14 speaks about proving the sonship of the sons of God.

On the last day, mere church certification or self-attestation cannot prove that we are Christians. Jesus warns, "Not everyone who says to me, 'Lord, Lord,' will enter the kingdom of heaven, but only he who does the will of my Father who is in heaven" (Matt. 7:21). To enter the kingdom of heaven, one must be a true son or daughter of God, born from above by the Holy Spirit. The proof of our sonship is godliness, being led by the Holy Spirit in accordance with the word of God.

There are some who believe in the universal fatherhood of God and, therefore, in universal salvation. They would assert that even fallen angels and the devil himself will be saved in the end, so there is no need for missions and evangelization. But Romans 8:14 proves such teaching to be false. God is the Creator of all, but he is the Father of only those who have become his sons and daughters by new birth and saving faith in Jesus Christ.

And those who are sons of God will have complete certainty of their final and full salvation.

A true child of God is indwelt by the Holy Spirit, who teaches and enables him to do God's will, to say no to sin and yes to righteousness. A believer who lives in sin is dead in sin. Such a person can have no assurance of final salvation and in fact will not be admitted to the kingdom of God.

Romans 8:14 explains verse 13, which tells us that only those who put sin to death will have eternal life. From this verse we want to examine two points: what it means to be led by the Holy Spirit and what it means to be a son of God.

Being Led by the Spirit of God

"For those who are being led by the Spirit of God, they and they alone are the sons of God" (Rom. 8:14, author's translation). The vital evidence of our salvation is not our profession or baptism or being born in a Christian home; it is whether or not we are daily being led by the indwelling Holy Spirit. Are we ruled and governed by the Spirit in our thinking, affections, and decisions? Simply put, do we obey God without arguing, murmuring, or complaining? Do we continually put to death sin in our bodies and live a holy life? If so, this will indicate that we are children of God who possess eternal life. We can therefore be completely assured of our final and entire salvation. Sons of God will live the life of God. They can never die.

If we claim to be Christians but continue to live in sin, then we are not under the government of the Holy Spirit. Rather, we are governed by the ruler of the kingdom of the air, the spirit that now works in the sons of disobedience (Eph. 2:2). We shall not live that eternal life which Jesus came to give us. Killing sin is the evidence of justification and the manifestation of the life of God in the soul of man.

Children Obey Their Father

"For those who are being led by the Spirit of God . . ." A Christian confesses by the Spirit that Jesus is his covenant Lord. This means that confessing Christians are obedient servants of God in all things. They obey the Holy Spirit, who is Lord, sent to dwell in us and govern us.

The gospel demands that we obey God. Consider the following Scriptures from Romans: "Through him and for his name's sake, we received grace and apostleship to call people from among all the Gentiles to the obedience that comes from faith" (1:5); "But thanks be to God that, though you used to be slaves to sin, you wholeheartedly obeyed the form of teaching to which you were entrusted" (6:17); "I will not venture to speak of anything except what Christ has accomplished through me in leading the Gentiles to obey God by what I have said and done" (15:18); "Everyone has heard about your obedience, so I am full of joy over you" (16:19). The Scriptures were given "by the command of the eternal God, so that all nations might believe and obey him" (16:26).

If we are Christians, we will obey God. The apostles were sent out to make disciples, teaching them to obey whatsoever things Jesus had commanded them, meaning the Bible (Matt. 28:20). The Christian life is a life of holiness, a life of obeying the Holy Spirit. When we read the book of Acts, we see that the apostles obeyed the Lord Jesus by obeying the Holy Spirit. When commanded by the Sanhedrin not to speak about Jesus, they replied, "Judge for yourselves whether it is right in God's sight to obey you rather than God. . . . We must obey God rather than men!" (Acts 4:19; 5:29). Some people misuse this, telling their parents, the civil authorities, or their church leaders, "We don't need to obey you! You are only men." But we are called to obey God's delegated authorities. The apostles also declared that the Holy Spirit is given by God "to those who obey him" (Acts 5:32). And the Hebrews writer says that Jesus is "the source of eternal salvation for all who obey him" (Heb. 5:9). We may try hard to remove obedience from the gospel, but we cannot.

The Holy Spirit is called the Spirit of holiness because he always leads us in righteousness, that is, in sanctification. He will never lead us into wickedness. He is also called the Spirit of truth: "But when he, the Spirit of truth, comes, he will guide you into all truth" (John 16:13). The Holy Spirit leads his people in the truth of the Bible, of which he is the author. So those who are being led by the Spirit will delight in reading, hearing, and doing what the Scriptures say. They will agree with everything the Scripture teaches. Therefore they will refuse to believe in the evolutionary hypothesis or the medical model that excuses away sin. They will vigorously oppose the killing of babies and will refuse to worship money or put their hope in this world.

The Holy Spirit does not glorify himself; he always glorifies Christ, in and through us. He testifies to us concerning Christ. Jesus said, "He will not speak on his own; he will speak only what he hears, and he will tell you what is yet to come. He will bring glory to me by taking from what is mine and making it known to you" (John 16:13b–14).

A son honors his father by obeying him. Likewise, we glorify our heavenly Father by obeying his will, which the Holy Spirit reveals to us in the Bible. "Those according to the Spirit think the things of the Spirit" (Rom. 8:5, author's translation). "The things of the Spirit" is the gospel, the word of God (see 1 Cor. 2). The Spirit enlightens our minds so that we understand, believe, and obey the gospel. The Spirit leads us in the word that we may bring glory to Christ.

Thus, the Spirit of God will guide us to honor and obey our parents and other delegated authorities who are God's ordained agents in the world. The Spirit will lead wives to submit to their husbands, and husbands to love their wives as Christ loved the church. The Spirit will instruct us to obey spiritual leaders and the just laws of the state, to love our children and teach them to obey God in everything, and to provide for our families by working six days a week. The same Holy Spirit will lead us to love especially the family of God and join a local church where the word is preached and Christ is exalted.

The Leading of the Spirit

The Holy Spirit determines the entire direction of our life: "The steps of a [righteous] man are ordered by the LORD" (Ps. 37:23, KJV). He directs whom we should marry and what vocation we should choose. He guides us in all these decisions through our Spirit-renewed reason. He prevents us from doing certain things and permits us to do certain other things. He can put it into our mind to take a certain course of action, as he did with Nehemiah:

"I set out during the night with a few men. I had not told anyone what my God had put in my heart to do for Jerusalem" (Neh. 2:12; see also 7:5). We also see the Spirit's guidance in the early church: "The Spirit told Philip, 'Go to that chariot and stay near it'" (Acts 8:29); and, "While Peter was still thinking about the vision, the Spirit said to him, 'Simon, three men are looking for you'" (Acts 10:19).

However, the fundamental way the Spirit leads us is not through extraordinary ways, but through the infallible written word of God. Those who are killers of sin and pursuers of righteousness are great students of God's word. They hunger and thirst after the Scriptures. God's word is light to them in dark places. It is food for them, sweeter than honey. It is treasure for them, more precious than fine gold. It is their companion and comfort in affliction. The Spirit leads us by the truth of the Scripture. So we are active in killing sin and pursuing the positive commands of the word.

We are active and passive at the same time. We are active in killing sin, but we are passive in being led by the Holy Spirit. John Murray notes, "The activity of the believer is the evidence of the Spirit's activity and the activity of the Spirit is the cause of the believer's activity."[1] We are led by the Spirit in the word as the Israelites were led by the pillar of fire and the pillar of cloud: "Whenever the cloud lifted from above the Tent, the Israelites set out; wherever the cloud settled, the Israelites encamped. At the LORD's command the Israelites set out, and at his command they encamped" (Num. 9:17–18).

Jesus himself was led by the Holy Spirit all his life. The Holy Spirit descended on him at his baptism. Later, the Spirit led him into the wilderness to be tempted and helped him to use the sword of the Spirit, the written word of God, to utterly defeat the devil. Christ's entire ministry was in the power of the Holy Spirit, and he always obeyed his Father by obeying the Holy Spirit. The Spirit led him to Gethsemane and to Calvary. It was "through the eternal Spirit" that Christ offered himself unblemished to God on Calvary's cross (Heb. 9:14).

This leading of the Holy Spirit is the mark of all God's children. They are obeyers who walk after the Spirit, thinking the things

---

1   Murray, *Epistle to the Romans*, 295.

of the Spirit. They are like Enoch, who walked with God in the direction of God (Gen. 5:22). They hear the Spirit's voice in the Scripture: "This is the way, walk ye in it" (Isa. 30:21, KJV). The people of God will walk in that way marked out for us by the Spirit in the Holy Scripture.

The Holy Spirit works in our minds, affections, and wills to think God's thoughts, love his ways, and will his will. He draws us, and we follow him irresistibly: "I have loved thee with an everlasting love; therefore with lovingkindness have I drawn thee" (Jer. 31:3, KJV). The leading of the Spirit does not often make us rich or famous. But only the leading of the Spirit in the highway of holiness will lead us home to God. It is the narrow way, leading us to life everlasting.

Joseph was led by the Spirit to reconcile with his brothers, who threw him into a pit. Though he cried out for deliverance, they did not listen, but sold him as a slave. He became a slave in the house of Potiphar in Egypt. Even there, he was falsely accused and was thrown into a prison. But every step of Joseph was ordered of the Lord, that his people might be saved: "You intended to harm me, but God intended it for good to accomplish what is now being done, the saving of many lives" (Gen. 50:20).

Israel was led by the Spirit out of Egypt, though the Egyptians followed them. Then Israel was led through the Red Sea, only to arrive at Marah with no food or water. Then the Amalekites came and opposed them. Yet we are told all along that God was guiding and testing his people to see whether they would behave as sons by their obedience.

Peter was led by the Holy Spirit to his crucifixion. Paul was led by the Spirit to go to Europe, only to be beaten and put in prison. But as a result of this leading, Lydia was saved and the jailer and his family and others were saved. And finally, Paul was led by the Holy Spirit to be beheaded, so that he could receive the crown of righteousness.

In the life of a true believer, the best things work for the good of the godly, as do also the worst things.[2] In all things, God works for the good of those who love him. He guides us through the

---

2   Summary from Thomas Watson, *All Things for Good* (Edinburgh: Banner of Truth, 1998).

seas, the rivers, and the mountains. We may experience illness, poverty, death, persecution, and even martyrdom; but we are on our way to the city of God our Father.

God's Ordinary Guidance

God sometimes leads us in extraordinary ways. Professor William Hendriksen tells a story that happened in the Netherlands in 1834 when the true church was being persecuted. A godly pastor was asked to call on a poor widow on the other side of a deep forest. Though it was late in the day, he went right away, ministered to her, and came back. After several years, two people came to know Christ through his ministry. One day they asked him, "On a Friday afternoon a few years ago, you went to visit a widow on the other side of the woods. We would like to know who were those two men in white shining armor on either side of you." The pastor replied, "I was alone." The men asserted, "No, there were two men. We were going to kill you, but we were afraid when we saw them and we ran."[3]

God can also guide us through visions and dreams, and angels are ministering spirits to us. But the normal way of the Spirit's leading is the way of the word of God and the way of suffering, the way of the cross. Jesus said, "Deny yourself and take up the cross daily and follow me." Through his leading, the Spirit enables us to mortify sin and conform ourselves to our Savior, that we may walk as he walked. Peter tells us, "To this you were called, because Christ suffered for you, leaving you an example, that you should follow in his steps. . . . He himself bore our sins in his body on the tree, so that we might die to sins and live for righteousness" (1 Pet. 2:21, 24).

The Holy Spirit's leading is not sporadic but constant. Because he dwells in us, he enables us to walk in his ways always. He protects, corrects, directs, and controls us. When we see the fruit of the Spirit in our lives, we know the Holy Spirit is leading us. He guides us in ways that glorify Christ and helps us take captive every thought to make it obedient to Christ.

---

3   Hendriksen, *Exposition of Romans*, 255–56.

Yield to the Holy Spirit as he speaks to you in the word. Do not argue, murmur, or complain. Do not insult the Holy Spirit; rather, obey him. The Hebrews writer says, "How much more severely do you think a man deserves to be punished who has trampled the Son of God under foot, who has treated as an unholy thing the blood of the covenant that sanctified him, and who has insulted the Spirit of grace?" (Heb. 10:29).

Do not quench the Holy Spirit (1 Thess. 5:19). Do not put out the Spirit's fire by saying no to him or doing the opposite of what he wants you to do. Do not grieve the Holy Spirit (Eph. 4:30). Do not rebel against the Holy Spirit: "Yet they rebelled and grieved his Holy Spirit. So he turned and became their enemy and he himself fought against them" (Isa. 63:10). Instead, be being filled with the Holy Spirit, that you might worship and serve him. The Spirit of God is working in us, both to will and to do his good pleasure.

Sons of God

The second point we want to examine is who are the sons of God: "*For those who are being led by the Spirit of God, they and they alone are the sons of God.*" Who are these sons? They are those who kill sin, not those who commit sin. They are dead to sin and alive in Christ. They are led by the Holy Spirit and taught in the word of God. They alone are the sons of God. They are sons by new birth and by adoption. They have the life of God in them. They have full assurance of eternal life. Neither death nor life nor anything else in all creation can separate them from the life and love of God.

Only holy and obedient people are the sons and daughters of God. Sons of God honor their Father by doing his will. They are like their heavenly Father in character and nature, because God has given us everything we need for life and godliness, and we participate in the divine nature (2 Pet. 1:3–4).

The unbelieving Jews claimed to be the children of Abraham, but Jesus said, "Your father is the devil. You behave like the devil, so you are his children" (see John 8:31–47). These people hated Jesus Christ and killed him. But Paul says, "Understand, then, that those who believe are children of Abraham" (Gal. 3:7). Abraham believed God; therefore, Abraham's children should believe God by believing in his Son. If we are like God and like his Son, we are sons of God. Preachers should preach this truth with all clarity. They should take away the false assurance that many people have and give full assurance to the true people of God.

Holiness is the hallmark of a true child of God. "'Therefore come out from them and be separate, says the Lord. Touch no unclean thing, and I will receive you.' 'I will be a Father to you, and you will be my sons and daughters, says the Lord Almighty'" (2 Cor. 6:17–18). Only holy people are sons and daughters of the holy God.

Today we have accurate genetic tests that can determine who the father of a child is. There are also spiritual tests we can apply to determine if we are truly Christians. If we claim to be sons and daughters of God, we must apply these tests to ourselves: Are we holy? Are we like Jesus Christ, who always pleased God and so God was well-pleased with him?

Objects of the Father's Affection

Sons of God are objects of God's peculiar affections. God's children enjoy not just common grace but especially special grace: Those to whom God once said, "You are not my people," shall now be called "sons of the living God" (Rom. 9:26). The Father did not spare his one and only Son, so that we might be made his sons. His love for us is beyond measure. All repenting prodigals will be received as sons by the Father with great celebration in heaven. Repent, return, and he will receive us.

As sons of God, we always have access to our heavenly Father. He is eager to see us, bless us, embrace us, and answer our prayers. "For through [Jesus Christ] we . . . have access to the Father by [the Holy] Spirit" (Eph. 2:18). Draw near to God and he will draw near to us.

Sometimes when my grandchildren come over, I go to my room and lie down on my bed. As I am resting, I can see the door handle moving as someone tries to open the door. What should I do? I must get up and open the door, allowing these little ones in to see me. How much more does our heavenly Father want to see us! The Father always has time for his sons.

And we are not afraid of him who loved us from all eternity! He saved us in time by the sacrifice of his Son, and he will love us through all eternity. So we read, "Let us then approach the throne of grace with confidence, so that we may receive mercy and find grace to help us in our time of need" (Heb. 4:16).

Jesus said his grace is sufficient, and he gives grace to his children. How many parents plan for their children, determining when to play, when to go to school, when to eat, when to do chores, when to go to bed, and when to worship God? They provide for them and protect them from all harm, including all wicked, worldly ideas. In the same way, our heavenly Father cares for us. He hears our prayers, for he knows what we need before we ask him (Matt. 6:8). He knows we need food, clothing, shelter, and medicine, and he provides for us, specifically by giving us work in which we excel by working as unto the Lord with all our might. Because we are his sons, our heavenly Father has compassion on us. When all forsake us, and even if our own father and mother disown us, the Lord will receive us (Ps. 27).

As sons of our heavenly Father, we necessarily and naturally love all those who are born of the same Father. A man from another country recently came to see me. I was blessed as he described how God by divine mercy led him to come to this church. As I sat listening to him quote scripture after scripture, I said, "You are my brother." We love all the children of the same heavenly Father. We love the household of faith. We love the church of Jesus Christ, not only in words, but in self-sacrificial deeds.

Children of God live in holy communion with the Father and the Son. They are not worried about anything. They are sure about their final salvation because they are fellowshipping with the Father daily. There is conversation. God speaks to us from the word and assures us that everything is going to be all right.

We are eternally loved and chosen by the Father. We are predestinated and effectually called in time. We are born of God, justified forever by faith, and adopted into the family of God. We are being led by the Spirit in sanctification, and we shall be glorified in soul and body to live with God forever. Our being led by the Spirit ministers to us full assurance of our final salvation, even though we may experience tribulations here and now.

As God's sons and daughters, we are given greater dignity than any other creatures. Consider what we were when God called us: We were not influential or of noble birth; we were foolish, lowly, and despised things; we were nothings, zeroes (1 Cor. 1:26–28). We were the publicans and prostitutes. We were blind, lost, dead wretches. We were in the slimy pit of mud and mire. But the Father sent his own Son into our pit, and he lifted us up out of the miry pit and made us stand on firm ground. He put a new song of praise to God in our mouth and seated us with Christ in heavenly places. He took us from the pit and placed us in God's family.

We are children of God, so let us behave as God's children. "How great is the love the Father has lavished on us, that we should be called children of God! And that is what we are!" (1 John 3:1). Noble people should behave nobly. Growing up, I was told, "Behave yourself. You must never bring shame to our family's noble name." Likewise, as children of God, may we do good works so that people will see them and glorify our Father in heaven.

As God's children, we are also disciplined by the Father so that we will be conformed to the image of Christ. This discipline comes especially when we refuse to be led by the Spirit. So we read, "My son, do not make light of the Lord's discipline, and do not lose heart when he rebukes you, because the Lord disciplines those he loves, and he punishes everyone he accepts as a son" (Heb. 12:5–6). Only true sons, not illegitimate children, are loved and disciplined. God disciplines us so that we may share in his holiness, for without holiness, no one will see God.

In this discipline, some may experience weakness and sickness, and some may even be called home by God so that they may sin no more. But our salvation is assured. He who leads his children by his Spirit will not abandon them on the way. Every true son and daughter of God will arrive in God's presence. "He who did not spare his own Son, but gave him up for us all—how will he not also, along with him, graciously give us all things?" (Rom. 8:32). This means we will be glorified.

Application

Let us then apply the test to ourselves. Do we kill sin daily? Then we are living the life eternal, the abundant life. Are we being daily led by the Holy Spirit? Everyone is led by something; no one is autonomous in this world. The unbeliever is a child of the devil, led by the evil spirit, "the ruler of the kingdom of the air, the spirit who is now at work in [the sons of disobedience]" (Eph. 2:2). An unbeliever strictly obeys the evil spirit, without complaining or arguing, because the devil will not tolerate opposition. The unbeliever is deceived by the momentary pleasures of sin.

But a believer is led by the Holy Spirit. He is a child of God, thus like God. He does not enjoy the momentary pleasures of sin but seeks after the eternal pleasures of being in God's presence.

Children of God are filled with the Spirit of God. The Spirit of God controls our thinking, our willing, and our affections. Therefore, we do not fight against being led by the Holy Spirit. And as we said earlier, the Holy Spirit always leads us in the way of the word of God. So a child of God will love God's word and meditate on it. The word of Christ will dwell in his heart richly. He will agree wholeheartedly with the word and walk in its ways. He will hope not in this world but in the God of the word.

As sons and daughters of God, we love God Triune and all God's legitimate children everywhere. What peace and joy we will have if we obey the Holy Spirit! We do so as individuals, and we do so in our marriages. When husbands and wives are led by the Spirit, what peace and joy they will have, for quarrels come from self-centeredness and unholy selfish desires. In our families, if the husband and wife and children are obedient to the word of God, what blessings we will experience! And in the church, if every believer is led by the Spirit, what joy, what peace, what unity, what revival we will enjoy!

John exhorts us, "Dear friends, do not believe every spirit, but test the spirits to see whether they are from God, because many false prophets have gone out into the world" (1 John 4:1). When you visit a church, test the spirits there. Test the preacher and see whether he preaches the Bible. See if the people practice holiness. And if you find such a church, enjoy great fellowship with them, because they are the people of God.

It is not difficult to test our paternity. We cannot say God is our father and behave like the devil. Test the spirits. The Holy Spirit always glorifies Christ, leads us into the Scripture, and makes us holy. I pray all of us will be led by the Holy Spirit and prove that we are sons of God.

46

Proof of Sonship, Part 2

[15]For you did not receive a spirit that makes you a slave again to fear, but you received the Spirit of sonship. And by him we cry, "Abba, Father." [16]The Spirit himself testifies with our spirit that we are God's children.

Romans 8:15–16

How can we know that we are saved from the wrath of God? How can we have certainty that we will go to paradise when we die? How can we know that we who were slaves of sin have become saints and sons of God? Can we truly sing, "Blessed assurance, Jesus is mine"?

Romans 8 speaks about assurance of salvation. Some teach that a Christian ought always to be in fear of condemnation and doubt the love of God. But Charles Hodge comments, "A spirit of fear, so far from being an evidence of piety, is an evidence of the contrary."[1] Yet it is also not enough to self-certify that we are saved. Anyone can claim to be a Christian without the saving work of the Spirit in his life. Romans 8:14–17 teaches that sons of God truly know that they are sons of God and therefore are guaranteed of eternal life.

From Romans 8:14 we learned that the first proof of sonship is that the sons of God are those who are being led by the Spirit of God.

In Romans 8:15–16, we will look at two further proofs of our sonship: the proof of adoption and the proof of the internal witness of the Holy Spirit.

---

1   Hodge, *Romans*, 282.

Proof of Adoption

"For you did not receive a spirit of a slave again to fear, but you received a spirit of sonship by whom we cry, 'Abba, Father'" (v. 15, author's translation). This verse speaks about the assurance of salvation that is the birthright of every believer, obtained through the proof of adoption. With John Murray I would translate it this way: "For you did not receive the Holy Spirit as a spirit of a slave [or slavery], to fear again."[2]

Unbelievers are anxious and fearful, worrying about what will happen today or tomorrow. Anti-depressants are in great demand.

The people of the world have much to fear. By nature they are children of wrath, sons of disobedience, and sons of the devil. As sons of Adam and slaves of sin, they live daily in fear of the wrath of God and in fear of death. All sinners, whether Jews under the law or Gentiles without the law, are fearful because of their guilt, though they mask it with money, false joy, or power. The Hebrews writer confirms this, saying, "[Christ came to] free those who all their lives were held in slavery by their fear of death" (Heb. 2:15).

Our pre-Christian life was a life of fear and slavery. Paul asks, "What benefit did you reap at that time from the things you are now ashamed of? Those things result in death!" (Rom. 6:21). Isaiah was afraid when he saw the Lord seated on the throne. He was afraid because of his guilt, so he cried out, "Woe to me! I am ruined! For I am a man of unclean lips" (Isa. 6:5). When people heard Peter's sermon on the day of Pentecost, they were cut to the heart and said, "Brothers, what shall we do?" (Acts 2:37). The Philippian jailer fell trembling before Paul and Silas, asking, "Sirs, what must I do to be saved?" (Acts 16:30).

Have you asked that question? May the Holy Spirit, who does not make us slaves to fear again, help you to do so even today.

The following verses are parallel to Romans 8:15:

1. "We have not received the spirit of the world but the Spirit who is from God, that we may understand what God has freely given us" (1 Cor. 2:12). The "spirit of the world" is the god of this world, "the spirit who is now at work in those who

---

2   Murray, *Epistle to the Romans*, 293.

550

are disobedient" (Eph. 2:2). The spirit of this world makes the people of this world live the life of slaves, a life of fear.

2. "For God did not give us a spirit of timidity [a spirit of fear, a spirit of cowardice], but a spirit of power, of love and of [sound thinking]" (2 Tim. 1:7). The Spirit we received does not make us slaves. This Holy Spirit is the Spirit of sonship. He is the Spirit of God's own Son. Slaves fear, not sons and daughters of God, whose sins are blotted out by Jesus Christ, who was sent by the Father "to rescue us from the hand of our enemies, and to enable us to serve him without fear" (Luke 1:74).

3. "But now . . . you have been set free from sin" (Rom. 6:22). The Holy Spirit is the spirit of liberty. We are former slaves who have been set free. "Where the Spirit of the Lord is, there is freedom" (2 Cor. 3:17). We did not receive the Holy Spirit as a spirit of a slave, but we received the Spirit of sonship by whom we cry, "Abba, *ho pater.*"

Spirit of Sonship

This Holy Spirit, the Spirit of God's Son, is the Spirit of sonship. Question 34 of the Westminster Shorter Catechism defines simply what adoption is: "Adoption is an act of God's free grace, whereby we are received into the number, and have a right to all the privileges, of the sons of God." Regeneration secures our membership in God's kingdom, but adoption secures our membership in God's family. Like justification, adoption is the Father's judicial act. Regeneration gives us new life and a new nature; adoption gives us new status, a new family, and new rights.

There is a family of God, and there is a family of the devil. Paul says, "For this reason I kneel before the Father, from whom his whole family in heaven and on earth derives its name" (Eph. 3:14–15). John articulates the same thing, "Yet to all who received him, to those who believed in his name, he gave the right to become children of God" (John 1:12).

Adoption is the highest privilege that the redeemed enjoy. It is our present possession with future implications. We *are* sons of God, and we *will* enjoy our adoption in its fullness when our bodies are transformed. Adopted sons are assured that they will be conformed to God's image and enjoy the beatific vision forever: "They will see [God's] face, and his name will be on their foreheads" (Rev. 22:4). The Spirit of adoption produces in us the highest confidence in God our Father.

The Greek word for adoption (*huiothesia*) means to be installed as a son. Of the New Testament writers, only Paul uses this word, which he does five times. This idea of adoption is based on Roman law, which the Roman Christians were well aware of. By this legal institution, one could adopt a child and confer on that child all the legal rights and privileges that would ordinarily accrue to a natural child. Roman law also required multiple witnesses for an adoption to be legal. Roman adoption applied only to boys; but, thank God, this is not so in the family of God. God the Father adopts boys and girls, men and women, even old people, and they are given full rights: "'Therefore come out from them and be separate, says the Lord. Touch no unclean thing, and I will receive you.' 'I will be a Father to you, and you will be my sons and daughters, says the Lord Almighty'" (2 Cor. 6:17–18).

Adoption follows regeneration and justification in the *ordo salutis*. It severs our legal and social relations to our natural family, the family of Adam, which is the family of the devil, and places us permanently into God's new family. Paul explains: "The Father . . . has qualified you to share in the inheritance of the saints in the kingdom of light. For he has rescued us from the dominion of darkness and brought us into the kingdom of the Son he loves, in whom we have redemption, the forgiveness of sins. . . . He forgave us all our sins, having canceled the written code, with it regulations, that was against us and that stood opposed to us; he took it away, nailing it to the cross" (Col. 1:12–14; 2:13–14). Our previous debts and obligations are canceled. Jesus paid it all.

We have been adopted, just as Julius Caesar adopted Octavian, who later became Emperor Caesar Augustus. "In the Roman world . . . an adopted son was deliberately chosen by his adoptive father to perpetuate his name and inherit his estate; he was no whit inferior in status to a son born in the ordinary course of nature, and might well enjoy the father's affection more fully and reproduce the father's character more worthily."[3]

---

3   Bruce, *Letter of Paul to the Romans*, 157.

Baptism in the Holy Spirit

This Spirit of sonship, the Spirit of God's Son, creates within our hearts great filial affection by which we love God and call him, "Abba, Father." Dr. Martyn Lloyd-Jones connects this experience to the baptism in the Holy Spirit, which is an experience that registers not only in our intellect but also in our feelings, in our emotions, in the depths of our being. Paul writes, "And hope does not disappoint us, because God has poured out his love into our hearts by the Holy Spirit, whom he has given us" (Rom. 5:5).

This is also known as sealing of the Holy Spirit. "Having believed, you were marked in him with a seal, the promised Holy Spirit" (Eph. 1:13). The seal gives us security. Paul speaks of it again in the same epistle, "Do not grieve the Holy Spirit of God, with whom you were sealed for the day of redemption" (Eph. 4:30).

Jesus Christ baptizes believers in the Holy Spirit. When Christ was glorified, he received the Holy Spirit from the Father and poured him out in abundance on the church, as Peter declared on the day of Pentecost: "Exalted to the right hand of God, [Jesus] has received from the Father the promised Holy Spirit and has poured out what you now see and hear" (Acts 2:33).

Baptism in the Holy Spirit, or sealing with the Holy Spirit, is experimental, not theoretical. Those who experience it are fearless and full of joy. The cure for fear is baptism in the Holy Spirit, which does not depress or disappoint us, but causes us to rejoice in the hope of the glory of God. It causes us to rejoice even in tribulations.

Paul was baptized in the Holy Spirit. Ananias was sent to pray for Paul that he might see again and be filled with the Holy Spirit (Acts 9:17). Later Paul wrote, "I thank God that I speak in tongues more than all of you" (1 Cor. 14:18). He prayed and sang in tongues in the Spirit. That means he prayed and sang without understanding what he was praying or singing; nevertheless, he was being edified as he spoke and sang to God.

Christ pours out his Spirit upon believers, and the Spirit in turn pours out divine love into our hearts in great abundance. With this mighty effusion of love power, we love God, we love Christ, we love our brothers and sisters, and we keep God's commandments. The Christian life is not legalism or moralism or sheer duty. It is love life. With this love we love God's people and gladly lay down our lives for them. With this same love we suffer martyrdom and persecution.

"How great is the love the Father has lavished on us, that we should be called children of God! And that is what we are!" (1 John 3:1). John later states, "God is love. Whoever lives in love lives in God, and God in him. In this way, love is made complete among us so that we will have confidence on the day of judgment, because in this world we are like him. There is no fear in love. But perfect love drives out fear, because fear has to do with punishment" (1 John 4:16–18). Jesus Christ has taken our punishment.

Paul writes, "For Christ's love compels us [motivates us, impels us, empowers us]" (2 Cor. 5:14). Peter says, "Though you have not seen him, you love him; and even though you do not see him now, you believe in him and are filled with an inexpressible and glorious joy" (1 Pet. 1:8). All this is because of the Holy Spirit at work in our hearts.

A theoretical Christianity that does not affect our emotions or feelings is not biblical Christianity. Rather, it is dead orthodoxy that will take its followers to hell. In Romans 8:15 Paul is speaking about something experimental and subjective that affects our feelings and emotions and causes us to rejoice in the hope of the glory of God. The Spirit of adoption creates within us such love and assurance that we as adopted children of God cry out spontaneously, "Abba, *ho pater.*" Charles Hodge says, "The Holy Spirit . . . produces the filial feelings of affection, reverence, and confidence, and enables us, out of the fulness of our hearts, to call God our Father."[4] Strangers do not call God "Abba, Father."

The Love of the Father

The Spirit of adoption causes us to know we have been adopted into God's family and blessed with the highest blessing. This has been God's plan from eternity: "Praise be to the God and Father of our Lord Jesus Christ, who has blessed us in the heavenly realms

---

4   Hodge, *Romans,* 266.

with every spiritual blessing in Christ. For he chose us in him before the creation of the world to be holy and blameless in his sight. In love he predestined us to be adopted as his sons through Jesus Christ, in accordance with his pleasure and will—to the praise of his glorious grace" (Eph. 1:3–6). That is what God has always wanted to do with us—adopt us and bring us into his family. Jesus Christ is the Son eternal by nature. We are sons by grace.

The Father loves us just as he loves his Son. So Jesus prayed, "May they be brought to complete unity to let the world know that you sent me and have loved them even as you have loved me" (John 17:23). In adoption, we are given a standing before God comparable to that of his unique Son.

Dr. Lloyd-Jones says, "The ultimate object of salvation is not merely to keep us from hell, not merely to deliver us from certain sins; it is that we may enjoy 'adoption', and that we may become 'the children of God' and 'joint-heirs with Christ'."[5] We were nobodies; but, having been loved by the Father from all eternity, we have now been adopted into his own family. We are children of God. What dignity we have! What wealth we have! What love we enjoy! We are not slaves; we are sons of God.

Not only are we sons of God, but we are also brothers of Christ. "For those God foreknew he also predestined to be conformed to the likeness of his Son, that he might be the firstborn among many brothers." (Rom. 8:29; see also Heb. 2:11–12). The risen Christ commanded Mary, "Do not hold on to me, for I have not yet returned to the Father. Go instead to my *brothers* and tell them, 'I am returning to my Father and your Father, to my God and your God'" (John 20:17).

Galatians 4:6 says the Spirit himself is crying, "Abba, Father." Here we cry by the Spirit's help, "Abba, Father." It is the right of a son to call out, "Abba, *ho pater*." *Krazomen* means that we continually cry out. The Spirit makes us very aware of our Father and enables us to converse and commune with him. In prayer and in singing we express our relationship to and our fellowship with God our Father and his Son, Jesus Christ.

The word Paul uses for fervent prayer (*krazō*) is used in the Old Testament Septuagint many times, especially in the psalms: "To

---

5   Lloyd-Jones, *Romans*, vol. 7, *Sons of God*, 245.

the Lᴏʀᴅ I cry aloud. . . . The Lᴏʀᴅ will hear when I call to him" (Ps. 3:4; 4:3). It is a cry of deep emotion, want, intimacy, love, security, fervency, confidence, importunity, faith, assurance, and power. Some theologians think this cry refers also to the ecstatic speech of 1 Corinthians 14, where Paul speaks about praying and singing in the Spirit. Douglas Moo says about this crying, "In using the verb 'crying out,' Paul stresses that our awareness of God as Father comes not from rational consideration nor from external testimony alone but from a truth deeply felt and intensely experienced. . . . In crying out, 'Abba, Father,' the believer not only gives voice to his or her consciousness of belonging to God as his child, but also to having a status comparable to that of Jesus himself."[6] The mission of Jesus Christ is to bring many sons to glory (Heb. 2:10).

"Abba" is the word children used in Jewish homes to call their fathers. The Talmud says that when a child is weaned, he learns to say "Abba" and "Imma," that is, "Daddy" and "Mommy." "Abba" is Aramaic, the language Jesus spoke; thus, he must have called Joseph "Abba." In his recorded prayers, Jesus almost always called his heavenly Father "Abba," and he authorized his disciples also to call his Father "Abba." He said, "This, then, is how you should pray: 'Our Father in heaven . . .'" (Matt. 6:9).

We know that God the Father of our Lord Jesus Christ is our Father also. Jesus said, "Whoever has my commands and obeys them, he is the one who loves me. He who loves me will be loved by my Father. . . . If anyone loves me, he will obey my teaching. My Father will love him, and we will come to him and make our home with him" (John 14:21, 23). He is no stranger to us.

As sons and daughters of God, we need not be afraid of anything. And we are not afraid of the Father either. We revere him, but we are not afraid of him. We approach his throne with freedom and confidence, for to us it is not a throne of judgment but of grace (Eph. 3:12; Heb. 4:16). Through Jesus we have access to the Father by the Holy Spirit (Eph. 2:18). We have freedom of speech and access to his presence through faith in him.

---

6   Moo, *Epistle to the Romans*, 502.

The prodigal son had nothing to eat and was afraid that his father would throw him out. Yet he returned home, saying, "I am not worthy to be called your son." What did his father say? "You are my son!" In the same way, our heavenly Father makes certain that we know we are his child and can call him "Abba" by the help of the Holy Spirit.

So we cry in prayer, "Abba, Father" (*Abba* in Aramaic, *ho pater* in Greek). Maybe Jesus used both. Father! Father! Daddy! Daddy! This is an expression of our certitude. God is not our judge but our loving Father who hears our prayers.

One cannot be an adopted child of God and not know it. Assurance of salvation is our birthright. The majority of Reformers, including Calvin and Luther, said that assurance of salvation is essential to salvation. By God's grace, I am assured that I am a child of God. I love God, believe in God, and can rejoice with joy unspeakable and full of glory.

The Proof of the Testimony of the Holy Spirit

"*The Spirit himself testifies with our spirit that we are sons of God*" (v.16, author's translation). This verse gives us the highest proof that we are sons of God. It speaks not only of our own witness, enabled by the Holy Spirit, to our sonship, but of the additional witness of the Holy Spirit himself, which is another aspect of the baptism of the Holy Spirit.

"A matter must be established by the testimony of two or three witnesses" (Deut. 19:15). So first is our own testimony that because God is our Father, we are God's sons. But we have an additional testimony so that the matter may be settled once and forever. God himself testifies by the Holy Spirit that we are children of God. There is no greater proof than God's own testimony to us. The Spirit himself bears joint witness with our spirit that we are children of God, and that settles it.

This is the highest proof of our sonship and the highest Christian experience. Think of the old father of the prodigal, running to his returning son, throwing his arms around him, and hugging and kissing him. All the prodigal's fears and doubts evaporated, and he said to himself, "My father loves me! Now I am fully persuaded that nothing can cut me off from my father's love."

The Holy Spirit is the Spirit of truth. He cannot lie; his testimony is true. He testifies along with our spirits' own testimonies that we are children of God now and forever. This perfect love casts out all fear. Such love of God is the engine of our lives, motivating us to love God and live for him alone in obedience.

We have been adopted by God into his own family. We were nobodies, but we now are given status, dignity, rights, and privileges. We have access to God the Father and freedom of speech in his presence. And this relationship is eternal.

When we pray, "Our Father in heaven," when we cry out with the Spirit's assistance, "Abba, *ho pater*," God from heaven replies, "My child, what do you want me to do for you?" The Spirit himself witnesses with our spirit that we are children of God. Don't ever doubt it.

This testimony of the Holy Spirit is called *testimonium Spiritus sancti internum* (the internal testimony of the Spirit). It fills us with great confidence. It is as if God himself were lifting us up and saying to us, "You are my son," and then putting us down, and we are happy.

I have experienced this several times in my life. It is the privilege of every child of God to enjoy this highest form of assurance. It is not talking to ourselves; it is the Holy Spirit speaking to us. This witness of the Spirit is an immediate witness. It is a direct operation of the Spirit of God into the depths of our being. It is not based on some logical deduction.

Study the experiences of those in the book of Acts who were baptized in the Holy Spirit, and you will be convinced it is an experience. We feel it and it produces happiness and certainty. Dr. James Boice tells us, "[It is] a direct witness of the Holy Spirit to believers that they are sons and daughters of God."[7] By this, a child of God experiences an overwhelming sense of God's presence that causes him to forget the things of this world and long for heaven. As a deer pants after water brooks, so also we pant, not after money or position or power, but after God. No wonder Paul wrote from his prison, "For to me, to live is Christ and to die is gain. . . . I desire to depart and be with Christ, which is better by far" (Phil. 1:21, 23).

---

7   Boice, *Romans*, vol. 2, *Reign of Grace*, 843.

Application

Do you want to experience these proofs of sonship? If so, you must do the following:

First, live an obedient life. The Holy Spirit leads us in the word of God. We are not to adjust it or argue about it; we are to obey it. As many as are being led by the Spirit, they are the sons of God.

Second, seek earnestly the Holy Spirit of God. Jesus promises, "If you then, though you are evil, know how to give good gifts to your children, how much more will your Father in heaven give the Holy Spirit to those who ask him!" (Luke 11:13). Our need is not more money, more power, or a bigger house. We need to recognize that our need is God himself. We need to confess that we are paupers. Jesus Christ himself promises that our heavenly Father will give the Holy Spirit to those who ask ("keep asking" in the Greek). When we keep asking, we express that we really need the Holy Spirit.

We should not come to God with a plan B. We have only one plan: we need the Holy Spirit. We want to be like Jacob, who wrestled all night with God. He recognized his opponent was God and said, "I will not let you go unless you bless me," and God blessed him (Gen. 32:26). The Syro-Phoenician woman was rebuffed, but she did not give up. She said, "Yes, I am a dog, but even dogs must live from the master's table," and she was heard (Matt. 15:27). Isaiah exhorts us, "You who call on the LORD, give yourselves no rest, and give him no rest till he establishes Jerusalem and makes her the praise of the earth" (Isa. 62:6–7). Jesus himself, speaking about the Holy Spirit, said, "Anyone who thirsts, let him come to me and drink. And out of your innermost being shall flow rivers of living water" (see John 7:37–39). Come and drink and be filled with the Holy Spirit.

Third, love the word of God. Begin by affirming the authority of God's word. If you are a child of God, that understanding will be birthed into you. The word of God is the truth. It should be obeyed. Do not seek experiences that are not consonant with the word of God.

Fourth, test the spirits. If the Holy Spirit comes upon you in such mighty power, he will cause you to confess that God is your

Father, and will witness to you that you are a child of God. If you have truly experienced baptism in the Holy Spirit:

1. Know that this experience always confirms the word, never contradicts it.

2. You will have a sense of reverence and unworthiness. You will not go around pretending you are someone important. The more you experience God, the more you fall prostrate before him.

3. There will be a great thankfulness to God. You will sing, "*Thank you, Lord, for saving my soul; thank you, Lord, for making me whole; thank you, Lord, for giving to me thy great salvation, so rich and free.*"

4. You will be filled with God's love, by which you obey God. Jesus said, "If you love me, you will keep my commandments."

5. The things of this world will grow strangely dim. Worldliness will be exorcised from you.

6. You will have great courage and fearlessness to witness to Jesus Christ. "You shall receive power after the Holy Spirit has come upon you, and you shall be my witnesses in Jerusalem, Judea, Samaria, and to the uttermost parts of the earth" (see Acts 1:8; also Luke 24:47–49). When the Holy Spirit comes upon us, we are emboldened. Fearful Peter's entire personality was changed. He became fearless. May God baptize us with the Holy Spirit that we may have courage to witness.

7. God gives us freedom of speech. There is a flow. Rivers of living water flow out of our mouths in words, in sentences. We are not scratching our heads to think of the next thing we should say. There is a freedom of speech.

8. There is freedom in prayer. Instead of two minutes of formal, ceremonial prayer, we will pour out our hearts for hours. The Spirit of God will help us to pour out petitions to God. "And I will pour out on the house of David and the inhabitants of Jerusalem a spirit of grace and supplication" (Zech. 12:10).

9. There will be great love for brothers and sisters, because they are children of the same heavenly Father. Those who leave the church are not of us (1 John 2:19). It is only natural for children of the same father to love each other, and in such a way that we lay down our lives for our brothers (1 John 3:16).

10. There is a spirit of joy in a Christian's life, no matter what he is going through. The kingdom of God is righteousness, peace, and joy in the Holy Spirit. Peter writes, "Though you have not seen [Jesus], you love him; and even though you do not see him now, you believe in him and are filled with an inexpressible and glorious joy" (1 Pet. 1:8).

11. You will be the light of the world. Jesus said, "In the same way, let your light shine before men," that means you live an obedient life, "that they may see your good deeds and praise your Father in heaven" (Matt. 5:16). The Father's children shine as light. "Do

everything without complaining or arguing, so that you may become blameless and pure, children of God without fault in a crooked and depraved generation, in which you shine like stars in the universe" (Phil. 2:14–15). When we are living in sin, we cannot have assurance. How can we? "This is how we know who the children of God are and who the children of the devil are: Anyone who does not do what is right is not a child of God; nor is anyone who does not love his brother" (1 John 3:10).

May God help us to know for sure that we are children of God! All we need is the assurance created within us by the Holy Spirit. It does not matter where we go; we are children of God. He is around us; he is in us.

The psalmist paints this word picture of the joy a child of God experiences: "I sing in the shadow of your wings" (Ps. 63:7). And as I was growing up, I saw this illustrated. Whenever a hawk came, the mother hen would give a signal, and her chicks would run to her. The hen would lift her wings, and the chicks would all gather underneath. The fight would be between the hawk and the hen. The chicks under the wings could sing, "Our mother will take care of us!" So we also can sing in the shadow of God's wings.

Friends, we are in God, under his wings. All our battles are between God and our enemies, including the devil. God wins, and thus we can truly sing. What a mighty God we serve!

47

The Proof of Suffering

And if children, and heirs, heirs of God, joint-heirs with Christ, if indeed we suffer with him in order that [or for the purpose that] we may be glorified together with him.

Romans 8:17, *author's translation*

On Palm Sunday, Jesus entered Jerusalem on his way to suffer and die on the cross. He did so to accomplish our redemption. The way of the cross is the way of our life as well. Why are God's children enrolled in the school of suffering? The answer is so they can graduate to glory. Cross now, crown later. That is the order.

We have been considering the proofs of sonship in Romans 8:14–17. Sons of God are, first, those who are being led by the Spirit of God; second, those who give witness to that fact by crying out, "Abba, Father," by the help of the Holy Spirit; and third, those to whom the Holy Spirit himself gives testimony that they are children of God. Now we want to study the fourth proof: that the children of God are called to suffer now in this world so that they may be glorified in the age to come.

God ordains suffering for the good of his children. So suffering is not a surprise for the people of God. I recently heard the testimony of a Roman Catholic priest who was sent from Texas to Spain to do his doctoral studies in the theology of the cross. This man had long suffered from migraine headaches. Once in a while they would go away. When that happened, he could work hard and excel in his studies. But this time, he became overwhelmed. Not only did he feel poorly, but also his classes were in Spanish, not English. So he called his superior and said he could not continue. His wise superior answered, "What are you researching?" This priest replied, "The theology of the cross." "Well, do it, then."

We walk the way of the cross. Dr. Martyn Lloyd-Jones said, "If you are suffering as a Christian, and because you are a Christian, it is one of the surest proofs you can ever have of the fact that you are a child of God."[1] Robert Haldane said, "The man professing Christ's religion, who meets with no persecution or opposition from the world for Christ's sake, may well doubt the sincerity of his profession."[2]

Suffering can only last until we die. What will endure forever for us is not suffering but our reigning in glory with Christ. Every child of God will suffer here and now. If you are suffering, then rejoice in hope of the glory of God and in the fact that you are truly a child of God.

And If Children

In the Greek, Paul begins, "And if children . . ." (v. 17). This phrase really means "because we are children." There is no doubt about it. We are children by the judicial action of God called adoption. John declares, "To all who received him, to those who believed in his name, he gave the right to become children of God" (John 1:12). In his first epistle he exclaims, "How great is the love the Father has lavished on us, that we should be called children of God! And that is what we are!" (1 John 3:1). Paul also speaks of this: "Be imitators of God, therefore, as dearly loved children" (Eph. 5:1). We are children of God! No longer are we sons of Adam or sons of the devil. Truly we are children of God by his special love shown in his adopting us. As children, we are being conformed to the image of his Son.

---

1   Lloyd-Jones, *Romans*, vol. 7, *Sons of God*, 433.
2   Haldane, *Exposition of Romans*, 366.

We Are Heirs

Paul continues, *"And if children, and heirs . . ."* If we are God's children, we are also his heirs. Sons are heirs, and heirs inherit, as God declares, "I myself said, 'How gladly would I treat you like sons and give you a desirable land, the most beautiful inheritance'" (Jer. 3:19). Paul writes, "So you are no longer a slave, but a son; and since you are a son, God has made you also an heir" (Gal. 4:7). Elsewhere he says, "After all, children should not have to save up for their parents, but parents for their children" (2 Cor. 12:14). The Spirit of God dwelling in us guarantees our inheritance of final and full salvation: "He anointed us, set his seal of ownership on us, and put his Spirit in our hearts as a deposit, guaranteeing what is to come" (2 Cor. 1:21–22).

All true believers are children of God, not just some; and *all* children are heirs, not just some. There is a great inheritance waiting for us. This is the greatest stimulus for God's children to live holy lives in this world even as we suffer. All believers, Jewish or Gentile, are heirs. Paul says, "You are all sons of God through faith in Christ Jesus. . . . There is neither Jew nor Greek, slave nor free, male nor female, for you are all one in Christ Jesus" (Gal. 3:26, 28).

We are heirs "according to the promise" (Gal. 3:29), which is the promise of God, who cannot lie, a promise that is made more sure by divine oath. We are heirs of salvation, full and free; heirs of the grace of life; heirs according to the hope of eternal life; heirs of righteousness; and heirs of the kingdom which God has promised. So Jesus assures us, "Do not be afraid, little flock, for your Father has been pleased to give you the kingdom" (Luke 12:32). He tells us, "Then the King will say to those on his right, 'Come, you who are blessed by my Father; take your inheritance, the kingdom prepared for you since the creation of the world'" (Matt. 25:34). If children, then heirs.

We Are Heirs of God

All true believers are not just heirs, but *"heirs of God,"* a unique phrase signifying that we are "heirs belonging to the Father."

So our inheritance is absolutely safe. Our Father is eternal and unchanging; he cannot lie, nor can any enemy defeat him and take away our inheritance. So Peter states, "In his great mercy he has given us new birth into a living hope through the resurrection of Jesus Christ from the dead, and into an inheritance that can never perish, spoil or fade—kept in heaven for you" (1 Pet. 1:3–4). We saints have a treasure in heaven, where moth and rust cannot destroy and where thieves do not break in and steal. We are not heirs of men, whose promises cannot be trusted. They can be killed or their wealth can fly away.

As heirs of God, all that God owns (i.e., the whole creation) belongs to us. As heirs of God, we need not fear that somehow we will perish before we arrive in his presence to enjoy our inheritance. That is not going to happen, for he keeps safe not only our inheritance but us as well. Jesus promised, "I give them eternal life, and they shall never perish; no one can snatch them out of my hand" (John 10:28). Nothing in all creation is able to cut us off from God our heavenly Father. What God begins, he also continues and completes. The salvation of God's heirs is absolutely certain.

This also means that we inherit not only all that the Father has, but also God himself. The Bible says that God is our portion, and we are God's portion: "Whom have I in heaven but you? And earth has nothing I desire besides you. My flesh and my heart may fail, but God is the strength of my heart and my portion forever" (Ps. 73:25–26). God is all-sufficient. We possess God and all God has.

We Are Joint-heirs with Christ

Paul next explains that all of God's adopted children are "*joint-heirs with Christ.*" There cannot be any adoption or inheritance outside of Christ. We were sons of Adam and sons of the devil, but God took us out of that family by a divine miracle. By faith we are now united with Christ. He is the head, and we are the body. He is the bridegroom, and we are the bride. He is the foundation, and we are the building. He is the vine, and we are the branches. He is the Son, and we are sons in him. So Paul writes, "Therefore, there is now no condemnation for those who are in Christ Jesus, because through Christ Jesus the law of the Spirit of life set me free from the law of sin and death" (Rom. 8:1–2).

566

We are inseparably and eternally in Christ. We are sons in God's Son and brothers in Jesus, our older brother. So all our inheritance comes to us in him also. God has appointed his Son to be "heir of all things" (Heb. 1:2). Since we are united with the Son, we too are appointed to inherit all things.

In the parable of the tenants, Jesus said, "Last of all, he sent his son to them. 'They will respect my son,' he said. But when the tenants saw the son, they said to each other, 'This is the heir. Come, let's kill him and take his inheritance'" (Matt. 21:37–38). But they could not take his inheritance. It is reserved for us who have put our trust in Jesus Christ.

So Paul says, "All things are yours . . . and you are of Christ, and Christ is of God" (1 Cor. 3:21–23). Jesus is seated on God's right hand, we are seated with him, and "God placed all things under [Christ's] feet" (Eph. 1:22). So we are joint-heirs with Christ, and Christ fills us with his fullness. All his inheritance belongs to the suffering children of God.

We Share in His Sufferings

Now Paul brings in more clarity: "*if indeed we suffer with him.*" Once again, this "if" does not signify any doubt. We will experience suffering. We can translate it this way: "since we are suffering with him" or "since we share in his sufferings." That is the meaning of the text.

Paul suffered daily for the gospel. He was also keenly aware of the sufferings of the Roman Christians. He knew that union with Christ not only entitles us to his inheritance, but also causes us to suffer with him in this present evil age. If the world hated Christ, it will hate Christians, because they confess his name. The Son himself, though sinless, learned obedience and became perfect by suffering (Heb. 5:8–9). He was not exempt from it. Christ's sufferings alone accomplished the atonement, the propitiation, on our behalf. Our sufferings contribute nothing to our redemption. But the path to glory for Christ was suffering, and for us suffering is also the path to glory.

The risen Lord asked, "Did not the Christ have to suffer these things and then enter his glory?" (Luke 24:26). And Peter says, "Concerning this salvation, the prophets, who spoke of the grace that was to come to you, searched intently and with the greatest care, trying to find out the time and circumstances to which the Spirit of Christ in them was pointing when he predicted the sufferings of Christ and the glories that would follow. . . . To this you were called, because Christ suffered for you, leaving you an example, that you should follow in his steps" (1 Pet. 1:10–11; 2:21).

We learn more of Christ and make greater progress in sanctification, not in prosperity, but when we are facing severe adversity. All of Christ's sheep are branded with the cross. We are persecuted because, as the light of the world, we expose the evil of the world.

The Proof of Suffering

Suffering as a Christian, suffering for Christ's sake, suffering because of righteousness, is proof that we are children of God. No son is exempt. If we are not suffering, we may not be shining as stars in the universe, holding forth the word of life. If we start shining by living obedient lives and proclaiming the gospel, we can rest assured that we will be persecuted.

There are many ways Christians suffer in our modern society. Suppose you are a university professor and do not believe in Darwinian evolution or in moral relativism, but in intelligent design and the Bible. You may not get tenure, and you may even lose your job. Suppose you are a student who believes the biblical view of reality and morality. You are against cheating and abortion and tell others that you are for sexual purity. You may end up with a lower grade. If you are an employee, you may be laid off for insisting on worshiping on the Lord's Day rather than working, or you may get fired for refusing to participate in a crooked business deal. If you are a pastor who preaches that Christians must live holy lives, keeping God's commandments, you may be persecuted, slandered, and even removed from your office.

Yet even as we suffer, we can be encouraged that we are not alone. Jesus Christ suffers with us and is touched with our grief, for we are vitally united with him. The resurrected Christ spoke to Saul in Aramaic, "Saul, Saul, why do you persecute me?"

indicating the unity between Christ and his church. We suffer with Christ, and he suffers with us.

Daniel 3 speaks of the persecution of the three Hebrew children who refused to fall down and worship the image of gold. As threatened, these three sons of God were thrown into a fiery furnace made seven times hotter than usual. But King Nebuchadnezzar then declared, "Look! I see four men walking around in the fire, unbound and unharmed, and the fourth looks like a son of the gods" (Dan. 3:25). Nebuchadnezzar was right: it was the Son of God. Christ is with us always, even to the end of the age. He is a wall of fire around us. We suffer with him, and he suffers with us. Jesus is truly our sympathizing high priest (Heb. 4:15).

"Sympathizing" means suffering with us. The Greek word *sumpaschō* is found in only one other place in the New Testament: "If one member suffers, every member suffers with him" (1 Cor. 12:26). Because we are united to all the members of the body of Christ, we truly suffer with our suffering brothers and sisters. It is like a mother who truly suffers with her suffering child. So also, when we suffer with Christ, Christ suffers with us and gives us grace to endure.

Jesus told us ahead of time that we must suffer for our faith: "If anyone would come after me, he must deny himself and take up his cross daily and follow me" (Luke 9:23); "In this world you will have trouble" (John 16:33); "Blessed are those who are persecuted because of righteousness, for theirs is the kingdom of heaven. Blessed are you when people insult you, persecute you and falsely say all kinds of evil against you because of me. Rejoice and be [exceedingly] glad, because great is your reward in heaven, for in the same way they persecuted the prophets who were before you" (Matt. 5:10–12; see also John 15:18–25).

Paul said the same thing: "We must go through many hardships to enter the kingdom of God" (Acts 14:22). Paul told Timothy, "In fact, everyone who wants to live a godly life in Christ Jesus will be persecuted. . . . If we endure [suffer], we will also reign with him" (2 Tim. 3:12; 2:12).

James, the brother of the Lord, said the same thing: "Consider it pure joy, my brothers, whenever you face trials of many kinds, because you know that the testing of your faith develops perseverance" (James 1:2–3). Then he declared, "Blessed is the man who perseveres under trial, because when he has stood the test, he will receive the crown of life that God has promised to those who love him" (James 1:12).

Peter spoke similarly: "Dear friends, do not be surprised at the painful trial you are suffering, as though something strange were happening to you. But rejoice that you participate in the sufferings of Christ, so that you may be overjoyed when his glory is revealed. If you are insulted because of the name of Christ, you are blessed, for the Spirit of glory and of God rests on you" (1 Pet. 4:12–14). John said the same thing: "Do not be surprised, my brothers, if the world hates you" (1 John 3:13).

Therefore, if any evangelist or minister tells sinners to receive Jesus so that all their problems may disappear, and promises that they will obtain health, wealth, power, and glory in this world, he is a fraud. He is lining his pocket with the money of the suffering of others. He is a pseudo-evangelist, and his gospel is a different gospel, a lie from Satan.

The Purpose of Suffering

Paul says, "We suffer with him in order that . . ." When Christians suffer, their afflictions are meaningful. The godly suffer for a purpose. Through God-ordained sufferings, God forms in them the character of his Son Jesus Christ. In other words, afflictions work for the good of conforming us to the image of Christ: "And we know that in all things God works for the good of those who love him, who have been called according to his purpose. For those God foreknew he also predestined to be conformed to the likeness of his Son" (Rom. 8:28–29).

God has purposed from all eternity to make us holy and blameless so that we can enjoy eternal holy communion with him. "He chose us in him before the creation of the world to be holy and blameless in his sight" (Eph. 1:4). Jesus Christ "loved the church and gave himself up for her to make her holy, cleansing her by the washing with water through the word, and to present her to himself as a radiant church, without stain or wrinkle or any other blemish, but holy and blameless" (Eph. 5:25–27). Paul elsewhere speaks of God as being "able to keep [us] from falling and to present [us] before his glorious presence without fault and with great joy" (Jude 24).

God has the following purposes in suffering:

1. *Suffering is educative.* God's sons are loved and disciplined for their good that they may share in his holiness (Heb. 12:7–14). Without holiness no one will see God.
2. *Suffering is productive.* It results in something. "We rejoice in sufferings also because we know sufferings produce endurance; endurance, proven character; and proven character, hope of the glory of God" (Rom. 5:3–5, author's translation). Sufferings help us hope for heaven and make us let go of the world and its allurements. "For our light and momentary troubles are achieving for us an eternal glory that far outweighs them all" (2 Cor. 4:17). It is time that we valued suffering. "You know that the testing of your faith develops perseverance" (James 1:3).
3. *Suffering is corrective.* The psalmist declares, "Before I was afflicted I went astray, but now I obey your word" (Ps. 119:67; see also 2 Cor. 1:5–9).
4. *Suffering is purificatory.* "I will refine them like silver and test them like gold. They will call on my name and I will answer them; I will say, 'They are my people,' and they will say, 'The LORD is our God'" (Zech. 13:9). Peter states, "In this you greatly rejoice, though now for a little while you may have had to suffer grief in all kinds of trials. These have come so that your faith—of greater worth than gold, which perishes even though refined by fire—may be proved genuine and may result in praise, glory and honor when Jesus Christ is revealed" (1 Pet. 1:6–7).
5. *Suffering reveals the faithfulness of God.* "I know, O LORD, that your laws are righteous, and in faithfulness you have afflicted me" (Ps. 119:75).
6. *Suffering causes us to discover the comfort of the Scriptures.* "If your law had not been my delight, I would have perished in my affliction" (Ps. 119:92). All kinds of commendations and get-well cards cannot help you. You finally must open the Book, and there you discover the comfort of the Scriptures.
7. *Suffering is also preparatory.* "If we [suffer with him], we will also reign with him" (2 Tim. 2:12). Suffering prepares us for glory.
8. *Suffering is preventive.* Paul writes, "To keep me from becoming conceited because of these surpassingly great revelations, there was given me a thorn in my flesh, a messenger of Satan, to torment me" (2 Cor. 12:7). He prayed three times for it to be removed, but God said no. But that is not all he said. He also said, "My grace is sufficient for you." Paul's suffering kept him from becoming arrogant. There are people who foolishly say that if we are suffering, we have no faith, and if only we believed, we would experience no suffering. In fact, our suffering proves the opposite. It proves we are sons who live by faith in Jesus Christ. Paul says the sufferings of Christ flow over into our lives (2 Cor. 1:5). "We always carry around in our body the death of

Jesus, so that the life of Jesus may also be revealed in our body. For we who are alive are always being given over to death for Jesus' sake, so that his life may be revealed in our mortal body" (2 Cor. 4:10–11). Paul also said he wanted "to know Christ and the power of his resurrection and the fellowship of sharing in his sufferings" (Phil. 3:10).

By what power can we endure these fiery trials? We can do so, not in our own power, but by the power of God. Paul speaks of God's "incomparably great power for us who believe" (Eph. 1:19). It is the power that raised Christ from the dead. That same power raised us spiritually and will raise us also physically. This resurrection power is given to us so that we can live in this world and endure affliction. So Paul prays, "Now to him who is able to do immeasurably more than all we ask or imagine, according to his power that is at work within us . . ." (Eph. 3:20).

Why must we experience all these troubles? Why all this heat? As Dr. Lloyd-Jones said, God uses troubles like a hot iron to remove all wrinkles in our character.[3] He will have a radiant bride without any stain, spot, or wrinkle, dressed in fine linen, bright and clean. Therefore, Paul calls us to rejoice in tribulations because they prepare God's children for glory. If we are suffering now, Jesus calls us blessed and says, "Rejoice and be [exceedingly] glad, because great is your reward in heaven" (Matt. 5:10–12). Peter says, "If you are insulted because of the name of Christ, you are blessed" (1 Pet. 4:14). James says, "Blessed is the man who perseveres under trial" (James 1:12). Jesus, Peter, Paul, and James all say we are blessed! We are the most blessed people on the face of the earth.

Disappointments are truly God's appointments. The believer's suffering is not eternal, for it will end with our death. Our sufferings are light and momentary. What is eternal is glory.

Glorified with Christ

Finally, Paul ends with two words: *hina sundoxasthōmen* ("in order that we may be glorified with him"). There is a necessary connection between our present suffering and our future glory.

---

3   Lloyd-Jones, *Romans*, vol. 7, *Sons of God*, 433.

As children of God, we now suffer with Christ so that we may be glorified together with him. No pain, no gain; no cross, no crown; no suffering, no glory. Our present suffering is a stepping stone, a step up to future glory. There is a necessary order, which cannot be reversed: first suffering, then glory. Any gospel that offers glory without suffering is not true and is an abomination to the Lord.

In the midst of their sufferings, God's children rejoice in the hope of the glory of God. We alone are people of hope. The people of the world are without hope and without God in the world (Eph. 2:12). A rich man may dress in purple and dine on fine foods and party every day, but bad things are waiting for him (Luke 16). But glory is waiting for us. God has a plan for our lives: "'For I know the plans I have for you,' declares the LORD, 'plans to prosper you and not to harm you, plans to give you hope and a future'" (Jer. 29:11). We must understand that God is planning a bright and glorious future of glory for those who trust in him.

We are predestinated to glory. God sent his Son to this world that he may bring many sons to glory, and he has done it. Jesus prayed to his Father, "I have given them the glory that you gave me, that they may be one as we are one. . . . Father, I want those you have given me to be with me where I am, and to see my glory, the glory you have given me because you loved me before the creation of the world" (John 17:22, 24).

From all eternity God loved and predestinated us to be conformed to the likeness of his Son. In time, he effectually called and justified us. And those whom he justified, he also will glorify. In other words, it is a done deal. Every child of God will be glorified. What God begins, he completes. We shall be made like his own Son, that we may be with him to see his glory.

We cannot see his glory without ourselves being glorified in soul and body. John says, "We know that when he appears, we shall be like him, for we shall see him as he is" (1 John 3:2). This is speaking about our glorification. Even now, through sanctification, we are being transformed: "And we, who with unveiled faces all reflect the Lord's glory, are being transformed into his likeness with ever-increasing glory, which comes from the Lord, who is the Spirit" (2 Cor. 3:18).

We are being transformed, though outwardly we waste away through suffering (2 Cor. 4:16). We do not need any proof of that. We can look at the mirror and see it. Yet inwardly we are being renewed day by day. There is real growth. All our sufferings are producing glory. And soon our bodies will be clothed with Spirit-engineered bodies, fit to dwell in glory with God, bodies like unto the glorious body of Jesus Christ, bodies of flesh and bones. For the dead in Christ will be raised imperishable. We will be raised in glory, power, and immortality.

Our mortal bodies must by divine decree put on immortality in a flash, in the twinkling of an eye, at the last trumpet. Then we will have bodies without sin, bodies that shine like the sun. So Paul declares that Christ by his death "has destroyed death and has brought life and immortality to light through the gospel" (2 Tim. 1:10).

Glory means no sin, no sickness, no wasting away, no tears, no death, and no separation. Glory means eternal life, eternal joy, eternal peace, and eternal fellowship.

All of God's children will enjoy this glory. So Paul prayed, "And I pray that you may have power, *together with all the saints,* to grasp how wide and long and high and deep is the love of Christ" (Eph. 3:18), and later declared, "Now there is in store for me the crown of righteousness, which the Lord, the righteous Judge, will award to me on that day—*and not only to me, but also to all who have longed for his appearing*" (2 Tim. 4:8, italics added).

All creation also shall be glorified. All creation is longing to see the children of God glorified. There will be a new heaven and a new earth where dwells no sin but only righteousness, where we dwell with God and Jesus and holy angels as well as trees, animals, birds, streams, and flowers. There shall not be any rebels there, who will slander and persecute and speak falsely all manner of evil against God's people. No, only God's glory awaits us.

> He is coming soon, he is coming soon,
> with joy we welcome his returning.
> It may be morn, it may night or noon,
> we know he is coming soon.

When Christ comes, he will give us a new name and a crown of gold (Rev. 3:12; 4:4). He will give us a crown of life, a crown of righteousness, and we shall reign with him forever. We shall sit with Jesus Christ on his throne. This glory is inalienable. All things are ours in Christ.

John Piper says, "Everything that exists will serve [our] happiness."[4] As children of God, we inherit God and Christ and all creation. And we will have a heavenly home. Christ ascended into the heavens to make a home for us. We will enjoy a heavenly banquet as we rule with Christ in our glorified bodies. Then we shall sing, "Hallelujah! For our Lord God Almighty reigns. Let us rejoice and be glad and give him glory! For the wedding of the Lamb has come, and his bride has made herself ready" (Rev. 19:7).

So rejoice in your sufferings! And as you suffer, see that the Son of God is with you. For he promises, "I will be with you always, even unto the end of the ages" (Matt. 28:20). He assures us, "My grace is sufficient for you" to live a victorious Christian life. The Lord guarantees, "Never will I leave you; never will I forsake you" (Heb. 13:5). If we suffer with him, we shall also be glorified together with him. Blessed be the Lord, who blessed us with all spiritual blessing in heavenly places in Christ Jesus. Soon our suffering will end, and God will take us to glory.

---

4   John Piper, "Children, Heirs, and Fellow Sufferers," sermon April 21, 2002, http://www.desiringgod.org/resource-library/sermons/children-heirs-and-fellow-sufferers

48

Our Hope of Glory

I consider that our present sufferings are not worth comparing with the glory that will be revealed in us.

Romans 8:18

In this world, all of us experience all kinds of troubles—financial problems, physical sickness, work difficulties, or marriage and family troubles. Paul reminds us about the hope of glory that Christians have in the midst of their problems: "*For I reason that our present sufferings are not worth comparing with the glory that will be revealed in us*" (v. 18, author's translation). The glory that will be revealed in us is incomparable. That is, our present sufferings cannot be in any way compared with the great and grand future God has planned for us from all eternity.

The Sufferings of Unbelievers

Ours is a fallen world of misery. All people suffer here because of sin. But the children of God wait eagerly to enter into the glory promised them by Christ, who died and rose again. Only the children of God possess this hope of glory. If a person refuses to bow down to King Jesus and treats Christ as a gnat, he has no hope. He is without hope because he is without the true and living God.

This life of suffering is the best life that unbelievers will ever experience. They may believe in the evolutionary hypothesis and inevitable progress of man, but the truth is that they are hopeless pessimists. So they go to parties to eat, drink, and be merry, for they are about to die. They cannot face death as believers can. Paul says, "Brothers, we do not want you to be ignorant about those who fall asleep, or to grieve like the rest of men, who have no hope" (1 Thess. 4:13). The rich man of Luke 16 dressed in purple and lived in luxury every day. But Jesus said that at death the rich man went to hell, where he was in torment and agony.

As unbelievers suffer here, they unknowingly are awaiting the greater sufferings of hell prepared for them. Unbelievers are objects of wrath prepared for destruction, while believers are objects of mercy prepared in advance for glory. If you have not believed in the only Savior, Jesus Christ, I counsel and command you to do so today. God commands all people everywhere to repent. He does not beg us: we beg him to show us mercy. Believe on the Lord Jesus Christ and join us in the way of the cross, which is also the way to glory.

For God's children, then, sufferings mark the way to glory. Sufferings prove that we are children of God. As Paul stated in verse seventeen, we are heirs of God and joint-heirs with Jesus Christ, if indeed we suffer with him in order that we may be glorified together. Now, in verse eighteen, Paul teaches us about the disproportionate sufferings and incomparable glory awaiting every Christian.

Our Disproportionate Sufferings

Our present sufferings cannot be compared to the future glory that awaits us. Only Christianity deals with the reality of the present sufferings and future glory yet to be revealed in us. Christianity alone deals with creation, fall, and redemption. Only Christians can interpret history correctly, for we have the mind of Christ. We have God's truth and renewed minds. Not all that man says is truth; only what God says is all truth and nothing but truth. Yet people do not want to read the Bible.

Paul begins, "For I reason . . ." The Greek word is *logizomai*. That means I exercise my Christian mind and I think! I am a thinking person, and I keep on thinking. Paul is saying, "I have applied my mind to study the gospel, and by reasoning I have arrived at this firm conviction and conclusion."

Remember how Paul later describes the Roman Christians: "I myself am convinced, my brothers, that you yourselves are full of goodness, complete in knowledge and competent to instruct one another" (Rom. 15:14). These believers were thinking Christians. May God help us also to think and reason, so that we may enjoy the comfort of the Scriptures.

This word is also used by the Hebrews author: "Abraham reasoned that God could raise the dead" (Heb. 11:19). He reasoned in light of what God had spoken to him, and his reasoning helped him conclude that God must raise Isaac from the dead. This is sound thinking.

The complaining Israelites in the desert were a burden to Moses. They moaned that they had no grain, no grapes, no figs, no pomegranates, and no water (Num. 20:5). But thinking Christians realize that they have God with them, who is able to provide water, bread, meat, and any other thing they could possibly need (Num. 11; see also Matt. 6:25–33). Are you a thinking Christian? The hope of glory belongs to thinking Christians; therefore, study the word of God.

Romans 8:18 speaks of the sufferings of the present age. There are two ages: this present evil age, and the glorious coming age. Jesus taught that the latter belongs only to the children of the resurrection: "The people of this age marry and are given in marriage. *But those who are considered worthy of taking part in that age* and in the resurrection from the dead will neither marry nor be given in marriage, and they can no longer die; for they are like the angels. They are God's children, since they are children of the resurrection" (Luke 20:34–36, italics added).

In this present evil age, all people experience sufferings. This will continue until the end of time. For believers, this suffering will only last until our deaths. Our sufferings include suffering for Christ, but we also experience all sorts of other sufferings in this fallen world. For example, the pain of childbirth is a direct result of sin entering into the world. Additionally, we can eat only by the sweat of our brow. Because of the intrusion of sin into the world, we now are subject to sickness, weakness, poverty, disappointments, betrayal, war, plagues, famine, and death.

Sin is so horrible. The one sin of one man, Adam, caused sin and death to come on all his descendants. Even now you may be reflecting on your sins and saying, "I should have listened. I should not have done it." But you did, and now you are paying the consequences. Sin never pays. Sin brought terrible suffering into this world, and Christians are not exempt from it. Some argue that Christians are exempt from sufferings. If you have not already, you will soon find out that this is not true.

Our Incomparable Glory

Paul concludes that the sufferings of this present age cannot be compared to the glory that is about to be displayed in us. There is no comparison. Soon God is going to put his suffering saints on display. Soon they will share in the glory of God's Son. We were in Adam, and we shared in his sin and death. Now we are in Christ, and we share in his life and in his glory.

Not all professing Christians will be glorified. Only God's elect true believers will share in the coming glory. "The Lord knows those who are his" (2 Tim. 2:19). There will be a final separation of sheep from goats, and false professors will be told by Jesus, "Depart from me; I never knew you." We are destined to glory in the coming age, while the unbelievers are destined to everlasting shame.

In Adam, all sinned and came short of the glory of God. In Christ, we share in his glory. Soon we shall be glorified together with him. In the meantime, we suffer. But these sufferings are nothing when weighed in a balance. Our sufferings are revealed to be very light and our future glory very heavy. The scale pan of suffering will go straight up and that of glory will come straight down.

Paul was realistic about suffering, having experienced a great deal of it:

> Are they servants of Christ? (I am out of my mind to talk like this.) I am more. I have worked much harder, been in prison more frequently, been flogged more severely, and been exposed to death again and again. Five times I received from the Jews the forty lashes minus one. Three times I was beaten with rods, once I was stoned, three times I was shipwrecked, I spent a night and a day in the open sea, I have been constantly on the move. I have been in danger from rivers, in danger from bandits, in danger from my own countrymen, in danger from Gentiles; in danger in the city, in danger in the country, in

danger at sea; and in danger from false brothers. I have labored and toiled and have often gone without sleep; I have known hunger and thirst and have often gone without food; I have been cold and naked. Besides everything else, I face daily the pressure of my concern for all the churches. Who is weak, and I do not feel weak? Who is led into sin, and I do not inwardly burn? (2 Cor. 11:23–29)

Yes, Paul suffered greatly. But he knew it was nothing compared with the great glory that was awaiting him. Therefore he wrote:

Who shall separate us from the love of Christ? Shall trouble or hardship or persecution or famine or nakedness or danger or sword? As it is written: "For your sake we face death all day long; we are considered as sheep to be slaughtered." No, in all these things we are more than conquerors through him who loved us. For I am convinced that neither death nor life, neither angels nor demons, neither the present nor the future, nor any powers, neither height nor depth, nor anything else in all creation, will be able to separate us from the love of God that is in Christ Jesus our Lord. (Rom. 8:35–39; see also 2 Cor. 4:16–18)

Think about these things. When we use our reasoning, we see our sufferings as light, temporary, and productive of glory. Glory is most heavy, solid, eternal, and unimaginable. So Paul says, "Not only so, but we also rejoice in our sufferings, because we know that suffering produces perseverance; perseverance, character; and character, hope. And hope does not disappoint us, because God has poured out his love into our hearts by the Holy Spirit, whom he has given us" (Rom. 5:3–5). This glory is guaranteed by the presence of the Holy Spirit in us: "And if the Spirit of him who raised Jesus from the dead is living in you, he who raised Christ from the dead will also give life to your mortal bodies through his Spirit, who lives in you" (Rom. 8:11).

This is not mere positive thinking. The Spirit of God dwells in us and points us toward our home in heaven and glory. "And hope does not disappoint us." In this world, hope disappoints us. We elect a president or governor who says he will take care of us, but he disappoints. Our spouses or children make promises, but we cannot count on them to fulfill them. All the promises of this world can disappoint us. But this hope will never disappoint us, because it is guaranteed by the indwelling Holy Spirit. Where the Holy Spirit dwells, there is hope, love, peace, power, confidence, faith, and joy. So Paul writes, "May the God of hope fill you with all joy and peace as you trust in him, so that you may overflow with hope by the power of the Holy Spirit" (Rom. 15:13). The Holy Spirit releases into us this great hope of the glory of God. We can look at ourselves and say, "I have glory waiting for me."

Soon Christians, who are despised by the world, will be honored by God as he puts us on display in glory in our glorious resurrection bodies. We are waiting for our manifestation and revelation as the glorious ones. "When Christ, who is your life, appears, then you will also appear with him in glory" (Col. 3:4). As the Lord asserts, "Then the righteous will shine like the sun in the kingdom of their Father" (Matt. 13:43).

Paul saw this shining glory in Christ when he appeared to Paul on the road to Damascus: "As I was on the road, I saw a light from heaven, brighter than the sun, blazing around me and my companions" (Acts 26:13). This same glory of Christ will be manifested in us when Christ comes again: "Our citizenship is in heaven. And we eagerly await a Savior from there, the Lord Jesus Christ, who, by the power that enables him to bring everything under his control, will transform our lowly bodies so that they will be like his glorious body" (Phil. 3:20–21). "This will happen when the Lord Jesus is revealed from heaven in blazing fire with his powerful angels" (2 Thess. 1:7). The ultimate end of our salvation in Christ is not suffering but glory. We shall be made perfect and glorious in body, soul, and spirit. In fact, in Christ we shall be made more glorious than Adam ever was before the fall.

Friends, if you are not suffering now, you will. Your Bible understanding and reasoning in the Scriptures should alert you that it is coming. Therefore, do not be surprised when it comes. Expect suffering, because it is productive of glory. Yet when it comes, do not doubt God's love for you, but know that he loves his people through sufferings. Do not be shaken and doubt God's power. Do not become bitter and hold a grudge against God. Understand that God is preparing you for glory by removing all impurities from you by these fiery tribulations.

As Peter writes, "In this you greatly rejoice, though now for a little while you may have had to suffer grief in all kinds of trials. These have come so that your faith—of greater worth than gold, which perishes even though refined by fire—may be proved genuine and may result in praise, glory and honor when Jesus Christ is revealed" (1 Pet. 1:6–7). Our sufferings are meaningful, therefore, because they produce glory. When Paul says, "All things work together for good" (Rom. 8:28, KJV), he is referring especially to sufferings, not prosperity.

On that day when Christ returns in glory the unbelievers will also be displayed, but in great shame. Those who believed in a godless, closed-system philosophy will suddenly see the Lord of the universe, whom they shut out from their thinking. "Then he will say to those on his left, 'Depart from me, you who are cursed, into the eternal fire prepared for the devil and his angels.' . . . Then they will go away to eternal punishment, but the righteous to eternal life" (Matt. 25:41, 46). Eternal shame and eternal fire.

Unbelievers, therefore, have a hellish prospect, but believers have a heavenly one. We enjoy the hope of glory. Abraham looked forward "to the city with foundations, whose architect and builder is God" (Heb. 11:10). Moses also shared this hope, as do all God's people living in this present age. Jesus himself had this hope, as the Hebrews writer declares: "Let us fix our eyes on Jesus, the author and perfecter of our faith, who for the joy set before him endured the cross, scorning its shame, and sat down at the right hand of the throne of God" (Heb. 12:2).

This hope of glory enables us to endure our present sufferings, as Jesus did. Dr. Martyn Lloyd-Jones says:

> Hope is the measure of true Christianity, which is through and through other-worldly. Pseudo-Christianity always looks chiefly at this world. Popular Christianity is entirely this-worldly and is not interested in the other world. But true Christianity has its eye mainly on the world which is to come. It is not primarily concerned even with deliverance from hell, and punishment, and all the things that trouble and worry us. That really belongs to the past. True Christianity 'sets its affection on things which are above, not on things which are on the earth'. It is that which says, 'We look not at the things which are seen, but at the things which are not seen: for the things which are

seen are temporal, but the things which are not seen are eternal'
(2 Cor. 4:17 and 18).[1]

We are people of hope, not of depression, fear, anxiety, misery, and complaining. We must reason from the Scriptures: sufferings are real, but glory is also real, and our sufferings will soon end. They are temporary, but glory is eternal. Glory means eternal fellowship with God and God's people in a new heaven and a new earth.

The sufferings we experience in this world—the slander and persecution, the pain and deprivation, the sickness and loneliness—all have purpose. They help us to pray. They cause us to not be worldly and trust in this fallen world. They prepare us to yearn for our true home, where Jesus has gone to prepare a place for us. He is coming again to take us to be with him and will clothe us with his glory, in which we share because we are his bride. He is coming again so that we may be with him to see his glory.

Jesus is coming again to give us a crown of righteousness: Paul writes, "Now there is in store for me the crown of righteousness, which the Lord, the righteous Judge, will award to me on that day—and not only to me, but also to all who have longed for his appearing" (2 Tim. 4:8). He is coming again to give us a crown of glory: "And when the Chief Shepherd appears, you will receive the crown of glory that will never fade away" (1 Pet. 5:4). He is coming again to give us a crown of life: "Do not be afraid of what you are about to suffer. I tell you, the devil will put some of you in prison to test you, and you will suffer persecution for ten days. Be faithful, even to the point of death, and I will give you the crown of life" (Rev. 2:10). Jesus wore a crown of thorns. He became a curse that we may wear a crown of glory.

Jesus is coming again to give us a kingdom and authority and rule and power and dignity: "Then the King will say to those on his right, 'Come, you who are blessed by my Father; take your inheritance, the kingdom prepared for you since the creation of the world'" (Matt. 25:34; see also Luke 12:32). So do not worry about sufferings. Look by faith to the coming glory.

---

1   Lloyd-Jones, *Romans*, vol. 8, *Final Perseverance of the Saints*, 104.

This glory comes to us from without. In Adam we sinned and lost all glory. But Jesus Christ, the obedient servant, dealt with all our sins on the cross to give us his glory. To this end God foreknew and predestinated us in eternity. To this end he called us effectually and justified us in time that we all may be glorified when Jesus comes again. He is coming again for the revelation of the sons of God. This glory is coming toward us and it will never miss us. This glory shall be in us. The Holy Spirit is already in us, pointing us daily toward this heavenly prospect through the Scriptures, sacraments, worship, and fellowship.

So Paul says, "[The Father's] intent was that now, through the church, the manifold wisdom of God should be made known to the rulers and authorities in the heavenly realms" (Eph. 3:10). The wisdom of God will be revealed in us. "Oh, the depth of the riches of the wisdom and knowledge of God! How unsearchable his judgments, and his paths beyond tracing out!" (Rom. 11:33). God's eternal intention is to bring us to glory.

Jesus said, "In this world you will have trouble. But take heart! I have overcome the world" (John 16:33). Therefore, while we suffer and groan, may our minds dwell on our heavenly prospect of glory. Then we can say with Paul: *"I reason that our present sufferings are not worth comparing with the glory that will be revealed in us."* There is no comparison.

49

The Coming Glorious Earth Day

¹⁹The creation waits in eager expectation for the sons of God to be revealed. ²⁰For the creation was subjected to frustration, not by its own choice, but by the will of the one who subjected it, in hope ²¹that the creation itself will be liberated from its bondage to decay and brought into the glorious freedom of the children of God.

²²We know that the whole creation has been groaning as in the pains of childbirth right up to the present time.

Romans 8:19–22

As we study this next passage in Romans 8, let us keep in mind that we are coming together to reason, consider, understand, and exercise our minds in the word of God. Possibly the greatest biblical expositor of the last century, Dr. Martyn Lloyd-Jones, said this about churchgoing people: "And they come to the church; all they want is a ministry of comfort, a pleasing, soothing atmosphere. They want a bright service, a spice of entertainment, something to help them, something to soothe and comfort them. Suddenly, they are confronted by a man standing in a pulpit who preaches about a holy God who hates sin and who is full of wrath against sin. And they say; 'Things were bad enough already; this is but making it worse. I wanted some comfort.' But that is the answer of the gospel; there is no comfort except to those who are in Christ Jesus. There is no comfort except to those who believe that Jesus is the Son of God, that He died to make atonement for our sins, that He was buried, that He literally rose triumphant o'er the grave, having conquered the last enemy, and that He has ascended through the heavens. If you do not believe that, this passage has nothing to say to you."[1]

Dr. Lloyd-Jones also stated, "The business of preaching is not merely to make the hearer to feel a little happier while he is listening or while he is singing particular hymns; it is not meant to be a way of producing an atmosphere of comfort. If I do that I am a quack and am a very false friend indeed. No, the business of preaching is to teach you to think."[2] So let us exercise our minds to understand the word of God.

Paul taught in Romans 8:18 that our present sufferings cannot in any way be compared to the magnitude of our future glory. Let us consider from Romans 8:19–22 about the coming glorious "Earth Day." This section teaches that the whole creation is going to share in this coming glory. This is the theology of the hope of creation. One sin of one man (Adam) brought death and destruction, not only to the whole human race, but also to the environment. So Paul speaks of the creation four times in these four verses. "Creation" here means animate and inanimate subhuman creation. "The creation" (*ktsis*) has particular reference especially to this earth, as we read in Genesis 1:1–2.

Redemption of Our Environment

In this passage, creation refers to our environment. God has a wonderful plan both for us and for our environment: "'For I know the plans I have for you,' declares the LORD, 'plans to prosper you and not to harm you, plans to give you hope and a future'" (Jer. 29:11). Paul declares, "And we know that in all things God works for the good of those who love him, who have been called according to his purpose. For those God foreknew he also predestined to be conformed to the likeness of his Son, that he might be the firstborn among many brothers. And those he predestined, he also called; those he called, he also justified; those he justified, he also glorified" (Rom. 8:28–30).

---

1   Lloyd-Jones, *Romans*, vol. 8, *Final Perseverance of the Saints*, 26.
2   Ibid., 24.

Professor John Frame says of God's plan of redemption for our environment, "Remember, the consummation of human existence does not take us above and beyond the physical. Rather, as with Jesus' resurrection body, our existence in the new heavens and the new earth will be physical. There will be eating and drinking (Luke 22:18; Rev. 19:9; 22:1–2) and travel through a city with streets (Rev. 21:10–11, 21–26)."[3]

God has a plan both for us and for our environment, and we should do everything we can to save trees and whales and the planet. But the truth is that sinful man cannot save his environment. Creation's hope of glory is not in man but in Christ. In a sense, then, creation believes in Jesus Christ to transform it. It is not human environmentalists but Jesus Christ who will ultimately save his planet.

There is a grand and glorious Earth Day celebration coming, when all creation, including this earth, will enjoy maximum salvation and glory together with the glory of God, for the destiny of creation is linked with the glorious destiny of the children of God. In contrast, the destiny of everyone who refuses to bow down to Jesus Christ is eternal suffering. If one does not bow his knees to Christ and confess him as Lord, he has no hope of glory. The creation hopes in Christ for its own liberation from futility.

Creation Eagerly Awaits

"*The creation is on tiptoes, creation is craning its neck, in eager anticipation of the glorious revelation of the sons of God*" (v. 19, author's paraphrase). As sons of God, we are led by the Holy Spirit. We are sons by divine adoption, heirs of God and co-heirs of Christ. We will suffer with Christ so that we may also be glorified together with him (see vv. 14–18).

In some sense it seems that creation is aware of the coming glorification of God's children. As the father of the prodigal son was eagerly looking out for his son to come home, the creation is expecting our imminent change. The sin of Adam affected all of creation, including all non-rational, subhuman creation.

---

3   Frame, *Salvation Belongs to the Lord*, 292–93.

But creation is not longing for self-liberation or liberation by man. Creation is longing for God to glorify it as he glorifies his children.

How hideous, repulsive, and destructive the original sin of Adam was! The effects of this one man's one sin extend to all humans and to the entire world. That is why we counsel people to avoid sin by all means. Flee from all kinds of sin! All the pleasures of sin are for a moment; then comes pain, misery, and destruction.

In Romans 8:19–22, creation is personified as an entity that is longing for, hoping for, and expecting from Jesus a glorious future for itself and for us. This personification of creation is an Old Testament phenomenon. We find it in Jeremiah's prophecy: "Therefore the earth will mourn and the heavens above grow dark, because I have spoken and will not relent, I have decided and will not turn back" (Jer. 4:28). Elsewhere the Lord says, "How long will the land lie parched and the grass in every field be withered? Because those who live in it are wicked, the animals and birds have perished" (Jer. 12:4). Here we see how creation suffers because of man's sin. Isaiah says, "You will go out in joy and be led forth in peace; the mountains and hills will burst into song before you, and all the trees of the field will clap their hands" (Isa. 55:12).

The psalmist says, "The grasslands of the desert overflow; the hills are clothed with gladness. The meadows are covered with flocks and the valleys are mantled with grain; they shout for joy and sing" (Ps. 65:12–13).

Here in Romans 8 Paul is personifying inanimate and animate non-rational creation, saying that creation itself is hoping for its redemption. Both creation and Christians are anticipating their coming glory. Creation is not hoping in man or in man's evolutionary hypothesis; it is hoping for its deliverance by Jesus Christ. Creation is eagerly looking for the now-despised Christians to be revealed in glory, that it also may be glorified.

Matter has never been evil, for God himself created it and called it very good. Therefore, the new paradise will consist of matter. There is going to be regeneration not only of God's elect but also of the entire universe.

Creation Subjected to Futility

"For to futility creation was subjected, not by its fault but by reason of him who subjected it in hope" (v. 20, author's translation). When man sinned, he was punished. As a result of Adam's sin, we must work hard to eat, women deliver children in pain, and all people must die. But man was also punished by God's subjecting all creation to futility.

Paul helps us define futility: "So I tell you this, and insist on it in the Lord, that you must no longer live as the Gentiles do, in the *futility* of their thinking" (Eph. 4:17). Unbelievers are incapable of thinking correctly, that is, they can never think God's thoughts after him.

God subjected creation to such futility to punish man. Because of this subjugation, creation itself cannot achieve its own God-intended destiny. According to Professor John Murray, Romans 8:19-22 is Paul's commentary on Genesis 3:17-19,[4] in which we read: "To Adam he said, 'Because you listened to your wife and ate from the tree about which I commanded you, "You must not eat of it," Cursed is the ground because of you; through painful toil you will eat of it all the days of your life. It will produce thorns and thistles for you, and you will eat the plants of the field. By the sweat of your brow you will eat your food until you return to the ground, since from it you were taken; for dust you are and to dust you will return.'"

God cursed the ground to punish Adam and all mankind. This subjection to frustration and futility was not God's original plan for his creation. Because of man's sin, it was cursed to emptiness, purposelessness, meaninglessness, and disappointment.

What is frustration? It is like climbing a greased pole; all attempts to reach the top fail. Yet in his common grace God enables the earth to produce food for man if he works hard. God's sun shines on it and his rain falls on it.

Notice certain facts from Romans 8:20:

1. God, not Satan or man, subjected creation to futility.
2. God subjected all subhuman creation to futility.
3. God subjected it in hope of a glorious future.

---

4   Murray, *Epistle to the Romans*, 303.

4. This subjection, therefore, is temporary, occurring between the fall and the second coming of Christ.
5. Creation will be glorified when Christ returns in manifest glory.
6. The children of God will also be revealed in glory at that time.
7. This subjection to futility was not due to creation's sin but to punish man who sinned. So when man is glorified, God will also glorify man's environment.

Because of the curse, creation is now filled with thorns, thistles, pests, plagues, infertilities, famines, dust bowls, global warming, global cooling, decay, and entropy. In fact, the universe itself is running down and dying. It is going from order to disorder. There are earthquakes, volcanoes, and tsunamis. Change and decay all around us we see.

But God subjected creation to this frustration in hope. The entire creation possesses an eschatological destiny of glory. Paradise will be restored. To understand this truth, we must read carefully the divine record as found in Genesis 1–11.

The Liberation of Creation

"The creation itself will be liberated from the slavery of decay [that is, slavery consisting in corruption]. It will be delivered into the freedom of the glory of the children of God" (v. 21, author's translation). Verse twenty told us that the creation was subjected to frustration *in hope*. Verse twenty-one reveals what that hope is: It is liberation from slavery to corruption and deliverance into the coming freedom of the glory of God's children. This hope will not make us ashamed.

Man's sin must be atoned for. But who can do it? No human or angel can, so God sent his own Son in the likeness of sinful man to be a sin offering. Christ died for our sins and was raised for our justification (Rom. 4:25). God in Christ solved our sin problem once and forever. So man is liberated from the penalty of sin. So too his environment will be set free from its subjection to futility, slavery, and decay. The ill effects of man's sin extended to all creation; therefore, the good effects of his God-given gracious salvation must also reach his environment, the whole of creation, especially this planet Earth. There is coming a day, an Earth Day, when there shall be no more ecological imbalance due to human greed. There shall only be beauty and harmony beyond all human imagination.

Isaiah foresaw this fulfillment of God's plan for creation:

> The wolf will live with the lamb, the leopard will lie down with the goat, the calf and the lion and the yearling together; and a little child will lead them. The cow will feed with the bear, their young will lie down together, and the lion will eat straw like the ox. The infant will play near the hole of the cobra, and the young child put his hand into the viper's nest. They will neither harm nor destroy on all my holy mountain, for the earth will be full of the knowledge of the LORD as the waters cover the sea. (Isa. 11:6–9)

> The desert and the parched land will be glad; the wilderness will rejoice and blossom. Like the crocus, it will burst into bloom; it will rejoice greatly and shout for joy. The glory of Lebanon will be given to it, the splendor of Carmel and Sharon; they will see the glory of the LORD, the splendor of our God. (Isa. 35:1–2)

> "Behold, I will create new heavens and a new earth. The former things will not be remembered, nor will they come to mind. But be glad and rejoice forever in what I will create, for I will create Jerusalem to be a delight and its people a joy. I will rejoice over Jerusalem and take delight in my people; the sound of weeping and of crying will be heard in it no more. Never again will there be in it an infant who lives but a few days, or an old man who does not live out his years; he who dies at a hundred will be thought a mere youth; he who fails to reach a hundred will be considered accursed. They will build houses and dwell in them; they will plant vineyards and eat their fruit. No longer will they build houses and others live in them, or plant and others eat. For as the days of a tree, so will be the days of my people; my chosen ones will long enjoy the works of their hands. They will not toil in vain or bear children doomed to misfortune; for they will be a people blessed by the LORD, they and their descendants with them. Before they call I will answer; while they are still speaking I will hear. The wolf and the lamb will feed together, and the lion will eat straw like the ox, but dust will be the serpent's food. They will neither harm nor destroy on all my holy mountain," says the LORD. (Isa. 65:17–25)

There will be no more killing, cruelty, hatred, or war. Jesus himself spoke of this new world order: "I tell you the truth, at the renewal of all things . . ." (Matt. 19:28). Things are not in order. Everything is dying. But there is going to be a renewal, a restoration, of all things, both of man and of his environment. Jesus' disciples asked the risen Lord, "Lord, are you at this time going to restore the kingdom to Israel?" (Acts 1:6). And Peter explained, "[Christ] must remain in heaven until the time comes for God to restore everything, as he promised long ago through his holy prophets" (Acts 3:21).

God has a wonderful plan for us and for the environment. Peter says, "But in keeping with his promise we are looking forward to a new heaven and a new earth, the home of righteousness" (2 Pet. 3:13). John writes:

> Then I saw a new heaven and a new earth, for the first heaven and the first earth had passed away, and there was no longer any sea. I saw the Holy City, the new Jerusalem, coming down out of heaven from God, prepared as a bride beautifully dressed for her husband. And I heard a loud voice from the throne saying, "Now the dwelling of God is with men, and he will live with them. They will be his people, and God himself will be with them and be their God. He will wipe every tear from their eyes. There will be no more death or mourning or crying or pain, for the old order of things has passed away.". . . No longer will there be any curse. (Rev. 21:1–4; 22:3)

The creation is going to share in the glorious destiny of man. A twelve-year-old Welsh Christian girl had this verse in mind when she wrote the following in the 1860s on the day her father died: "Today Dada has left us. He has gone into the glorious liberty of the children of God."[5] She lived at a time when people thought biblically. But the truth is, her Dada is still waiting for the fullness of his glory. He will be soon glorified together with her and with us. All God's people and all creation will enter into the freedom of the glory destined for the sons of God. Christ's glory will be shared by us and our environment, this planet Earth. This is the blessed hope of the children and creation. So Paul says, "We wait for the blessed hope—the glorious appearing of our great God and Savior, Jesus Christ" (Titus 2:13), and Peter says, "Look forward to the day of God and speed its coming" (2 Pet. 3:12). We are looking forward, not to the next election, but to the coming of Christ and to our glorification and the renewal of our environment.

---

5   Lloyd-Jones, Romans, vol. 8, Final Perseverance of the Saints, 118.

We are already delivered partially. Christians "have been set free from sin and have become slaves to righteousness" (Rom. 6:18). But we shall be fully delivered from all effects of sin when God gives us the glorious body that he promised: "And if the Spirit of him who raised Jesus from the dead is living in you, he who raised Christ from the dead will also give life to your mortal bodies through his Spirit, who lives in you" (Rom. 8:11). At that time the new and glorious people of God will dwell with God in a new and glorious earth, complete with plants, flowers, birds, animals, and so on, in all its explosive beauty. There shall be no more death, no more tears, and no more bad news. Our destiny is not misery or frustration. It is glory and beauty beyond imagination. It is liberation and life. And the same is true for planet Earth. Then the glory of God shall fill the earth as the waters cover the sea, and God's original plan for us and for the planet will come to pass.

> O that will be glory for me, glory for me, glory for me.
> When by his grace I shall look at his face,
> That will be glory, be glory for me.

The Creation Groans

"*For we know that the whole creation is groaning and travailing together until now*" (v. 22, author's translation). Creation is groaning. This began at the fall, when God subjected creation to futility, slavery, and corruption because of one sin of one man one time. This groaning and travailing continues until now. It will go on until the end of this age, when Christ shall come to inaugurate the new glorious age of life, liberation, and sheer happiness.

But because God subjected creation in hope, this groaning is also in hope. John Murray said the travail of creation is "not death pangs but birth pangs."[6] Destruction of creation is not God's ultimate plan; rather, renewal and restoration are. The creation shall by God's power give birth to a new creation, a new heavens and a new earth, wherein dwells righteousness.

When man sinned, creation was cursed and man lost his rule over creation. But all this will change. The sons of God shall

---

6   Murray, *Epistle to the Romans*, 305.

share in the Son's glory, as will creation, and God shall dwell with man. Redeemed people, once again under God, will have rulership over the earth, a rulership which Adam lost. Jesus said, "Blessed are the meek, for they will inherit the earth" (Matt. 5:5). We shall inherit the earth. Rulership and authority shall be restored to us. So the writer to the Hebrews says:

> It is not to angels that he has subjected the world to come, about which we are speaking. But there is a place where someone has testified: "What is man that you are mindful of him, the son of man that you care for him? You made him a little lower than the angels; you crowned him with glory and honor and put everything under his feet." In putting everything under him, God left nothing that is not subject to him. Yet at present we do not see everything subject to him. But we see Jesus, who was made a little lower than the angels, now crowned with glory and honor because he suffered death, so that by the grace of God he might taste death for everyone. In bringing many sons to glory, it was fitting that God, for whom and through whom everything exists, should make the author of their salvation perfect through suffering. Both the one who makes men holy and those who are made holy are of the same family. So Jesus is not ashamed to call them brothers. (Heb. 2:5–11)

In Jesus Christ our authority will be restored to us. Once again we will rule the planet. In Christ, God is bringing us and the creation to glory.

If you have not bowed down to Jesus Christ, I urge you to do so today. Outside of Christ you have no hope nor prospect of glory. God commands all people everywhere to repent. The psalmist says, "Kiss the Son, lest he be angry and you be destroyed in your way, for his wrath can flare up in a moment. Blessed are all who take refuge in him" (Ps. 2:12).

In the meantime, believers are not exempt from sufferings. But thank God, the Holy Spirit, the Comforter, is given to us. He helps us in all our sufferings and causes us to rejoice always, even in tribulations.

We must aim for perfection, but do not expect it. Do not expect your computer or iPhone to work perfectly. Do not expect to have a perfect marriage, since we are still sinners. Be happy with less than perfect. Do not expect to hear a perfect sermon or find a perfect pastor. Do not expect the price of your house to always go up. Do not trust others to improve your conditions or the conditions of the planet, for not even brilliant scientists, philosophers, politicians, artists, televangelists, environmentalists, prime ministers, presidents, or those in science and technology can do it. Do not expect not to die. Do not expect any exemption from sufferings because we are believers. In fact, expect more. But do not worry: fix your eyes on Jesus, the author and finisher of our faith, who endured the cross because of the joy that was set before him.

God has a wonderful plan for us and for our environment. What a future! What a hope! I pray that we will all trust in Jesus Christ and participate in this great, grand plan of salvation.

50

Patient Waiting

23Not only so, but we ourselves, who have the firstfruits of the Spirit, groan inwardly as we wait eagerly for our adoption as sons, the redemption of our bodies. 24For in this hope we were saved. But hope that is seen is no hope at all. Who hopes for what he already has? 25But if we hope for what we do not yet have, we wait for it patiently.

Romans 8:23–25

Romans 8:23–25 teaches us about waiting with endurance, or waiting patiently. Most of us today do not know how to wait because we do not experience sufferings. We are loaded with money and comforts. We cannot even tolerate a little headache without grabbing medicine. We do not know hunger pains because we eat before we hunger.

But our God does not spoil his children. He will teach us endurance through God-ordained troubles and trials, whether we like it or not. If we are complaining and murmuring about our problems, we must learn what it means to wait with endurance. That is what Paul is telling us: "*But if we are hoping for that which we do not see, we wait for it patiently*" (v. 25, author's translation).

In paradise, Adam was warned that he must not eat from the tree of the knowledge of good and evil, "for when you eat of it you will surely die" (Gen. 2:17). But he ate from it and he died, groaning. Furthermore, all his descendants also die groaning. The second law of thermodynamics attests to the fact that the creation itself is dying. God himself subjected it to futility, slavery, and decay to punish man the sinner. But God subjected creation and the elect children of God in hope of deliverance. William Hendriksen says that temporal suffering is the result of sin, but eternal glory is the result of God's grace.[1] The proto-euangelion found in Genesis 3:15 gives hope to creation and to the children of God: "And I will put enmity between you and the woman, and between your offspring and hers; he will crush your head, and you will strike his heel."

The offspring of the woman is Jesus Christ. The Scriptures tell us that even Christ groaned and died. His substitutionary death destroyed our death and the decay of creation, and so creation and the children of God are all craning their necks, patiently awaiting the incomparable glory and splendor coming to them.

In this present age the children of God are not exempt from sufferings. But even as we together with creation groan, we do so in hope of the glory of God, which is sure and beyond all imagination in its magnitude and luminosity.

The major points in Romans 8:23–25 can be summarized by five Greek words found in the text: *stenazomen* (we groan), *echomen* (we have), *elpizomen* (we hope), *apekdechometha* (we wait), and *hupomenomen* (we endure).

We Groan

As we said in our previous study, creation is groaning and travailing in pain, in hope of giving birth to a new heaven and new earth. And Paul says that not only does creation groan, but also the children of God. We all experience the effects of sin in our lives, especially as we suffer for Christ's sake. We are hated, persecuted, and slandered. The people of God have experienced torture, jeers, flogging, and stoning. They have been chained and thrown to lions. Stephen was stoned to death, James beheaded, Paul cut down by the sword, and Peter crucified.

Our own bodies are wasting away, and soon they will die. Moses, who witnessed the deaths of thousands of his people, said, "The length of our days is seventy years—or eighty, if we have the strength; yet their span is but trouble and sorrow, for they quickly pass, and we fly away" (Ps. 90:10).

---

1   Hendriksen, *Exposition of Romans*, 264.

We must not believe televangelists who promise to heal us in exchange for a generous contribution. They do not heal, nor can they. Paul says that we suffer with Christ in order that we may be glorified together with him (Rom. 8:17). Therefore, we groan and sigh all our lives, as the Greek text indicates. We groan because of pain and persecution; but we do so privately. We keep our sighs to ourselves and God, who comforts us in all our troubles.

The Son of God groaned at the tomb of Lazarus. He groaned as he encountered death; he groaned at the great sorrow caused by death; and he groaned at the wicked unbelief of the people. "When Jesus saw [Mary] weeping, and the Jews who had come along with her also weeping, he groaned in the spirit and was troubled" (John 11:33, author's translation). At Gethsemane he also groaned: "And being in anguish, he prayed more earnestly, and his sweat was like drops of blood falling to the ground" (Luke 22:44).

Paul speaks of his own groaning as he faced the prospect of death: "Now we know that if the earthly tent we live in is destroyed, we have a building from God, an eternal house in heaven, not built by human hands. Meanwhile we groan, longing to be clothed with our heavenly dwelling, because when we are clothed, we will not be found naked. For while we are in this tent, we groan and are burdened" (2 Cor. 5:1-4).

We Have

Both believers and unbelievers groan. But believers have something unbelievers do not have. The next word Paul uses is *echomen*, "we have" or "we possess." What is it we possess? The Holy Spirit.

Unbelievers are without God, without hope, and without eternal life. Like believers, they may grieve when someone dies, but they grieve without the hope of ever seeing the person again.

Paul says that God's children, though they possess the Holy Spirit, groan daily. This is surprising. We might expect believers, in whom the Holy Spirit dwells, not to groan at all, but to always smile and be happy. But believers in Jesus Christ, Spirit-filled believers, also groan in this life.

We desire to reach the end of our groaning and to enter the new age of perfect peace and happiness. Unlike the children of this age, the citizens of heaven groan eagerly, waiting in expectation of their full inheritance as God's sons. As children of God, who have the Holy Spirit, we are waiting for the redemption of our bodies. This is the right of God's adopted sons. We have received the spirit of adoption. And because we are sons of God, our bodies are dead because of sin but our spirits are alive because of the righteousness of Christ. But, thank God, God has a salvation plan for our bodies also.

As God raised Jesus from the dead by the power of the Holy Spirit, so will he also raise us up by the operation of the indwelling Spirit of Christ. The resurrection of Christ is the guarantee of our resurrection. The indwelling Holy Spirit also guarantees our resurrection and transformation. Take heart, friends, our groaning is temporal. Our final destiny is not groaning but glory. We suffer now that we might be glorified later.

Romans 8:23 tells us we are children of God by adoption. Adoption has three phases. First, God elects us to adoption from all eternity: "For he chose us in him before the creation of the world to be holy and blameless in his sight. In love he predestined us to be adopted as his sons through Jesus Christ" (Eph. 1:4–5). In time and history, God adopts us by giving us his Holy Spirit: "For you did not receive a spirit that makes you a slave again to fear, but you received the Spirit of [adoption, by whom] we cry, 'Abba, Father'" (Rom. 8:15). That is the second phase. But the third phase is coming. When Christ is revealed in all his glory, we shall also be revealed in glory. We shall be revealed as sons when we inherit the Son's full inheritance of a glorified body.

Yet now we are groaning. Even though we have the Holy Spirit, we groan, earnestly anticipating our adoption, the redemption of our bodies.

There are several implications of this wonderful truth that we have the Holy Spirit.

1. We have the Holy Spirit as a seal, *sphragis*. "And you also were included in Christ when you heard the word of truth, the gospel of your salvation. Having believed, you were marked in him with a seal, the promised Holy Spirit" (Eph. 1:13). There is a mark on us, identifying that we belong to God. "[God] set his seal of

ownership on us, and put his Spirit in our hearts as a deposit, guaranteeing what is to come" (2 Cor. 1:22). God has sealed all his children with the Holy Spirit. We cannot belong to Christ without this mark, this seal, this branding. In other words, we cannot be Christians without the Holy Spirit dwelling in us.

a. This seal of the Holy Spirit shows we are God's portion and inheritance. "For the LORD's portion is his people, Jacob his allotted inheritance" (Deut. 32:9). We are God's treasure, and he is ours. "And they shall be mine, saith the LORD of hosts, in that day when I make up my jewels; and I will spare them, as a man spareth his own son that serveth him" (Mal. 3:17, KJV). Think about it. We are God's precious jewels.

b. This Spirit-seal shows that God is our owner. Once we belonged to Satan, but no more. Oh, what dignity we now have! We belong to God.

c. This seal of the Holy Spirit also shows that we are secure in God. Our heavenly Father sees to it that no harm can come to us. God's treasured jewels are forever secure. May we rejoice in our secure salvation!

d. The seal of the Holy Spirit also distinguishes us from the godless and wicked people of the world, and authenticates us as God's true children. Holy Spirit-filled children of God will live holy lives.

2. We have the Holy Spirit as the *aparchē*, the "firstfruits" (v. 23). This is an agricultural metaphor. Firstfruits points to and guarantees a harvest, in this case a harvest consisting of the full salvation not only of our spirits but also of our bodies. God will give us glorious, sinless, physical bodies. Jesus himself is spoken of as the firstfruits in 1 Corinthians 15:20 and 23, and the resurrection of Christ guarantees the resurrection of all who belong to him.

3. Not only that, the Holy Spirit is also described as a deposit, *arrabōn*. This is a commercial metaphor. The Holy Spirit is a down payment guaranteeing the final payment that will complete the transaction. As the down payment, the Holy Spirit guarantees the full salvation of our spirits, souls, and bodies when Jesus comes again.

Therefore, as believers in Christ, who have the seal, the firstfruits, and the deposit consisting in the Holy Spirit, we are guaranteed of our full inheritance, the redemption of our bodies. This is why we rejoice in the hope of the glory of God. "And hope does not disappoint us, because God has poured out his love into our hearts by the Holy Spirit, whom he has given us" (Rom. 5:5).

The Holy Spirit has set us free from the law of sin and death, and we now walk according to the Spirit. The Holy Spirit permanently dwells in us and leads us in our spiritual journey. "For as many as are being led by the Spirit of God, they are the sons of God" (Rom. 8:14, author's translation). We are the temple of the Holy Spirit, who is the Spirit of the Lord—the Spirit of wisdom and counsel, the Spirit of knowledge and understanding, the Spirit of power, and the Spirit who produces in us true fear of God that keeps us from sinning (Isa. 11:2–3).

This Holy Spirit we possess is our other Comforter and Shepherd. He is the one who convicts us when we sin. He always glorifies Jesus Christ. So even though we groan in our present sufferings, that is not all we do. By the Spirit of God, we rejoice in tribulations also. We rejoice always, for the joy of the Lord is our strength, and the fruit of the Spirit is joy. Even now in our suffering, we are filled with an inexpressible and glorious joy in view of the coming redemption of our bodies.

We Hope

The third word Paul uses is *elpizomen*, "we hope." Christians are people of hope, and our hope will not disappoint us. The Philippian jailer asked, "What must I do to be saved?" Paul replied, "Believe in the Lord Jesus, and you will be saved—you and your household" (Acts 16:30–31). Paul declares, "*For in this hope we were saved*" (v. 24). Our salvation comes to us in installments. Our spirits are alive now, but our bodies are dying. For the second installment of body-salvation we must wait. But we are saved in hope of it.

Salvation has three tenses. Paul uses the past tense in verse 24: "We *were saved* in hope." Elsewhere he speaks of our present salvation: "For the message of the cross is foolishness to those who are perishing, but to *us who are being saved*, it is the power of God" (1 Cor. 1:18). But our salvation is also future: "Since we have now been justified by his blood, how much more *shall we be saved* from God's wrath through him! For if, when we were God's enemies, we were reconciled to him through the death of his Son, how much more, having been reconciled, *shall we be saved* [in] his life!" (Rom. 5:9–10).

Therefore, if someone asks us if we are saved, we can answer, "I am saved, I am being saved, and I will be saved. I have been justified, I am being sanctified, and I will be glorified." Look at the argument: If Christ loved us and died for us when we were powerless and ungodly, when we were terrible sinners and enemies of God, how much more shall we be saved in his life now that we are justified, reconciled, and adopted as God's sons!

Jesus died to save us and he lives to save us. This hope was revealed in Genesis 3:15, when God revealed that the seed of the woman would crush Satan. Now the stronger one, Jesus, has come. He has defeated the strong one, Satan, and set us free. By his death and resurrection, Jesus defeated sin, Satan, the world, and the flesh. Soon we shall also be redeemed in our bodies, for we are saved in hope of this full salvation, which Christ has purchased for us.

Our hope is certain. There is no condition or contingency about it. And this hope shall never disappoint us, for God has guaranteed it by sending the Holy Spirit into our hearts, who daily points us to this glorious future of our full salvation.

Our present salvation is incomplete. We are half-saved, in a sense, because sin is still in us. Our outward man is wasting away. Yes, we have received the engagement ring of the Holy Spirit, but we are waiting eagerly for the wedding ring. Soon our Bridegroom will come to take his glorious bride to himself, a radiant bride without stain or wrinkle or any other blemish, but holy and blameless. Soon we shall hear the heavenly shouting:

> Then I heard what sounded like a great multitude, like the roar of rushing waters and like loud peals of thunder, shouting: "Hallelujah! For our Lord God Almighty reigns. Let us rejoice and be glad and give him glory! For the wedding of the Lamb has come, and his bride has made herself ready. Fine linen, bright and clean, was given her to wear." (Fine linen stands for the righteous acts of the saints.) Then the angel said to me, "Write: 'Blessed are those who are invited to the wedding supper of the Lamb!'" And he added, "These are the true words of God." (Rev. 19:6-9)

As our marriage approaches, we wait, not in anguish but in eagerness. Man's promise disappoints, but God will fulfill his word. Let God be true and every man a liar. So we hope in God, whose promise fills us with hope.

Our triune God is a God of hope. Paul writes, "May the God of hope fill you with all joy and peace as you trust in him, so that you may overflow with hope by the power of the Holy Spirit" (Rom. 15:13). Elsewhere Paul says he is "an apostle of Christ Jesus by the command of God our Savior and of Christ Jesus our hope" (1 Tim. 1:1).

Our God cannot lie. He is truth, and his word is truth (John 17:17). God not only promises our eternal salvation, but because we are still sinners, he confirms his promises with an oath so that we may be doubly certain of their fulfillment, as we read in Hebrews 6:

> When God made his promise to Abraham, since there was no one greater for him to swear by, he swore by himself, saying, "I will surely bless you and give you many descendants." And so after waiting patiently, Abraham received what was promised.
>
> Men swear by someone greater than themselves, and the oath confirms what is said and puts an end to all argument. Because God wanted to make the unchanging nature of his purpose very clear to the heirs of what was promised, he confirmed it with an oath. God did this so that, by two unchangeable things [promise and oath] in which it is impossible for God to lie, we who have fled to take hold of the hope offered to us may be greatly encouraged. We have this hope as an anchor for the soul, firm and secure. It enters the inner sanctuary behind the curtain, where Jesus, who went before us, has entered on our behalf. He has become a high priest forever, in the order of Melchizedek. (Heb. 6:13–20)

We were saved in hope. Our hope is based on faith in God's promises of our future final salvation. Faith substantiates hope.

This hope is not like a kite, driven by uncertain winds. Rather, it is an anchor that secures us in the eternal world. This anchor is Jesus, the Son of God, who died for our sins and was raised for our justification. Our anchor of hope has gone into the heavens into the presence of the Father to make intercession for us as high priest, and he is seated on the Father's right hand. It is his mission to save us fully, for which he is coming again. Christ our anchor stabilizes our souls and keeps them in hope. Even amid the storms of this present life, our anchor holds. Jesus Christ, who is moored to God himself, will keep our souls safe and steady. So we have great calm in the depths of our hearts. No wonder Jesus said, "Do not let your hearts be troubled" (John 14:1), and we are commanded, "Do not be anxious about anything" (Phil. 4:6).

Paul says, "In all these things we [super-conquer] through him who loved us. For I am convinced that neither death nor life, neither angels nor demons, neither the present nor the future, nor any powers, neither height nor depth, nor anything else in all creation, will be able to separate us from the love of God that is in Christ Jesus our Lord." (Rom. 8:37–39).

Dr. Martyn Lloyd-Jones says, "Hope is the measure of true Christianity, which is through and through other-worldly."[2] Paul says the hope of salvation is our helmet (1 Thess. 5:8). We think in hope, meditate in hope, labor in hope, and die in hope. We hope in God, who will grant to us the redemption of our bodies. So Paul speaks of "the faith and love that spring from the hope that is stored up for you in heaven and that you have already heard about in the word of truth, the gospel" (Col. 1:5). Peter writes, "Praise be to the God and Father of our Lord Jesus Christ! In his great mercy he has given us new birth into a living hope through the resurrection of Jesus Christ from the dead, and into an inheritance that can never perish, spoil or fade—kept in heaven for you" (1 Pet. 1:3–4). Yes, we groan, but we have the Holy Spirit, and we have hope.

We Wait

The fourth word is *apekdechometha*, "we wait." Paul writes, "*But if we hope for what we do not see, we wait for it through patience*" (v. 25, author's translation).

Pseudo-Christianity looks to this world for its fulfillment and glory. True Christians do not. We refuse to invest in the real estate of Sodom, because we are convinced that the fashion of this world is passing away. Paul declares, "This world in its present form is passing away" (1 Cor. 7:31). John says, "The world and its desires pass away, but the man who does the will of God lives forever" (1 John 2:17). Peter writes, "But in keeping with his promise we

---

2   Lloyd-Jones, *Romans*, vol. 8, *Final Perseverance of the Saints*, 104.

are looking forward to a new heaven and a new earth, the home of righteousness" (2 Pet. 3:13).

Many evangelicals today focus only on telling people how to make money. They have no interest in the world to come. But we are citizens of heaven whose hope is in the coming world. We are already seated with Christ, and even now we are storing up our treasure in heaven. Christ is our life, and we think heavenly things.

Creation waits patiently, and God's children also wait. We wait in eager expectation, as people wait expectantly for holidays to come, for their final examinations to be over, for graduation from the university, for their wedding day, or for the birth of a child.

Notice, our waiting is not passive, lazy waiting. Some Thessalonian believers were waiting for Christ to come, so they stopped working for a living. The apostle rebuked them: "If a man will not work, he shall not eat" (2 Thess. 3:10).3 We work hard while we wait, laboring six days a week, twelve hours a day.

We do business with God's talents and make a profit. To the lazy servant Jesus said, "You wicked, lazy servant! So you knew that I harvest where I have not sown and gather where I have not scattered seed? Well then, you should have put my money on deposit with the bankers, so that when I returned I would have received it back with interest" (Matt. 25:26–27). The king's business requires haste. Paul says we must not be "slothful in business" (Rom. 12:11, KJV).

Therefore, at the end of Paul's argument for the reality of the physical resurrection of Jesus Christ and our future resurrection, the apostle exhorts: "Therefore, my dear brothers, stand firm. Let nothing move you. Always give yourselves fully to the work of the Lord, because you know that your labor in the Lord is not in vain" (1 Cor. 15:58).

We wait actively. The Hebrews writer says, "And so after waiting patiently, Abraham received what was promised" (Heb. 6:15). Abraham waited twenty-five years for Isaac. Paul says, "Not that I have already obtained all this, or have already been made perfect,

---

3   This is a sound principle for governments to apply. Otherwise, those who are lazy depend on the hardworking people to support them.

but I press on to take hold of that for which Christ Jesus took hold of me. Brothers, I do not consider myself yet to have taken hold of it. But one thing I do: Forgetting what is behind and straining toward what is ahead, I press on toward the goal to win the prize for which God has called me heavenward in Christ Jesus" (Phil. 3:12–14). We must occupy until he comes.

We Endure

The last point Paul makes is that we endure. The Greek word *hupomenō* means "to stand up under" or "to bear up under" intense pressure. We can do so only by the Spirit's presence and power. Tribulations and pressures develop our spiritual muscle power. Without trials, we do not develop the ability to endure hardship. Instead, we begin to murmur, become anxious, and quit. Paul says we are to endure hardship as a good soldier (2 Tim. 2:3).

God ordains troubles. So Paul says, "Therefore put on the full armor of God, so that when the day of evil comes, you may be able to stand your ground, and after you have done everything, to stand" (Eph. 6:13). It is the idea of a wrestling match. Satan is down, but the saints of God are standing, because we are super-conquerers in the Spirit's power.

Trials produce endurance (James 1:2–3). When we lose our job, it is an opportunity to grow more in the grace and knowledge of God than ever before. Trials produce endurance and endurance produces hope. Those who suffer much endure much, hope much, and praise God much.

The Bible says many things about endurance. In fact, it says we need endurance: "You have need of endurance so that when you have done the will of God, you will receive what he has promised, the full salvation" (Heb. 10:36, author's translation). We need endurance for spiritual fruitfulness. Jesus taught, "But the seed on good soil stands for those with a noble and good heart, who hear the word, retain it, and by [endurance] produce a crop" (Luke 8:15). If we are not bearing fruit, it means we do not have endurance. God wants us to bear fruit, more fruit, and much fruit. And as we bear fruit, God will prune us so that we can bear even more fruit for him. That is what trials are designed for.

When believed, Scripture itself gives us endurance. Paul writes, "For everything that was written in the past was written to teach us, so that through endurance and the encouragement of the Scriptures we might have hope" (Rom. 15:4). We cannot read the Bible without receiving encouragement to persevere. As we see how all God's people went through the trials they endured, we also see that the Holy Spirit helps us endure. Paul wrote to Timothy, "So do not be ashamed to testify about our Lord, or ashamed of me his prisoner. But join with me in suffering for the gospel, by the power of God" (2 Tim. 1:8). He also says, "For God did not give us a spirit of timidity, but a Spirit of power, of love and of self-discipline" (2 Tim. 1:7). Peter exhorts: "Dear friends, do not be surprised at the painful trial you are suffering, as though something strange were happening to you. But rejoice that you participate in the sufferings of Christ, so that you may be overjoyed when his glory is revealed. If you are insulted because of the name of Christ, you are blessed, for the Spirit of glory and of God rests on you" (1 Pet. 4:12–14). The Holy Spirit rests on us and helps us to endure.

The Bible tells us endurance is the prerequisite for reigning with Christ. Paul says if we endure, we will also reign with him (2 Tim. 2:12). The Bible says the elect shall endure to the end. That is the doctrine of the perseverance of the saints. Jesus declared, "All men will hate you because of me, but he who stands firm to the end will be saved" (Matt. 10:22). God will help us to persevere to the end. When Jesus spoke to the church in Smyrna, he told them, "Do not be afraid of what you are about to suffer. . . . Be faithful, even to the point of death, and I will give you the crown of life" (Rev. 2:10)

Christ himself is with us always to help us endure: "And surely I am with you always, to the very end of the age" (Matt. 28:20). When Nebuchadnezzar looked at the fiery furnace, he said, "Look! I see four men walking around in the fire, unbound and unharmed, and the fourth looks like a son of the gods" (Dan. 3:25). The pre-incarnate Christ was in the fire with the three Hebrew children. Paul said, "I can do all things through Christ who strengthens me" (Phil. 4:13, KJV).

To enable us to endure and wait patiently, God gives us grace that is sufficient for all our needs. Paul declares, "And God is able to make all grace abound to you, so that in all things at all times, having all that you need, you will abound in every good work" (2 Cor. 9:8). He gives grace to humble saints. Paul writes,

> To keep me from becoming conceited because of these surpassingly great revelations, there was given me a thorn in my flesh, a messenger of Satan, to torment me. Three times I pleaded with the Lord to take it away from me. But he said to me, "My grace is sufficient for you, for my power is made perfect in weakness." Therefore I will boast all the more gladly about my weaknesses, so that Christ's power may rest on me. That is why, for Christ's sake, I delight in weaknesses, in insults, in hardships, in persecutions, in difficulties. For when I am weak, then I am strong. (2 Cor. 12:7–10)

Whatever trials you are facing, do not tell the Lord they are too burdensome. Get on your knees and cry out to God for grace.

Not only that, God may send angels to help us in our trials. "Are not all angels ministering spirits sent to serve those who will inherit salvation?" (Heb. 1:14). The Bible speaks about angels and their ministry. After tempting Jesus in the desert, the devil left him and "angels came and attended him" (Matt. 4:11). An angel from heaven appeared to Jesus as he prayed in the garden of Gethsemane, and strengthened him (Luke 22:43). The psalmist says, "For he will command his angels concerning you to guard you in all your ways; they will lift you up in their hands, so that you will not strike your foot against a stone" (Ps. 91:11–12). The ministry of angels appears throughout the Scriptures. We do not usually see angels, but they help us. Paul tells us they are present when the church gathers to worship (1 Cor. 11:10).

What Are You Waiting For?

Creation groans and travails in hope of giving birth to a new heaven and a new earth, and as God's children, we also groan in hope of the redemption of our bodies. We suffer that we may be glorified with an unimaginable glory. The sufferings of the present time can only contribute to our glory and holiness. Suffering produces endurance and endurance hope. We may pray, "O Lord, take my troubles away," and God may say, "No, the time is not yet." But when the time comes, he relieves us of our burdens.

As children, we are given the Holy Spirit, guaranteeing our final and full salvation. The Holy Spirit, the holy Scripture, and the fellowship of God's holy church all help us to wait patiently for our glorification, which, though future, yet is certain. As we wait eagerly, we will labor for the Lord, for he rewards those who are good and faithful servants. So we wait and we endure. Professor John Murray said, "Impatience spells dispute and dissatisfaction with God's design."[4]

What about you? Do you have hope? Are you waiting patiently for the redemption of all things? Those who are hopeless are fearful, anxious, and depressed. If this describes you, I counsel you to repent and believe on the Lord Jesus Christ, who died and rose again. Come to Christ in true repentance and saving faith. Then you also can enjoy the hope of the glory of God.

---

4 Murray, *Epistle to the Romans*, 310.

51

The Holy Spirit, Our Helper

26In the same way, the Spirit helps us in our weakness. We do not know what we ought to pray for, but the Spirit himself intercedes for us with groans that words cannot express. 27And he who searches our hearts knows the mind of the Spirit, because the Spirit intercedes for the saints in accordance with God's will.

Romans 8:26–27

As people of God, we all need help, because this age is one of sufferings. Paul told us to wait for the life of the age to come with endurance (Rom. 8:25). So we are waiting in hope of the glory of God—waiting for our resurrection bodies and for the new heaven and new earth, the home of righteousness.

But this hope is not the only thing that sustains us in our present sufferings. Paul tells us the Holy Spirit himself also helps us in all our weaknesses. God never leaves us nor forsakes us: "God is our refuge and strength, an ever-present help in trouble. Therefore we will not fear" (Ps. 46:1–2). Paul declares, "If God is for us, who can be against us?" (Rom. 8:31). Then he states, "In all these things we are more than conquerors through him who loved us" (Rom. 8:37). Nothing can separate us from the love of God, not even death, because God has given us the Holy Spirit.

In our previous studies of Romans 8 we learned a few things about the Holy Spirit: The law of the Spirit of life regenerated us and set us free from the law of sin and death so that we now live according to the rule of the Holy Spirit *[kata pneuma]*. As children of God, we delight in what the Holy Spirit desires; we are now controlled, not by our old sin nature, but by the Holy Spirit. The Spirit of Christ who dwells in us guarantees that he will raise us up on the last day, and even now by the power of the Spirit of God we can daily put sin to death. The Holy Spirit guides us in the way of righteousness. This Spirit is the Spirit of our adoption as sons of God and by him we boldly cry, "Abba, Father." The Holy Spirit witnesses to our spirits that we are children of God, heirs of God, and joint-heirs with Christ. The Holy Spirit is the firstfruits, pointing us to the harvest of our full and final salvation.

Now we learn from Romans 8:26–27 that this Holy Spirit who is dwelling in us is continually helping us in all the weaknesses we experience in this life, especially with our weakness in prayer. He intercedes for us, and his intercession is always effectual. Therefore, just as the hope of the coming glory sustains us to wait with patience, so also the Holy Spirit helps us to endure our sufferings.

The Holy Spirit Helps Us

"In the same way, the Spirit helps us in our weakness," that is, in all our infirmities (v. 26). Paul here tells us something more about the Holy Spirit to assure us of our final salvation: The Spirit helps us in our present weakness. Notice, he does not remove our weakness, but he helps us in it. The Spirit helps us to go through our sufferings triumphantly. Our weaknesses include all the suffering of this present age—physical pain, mental depression, spiritual conflicts, groanings peculiar to pastors (Heb. 13:17), slander, persecution, martyrdom, sickness, lack of physical strength as we grow older, frustration, ignorance, dullness of mind to understand the Scriptures, terminal diseases, tragedies, being dragged to court, and finally facing death itself.

But the particular weakness Paul cites that affects all aspects of our life is our inability to discern clearly the will of God, especially in unusual circumstances and crisis situations. We do not know what to pray for in such circumstances. For instance, suppose your wife is sick with cancer. You pray for her healing, yet you do not know what God's will is for her—to live, or to die and be with Christ, which is far better.

Many people in the Scriptures experienced this problem. Moses prayed for God to let him go over and see the good land beyond the Jordan. But he was not praying in the will of God. The Lord said, "That is enough! My will is for you to die, and you will not enter Canaan" (see Deut. 3:23–27). Elijah grew tired of the ministry and prayed, "I have had enough, Lord. Take my life" (1 Kings 19:4). He did not know what to pray. Instead of fulfilling his desire, God took him to heaven and he never died. When Jesus was suffering, he prayed, "Now my heart is troubled, and what shall I say? 'Father, save me from this hour'? No, it was for this very reason I came to this hour" (John 12:27).

Paul himself did not always know how to pray. When God gave Paul a thorn in his flesh to torment him, Paul prayed for its removal: "Three times I pleaded with the Lord to take it away from me." But God did not grant Paul's request. He said, "My grace is sufficient for you, for my power is made perfect in weakness" (2 Cor. 12:8–9). Another time Paul had to leave Trophimus sick in Miletus (2 Tim. 4:20). I am certain Paul prayed for his healing. But although God had used Paul to perform great miracles in many places, there was no miraculous healing of Trophimus.

Because of our present weakness and our limited horizons, sometimes we do not know what we should pray for and what we should not pray for. This weakness to discern the will of God is not sin. It is part of our present imperfect existence.

Since we do not know the secret will of God, we often add to our prayers, "If it is your will." The apostles did this. Paul spoke like this in his letter to the Romans: "I pray that now at last by God's will the way may be opened for me to come to you . . . so that by God's will I may come to you with joy and together with you be refreshed" (Rom. 1:10; 15:32). He also told the Corinthian church, "I will come to you very soon, if the Lord is willing" (1 Cor. 4:19). Paul promised the Ephesians, "I will come back if it is God's will" (Acts 18:21). James instructs us, "Instead, you ought to say, 'If it is the Lord's will, we will live and do this or that'" (James 4:15). Jesus himself prayed, "Father, if you are willing, take this cup from me; yet not my will, but yours be done" (Luke 22:42).

We have weakness and problems, and do not always know what to pray in times of crisis. But the Holy Spirit comes to our aid in all such situations. He comes to help bear our burdens. He comes as the heaven-sent Comforter, Counselor, and ever-prevailing Advocate, who has never lost a case and never will. He is our *paraklētos*, one called alongside us to help us.

Paul uses the word *sunantilambanetai*, which means "continually helping." The Holy Spirit comes at just the right time to help us. He comes to take up one end of the burden, and he strengthens us to carry the other end of the load. This word is used in the Septuagint to describe easing the burden of God's people, especially of leaders. Moses was told to appoint leaders for groups of tens, fifties, hundreds, and thousands: "That will make your load lighter, because they will share it with you" (Exod. 18:22). Another time in reference to the seventy elders, God said, "They will help you carry the burden of the people so that you will not have to carry it alone" (Num. 11:17). It is good to have a plurality of leaders so that one man does not have to bear the burden alone. In the New Testament, the overburdened Martha used this word when she requested, "Lord, . . . tell [Mary] to help me!" (Luke 10:40).

When troubles come that we cannot bear, the Holy Spirit will come and share the burden. Jesus declares, "Come to me, all you who are weary and burdened, and I will give you rest. Take my yoke upon you and learn from me, for I am gentle and humble in heart, and you will find rest for your souls" (Matt. 11:28–29). In eastern countries we still see plows with two oxen attached to a yoke. The idea is that we are one ox, Jesus is the other, and together we do the job. We bear the yoke with Jesus. He bears our burdens with us and enables us to bear them also. He promises to be with us always, even unto the end of the age. He is our high priest who sympathizes with all our troubles and helps us: "For we do not have a high priest who is unable to sympathize with our weaknesses, but we have one who has been tempted in every way, just as we are—yet was without sin" (Heb. 4:15).

So Paul said, "I can do everything through [Christ] who gives me strength" (Phil. 4:13). We are weak and need strength. Jesus promises, "You will receive power when the Holy Spirit comes on you" (Acts 1:8). Christ helps us by sending the Spirit of God to empower us.

The Spirit Intercedes for Us

It is not that we never know what to pray for. Most of the time we do know, because the Scripture instructs us to pray according to the will of God. And as we pray believing in God's promises, God answers such prayers of faith.

Some would ask that if the Holy Spirit prays for us in the will of God, why should we bother praying? There are several answers to this question:

1. God commands us to pray.
2. God taught us to pray.
3. Just as God ordains the ends, he also ordains the means of prayer to those ends.
4. Jesus himself prayed.
5. God tells us to pray to him in the name of Christ to receive mercy and grace to help us in our time of need.
6. God wants us to know his will and pray in that will. Paul says, "Therefore do not be foolish, but understand what the Lord's will is" (Eph. 5:17).
7. God promises to hear our prayers. God does not hear the prayers of sinners but he hears the prayers of his saints.
8. The more godly we become, the more we will be in the word of God and the more we will pray in the will of God.
9. We know that spiritual requests are always in God's will, and we should make such requests, like the prayer of Paul for the church: "I pray that out of his glorious riches he may strengthen you with power through his Spirit in your inner being, so that Christ may dwell in your hearts through faith. And I pray that you, being rooted and established in love, may have power, together with all the saints, to grasp how wide and long and high and deep is the love of Christ, and to know this love that surpasses knowledge—that you may be filled to the measure of all the fullness of God " (Eph. 3:16–19).
10. We know that when we pray based on God's promises, he will hear us. David prayed, "You promised. . . . Please do it" (see 2 Sam. 7:25–29). That is what children say to their parents: "You promised; please do it."

However, we must make two cautionary notes about our prayers. First, we must never demand anything from God. Second, we must use caution when praying for personal things. The nation of Israel provides a warning in this regard: "In the desert they gave in to their craving; in the wasteland they put God to the test.

So he gave them what they asked for, but sent a wasting disease upon them" (Ps. 106:14–15).

"We do not know what we ought to pray for, but the Spirit himself intercedes for us with groans that words cannot express" (v. 26). Romans 8:26–27 is especially speaking about the weakness of our ignorance as to what to pray for in crisis situations. The Spirit intercedes to the Father in heaven in behalf of his weak saints. He intercedes *stenagmois alalētois*, "with groanings unspoken," which is a difficult phrase to interpret.

What is the meaning of groanings? When Paul writes about creation groaning (Rom. 8:22), we know that is metaphorical. But when he says we groan within ourselves (v. 23), is that literal or metaphorical? In Romans 8:26, who is groaning? Does the Holy Spirit, who is eternal God, groan under pressure? Dr. Martyn Lloyd-Jones says no: "He never groans, He never sighs; that is inconceivable."[1]

The word "groaning," *stenagmos*, or its verb *stenazō*, is used in the Septuagint and the New Testament to refer to groanings of creatures who are suffering under severe burdens. God told Moses, "I have indeed seen the oppression of my people in Egypt. I have heard their groaning and have come down to set them free" (Acts 7:34). Paul says that "while we are in this tent, we groan and are burdened" because our outward man is wasting away (2 Cor. 5:4). The word is also used in Hebrews 13:17: "Obey [your leaders] so that they do their work with joy and not groaning" (author's translation).

If this groaning is not metaphorical, who groans—the Holy Spirit or the saints? I believe it is neither alone, but the saints groaning under the direction of the Holy Spirit.

What is the nature of this groaning? Is *alalētois* to be defined as "wordless," meaning these groanings are silent sighs too deep for words? Is it "ineffable," incapable of being expressed in human language? Or does it mean "inarticulate," that the sounds make no sense either to the hearers or to the one who groans?

Whatever the meaning is, the content of the groaning is the intercession of the Holy Spirit, so this groaning has meaning and purpose. As well, the sighs assume a degree of distress and anguish.

---

1   Lloyd-Jones, *Romans*, vol. 8, *Final Perseverance of the Saints*, 136.

But are these groanings perceptible or imperceptible to the saints? C. H. Spurgeon says, "A groan then is a part of prayer which we owe to the Holy Ghost."[2] I say we groan under the direction of the Holy Ghost. In Galatians 4:6 Paul says, "Because you are sons, God sent the Spirit of his Son into our hearts, crying, 'Abba, Father'" (author's translation). In Romans 8:15 we read: "And by him we cry, 'Abba, Father.'" The conclusion, then, is that we cry, "Abba, Father," by the direction of the Holy Spirit. So also we groan under the direction of the Spirit.

Let me prove it in this way. Jesus said, "But when they arrest you, do not worry about what to say or how to say it. At that time you will be given what to say, for it will not be you speaking, but the Spirit of your Father speaking through you" (Matt. 10:19–20). However, elsewhere Jesus says, "When you are brought before synagogues, rulers and authorities, do not worry about how you will defend yourselves or what you will say, for the Holy Spirit will teach you at that time what you should say" (Luke 12:11–12). John says, "The Spirit and the bride say, 'Come!'" (Rev. 22:17). It is not the Spirit speaking, "Come!" Rather, the Spirit speaks through the church, "Come!" Therefore, I say, we groan by the direction of the Spirit.

A number of scholars, including Origen, Chrysostom, Ernst Käsemann, Gordon Fee, and F. F. Bruce,[3] argue that this groaning is the private praying in tongues Paul speaks of in 1 Corinthians 14: "For anyone who speaks in a tongue does not speak to men but to God. Indeed, no one understands him; he utters mysteries [by the] Spirit" (v. 2).

A person who prays in tongues prays to God by the Holy Spirit. He speaks by the Spirit mysteries to God. When he

---

2   C. H. Spurgeon, "The Holy Spirit's Intercession" (No. 1532), delivered on Lord's-Day Morning, April 11th, 1880, at the Metropolitan Tabernacle, Newington (accessed at http://www.spurgeon.org/sermons/1532.htm, May 15, 2010).

3   Bruce, Letter of Paul to the Romans, 165; Ernst Käsemann, Commentary on Romans (Grand Rapids: Eerdmans, 1980), 239–243; Robert L. Saucy, "An Open but Cautious Response" in Are Miraculous Gifts for Today? Four Views, Wayne A. Grudem, ed., (Grand Rapids: Zondervan, 1996), 233; Gordon Fee, God's Empowering Presence (Peabody, MA: Hendrickson, 2002), 575–586 (including note 323 on p. 586 concerning Origen); Moo, Epistle to the Romans, 524–526 (including note 92 on p. 525 concerning Chrysostom).

prays privately, he edifies himself, even though he does not understand what he is saying. The Holy Spirit prays, but his mind does not understand. But God who searches our hearts knows the mind of the Spirit. So these scholars conclude that what Romans 8:26–27 says has reference to the phenomenon in the early church of saints praying in private in tongues, as Paul himself did (1 Cor. 14:18).

The saints pray, but the Holy Spirit gives them the content of their utterance. It is the Spirit's intercession in behalf of the saints. And whether this has to do with our groans or with praying in tongues, one thing is certain: it is the intercession of the Holy Spirit in behalf of us according to the will of God.

The Spirit's Effectual Intercession

The intercession of the Holy Spirit is always effectual. This is because God, who examines our hearts, knows the mind of the Holy Spirit and what his desire for us is.

God knows our hearts. David said, "And you, my son Solomon, acknowledge the God of your father, and serve him with wholehearted devotion and with a willing mind, for the LORD searches every heart and understands every motive behind the thoughts. If you seek him, he will be found by you" (1 Chron. 28:9). He also prayed, "Search me, O God, and know my heart; test me and know my anxious thoughts" (Ps. 139:23).

The prayer of the Spirit is always effectual because he prays according to the will of God in our behalf. The Father is God and the Holy Spirit is God, so there exists perfect harmony between the Father who searches our hearts and the mind of the Holy Spirit.

Yes, we do not always know how to pray in accordance with God's will in specific situations. But Paul tells us, "*According to God the Spirit intercedes for the benefit of the saints*" (v. 27, author's translation). The Holy Spirit always prays according to the will of God. His intercession is always effectual because he intercedes according to God's perfect will. He is our *paraklētos*, one who comes alongside to help us in all our weaknesses.

Moses prayed to enter Canaan. The Spirit interceded that he not enter, and the Spirit's intercession was effectual. Elijah prayed that he might die, but the Spirit interceded that he never die, and his intercession was effectual. Paul prayed that his thorn in the flesh be removed immediately; the Holy Spirit interceded that the thorn remain in his flesh, and the Spirit's intercession was effectual. As a church we prayed for the healing of a cancer-stricken sister. The Holy Spirit prayed that she instead die and enter the presence of God, and the Spirit's blessed intercession prevailed.

Saints, do not worry when you do not know what to pray for at certain difficult times. The Holy Spirit prays for us, and his prayer always prevails. The will of God will be done. Listen to Douglas Moo's comforting words: "When we do not know what to pray for—yes, even when we pray for things that are not best for us—we need not despair, for we can depend on the Spirit's ministry of perfect intercession 'on our behalf.'"[4] Martin Luther said, "It is not an evil sign, but indeed the very best, if upon our petitions the very opposite happens to us. Conversely, it is not a good sign if everything is granted to us for which we pray. The reason for this is the following: God's counsel and will tower high above our own counsel and will, as we read in Isaiah 55:8, 9."[5]

Conclusion

We are weak, but God is strong to help us in all our weaknesses. We can rejoice, knowing that we have a number of intercessors.

1. Christ in heaven is interceding for us (Rom. 8:34), guaranteeing our justification based on his blood atonement. His intercession is effectual.
2. The Holy Spirit intercedes for us in our hearts according to the will of God. His intercession is always effectual for our sanctification.
3. God's holy church intercedes for us. After James, the brother of John, was put to the sword, Peter was arrested and put in prison. The church was interceding for Peter in the house of Mary the mother of Mark (Acts 12:5), and the intercession was effectual. God sent an angel and let Peter out of prison to continue his

---

4   Moo, *Epistle to the Romans*, 526.
5   Luther, *Commentary on Romans*, 126.

ministry. Paul says that if one member suffers, the whole body suffers (1 Cor. 12:26). Elsewhere, he says, "Bear one another's burdens, and so fulfill the law of Christ" (Gal. 6:2, KJV).

May we therefore not worry as we face problems, weaknesses, sufferings, and trials. God the Father is for us, Christ the Son is for us, the Holy Spirit is for us, and the holy church is for us. We are well taken care of, and in his time, the Lord will bring us safely home.

52

God Guarantees Our Good

And we know that in all things God works for the good of those who love him, who have been called according to his purpose.

Romans 8:28

God guarantees our good. What is our good? Our eternal happiness, salvation, and glory. Along with Psalm 23 and John 3:16, Romans 8:28 is one of the most well-known verses of the Bible. It speaks of the absolute certainty of the final salvation of a true believer in Jesus Christ. The proposition regarding our assurance made in this verse is explained further in Romans 8:29-30. If you are a child of God, you may derive great comfort from this scripture. God is speaking to all his suffering children. Dr. John Stott says of Romans 8:28: "It has been likened to a pillow to rest our weary heads."[1]

Why do God's children suffer afflictions? Why doesn't God eliminate all sufferings in answer to our prayers? If the Holy Spirit intercedes with God the Father in behalf of us according to God's will, why do God's people still suffer? Why do bad things happen to God's good people?

Paul assures us that afflictions are salutary and profitable. God makes them work for our ultimate good. God directs all things, good and bad, to bring about God's ultimate purpose for our lives—our glory for God's glory.

---

1   Stott, *Romans: God's Good News,* 246.

"And We Know"

Paul begins, "And we know . . ." In other words, we know something for certain; we have unshakable knowledge. Romans 8:26 stated that true believers "do not know" what to pray for in the will of God, especially in unusual and crisis situations, and therefore the Holy Spirit intercedes in behalf of us according to the perfect will of the Father. But in this verse we are told something we do know.

There are many things we do not know in this life, especially why certain negative things are happening to us. Joseph did not know why his brothers hated him, threw him into a pit, sold him to the Midianite merchants for twenty shekels, and why the merchants then sold him as a slave to Potiphar of Egypt. He did not know why Mrs. Potiphar accused him of rape, why he was put in prison, or why the butler of Pharaoh completely forgot to help him get out of the prison, as promised. "The secret things belong to the LORD our God" (Deut. 29:29). We do not know everything now, but we will know by and by. But we do know the ultimate things. We know for certain that we are destined for glory. God will bring all his people to final and full salvation through the valley of the shadow of death.

How do we know what we know? We know by faith. We know by the Holy Spirit's illumination. We know from God's propositional revelation, the Bible.

> Jesus loves me, this I know,
> for the Bible tells me so.

So we know God brings good out of bad things. Thus the psalmist declares, "Before I was afflicted I went astray, but now I obey your word. . . . It was good for me to be afflicted so that I might learn your decrees" (Ps. 119:67, 71).

It is not "we feel," but "we know." Therefore, God's people engage in serious daily Bible study to know God and his plan for our lives. The Lord promises to rescue and protect those who love him and honor his name (Ps. 91:14). We are the Lord's portion, his allotted inheritance; he shields and cares for us, and he guards us as the apple of his eye (Deut. 32:9–10; see also Zech. 2:8). He is for us, and he will save us.

God is our portion and inheritance. Therefore, we know that no harm will ultimately come to us, because from the Scriptures we know the ultimate reality that God saves his people. All Scripture is written for our comfort: "For everything that was written in the past was written to teach us, so that through endurance and the [comfort] of the Scriptures we might have hope" (Rom. 15:4). God gave us his word to teach us that we may have endurance, comfort, and hope. Therefore, can you say with Paul, "We know"?

God Works for Our Salvation

Our great and good God works for our salvation. He weaves together all experiences in this life—good and bad, pain and laughter, prosperity and adversity—for the good of his children. The lie of the evolutionary hypothesis is that things work of themselves. No, God works in all things.

I translate Romans 8:28 as follows: *"And we know that to those who love God, he works together all things for good to those who are called according to his purpose."*[2] God is the subject and *panta* (all things) is the object. "'All things' do not tend toward good in and of themselves, as if Paul held to a 'naively optimistic' interpretation of history.[3] No, in all things God works.

God is always at work in our lives. He ceaselessly, energetically, and purposefully works in us moment by moment. He never sleeps nor slumbers. Jesus said, "My Father is always at his work to this very day, and I, too, am working" (John 5:17). It is against Christianity for a person to be lazy, unproductive, a failure in school, or living off parents and the government. God the Father, God the Son, and God the Holy Spirit, as well as God's holy angels and his holy church, are all at work to save God's people through the preaching of the gospel. And God never fails.

There is no equal ultimacy of good and evil. God is almighty, all holy, and all wise. So no evil can frustrate God's purpose to save us. Everything is under God's control. Satan could not tempt Job without God's permission. God puts a hedge, a wall of fire,

---

2   See also NIV, RSV, and NASB translations, and mss. P46, B, A, and 81.

3   Moo, *Epistle to the Romans*, 528.

around his people. So Job did not curse God; rather, by God's grace, he blessed God, despite his tragedies. How could he do so? Because God works in everything for our salvation.

He Works for Good

God works for or "unto" good *(eis agathon)*. Our triune God works in everything for our ultimate good, not necessarily to give us the earthly goods of health, wealth, power, or fame. Recall the experiences of the saints: "Others were tortured and refused to be released, so that they might gain a better resurrection. Some faced jeers and flogging, while still others were chained and put in prison. They were stoned; they were sawed in two; they were put to death by the sword. They went about in sheepskins and goatskins, destitute, persecuted and mistreated—the world was not worthy of them. They wandered in deserts and mountains, and in caves and holes in the ground" (Heb. 11:35b–38). Or listen to Paul: "Are they servants of Christ? (I am out of my mind to talk like this.) I am more. I have worked much harder, been in prison more frequently, been flogged more severely, and been exposed to death again and again. Five times I received from the Jews the forty lashes minus one. Three times I was beaten with rods, once I was stoned, three times I was shipwrecked, I spent a night and a day in the open sea" (2 Cor. 11:23–25).

God works for the ultimate good of conforming us to the image of his Son. We were once wrath-filled enemies of God, dead in trespasses and sins. But he took us ungodly, powerless nobodies of the world and made us glorious saints who now praise God for his grace.

God uses all measures at his disposal to do good to his people, including the discipline of expelling them from the church and giving them over to Satan that he may work on them. Paul speaks of this in his letter to the Corinthians: "When you are assembled in the name of our Lord Jesus and I am with you in spirit, and the power of our Lord Jesus is present, hand this man over to Satan, so that the [flesh] may be destroyed and his spirit saved on the day of the Lord" (1 Cor. 5:4–5). To the same church Paul wrote, "That is why many among you are weak and sick, and a number of you have fallen asleep," because God's judgment had come upon them. But then he explained, "When we are judged by the Lord, we are being disciplined so that we will not be condemned with the world" (1 Cor. 11:30, 32).

The goal of God's good work in us is our eschatological glory of final salvation. The people of God are destined to shine like the sun in the kingdom of God the Father.

Fear not, little flock; our God is at work in us for our good. To the rich young ruler who worshiped money and called him "good teacher," Jesus said, "No one is good—except God alone" (Luke 18:19). God is good, and he works good. God permits evil, but he is never the author of it. Jesus said, "If you, then, though you are evil, know how to give good gifts to your children, how much more will your Father in heaven give good gifts to those who ask him!" (Matt. 7:11). God alone is good, and he gives good gifts.

God works for our good and our glory. Our good is the goal of all God's providential dealings. Out of all things God brings good. Look at a watch. One wheel moves in one direction, the other goes in the opposite direction, yet the watch shows correct time. Look at bread. Wheat is made into flour by crushing it; then water and yeast are added to it. More pressure is applied through kneading and then it is put in a hot oven to bake. The result is good bread. Likewise, God works with us through positive as well as negative experiences to bring about our good ultimate end.

Professor John Murray called the crucifixion of the sinless Son of God "the arch-crime of history."[4] Yet through this arch-crime God brought about our salvation. Peter declared, "This man was handed over to you by God's set purpose and foreknowledge; and you, with the help of wicked men, put him to death by nailing him to the cross" (Acts 2:23), and Paul says, "He was delivered over to death for our sins and was raised to life for our justification" (Rom. 4:25).

Not even one small thing in our lives can ultimately work for our destruction. Everything is working, and God works through everything, for our good. Moses said, "He gave you manna to eat in the desert, something your fathers had never known, to humble and to test you so that in the end it might go well with you" (Deut. 8:16). Since God is at work, everything will work for our good by God's providence.

---

4   Murray, *Collected Writings*, vol. 2: *Systematic Theology*, 73.

In All Things

"In all things" means in both good and bad experiences of God's people, but the emphasis is on our present sufferings. We are weak and suffer daily. We may go through many fiery trials. Yet these cannot destroy us. Instead, they serve to purify our faith by removing the filth, dross, and impurities of our lives, and produce in us endurance and proven character. So our trials are achieving for us an eternal weight of glory (2 Cor. 4:17). In other words, they bring about our sanctification. Sufferings under God's providence are our servants, though they are evil in themselves.

We do not court sufferings. We are not ascetics who mutilate our bodies. But the shocking truth is that even our sins and our backslidings contribute to our final good. The prodigal came to a better knowledge of his father when he returned. Nothing can prevent God from saving us, not even our sins. Bishop Anders Nygren says, "Thus all that is negative in this life is seen to have a positive purpose in the execution of God's eternal plan."[5] John Stott declares, "Nothing is beyond the overruling, overriding scope of his providence."[6]

God permits terrible things to happen to us. Study the lives of Joseph, Job, Jacob, Jeremiah, and Jesus. Listen to Paul, who says, "To keep me from becoming conceited because of these surpassingly great revelations, there was given me a thorn in my flesh, a messenger of Satan, to torment me. Three times I pleaded with the Lord to take it away from me. But he said to me, 'My grace is sufficient for you, for my power is made perfect in weakness.' Therefore I will boast all the more gladly about my weaknesses, so that Christ's power may rest on me" (2 Cor. 12:7–9).

Not only does God allow terrible things to happen to us, but he also leads us directly into bitter experiences: "He humbled you, causing you to hunger and then feeding you with manna, which neither you nor your fathers had known, to teach you that man does not live on bread alone but on every word that comes from the mouth of the LORD" (Deut. 8:3).

---

5   Nygren, *Commentary on Romans*, 338.
6   Stott, *Romans: God's Good News*, 247.

In 1841, the family bank of J. C. Ryle failed in one day. His family lost everything. Of that time Ryle, who later became one of the great evangelical theologians in nineteenth-century England, wrote:

> I have not the least doubt it was all for the best. If my father's affairs had prospered and I had never been ruined, my life, of course, would have been a very different one. I should have probably gone into Parliament very soon and it is impossible to say what the effect of this might have been upon my soul. I should have formed different connections, and moved in an entirely different circle. I should never have been a clergyman, never have preached, written a tract or book. Perhaps I might have made shipwreck in spiritual things. So I do not mean to say at all, that I wish it to have been different to what it was. All I mean to say is that I was deeply wounded by my reverses, suffered deeply under them, and I do not think I have recovered in body and mind from the effect of them.[7]

My family suffered a similar economic collapse. This circumstance was ultimately used by God to bring my parents to evangelical faith. In a sense, I preach the gospel today because of the economic deprivation suffered by my grandparents a hundred years ago. God works in all things for our good.

Moreover, God may also withhold blessings. He turns his face away from us and may not smile on us for a season. He scolds and rebukes: "On that day I will become angry with them and forsake them; I will hide my face from them, and they will be destroyed. Many disasters and difficulties will come upon them, and on that day they will ask, 'Have not these disasters come upon us because our God is not with us?' And I will certainly hide my face on that day because of all their wickedness in turning to other gods" (Deut. 31:17–18; see also Deut. 32:20). The psalmist cries, "Answer me quickly, O LORD; my spirit [faints with longing]. Do not hide your face from me or I will be like those who go down to the pit" (Ps. 143:7). But through all these things God brings about our repentance and correction.

Through the high pressure and heat of difficult experiences, he creates many sons of glory. So Paul writes,

---

7   Quoted by Eric Russell in *That Man of Granite with the Heart of a Child: Biography of J. C. Ryle* (Ross-Shire, Great Britain: Christian Focus, 2001), 32.

Who is he that condemns? Christ Jesus, who died—more than that, who was raised to life—is at the right hand of God and is also interceding for us. Who shall separate us from the love of Christ? Shall trouble or hardship or persecution or famine or nakedness or danger or sword? . . . No, in all these things we are more than conquerors through him who loved us. For I am convinced that neither death nor life, neither angels nor demons, nor the present nor the future, nor any powers, neither height nor depth, nor anything else in all creation, will be able to separate us from the love of God that is in Christ Jesus our Lord. (Rom. 8:34–39)

To Those Who Love God

"*To those who love God*" is a limiting clause. The comfort of Romans 8:28 is limited to a minority, a remnant of people who are characterized by love for God. God does not work in all things for the good of the vast majority of people. Of such people Paul says, "What if God, choosing to show his wrath and make his power known, bore with great patience the objects of his wrath—prepared for destruction?" (Rom. 9:22). The comfort of Romans 8:28 is for those who love the true and living God, that is, the triune God who has revealed himself in nature and especially in the Holy Bible.

Most religious people of the world do not love the God and Father of the Lord Jesus Christ. Rather, they are devil worshipers who hate the true God. They sacrifice to demons, which are not God (Deut. 32:17; 1 Cor. 10:20). They will not repent and believe on Jesus Christ, because they worship Satan, the god of this world. They would rather believe in the lie of religious pluralism.

But Paul writes, "*to those who love God* . . .*"* Do you love God? Consider this carefully so you can arrive at the correct conclusion. There is emphasis in the Greek text. It does not say "to those who *believe* God," but "to those who *love* God." We love God because he first loved us (1 John 4:19). By his love, God transforms his enemies into lovers of God. Jesus said that the first commandment is to "love the Lord your God with all your heart and with all your soul and with all your mind and with all your strength" (Mark 12:30). And Paul says, "Hope does not disappoint us, because God has poured out his love into our hearts by the

Holy Spirit, whom he has given us" (Rom. 5:5). The Holy Spirit floods our souls with love, that we may love God.

So Paul writes to the Corinthians, "However, as it is written: 'No eye has seen, no ear has heard, no mind has conceived what God has prepared for those who love him'"; "But the man who loves God is known by God."; "If anyone does not love the Lord—a curse be on him" (1 Cor. 2:9; 8:3; 16:22). He writes elsewhere, "Grace to all who love our Lord Jesus Christ with an undying love" (Eph. 6:24).

Jesus said, "If you love me, keep my commandments" (John 14:15, KJV). So God works in all things for the good of those who love him, that is, those who obey him. Or we could say, God works for the good of those who are being sanctified. If we believe in God, we will love God. And if we love God, we will obey God with delight.

This verse speaks against universalism, as taught by theologians like Karl Barth, who taught that because God is love, all will be saved in the end, including all wicked people, all evil angels, and the devil himself. This is the danger of speaking about unconditional love at the expense of the justice and holiness of God.

The Scriptures condemn such universalism. God works in all things for the good of those who love him. The devil believes that God exists and even trembles at this thought, but he does not love God. In fact, he is at war with God, even though he always loses. Jesus said, "My sheep hear my voice." That means they hear and do. Jesus prayed for his sheep, who are the Father's gifts to him. He did not pray for the world (John 17:9). The Lord knows those who are his. The visible church is always a mixture of people who love God and those who pretend to love God. But eventually the God-haters will stop pretending and will fall away. So John says, "They went out from us, but they did not really belong to us. For if they had belonged to us, they would have remained with us; but their going showed that none of them belonged to us" (1 John 2:19).

What do you love from the depths of your heart? What do you love when you are alone? What do you love with all your heart, soul, mind, and might? Do you love the goods of the world? Or do you love God, the Creator and Redeemer, the Lover of our souls? John tells us, "Do not love the world or anything in the world. If anyone loves the world, the love of the Father is not in him. For everything in the world—the cravings of sinful man, the lust of his eyes and the boasting of what he has and does—comes not from the Father but from the world. The world and its desires pass away, but the man who does the will of God lives forever" (1 John 2:15–17).

John Piper said this is how we know if we love God: Do we desire God? Do we treasure God? Are we satisfied with God? The word "love" is in the present tense. Do we love God always, not once in a great while? And especially do we love God in the midst of adversity? Assurance of our full, final, and glorious salvation belongs only to the lovers of God who obey him. They love and obey God because God loved them and sent his Son to die on the cross for their salvation.

To Those Who Are Called

"To those who are called . . ." Our love for God springs from our being effectually called by God with the gospel. Our love for God is subjective, but the objective basis of our love is God's call. So Paul writes, "Through him and for his name's sake, we received grace and apostleship to call people from among all the Gentiles to the obedience that comes from faith. And you also are among those who are called to belong to Jesus Christ. To all in Rome who are loved by God and called to be saints: Grace and peace to you from God our Father and from the Lord Jesus Christ" (Rom. 1:5–7).

Through the gospel preaching, God calls sinners to repentance. "How beautiful on the mountains are the feet of those who bring good news, who proclaim peace, who bring good tidings, who proclaim salvation, who say to Zion, 'Your God reigns!'" (Isa. 52:7). It is time we appreciated preachers of the gospel. Bad heads of state and bad physicians can only kill us, but a bad preacher can send us to hell. That is why we must be careful about what church we attend. The question is whether the preacher preaches the word of God or not. If a minister does not preach the gospel, then run from that place and find a place where it is preached.

We are called to be holy. Paul writes, "To the church of God in Corinth, to those sanctified in Christ Jesus and *called to be holy*, together with all those everywhere who call on the name of our Lord Jesus Christ—their Lord and ours" (1 Cor. 1:2). Many who call themselves Christians are mere pretenders. But do they truly love God? Are they living holy lives? We are called to be saints. God is calling people to come to him and enjoy fellowship with him. "God, who has called you into fellowship with his Son Jesus Christ our Lord, is faithful" (1 Cor. 1:9). God is calling us to come to live with him.

God calls those who are dead in trespasses and sins to come to him. He calls those who are weary of sin to come to Jesus and he will give them rest. He is life and he gives life. He is the light that enlightens the blind. The call of the gospel has to do with the person and saving work of Christ. The gospel is the medicine for sinners' health.

Because of our moral inability, we cannot come to God unless he enables us. Jesus says, "No one can come to me unless the Father who sent me draws him, and I will raise him up at the last day" (John 6:44; see also v. 65). By nature we are dead in trespasses and sins (Eph. 2:1). But when Jesus calls, we come through his powerful, divine drawing. When Jesus called the dead and decomposing Lazarus, "Lazarus, come forth!" he came. Elsewhere Jesus said, "But I, when I am lifted up from the earth, will draw all men to myself" (John 12:32). So the Father draws, the Son draws, the Holy Spirit regenerates us, and we come.

When God calls, we come. If a person has not come to Christ, God did not call him effectually. There is a general call and there is a specific, particular call; an outward call and an interior call by the Holy Spirit. Yet many people do not come to Jesus. They have excuses: "I bought a new field"; "I bought a new tractor"; "I got married." Many people may hear the gospel, but they go to their deaths never having come to Christ. Such people were never called by the Spirit in the interior of their being.

Jesus said, "Many are called, but few are chosen" (Matt. 22:14, KJV). There is the general call, which offers life, and there is the call of the Holy Spirit, which gives us life. There is the general call, which offers hope, and there is the call of the Spirit, which gives hope.

God's particular, effectual, and internal call of the gospel comes to the poor, crippled, blind, and lame (Luke 14:21). God effectually calls not many who are wise or noble; rather, he calls the foolish, the weak, the lowly, the despised, and the nothings of this world (1 Cor. 1:26ff). This general call is to be given to all. We are to go into all the world and preach the gospel.

The effectual call comes only to the elect. And when God's powerful, effectual call comes, we cannot sit still. We will say, "God is calling me, and I am going to him." Through the effectual call of the Spirit, a sinner is regenerated and given the gift of repentance and faith, so he will repent and believe in Christ.

When Jesus called, the blind Bartimaeus received his sight and followed Jesus (Mark 10:46–52). When Jesus commanded, the legion of demons were cast out of the miserable man, and he began to proclaim the gospel to his own people (Luke 8:26–39).

God's effectual call came to Saul of Tarsus, a murderer and blasphemer, and he began to preach the gospel. Then he was directed to go to Europe, where he preached to some women in Philippi, a Roman colony. All of a sudden the Lord opened the heart of the businesswoman Lydia, and she and her entire household were effectually called and regenerated. They repented of their sins, believed in Jesus Christ, and were baptized and saved (Acts 16:11–15). God directed the feet of Paul from Asia all the way to Europe so that Lydia could be saved!

Paul then was beaten up and put in prison. There in the prison at midnight the jailer heard the gospel call from Paul, and he and his family were saved. Paul was beaten and thrust into prison so that this jailer could hear the gospel and be saved.

Later, when Paul was on his way to Rome as a prisoner, there was a shipwreck, but all 276 passengers landed safely on the island of Malta (Acts 27–28). Why did this happen? God engineered this shipwreck so Paul could preach the gospel in Malta. And the people of Malta whom God loved from all eternity heard the gospel, believed the gospel, and were saved.

Think about how you heard the gospel. God engineered it all. So Jude writes, "To those who have been called, who are loved by God the Father and kept by Jesus Christ" (v. 1). Why are we called? Because God the Father loved us. And we are "kept by Jesus Christ." We are loved, called, and kept.

According to Purpose

Finally, Paul says, we are called *"according to purpose."* It is God's purpose, not ours. We love God because we are called, and we are called because of God's eternal purpose. In Romans 8:29–30 Paul explains this great, grand, glorious purpose of God.

God purposed our salvation from all eternity, and his call came to us in time in our personal history. We remember when the call came to us and interrupted our lives, just as it interrupted the lives of the tax collector Matthew, the fisherman Peter, and the prosecutor Paul. After God called, they were never the same. What a glorious interruption and intervention! Those who are effectually called will rise to follow Jesus.

God's purpose is behind it all. What is his purpose? It is to save us, to conform us to the image of Christ, and to glorify us, that Jesus Christ may have pre-eminence and the Father may be glorified. The ultimate purpose is for the praise of his glorious grace.

This purpose of God is unchanging. Nothing in all creation can prevent it from happening. To accomplish this purpose in the fullness of time, God sent his Son to die in our place for our sins on the cross: "For what the law was powerless to do in that it was weakened [in the flesh], God did by sending his own Son in the likeness of sinful man to be a sin offering" (Rom. 8:3).

In the fullness of time, God sent his own Son to accomplish redemption. "But when the time had fully come, God sent his Son, born of a woman, born under law, to redeem those under law" (Gal. 4:4–5). Then God sent his Holy Spirit to apply this redemption to us. "Because you are sons, God sent the Spirit of his Son into our hearts, the Spirit who calls out, 'Abba, Father'" (Gal. 4:6). In Romans 8:29–30, Paul uses five verbs in the past (aorist) tense: God foreloved, predestinated, called, justified, and glorified. God purposed and God accomplished his purpose, and we now enjoy this great salvation. His purpose is the guarantee of our full and final salvation.

God's purpose is his will, plan, and good pleasure. Elsewhere Paul states, "In him we were also chosen, having been predestined according to the plan of him who works out everything in conformity with the purpose of his will" (Eph. 1:11). God alone does what he wills. Paul also says, "The manifold wisdom of

God [is being] made known . . . according to his eternal purpose which he accomplished in Christ Jesus our Lord" (Eph. 3:10–11). So God's purpose is behind our calling. We love God because of his purpose, and we repent and believe because of God's purpose.

Paul also explains, "[God] has saved us and *called us to a holy life*—not because of anything we have done but because of his own purpose and grace. This grace was given us in Christ Jesus before the beginning of time" (2 Tim. 1:9). If people do not live holy lives, they are not called and are not in God's purpose. Why are true pastors persecuted? Because they preach that Christians are called to live holy lives. The simple reason is that people like to sin. But we are not called to conform to our modern ungodly culture. We are called to be saints. I pray that we will never get accustomed to moral filth, but will oppose it and show people the way out of it.

On the day of Pentecost, Peter declared, "[Jesus] was handed over to you by God's set purpose and foreknowledge; and you, with the help of wicked men, put him to death by nailing him to the cross" (Acts 2:23). God purposed in eternity past, before creation and before the fall, to save a people and glorify them. Friends, we have been in the mind of God from all eternity! That is all we need to know. God loved us from eternity past, he loves us in time, and he will love us in eternity future. Therefore, we have no reason to doubt. Not even our death can threaten our salvation. God's purpose will be done; neither Satan nor sin nor the world can prevent our glorious eternal happiness. If God is for us, who can be against us?

Conclusion

Let us further examine the life of Joseph in light of Romans 8:28. Joseph's father sent him to his brothers, who hated him and threw him into a pit. Then his own brothers sold him for twenty pieces of silver, though he cried and pleaded with them not to do it. Potiphar of Egypt bought him from the Midianite traders to be his slave. At Potiphar's house, Joseph was falsely accused of rape and thrown into prison. Then he helped a fellow prisoner, Pharaoh's butler, interpret his dream, and told the butler he was innocent. Yet for two years after his release, the butler forgot to help Joseph by speaking to Pharaoh. All this time Joseph did not know why these terrible things were happening to him. Yet God was working in all things for his good.

In Genesis 39 we find the secret of Joseph's life: God was with him. So we read, "The LORD was with Joseph and he prospered. . . . His master saw that the LORD was with [Joseph] and that the LORD gave him success in everything he did. . . . From the time [that Potiphar] put [Joseph] in charge of his household and of all that he owned, the LORD blessed the household of the Egyptian. . . . [Joseph told Potiphar's wife,] 'No one is greater in this house than I am. My master has withheld nothing from me except you, because you are his wife. How then could I do such a wicked thing and sin against God?' . . . But while Joseph was there in the prison, the LORD was with him. . . . The warden paid no attention to anything under Joseph's care because the LORD was with Joseph" (Gen. 39:2–3, 5, 9, 20–21, 23).

This is the secret of our lives as well: God is with us. We do not see him, but he is with us. David declared, "Yea, though I walk through the valley of the shadow of death, I will fear no evil; *for thou art with me*; thy rod and thy staff they comfort me" (Ps. 23:4, KJV).

We may not understand certain things that happen to us, but we will understand by and by. Finally, Joseph was able to tell his brothers: "You purposed to destroy me, but God purposed it for good to save his people" (see Gen. 50:20).

God's purpose is to save us. To do so, he did not spare his own Son, but gave him up for us all. How will he not, along with him, graciously give us all things? So do not worry; God is with us. He has purposed to save us, and he always wins.

53

Salvation Is of the Lord

²⁹For those God foreknew he also predestined to be conformed to the likeness of his Son, that he might be the firstborn among many brothers. ³⁰And those he predestined, he also called; those he called, he also justified; those he justified, he also glorified.

Romans 8:29–30

From the inside of the big fish, the prophet Jonah prayed, "Salvation is of the LORD" (Jonah 2:9, KJV). Man cannot save himself. He is a helpless, ungodly sinner. He is dead in sins. More than that, he is an enemy of God. Only God in his mercy can save the ungodly sinner.

God has purposed to save sinners. Paul declared, "In all things God works for the good of those . . . who have been called according to his purpose" (Rom. 8:28). There is no contingency in God's eternal purpose. Man often cannot fulfill what he purposes. He cannot do so because his situation changes, or he may even die. But what God purposes, he is able to do. What he begins, he completes. He is the Alpha and the Omega, the beginning and the end.

Romans 8:29–30 explains God's purpose that Paul referred to in Romans 8:28. Here God is revealed as the ultimate ground of the promise of Romans 8:28. He is the supreme guarantee of our full and final salvation. Here Paul discloses in five verbs how God works for our glory. What is emphasized is not man's response of faith, but God's actions in our election, predestination, effectual calling, justification, and glorification.

Dr. James Boice cites a story of a Hindu holy man, a mystic named Rao,[1] who announced to the people of Bombay in 1966 that he was going to walk on water on a certain date. Many people gathered around a pool in the city on that day. When the time came, Rao looked to heaven in prayer, stepped onto the water, and promptly sank. When he surfaced, he explained why he failed. Like our modern healing evangelists, he said, "One of you is an unbeliever." Rao failed. Man fails. But God never fails, and Jesus never fails.

Romans 8:29–30 consists in five unbreakable links of a golden chain, five steps of divine salvation.

1. Election

Paul begins, *"For those God foreknew."* The foreknowledge of God is the basis of the rest of God's saving actions. In God's plan of salvation, he foreknew a certain specific number of people only, meaning they are distinguished from all others. They include Jews and Gentiles from all nations and tribes on earth. These foreknown by God do not comprise the majority of mankind; in fact, they are few. Jesus called them "little flock" (Luke 12:32). Yet they also are a multitude which no man can number, as John describes: "After this I looked and there before me was a great multitude that no one could count, from every nation, tribe, people and language, standing before the throne and in front of the Lamb" (Rev. 7:9). God foreknew these people from eternity past.

What does "foreknow" mean? It can mean pre-vision, that God knows everyone and everything because he is omniscient. But such a definition does not fit the context of Romans 8. Here Paul is saying that God foreknows some people who are distinguished from all others. What is the reason for this distinction? Some would say that God foresees the faith of people and sees that only certain people will believe in him. But if this is the meaning, then the ground of our salvation is our faith. This does not give any basis of assurance of salvation, for man is fickle and unreliable. He is by nature a covenant breaker. Besides, how can sinful man, an enemy of God, believe in God?

---

1   Boice, *Romans*, vol. 2, *Reign of Grace*, 911–12.

If any sinner believes in God, it is a miracle. He believes because he is given the gift of faith. "For it is by grace you have been saved, through faith—and this not from yourselves, it is the gift of God" (Eph. 2:8). Jesus himself said, "No one can come to me unless the Father who sent me draws him" (John 6:44). Paul writes, "For who makes you different from anyone else? What do you have that you did not receive? And if you did receive it, why do you boast as though you did not?" (1 Cor. 4:7). Elsewhere, he says, "For it has been granted to you on behalf of Christ not only to believe on him, but also to suffer for him" (Phil. 1:29). This gift of faith is a grant by God to us.

So God foreknows some people individually from eternity past, before creation, before the fall, before our birth, before we did anything good or bad. Yet God foreknows us as fallen sinners. We must look to the Old Testament to discover the meaning of this word "foreknow."

The Hebrew word is *yada*. So from Hebrew we translate God's words about Abraham: "For I have *known* [chosen] him, so that he will direct his children and his household after him to keep the way of the LORD" (Gen. 18:19). The psalmist says, "For the LORD *knows* [watches over] the way of the righteous, but the way of the wicked will perish" (Ps. 1:6); "O LORD, what is man that you *know* [care for] him, the son of man that you think of him?" (Ps. 144:3). In Jeremiah 1:5 we read, "Before I formed you in the womb I *knew* [chose] you, before you were born I set you apart." In Amos 3:2 we read, "You only have I *known* [chosen] of all the families of the earth." In Hosea 13:5 the Lord says, "I *knew* [cared for] you in the desert, in the land of burning heat."

The Hebrew word *yada* in these verses means God's taking delight in and caring for some people. It is not speaking about intellectual knowledge of the person, but of God's loving relationship with that person, as we read in Deuteronomy 7:7–8: "The LORD did not set his affection on you and choose you because you were more numerous than other peoples, for you were the fewest of all peoples. But it was because the LORD loved you." In other words, foreknowledge means God's eternal love for us.

So foreknew means foreloved. From eternity, God loved us individually. This foreknowledge of God is a synonym for divine election. God loved us; therefore, he chose us (Eph. 1:4). Those whom God loves, he chooses to save so that they may enter into eternal fellowship with him.

We find the same idea in the New Testament. Paul uses the word *proginoskō*: "God did not reject his people, whom he foreknew" (Rom. 11:2), meaning whom he loved before in eternity. Jesus says, "Then I will tell them plainly, 'I never knew you. Away from me, you evildoers!'" (Matt. 7:23). In other words, "I never loved you. I never cared for you." Paul also declares, "But the man who loves God is known by God" (1 Cor. 8:3) and, "But now that you know God—or rather are known by God . . ." (Gal. 4:9). To Timothy he says, "[God] has saved us and called us to a holy life—not because of anything we have done but because of his own purpose and grace. This grace was given us in Christ Jesus before the beginning of time" (2 Tim. 1:9). Peter says we "have been chosen according to the foreknowledge of God the Father" (1 Pet. 1:2).

Professor John Murray says, "It is not the foresight of difference but the foresight that makes difference to exist, not foresight that recognizes existence but the foreknowledge that determines existence. It is the sovereign distinguishing love."[2] So the foreknowledge of God stands for the gracious election of sinners to glory in eternity past.

Paul refers to the Thessalonians as "brothers loved by the Lord" (2 Thess. 2:13–14). In the Greek it is a perfect passive participle. When did God start loving us? In eternity past. Additionally, he loves us in time, and will love us in eternity future. Count on it: we are loved by God. And nothing in all creation will be able to separate us from the love of God. So Paul writes, "But we always thank God for you, brothers loved by the Lord, because from the beginning God chose you unto salvation through the sanctification of the Spirit and through belief of the truth" (author's translation).

What differentiates the elect from the non-elect? Not our faith nor our merit, for we have none. God's foreknowledge alone, his electing love, differentiates us from everyone else. God's delight in us, his personal care and affection for every one of us, distinguishes us. Before our parents began to love us, our heavenly Father loved us. We have been in the heart of God always. We are loved forever. We love God because he has loved us first.

---

2   Murray, *Epistle to the Romans*, 318.

When did God start loving us? "He chose us in him *before the creation of the world*" (Eph. 1:4); "We speak of God's secret wisdom, a wisdom that has been hidden and that God destined for our glory *before time began*" (1 Cor. 2:7). What glorious truth! God loved us in eternity past with an everlasting love from which nothing can separate us. The angel told John, "The beast, which you saw, once was, now is not, and will come up out of the Abyss and go to his destruction. The inhabitants of the earth whose names have not been written in the book of life *from the creation of the world* will be astonished" (Rev. 17:8). This means our names are written in the book of life from the creation of the world. God loved us first, so we love him now. God chose us first, so we choose him now. God called us first, so we call upon him now. God works in us to will and to do his good pleasure; so we work out his good pleasure.

"For those God foreknew" means those whom God foreloved, even us, his beloved people. The church of Jesus Christ has existed in all eternity in the heart of God, and it consists of individuals like you and me.

Salvation is of the Lord. This excludes all human boasting. The ground of our full and final salvation is not our faith, not even our holiness and righteousness. The ground is God's eternal love for us in Jesus Christ. "The LORD appeared to us in the past, saying: 'I have loved you with an everlasting love'" (Jer. 31:3).

This is why I do not stay depressed. I always come back to this: I belong to God. I was always in the heart of God. He always loved me and he loves me now. Therefore, rise up and praise God! "Rejoice in the Lord always. I will say it again: Rejoice!" (Phil. 4:4). God is for us; who can be against us? Even when we fall down, he loves us. He comes to our aid and plants our feet on Jesus Christ, the solid rock. "The joy of the LORD is your strength" (Neh. 8:10).

2. Predestination

The second link in the chain of salvation is predestination: *"For those God foreknew he also predestined to be conformed to the likeness of his Son, that he might be the firstborn among many brothers"* (v. 29). The foreknowledge of God has regard to the people of God; predestination has to do with God's purpose for those people.

God's purpose is that all of his people be blessed, glorified, and conformed to the image and likeness of his one and only Son. The elect are appointed from eternity to arrive at the destination, which is conformity to Christ. God's good purpose for us is that we be glorified in spirit and body. We shall be holy, even as God is holy.

God will have a holy people. To this end God has predestinated us. To predestinate means to decide upon beforehand: "They did what your power and will had decided beforehand should happen" (Acts 4:28). What God has decided upon beforehand will surely happen, in spite of our sin, stubbornness, failure, and rebellion. God will have a holy people to enjoy communion with him for all eternity.

Dr. John Stott makes these observations regarding predestination:[3]

1. *Predestination excludes human boasting.* The praise belongs to God alone. Paul says, "In love he predestined us to be adopted as his sons through Jesus Christ, in accordance with his pleasure and will—to the praise of his glorious grace" (Eph. 1:4–6; also 12, 14).
2. *Predestination produces certainty of salvation.* Not even a shadow of doubt exists as to our destiny.
3. *Predestination causes God's people not to be lazy or passive but to work harder in the service of Christ.* God saves his people through his appointed means of human, not angelic, witnesses to the gospel. God is a worker, and his people are workers. Jesus said, "My Father is always at his work to this very day, and I, too, am working" (John 5:17). Those who believe in predestination are the people who work the hardest. Paul says, "But by the grace of God I am what I am, and his grace to me was not without effect. No, I worked harder than all of them—yet not I, but the grace of God that was with me" (1 Cor. 15:10). Be a productive worker. God gives us grace to work. "God is able to make all grace abound to you, so that in all things at all times, having all that you need, you will abound in every good work" (2 Cor. 9:8). Put away laziness. From this day forward, work, saying, "I can do all things through Jesus Christ who gives me strength" (see Phil. 4:13).
4. *Predestination produces holy living, not antinomianism.* "For he chose us in him before the creation of the world to be holy and blameless in his sight" (Eph. 1:4). In the same epistle Paul says,

---

3   Stott, *Romans: God's Good News,* 248.

"Christ loved the church and gave himself up for her to make her holy, cleansing her by the washing with water through the word, and to present her to himself as a radiant church, without stain or wrinkle or any other blemish, but holy and blameless" (Eph. 5:25–27). God will have a bride who is holy, pure, radiant, and glorious. "[God] has saved us and called us to a holy life" (2 Tim. 1:9). Those who live sinful lives are not Christians. God's people will live holy lives. "For the grace of God that brings salvation has appeared to all men. It teaches us to say 'No' to ungodliness and worldly passions, and to live self-controlled, upright and godly lives in this present age" (Titus 2:11–12).

5. *Predestination delivers us from narrow-mindedness.* Peter was a narrow-minded person who did not want to have anything to do with the Gentiles. He forgot the Bible, which teaches broad-mindedness. God told Abraham, "In thee shall all families of the earth be blessed" (Gen. 12:3, KJV). The Lord said of Jesus, "I will also make you a light for the Gentiles, that you may bring my salvation to the ends of the earth" (Isa. 49:6b), which Paul quoted in Acts 13:47–48. Paul writes of this plan of God: "This mystery is that through the gospel the Gentiles are heirs together with Israel, members together of one body, and sharers together in the promise in Christ Jesus. . . . Consequently, you are no longer foreigners and aliens, but fellow citizens with God's people and members of God's household" (Eph. 3:6; 2:19). God's church is broad-minded.

Dr. Martyn Lloyd-Jones says, "Predestination is simply a description of the destiny that God has determined and decided upon for the people whom he has foreknown."[4] Friends, we have a glorious destiny, and God will bring us into it. "'For I know the plans I have for you,' declares the LORD, 'plans to prosper you and not to harm you, plans to give you hope and a future'" (Jer. 29:11). We are predestinated to a glorious hope and future.

A. The First Purpose of Predestination: Conformity to Christ

Predestination has two purposes: one is proximate, or penultimate, and the other is ultimate. The proximate purpose is to be conformed to the image of God's one and only eternal Son who himself is the image of the Father. The Father has predestinated us for the proximate purpose of conformity to Jesus Christ in holiness.

---

4   Lloyd-Jones, *Romans,* vol. 8, *Final Perseverance of the Saints,* 242.

Consider the following:

1. We are predestinated not just to receive forgiveness.
2. We are predestinated not just to avoid hell and go to heaven when we die.
3. We are predestinated not to get rich or have health and fame in this life.
4. We are predestinated not to avoid sufferings. Jesus suffered, and we must suffer too (Acts 14:22).
5. We are predestinated not to be conformed to the culture of the wicked world. Paul describes this culture: "At one time we too were foolish, disobedient, deceived and enslaved by all kinds of passions and pleasures. We lived in malice and envy, being hated and hating one another" (Titus 3:3). Thank God, he called us out of this world. That is what *ekklēsia* means—the company of the called-out ones. Paul warned, "But mark this: There will be terrible times in the last days. People will be lovers of themselves, lovers of money, boastful, proud, abusive, disobedient to their parents, ungrateful, unholy, without love, unforgiving, slanderous, without self-control, brutal, not lovers of the good, treacherous, rash, conceited, lovers of pleasure rather than lovers of God—having a [show] of godliness but denying its power. Have nothing to do with them" (2 Tim. 3:1–5). We are to have nothing to do with such people because we are predestinated to be conformed to be like Jesus Christ. We read in Exodus 23:2, "Do not follow the crowd in doing wrong. When you give testimony in a lawsuit, do not pervert justice by siding with the crowd." Don't say, "Everybody is doing it." We are not everybody. We are foreknown, predestinated, called, justified, and glorified people of God!
6. We are predestinated not to be conformed to the culture of the ungodly church of professing Christians. Don't come and say, "This church does it this way, so we must do it this way." We are called to conform to the Scriptures and to Christ. We may hear of pastors divorcing their wives. Does that mean I can divorce my wife? No! I belong to the body of Christ, which is called out from the wicked world to be holy, blameless, separate, and devoted to Christ and truth.

Paul exhorts, "Therefore, I urge you, brothers, in view of God's mercy, to offer your bodies as living sacrifices, holy and pleasing to God—this is your spiritual act of worship. Do not conform any longer to the pattern of this world, but be transformed by the renewing of your mind" (Rom. 12:1–2).

We were conformed to Adam in his sin and death. We bore his image. But now we are destined to be conformed to the last

Adam, Jesus Christ, in righteousness and true holiness. This process of conformation begins at conversion and reaches its consummation in glory. F. F. Bruce says, "Sanctification is glory begun; glorification is sanctification consummated."[5] We were created in the image and likeness of God. This image was distorted because of Adam's sin. It is God's eternal plan that this image of God be restored in the elect of God.

This image, Dr. Lloyd-Jones says, is a derived likeness. A Roman coin has the image of the emperor, an exact derived likeness. A stamp has the exact derived likeness of the person in whose honor it is issued. A child has the derived likeness of his parents.[6] Jesus Christ is the image of the Father. So Jesus said, "Anyone who has seen me has seen the Father" (John 14:9). Jesus always delighted in his Father's will and always did it.

Even so, a Christian is the image of Christ. Do people see Christ when they see you? This is God's proximate plan. He predestinated us to this end. Paul speaks often of this end: "For we are God's workmanship, created in Christ Jesus to do good works, which God prepared in advance for us to do" (Eph. 2:10); "[We] have put on the new self, which is being renewed in knowledge in the image of its Creator" (Col 3:10); "[You were taught] to be made new in the attitude of your minds; and to put on the new self, created to be like God in true righteousness and holiness" (Eph. 4:23–24); "And just as we have borne the likeness of the earthly man [that is, Adam], so shall we bear the likeness of the man from heaven" (1 Cor. 15:49).

John writes, "Dear friends, now we are children of God, and what we will be has not yet been made known. But we know that when he appears, we shall be like him, for we shall see him as he is" (1 John 3:2). Even now it is happening. Paul says, "And we, who with unveiled faces all reflect the Lord's glory, are being transformed into his likeness with ever-increasing glory, which comes from the Lord, who is the Spirit. . . . For God, who said, 'Let light shine out of darkness,' made his light shine in our hearts to give us the light of the knowledge of the glory of God in the face of Christ" (2 Cor. 3:18, 4:6). From glory to glory he is changing us.

---

5   Bruce, *Letter of Paul to the Romans*, 168.
6   Lloyd-Jones, *Romans*, vol. 8, *Final Perseverance of the Saints*, 222–23.

The Holy Spirit is working in us right now. Paul declares, "And hope does not disappoint us, because God has poured out his love into our hearts by the Holy Spirit, whom he has given us" (Rom. 5:5). A Christian is a Spirit-indwelt, Spirit-empowered, Spirit-directed person. The Spirit transforms us from one degree of glory to another to achieve the predestinated purpose of God. So the Holy Spirit is working in us, transforming us daily into the likeness of Christ, imprinting on our soul and body the image of Christ.

Those who profess Christ yet live sinful lives are not the people of God. We experience pressure every day to compromise and sin. People do not like those who oppose sin in the church. But read the first three chapters in Revelation. Jesus Christ himself does not like sin in the church. How dare people want us to welcome sin into the church! The church denies its very existence when it becomes like the world.

Professing Christians who live sinful lives are chaff, which the wind blows away. They are the foolish virgins, who will hear these words from the Lord of the church: "I tell you the truth, I do not know you." They may call Jesus, "Lord, Lord," but the Lord will say to them, "Depart from me, you evildoers. I never knew you!"

What about you? Are you holy? Are you presently being conformed to the image of Christ? Do you love God and his ways? Then you are God's beloved in God's eternal plan, and you can rejoice in this knowledge. If not, then consider this truth: "Without holiness no one will see the Lord" (Heb. 12:14). Let us make every effort to be holy, beginning today.

B. The Final Purpose of Predestination: Pre-eminence of Christ

Our conformity to the image of Christ is not the ultimate purpose. The ultimate purpose is the pre-eminence of his Son, *"that he might be the firstborn among many brothers"* (v. 29). Paul writes, "Therefore God exalted him to the highest place and gave him the name that is above every name, that at the name of Jesus every knee should bow, in heaven and on earth and under the earth, and every tongues confess that Jesus Christ is Lord, to the glory of God the Father" (Phil. 2:9–11). It is God's ultimate purpose that his Son will have pre-eminence: "And he is the head of the body, the church; he is the beginning and the firstborn from among the dead, so that in everything he might have the supremacy" (Col. 1:18).

God's eternal plan is to have a family consisting in Jesus Christ, his Son by nature, and the elect people of God, sons and daughters by grace and adoption. This family of God consists of Jesus Christ as older brother and us as his younger brothers. The Father's family consists of the firstborn son and later born sons. Jesus is the firstborn: "He is the image of the invisible God, the firstborn over all creation" (Col. 1:15; see also Heb. 1:6).

Paul says Jesus is the firstborn among many brothers. "Brothers" includes Jews and Gentiles, men and women, from all the families of the earth. Christ has many brothers throughout the world, all on equal footing in the family of God.

What does firstborn mean? It points to the priority, supremacy, and pre-eminence of Christ. Psalm 89:27 clearly teaches this: "I will also appoint him [David] my firstborn, the most exalted of the kings of the earth." In his natural family, David was the lastborn. But God appointed him as firstborn, that is, he gave him supremacy and pre-eminence.

In some Christian homes you may see a plaque on the wall: "That in all things Jesus Christ might have pre-eminence." The owners are declaring that in their house, in all they do, Jesus Christ has pre-eminence. It is the will of the Father that the people of God live for the glory of Christ. He is to be worshiped and served as Lord.

In the family of God, Jesus Christ is pre-eminent. This tells us that we are eminent. He is King of kings, and we are kings in him.

The Father has put all things under his feet. If you are his enemy, Christ's feet are on your neck, and you shall be destroyed. But we who are God's people are not placed under his feet. We are the bride of Christ, clothed in radiant beauty and seated with him in the heavenly realms. Christ is the most glorious, and we are glorious in him. So the Hebrews writer explains, "In bringing many sons to glory, it was fitting that God, for whom and through whom everything exists, should make the author of their salvation perfect through suffering. Both the one who makes men holy and those who are made holy are of the same family. So Jesus is not ashamed to call them brothers. He says, 'I will declare your name to my brothers; in the presence of the congregation I will sing your praises'" (Heb. 2:10–12). We are Christ's brothers, sons of glory, eminent, and famous. Jesus Christ is pre-eminent and most famous. And in all of this, God the Father is glorified.

3. Effectual Calling

"And those he predestined, he also called" (v. 30). Those whom God chose in love and predestinated in eternity he calls effectually in time, in the personal history of the individual. The call of the gospel comes to every elect. It does not come as a general invitation, which the hearer can refuse. This call is effectual. It is a divine summons, and the elect are enabled to come to Jesus, believe in him, and be united with him. He may be calling you today. If so, I urge you to come to him, believe in him, be saved, and go in peace.

How does the call come? Paul explains, "How, then, can they call on the one they have not believed in? And how can they believe in the one of whom they have not heard? And how can they hear without someone preaching to them? And how can they preach unless they are sent? As it is written, 'How beautiful are the feet of those who bring good news!'" (Rom. 10:14–15). A true preacher is called, commissioned, and sent in the power of the Holy Spirit and in the knowledge of the gospel. He preaches Jesus Christ and him crucified, dead, buried, raised from the dead, and seated on the right hand of God as Sovereign Lord. As the gospel is being preached, an elect sinner's heart is opened by the Holy Spirit, who regenerates the sinner and enables him to repent and believe the gospel.

No one is saved without faith. Faith requires the hearing of the word; therefore, we must share the gospel so that elect sinners can be called.

The Sovereign God works primarily through his people. Cornelius was saved by hearing the gospel through Peter, not through an angel. We are important in God's plan of saving elect sinners. If we are called by the gospel, we must call others by the same gospel. The book of Revelation concludes, "The Spirit and the bride say, 'Come!' And let him who hears say, 'Come!' Whoever is thirsty, let him come; and whoever wishes, let him take the free gift of the water of life" (Rev. 22:17). The Spirit says come. The church says come. And every believer says come. Come, take the water of life, and live.

Call your spouse in this way. Call your children. Call your parents and relatives. Call your neighbors. Call your colleagues. Call those whom God sends your way, and call those to whom you are sent. God called me and sent me, and I came to proclaim the gospel to you.

Paul preached the gospel in Pisidian Antioch: "When the Gentiles heard this, they were glad and honored the word of the Lord; and all who were appointed for eternal life believed" (Acts 13:48). Paul told the Thessalonians, "For we know, brothers loved by God, that he has chosen you, because our gospel came to you not simply with words, but also with power, with the Holy Spirit and with deep conviction. . . . And we also thank God continually because, when you received the word of God, which you heard from us, you accepted it not as the word of men, but as it actually is, the word of God, which is at work in you who believe. . . . He called you to this through our gospel, that you might share in the glory of our Lord Jesus Christ" (1 Thess. 1:4–5, 2:13; 2 Thess. 2:14). God loved, he chose, and he called through the gospel all his elect to share in the glory of our Lord Jesus Christ.

I pray we will be baptized in the Holy Spirit and clothed with the Spirit of power, love, and a sound mind. May we be filled with the Spirit and speak the gospel with boldness, that we may call people from death to life, from eternal shame to eternal glory. Remember, we speak in the name of the one who has received all authority in heaven and on earth. He is with us always, and not even death can separate us from the love of God. The end of the world will come when every elect has been called to life (Matt. 24:14).

4. Justification

The sons of Adam find themselves already condemned. They are under the wrath of God every day and are on their way to hell. Yet they try to clothe themselves with the stinking fig leaf contraption of self-righteousness. But it is useless. By the works of the law no flesh can be justified (Rom. 3:20). We need to be clothed in the righteousness of another. We need a man who is sinless and at the same time eternal God, whose merit is infinite.

So God sent his own Son from heaven to be incarnate in the womb of the virgin Mary. The wages of sin is eternal death. Jesus Christ came to die in behalf of those whom the Father loved from eternity. He who knew no sin became sin for us that in him we might become the righteousness of God. God can now justify the ungodly justly—anyone who trusts in Jesus Christ alone.

Jeremiah declares, "This is the name by which [Jesus] will be called: The LORD Our Righteousness" (Jer. 23:6). And Paul tells us, "It is because of [God the Father] that you are in Christ Jesus, who has become for us wisdom from God—that is, our righteousness, holiness and redemption" (1 Cor. 1:30). Jesus Christ died for our sins and was raised for our righteousness (Rom. 4:25). We are now justified freely by God's grace alone (Rom. 3:24). We are justified by faith in Jesus. Salvation is by grace alone through faith alone (Rom. 3:26). We are justified by the blood of Jesus (Rom. 5:9).

Without the cross of Christ, there is no justification for the ungodly. If one denies the cross, one denies salvation. We must lift high the cross of Calvary. We confess Christ who died for our sins. Having been justified by the Father, we have peace with God. We are reconciled to God and stand by grace in God's presence. God has moved us from our former state of condemnation to our new state of justification.

It is God the Father who justifies (Rom. 8:33). No appeal is possible to another court, and our justification cannot be reversed. We who were enemies of God are reconciled to him through Jesus Christ our Lord.

Grace is the *source* of our justification. The work of Christ is the *ground* of our justification. Faith is the *means* of our justification, and that faith is a divine gift. The *effect* of our justification is nothing less than vital union with Christ. This is the mother of all doctrines. God the Father is the one who has justified us. And so we wait in hope of the glory of God.

5. Glorification

"Those he justified, he also glorified" (v. 30). What is emphasized is not our response of faith, but God's action. We believe and live an obedient life because of the divine life he gives us. So we do not boast; we praise God for his work in our lives.

Note the divine monergism in our salvation:

- God foreloved a specific number of sinners in eternity past;
- God predestinated these ones to become like Christ, holy and blameless;
- God effectually called these people in time, in our personal history, by the preaching of the gospel; he called us to life even as Lazarus was called to life from the tomb of death;
- God justified the ungodly, declaring us righteous;
- God not only forgave our sins, but he also clothed us with the perfect righteousness of Christ.

Divine monergism continues to the end. Those whom God justified, these he also glorified. Here Paul deliberately uses the aorist tense because it is so certain. He says, "He glorified," not, "He shall glorify" us in the future. It is as good as done. There is no contingency. God who acted first in loving us moves from step to step until he comes to our glorification. No power in the world can stop him from glorifying in the future those whom he foreloved and predestinated in eternity, those whom he called and justified in time. God alone works from eternity past through time to eternity future.

Even now Christ is in us, the hope of glory. We have already been raised with Christ and are seated with Christ (Eph. 2:6). Our spirit is alive because of righteousness, and the God who raised Jesus Christ from the dead will make alive our mortal bodies through the Holy Spirit who indwells us now (Rom. 8:11). Our new federal head, Jesus Christ, has already been glorified. And we are united with him. We are in him. So soon we also must be glorified.

Paul declares, "But Christ has indeed been raised from the dead, the firstfruits of those who have fallen asleep. . . . So in Christ all will be made alive. But each in his own turn: Christ, the firstfruits; then, when he comes, those who belong to him" (1 Cor. 15:20–23). Our glorification is certain. Elsewhere he writes, "[Christ], by the power that enables him to bring everything under his control, will transform our lowly bodies so that they will be like his glorious body" (Phil. 3:21). Again, he declares, "And just as we have borne the likeness of the earthly man, so shall we bear the likeness of the man from heaven" (1 Cor. 15:49). All have sinned in Adam and lost the glory of God. In Jesus Christ, the glory of our spirit and body is restored to us. So we shall bear the likeness of the man from heaven. "He called you to this through [the] gospel, that you might share in the glory of our Lord Jesus Christ" (2 Thess. 2:14).

God sent his Son into this world not just that our sins may be forgiven and we be justified, but that he may bring many sons, every elect, to glory and so that every elect would be made like our glorious Lord Jesus Christ. As we share in his life, we also shall share in his glory.

Sanctification is glory begun and glorification is the consummation of sanctification. Right now it is happening. We are being transformed into Christ's likeness with ever-increasing glory. Even now, from glory to glory he is changing us. "Therefore we do not lose heart. Though outwardly we are wasting away, yet inwardly we are being renewed day by day" (2 Cor. 4:16). We cannot deny that we are wasting away as we get older. But that is not all. Even now we are being renewed daily in our inward man. Jesus not only restores to us the glory we lost in Adam, but he also gives us greater glory, because the glory of Christ, the man from heaven, is greater than the glory of the man from earth.

God moves irresistibly from the first step of foreknowledge to the last step of our glorification. We can be absolutely confident of this: "that he who began a good work in you will carry it on to completion until the day of Christ Jesus" (Phil. 1:6). What God began, he shall complete, and in Christ our glorification is an accomplished fact. Even now we experience some of this. Paul exhorts, "Do everything without complaining or arguing, so that you may become blameless and pure, children of God without fault in a crooked and depraved generation, in which you shine like stars in the universe as you hold out the word of life" (Phil. 2:14–16). But soon we shall shine with far greater brightness, for when we see him, then we shall be like him

(1 John 3:2). Then we shall shine like the sun in the kingdom of our Father (Matt. 13:43), just as our older brother's face is like the sun shining in all its brilliance (Rev. 1:16).

That is our destiny, and we shall reach the goal. We shall be conformed to Christ, that he may have pre-eminence among many brothers. All this is for the Father's glory. Then shall eternity future begin in a creation that is glorified too. God will dwell with us, and we with him. That is life eternal. That is joy unspeakable and full of glory.

Conclusion

Salvation is of the Lord from beginning to end. He does all the work. What did we do? We ran away from God. We became prodigals and rebels, enemies of God. But God came after us and apprehended us. He transformed us, and from glory to glory he is changing us. Now we love God and delight in doing his will. We worship God and live for his glory. God is working one hundred percent, and we also work one hundred percent. But we work because of God's grace. The Spirit of God enables us to think God's thoughts and to do his will.

Ask the question: "For who makes you different from anyone else? What do you have that you did not receive? And if you did receive it, why do you boast as though you did not?" (1 Cor. 4:7). Salvation is of the Lord. Therefore we can depend on it. God works in us and through us, and God receives all praise.

Remember this also: The visible church is always a mixture of wheat and chaff. If you are not living a holy and obedient life, then you must draw the conclusion that you may not be God's chosen. Call upon the name of the Lord that you may be saved. But if you live by repentance and faith, then you are God's chosen. Romans 8:28 told us, "We know that to those who love God, in all things God works for good, to those who according to purpose are called." So our love for God, which is a response to God's love for us, is a proof that we are in the company of those whom God foreknew, God predestinated, God called, God justified, and God glorified. To God be the glory! To such people Romans 8:29–30 gives the ultimate and supreme guarantee of their final salvation in glory.

54

God Is for Us

What, then, shall we say in response to this? If God is for us, who can be against us?

Romans 8:31

Sometimes people try to encourage me by saying, "Pastor, don't worry. I am for you." But I do not put too much confidence in such a statement. Why? Because man is a sinner, and man can change. God alone is unchangeable; therefore, I want to make certain that God is for me. Saints of God, we have great reason for confidence in God for our full and final salvation. What is that reason? God is for us!

In Romans 8:31–39, Paul challenges any creature opposed to our salvation to answer and deny the truth of five unanswerable questions.[1] These questions are:

1. *If God is for us, who can be against us?* (v. 31)
2. *He who did not spare his own Son, but gave him up for us all—how will he not also, along with him, graciously give us all things?* (v. 32)
3. *Who will bring any charge against those whom God has chosen? It is God who justifies.* (v. 33)
4. *Who is he who condemns? Christ Jesus, who died—more than that, who was raised to life—is at the right hand of God and is also interceding for us.* (v. 34)
5. *Who shall separate us from the love of Christ?* (v. 35ff) What is the answer? Nothing and no one in God's universe is able to separate us from the love of God. In Christ, we are super-

---

1   Stott, *Romans: God's Good News,* 253–58.

conquerors. Nothing can destroy or defeat us in this life or in the life to come.

What Shall We Say?

Paul begins this section: "What shall we say to these things?" In other words, what should we say to what God has done for us as stated so far in this epistle, particularly in the previous three verses (Rom. 8:28–30)?

As sinners, we were under God's wrath. We were not lovers of God or keepers of his law. We were ungodly, helpless sinners, enemies of God, dead in trespasses and sins. Yet God from all eternity loved us and chose us. He predestinated us to be conformed to the image of his Son, that he might be the firstborn among the many brethren in God's family. In time, he effectually called us by the gospel and regenerated us, granting us true repentance and saving faith to trust in Jesus Christ alone for our eternal salvation.

God justified us, declaring us just because of Christ's atoning death in behalf of us. God is sanctifying us and will glorify us. Forgiven of all sins, we are clothed in divine righteousness. We are united with Christ and live his resurrection life every day. As adopted children of God, we are heirs of God and joint-heirs with Christ. Having been freed from the dominion of sin, law, and death, we are now outside of their reach and authority.

Friends, we are in Christ and in God. What shall we say to these things? In other words, what must be the logical conclusion we draw from this truth? As Christians, we must be logical and doctrinal. We should know what God has done for us, and be impressed with the divine monergism.

Doctrine is detested today in favor of entertainment and the priority of emoting. We must recognize that doctrine is fundamental for us to stand against all the wiles of the devil. I have seen people fall away because they refused to study the Scriptures and know doctrine. How can we resist the devil unless we know what the Scripture declares as to what God has done for us? John writes of this, saying, "They overcame [the devil] by the blood of the Lamb and by the word of their testimony" (Rev. 12:11).

Jesus himself overcame the devil by the Scripture. I pray that we all will study and know the Scripture, so that we may live confident, assured, happy, and steady lives in this world, in the midst of all troubles, tribulations, pains, and persecutions.

The God Who Is for Us

"If God is for us, who can be against us?" The word "if" does not introduce any doubt. It means "since" or "because" of this reality of divine monergism in our salvation. The meaning is, *"Since God is for us."* But what God is he talking about? Question 4 of the Westminster Shorter Catechism asks, "What is God?" The answer: "God is a Spirit, infinite, eternal, and unchangeable in his being, wisdom, power, holiness, justice, goodness and truth."

So Paul is speaking not of the many gods of the world religions. No, he is talking about the true and living God, who has revealed himself in creation, in the human conscience, in the holy Scriptures, and especially in the person of Jesus Christ.

He is the one God who exists in three persons—the Father, the Son, and the Holy Spirit. Paul states, "We know that an idol is nothing at all in the world and that there is no God but one. For even if there are so-called gods, whether in heaven or on earth (as indeed there are many 'gods' and many 'lords'), yet for us there is but one God, the Father, from whom all things came and for whom we live; and there is but one Lord, Jesus Christ, through whom all things came and through whom we live" (1 Cor. 8:4–6). There is none greater than or equal to this God of the holy Scriptures. He created and sustains all things, and he is the redeemer of his elect people.

We can know this God better through studying his attributes:[2]

1. *Eternal.* God has no beginning and no end. He is above time, space, and matter. He declares and ordains the end from the beginning. That is why we have prophecy in the Bible.
2. *Unchangeable.* God is unchangeable in his being, perfections, purposes, and promises. What he promises he fulfills. He tells

---

2   For further study on the attributes of God, see Louis Berkhof, *Systematic Theology* (Part I, sections v–vii); Frame, *Doctrine of God* (ch. 19); Wayne Grudem, *Systematic Theology* (chs. 11–13); Charles Hodge, *Systematic Theology* (Part I, section v).

us, "Remember the former things, those of long ago; I am God, and there is no other; I am God, and there is none like me. I make known the end from the beginning, from ancient times, what is still to come. I say: My purpose will stand, and I will do all that I please" (Isa. 46:9–10). Man lies and breaks his covenant, but God does not change: "I the LORD do not change. So you, O descendants of Jacob, are not destroyed" (Mal. 3:6). He does not lie. He does not "become."

3. *Omnipresent.* God is present everywhere in his fullness, to punish, to sustain, and to bless. "'Am I only a God nearby,' declares the LORD, 'and not a God far away? Can anyone hide in secret places so that I cannot see him?' declares the LORD. 'Do not I fill heaven and earth?' declares the LORD" (Jer. 23:23–24).

4. *Independent.* God is from himself. He has no need; he is not served by human hands. "The God who made the world and everything in it is the Lord of heaven and earth and does not live in temples built by hands. And he is not served by human hands, as if he needed anything, because he himself gives all men life and breath and everything else" (Acts 17:24–25). Creation does not contribute to God's glory; rather, it manifests and declares it.

5. *Spirit.* God is not made of matter. He is uncreated Spirit, not perceivable by our senses.

6. *Invisible.* God in his essence cannot be seen by creatures, though he has manifested himself to us in visible forms, such as theophanies. In heaven we will see God, but not exhaustively. We will see him only to the degree a sinless creature can see him.

7. *Omniscient.* God knows all things always in one simple, eternal act. He knows himself and all things. Adam, Achan, Ananias, Jonah, Judas, and others thought they could hide matters from God, but we all stand stripped naked before him. God never has to learn anything. He can never increase his knowledge. He knows everything, including our every thought.

8. *Wise.* God always chooses the best goals and the best means to achieve those goals. Therefore, the cross reveals the wisdom of God, for it was the best means to redeem us for his glory. Our God is the only wise God. "Oh, the depth of the riches of the wisdom and knowledge of God!" (Rom. 11:33).

9. *Truthful.* God cannot lie. He alone is reliable and true. Thus, God's revelation, the holy Bible, is true, because God is truth. As well, his children must speak and do truth. All liars will be cast into the lake of fire.

10. *Loving.* God is love, so God gives himself. God gave his Son to the death of the cross because he loved us. God from eternity foreloved us and chose us to glory.

11. *Holy.* God is holy; he is separated from sin and seeks his own glory. So we also must live holy lives, separating ourselves from

sin and always seeking God's glory, for "without holiness no one will see the Lord" (Heb. 12:14). Antinomians and libertines are children of the devil, the lawless one.

12. *Righteous.* God always acts in accordance with what is right. He is the ultimate standard of right and, therefore, he intently hates all sin. "The wrath of God is being revealed from heaven against all the godlessness and wickedness of men" (Rom. 1:18). Hell is prepared for all sinners who will not repent and believe in Jesus Christ. His wrath is being revealed against them even now.

God Is for Us

This God is for us. The word "for" (*huper*) is very important. God is for us, not against us. The wrath of God is revealed against all sinners, but God poured out the wrath that was due us on his own Son on the cross. God was *against* Jesus Christ so that he could be *for* us.

"For us" means "in our place" and "for our eternal benefit." Paul writes, "Christ died for [*huper*] the ungodly" (Rom. 5:6). In other words, he died in our place, for our benefit. And because of this, we do not die under God's wrath. There is no longer wrath against us, but only love for us. So Paul writes, "But God demonstrates his own love for us in this: While we were still sinners, Christ died for [*huper*] us" (Rom. 5:8). We deserved to die, for the wages of sin is death, but Christ died vicariously. He died a substitutionary death in our place and for our eternal salvation, so now we live by his resurrection life. Christ died for us because God the Father is for us. "God made him who had no sin to be sin for [*huper*] us, so that in him we might become the righteousness of God" (2 Cor. 5:21).

God is not for us as a subservient ally. Some people think God is for us as a waiter, that we can snap our fingers and he will come to help us. But God's purpose is not to do everything we say. He is the Sovereign; we are the servants. This Sovereign is for us now and forever. In one sense, God was for us from eternity, when he foreloved and predestinated us. God is not, however, for everybody. He is for the elect only, for those who love him. He is against all others. The fact that God is for us spells hope and full assurance; the fact that God is against his enemies spells eternal doom.

Is God for you? Do you love God? Do you love his Son? Do you trust in Christ and serve him only? Or do you presume that God is for you, no matter how you live?

Eli's sons and all Israel presumed that God was for them when they fought against the Philistines. After four thousand Israelites were killed in battle, they brought the ark into the battlefield with a great shout. They presumed that now God would defeat the Philistines totally:

> So the people sent men to Shiloh, and they brought back the ark of the covenant of the LORD Almighty, who is enthroned between the cherubim. And Eli's two sons, Hophni and Phinehas, were there with the ark of the covenant of God. When the ark of the LORD's covenant came into the camp, all Israel raised such a great shout that the ground shook. . . . So the Philistines fought, and the Israelites were defeated and every man fled to his tent. The slaughter was very great; Israel lost thirty thousand foot soldiers. The ark of God was captured, and Eli's two sons, Hophni and Phinehas, died. . . . The man who brought the news replied, "Israel fled before the Philistines, and the army has suffered heavy losses. Also your two sons, Hophni and Phinehas, are dead, and the ark of God has been captured." When he mentioned the ark of God, Eli fell backward off his chair by the side of the gate. His neck was broken and he died, for he was an old man and heavy. He had led Israel forty years. (1 Sam. 4:4–5, 10–11, 17–18)

Presumption led to the deaths of thirty-four thousand Israelites, including Hophni and Phinehas. The ark was taken, and God broke Eli's neck. The wife of Phinehas died in childbirth, and her son was given the terrible name Ichabod, "Glory gone."

Apostate evangelicals and charismatics presume that God is for them. But God is not for apostate Israel nor for apostate Christians. God is for the elect only, for those who love God and live for his glory. God the Father, Jesus Christ, and the Holy Spirit are for us. Holy angels are also for us, as is the holy church.

God was for young David in another battle between Israel and the Philistines. The enemies of God were winning under the leadership of the champion Goliath, who was nine feet tall and fully armed. But young David came forward, full of wisdom, faith, and the Holy Spirit. He declared, "The LORD who delivered me from the paw of the lion and the paw of the bear will deliver me from the hand of this Philistine" (1 Sam. 17:37). David trusted in the Lord. Then he boldly proclaimed to the Philistines, "You come against me with sword and spear and javelin, but I come against you in the name of the LORD Almighty, the God of the armies of Israel, whom you have defied. This day the LORD will hand you over to me, and I'll strike you down and cut off your head. Today I will give the carcasses of the Philistine army to the birds of the air and the beasts of the earth, and the whole world will know that there is a God in Israel" (vv. 45–46). After David stood over the defeated giant and cut off his head with Goliath's own sword, "the Philistines saw that their hero was dead [and] they turned and ran" (v. 51). Here God was for David and Israel, and God was against the Philistines. If God is for us, our final victory is certain and sure.

God was also for Jesus. Though he gave him up to be crucified for our salvation, he was for him in his conception, birth, and life. He forsook him briefly on the cross, and then Jesus died and was buried. Yet God raised him from the dead. "And if the Spirit of him who raised Jesus from the dead is living in you, he who raised Christ from the dead will also give life to your mortal bodies through his Spirit, who lives in you" (Rom. 8:11). In fact, God highly exalted Jesus "when he raised him from the dead and seated him at his right hand in the heavenly realms, far above all rule and authority, power and dominion, and every title that can be given, not only in the present age but also in the one to come. And God placed all things under his feet and appointed him to be head over everything for the church" (Eph. 1:20–22; see also Phil. 2:9–11).

It is also true that when all others forsook Paul, God was for him. At that time Paul wrote, "You know that everyone in the province of Asia has deserted me, including Phygelus and Hermogenes. . . . Demas, because he loved this world, has deserted me and has gone to Thessalonica. Crescens has gone to Galatia, and Titus to Dalmatia. . . . At my first defense, no one came to my support, but everyone deserted me. May it not be held against them. But the Lord stood at my side and gave me strength, so that through me the message might be fully proclaimed and all the Gentiles might hear it. And I was delivered from the lion's mouth" (2 Tim. 1:15; 4:10, 16–17). God is for us, with us, in us, and we are in God. If God is for us, who can be against us?

Who Can Be against Us?

We have many enemies, but they are all finite creatures. No power can prevail against the infinite God, who has purposed to save us. No one can resist him. What about the devil and demons? God in Christ has defeated the devil on the cross and liberated us from his clutches. The stronger one, Jesus Christ, defeated the strong one, the devil, and set us free.

What about the world? Jesus said, "Rejoice, I have overcome the world." The world of Pharaohs and Caesars and dictators and presidents cannot harm us. Jesus Christ has defeated them all.

What about the apostate church? Again, the answer is no. It cannot harm us. Why is that? Paul writes, "Having disarmed the powers and authorities, he made a public spectacle of them, triumphing over them by the cross" (Col. 2:15). Jesus Christ by his death has defeated all our enemies and all his enemies.

What about the flesh, that sin which still dwells in us? Yes, it is against us, but it is not the only thing in us. God's Holy Spirit is also in us. He is the Spirit of holiness, who gives us victory over sin. Therefore, sin cannot have dominion over us. We are not under sin or law or death, nor are we under the devil, the world, or the apostate church.

Is there any power equal to or above God's power? No! Therefore, if God is for us, who can be against us? The Scriptures emphasize this point throughout.

Jesus is still waging war against all our defeated enemies; it is his business to fight such a war. So the psalmist declares, "The LORD says to my Lord: 'Sit at my right hand until I make your enemies a footstool for your feet'" (Ps. 110:1). "Then the end will come, when he hands over the kingdom to God the Father after he has destroyed all dominion, authority and power. For he must reign until he has put all his enemies under his feet. The last enemy to be destroyed is death. For he 'has put everything under his feet.' Now when it says that 'everything' has been put under him, it is clear that this does not include God himself, who put everything under Christ" (1 Cor. 15:24–27). The Father commissioned his Son to defeat all his enemies, angelic and human. And he will destroy you unless you repent and believe on the Lord Jesus Christ.

Who do you think Jesus is? People sing, "Jesus, sweet Jesus, what a wonder you are." But did you know that he is also the Judge of the whole world? Did you know that he has wrath against all evildoers? Listen to John's words:

> Then the kings of the earth, the princes, the generals, the rich, the mighty, and every slave and every free man hid in caves and among the rocks of the mountains. They called to the mountains and the rocks, "Fall on us and hide us from the face of him who sits on the throne and from the wrath of the Lamb! For the great day of their wrath has come, and who can stand?" (Rev. 6:15–17)

> I saw heaven standing open and there before me was a white horse, whose rider is called Faithful and True. With justice he judges and makes war. His eyes are like blazing fire, and on his head are many crowns. He has a name written on him that no one knows but he himself. He is dressed in a robe dipped in blood, and his name is the Word of God. The armies of heaven were following him, riding on white horses and dressed in fine linen, white and clean. Out of his mouth comes a sharp sword with which to strike down the nations. "He will rule them with an iron scepter." He treads the winepress of the fury of the wrath of God Almighty. On his robe and on his thigh he has this name written:

> KING OF KINGS AND LORD OF LORDS.

> And I saw an angel standing in the sun, who cried in a loud voice to all the birds flying in midair, "Come, gather together for the great supper of God, so that you may eat the flesh of kings, generals, and mighty men, of horses and their riders, and the flesh of all people, free and slave, small and great." Then I saw the beast and the kings of the earth and their armies gathered together to make war against the rider on the horse and his army. But the beast was captured, and with him the false prophet who had performed the miraculous signs on his behalf. With these signs he had deluded those who had received the mark of the beast and worshiped his image. The two of them were thrown alive into the fiery lake of burning sulfur. The rest of them were killed with the sword that came out of the mouth of the rider on the horse, and all the birds gorged themselves on their flesh. (Rev. 19:11–21)

> And the devil, who deceived them, was thrown into the lake of burning sulfur, where the beast and the false prophet had been

thrown. They will be tormented day and night for ever and ever. . . . If anyone's name was not found written in the book of life, he was thrown into the lake of fire. (Rev. 20:10, 15)

Jesus said, "I will build my church, and the gates of hell shall not prevail against it" (Matt. 16:18, KJV). In Christ, Christ's church triumphs over the gates of hell. All Jericho's walls shall fall, and Jericho will be destroyed.

We are more than conquerors in and through Jesus Christ. Paul writes,

> Finally, be strong in the Lord and in his mighty power. Put on the full armor of God so that you can take your stand against the devil's schemes. For our struggle is not against flesh and blood, but against the rulers, against the authorities, against the powers of this dark world and against the spiritual forces of evil in the heavenly realms. Therefore put on the full armor of God, so that when the day of evil comes, you may be able to stand your ground, and after you have done everything, to stand. Stand firm then, with the belt of truth buckled around your waist, with the breastplate of righteousness in place, and with your feet fitted with the readiness that comes from the gospel of peace. In addition to all this, take up the shield of faith, with which you can extinguish all the flaming arrows of the evil one. Take the helmet of salvation and the sword of the Spirit, which is the word of God. And pray in the Spirit on all occasions with all kinds of prayers and requests. With this in mind, be alert and always keep on praying for all the saints. (Eph. 6:10–18)

Onward, Christian soldiers! Fight the good fight against all defeated enemies and spiritual forces of evil. Pray in the Spirit and stand firm. Fight, and stand in victory. "Submit yourselves, then, to God. Resist the devil, and he will flee from you" (James 4:7). "Be self-controlled and alert. Your enemy the devil prowls around like a roaring lion looking for someone to devour. Resist him, standing firm in the faith" (1 Pet. 5:8–9). How do you resist the devil? Tell him, "Christ died for my sins and is raised for my justification."

I hope we will believe that God is for us forever! He alone is for our eternal salvation. God is all we need. For, if God is for us, who can be against us?

God Is with Us

Not only is God for us, but he is also with us. He is our portion and cup. Listen to what God said to the worried Abraham: "Do not be afraid, Abram. I am your shield, your very great reward" (Gen. 15:1). God is our reward and shield—not the small shield, but the large shield that covers a person completely. In Exodus 14 we read, "Moses answered the people, 'Do not be afraid. Stand firm and you will see the deliverance the LORD will bring you today. The Egyptians you see today you will never see again. The LORD will fight for you; you need only to be still'. . . . Then the angel of God, who had been traveling in front of Israel's army, withdrew and went behind them. The pillar of cloud also moved from in front and stood behind them, coming between the armies of Egypt and Israel. Throughout the night the cloud brought darkness to the one side and light to the other side; so neither went near the other all night long" (vv. 13–14, 19–20).

God is with us, and he is the one who is dealing with our enemies. We are shielded by him. Moses declared, "The eternal God is your refuge, and underneath are the everlasting arms. He will drive out your enemy before you, saying, 'Destroy him!'" (Deut. 33:27). Elsewhere we read, "Now when Joshua was near Jericho, he looked up and saw a man standing in front of him with a drawn sword in his hand. Joshua went up to him and asked, 'Are you for us or for our enemies?' 'Neither,' he replied, 'but as commander of the army of the LORD I have now come.' Then Joshua fell facedown to the ground in reverence, and asked him, 'What message does my Lord have for his servant?' The commander of the LORD's army replied, 'Take off your sandals, for the place where you are standing is holy.' And Joshua did so" (Josh. 5:13–15). We have a commander who goes with us into battle.

So David said, "Even though I walk through the valley of the shadow of death, I will fear no evil, for you are with me" (Ps. 23:4); "The LORD is my light and my salvation—whom shall I fear? The LORD is the stronghold of my life—of whom shall I be afraid?" (Ps. 27:1). The answer is, "No one!" Elsewhere David proclaims, "The LORD is with me; I will not be afraid. What can man do to me? The LORD is with me; he is my helper. I will look in triumph on my enemies" (Ps. 118:6–7).

The servant of Elisha was troubled when the Arameans came to attack them, and we read, "When the servant of the man of God got up and went out early the next morning, an army with horses and chariots had surrounded the city. 'Oh, my lord, what shall we do?' the servant asked. 'Don't be afraid,' the prophet answered. 'Those who are with us are more than those who are with them.' And Elisha prayed, 'O Lord, open his eyes so he may see.' Then the Lord opened the servant's eyes, and he looked and saw the hills full of horses and chariots of fire all around Elisha" (2 Kings 6:15–17). We are well surrounded by the horses and fiery chariots of heaven.

Isaiah declares,

> See, the Sovereign Lord comes with power, and his arm rules for him. See, his reward is with him, and his recompense accompanies him. . . . Who has measured the waters in the hollow of his hand, or with the breadth of his hand marked off the heavens? Who has held the dust of the earth in a basket, or weighed the mountains on the scales and the hills in a balance? Who has understood the mind of the Lord, or instructed him as his counselor? Whom did the Lord consult to enlighten him, and who taught him the right way? Who was it that taught him knowledge or showed him the path of understanding? . . . Do you not know? Have you not heard? The Lord is the everlasting God, the Creator of the ends of the earth. He will not grow tired or weary, and his understanding no one can fathom. He gives strength to the weary and increases the power of the weak. (Isa. 40:10, 12–14, 28–29)

The Lord is with us. Elsewhere Isaiah says, "'No weapon forged against you will prevail, and you will refute every tongue that accuses you. This is the heritage of the servants of the Lord, and this is their vindication from me,' declares the Lord" (54:17). And in Zechariah we read, "'And I myself will be a wall of fire around [Jerusalem],' declares the Lord, 'and I will be its glory within'" (2:5).

After his resurrection, Jesus told his disciples he would be with them: "And surely I am with you always, to the very end of the age" (Matt. 28:20). And if Jesus is with us and for us, then we cannot be defeated. Jesus says, "I give them eternal life, and they shall never perish; no one can snatch them out of my hand. My

Father, who has given them to me, is greater than all; no one can snatch them out of my Father's hand" (John 10:28–29). John writes, "You, dear children, are from God and have overcome them, because the one who is in you is greater than the one who is in the world" (1 John 4:4). The infinite, almighty, omnipresent, all-holy, all-wise, eternal, sovereign God is with us and for us.

Think about this: even our sin cannot keep us from God's purpose to save us. God will deal with his children. Paul writes, "Hand this man over to Satan, so that the [flesh] may be destroyed and his spirit saved on the day of the Lord" (1 Cor. 5:5). In the same epistle he writes, "That is why many among you are weak and sick, and a number of you have fallen asleep. . . . When we are judged by the Lord, we are being disciplined so that we will not be condemned with the world" (1 Cor. 11:30, 32). God may even have to kill us so that we will go to heaven. This is called "mercy killing"!

If God is for us, who can be against us? The world, the flesh, the devil, death, the law, and sin are all formidable adversaries. But they are finite, not almighty. For us is God our Father, Christ our Redeemer, and the Holy Spirit as our divine empowering advocate. In all things God works for our good, and since God never fails, we will always win.

The Hebrews writer tells us there is a great cloud of witnesses surrounding us, who testify to God's ability to save us. "Therefore, since we are surrounded by such a great cloud of witnesses, let us throw off everything that hinders and the sin that so easily entangles, and let us run with perseverance the race marked out for us" (Heb. 12:1). For us there is no condemnation and no separation from God's everlasting love.

Let me ask you: Is God for you? Have you trusted in Jesus Christ, God's sacrifice for our sins? If you have done so, you can rejoice—God is for you! But if you have not, know that God is against you even now. God commands all people to repent of their sins and trust in Jesus. Do this right now, so that you may know for certain that God is for you. Remember, we will live forever—either with God being for us or with God being against us. May God help us trust in Christ and be saved.

55

The Wondrous Cross

He who did not spare his own Son, but gave him up for us all—how will he not also, along with him, graciously give us all things?

Romans 8:32

The wondrous cross of Christ is the theme of Romans 8:32. Paul declared that "the message of the cross is foolishness to those who are perishing, but to us who are being saved it is the power of God" (1 Cor. 1:18). When he was in Corinth, he said he "resolved to know nothing . . . except Jesus Christ and him crucified" (1 Cor. 2:2). To the Galatians he said, "Before your very eyes Jesus Christ was clearly portrayed as crucified" (Gal. 3:1).

Without the gospel of the cross, there is no forgiveness of sins. Paul tells us, "May I never [glory] except in the cross of our Lord Jesus Christ, through which the world has been crucified to me, and I to the world" (Gal. 6:14). Jesus himself foretold, "But I, when I am lifted up from the earth, will draw all men to myself," that is, "I will save them from all their sins" (John 12:32). May we get out of the mud of gloom, misery, depression, and self-justification, and be freed as we look to the wondrous cross.

Christians suffer all the afflictions common to man, such as sickness, famine, accidents, and death. They also suffer troubles peculiar to being believers in Christ, whom the world hates. Jesus calls us to deny ourselves daily, take up the cross, and follow him. Paul says, "In fact, everyone who wants to live a godly life in Christ Jesus will be persecuted" (2 Tim. 3:12). Paul himself was persecuted all his life and was finally beheaded. We are also daily tempted by the devil. We may be plagued by the question: "What about the sins I have committed after trusting in Jesus Christ?" Not only that, we are also viciously hated by false Christians who profess Christ and call him "Lord, Lord," but who are ravenous wolves and servants of Satan.

When we are so afflicted and persecuted, we may be tempted to doubt God's love for us. While in prison, John the Baptist questioned whether Jesus was the Messiah, or should he wait for another. Jesus assured him that he was the true Messiah. Yet John was beheaded.

In Romans 8:32 Paul puts forward the second of five unanswerable questions to assure us that God's infinite love toward his elect shall never diminish. It remains constant, from eternity past to eternity future. The apostle provides the most powerful argument he can for this assurance. We must therefore know this argument from the wondrous cross and meditate on it. Then we too can live and die for the glory of God in triumph.

This argument is the ground of all our confidence in life and in death. Before he died, Paul said, "For I am already being poured out like a drink offering, and the time has come for my departure. I have fought the good fight, I have finished the race, I have kept the faith. Now there is in store for me the crown of righteousness, which the Lord, the righteous Judge, will award to me on that day—and not only to me, but also to all who have longed for his appearing" (2 Tim. 4:6–8).

The Father Spared Not

"He who did not spare his own Son . . ." In the Greek text, Paul uses a two-letter intensive particle (*ge*), which is not translated in the New International Version. It means "indeed" or "surely." So this verse begins, "He who *indeed* did not spare his own Son." This intensive particle is intended to magnify the great generosity of God's love for us in his saving act of handing over his Son to be crucified.

We must understand the significance of the term "his own Son." Paul used this phrase earlier: "For what the law was powerless to do . . . God did by sending his own Son" (Rom. 8:3). We are adopted sons by grace, but God did not spare his *own* Son, his one and only Son *by nature*, the second Person of the holy Trinity. He is the beloved Son, with whom the Father is well pleased.

Theological liberals do not believe Jesus is God's own Son. For them, Jesus was a mere man, the son of Joseph and Mary by natural generation, a sinner who thought he was God. They would say, "Jesus was a moral teacher, a reformer, a revolutionary, the first Marxist, a friend of the poor and the downtrodden, and a community organizer. He was a good man, though somewhat deluded. But he died and never rose again."

No! The Scriptures say the Father did not spare *his own Son*. Jesus is God's Son, and the Jews tried to kill him because of it: "For this reason the Jews tried all the harder to kill him; not only was he breaking the Sabbath, but he was even calling God his own Father, making himself equal with God" (John 5:18). Later on Jesus said, "I and the Father are one" (John 10:30). The Jews reacted to Jesus' words, saying, "We are not stoning you for any of these [miracles], but for blasphemy, because you, a mere man, claim to be God" (John 10:33). They concurred with the liberal view that Jesus was a mere man.

But Jesus is not a mere man; he is God incarnate. John writes, "In the beginning was the Word, and the Word was with God, and the Word was God. . . . The Word became flesh and made his dwelling among us. We have seen his glory, the glory of the One and Only, who came from the Father, full of grace and truth. . . . No one has ever seen God, but God the One and Only, who is at the Father's side, has made him known" (John 1:1, 14, 18). Thomas finally confessed and said to Jesus, "My Lord and my God!" (John 20:28).

God did not spare his own unique Son, who is eternal Deity: "The Son is the radiance of God's glory and the exact representation of his being, sustaining all things by his powerful word. After he had provided purification for sins, he sat down at the right hand of the Majesty in heaven" (Heb. 1:3). Paul writes, "For in Christ all the fullness of the Deity lives in bodily form" (Col. 2:9). This Son is the one "who through the Spirit of holiness was declared with power to be the Son of God by his resurrection from the dead: Jesus Christ our Lord" (Rom. 1:4).

The Father did not *spare* the only Son of his bosom. Paul is here reflecting on Genesis 22, which speaks of the sacrifice of Isaac when God tested Abraham's love. It is not enough for us to profess love for God; that love must be tested, and God himself does it. So God demanded that Abraham prove his love by sacrificing his son, his only son, his beloved son Isaac—not Ishmael, but Isaac, the son of promise through whom nations and kings were to come, and through whom the Messiah was eventually to come. And in reality, Abraham did not spare his son. It was God who intervened and spared Isaac from instant execution.

The Greek word *pheidomai* (spare) is used in the Septuagint version of Genesis 22:12 and 16. It is the same word Paul uses in Romans 8:32, as well as in Acts 20:29: "I know that after I leave, savage wolves will come in among you and will not spare the flock." Peter also used this word: "God did not spare angels when they sinned" (2 Pet. 2:4).

Juries and judges in this world spare criminals, for there is no perfect justice in this sinful world. Perfect justice will come only when Christ comes again to judge the living and the dead. But to satisfy the justice of God, the Father did not spare his own Son. No other substitute could make atonement for the sins of the whole world. Isaac was spared because his death could not atone for his own sin, let alone the sins of the world. No rams or bulls or any other animals can atone for our sins. The Hebrews writer declares, "Without the shedding of blood there is no forgiveness" (Heb. 9:22). Yet he then states, "It is impossible for the blood of bulls and goats to take away sins" (Heb. 10:4). Not even the holy angel Gabriel can atone for our sins. Whose blood, then, can make atonement?

We needed the incarnate Son of God to atone for our sins. His blood alone avails. And the Father loved us so much that he did not spare his own Son, but gave him up for us on the cross. Think about this: Had he spared his Son, he would have had to destroy us.

Abraham asked God, "Will not the Judge of all the earth do right?" (Gen. 18:25). To be just in justifying sinners, it was necessary that the Father not spare the only One who was qualified to make atonement in behalf of his elect. Peter says, "For you know that it was not with perishable things such as silver or gold that you were redeemed . . . but with the precious blood of Christ, a lamb without blemish or defect. He was chosen before the creation of the world, but was revealed in these last times for your sake" (1 Pet. 1:18–20). Paul states, "This grace was given us in Christ Jesus before the beginning of time, but it has now been revealed through the appearing of our Savior, Christ Jesus, who has destroyed death and has brought life and immortality to light through the gospel" (2 Tim. 1:9–10).

To spare us from eternal damnation, the Father spared not his own Son. Jesus is our Passover lamb. The Lord told the Israelites, "The blood [of the Passover lamb] will be a sign for you on the houses where you are; and when I see the blood, I will pass over you. No destructive plague will touch you when I strike Egypt" (Exod. 12:13). If we have trusted in Jesus Christ and his blood, then we are spared, for "we have now been justified by his blood" (Rom. 5:9). Let us rejoice in God who spared us in Christ!

The Father Gave Him Up

"He . . . did not spare his own Son, *but gave him up for us all.*" The adversative "but" (*alla*) is a strong contrast. Negatively, the Father did not spare his own Son; positively, he gave him up to the death of the cross.

People make and break promises all the time. In the presence of God and witnesses, they lie. But what God promises, he fulfills. He purposed in eternity and promised in Genesis 3:15 that the Seed of the woman would crush the head of the serpent, the devil. This promise has been fulfilled in Christ. It is not a promise anymore; God the Father fulfilled it when he handed his Son over to be sacrificed. "When the time had fully come, God sent his Son, born of a woman, born under law, to redeem those under law, that we might receive the full rights of sons" (Gal. 4:4–5). The eternal became temporal; the immortal became mortal; God became man. He humbled himself as a servant and became obedient to death, even the death of the cross.

On the cross, Jesus experienced the hell of our death, which is the wages of sin. God the Father so loved us that he gave up his own Son to such a death to save us. Love gives the best, the most precious. The Father's best was his one and only Son. He gave him up to save us through his substitutionary death. The cross of Christ preaches God's eternal, undying, never-failing love to us. Our love for God may fail, but the Father's love never fails.

To whom did the Father give up his Son? He handed him over to the powers of darkness. Jesus said, "Every day I was with you in the temple courts, and you did not lay a hand on me. But this is your hour—when darkness reigns" (Luke 22:53). God handed him over to the prince of this world. Jesus told his disciples, "I will not speak with you much longer, for the prince of this world is coming. He has no hold on me, but the world must know that I love the Father and that I do exactly what my Father has commanded" (John 14:30–31). God handed his Son over to powers and authorities. Paul explains, "Having canceled the written code, with its regulations, that was against us and that stood opposed to us, [Christ] took it away, nailing it to the cross. And having disarmed the powers and authorities, he made a public spectacle of them, triumphing over them by the cross" (Col. 2:14–15). God also handed Jesus over to the Jews, the Gentiles, the Pharisees, the Sadducees, Caiaphas, Pilate, and all the forces of darkness. Jesus told Pilate, "You would have no power over me if it were not given to you from above" (John 19:11). Peter declared, "This man was handed over to you by God's set purpose and foreknowledge; and you, with the help of wicked men, put him to death by nailing him to the cross" (Acts 2:23). These wicked men only did what the Father had decided beforehand should happen (Acts 4:28).

The cross reveals the wisdom of God. By wisdom, God uses the best means to achieve his best goal. The best means to achieve our redemption was the death of his Son on the cross. This brings greater glory to God. The cross is foolishness, a stumbling block, and an offense to those who are perishing. But to us who are being saved, it reveals the power, wisdom, and surpassing love of God. So we glory in the wondrous cross! It is a stumbling block to the Jews and foolishness to the Gentiles, but to us it is life eternal.

If there were no cross of Christ, there would be no eternal life. May we therefore glory in this truth—because Jesus suffered the full penalty of God's holy law, we are now outside of the reach of God's holy law, and, therefore, outside of death and sin. These things cannot touch us, because Christ died for our sins. Paul declares, "The sting of death is sin, and the power of sin is the law.

But thanks be to God! He gives us the victory through our Lord Jesus Christ" (1 Cor. 15:56–57). Praise the Lord for our victory in Jesus Christ!

Christ, who obeyed the Father perfectly in life and death, prayed three times that the Father would remove the cup of his wrath from him. But finally he said, "Yet not my will but thine be done." It was God's will to spare us by crucifying his own Son. This purpose of God was unchangeable. Yet Christ's death was not the death of a martyr, for not only is Jesus true man, but he is also very God. Christ was without sin, but he died for our sins. He who knew no sin became sin for us that we sinners might become nothing less than the righteousness of God in him (2 Cor. 5:21). The Father did not count our sins against us; he counted them against his Son.

In the Old Testament sacrificial system, a sinner would bring a prescribed animal to the priest to make atonement for his sins. As the sinful worshiper would lay his hands on the animal's head and confess his sins, his sins would be transferred to the animal. Then the animal would be killed in the place of the sinner, and its blood would be sprinkled before the Lord. The worshiper's sins would thus be forgiven in view of the Messiah's sacrificial death to which the sacrifice of the animal pointed. Yes, Christ died for the sins of all his elect of all times.

The Father gave his Son the cup of his foaming wrath that was against us. Paul writes, "The wrath of God is being revealed from heaven against all the godlessness and wickedness of men who suppress the truth by their wickedness" (Rom. 1:18). And the psalmist says, "In the hand of the LORD is a cup full of foaming wine mixed with spices; he pours it out, and all the wicked of the earth drink it down to its very dregs" (Ps. 75:8). Isaiah calls, "Awake, awake! Rise up, O Jerusalem, you who have drunk from the hand of the LORD the cup of his wrath, you who have drained to its dregs the goblet that makes men stagger" (Isa. 51:17).

The Father would not remove this cup from his Son. He must drink it, and he drank it to the very dregs. No more wrath remains to be poured out upon us. Why did he drink it? Because he loved his Father. Why did he drink it? Because he loved the church. "Christ loved the church and *gave himself up for her*" (Eph. 5:25). Why did he drink it? Because he loved each one of us individually. So we can exult with Paul: "I have been crucified with Christ and I no longer live, but Christ lives in me. The life I live in the body, I live by faith in the Son of God, who loved me and *gave himself for me*" (Gal. 2:20).

Oh, the high price of our redemption! We were not redeemed with silver or gold or thousands of lambs. The prophet Hosea redeemed his sinful wife from the slave market for fifteen shekels of silver plus a homer and a lethek of barley. But the price of our redemption was the death of God's beloved, eternal Son.

The Father abandoned his Son on the cross, laying on him all our sins. So Jesus cried out, "My God, my God, why hast thou forsaken me?" (Matt. 27:46, KJV). The answer is, "Because I love every elect sinner personally with everlasting love. There is no other way to redeem them but by your death in their stead."

The cup of God's wrath is empty; no more wrath can be poured out against us. All our sins have been forgiven, and Christ's righteousness has been imputed to us. Oh, the glory of this double transaction! All our sin is imputed to God's own Son, and all his righteousness is imputed to us. Now we are given a different cup. It is the cup of salvation (Ps. 116:13), the cup of blessing (1 Cor. 10:16), the cup that runneth over (Ps. 23:5). Jesus said, "I give them eternal life. I have come that they may have life, and that more abundant and overflowing" (John 10:10, 28).

There is expiation and propitiation. God not only forgives our sins, but he is also reconciled to us. He is not angry with us anymore; he is gracious to us. Now we can come boldly to the throne of grace. Now we can have fellowship with the Father, the Son, and the Holy Spirit.

Jesus did not die on the cross to change the Father's mind. It was always the Father's plan to save us this way. His love for us spared not his Son. The Father loved us and therefore gave his Son up to the death of the cross. Isaiah prophesied: "We all, like sheep, have gone astray, each of us has turned to his own way; and the LORD has laid on him the iniquity of us all. . . .Yet it was the LORD's will to crush him and cause him to suffer" (Isa. 53:6, 10). Paul says, "God presented him as a sacrifice of atonement. . . . But God demonstrates his own love for us in this: While we were still sinners, Christ died for us" (Rom. 3:25; 5:8). In his commentary, Professor John Murray quotes Octavius Winslow: "Who delivered up Jesus to die? Not Judas, for money; not Pilate, for fear; not the Jews, for envy;—but the Father, for love!"[1]

The law stated, "Cursed is the man who does not uphold the words of this law by carrying them out" (Deut. 27:26), but "Christ redeemed us from the curse of the law by becoming a curse for us" (Gal. 3:13). Psalm 22 speaks of the suffering of Christ: "Many bulls surround me; strong bulls of Bashan encircle me. Roaring lions tearing their prey open their mouths wide against me. . . . Dogs have surrounded me; a band of evil men has encircled me, they have pierced my hands and my feet" (vv. 12–13, 16), yet it ends on this glorious note: "They will proclaim his righteousness to a people yet unborn—for he has done it" (v. 31). From the cross Jesus pronounced, "Tetelestai—it is finished." The work of redemption was finished. Murray says, "There was only one . . . who bore the full weight of the divine judgment . . . and bore it so as to end it."[2]

In view of the Father's action and Christ's obedience displayed by the wondrous cross, how can we ever doubt God's love for us in life and in death! The Father gave him up *for us all*. "For us all" means in our place and for our salvation. Christ's life and death were substitutionary. He actively and passively obeyed in our place and for our eternal salvation. Forgiveness of sins and perfect righteousness now come to all who trust in the person and work of this divine substitute. Isaac asked his father, "Where is the lamb for the burnt offering?" Abraham said, "*Jehovah Jireh*: the Lord will provide." Jesus Christ, God's own Son, is our Jehovah Jireh. In Jesus, the Lord will provide everything that we need.

Christ is our only vicar. His death was vicarious *in behalf of us all*. Note, this is not speaking of universalism. Jesus did not die for every person in the world; he died only for those whom the Father foreloved, predestinated, called, justified, and glorified. That is a definite number of people from all the families of the earth. The "us" of verse 31 is the "those" of verses 29–30. It is the same as the "us" of verses 32, 34, 35, 37, and 39. Paul is speaking of the elect of God, not everybody in the world. God gave his Son up for all who repent and trust in Jesus Christ alone for their

---

1   Murray, *Epistle to the Romans*, 324.
2   Murray, *Redemption Accomplished and Applied*, 77.

salvation. If you refuse to repent truly, trust savingly, and live in obedience to Christ, then he did not die for you.

The Blessings That Flow to Us

"How shall he not, together with him, freely give us all things?" The argument is, if God did not spare his own Son but gave him up for us all, if he already did the most difficult thing and paid the highest price for our redemption, if he has given us the greatest and most precious gift he possessed, then it is absolutely impossible for him not to give us all lesser things.

It is an argument from the greater to the lesser. It is sound reasoning and pure doctrine. We see similar logic illustrated in Judges 13. God revealed himself to Manoah's wife and later came to speak to her husband. They realized that this person speaking to them was neither a man nor an angel, but God himself. Manoah, speaking emotionally, exclaimed, "We are doomed to die! . . . We have seen God!" (Judg. 13:22). But Manoah's unnamed wife exercised logic and answered her husband, "If the LORD had meant to kill us, he would not have accepted a burnt offering and grain offering from our hands, nor shown us all these things or now told us this" (Judg. 13:23). What a mind! In other words, she was reasoning, "God did not come to kill us. He brought us good news, the gospel, that we would have a son who would be a judge to deliver his people from foreign domination."

A parallel argument from the greater to the lesser is found in Romans 5:8–10. If helpless, sinful, ungodly enemies can be reconciled to God through the death of his Son, how much more, having been reconciled, shall we be saved through his life! As we resist the devil through such powerful biblical arguments, he shall flee from us. Therefore, we must think logically. We are living at a time when irrationalism rules. Irrationalism is the very heart of postmodernism. No one wants to think. People would rather ask, "How do you *feel* about it?" But we must exercise our minds. We can be delivered from all our shackles of sin and misery if we understand biblical arguments and believe them.

We can make a similar argument based on our union with Christ. Paul says, "Or don't you know that all of us who were baptized into Christ Jesus were baptized into his death? We were therefore buried with him through baptism into death in order that, just as Christ was raised from the dead through the glory of the Father, we too may live a new life" (Rom. 6:3–4). By faith we died with Christ, were buried with Christ, and were raised with Christ to live the resurrection life of Christ. Christ never dies again; he lives forever. And because he lives, we shall also live forever. He is the vine; we are the branches, and the branches live by the life of the vine. Christ is our life, and with him, the Father gives us all things. This is the type of thinking we must engage in.

We also find in the Bible arguments from the lesser to the greater. Read Matthew 6:25–34 from this point of view and see the substantial arguments Jesus makes. If God cares for the birds and the lilies of the field—those are the lesser things—how much more will he care for his children of grace! So Jesus asks, "Are you not much more valuable to God than birds?" The answer is "Yes," for we are created in the image and likeness of God, and for us Christ died. So Jesus exhorts us in that passage not to worry about temporal things—food, clothing, housing, and all other things our physical bodies need. In fact, he says, "Do not worry" four times in that passage (Matt. 6:25, 28, 31, 34).

But realize that God provides these things to us through our work. An idle, lazy man is a sinner who every day lives against God and his law. Work six days a week, and the Lord will bless your work, and all your needs will be met. Did you ever think about the fact that birds work to get their food? Even the lilies of the field work.

God freely gives us all things; everything we have, we receive by grace, not by our merit. Even God's enemies live because of his common grace. They are given daily bread through their work. God's sun shines upon them, the rain comes upon them, and the earth produces food for them.

But in Jesus Christ we are given also special grace, which flows to us from the cross of Christ—the blessings of regeneration, repentance, saving faith, righteousness, the Holy Spirit, the knowledge of God, adoption as sons, and glorification.

What is Paul's argument? If God has already given us his most precious, indescribable gift in Jesus Christ, how much more will he lavish every other gift upon us freely! The cross proves the Father's super-generosity of love toward his children. No wonder

Mary was generous in taking all her money to buy the most precious perfume and pour it on Jesus! Those who give generously to God and his church are those who have appreciated the super-generosity of divine grace.

Dr. John Stott says the cross "is the guarantee of the continuing, unfailing generosity of God."[3] Dr. Douglas Moo says God's giving up of his Son guarantees his all-future blessings.[4]

We find promises of these blessings in the psalms:

– *Psalm 23:1:* "The LORD is my shepherd, I shall not be in want."
– *Psalm 84:11:* "For the LORD God is a sun and shield; the LORD bestows favor and honor; no good thing does he withhold from those whose walk is blameless."
– *Psalm 85:12:* "The LORD will indeed give what is good, and our land will yield its harvest."
– *Psalm 86:17:* "Give me a sign of your goodness, that my enemies may see it and be put to shame, for you, O LORD, have helped me and comforted me."
– *Psalm 103:1–5:* "Praise the LORD, O my soul; all my inmost being, praise his holy name. Praise the LORD, O my soul, and forget not all his benefits—who forgives all your sins and heals all your diseases, who redeems your life from the pit and crowns you with love and compassion, who satisfies your desires with good things so that your youth is renewed like the eagle's."

In Christ we are given all things, spiritual and temporal, that we need to live. Paul exclaims, "Praise be to the God and Father of our Lord Jesus Christ, who has blessed us in the heavenly realms with every spiritual blessing in Christ" (Eph. 1:3). In Christ we are given all things necessary for our preservation, perseverance, and final glorification. So Paul writes, "I can do everything through him who gives me strength. . . . And my God will meet all your needs according to his glorious riches in Christ Jesus" (Phil. 4:13, 19; see also 1 Cor. 4:7; 2 Cor. 9:8; 12:9).

What about temptation? Does God provide for us in that? This week I was tempted not to exercise. But I resisted the devil and said, "I am going to spend even more minutes today exercising because you tempted me." Paul declares, "No temptation has seized you except what is common to man. And God is faithful;

---

3   Stott, *Romans: God's Good News*, 255.
4   Moo, *Epistle to the Romans*, 539.

he will not let you be tempted beyond what you can bear. But when you are tempted, he will also provide a way out so that you can stand up under it" (1 Cor. 10:13).

God also gives us much needed instruction and counsel. He says, "I will instruct you and teach you in the way you should go; I will counsel you and watch over you" (Ps. 32:8). Our problem is that too often we do not want to heed the counsel.

The late Dr. James Boice says Romans 8:32 "is a blank check for our true needs."[5] Professor John Murray says, "The costliness of the sacrifice assures us of the greatness of the love and guarantees the bestowal of all other free gifts."[6] John Flavel remarks,

> How is it imaginable that God should withhold, after this [giving up his Son for the death of the cross], spirituals or temporals, from his people? How shall he not call them effectually, justify them freely, sanctify them thoroughly, and glorify them eternally? How shall he not clothe them, feed them, protect and deliver them? Surely if he would not spare this own Son one stroke, one tear, one groan, one sigh, one circumstance of misery, it can never be imagined that ever he should, after this, deny or withhold from his people, for whose sakes all this was suffered, any mercies, any comforts, any privilege, spiritual or temporal, which is good for them.[7]

Now we do not have all things, but they shall come to us in due time. As for now, God's mercies are new every morning. Soon we shall put on also immortality and glory.

All blessings, spiritual and temporal, flow to us from the Father, in and through his Son, Jesus our Lord, who loved us and gave himself for us on the cross. He is our Savior. But he is also the Judge of all who will not surrender to his lordship. All judgment is given to him by his Father. "Kiss the Son, lest he be angry and you be destroyed in your way, for his wrath can flare up in a moment. Blessed are all who take refuge in him" (Ps. 2:12).

Either God's own Son bears God's wrath for us, or we must bear it ourselves. That is the choice we all face. John Murray says,

---

5   Boice, *Romans*, vol. 2, *Reign of Grace*, 954.

6   Murray, *Redemption Accomplished and Applied*, 17.

7   Quoted by John Piper, "God Did Not Spare His Own Son," sermon Aug. 18, 2002, http://www.desiringgod.org/resource-library/sermons/god-did-not-spare-his-own-son

"The lost in perdition will everlastingly bear the unrelieved and unmitigated judgment due to their sins; they will eternally suffer in the exaction of the demands of justice."[8]

God's people alone confess, "Christ died for our sins and was raised for our justification." God's people alone can say, "Jesus Christ loved me and gave himself for me." God's people alone declare, "There is therefore now no condemnation for those who are in Christ Jesus." May God help all of us to trust in Jesus Christ today, that we may be saved and enjoy this glorious freedom from the wrath of God. Jesus said, "If you know these things, blessed are you if you do them." May we live in obedience to God and enjoy eternally the sunshine of his love.

---

8   Murray, *Redemption Accomplished and Applied*, 77.

56

No Accusation and No Condemnation

33Who will bring any charge against those whom God has chosen? It is God who justifies. 34Who is he that condemns? Christ Jesus, who died—more than that, who was raised to life—is at the right hand of God and is also interceding for us.

Romans 8:33–34

Is there a possibility that believers in Jesus Christ can find themselves ultimately condemned by God? Is there a possibility of God saying to them on that day, "I never knew you. Depart from me"? Is there a possibility that believers can lose their salvation, or that some new charges will be brought against them, reversing their justification? The answer to all of these questions is, "Not at all!"

In Romans 8:33–34 Paul gives us five solid reasons for our total security and final salvation on the last day: 1) God the Father justified us; 2) Christ died for us; 3) Christ has been raised; 4) Christ is seated at the right hand of God in heaven; and 5) Christ is making intercession for us in heaven.

1. God Who Justifies

"Who will bring any charge against God's chosen ones?" (v. 33). The idea is that there are many who will bring charges against us, but the charges cannot stick. For instance, our enemy Satan brings charges against us. He is called the accuser of the brethren: "For the accuser of our brothers, who accuses them before our God day and night, has been hurled down" (Rev. 12:10). Job was blameless, yet Satan accused him before God as being full of blame: "Then the LORD said to Satan, 'Have you considered my servant Job? There is no one on earth like him; he is blameless and upright, a man who fears God and shuns evil.' 'Does Job fear God for nothing?' Satan replied" (Job 1:8–9). Satan had a sound argument. Most Christians serve God to get something, for some temporal benefit. But God argued that this was not true of Job.

The devil hates our salvation. He hates our justification, sanctification, and glorification. Therefore he tempts us and accuses us to God himself. When God tests us, he wants us to succeed, and he helps us do so. But the devil only wants us to fail.

See what Satan did in reference to Peter. Jesus told Peter, "Simon, Simon, Satan has asked to sift you as wheat. But I have prayed for you, Simon, that your faith may not fail. And when you have turned back, strengthen your brothers" (Luke 22:31–32). Satan wants to sift us as wheat. He tells God that we are not really the wheat, that we are not children of God, but that we are just chaff.

Remember what Satan did to Joshua the high priest:

> Then he showed me Joshua the high priest standing before the angel of the LORD, and Satan standing at his right side to accuse him. The LORD said to Satan, "The LORD rebuke you, Satan! The LORD, who has chosen Jerusalem, rebuke you! Is not this man a burning stick snatched from the fire?" Now Joshua was dressed in filthy clothes as he stood before the angel. The angel said to those who were standing before him, "Take off his filthy clothes." Then he said to Joshua, "See, I have taken away your sin, and I will put rich garments on you." (Zech. 3:1–4)

Satan accused the high priest Joshua of being full of sin and guilt, so how can he function as high priest? But God gave Joshua new garments, standing for righteousness.

Not only does Satan accuse us, but false brothers also accuse and slander us (e.g., see 3 John 9–10). Paul said he had often been "in danger from false brothers" (2 Cor. 11:26), and he experienced opposition "because some false brothers had infiltrated our ranks to spy on the freedom we have in Christ Jesus and to make us slaves" (Gal. 2:4).

The world of unbelievers also accuses God's people all the time (e.g., see Acts 6:13; 1 Pet. 2:12). Jesus told his disciples, "If the world hates you, keep in mind that it hated me first. If you belonged to the world, it would love you as its own. As it is, you do not belong to the world, but I have chosen you out of the world. That is why the world hates you. . . . I have told you these things, so that in me you may have peace. In this world you will have trouble. But take heart! I have overcome the world" (John 15:18–19; 16:33).

Moreover, our own consciences can accuse us—sometimes correctly, but other times falsely. What do we do when we are falsely accused by our own consciences? John writes, "This then is how we know that we belong to the truth, and how we set our hearts at rest in his presence whenever our hearts condemn us. For God is greater than our hearts, and he knows everything" (1 John 3:19–20). We must argue to our consciences that, having known everything about us, God still justified us.

What, then, should we do when we are accused by Satan, by false brothers, by the world, and by our consciences? We must resist them by doctrine, through understanding God's declaration concerning us. We must resist them by the truth of the word of God. That is why those who refuse to learn the truth of the gospel cannot stand when they face such accusations. Resist the devil, who comes as a roaring lion to devour us. Resist him by faith in God. John writes, "They overcame him by the blood of the Lamb and by the word of their testimony" (Rev. 12:11). Resist him by remembering the facts of our salvation, the great indicatives of doctrine. Tell him, "Yes, I was guilty as charged, but my sins have been blotted out." The Lord himself says, "I, even I, am he who blots out your transgressions, for my own sake, and remembers your sins no more. . . . I have swept away your offenses like a cloud, your sins like the morning mist. Return to me, for I have redeemed you" (Isa. 43:25; 44:22).

In Jeremiah 50:20 we read, "'In those days, at that time,' declares the LORD, 'search will be made for Israel's guilt, but there will be none, and for the sins of Judah, but none will be found, for I will forgive the remnant I spare.'" Who is searching? It may be Satan or false brothers or the world, or maybe even our own consciences. But they will find nothing; the case is closed. No charge brought against us will stick, either now or on the last day, because we are God's beloved, foreloved and chosen in his beloved Son. Who shall bring a charge against God's elect? Absolutely no one.

We are God's peculiar people, a people of God's own possession. We are God's portion and inheritance. We are God's treasure. Therefore, any charges brought against us are against God himself, who chose us to salvation. God loves us with everlasting love, and many waters cannot quench this love of God for us. How can our enemies bring charges against us when God the Judge is for us? He chose us in Christ before the foundation of the world to be holy and blameless and blessed with every spiritual blessing in Christ. This God who chose us is the Judge of the Supreme Court of the universe, and he has already justified us. He made a judicial declaration about us, as he did about Job, that we are just, righteous, and holy. We are as righteous as his beloved Son. He justified us justly because his righteous law has been fully kept by his Son, our representative, redeemer, and mediator.

All our sins are pardoned forevermore. More than that, we have been clothed in divine righteousness. This justification is once for all; it cannot be reversed. God has justified the ungodly, and no new charge can be brought against us by anyone. We died to the law and are married to Christ. Now we are outside of the reach of God's law; we are under grace.

All sin is against God, and God himself justifies us. So Paul's statement, "It is God who justifies," paralyzes all our accusers. We are in God, in Christ Jesus. "Therefore, there is now no condemnation for those who are in Christ Jesus" (Rom. 8:1). Know this doctrine of justification so that you can resist all the accusations of your enemies. God promised, "When I see the blood, I will pass over you."

2. Christ Who Died

"It is God who justifies. Who is he that condemns?" (vv. 33–34). Condemnation is the opposite of justification. Since we are justified, who can condemn us on the last day? God the Father has given Jesus Christ all authority to judge on the last day. Peter declared,

"[Christ] commanded us to preach to the people and to testify that he is the one whom God appointed as judge of the living and the dead" (Acts 10:42). Paul proclaimed, "For [God] has set a day when he will judge the world with justice by the man he has appointed. He has given proof of this to all men by raising him from the dead" (Acts 17:31); "For we must all appear before the judgment seat of Christ, that each one may receive what is due him for the things done while in the body, whether good or bad" (2 Cor. 5:10).

Can anyone condemn us on the last day? How can anyone curse those who are blessed? Balaam wanted to curse the people of God. But he found that he could not do it, because they were blessed. So he said, "God is not a man, that he should lie, nor a son of man, that he should change his mind. Does he speak and then not act? Does he promise and not fulfill? I have received a command to bless; he has blessed, and I cannot change it" (Num. 23:19-20). We are blessed and no one can change it. So in Isaiah 50:8-9 we read, "He who vindicates me is near. Who then will bring charges against me? Let us face each other! Who is my accuser? Let him confront me! It is the Sovereign LORD who helps me. Who is he that will condemn me?" The answer is, "No one."

Will Judge Jesus condemn us on the last day? No, Jesus Christ does not condemn us. The works of Christ have freed us from all condemnation. So the second reason for our security is *"Christ who died."* The wages of sin is death, and Jesus died in our place and for our sin. He came to give his life as a ransom for many. He is our Boaz, our kinsman-redeemer. The sinless Son of God died for the sinful sons of men. He obeyed and suffered as our representative. So God's faithfulness and justice demand that we be not punished, but pardoned and justified.

God incarnate, not a bull, was sacrificed. Jesus cried from the cross, "It is finished!" Nothing can be added to Christ's finished work of atonement. God condemned our sin in Christ's flesh. Christ defeated all our enemies by his death—the devil, death, the world, sin, the law, and hell. The blood of Christ cleanses us from all our sins.

A theologian was once asked what the most important word in the Bible is. He responded that it is the preposition *huper* ("on behalf of" or "for"). Christ died *for* our sins. He died in our place, for our salvation. So Paul writes, *"Christos huper hēmōn apethanen*—Christ in behalf of us died" (Rom. 5:8).

3. Christ Who Was Raised

The third solid ground for our assurance of salvation is that not only did Christ die, but he also was raised by the Father (see Rom. 1:4; 4:25; 6:4; 8:11). Paul says that God's "incomparably great power for us who believe . . . is like the working of his mighty strength, which he exerted in Christ when he raised him from the dead" (Eph. 1:19–20). In celebrating the resurrection of Christ, Paul writes, "And if Christ has not been raised, our preaching is useless and so is your faith. . . . And if Christ has not been raised, your faith is futile; you are still in your sins" (1 Cor. 15:14, 17).

The resurrection of Jesus Christ proves several things:

1. Christ was sinless. No resurrection would have shown that Jesus was a sinner just like us, in need of a Savior. The resurrection shows that he was, as he said, sinless.
2. Christ's atoning sacrifice was accepted by God the Father. The resurrection was the Father's "Amen" to Christ's cry, "It is finished."
3. God's law and justice have been fully satisfied (Rom. 3:25–26).
4. Jesus Christ, as he declared, was and is the Son of God (Rom. 1:4).
5. Jesus will judge the world on the last day (Acts 17:31).
6. Jesus Christ is the author of salvation to all who obey him. He is raised Prince and Savior (Acts 5:31).

Dr. Martyn Lloyd-Jones says that the resurrection does not justify us. Rather, he states, "The resurrection is the proof to us that we have been justified by our Lord's death."[1] Look to the cross and know that atonement has been made. Then look at the risen Christ and know that his atonement has been accepted. A dead Savior is a contradiction in terms. "But Christ has indeed been raised from the dead, the firstfruits of those who have fallen asleep" (1 Cor. 15:20).

4. Christ Is at the Right Hand of God

Jesus has been glorified in answer to his high priestly prayer: "And now, Father, glorify me in your presence with the glory I

---

1 Lloyd-Jones, *Romans*, vol. 8, *Final Perseverance of the Saints*, 420.

had with you before the world began" (John 17:5). He has been exalted to the right hand of God: "God exalted him to his own right hand as Prince and Savior that he might give repentance and forgiveness of sins to Israel" (Acts 5:31). Peter speaks of "the resurrection of Jesus Christ, who has gone into heaven and is at God's right hand—with angels, authorities and powers in submission to him" (1 Pet. 3:21–22). Even now Jesus is seated on the right hand of God. His Father has given him the place of supreme honor. Christ Jesus is exalted to universal dominion as King of kings and Lord of lords. He has all authority in heaven and on earth.

Jesus is in God's presence also as our high priest. Once a year the high priest entered the Holy of Holies with the blood of sacrifice so that he could sprinkle it on and before the mercy seat. He did this as the representative of the twelve tribes of Israel, whose sins needed to be atoned for. And when he came out with the good news that their sins had been covered by the blood, those waiting outside rejoiced.

But Jesus entered the heavenly tabernacle by his own blood. In God's presence Christ's sacrifice of himself obtained for us full pardon and justification. So in Hebrews 9:24 we read, "For Christ did not enter a man-made sanctuary that was only a copy of the true one; he entered heaven itself, now to appear for us in God's presence" as our high priest to represent us and pray for us.

Thus there is no more accusation and condemnation. Christ our high priest is in God's presence for us, and he is seated. "The Son is the radiance of God's glory and the exact representation of his being, sustaining all things by his powerful word. After he had provided purification for sins, he sat down at the right hand of the Majesty in heaven. So he became as much superior to the angels as the name he has inherited is superior to theirs" (Heb. 1:3–4). Look at Psalm 110, one of the oft-quoted passages from the Old Testament: "The LORD says to my Lord: 'Sit at my right hand until I make your enemies a footstool for your feet'" (Ps. 110:1).

We are told that God rested after creation because the work of creation was finished. Now in heaven Christ is seated, resting from his redemption work. There were no chairs for the priests in the tabernacle or in the temple, because their work was never finished. But now the work is finished. Jesus, therefore, is seated in his glorious body in heaven. Stephen, Paul, and John saw him in such glory.

Jesus Christ is Lord over all creation. Now his job is to destroy all his enemies, whom he already destroyed in principle on the cross. We read, "Since that time he waits for his enemies to be made his footstool" (Heb. 10:13). Paul writes, "Then the end will come, when he hands over the kingdom to God the Father after he has destroyed all dominion, authority and power. For he must reign until he has put all his enemies under his feet. The last enemy to be destroyed is death. For he 'has put everything under his feet.' Now when it says that 'everything' has been put under him, it is clear that this does not include God himself, who put everything under Christ" (1 Cor. 15:24–27). Jesus works to destroy every enemy.

If you are an unbelieving enemy of Christ, listen to this warning: "Therefore, you kings, be wise; be warned, you rulers of the earth. Serve the LORD with fear and rejoice with trembling. Kiss the Son, lest he be angry and you be destroyed in your way, for his wrath can flare up in a moment. Blessed are all who take refuge in him" (Ps. 2:10–12).

Not only is Christ seated, but so too are we the church, his bride, seated with him. Christ is our head. He loves and protects us. This is our security. He is no longer in a state of humiliation. He has been glorified as the Prince and Savior of his people.

5. Christ Is Interceding for Us

What is Jesus doing in heaven? He is ever-interceding *huper* ("in behalf of") us. He died, he was raised, and he was seated. That is all in the past. Now Paul uses a present tense verb: *"Christ Jesus . . . is also interceding for us."* To put it simply, Jesus is praying for us.

All that Jesus did was in behalf of us—his death, his resurrection, his ascension, his session, and now his intercession. Jesus will never die again. He lives forever and, therefore, he will intercede for us forever.

While on earth, he prayed for Peter. He also prayed for the other disciples, and he prayed for us: "I pray for them. I am not praying for the world, but for those you have given me, for they are yours. . . . My prayer is not that you take them out of the world but that you protect them from the evil one" (John 17:9, 15). Now he prays for us in heaven.

Moreover, his prayer is always effectual: "Father, . . . I knew that you always hear me" (John 11:42). He prayed to the Father that the Holy Spirit be sent to us to be with us forever as another Comforter: "And I will ask the Father, and he will give you another Counselor to be with you forever—the Spirit of truth" (John 14:16–17). This Holy Spirit was outpoured on the Day of Pentecost, and he is in us now to guide us in triumph all the way to the city of God, the new Jerusalem.

We read in Hebrews 7, "But because Jesus lives forever, he has a permanent priesthood. Therefore he is able to save completely those who come to God through him, because he always lives to intercede for them" (vv. 24–25). Jesus lives forever and saves us totally. He lives for the purpose of interceding for us. Christ's presence before his Father itself is intercession. Based on his atoning work, he secures for us the full benefits of redemption, including our future glorification.

He is our sympathizing high priest. It is not the angels he helps. He helps us now, even while we are being tempted and harassed by our enemies. So we approach the throne of grace in Jesus' name "with confidence, so that we may receive mercy and find grace to help us in our time of need" (Heb. 4:16). In Jesus Christ we are blessed with every spiritual blessing. All blessings flow to us through Jesus Christ, the vine, our heavenly intercessor.

John says, "My dear children, I write this to you so that you will not sin. But if anybody does sin, we have one who speaks to the Father in our defense—Jesus Christ, the Righteous One. He is the atoning sacrifice for our sins, and not only for ours but also for the sins of the whole world" (1 John 2:1–2). Our Lord Jesus Christ is our advocate with the Father, and he will win our case every time. His prayer is heard because it is based on his atoning sacrifice. And our prayers are answered when we pray in his name, based on his person and his work. Isaiah tells us, "For he bore the sin of many, and made intercession for the transgressors" (Isa. 53:12). Christ's intercession is based on his atonement.

Through Christ, the Father himself loves us. Jesus declared, "The Father himself loves you because you have loved me and have believed that I came from God" (John 16:27). How much does he love us? In his high priestly prayer, Jesus prayed "that they may be one as we are one: I in them and you in me. May they be brought to complete unity to let the world know that you sent me and have loved them even as you have loved me" (John 17:22–23). Same degree, same extent, same manner.

Friends, God is not our Judge; he is our loving heavenly Father. And he is eager to bless us in view of his Son's triumphant, mediatorial work. Therefore, we have an intercessor in heaven, Jesus Christ, who prays for us. We also have an intercessor on earth, the Holy Spirit, who prays for us: "In the same way, the Spirit helps us in our weakness. We do not know what we ought to pray for, but the Spirit himself intercedes for us with groans that words cannot express. And he who searches our hearts knows the mind of the Spirit, because the Spirit intercedes for the saints in accordance with God's will" (Rom. 8:26–27). Moreover, we have God's holy church praying for us: "Therefore confess your sins to each other and pray for each other so that you may be healed. The prayer of a righteous man is powerful and effective" (James 5:16).

Conclusion

Paul gives us five solid arguments in Romans 8:33–34 so that we may enjoy the full security of our final salvation, especially when we face death. Jesus said, "Do not be anxious. Do not be afraid." So rejoice, God is for us, Jesus Christ is for us, and the Holy Spirit is for us. The holy angels are for us, and the holy church is for us. Our salvation is secure, built on the solid rock of Jesus Christ.

But if you are not a believer in Jesus Christ, you should be anxious and worried. You are right to be afraid of God, whose wrath is revealed against you, and afraid of Jesus Christ, the supreme Lord and Judge of all. Those who refuse to repent and embrace Jesus Christ are denying that they are sinners and that God's wrath is being revealed against them. Such people despise the person and saving work of Christ. They deny that he is coming again in glory to judge the ungodly. They deny that there is eternal life in heaven for true believers and eternal punishment in hell for Christ-haters.

If you are outside of Christ, I urge you to come to him with all your burden of guilt, and he will give you rest. Do it now; do it today. Jesus said, "All that the Father gives me will come to me, and whoever comes to me I will never drive away" (John 6:37). Those who come to him will eat of the living bread and will never go hungry. They will drink the living water of life and will never go thirsty.

57

Jesus Loves Me, This I Know

³⁵*Who shall separate us from the love of Christ? Shall trouble or hardship or persecution or famine or nakedness or danger or sword?* ³⁶*As it is written:*

> *"For your sake we face death all day long;*
> *we are considered as sheep to be slaughtered."*

³⁷*No, in all these things we are more than conquerors through him who loved us.* ³⁸*For I am convinced that neither death nor life, neither angels nor demons, neither the present nor the future, nor any powers,* ³⁹*neither height nor depth, nor anything else in all creation, will be able to separate us from the love of God that is in Christ Jesus our Lord.*

Romans 8:35–39

"Jesus loves me, this I know." This is, in essence, how Paul concludes this great chapter of Romans 8. Thank God, Jesus loves us. We are weak, but he is strong to make us strong, to make us alive, and to make us lose our depression, misery, and death. He is strong to give us life eternal, that we may rejoice with joy unspeakable and full of glory.

Some people love their misery and do not want it to be taken away. They revel in it. Such people have no hope. But Jesus invites all who are burdened, weary, and sick of their misery to come to him, and he will save them. Little ones, old ones, middle-aged ones, men and women, come to him and be saved.

First, Paul makes this final challenge: "*Who shall separate us from the love of Christ?*" (v. 35). Then he makes a list of our enemies, naming seventeen of them. Finally, he concludes by speaking of the great victory we have in Christ over all our enemies.

The Challenge

From verse one of Romans 8 we have been steadily climbing until, now, in Romans 8:35–39, we have arrived at the Mount Everest of the eternal security of true believers. The Westminster Confession of Faith speaks about this eternal security of the children of God: "They whom God hath accepted in his beloved, effectually called and sanctified by his Spirit, can neither totally nor finally fall away from the state of grace, but shall certainly persevere therein to the end, and be eternally saved."[1]

This truth of the full assurance of our salvation in Jesus Christ is clearly taught in Romans 8:35–39. Here Paul poses the fifth and final unanswerable question: "Who shall separate us from the love of Christ?" This passage finishes the argument Paul began in Romans 8:31: "If God is for us, who can be against us?" The answer is, "No one." The very gates of hell shall not prevail against the church, which Christ is building upon the rock foundation of himself, with us as the living stones. We are in God and in Christ Jesus. We are born of the Spirit, led by the Spirit, and kept by the mighty power of the Spirit. Because Jesus lives, we live forever, for he has given us eternal life and we shall never perish. We are gripped by his crucified hands; no one is able to snatch us out of them. We are gripped also by the Father's hand. Who can snatch us out of his hand? We are held by the Father and the Son in the Holy Spirit.

We are not like Esau, Achan, Saul, Judas, Ananias, or Demas, who were not born of God. Such people fell away because they "trampled the Son of God under foot, . . . treated as an unholy thing the blood of the covenant . . . [and] insulted the Spirit of grace" (Heb. 10:29). But the people of God will persevere to the end in the power of God. Therefore there is now no condemnation or separation for those who are in Christ Jesus.

We have been taken out of Adam and the world, and have been joined to Jesus Christ, our beloved bridegroom, by the

---

1   Westminster *Confession of Faith*, Chapter XVII: Of the *Perseverance of the Saints*, section 1.

divine glue of Christ's love. Separation from him, therefore, is absolutely impossible. In fact, God hates divorce (Mal. 2:16). Jesus Christ never divorces his bride, the church, for whose sake he died.

Who, then, shall separate us, the church, from the love of Christ? Who shall cut us off? That is the challenge. Who shall put a distance between Christ and his church?'

The phrase *"the love of Christ"* is an objective genitive, indicating not our changing love for Christ, but Christ's infinite, unchanging love for us. This Jesus died for us, was raised for us, is seated at the right hand of God for us, and ever lives to make intercession for us.

Who can separate us from Christ's love? Or, to put it differently, can anyone or anything cause Christ to hate us? The answer is no. It is impossible. Not even our own sin can separate us from the love of Christ.

We are justified by God, not on the basis of our righteousness, but on the sole basis of Christ's perfect righteousness. If we sin, God will discipline us (Heb. 12:7–11), for he is making us holy and blameless, and he knows how to do it. But he will never cast us off. No one and no thing can do that. The Holy Spirit dwells in us forever. The Holy Spirit departed from Saul but not from David. We died with Christ, were buried with Christ, were raised with Christ, and are seated with Christ. He is the vine and we are the fruit-bearing branches, vitally united to him forever. No one can cut us off. Christ loved us from eternity, loves us now, and will love us forever.

Of Christ's love we read, "Greater love has no one than this, that he lay down his life for his friends" (John 15:13). "But God demonstrates his own love for us in this: While we were still sinners, Christ died for us" (Rom. 5:8). Even now, Christ is loving us by sanctifying us by his word to make us shine as the sun, that he may present us to himself as a radiant church, perfect in glory.

We have enemies who would like to cut us off from the love of Christ, but they cannot and will not succeed. How can creatures frustrate the purpose of the sovereign God? It is God's purpose to conform us to the image of his Son, and we are called according to this purpose.

Our Enemies

There are seventeen possible enemies listed in this passage:

1. Trouble (*thlipsis*). In Latin, it is *tribulum*, from which we derive the word "trouble." A *tribulum* was a kind of sledge or wooden platform, studded underneath with sharp pieces of flint or iron teeth. Farmers used this tool to thresh corn. The idea is of applying severe pressure, such as the pressure applied to grapes to get juice or to olives to produce olive oil.

Christians are not exempt from pressures in this life. In fact, we experience more troubles because we belong to Christ, whom the world hates. Paul said, "We must go through many hardships to enter the kingdom of God" (Acts 14:22). He wrote to Timothy, "In fact, everyone who wants to live a godly life in Christ Jesus will be persecuted" (2 Tim. 3:12). We can count on it. Jesus said, "Blessed are those who are persecuted because of righteousness, for theirs is the kingdom of heaven. Blessed are you when people insult you, persecute you and falsely say all kinds of evil against you because of me. Rejoice and be glad, because great is your reward in heaven, for in the same way they persecuted the prophets who were before you" (Matt. 5:10–12). Jesus told the Pharisees, "Therefore I am sending you prophets and wise men and teachers. Some of them you will kill and crucify; others you will flog in your synagogues and pursue from town to town" (Matt. 23:34). Persecution of God's people is not new. Therefore, do not moan, complain, and argue, but understand this truth.

2. Hardship (*stenochōria*). The Greek word indicates that the way of Jesus is very narrow. We are to take Christ's yoke and our cross, and follow Jesus. We will experience anguish, straitness, and distress in our Christian life. Paul used this word in Romans 2:9: "There will be trouble and *distress* for every human being who does evil: first for the Jew, then for the Gentile."

3. Persecution (*diōgmos*). Ishmael persecuted Isaac. Centuries later, Jews persecuted early Christians: "On that day a great persecution broke out against the church at Jerusalem, and all except the apostles were scattered throughout Judea and Samaria" (Acts 8:1). Study the history of Christian martyrs; you will find much about persecution.

4. Famine (*limos*). The people of God may suffer hunger. I have known ministers' children who suffered and died because they

did not have food. Read the story of Indian saint Pandita Ramabai and you will see the results of famine. Paul also experienced severe hunger (see 2 Cor. 11:27). Jesus also speaks about it: "For I was hungry and you gave me nothing to eat, I was thirsty and you gave me nothing to drink" (Matt. 25:42).

5. Nakedness (*gumnotēs*). This means Christians may lack clothing to cover their nakedness fully. Jesus says, "I needed clothes and you did not clothe me" (Matt. 25:43). James says, "Suppose a brother or sister is without clothes and daily food. If one of you says to him, 'Go, I wish you well; keep warm and well fed,' but does nothing about his physical needs, what good is it?" (James 2:15-16). Not helping one's brother is hypocrisy and a denial of Christianity.

6. Danger (*kindunos*). As Christians, we may experience all kinds of dangers, for we are not exempt from them. Just read Paul's list of dangers (2 Cor. 11:26). He speaks about dangers from rivers, from bandits, from countrymen, and from Gentiles; dangers in the city, in the country, and at sea; and, finally, danger from false brothers. We must realize that the Holy Spirit does not always prevent us from experiencing dangers.

7. Sword (*machaira*). This speaks of violent death. Someone may try to kill us. Paul had not experienced the sword at the time of this writing, but he was later killed by the sword. This is still happening today. So Paul quotes Psalm 44:22 to show how God's people have always suffered for their faith in God: "*For your sake we are being put to death all day long, we are counted and marked off as sheep for the slaughter*" (v. 36, author's translation). What are we complaining about? Superficial, synthetic evangelism says, "Believe Jesus and your troubles shall disappear. You will have wealth and health and fame." That is utterly false and has nothing to do with the gospel.

8. Death (*thanatos*). Believers may die a natural death or be put to death. But do not worry: Christ destroyed death for us by his death on the cross. Paul declares, "Then the saying that is written will come true: 'Death has been swallowed up in victory.' . . . The sting of death is sin, and the power of sin is the law. But thanks be to God! He gives us the victory through our Lord Jesus Christ. . . . We will all be changed—in a flash, in the twinkling of an eye, at the last trumpet. For the trumpet will sound, the

dead will be raised imperishable, and we will be changed" (1 Cor. 15:54, 56–57, 51–52). Elsewhere he says, "[Grace] has now been revealed through the appearing of our Savior, Christ Jesus, who has destroyed death and has brought life and immortality to light through the gospel" (2 Tim. 1:10). The gospel tells us how to obtain life and immortality. Think of the killing of thousands of Scottish Covenanters by the so-called Christian rulers, or read about Nero, who burned Christians as living torches to light the city of Rome at night. But for us, to die is gain, for death opens the door to paradise.

9. Life (*zōē*). Our lives are full of problems in this fallen world, and every day people try to escape their problems. Some even commit suicide. But to us, life here means fruitful service to God. Paul writes, "If I am to go on living in the body, this will mean fruitful labor for me" (Phil. 1:22). We must redeem the time, for we have work to do for God. And God, who formed us in our mothers' wombs, will sustain us all through life. He will be with us in life, in death, and beyond the grave. So Paul declares, "For none of us lives to himself alone and none of us dies to himself alone. If we live, we live to the Lord; and if we die, we die to the Lord. So, whether we live or die, we belong to the Lord" (Rom. 14:7–8).

10 and 11. Angels (*angeloi*) and demons (*archai*, lit. "rulers") are against us. But don't worry: all evil angels and evil rulers have been defeated by Christ's death on the cross. Paul exults, "And having disarmed the powers and authorities, he made a public spectacle of them, triumphing over them by the cross" (Col. 2:15). What about Jesus himself? He "has gone into heaven and is at God's right hand—with angels, authorities and powers in submission to him" (1 Pet. 3:22). So Paul says, "We demolish arguments and every pretension that sets itself up against the knowledge of God, and we take captive every thought to make it obedient to Christ" (2 Cor. 10:5). We resist the devil, wrestling against him. He flees, and we stand in triumph.

12 and 13. Things present (*enestōta*) and things future (*mellonta*). What of the present time and the unknown future? Jesus has all authority in heaven and on earth. He said to his disciples, "I have told you these things, so that in me you may have peace. In this world you will have trouble. But take heart! I have overcome

the world" (John 16:33). God exalted him "far above all rule and authority, power and dominion, and every title that can be given, not only in the present age but also in the one to come. And God placed all things under his feet and appointed him to be head over everything for the church, which is his body, the fullness of him who fills everything in every way" (Eph. 1:21–23).

Faith is the victory that overcomes the world. So John writes, "For everyone born of God overcomes the world. This is the victory that has overcome the world, even our faith" (1 John 5:4), meaning faith in Christ, faith in God, faith in the gospel. Paul says, "We live by faith, not by sight" (2 Cor. 5:7).

Jesus is the same yesterday, today, and forever. He knows the end from the beginning. He is with us. He never leaves us, and we are the temple of his Holy Spirit. We do not know what tomorrow will bring. But Jesus is the Lord of the present and the future. So we can sing with confidence:

Many things about tomorrow
I don't seem to understand.
But I know who holds tomorrow,
and I know who holds my hand.

14. Powers (*dunameis*) that are against us. This may refer to miracles performed in the power of the devil to deceive people. Will we be deceived by counterfeit miracles and spiritual charlatans, as many people are deceived today? Jesus himself warned, "For false Christs and false prophets will appear and perform great signs and miracles to deceive even the elect—if that were possible" (Matt. 24:24). But it is not possible to deceive God's elect. Paul says, "The coming of the lawless one will be in accordance with the work of Satan displayed in all kinds of counterfeit miracles, signs and wonders, and in every sort of evil that deceives those who are perishing" (2 Thess. 2:9–10).

15 and 16. Height (*hupsōma*) and depth (*bathos*). Do not worry: Jesus Christ is the Lord of all space. He is in the highest heights and the deepest depths. The psalmist asked, "Where can I go from your Spirit? Where can I flee from your presence? If I go up to the heavens, you are there; if I make my bed in the depths, you are there" (Ps. 139:7–8). Can we go away from God's presence to someplace else? No, he is everywhere.

17. Anything else in creation (*tis ktisis hetera*, "any other created thing"). That is the final challenge: Is there any other created thing in God's universe that can separate us from the love of Christ? The answer is "No." Nothing in all creation can separate us from the love Christ has for us.

Friends, what should we conclude? We are eternally secure. We have reached the Mount Everest of our security. We are not victims of our circumstances, but victors over them. Christ has defeated all our enemies. He defeated death and the devil by his death.

What are we complaining about? Consider some of the troubles the Hebrew believers and Paul himself suffered:

> Remember those earlier days after you had received the light, when you stood your ground in a great contest in the face of suffering. Sometimes you were publicly exposed to insult and persecution; at other times you stood side by side with those who were so treated. You sympathized with those in prison and joyfully accepted the confiscation of your property, because you knew that you yourselves had better and lasting possessions. (Heb. 10:32–34)

> Others were tortured and refused to be released, so that they might gain a better resurrection. Some faced jeers and flogging, while still others were chained and put in prison. They were stoned; they were sawed in two; they were put to death by the sword. They went about in sheepskins and goatskins, destitute, persecuted and mistreated—the world was not worthy of them. They wandered in deserts and mountains, and in caves and holes in the ground. (Heb. 11:35–38)

> Are they servants of Christ? (I am out of my mind to talk like this.) I am more. I have worked much harder, been in prison more frequently, been flogged more severely, and been exposed to death again and again. Five times I received from the Jews the forty lashes minus one. Three times I was beaten with rods, once I was stoned, three times I was shipwrecked, I spent a night and a day in the open sea, I have been constantly on the move. I have been in danger from rivers, in danger from bandits, in danger from my own countrymen, in danger from Gentiles; in danger in the city, in danger in the country, in danger at sea; and in danger from false brothers. I have labored and toiled and have often gone without sleep; I have known hunger and thirst and have often gone without food; I have been cold and naked. Besides everything else, I face daily the pressure of my concern for all the churches. (2 Cor. 11:23–28)

Saints do not just endure hardship but glory in it. So Paul declares, "Not only so, but we also rejoice in our sufferings, because we know that suffering produces perseverance; perseverance, character; and character, hope. And hope does not disappoint us, because God has poured out his love into our hearts by the Holy Spirit, whom he has given us" (Rom. 5:3–5). We glory and boast in our sufferings because sufferings produce in us Christ's likeness. Elsewhere Paul wrote, "But [God] said to me, 'My grace is sufficient for you, for my power is made perfect in weakness.' Therefore I will boast all the more gladly about my weaknesses, so that Christ's power may rest on me" (2 Cor. 12:9).

The Victory

"In all these things we are more than conquerors" (v. 37). We are super-conquerors in all things. Christians are realists. We expect troubles and persecutions. But they cannot harm or defeat us. On the contrary, "in all these things" we enjoy daily overwhelming victory. For instance, "Just as the sufferings of Christ flow over into our lives, so also through Christ our comfort overflows" (2 Cor. 1:5). When there is trouble, there is also comfort.

Moreover, we learn to trust in Christ alone because of sufferings. Paul says, "Indeed, in our hearts we felt the sentence of death. But this happened that we might not rely on ourselves but on God, who raises the dead" (2 Cor. 1:9). Troubles make us trust only in Christ. We hope not in this world but in the world to come. Sufferings for Christ's sake cause the things of this world to grow strangely dim. These sufferings focus our spiritual eyes on Jesus, the author and finisher of our faith, who is at the right hand of the Father, making intercession for us right now.

True believers are filled with the Spirit, thus are full of faith and wisdom. They are clothed with the Spirit and the power of God. The church of Christ follows Jesus, who goes out conquering and to conquer. By faith we overcome the world, the devil, the flesh, and hell. We do so by the blood of the Lamb and the word of our testimony.

The church super-conquers all her enemies. Like Samson, who destroyed the gates of Gaza, the church in Christ's strength takes the battle to the gates of hell, and those gates are destroyed. The walls of Jericho crumble before the church; Goliath is killed by his own sword. Like David, the church goes against all Christ's enemies in the name of the Lord Almighty, the God of the armies of Israel. Like Joshua, we fight and win because our God is a warrior, the commander of the army of the Lord.

Onward, Christian soldiers! We never retreat in defeat, for God is with us. And we will sing the song of Moses:

> I will sing unto the Lord,
> for he has triumphed gloriously,
> the horse and the rider thrown into the sea.
> The Lord, my God, my strength, my song,
> has now become my victory.
> The Lord is God, and I will praise him,
> my Father's God, and I will exalt him.

We do not just overcome our enemies: we super-overcome (*hupernikōmen*), and we do so daily. The Lord is with us. In all things God works for our good, for our final salvation, our glorification. So we read in Isaiah 43:

> But now, this is what the LORD says—he who created you, O Jacob, he who formed you, O Israel: "Fear not, for I have redeemed you; I have summoned you by name; you are mine. When you pass through the waters, I will be with you; and when you pass through the rivers, they will not sweep over you. When you walk through the fire, you will not be burned; the flames will not set you ablaze. For I am the LORD, your God, the Holy One of Israel, your Savior." (vv. 1–3)

Paul says, "I can do all things through Jesus Christ who gives me strength daily, who makes me strong. When I am weak, then I am strong. His grace comes to me and is sufficient for me to do every good work" (see Phil. 4:13; 2 Cor. 12:9–10).

Dr. Martyn Lloyd-Jones speaks of Thomas Browning, a seventeenth-century pastor who was put in Northampton prison by Charles II. From there, he wrote to his flock, "The cup of afflictions for the gospel is the sweeter the deeper, . . . a stronger cordial the nearer the bottom." In other words, Lloyd-Jones says, "The deeper the affliction, the sweeter it is."[2] Dr. John Stott says,

---

2   Lloyd-Jones, *Romans*, vol. 8, *Final Perseverance of the Saints*, 447.

"Christian people are not guaranteed immunity to temptation, tribulation or tragedy, but we are promised victory over them. God's pledge is not that suffering will never afflict us, but that it will never separate us from his love."[3]

No suffering can separate us from our union with Christ, which is our union with his life and love. We will go with the Lord through the valley of the shadow of death, but we will also arrive at the city of the living God to enjoy everlasting life. In all things, including sufferings, we daily super-conquer, not in our strength, but through him who loved us, who died for our sins on the cross.

Christ loved us and died for us. If we want a demonstration of Christ's love, look to the cross and be fully convinced that nothing can destroy our salvation. Paul says, "I am persuaded" (v. 38). The word *pepeismai* is the perfect passive indicative of *peithō*, meaning "I have arrived at this unshakable conviction." It is not an emotional feeling. Paul stood convinced, and his was a conviction brought about by the facts of the gospel as a result of the Spirit's enlightening his rational mind. So he came to a settled conclusion. He was not deceived or deluded, but had absolute certainty. So finally Paul obediently and confidently went out to the place of execution, because he was absolutely certain that nothing could cut him off from the love of Christ. He was beheaded, as was also James the apostle. Stephen was stoned to death and Peter crucified. All these were convinced beyond a shadow of doubt of the enduring love of God manifested in Jesus Christ. In fact, the Scripture records the assurance God gave the dying Stephen of his love: "But Stephen, full of the Holy Spirit, looked up to heaven and saw the glory of God, and Jesus standing at the right hand of God. 'Look,' he said, 'I see heaven open and the Son of Man standing at the right hand of God'" (Acts 7:55–56). Stephen saw Jesus Christ and the Father in paradise. He was going where the thief on the cross went in his spirit.

Death cannot separate us from the love of the triune God. It can only help us to reach his paradise, a paradise of inexpressible joy. God gives us grace to live, grace to suffer, grace to die, and grace to arrive in paradise. No wonder Paul said, "For to me, to

---

3   Stott, *Romans: God's Good News*, 259.

live is Christ and to die is gain" (Phil. 1:21). Earlier in this chapter he said, "And *we know* that to those who love God, God works in all things for good" (Rom. 8:28). In other words, we know for certain. Now he says, "I am convinced." God's love in Christ never fails. You have heard it sung,

> Jesus never fails, Jesus never fails.
> Heaven and earth may pass away,
> but Jesus never fails.

Are You in Christ?

All seventeen enemies listed in this passage are powerless to separate us from the love of God. Yes, they are super-human and mighty. But God is almighty. So we read in Revelation 20 that the devil, the antichrist, the false prophet, all evil spirits, and every unbeliever in Jesus Christ will be cast out into the lake of fire by Christ, the Judge of all. After that, we who are God's people will dwell with God in the new heaven and the new earth, where there are no enemies, no death, and no tears.

Absolutely nothing can separate us from the love of Christ, which is the love of God our Father. The love of the Father is the love Christ displayed on the cross. It is the love the Holy Spirit sheds abroad in our hearts in super-abundance. It is great, everlasting, undying love, which many waters cannot quench. It is the love with which the Father loves his own Son. It is beyond all human comprehension, yet Paul prays that we can grow in our knowledge of this love: "I pray that out of his glorious riches he may strengthen you with power through his Spirit in your inner being, so that Christ may dwell in your hearts through faith. And I pray that you, being rooted and established in love, may have power, together with all the saints, to grasp how wide and long and high and deep is the love of Christ, and to know this love that surpasses knowledge—that you may be filled to the measure of all the fullness of God" (Eph. 3:16–19).

Therefore we can conclude that the question of Romans 8:35, "Who can separate us from the love of Christ?" is answered in the negative: Nothing and no one in the entire universe, including ourselves and our sin, can separate us from his love. And so Paul concludes by saying that nothing in all creation *"will be able to separate us from the love of God that is in Christ Jesus our Lord"* (Rom. 8:39). This is eternal security! Notice, however, that this love of God is *"in* Christ Jesus our Lord." No one can know the love of God without knowing and trusting in Jesus Christ, who died on the cross. Full assurance of our final salvation is only for those who confess, "Jesus is Lord."

Have you done that? "If you confess with your mouth, 'Jesus is Lord,' and believe in your heart that God raised him from the dead, you will be saved" (Rom. 10:9). Anyone who trusts in him will never be put to shame. Jesus said, "I am the bread of life. He who comes to me will never go hungry, and he who believes in me will never be thirsty" (John 6:35).

Those who are in Christ, rejoice! Those who are outside of Christ, come! Come to him, confess him, trust in him, and be eternally secure in the love of God and the love of Christ.

Select Bibliography

Barnhouse, Donald Grey. *Romans.* Vol. 1, *Man's Ruin; God's Wrath.* Vol. 2, *God's Remedy; God's River.* Vol. 3, *God's Grace; God's Freedom; God's Heirs.* Vol. 4, *God's Covenants; God's Discipline; God's Glory.* Grand Rapids: Eerdmans, 1952–1964.

Barth, Karl. *The Epistle to the Romans.* Translated by Edwyn C. Hoskyns. Oxford: Oxford University Press, 1968.

Boice, James M. *Romans.* Vol. 1, *Justification by Faith (Romans 1–4).* Grand Rapids: Baker, 1991.

_____. *Romans.* Vol. 2, *The Reign of Grace (Romans 5–8).* Grand Rapids: Baker, 1992.

_____. *Romans.* Vol. 3, *God and History (Romans 9–11).* Grand Rapids: Baker, 1993.

_____. *Romans.* Vol. 4, *The New Humanity (Romans 12–16).* Grand Rapids: Baker, 1995.

Bruce, F. F. *The Letter of Paul to the Romans.* Rev. ed., 1985. Tyndale New Testament Commentaries. Grand Rapids: Eerdmans, reprinted 2000.

Cranfield, C. E. B. *Romans: A Shorter Commentary.* Grand Rapids: Eerdmans, 1992.

Denney, James. "St. Paul's Epistle to the Romans" in *The Expositor's Greek Testament,* Vol. 2. Edited by W. Robertson Nicoll. Grand Rapids: Eerdmans, reprinted 1970.

Frame, John. *The Doctrine of God*. Phillipsburg, NJ: Presbyterian and Reformed, 2002.

_____. *Salvation Belongs to the Lord*. Phillipsburg, NJ: Presbyterian and Reformed, 2006.

Garlington, Donald B. *Faith, Obedience and Perseverance: Aspects of Paul's Letter to the Romans*. Tübingen: J. C. B. Mohr (Paul Siebeck), 1994.

Godet, Frederic L. *Commentary on St. Paul's Epistle to the Romans*. Translated by A. Cusin. 2 vols. Edinburgh: T & T Clark, 1888–89.

Haldane, Robert. *Exposition of the Epistle to the Romans*. 1958. Geneva Series of Commentaries. Edinburgh: Banner of Truth, reprinted 1996.

Hendriksen, William. *Exposition of Paul's Epistle to the Romans*. New Testament Commentary Series. Grand Rapids: Baker Books, 1990.

Hodge, Charles. *Romans*. Geneva Series of Commentaries. Edinburgh: Banner of Truth, reprinted 1989.

Lloyd-Jones, D. Martyn. *Romans*. Vol. 1, *An Exposition of Romans 1: The Gospel of God*. Grand Rapids: Zondervan, 1986.

_____. *Romans*. Vol. 2, *An Exposition of Romans 2:1–3:20: The Righteous Judgment of God*. Grand Rapids: Zondervan, 1989.

_____. *Romans*. Vol. 3, *An Exposition of Romans 3:20–4:25: Atonement and Justification*. Grand Rapids: Zondervan, 1971.

_____. *Romans*. Vol. 4, *An Exposition of Romans 5: Assurance*. Grand Rapids: Zondervan, 1972.

_____. *Romans*. Vol. 5, *An Exposition of Romans 6: The New Man*. Grand Rapids: Zondervan, 1973.

_____. *Romans*. Vol. 6, *An Exposition of Romans 7:1–8:4: The Law: Its Functions and Limits*. Grand Rapids: Zondervan, 1973.

_____. *Romans*. Vol. 7, *An Exposition of Romans 8:5–17: The Sons of God*. Grand Rapids: Zondervan, 1975.

_____. *Romans.* Vol. 8, *An Exposition of Romans 8:17–39: The Final Perseverance of the Saints.* Grand Rapids: Zondervan, 1976.

_____. *Romans.* Vol. 9, *An Exposition of Romans 9: God's Sovereign Purpose.* Grand Rapids: Zondervan, 1992.

_____. *Romans.* Vol. 10, *An Exposition of Romans 10: Saving Faith.* Edinburgh: Banner of Truth, 1997.

_____. *Romans.* Vol. 11, *An Exposition of Romans 11: To God's Glory.* Edinburgh: Banner of Truth, 1998.

_____. *Romans.* Vol. 12, *An Exposition of Romans 12: Christian Conduct.* Edinburgh: Banner of Truth, 2000.

_____. *Romans.* Vol. 13, *An Exposition of Romans 13: Life in Two Kingdoms* Edinburgh: Banner of Truth, 2002.

_____. *Romans.* Vol. 14, *An Exposition of Romans 14:1–17: Liberty and Conscience.* Edinburgh: Banner of Truth, 2003.

Luther, Martin. *Commentary on Romans.* Translated by J. Theodore Muller. Grand Rapids: Kregel, 1993.

MacArthur, John. *Romans 1–8.* The MacArthur New Testament Commentary series. Chicago: Moody, 1991.

Moo, Douglas. *The Epistle to the Romans.* The New International Commentary on the New Testament. Grand Rapids: Eerdmans, 1996.

Morris, Leon. *The Epistle to the Romans.* Grand Rapids: Eerdmans, reprinted 1992.

Murray, John. *Collected Writings of John Murray.* 4 vols. Edinburgh: The Banner of Truth Trust, 1977.

_____. *The Epistle to the Romans.* The New International Commentary on the New Testament. Grand Rapids: Eerdmans, reprinted 1979.

_____. *The Imputation of Adam's Sin.* Grand Rapids: Eerdmans, 1959. Reprint, Philipsburg, NJ: Presbyterian and Reformed, n.d.

_____. *Principles of Conduct*. Grand Rapids: Eerdmans, reprinted 1974.

_____. *Redemption Accomplished and Applied*. Grand Rapids: Eerdmans, 1980.

Nygren, Anders. *Commentary on Romans*. Translated by Carl Rasmussen. London: SCM Press, 1958.

Sandlin, P. Andrew, ed. *A Faith That Is Never Alone*. LaGrange, CA: Kerygma Press, 2007.

Stott, John R. W. *Romans: God's Good News for the World*. Downers Grove, IL: InterVarsity, 1994.

Wilson, Geoffrey B. *Romans: A Digest of Reformed Comment*. London: Banner of Truth, 1969.

Grace and Glory Ministries

GRACE & GLORY
MINISTRIES

Grace and Glory Ministries is an extension of Grace Valley Christian Center. We are committed to the teaching of God's infallible word. It is our mission to proclaim the whole gospel to the whole world for the building up of the whole body of Christ.

For more information on the ministries of Grace Valley Christian Center, please visit:

http://www.gracevalley.org

To obtain additional copies of this book, please e-mail:

gvcc@gracevalley.org